D1021995

THE ENGLISH OPIUM EATER

THE ENGLISH OPIUM EATER

A BIOGRAPHY OF THOMAS DE QUINCEY

ROBERT MORRISON

PEGASUS BOOKS
NEW YORK

THE ENGLISH OPIUM EATER

Pegasus Books LLC
80 Broad Street, 5th Floor
New York, NY 10004

Copyright © 2010 by Robert Morrison

First Pegasus Books cloth edition 2010

Library of Congress Cataloging-in-Publication Data is available.

ISBN: 978-1-60598-132-1

10 9 8 7 6 5 4 3 2 1

Printed in the United States of America
Distributed by W. W. Norton & Company, Inc.
www.pegasusbooks.us

To Carole

The love of you will never from my heart

Contents

Illustrations

Acknowledgements

My research for this book was generously funded by the Office of Research Services at Queen's University, and the Social Sciences and Humanities Research Council of Canada. I was advanced a full-year sabbatical leave to enable me to complete this project to mark the one hundred and fiftieth anniversary of De Quincey's death, and I gratefully acknowledge Alistair MacLean, Ramneek Pooni, and Marta Straznicky for their support of my application.

For permission to quote from manuscript material in their collections, I am indebted to Charles Agvent and Frederick Burwick, as well as to the following institutions: the Henry W. and Albert A. Berg Collection of English and American Literature, the New York Public Library, Astor, Lenox, and Tilden Foundations; the Beinecke Library, Yale University; the Bodleian Library, Oxford University; the Boston Public Library; the British Library; the Cornell University Library; the Trustees of the Dove Cottage Library; the Trustees of Dr Williams's Library; the Ella Strong Denison Library, Scripps College; the Edinburgh University Library; the General Register Office for Scotland; the Harry Ransom Center, University of Texas at Austin; the Houghton Library, Harvard University; the Huntington Library, San Marino, California; the Lee Kohns Memorial Collection, Manuscripts and Archives Division, the New York Public Library, Astor, Lenox, and Tilden Foundations; the Division of Special Collections and Digital Programs, University of Kentucky Libraries; the Liverpool Record Office; the Manchester Central Library; the Trustees of the National Archives of Scotland; the National Library of Ireland; the National Library of Scotland; the Carl H. Pforzheimer Collection of Shelley and His Circle, the New York Public Library, Astor, Lenox, and Tilden Foundations; the Pierpont Morgan Library; the Robert H. Taylor Collection, Manuscripts Division, Department of Rare Books and Special Collections, Princeton University Library; Rare Books and Special Collections, University of Rochester Library; the Trinity College Library, Cambridge University; the Tennyson Research Centre, Lincolnshire County Council; the University of Iowa Libraries; and the Provost and Fellows of Worcester College, Oxford.

I would like to thank the following librarians and archivists for providing extra information and guiding me to new sources: Paul Wiens and Bonnie S. Brooks at the Stauffer Library, Queen's University; William J. Marshall at the University of Kentucky; Gayle Richardson at the Huntington Library; Grace Timmins at the Tennyson Research Centre; Rachel Foss at the British Library; Paul Parr at the General Register Office for Scotland; Derek Oliver at the National Library of Scotland; and Joanna Parker and Owen Massey McKnight at Worcester College, Oxford. For his indispensable assistance throughout this project, I would especially like to record my thanks to Jeff Cowton at the Dove Cottage Library.

Writing a biography is a complicated and exhilarating task, and I have benefited enormously from the expertise and support of a number of scholars and friends. I am grateful to Peter Bell, Ben Colbert, Michael S. Cummings, Patrick Deane, Sheila Deane, Richard Downing, the late Bob Freeman, Peter Haining, Christopher Hallam, Roger Hamilton, William Hughes, Heather Jackson, Robin Jackson, Allan Jefferis, Larry Krupp, John Kulka, Charles Mahoney, Jonathan McKay, Barry Milligan, Pam Perkins, Tinka Markham Piper, David Punter, Michael Rauth, William C. Reeve, Nicholas Roe, Charles Rzepka, Michael Silverman, Jonathan Smith, John Strachan, the late John D. Thomas, Eirian Youngman, Duncan Wu, and Sue Zlosnik.

I have learned a great deal from De Quincey's previous biographers: Alexander Japp, Edward Sackville-West, Horace Eaton, and Grevel Lindop. Indeed, at the outset of this project, I sat down in an Oxford pub with Grevel, who generously shared with me his experience of writing a life of De Quincey. Shortly thereafter, I also sat down with Barry Symonds, who gave me complete access to his extensive De Quincey archive of letters and manuscript transcriptions, and who responded with great incisiveness on the many occasions when I consulted him. Without Barry's expertise and great generosity, this biography could not have been written.

I have other specific debts. Helen Tiffin provided invaluable guidance as I began this project; Ian Reed walked me all over De Quincey's Lake District, and answered my many questions about the area; Richard Hamilton accompanied me on visits to De Quincey's cottages at Duddingston and Lasswade; Harri Parry supplied me with a great deal of information about Glanllynnau farm; Billy Jackson kindly showed me around Lingstubbs; Cella Olmstead shared with me her vast knowledge of opiate addiction; David Hedley read all the available information, and then diagnosed the disease that killed De

Quincey's son William; Matthew Strohack did a superb job of transcribing hundreds of De Quincey letters; Penny Clutton entered hundreds of other De Quincey letters into a database; James Crowden generously sent me a steady stream of information, from photographs of Westhay to a copy of De Quincey's death certificate; and Daniel Sanjiv Roberts provided warm friendship, and – with my deadline fast approaching – kindly dashed into the Bodleian to check one last source. Finally, I would like to thank five scholars whose confidence and friendship have meant so much to me: Chris Baldick, Geoffrey Carnall, Thomas McFarland, Christopher Ricks, and the late Jonathan Wordsworth.

My friend Anthony Holden and my publisher Alan Samson both believed in this project right from the start, and I am deeply grateful for their advice and support. Bea Hemming read the entire manuscript with great care and insight, and offered many helpful suggestions.

For their love and constant encouragement, I would like to thank Joyce and Glenn, and Zachary and Alastair.

This book is for Carole.

Leigh House
Brewer's Mills
April 2009

Introduction

Thomas De Quincey wrote some of the most eloquent and searching prose of the nineteenth century. The mass media that now dominates our lives developed during his lifetime, and he was a popular and prolific contributor to it for more than forty years, whether writing for liberal-minded publications such as the *London Magazine* or *Tait's*, or for conservative journals such as the immensely successful *Blackwood's*. He was close to some of the key literary figures of his era, including William Wordsworth and Samuel Taylor Coleridge, and his biographical accounts of both poets continue to inform our understanding of them. His essays 'On Murder Considered as One of the Fine Arts' range from brilliantly funny satiric high jinks to penetrating cultural criticism, and had a remarkable influence on crime, terror, and detective fiction, as well as on the rise of nineteenth-century decadence. His *Confessions of an English Opium-Eater*, published in 1821 and revised in 1856, is the first account of drug euphoria and addiction that was consciously aimed at a broad commercial audience. The work has had an enormous impact on popular culture from De Quincey's day to ours, and has inspired a long line of writers, from Edgar Allan Poe, Charles Baudelaire, and Arthur Conan Doyle to Jean Cocteau, W. S. Burroughs, Ann Marlowe, and beyond. As long ago as 1975, the social psychologist Stanton Peele remarked that 'addiction is not, as we like to think, an aberration from our way of life. Addiction is our way of life'. De Quincey's *Confessions* signal the birth of the modern age, and speak directly to our ongoing fascination with habit, desire, commercialism, and consumption.

This is the first biography of De Quincey in nearly three decades, and it takes into account a vast array of new material that has come to light in recent years. For more than a century, David Masson's fourteen-volume edition of *The Collected Writings of Thomas De Quincey* was the standard edition, and by far the best edition available. But it was woefully incomplete: a great deal of material was missing altogether; most essays – including the *Confessions* – were printed only in their revised form; there was no manuscript material; and Masson sometimes silently tampered with essays by removing whole sections of prose. In 2000–03, this situation improved dramatically when Grevel Lindop and an international team of editors produced *The Works of Thomas De Quincey*, a new, fully-annotated, twenty-one-volume edition that reprinted virtually everything De Quincey published, together with all known manuscript material, and an extensive series of textual variants that charted the substantive differences between his essays in their original and revised versions. For the first time, everything that De Quincey published is easily accessible.

The situation with De Quincey's letters is very different. There are several editions of his correspondence, but none of them approaches completeness, and many of his letters have still not been published. My solution to this problem was to compile – with the crucial assistance of Barry Symonds – a database which contains transcriptions of, as far as I know, all of the De Quincey letters housed in public archives, and as many as possible of those housed in private collections. This database is the most comprehensive archive of De Quincey's correspondence ever assembled, and it contains an abundance of hitherto unknown or neglected material.

In the past twenty-five years, valuable new information on his life has also come from a variety of other sources. Scholarly editions of writings by Charlotte Brontë, Elizabeth Barrett Browning, John Clare, James Hogg, Richard Woodhouse, and William and Dorothy Wordsworth have all brought fresh material to light. In March 2009, the British Library purchased 119 previously unknown letters written by De Quincey's three daughters, all of whom comment with often disarming frankness on their father during the final decade of his life. The critical writings of a number of fine scholars, including John Barrell, Patrick Bridgwater, David Groves, Grevel Lindop, Barry Milligan, Daniel Sanjiv Roberts, Charles Rzepka, and Barry Symonds, have exposed a host of new perspectives on De Quincey's life and autobiographical writings.

This diverse and fascinating body of material has enriched our understanding of almost every aspect of De Quincey's life and career: his enduring sorrow over the loss of his beloved sister Elizabeth; his masochistic desire for humiliation; his association with prostitutes; his pursuit of and subsequent alienation from Wordsworth and Coleridge; his struggle with drugs and alcohol; his exhilarating engagement with the *London Magazine* circle of William Hazlitt, Charles Lamb, Edward Irving, John Clare, and Thomas Carlyle; his complicated and sometimes hostile relationship with John Wilson, his *Blackwood's* colleague and closest friend; his horrendous battles with debt; his imprisonment in Edinburgh gaols; his meeting with Ralph Waldo Emerson; his interest in the Brontës; and much else.

Yet despite the wealth of new information, De Quincey remains in many ways a remarkably elusive figure. To some extent, this is simply the nature of biography: it is difficult in any study of another person to gain access to what De Quincey himself once described as 'that inner world – that world of secret self-consciousness – in which each of us lives a second life apart and with himself alone'. Access to De Quincey is additionally complicated by the fact that opium was one of the central features of his existence, and that in innumerable instances he prevaricated in an attempt to keep his abuse of it hidden from others and, more importantly, from himself, his many public celebrations of the drug notwithstanding. Of his fellow opium *habitué* Coleridge, Dorothy Wordsworth once observed that 'his whole time and thoughts ... are employed in deceiving himself, and seeking to deceive others'. The same might often be said of De Quincey. Finally, in his autobiographical writings, it is clear that De Quincey often worked hard to disguise, rather than to reveal, his own experience. As Virginia Woolf once discerningly put it, in his many pieces of autobiography De Quincey tells us 'only' what he 'wished us to know; and even that has been chosen for the sake of some adventitious quality – as that it fitted here, or was the right colour to go there – never for its truth'. De Quincey's accounts of his past, in the *Confessions* and elsewhere, are powerfully seductive. But they need to be resisted. This biography points on several occasions to the gaps and inconsistencies that lie both within and between his various accounts of his past, and highlights the ways in which, for De Quincey, self-representation was often the subtlest form of self-concealment.

The portrait that emerges in these pages is of a man of enormous gifts who was both damaged and inspired by his fate. I have attempted to reveal De Quincey in all his complexity, to strip away the notion of him as simply a 'disciple' of Wordsworth and Coleridge, or a 'hack' writer who spent his career churning out respectable padding for the magazines, or a famous 'addict' who happened also to be a writer, or a Tory 'bigot' who despised radicalism and – especially – the East. As this book argues, De Quincey transcends these reductions. He was a supreme stylist with a remarkably diverse repertoire that extended from the impassioned and the humorous to the conversational and the taut. He was an iconoclast who repeatedly confounded his own sometimes virulent conservatism with both public acts of defiance and unconventionality, and with profound expressions of sympathy for the disenfranchised, the impoverished, and the abused. He made valuable contributions to political economy, biography, auto-biography, philosophy, satire, translation, history, classical scholarship, and terror fiction. He is commonly thought of as a 'Romantic' essayist, but he produced some of his finest work – including *Suspiria de Profundis*, *The English Mail-Coach*, 'A Sketch from Childhood', the 'Postscript' to 'On Murder', and the revised version of the *Confessions* – in the Victorian age, and while he remained deeply invested in the genius of Wordsworth and Coleridge, his work is often most revealingly read alongside the writings of Poe, Barrett Browning, the Brontës, Nathaniel Hawthorne, Wilkie Collins, and Charles Dickens, all of whom read and admired him. Far more than the other great essayists who were his contemporaries – Lamb, Hazlitt, Emerson, and Carlyle – De Quincey speaks to us directly about our divisions, our addictions, our losses, our selves. This is the first biography to take account of the complete range of his published and unpublished writings, and to demonstrate both the vital role he played in shaping his own age, and his enduring relevance in ours.

A Note on the Text

De Quincey filled his letters and manuscripts with abbreviations, which I have expanded for the sake of clarity. Thus, for example, I have amended his 'hitt^g him a dab on his disgust^g face' to read 'hitting him a dab on his disgusting face'; his '*the Rel^s of X^{ty} to man*' to read '*the Relations of Christianity to man*'; and his 'y^t I am thus made a party . . . to the ill-treatm^t, ye undervalu^n of my own truth' to read 'that I am thus made a party . . . to the ill-treatment, the undervaluation of my own truth'.

De Quincey wrote his last name with both an upper and a lower case 'd', and friends, correspondents, and critics regularly produced other variations: 'Quince', 'Quincy', 'De Quincy', 'Dequincey', and so on. I have allowed all of these inconsistencies to stand, though he appears as 'De Quincey' in my own references to him, in accordance with long-established custom and the precedent of his four previous biographers.

In the Notes and Bibliography, references to some nineteenth-century magazine articles contain a question mark in square brackets to indicate that the authorship of those articles is conjectural.

The Sphinx's Riddle

Edinburgh. A spring morning in 1850. An elderly man walks towards the city from Mavis Bush Cottage, a handsome, grey-stone building situated on the steep road that winds between the villages of Polton and Lasswade. It is a seven-mile journey and he knows the route intimately. It takes him about three hours. This morning he sets off before nine and travels steadily and alone, as he usually does. He is a short man, under five feet tall, yet his features are striking. His head retains the same beautiful shape of his youth, though the lines of his face have become pinched and drawn. His fine brown hair is greying but only just beginning to recede. The steep and prominent cliff of his forehead gives the appearance of deep thought, while his pale blue eyes combine scrutiny with weariness. He has lost most of his teeth so that his upper lip has all but disappeared and his lower projects like a little shelf. His clothing is careless. This morning he wears an Inverness cape which is much too large, and which serves him as both an under- and an overcoat. He has an air of gentlemanly refinement, despite his unkempt appearance.

His destination is 4 Nicolson Street, near the looming Old College of the University of Edinburgh, where the publisher James Hogg has recently established his headquarters. It is approaching midday before he reaches the front door and passes into the building. Mr Hogg, he is told, is not in. An accident at the printing office has forced him to take temporary premises in the suburb of Canonmills, and he is working there this morning. Undaunted, the man journeys an additional mile north across the Bridges, down through the New Town, and into Canonmills, where he enters Mr Hogg's office and explains to him the purpose of his visit. He wishes to become an occasional contributor to *Hogg's Instructor*, a monthly magazine of topical reviews, essays, and new fiction. Hogg greets the proposal with enthusiasm, for he has been quick to realize who his visitor is. The two men discuss payment and an agreement is soon reached. Tucking a hastily pencilled note from Hogg into his large coat, the man leaves the office, labours back up the New Town hill, and returns to the Nicolson Street headquarters shortly after four o'clock.

Now considerably fatigued, he asks to see Mr James Hogg junior, the proprietor's son. The younger Hogg is notified and descends from an upper office. With an air of quiet good breeding, the man introduces himself. He is Thomas De Quincey. Like his father, Hogg junior knows him immediately as the author of the *Confessions of an English Opium-Eater*, a work that had first appeared nearly thirty years earlier, and that had launched De Quincey on a distinguished, sometimes scandalous career in the mass media, where he had published on everything from philosophy, politics, history, economics, and literary theory to the lives of famous contemporaries, the pleasures and pains of opium, the afflictions of childhood, and the fine art of murder. In a voice gentle, clear, and silvery, De Quincey explains that he has a manuscript called 'The Sphinx's Riddle', which Mr Hogg senior has already seen and accepted for publication. Then, drawing the manuscript from one pocket and a small brush from another, De Quincey proceeds to dust each sheet before handing it to Hogg.

The pencilled note from Hogg senior is now produced. It contains instructions on payment. Hogg observes that De Quincey looks tired, and invites him into his office, where De Quincey takes a chair by the desk and is paid. As he rests, De Quincey begins to discourse on the subject of his manuscript. To the sphinx's riddle about which creature moves on four feet in the morning, two at noon-day, and three in the evening, Oedipus had correctly answered 'Man'. De Quincey, however, suggests that the full and final answer is Oedipus himself, who 'drew his very name ... from the injury done to his infant feet', who 'walked upright by his own masculine vigour', and who was 'guided and cheered' by 'holy Antigone', as 'the *third* foot that should support his steps'. De Quincey speaks with fervour on the grandeur and gloom of the ancient mystery until it seems to possess him. Time slips away as evening closes in, and it is more than an hour before he brings the discussion to a close. Rising refreshed, he prepares to depart, with his money and his brush in his coat. Hogg wonders how he will return to Mavis Bush. 'I shall, as usual, walk,' De Quincey replies. 'It is now only six o'clock, and I shall reach home about nine.' He bids Hogg farewell and makes his way out of Edinburgh.

'The Sphinx's Riddle' appeared shortly thereafter in *Hogg's Instructor*, and De Quincey became a valued contributor to the magazine. By the time he began to work for the Hoggs, his life had been ravaged by drug addiction, poverty, and despair. But his remarkable resilience meant that his conversation and his prose rarely showed these strains. In the years that followed, the Hoggs worked closely with him as he produced the first multi-volume edition of his writings. They saw him despondent, ill, irritable, and run aground. Nevertheless, every time he turned a manuscript over to them he brandished his 'famous *brush*,' and carefully cleaned each sheet, holding it 'first one way, and then the other'. In a life in which chaos so often reigned, it was a vivid token of the pride he took in what he wrote.

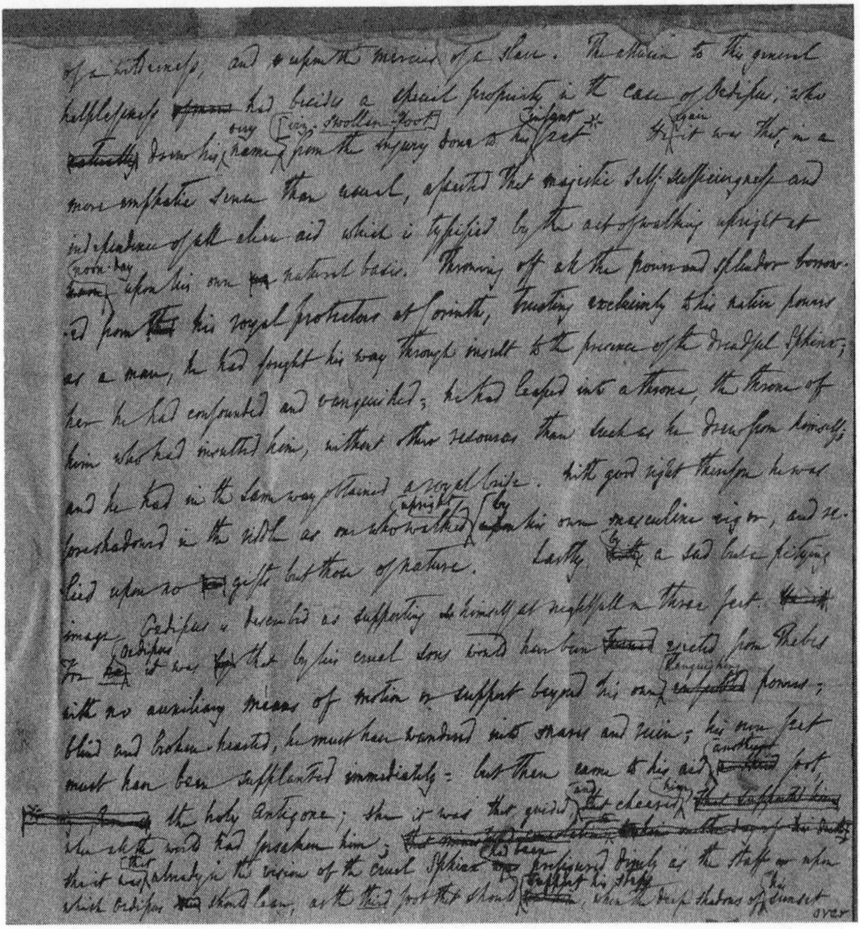

Figure 1: The only extant manuscript page from De Quincey's essay on 'The Sphinx's Riddle'. Beginning towards the end of the top line, De Quincey writes that 'The allusion to this general helplessness had besides a special propriety in the case of Oedipus, who drew his own name (viz. Swollen-Foot) from the injury done to his infant feet.'

PART ONE
DREAMS
1785–1804

ONE

Life is Finished

[i]

During a chance meeting at Windsor, King George III asked a teenage Thomas De Quincey about his descent. It was a tender point. 'Please your majesty, the family has been in England since the Conquest.' De Quincey was proud of his family lineage, and always anxious to dispel the notion that his last name was either 'foreign or outlandish'.[1] The story he liked to tell runs as follows. Originally Norwegian, 'the family of De Quincey, or Quincy, or Quincie' migrated south to Normandy, where it threw off 'three separate swarms – French, English, and Anglo-American'. De Quincey's kin attached themselves to William the Conqueror, following him into England, producing the earls of Winchester, and branching out splendidly into Scotland. More recently, from the same English stock had grown the distinguished American family of Quincy, while in Britain the remains of the Winchester estates were home to several squires, the last of whom was an elder kinsman of De Quincey's father. This account was undoubtedly part of family lore, and De Quincey rehearsed it with conviction. It gave him a strong sense of nobility and achievement, evident most clearly in his insistence that his last name was to be spelled with what he called 'the aristocratic *De*'.[2]

Genealogical investigation, however, has revealed that De Quincey's claims about his grand ancestry cannot be proven, and are almost certainly apocryphal.[3] At the same time, what is known of his origins is actually very slight. On his paternal side, there is a very dubious report that his grandfather was a wine-drinking, fox-hunting country gentleman who hailed from Ashby-de-la-Zouche in Leicestershire, and who fathered nearly two dozen children. The information concerning his father is more reliable. He was plain Thomas Quincey, born in 1753 or 1754, and most probably in or near Boston in Lincolnshire.[4] Beginning with a patrimony of £6000, he went into trade, and before long he and his brother John had found their way to London, where by 1775 they had established themselves as linen drapers in Cheapside.[5]

Early in the following year, however, the brothers migrated to Manchester, the centre of cotton manufacture in England, and in an 18 March advertisement in the *Manchester Mercury* respectfully informed 'the Ladies and Gentlemen, and the inhabitants of the town and neighbourhood (as well as the public in general)' that they had 'opened a shop, No. 10, at the Bottom of Market-Street Lane'. The business was clearly a success from the start, for within a month the brothers announced that they had 'now added to their stock a regular assortment of Haberdashery goods', and had also received from London 'a capital choice of printed Linens, Musslins, Furnitures, and other Cottons, all of the most approved spring patterns'. In July, they begged leave, 'once more, to remind Ladies of their Chip Hats, and especially of their Open Chips, which they sell so remarkably low', while in August 'an immense importation' of Drogheda linens was 'hourly expected'. More advertisements – or 'literary addresses', as Thomas Quincey referred to them – kept the public informed of buying trips to London and Chester, as well as '3 annual voyages to Ireland'. By 1780 the brothers were thriving both as linen drapers and as importers of Irish linen and West Indian cotton.[6]

On the maternal side, De Quincey's grandparents were Sarah and Samuel Penson. She was 'gentle', in De Quincey's only recollection, while he was 'very aristocratic', and 'at one time held an office under the king ... which conferred the title of *Esquire*'. 'Traditional prejudice' in the family had 'always directed their views to the military profession', so he may well have been a soldier. The couple had two sons, Edward and Thomas, both of whom obtained lieutenancies in the East India Company's service in Bengal, where Edward died of sunstroke shortly after arriving, and Thomas went on to enjoy a lucrative career.[7] The Pensons also had a daughter, Elizabeth, who seems to have been born in the late 1740s or early 1750s, and who lived with her parents in North Street, London.[8] Elizabeth occupied a 'more elevated' social position than Thomas Quincey, and how and where she met him is unknown. But in November 1780 the couple were married at St George's, Queen Square in London, and began their life together, most probably in the rooms over Quincey's shop in Cromford Court, Market-Street Lane.[9]

Within weeks of the wedding, the Quincey brothers dissolved their partnership for reasons that are not known, and Thomas ventured out on his own.[10] Eighteen months later he was operating from at least two different locations – one in Manchester and the other at 'Linen Hall, Chester' – and in 1783, he announced his decision 'to decline all retail trade', and concentrate on the wholesale side of his business.[11] 'My father was a merchant

... in the English sense,' De Quincey declared; '... that is, he was a man engaged in *foreign* commerce, and no other.'[12] This may have been the case from 1783 onward, but Thomas Quincey began as a 'shopkeeper' who then worked his way up to the respectability of 'merchant'.

De Quincey conceded that his father was not clever, but he was a man of great moral integrity. At a time when many West Indian merchants were making a fortune from the slave trade, he not only avoided any connection with it, but was so far 'from lending himself even by a *passive* concurrence to this most memorable abomination, that he was one of those conscientious protesters who ... strictly abstained from the use of sugar in his own family'. Years later a stranger would occasionally say to De Quincey, 'Sir, I knew your father: he was the most upright man I ever met with in my life.'[13]

Before long there were children. William (born 1781/82) was followed by Elizabeth (1783), Mary (1784), and then Thomas, who was born on 15 August 1785. The exact location has long been a matter of debate, but it was almost certainly in a building later known as the Prince's Tavern (which stood formerly at the corner of Cross and John Dalton Streets), or at the house in Market-Street Lane (now under the present Arndale Shopping Centre).[14] He was baptized on Friday, 23 September at St Ann's Church by the Reverend Samuel Hall, a close family friend, and named Thomas Penson, after his mother's brother. Four more children followed: Jane (1786–90); Richard, always known in the family as 'Pink' because of his beautiful complexion (1789); another Jane (1790/91); and Henry (1793/94).[15]

Little of Thomas's childhood was spent in the city of Manchester, for shortly after his birth his father seems to have taken a town residence in Fountain Street, and moved his family outside the city limits to a place at Moss Side known as The Farm, 'a pretty rustic dwelling', as Thomas himself recalled, though elsewhere he more accurately refers to it as a 'country-house'.[16] His earliest memories date from here, and occurred, he claimed, before he was two years old. One concerned feelings of 'a powerful character ... connected with some clusters of crocuses in the garden'; another involved a 'passion of grief' felt in 'a profound degree, for the death of a beautiful bird, a king-fisher'; and a third was 'a remarkable dream of terrific grandeur about a favourite nurse' that Thomas particularly valued because it demonstrated his 'dreaming tendencies to have been constitutional', and not dependent upon opium.[17]

More distinctly, at three and a half years old, he recalled witnessing the illuminations to celebrate the recovery of George III from his first attack of insanity, and a year later he could remember trying to save vagrant spiders from the wrath of the housemaids.[18] Perhaps his most revealing memory from these early years, however, was a recurrent dream about 'meeting a lion, and, from languishing prostration in hope and vital energy, that constant sequel of lying down before him'. Thomas came later to think that maybe all children had such a dream, and that it enacted 'the original temptation in Eden', where 'every one of us' has a bait offered to an infirm place in our will, and all of us completed for ourselves 'the aboriginal fall'. He set great store upon these early recollections. Children, he believed, were 'endowed with a special power of listening for the tones of truth – hidden, struggling, or remote'.[19]

When Thomas was six years old, his family left The Farm for a much larger house about a mile outside of Manchester, on the edge of what is now Hulme. Christened 'Greenhay' by Mrs Quincey, it was designed almost entirely according to her views 'of domestic elegance and propriety', and gave its name to the district which is still known as Greenheys. Thomas remembered the home as 'elegant but plain, and having nothing remarkable about it but the doors and windows of the superior rooms, which were made of mahogany, sent as a present from a foreign correspondent'. Elsewhere, however, he referred to 'such circumstances of luxury or aristocratic elegance as surrounded' him in childhood.[20] A contemporary painting of Greenhay shows it to be a handsome square box of a house, with a characteristically eighteenth-century façade of five windows and a portico, fronted by a sweeping drive and backed by trees and various outbuildings, including offices, a gardener's house, stables, and a coachhouse.[21] It cost Quincey £6000, and clearly reflected his burgeoning prosperity. Indeed, in the 'internal economy' of Greenhay, Thomas claimed that his parents 'erred by too much profusion'. There were 'too many servants; and those servants were maintained in a style of luxury and comfort, not often matched in the mansions of the nobility'.[22]

A small and shy child, Thomas was often ill 'with ague', a well-established, if vague, medical term usually associated with acute or violent fevers. At three he suffered too from 'hooping-cough', and was 'carried for change of air to different places on the Lancashire coast'. Riding on horseback was 'the remedy chiefly employed' for curing these maladies, and as a very young boy he was 'placed on a pillow, in front of a cankered old man, upon a large white horse'.[23] Arsenic – widely prescribed by physicians throughout the nineteenth century – was 'then never administered', but opium was an ingredient in many conventional medicines for a large number of complaints, and as a young child Thomas may well have taken it, though he was confident that no medicine prescribed during his first twenty-one months contained the drug. Up until the completion of his sixth year, he was 'a privileged pet' who 'naturally . . . learned to appreciate the indulgent tenderness of women'.[24] Rather more dangerously, he came both to crave the attention that sickness brought him, and to use it as a device to avoid tasks that he disliked.

In 1788, the elder Quincey took on a new partner, Robert Duck, who managed the business affairs in Manchester, while Quincey himself began to spend more time travelling abroad, both to pursue trade opportunities and to seek out warmer climates, for he had begun to show early signs of tuberculosis.[25] 'He lived for months in Portugal, at Lisbon, and at Cintra; next in Madeira; then in the West Indies; sometimes in Jamaica, sometimes in St Kitt's,' though he returned repeatedly to England, where he met his wife and children 'at watering-places on the south coast of Devonshire'. Thomas, however, was not 'one of the party selected for such excursions from home', and by the time he was seven he doubted – with evident exaggeration – whether his father 'would have been able to challenge me as a relative; nor I *him*, had we happened to meet on the public roads'.[26]

Yet while health concerns forced him to spend more and more time away from home, Quincey had cultural and literary interests which made a deep impression on his son. Frequent guests to the house included the Reverend Hall, and the distinguished physicians Thomas Percival and Charles White, who served as the family doctor. All three men were founding members of the Manchester Literary and Philosophical Society, suggesting that Quincey was at least on the cusp of an intellectual coterie.[27] What is more, like many members of the merchant class, he 'applied a very considerable proportion' of his income to 'intellectual pleasures'. Large gardens and a greenhouse provided a good deal of enjoyment. His small collection of paintings by the old Italian masters was scattered through the principal rooms of his home. He 'loved literature with a passionate love', especially the writings of William Cowper and Samuel Johnson.[28]

His library was rather more modest than Thomas remembered, but it laid the foundation for a number of his subsequent interests, and contained sections devoted to theology, biography, history, geography, travels, 'Novels and Romances' (including works by Fielding, Goldsmith, Lesage, Smollett, and Mackenzie), 'Poetry and Plays' (editions of Ovid, Shakespeare, Congreve, Swift, Pope, Gray, Young, and many others), and a wide range of titles listed under 'Miscellaneous' (such as Sterne's *Tristram Shandy* and Burke's *A Philosophical Enquiry into the Origin of Our Ideas of the Sublime and Beautiful*).[29] Quincey even published a book, *A Short Tour in the Midland Counties of England* (1775), in which he moves rather prosaically over such topics as drainage, emigration, architecture, and inclosures, but in which he also quotes Milton, surveys Oxford University with enthusiasm, and – 'growing poetical' – links the pioneer canal builder James Brindley with Shakespeare as 'the darling heirs of fame'. Looking back, Thomas had only two complaints: his father did not introduce enough music into the home, and he was rather too deferential of a college education.[30]

Thomas's mother had a more profound and less positive impact. She was attentive, tranquil, generous, and devout. But she was cold. The intense and often Calvinistic piety which governed her actions led her to assume guilt in those around her, and eventually culminated in her enduring commitment to Evangelicalism, a movement that had begun within the Church of England only a few decades earlier, and that emphasized biblical faith, personal salvation, and social welfare.[31] 'Amongst her faults never was numbered any levity of principle, or carelessness of the most scrupulous veracity; but, on the contrary, such faults as arise from austerity, too hard perhaps, and gloomy – indulgent neither to others nor herself.' To her friends, she was an 'object of idolizing reverence'. To the servants at Greenhay, however, she was a source of both trepidation and amusement, for her insistence on the marked difference between her social position and theirs meant that she 'never communicated with them directly but only through a housekeeper'. One maid was asked 'why in a case of supposed wrong she had not spoken to her mistress'. 'Speak to mistress?' she retorted. 'Would I speak to a ghost?'[32]

When it came to her role as a mother, Mrs Quincey was similarly severe. To some extent, the situation demanded it: there were eight children in thirteen years, and she was often forced to parent them without the assistance of her ailing husband. Yet at the same time, she clearly found little pleasure in motherhood: 'she delighted not in infancy, nor infancy in her', as Thomas memorably put it. Her approach was to govern the nursery with a combination of detachment and regimentation that undoubtedly owed a good deal to her family's military background. Every morning for some six years she had her children marched or carried into her dressing room, where they were minutely reviewed in succession for posture, dress, cleanliness, and health, before being dismissed with 'two ceremonies that to us were mysterious and allegorical – first that our hair and faces were sprinkled with lavender-water and milk of roses, secondly that we received a kiss on the forehead'.[33]

Thomas, even at that early age, seems to have known that something was missing in his relationship with his mother. He wanted love. She wanted duty. He wanted understanding. She wanted discipline. He wanted praise.

She wanted humility. 'Usually mothers defend their own cubs right or wrong ... Not so my mother ... Did a visitor say some flattering thing of a talent or accomplishment by one or other of us? My mother protested so solemnly against the possibility that we could possess either one or the other, that we children held it a point of filial duty to believe ourselves the very scamps and refuse of the universe.' In retrospect, Thomas could see only two qualities in his mother that he was able to turn to advantage: her 'polished manners', and the 'singular elegance' with which she 'spoke and wrote English'.[34]

Given his father's many absences and his mother's relentless austerity, it is perhaps not surprising that Thomas retreated into the feminine world of the nursery, where he bonded more closely with his three sisters – Mary, Jane, and especially Elizabeth – than he did with either of his parents.[35] He basked too in the pleasure of being the only boy in this world. His elder brother William had at 'an early stage of his career ... been found wholly unmanageable', and his parents had sent him away to Louth Grammar School in Lincolnshire, while his younger brother 'Pink' was still an infant, and unable to join in the activities of the group. 'With three innocent little sisters for playmates, sleeping always amongst them, and shut up for ever in a silent garden from all knowledge of poverty, or oppression, or outrage', Thomas recalled this existence as a kind of paradise.[36]

He and Elizabeth read a great deal, though 'she was much beyond me in velocity of apprehension, and many other qualities of intellect'.[37] Their favourite books included *The Arabian Nights*, Anna Laetitia Barbauld's *Hymns in Prose for Children*, Thomas Bewick's *General History of Quadrupeds*, and Thomas Percival's *A Father's Instructions*, which contained a tale of 'noble revenge' that made Elizabeth weep.[38] It was an illustrated Bible, however, especially as read to the four children by a young nurse, which was most frequently in demand. 'The fitful gloom and sudden lambencies of the room by firelight suited our evening state of feelings; and they suited, also, the divine revelations of power and mysterious beauty which awed us. Above all, the story of a just man – man and yet *not* man, real above all things, and yet shadowy above all things – who had suffered the passion of death in Palestine, slept upon our minds like early dawn upon the waters.' Several decades later, when he came to review his nursery experience, Thomas counted four central blessings: 'that I lived in the country; that I lived in solitude; that my infant feelings were moulded by the gentlest of sisters, not by horrid pugilistic brothers; finally, that I and they were dutiful children of a pure, holy, and magnificent church'.[39]

[ii]

Death shattered this calm in a terrible series of crescendoing blows. His maternal grandmother, Sarah Penson, who by this time was living at Greenhay, died on 16 January 1790, aged sixty-nine years. 'Our nursery party knew her but little', and Thomas was only vaguely aware of her passing.[40] Two months later he lost his sister Jane. But again, at only four and a half years old, her death was 'scarcely intelligible to me, and I could not so properly be said to suffer sorrow as a sad perplexity'. Indeed, more upsetting for Thomas than the loss of one of his 'nursery playmates' was the rumour that spread about a servant who had lost her temper with the sick child, perhaps to the point of striking her. The story seems never to have reached Mrs Quincey, but its effect upon Thomas 'was terrific', especially on those rare occasions when he actually saw the servant in question. 'The feeling which fell upon me was a shuddering horror, as upon a first glimpse of the truth that I was in a world of evil and strife.'[41]

If Jane's death left Thomas with the sense that she would come again – 'summer and winter came again ... why not little Jane?' – the death two years later of his beloved sister Elizabeth awakened him from that delusion, and 'launched God's thunderbolt' at his heart. A prodigy in the 'large and comprehensive' grasp of her intellect, Elizabeth had otherwise 'the usual slowness of a melancholy child'.[42] Thomas idolized her. She was his confidante: 'never but to thee only, never again since thy departure, *durst* I utter the feelings which possessed me'. She was his security: 'for me ... where my sister was, there was paradise.' She was his second self: 'having that capacious heart overflowing, even as mine overflowed, with tenderness, and stung, even as mine was stung, by the necessity of being loved'. Her illness set in one Sunday evening in spring after she walked home with a servant through some meadows. Soon she was confined to her bed. Percival and White attended her, but on 2 June 1792, she died.[43] Thomas believed that the cause was what was known as 'hydrocephalus', but it was most probably cerebro-spinal meningitis. When a nurse came to tell him the news, he simply could not take it in. 'Rightly it is said of utter, utter misery, that it "cannot be remembered" ... Mere anarchy and confusion of mind fell upon me.'[44] Thomas was just six years old.

On the day following Elizabeth's death, he determined to see her again. About one o'clock in the afternoon he crept up the stairs and to the door of her chamber. It was locked, but the key was there, and he stole in, closing the door behind him 'so softly, that, although it opened upon a hall which ascended through all the stories, no echo ran along the silent walls'. Turning round, he sought his sister's face, but her bed had been moved, and nothing met his eyes 'but one large window wide open, through which the sun of midsummer at noonday was showering down torrents of splendour'. He walked towards the 'gorgeous sunlight', and then turned round again.[45] There lay the corpse.

People in the house had said that Elizabeth's features had not suffered any change. 'Had they not? The forehead indeed, the serene and noble forehead, *that* might be the same; but the frozen eyelids, the darkness that seemed to steal from beneath them, the marble lips, the stiffening hands, laid palm to palm, as if repeating the supplications of closing anguish, could these be mistaken for life?' Not fear, but awe, possessed him as 'a solemn wind began to blow – the most mournful that ear ever heard ... It was a wind that had swept the fields of mortality for a hundred centuries.' Instantly a trance fell upon him.

A vault seemed to open in the zenith of the far blue sky, a shaft which ran up for ever. I in spirit rose as if on billows that also ran up the shaft for ever; and the billows seemed to pursue the throne of God; but *that* also ran before us and fled away continually. The flight and the pursuit seemed to go on for ever and ever. Frost, gathering frost, some Sarsar wind of death, seemed to repel me; I slept – for how long I cannot say; slowly I recovered my self-possession, and found myself standing, as before, close to my sister's bed.

Almost at that moment he heard a footstep on the stair. Alarmed that, if discovered, he would be prevented from coming again, he leaned forward hastily, kissed Elizabeth's lips, and then 'slunk like a guilty thing with stealthy steps from the room'.[46]

The following day the medical men came. There had been some anomalies in Elizabeth's condition, and they decided that 'her head ... should be opened'. The procedure was performed by White, who afterwards 'declared often that the child's brain was "the most beautiful" he had ever seen'. Some hours after the men had withdrawn, Thomas crept again to his sister's bedchamber. Again the door was locked, but this time the key was taken away, and he was shut out for ever. At least Thomas never admitted that he had gained entry to Elizabeth's room after the autopsy. Indeed, he claimed that he was 'happy' to have failed in his attempt, for if the doctor's bandages had not covered all the wounds in his sister's head, he would have had to endure the 'shock' of 'disfiguring images'. Yet at the same time it seems clear that Thomas did suffer some kind of trauma, as he hints in this passage and in several others. He denied it, but perhaps he did see 'the cruel changes' wrought in his sister's head, or thought he saw them, or at least imagined himself as seeing them.[47] Certainly he was haunted several decades later by the image of a skull in ruins.

Next came the funeral. Thomas was put in a carriage with some gentlemen he did not know and taken to St Ann's Church, where he was instructed to hold a white handkerchief to his eye as a token of his sorrow. But 'what need had *he* of masques or mockeries, whose heart died within him at every word that was uttered?' During the service, he sank back continually into his own darkness, and heard little 'except some fugitive strains from the sublime chapter of St Paul'. Thereafter, people moved outside for 'the magnificent service which the English church performs at the side of the grave'. All eyes surveyed 'the record of name, of sex, of age, and the day of departure from earth – records how useless!' Finally, as the sacristan stood ready with his shovel of earth and stones, the priest's voice was heard – '*earth to earth*', and the dreaded rattle ascended 'from the lid of the coffin'; '*ashes to ashes*', and again 'the killing sound' was heard; '*dust to dust*', and the 'farewell volley' announced that 'the grave – the coffin – the face' were 'sealed up for ever'.[48]

Thomas represented the death of Elizabeth as the most harrowing episode of his life. He rehearsed it over and over again in a formative but fruitless attempt to master his sorrow. He never did. The 'desolating grief' he felt at her death marked his terrible fall from Eden into self-consciousness, and stayed with him until the end.[49] In the months that followed, he roamed the grounds of Greenhay, or walked through the neighbouring fields, wearying 'the heavens with my inquest of beseeching looks'. He sat in church and 'wept in secret', while his 'sorrow-haunted eye' saw 'visions of beds with white lawny curtains; and in the beds lay sick children, dying children, that were tossing in anguish'. He sought relief in 'the consolations of ... solitude, which, when acting as a co-agency with unresisted grief, end in the paradoxical result of making out of grief itself a luxury; such a luxury as finally becomes a snare, overhanging life itself, and the energies of life, with growing menaces'. For Thomas, Elizabeth was 'the peace, the rest, the central security which belong to love that is past all understanding'. When she dies, he cannot escape the feeling that '*Life is Finished! Finished it is!*'[50]

But in what sense 'could *that* be true?' For a boy who was not yet seven years old, 'was it possible that the promise of life had been really blighted? or its golden pleasures exhausted?' No, he confessed. There were raptures still to come, and many of them would bring him happiness. 'Had I read Milton? Had I heard Mozart?' Even raptures, though, were 'modes of *troubled* pleasure', and they could in no way replace the 'unfathomable' love that had 'brooded over those four latter years of my infancy'.[51] Later, he tried to rationalize his misery. He told himself that he had been elected by grief: 'upon me, as upon others scattered thinly by tens and twenties over every thousand years, fell too powerfully and too early the vision of life'. He told himself that the afflictions of his childhood had stripped away affectation to reveal what was primary in the self: he stood 'nearer to the type of the original nature in man', and was 'truer than others to the great magnet in our dark planet'. He told himself that sorrow brought wisdom: 'either the human being must suffer and struggle as the price of a more searching vision, or his gaze must be shallow and without intellectual revelation'.[52] He constructed these myths of his past as an attempt at salvation, and he repeated them often, but in the end they did little to heal the terrible puncture of Elizabeth's death.

There was one more blow to come – a kind of grim coda. Two and a half weeks after Elizabeth passed away, Thomas Quincey made his will, and the following spring he boarded a West India packet back to England to die. Mrs Quincey went to meet him, and the two then travelled together to Greenhay. They were expected on an evening of 'unusual solemnity', and the children and servants waited on the lawn for several hours, before moving out of the grounds near midnight to take one last look for the returning couple. Almost immediately, to their general surprise, they saw horses' heads emerging 'from the deep gloom of the shady lane', moving at a 'hearse-like pace', and drawing a carriage in which 'the dying patient was reclining' against a 'mass of white pillows'.[53]

Quincey lingered for weeks on a sofa, and Thomas, from his 'repose of manners', was allowed often to go and visit him. On 29 June, Quincey added three codicils to his will, but by 4 July the consumption was far advanced, and he was 'in too ill a state of bodily infirmity to dictate much at large', though he was calmed by the knowledge that his wife and his principal clerk, John Kelsall, were in 'full possession of all particulars' related to 'the management of the trade'. Exactly two weeks later, on 18 July 1793, he died.[54] Thomas was 'present at his bedside in the closing hour of his life, which exhaled quietly, amidst snatches of delirious conversation with some imaginary visiters'. 'I was greatly affected at hearing him moan out to my mother a few minutes before he died – Oh Betty Betty! why will you never come and help me to raise this weight?'[55]

The will was detailed and thoughtful. Quincey left an unburdened estate producing exactly £1600 a year. When his four sons respectively attained the age of twenty-one, they were to have a yearly allowance of £150 each;

his two daughters, when they respectively reached majority, were to have £100 each. The remainder of the assets – including Greenhay itself and a share in the New Linen Hall in Chester – were put at the disposal of his widow. He saw 'no reason' why she and the children should not live at Greenhay, but if the decision was made to sell the property, Mrs Quincey should wait until 'better times have raised' its value.[56] In addition to their mother, the children were left in the care of four guardians, all of whom also served as executors: Thomas Belcher, a merchant; James Entwhistle, a rural magistrate; the Reverend Hall; and Henry Gee, a Lincolnshire banker and 'the wisest of the whole band'. Quincey's death 'made little or no change in the household economy, except that my mother ever afterwards kept a carriage; which my father, in effect, exacted upon his death-bed'.[57]

[iii]

'The deep deep tragedies of infancy' drove a shaft for the young boy 'into the worlds of death and darkness which never again closed'. On the surface, however, he carried on with the routines of Greenhay. At eight years old he was 'passionately fond of study' to the exclusion of childish 'play', though he made two exceptions: he 'invented a sport called *Trojd* (the details of which are not known), and he enjoyed gunpowder, which brought him 'the common boyish pleasure'. Whenever it was 'unavoidable to play at something, gunpowder was always my resource'.[58]

Greenhay often welcomed visitors, including his uncle Penson from Bengal, other relatives from Boston, and Mrs Quincey's friend Mrs Schreiber and her wards, Miss Smith and Miss Watson, both of whom carried Thomas about 'like a doll' until his eighth or ninth year. At one point Thomas 'met a niece of John Wesley, the Proto-Methodist', and at another he engaged in daily disputes with an unknown old lady 'whose *forte* was not logic'.[59] Most memorably, Mrs Quincey invited Rachel Fanny Antonina Lee to spend a few days at the house as a way of thanking her for conveying Thomas's sister Mary to a mutual acquaintance. Beautiful, talented, and wealthy, Lee was an illegitimate daughter of the notorious libertine Francis Dashwood, and boldly disputatious in her anti-Christian views. During dinner one day, she engaged in debate with both Hall, and another close family friend, the Reverend John Clowes, running theological circles around both, and shocking Mrs Quincey so thoroughly that, 'for the first and the last time in her long and healthy life', she succumbed to an 'alarming nervous attack'.[60]

Thomas spent some time away from Greenhay. On rare occasions he went with his family to the theatre. More commonly he was taken to see a picture gallery in a nearby house. Once he was given a tour of White's personal museum, where he 'gazed ... with inexpressible awe' upon an English clock-case that he was told housed the mummified body of a wealthy old lady. As a guest in the home of his guardian, Thomas Belcher, he first heard the music of Arcangelo Corelli, Niccolò Jommelli, and Domenico Cimarosa. 'But, above all ... at the house of this guardian, I heard sung a long canon of Cherubini's ... It was sung by four male voices, and rose into a region of thrilling passion, such as my heart had always dimly craved and hungered after, but which now first interpreted itself, as a physical possibility, to my ear.'[61]

When he was seven years old, Thomas was allowed to travel down into Lincolnshire to visit relatives, accompanied only by an arrogant eighteen-year-old 'blood' who had advertised for a travelling companion. On the morning of Thomas's departure, his mother 'shed more milk of roses, I believe, upon my cheeks than tears', whereas the servants fussed over him, and kissed him 'without check or art'. Thomas and his companion were on the road for several hours before they stopped to dine at Chesterfield, where both consumed a good deal of wine, and the landlord plied them with facetious reports of desperate highwaymen on the road ahead. Flushed and excited, the boys set out again, Thomas's companion priming his travelling pistols in anticipation of the danger. Soon, however, the wine 'applied a remedy to its own delusions', and by the time the boys' carriage reached Mansfield, both were fast asleep.[62] Thomas was drinking from a very early age, and his first known experience of alcohol revealed to him its paradoxical effects.

There were plenty of pets at Greenhay, and Thomas had a great fondness for them. In the evenings he often helped to walk two of the family dogs, Turk and Grim: 'always we took them through the fields ... and closed with giving them a cold bath in the brook which bounded my father's property'. When he was eight years old, Thomas was also given a kitten, which he loved passionately, and which Turk unfortunately killed. When shown the 'little creature dead', Thomas sat down upon a 'huge block of coal' and burst into tears. He could not, however, blame Turk, for the dog boiled with so much life that Thomas could not endure to see its misery when it was rechained at the end of its evening walk. Within a year, Turk and Grim were also dead, poisoned by a party of burglars. The episodes left behind in Thomas a conviction that 'brute creatures' had a right 'to a merciful for-bearance on the part of man', as well as 'a gloomy impression, that suffering and wretchedness were diffused amongst all creatures that breathe'.[63]

Thomas now had pocket money. And almost simultaneously, he now had debt. To some degree, the allowance was 'safely entrusted' to him because he 'never spent or desired to spend' even a fraction of it 'upon any thing but books', which inspired within him a need to consume that was 'absolutely endless and inexorable as the grave'.[64] 'Had the Vatican, the Bodleian, and the *Bibliothèque du Roi* been all emptied into one collection for my private gratification, little progress would have been made towards content in this particular craving.' Very soon he had run ahead of his weekly stipend by 'about three guineas'. Somebody was going to have to pay this debt. But 'who *was* that somebody?' With no 'confidential friend' to speak to, and a 'mysterious awe of ever alluding to it', Thomas gradually passed from a 'state of languishing desire' following the death of Elizabeth, to one of 'feverish irritation' as he attempted to cope with his arrears. It was not the amount to be paid. It was the principle of 'having presumed to contract debts on my own account, that I feared to have exposed'. In the event, no one even detected that the money was owed, but 'such was my simplicity, that I lived in constant terror'.[65]

A second item in this same case further exacerbated his anxieties about money. Thomas ordered 'a general history of navigation, supported by a vast body of voyages' from the bookseller, and then began to fret that such a work might tend to an infinite number of volumes, given how large the ocean was, and how many ships were 'eternally running up and down it'. Determined to know the worst, he went back to the bookseller to make enquiries, but his usual contact was busy and so he ended up speaking to a young clerk who was 'full of fun'. After describing the work he had ordered, Thomas asked the question that was to decide 'whether for the next two years I was to have an hour of peace': 'how many volumes did he think it would extend to?' 'Oh! really I can't say', the clerk replied in mock seriousness; 'maybe a matter of 15,000, be the same more or less.' Thomas missed the joke and was petrified. Without meaning to do so, he had contracted an obligation that was inexhaustible. His mind filled with panicked imaginings. In one, 'powerful men' pulling at a rope found his 'unhappy self hanging at the other end'. In another, waggoners brought cartloads of books to Greenhay and dumped them on the front lawn so that everyone could see his guilt and avarice.[66] The incident seems to mark the moment when Thomas first confronted the perverse logic of addiction, a logic which demanded that he negotiate an insatiable consumption that he both craved and loathed.[67] Books would later be replaced by more powerful stimulants.

The strife building within the boy was soon matched by equal pressures from without. Shortly after the death of her husband, Mrs Quincey decided to bring Thomas's older brother William home from Louth Grammar School, perhaps for financial reasons, perhaps in an attempt to incorporate him back within the family. The combative world of a public school, however, seems if anything to have intensified William's ungovernable spirit, and he exploded back into the Greenhay nursery, flying fire balloons, dropping cats by parachutes, building a 'humming-top' in an attempt to defy gravity, and declaiming to his siblings on all manner of topics, from the Thirty-Nine Articles of the English Church to 'How to raise a Ghost; and when you've got him down, how to keep him down.' At one point he gave a series of lectures on natural philosophy. At another he decided to dedicate himself to the tragic drama, and composed 'Sultan Selim', a title he promptly changed to 'Sultan Amurath', 'considering *that* a much fiercer name'.[68] All the children were given parts in the drama, but the first act was so bloody that scarcely any of the characters remained alive at the end of it.

William bullied Thomas. Roughly four years older, he was almost instantly contemptuous of the small, withdrawn, effeminate boy who had lived in the comfort of Greenhay while he had endured exile in Louth, who shed 'girlish tears' over the loss of his sister, and who had – as William sneered with some justice – 'always been tied to the apron-string of women or girls'. Thomas's response to these attacks was complicated. To a certain extent, he resisted them by occasionally displaying those powerful intellectual gifts that were clearly beginning to manifest themselves, and that undermined William's attempts to dismiss him as a nullity. Yet more commonly, he submitted to his brother, though he did so in two starkly different ways. On the one hand, when William demanded that he take part in even 'the most audacious of ... warlike plans', Thomas did it, for while he 'abominated' his brother's schemes, '*that* made no difference in the fidelity with which I tried to fulfil them'. On the other hand, when William berated him as useless, Thomas eagerly embraced his own humiliation, for in doing so he hoped to be left out of his brother's plans altogether. 'I had a perfect craze for being despised,' he confessed. '... Why not? Wherefore should any rational person shrink from contempt, if it happen to form the tenure by which he holds his repose in life?'[69]

Open hostilities were soon a part of Thomas's daily routine. His mother had decided to send him and William to be tutored by their guardian Hall, and their route to his home nearly two miles away in Salford involved crossing a bridge over the River Medlock, beside which stood a cotton factory full of working-class boys. As children of an 'opulent family', decked out in fashionably knee-high Hessian boots, the brothers were an obvious mark. One morning, just shortly after they had started with Hall, a factory boy saluted them with 'Holloa, Bucks', followed in a moment by a spiteful cry of 'Boots! boots!' That was all William needed to launch a shower of stones at the obstreperous enemy, and himself and his brother into a class warfare that involved running pitched battles on every morning and evening that they passed to and from Hall's. In a typical late-afternoon fracas, the brothers stuffed their pockets with stones and brickbats on the Greenhay side of the bridge as they waited for the 'smoky hive' to release its 'hornets', whereupon William moved to occupy the main high road, while Thomas deployed forty yards to the right. Most of these skirmishes ended with the Quincey boys fleeing, but in defiance of such gloomy news, William insisted 'twice, at the least, in every week, but sometimes every night' that he and his brother sing 'Te Deums' to commemorate their 'supposed victories'.[70]

On three occasions Thomas was captured by the enemy. Once he escaped. Once he was kicked and sent back with a menacing message for his brother. And once he was delivered over into the custody of young girls and women, one of whom snatched him up in her arms and kissed him, to which he responded with kisses of his own. Set free under the cover of petticoats and aprons, Thomas returned to Greenhay to discover that William had witnessed the entire reprehensible affair, and was preparing a bulletin which reported that his brother had 'for ever disgraced himself' by submitting to the caresses of the enemy. More bulletins followed in the form of a twice-weekly gazette, and Thomas found his military career the subject of wildly oscillating commentary. 'I suppose that no creature ever led such a life as *I* did in that gazette. Run up to the giddiest heights of promotion on one day, for merits which I could not myself discern, in a week or two I was brought to a court-martial for offences equally obscure.' The feud at the Oxford Road Bridge lasted until one day the boys' guardian, Belcher, happened to witness one of the clashes and saw to it that a truce was effected.[71] It is a measure of just how removed both their mother and their guardians were from their daily lives that these battles lasted for two years before being brought to a close.

Meanwhile, William was also engaging Thomas in psychological warfare. The boys invented imaginary kingdoms. William ruled over Tigrosylvania. Thomas was the king of Gombroon. When William announced that his capital city was located 65 degrees north of the line, Thomas, desperate to keep the peace, immediately situated his little island kingdom in the tropics, 10 degrees south of the line. Not to be outdone, William declared that 'his dominions swept southwards through a matter' of 80 or 90 degrees, placing parts of Tigrosylvania right on Gombroon's doorstep.[72] Thomas knew what that meant, and attempted to parry the threat of invasion by assuming the familiar guise of abjection. Gombroon, he asserted, was so impoverished that it could not possibly be of interest to the Tigrosylvanian empire. But William cut off this exit with the news that Gombroon contained diamond mines, which its inhabitants, in their barbaric state, neither valued nor had any means of working.

The game went back and forth – and Thomas's wiggle room got smaller and smaller – until William stepped forward with the most shocking news of all. So base were the natives of Gombroon that they still had tails! The humiliation of this discovery staggered Thomas, and thoroughly confounded his loyalties. He could not cut himself off from his 'poor abject' Gombroonians, yet he writhed with disgust at their 'ignominious appendage'. 'I lived for ever under the terror of two separate wars in two separate worlds,' he later exclaimed: 'one against the factory boys, in a real world of flesh and blood ... the other in a world purely aerial, where all the combats and the sufferings were absolute moonshine.'[73] In both realms, though, William initiated Thomas into schemes of mastery and dependence that would go on to shape one of the central tensions in his work: he is fascinated by power but feels a profound sympathy for the exile. The games of Tigrosylvania and Gombroon ended without resolution.

[iv]

In addition to serving as his guardian, Hall tutored Thomas from the autumn of 1793 through to late in 1796. He was a 'good and conscientious man', but as a religious thinker, he was sincere rather than earnest, or as Thomas once put it rather less charitably, he was 'dull, dreadfully dull'. Every Sunday, Thomas rode in a carriage to St Ann's Church to hear Hall deliver his sermon, which ran to sixteen minutes in length, and which rose no higher than a commonplace such as 'the danger from bad companions' or 'the importance of setting a good example'. Other members of the congregation could let the sermon flow over them 'like water over marble slabs', but Thomas had to listen intently, for on Monday morning, as part of his lesson, he had to present to Hall a 'mimic duplicate' of the sermon, 'preserving as much as possible of the original language; and also (which puzzled me painfully) preserving the exact succession of the thoughts'.[74]

Thomas claimed that these exercises were beneficial to him because they strengthened his memory, and forced him to concentrate on something other than his own brooding thoughts, which ran 'too determinately towards the sleep of endless reverie'. Yet at the same time, Hall's demands were an additional burden on a young boy already racked by anxiety and grief.

Thomas slept poorly on Saturday night 'under sad anticipation' of the trial to come, and worse on Sunday night 'under sadder experimental knowledge' of trying to remember and rehearse what he had heard. By Monday morning he 'felt like a false steward summoned to some killing audit', and the stress was not relieved until he stood before Hall and delivered the sermon. Hall, he was convinced, enjoyed the infliction of these fears. 'It gave him pleasure that he could reach me in the very recesses of my dreams, where even a Pariah might look for rest.'[75]

As a tutor in the classics, Hall's abilities were mixed. He was an 'indifferent Grecian', and raised Thomas to a reasonable competence for his age, but no further.[76] As a Latinist, however, he accomplished much more. To be sure, Thomas complained that he passed some 'wretched and ungenial days ... "learning by *heart*"' various grammatical rules, but Hall also did a great deal to encourage and hone his pupil's remarkable talent.[77] One day in a bookshop after three or four months of study under Hall, an elderly man gave Thomas the task of translating from Latin into English the chapter in St Paul on the grave and resurrection. Thomas knew the English chapter intimately, and while he had never seen a Latin version, he 'read it off with a fluency and effect like some great opera-singer uttering a rapturous *bravura*', for his 'deep memory of the English words' forced him 'into seeing the precise correspondence of the two concurrent streams – Latin and English'.[78] As a scholar of Latinity, he never looked back.

Hall introduced Thomas to a number of Latin authors, including Phae-drus, who initiated 'a great epoch in the movement' of Thomas's intellect when in his *Fables* he mentioned that the Athenians raised a 'mighty statue' to Aesop, a slave who became a fabulist. Thomas could not articulate his emotions at the time, but he was awed by the notion of a Greek king looking up to a Greek pariah, of a man without the rights of a man moving from 'the pollution of slavery' to the 'starry altitude' of emancipation through the application of his own 'intellectual power'. Only later did he recognize the passage as his first experience of a 'grand and jubilant sense of the moral sublime'.[79]

Over the course of more than three years, Thomas learned swiftly and comprehensively under Hall's tutelage. Yet perhaps his most powerful memory of his lessons in the 'quiet household' involved, not Hall himself, but Hall's twin daughters, Sarah and Mary, aged between twelve and four-teen, and both deaf, very plain, and 'obscurely reputed to be idiots'.[80] Hall's wife hated the two girls, and forced them to perform menial tasks, while Hall contented himself for the most part with looking the other way. What won Thomas's pity for the twins was, firstly, 'their affection for each other, united to their constant sadness; secondly, a notion which had crept into my head, probably derived from something said in my presence by elder people, that they were destined to an early death; and, lastly, the incessant persecutions of their mother'. When he met them intermittently in the back passages of the Hall house he exchanged kisses with them, and his wish had 'always been to beg them, if they really *were* idiots, not to mind it, since I should not like them the less on that account'. The last time he saw Sarah and Mary they were resting from their chores when an angry voice yelled at them from below stairs. Both rose instantly, flung their arms around each other, and then parted to their separate labours. Shortly thereafter they both died of scarlet fever.[81] Thomas knew that his upbringing and his intellect put a good deal of distance between him and the two girls. Yet their situation seems also to have reminded him vividly of his own feelings of alienation and shame.

Near the end of his time with Hall, Thomas went to stay at the Lincolnshire home of another one of his guardians, Henry Gee. Here, 'in the most chivalrous sense', he fell in love with Gee's daughter, who was one year his junior, and whom he refers to only as 'M'. At the dinner table Thomas usually sat beside her, but one day Gee seemed to object to the pleasure he took in touching her hand 'at intervals', and on the following day he saw to it that his daughter was seated on the opposite side of the table. Thomas realized that the new arrangement gave him a better view of M's 'sweet countenance', but he resented his guardian's interference, and exacted vengeance in a poem of Latin hexameters in the manner of the great Roman satirist Juvenal. 'Te nimis austerum, sacrae qui foedera mensae / Diruis, insector Satyrae reboante flagello,' he stormed at the opening: 'You, over-harsh one, who destroy the sacred covenants of the table, I pursue with the resounding whip of satire.' Thomas never showed the poem to Gee, but he was proud of the 'Roman strength' of some of what he had written.[82] Perhaps, too, for the first time he caught sight of himself as an author.

At some point during these months, Mrs Quincey again made the decision to send William away from the family. His bellicosity undoubtedly played a part, but he also showed a considerable talent for drawing, and when the distinguished painter and Royal Academician Philip James de Loutherbourg agreed to take him as a pupil, his mother and guardians paid a fee of one thousand guineas and sent him to London. Thomas remembered the morning of William's departure as a liberation from tyranny. But that same morning was also memorable to him for another reason. As his brothers and sisters gathered on the Greenhay lawn, a rabid dog ran up to the locked front gates, and then pursued his course along the brook which bordered the property. Thomas happened to be standing away from the other children, near the water, and the dog made a dead stop directly opposite him. 'I looked searchingly into his eyes, and observed that they seemed glazed, and as if in a dreamy state, but at the same time suffused with some watery discharge, while his mouth was covered with masses of white foam.' Later the family learned that only a short time before the dog had appeared at Greenhay it had bitten two horses, one of which died from rabies. In Thomas's mind, the two unrelated incidents came to represent a kind of double deliverance. 'Freedom won and death escaped, almost in the same hour.'[83] It seemed to him to signal the end of an epoch, though other tyrannies would soon replace William's, and death would continue to stare him in the eye.

TWO

The Ray of a New Morning

[i]

Mrs Quincey was selling Greenhay. Her dead husband had strongly advised against such a move until prices improved, but it had been three years since his passing, and a number of factors were pushing her to make a change. 'No motive existed any longer' for being near Manchester, 'so long after the commercial connection with it had ceased'. Greenhay was very expensive to run, as the gardens and grounds alone required at least three labourers. The Quincey estate was producing substantially smaller returns in the hands of the four executors, all of whom were 'men of honour', but all of whom were also busy with their own lives.[1] And finally, housing prices were not going to improve any time soon, as Britain had entered the French Revolutionary Wars in the year of Quincey's death, and its involvement in the conflict continued to generate widespread instability.

Greenhay went up for sale by auction on a rainy night in August 1796. Quincey had paid £6000 for the property. There was only one offer, for £2500, and the executors accepted it. Remarkably, one of the two buyers was the socialist and philanthropist Robert Owen, who lived in the house for the next three years, and who passed his honeymoon there. 'We soon drove into the grounds of Greenheys,' he recollected, 'and entering into the house through a part well contrived and neatly arranged as a greenhouse, and the interior being well constructed, furnished, and nicely arranged, both my wife and her servant were uncommonly well pleased.'[2]

Mrs Quincey soon decamped for Bath, the most elegant of Georgian cities, and one brought clearly into view in Jane Austen's *Northanger Abbey*, which is set during the years Mrs Quincey and her family lived there. The city is enthusiastically praised by Austen's heroine Catherine Morland: 'Here are a variety of amusements, a variety of things to be seen and done ... Oh! who can ever be tired of Bath?' On the look-out for a good address, Mrs Quincey settled on fashionable lodgings at Number 11, North Parade, which she moved into on or just after 13 September. The previous occupant of the house had been Edmund Burke, the great statesman and political thinker, who vigorously opposed the French Revolution, and whose *Reflections on the Revolution in France* (1790) is usually regarded as the epitome of conservatism.[3] Revealingly, it was in Bath that Mrs Quincey changed the family surname to 'De Quincey', for one of the main reasons she had chosen the city was the many opportunities it provided for her and her children to move in more refined social circles, and her adoption of the genteel prefix 'De' was undoubtedly an attempt to smooth their way.

The North Parade lodgings were of course much smaller than Greenhay, and while they seemed 'on all accounts' the 'natural station for a person' in Mrs De Quincey's position, the move was a big change for her children.[4] In the first instance, she took only Mary, Jane, and Henry – who had been born shortly after his father's death – down to Bath, leaving Thomas and Richard ('Pink') behind in Manchester, where they were placed under the care of Hall, but lived in the home of John Kelsall, Quincey's former principal clerk and now a successful merchant. In many respects, the following three months were 'without results', yet Thomas looked back on them with feelings 'inexpressibly profound', for the 'distinguishing feature' of the Kelsall household was 'the spirit of love which ... diffused itself through all its members'. Mrs Kelsall was 'a pretty and amiable young woman' who treated the servants with respect, who doted on her two-year-old daughter, and who waited eagerly each evening to greet her husband. After the strife and despair of so much of his time at Greenhay, Thomas's peaceful autumn was 'a jewelly parenthesis of pathetic happiness – such as emerges but once in any man's life'.[5]

In November, the two boys were summoned to join the rest of the family in Bath, where they were soon enrolled as day boarders in the prestigious Bath Grammar School, founded by Royal Charter in 1552, and known today as King Edward's School. Always competitive when it came to learning, Thomas was dismayed to find that his middling performance in Greek on the entrance exam meant that he was placed with Mr Wilkins, 'the second master out of four', rather than with the Reverend Nathaniel Morgan, the Master of the school, and the instructor in charge of the two upper classes. Yet within a month, Thomas's talent for Latin verse, 'which had by this time gathered strength and expansion', placed him on weekly parade before 'the supreme tribunal of the school'. What is more, as a Grecian Thomas quickly made up lost ground, for he flourished when placed under Morgan, a 'ripe and good' scholar, and 'of all my tutors ... the only one whom I loved or reverenced'. By the time he was thirteen years old he wrote Greek 'with ease', and Morgan had the pleasure of pointing him out to a stranger as a boy who could 'harangue an Athenian mob, better than you or I could address an English one'.[6]

Long starved of attention, Thomas delighted to shine in front of his new schoolmates. Morgan, however, inadvertently caused a backlash against him in the upper-year Latin classes by 'continually throwing in their teeth the brilliancy of my verses at eleven or twelve', as compared 'with theirs at seventeen, eighteen, and even nineteen'. One day in the playground an older boy strode up to him and, delivering a blow 'which was not intended to hurt me, but as a mere formula of introduction, asked me, "What the devil I meant by bolting out of the course, and annoying other people in that manner?"' Thomas was given two choices: either 'I wrote worse for the future, or else ... he would "annihilate" me'. But Thomas had pluck, and he tried even harder on the next exercise, with the result that he brought down 'double applause' upon himself. Riled by his defiance, his enemies stepped up their offensive, while Thomas 'hated and loathed' the fact that he once again found himself trapped in an 'eternal feud', especially as he could not '*altogether* condemn' the upper boys for despising him as 'a handle of humiliation'. The battle dragged on for over a year, until Thomas gradually won them over, in part for the 'splendour' of his Latin, but in the main for his courage. The ordeal concluded with him writing verses for many of the older boys, a practice which produced an overall decline in his workmanship, for 'as the subjects given out were the same for the entire class, it was not possible to take so many crops off the ground without starving the quality of all'.[7]

Thomas had been at Bath Grammar School for just over a year when his brother William contracted typhus fever and died at the London home of his painting instructor, de Loutherbourg.[8] Not yet sixteen years old, he was the third sibling Thomas had lost in the past seven years, but in this instance it is difficult to believe that he was very upset. William '*had* controlled, and for years to come *would have* controlled, the free spontaneous movements of a contemplative dreamer like myself'. The recent battles between Thomas and the older boys at Bath had been a too vivid reminder of what life was like under William's tyranny. Perhaps there was a spasm of remorse when he heard the news, but Thomas was glad to be free of him: 'I acknowledge no such tiger for a friend of mine.'[9]

The months that followed brought the happiness of socialization and broadening horizons. Despite his declared preference for solitude and the country, twelve-year-old Thomas liked Bath, and the more he got to know it, the more he enjoyed it. He went dancing. He drank wine.[10] He visited in the famous Pump Room, or took in concerts in the Upper

Rooms. Prior Park, a beautiful landscape garden complete with lakes, a grotto, a Palladian bridge, and a mansion, was 'a place well known to me. We, that is, myself and a schoolfellow, had the privilege of the *entrée* to the grounds.' Best of all, Thomas liked to visit Sydney Gardens, which contained a labyrinth that stirred his love of mystery. It was perhaps in games of hide-and-seek with his friends, or during afternoons spent by himself among strangers, that he was struck by how securely he could conceal himself at the heart of the labyrinth. More distressingly, in later years this 'literal' form came back to haunt him in abstract shapes, as he sought sanctuary amidst 'labyrinths of debt, labyrinths of error, labyrinths of metaphysical nonsense'.[11]

Bath was full of interesting people. Mrs De Quincey's acquaintance with 'several leading families' amongst its sizeable French emigrant community enabled Thomas to gain 'a large experience of French calligraphy'. At a concert given by the great German soprano Gertrud Elisabeth Mara, one of Thomas's party pointed out to him the eccentric philosopher and traveller John 'Walking' Stewart. In the spring of 1798, Thomas met the British naval officer Sir Sidney Smith, who had recently escaped from a French prison. Thomas and Pink were two of the three Bath Grammar School boys allowed to call on Smith 'formally', presumably as '*alumni* of the school' at which he had received his own education. Smith greeted the boys with 'great kindness', and then allowed them to accompany him down to the Pump Room, where they burdened him with their 'worshipful society', but also shielded him from the embarrassing curiosity of the crowds.[12]

Talking with a 'naval hero' such as Smith gave Thomas his first direct knowledge of Britain's war with Revolutionary France, and it undoubtedly confirmed him in his detestation of French radicalism, and his growing attachment to virulent forms of British nationalism and British imperialism. To be sure, there was a strong liberal streak in him, as there had been in his father, but in the heady political atmosphere of the 1790s he was deeply swayed by those who argued in favour of the war, and he aligned himself firmly on their side. 'I had a keen sympathy with the national honour, gloried in the name of Englishman, and had been bred up in a frenzied horror of Jacobinism,' he recollected. 'Not having been old enough, at the first outbreak of the French Revolution, to participate (as else, undoubtedly, I should have done) in the golden hopes of its early dawn, my first youthful introduction to foreign politics had been in seasons and circumstances that taught me to approve of all I heard in abhorrence of French excesses, and to worship the name' of the British Prime Minister William Pitt.[13] Sitting with Smith in the Pump Room – to say nothing of living in a house formerly occupied by Edmund Burke – could only have heightened Thomas's patriotic fervour.

He continued to study hard. Writing formed a central part of his daily routine, as he excelled at his Greek and Latin school exercises, and composed a tragedy 'on a certain Ethelfrid ... who cut the throats of the abbot and all his monks'. Reading, too, absorbed him, and while his favourite books ranged from a beautiful Glasgow reprint of Thomas à Kempis's *De Imitatione Christi* to Thomas James Mathias's celebrated contemporary satire on *The Pursuits of Literature*, he was the most fully engaged by two recent studies of secret societies: Augustin de Barruel's *Memoirs, Illustrating the History of Jacobinism*, and John Robison's *Proofs of a Conspiracy against all the Religions and Governments of Europe*.[14] Thomas was disturbed by these sects because of their alleged desire to overthrow Christianity and Monarchy, yet at some level he seems also to have studied them because of his growing sense that he himself belonged to a secret society, to a group of exiles and innocents who were inexplicably chosen to suffer, and who dwelled apart from the commonplace flow of daily life. Interestingly, Thomas's fascination with secret societies throws into relief the two powerful and often competing interests at the core of his intellect: an Enlightenment-based investment in classicism, and an anti-Enlightenment enthusiasm for mystery, mystification, and disorder. The tension between these two viewpoints produced some of his most characteristic insights, and he rendered it with memorable concision when he summarized his response to Barruel: 'I believed in [him] by necessity, and yet everywhere my understanding mutinied against *his*.'[15]

On 29 January 1799, as Thomas settled into his third year at Bath Grammar School, he was involved in an accident that sent him home for several weeks. A Mr Collins was briefly left in charge of Morgan's classroom, and when a couple of the boys became rambunctious, he attempted to enforce his authority with the use of a cane, as was routine at the time. But instead of striking his intended target – young Wilbraham – Collins missed and hit Thomas on the head. The blow was not serious enough to prevent him from going on with his lesson, but when he got home his mother promptly sent for a doctor, Mr Grant, who examined his head, shaved the area around the wound, and then bled him with six leeches, a procedure that was repeated the following morning. Thomas, however, did not improve, and for three weeks 'I neither read, nor wrote, nor *talked*, nor eat meats, nor went out of the back drawing-room, except when I went to bed.'[16]

It is difficult to determine the exact nature of this injury. Grant apparently thought that Thomas's 'skull had been fractured', and at one time considered trepanning. But as Thomas later acknowledged, his fears for his head were very largely fears in his head. 'I doubt whether in reality anything very serious had happened. In fact, I was always under a nervous panic for my head; and certainly exaggerated my internal feelings without meaning to do so; and this misled the medical attendants.' At issue here seems to be his identification with Elizabeth, and his ongoing grief over her death. He felt certain that hydrocephalus – a condition characterized by enlargement of the skull and atrophy of the brain – had killed her, and as he worried himself about his own head wound, he grew convinced that he was in real danger, as did his mother and his doctors. Months later Thomas 'fancied that he still suffered' from the blow, but as one school friend recollected, 'I think the injury was purely imaginary, and that his pains arose from irritation in his too active and susceptible brain.'[17]

Confinement at home did not slow his pursuit of knowledge. His mother read to him 'books past all counting', including John Hoole's popular translation of Ariosto's *Orlando Furioso,* while Thomas himself read John Milton's *Paradise Lost* for the first time.[18] Further, in a 12 March letter to his older sister Mary, he reported on the arrival of 'some ... new Books': Sir William Jones's *Asiatic Researches,* Samuel Ogden's *Sermons,* Joseph and Isaac Milner's *Ecclesiastical History of the Church of Christ,* Henry Venn's *The Complete Duty of Man,* Samuel Johnson's *The Rambler,* and Oliver Goldsmith's *History of England,* among others. Thomas may or may not have actually read all of these volumes, but it is easy to see mother and son compiling the order for them. Her piety was deepening under the influence of a new and firm friendship with Hannah More, one of the leading Evangelical writers of the day, while his intelligence was rapidly expanding under a largely self-directed course of reading in literature and history. Thomas closed this letter to Mary by signing himself 'Tabitha Quincey', a pseudonym in keeping with the letter's playful, patronizing and affectionate humour.[19] From the start he was intrigued by persona, and he was already experimenting with the ways in which his own identity might be extended and subverted.

With his recovery fully under way, Mrs De Quincey hired a French tutor for Thomas. But instead of doing his lessons he sat in the window with Pink and Henry and made faces at an old lady who lived across the street. 'Now, Monsieur Tomma, oh, do be parsuaded! Oh, do be parsuaded!' cried the tutor. 'Monsieur Tomma', however, would not be 'parsuaded', and his unruly behaviour continued. When Mrs De Quincey discovered what was going on, she ordered Thomas to call on the old woman and apologize, which he did so handsomely that she afterwards spoke of him as 'the cleverest and nicest little boy she ever saw'.[20] Thomas would certainly have been happy to appease both his mother and their neighbour. One word in the old woman's praise would have stung, though. Now a teenager, he was increasingly conscious of his physical appearance, and especially of the fact that he was short for his age. He would not have appreciated being referred to as 'little'.

During the spring, Mrs De Quincey began to consider Thomas's return to Bath Grammar School. She had some reservations. Thomas and a school friend named Bowes had been involved in some incident that had been at least partially witnessed by Mrs De Quincey's close friends, Mr and Mrs Pratt. His offence was certainly not flagrant, but his mother reminded him that 'appearances unfortunately are often all we have to judge of actions by; and those in the particular action in question were really against you'. Her unease was exacerbated when Morgan, his son-in-law and colleague Wilkins, and Bowes's father called in to enquire after Thomas, and made the fatal mistake of praising him. 'It illustrates my mother's moral austerity, that she was shocked at my hearing compliments to my own merits, and was altogether disturbed at what doubtless these gentlemen expected to see received with maternal pride. She declined to let me continue at the Bath School.'[21]

Though Morgan expressed 'great indignation' at Mrs De Quincey's decision, and Thomas deeply resented it, she was unmoved. By June he was a student at a school in the nearby village of Winkfield (now Wingfield) in Wiltshire, as were 'Pink and Hal'.[22] For Mrs De Quincey, 'the chief recommendation' of the school 'lay in the religious character of the master', the Reverend Edward Spencer. For Thomas, however, the new school was a decided step downward. Not only was Spencer a 'blockhead, who was in a perpetual panic, lest I should expose his ignorance', but Thomas was now a very big fish in a tiny pond of only thirty students. 'The consequence was that my powers entirely flagged, my mind became quite dormant in comparison of what it was at Bath Grammar School. I had no one to praise me, to spur me on, or to help me.'[23]

Yet despite these reservations, Thomas benefited far more from Winkfield than he remembered. He grew much closer to Pink, who inspired in him 'great affection', and who played Paris to his Ulysses in organized marches between 'a *Grecian* and a *Trojan* band'.[24] He was singled out as a 'special favourite' by Spencer's daughters, and with them and some of his schoolmates he set up a 'periodical work' called *The Observer*, for which he wrote a series of 'clever, funny things', including a spirited response to a challenge issued by a neighbouring school:

Since Ames's skinny school has dared
    To challenge Spencer's boys,
We thus to them bold answer give
    To prove ourselves 'no toys'.

Full thirty hardy boys are we,
    As brave as e'er was known;
We will nor threats nor dangers mind
    To make you change your tone![25]

Most impressively, while a student at Winkfield, Thomas entered a competition in *The Monthly Preceptor, or Juvenile Library* to translate two set passages, one from Cicero and the other from Horace. His translation of Cicero placed seventh and was not published, but his translation of Horace placed third and was:

Send me to dreary barren lands
    Where never summer zephyrs play,
Where never sun dissolves the bands
    Of ice away:

Send me again to scorching realms
    Where not one cot affords a seat,
And where no shady pines or elms
    Keep off the heat.[26]

The radical essayist and poet Leigh Hunt, Thomas's senior by ten months and then a student at Christ's Hospital, came first in the Horace competition, and the distinguished historian George Ormerod second. But Thomas later had the satisfaction of hearing that several people considered his rendering the finest of the three. At fourteen years old he was in print, and 'for the first time in my life, I found myself somewhat in the situation of a "*lion*"'.[27]

[ii]

He called it 'the greatest event in the unfolding of my own mind'. In 'about the year 1799' he read a manuscript copy of William Wordsworth's short poem 'We Are Seven' in Bath during one of his school holidays. Shortly thereafter he read the *Lyrical Ballads* (1798), the joint and anonymous publication of Wordsworth and his close friend Samuel Taylor Coleridge. In these poems Thomas instantly identified '"the ray of a new morning", and an absolute revelation of untrodden worlds, teeming with power and beauty, as yet unsuspected amongst men'.[28] At just fifteen years old, his remarkable recognition of Coleridge and Wordsworth as two of the predominant literary and cultural voices of his age dramatically altered the course of his life.

What attracted him to the *Lyrical Ballads*? The title points to a paradox, for 'lyric' suggests introspection and emotion, while 'ballad' implies action and story. The collection itself focuses on feeling, and most often when it has reached the extremes of confusion, passion, or despair. Coleridge contributed 'The Rime of the Ancyent Marinere' and three other shorter works, while Wordsworth published nineteen poems in the volume, including 'We Are Seven', 'Anecdote for Fathers', 'Goody Blake and Harry Gill', 'Simon Lee', 'The Last of the Flock', 'The Complaint of a Forsaken Indian Woman', and 'Lines Written a Few Miles Above Tintern Abbey'. Taken as a whole, the poetry of the *Lyrical Ballads* breaks decisively from the heroic couplet, the verse form most readily associated with the poetry of the eighteenth century, and instead uses straightforward (or 'simple') language to explore the relationship between humankind and the natural world, and to give voice to the plight of people who have been dismissed by their society as odd or insignificant. Characteristically, 'Her eyes are wild, her head is bare', writes Wordsworth in 'The Mad Mother':

> The sun has burnt her coal-black hair,
> Her eye-brows have a rusty stain,
> And she came far from over the main.
> She has a baby on her arm,
> Or else she were alone.[29]

Why did this poetry have such an immense impact on Thomas? One reason was its thoroughgoing challenge to his mother's Evangelicalism, especially in its emphasis on doubt (as opposed to moral certainties), its celebration of the vision of the child (as opposed to expectations of subservience and duty), and its insistence on the value of an education directed by 'the loveliness and the wonders of the world before us' (as opposed to education delivered in dogmatic and institutional forms).[30] Further, the volume's cast of convicts, exiles, idiot boys, and female vagrants was deeply congruent with Thomas's compassion for pariahs like Sarah and Mary Hall, and further complicated that divide in his sympathies between the value of the individual and the privileges of rank.[31] Finally, Coleridge and Wordsworth, in their shared fascination with obstinacy, grief, and solitude, must at times have seemed to Thomas to be speaking directly to him, legitimizing the sorrows of his past experience, and offering him strategies for self-preservation that – for the first time in the six years since Elizabeth's death – provided both solace and hope.[32] In 'We Are Seven', death visits but does not divide a family. In 'The Ancyent Marinere', 'strange power of speech' is used both to mollify and exploit a soul *in extremis*. In 'Tintern Abbey', a brother's love for his 'dear, dear sister' is as vital as Thomas knew such a love to be.[33]

Over the course of the ensuing months, Thomas planned a number of literary projects clearly indebted to his understanding of the *Lyrical Ballads*. One was a '*poetic and pathetic ballad* reciting the wanderings of two young children (brother and sister) and their falling asleep on a frosty – moonlight night among the lanes ... and so perishing'. Another was a '*Pathetic poem* describing the emotions (strange and wild) of a man dying on a rock in the sea ... which he had swum to from a shipwreck ... within sight of his native cottage and his paternal hills'. A third was '*An ode*, in which two angels or spirits were to meet in the middle of the Atlantic'.[34] None of these projects seems to have come to fruition, but all three show Thomas reading himself into the poetry of Wordsworth and Coleridge in ways that were repeatedly to shape his literary aspirations and many self-representations.

Issues of self-representation were also at the heart of another decision that Thomas made at this time. It is unclear to what extent his mother ever adopted the signature 'De Quincey'. Certainly in Bath she instructed her children to use the name, and she herself no doubt employed it for a couple of years when she thought that it would be an advantage to do so. But by early 1800 – at least in all her extant letters to Thomas – she is signing herself plain 'Quincey', and that was the name she used for the rest of her life, having apparently come to accept the argument of her friend Mrs Pratt, and perhaps of Hannah More as well, that 'the use of the "De" was a worldly vanity which she ought to lay aside' as incompatible with her religious views.[35]

Thomas's response to his mother's decision is highly revealing. From her Evangelicalism he took a belief in the educative power of suffering, a commitment to anxious self-scrutiny, and a fascination with sin and guilt. But much of her piety he found simple-minded and disingenuous, and when she made the decision to revert permanently to 'Quincey', he refused to follow her, retaining the 'De' for the rest of his life.[36] Beginning in 1800, she wrote to him as 'Thomas Quincey' and signed herself 'E. Quincey', while he responded by addressing her as 'Mrs Quincey', but signing himself 'Thomas de Quincey'.[37] As his own sense of self grew stronger, it was the clearest sign of his intention to mark himself out and off from his mother.

[iii]

In the early summer of 1800, as Thomas neared the end of his first year at Winkfield, he received an invitation to holiday in Ireland with a new friend. Lord Westport (later the second Marquess of Sligo) was the only son of Lord Altamont, an Irish peer who owned an estate in County Mayo, and who seems to have had some contact with Thomas's father during one of his many buying trips to Ireland.[38] Westport is best known as the boon companion of Lord Byron, who travelled with him in Greece, and who hailed him as 'the Marchesa' for his lasciviousness and extravagance. 'Sligo has told me some things, that ought to set you and me by the ears, but they shan't, and as a proof of it, I wont tell you what they are till we meet,' Byron wrote tantalizingly to John Cam Hobhouse on 29 July 1810.[39] Back in the spring of 1799, however, when Thomas first met him, Westport was an eleven-year-old Eton schoolboy on holiday in Bath who was not only 'very nice' to Thomas, but who – crucially for Thomas's ease – was 'about my size'. There was a two and a half year difference in their ages, so the plan was that Thomas would accompany Westport, not so much as a friend, but as an older companion whose learning, manners, and eloquence might guide and even inspire the younger boy.[40] Mrs Quincey's hard climbing on the social ladders of Bath was paying dividends.

Westport's private tutor, the Reverend Thomas Grace, was pleased that the two boys would be travelling together, for he had chaperoned Westport in Bath when they had first met, and he already thought 'very highly' of Thomas.[41] The same, however, cannot be said of Westport's mother. Lady Altamont had never met Thomas, but she was deeply suspicious of him, not because his social standing was much lower than her son's, but because she shared Mrs Quincey's distrust of his precocity. 'I do not like the Expression quoted by Grace out of Quincy's Letter which leads me to judge of Him very differently from what Mr Grace does,' she wrote snippily to her husband. 'I mean the words "My Mind is more athirst for knowledge than ever". You know I hate canting of every sort & from that in corroboration of some other circumstances which I have heard from Westport such as His attempting to write a Book at his Age ... I am rather inclined to think Quincy is a Pedant which I think is as disgusting in a Child as Methodism in a Man.'[42] Pedantry was a charge often levelled at him, but there can be little doubt that Thomas was eager to distinguish himself intellectually, and that he had talked of producing a book, perhaps one that included the poetry he had projected along the lines of the *Lyrical Ballads*. Lord Altamont's response to his wife is not known, but her objections to Thomas were not enough to upend the holiday plans, and on Monday, 14 July 1800, he boarded an early-morning coach in Bath and journeyed the twelve hours to Eton.[43]

Westport and Grace did not greet him on his arrival, as they had already set off for a *fête* given at nearby Frogmore, the Queen's country retreat at Windsor. They left instructions for him on their whereabouts, though, and he soon joined them at the party, where he and Westport stayed 'a little in the Ball-room' and then walked 'about the Gardens' with 'Lord Percy (the Duke of Northumberland's son)'. A short time later Thomas's mother discovered that he had gone to the royal gathering without first going to his rooms and changing his clothes. She was horrified. 'I certainly *did* go there in my travelling Dress,' he confessed to her, 'but then my travelling Dress was a very good one (*much* better than what Lord Westport had on) and my Boots were cleaned.'[44] Thomas was undoubtedly exhilarated at the thought of holidaying away from home for the first time. But his mother still had a close eye on him.

The next morning Grace drove Thomas and Westport to London in an open carriage, winding along rural lanes and by-roads for as long as possible, before falling in with 'the tumult and the agitation', which grew continually until they reached the heart of the city, where all Thomas could remember of his initial impression was 'one monotonous awe and blind sense of mysterious grandeur and Babylonian confusion'. The two boys had only a few hours to themselves, and decided to visit St Paul's Cathedral. They were both deeply impressed by the building, and Thomas especially by the Whispering Gallery, a circular structure running round inside the base of the dome which is famous for its ability to carry a whisper from one part of the wall to any other part of the wall at almost its original volume. Thomas, however, remembered the wall as being capable of amplifying sound, for when Westport whispered 'a solemn but not acceptable truth', Thomas claimed that it reached him 'as a deafening menace in tempestuous uproars'.[45] This cannot be accurate, but Thomas was not about to let physical fact impede imaginative truth, and in his memory Westport's whisper became a powerful metaphor of quiet circumstances surging into dangerous tumult.

After rejoining Grace, Thomas and Westport were taken to Porter's Lodge, near St Albans, in Hertfordshire, where they were received by Lady

Howe (Westport's grandmother), Lady Altamont, and George Douglas, the sixteenth Earl of Morton. Lady Altamont left no record of this meeting with Thomas, but certainly his recollections of it suggest that she was persuaded to abandon her initial mistrust of him. Lord Morton, the 'only gentleman who appeared at the dinner table', somehow knew of the recent competition in *The Monthly Preceptor*, and 'protested loudly' that Thomas's translation of Horace should have placed first, not third. Morton's high opinion 'elated' a boy who was so anxious for such praise at home, and greatly influenced both Lady Howe and Lady Altamont, so that Thomas 'came, not only to wear the laurel in their estimation, but also with the advantageous addition of having suffered some injustice'.[46]

The boys returned to Eton the following evening, and Thomas spent the next day writing letters, before he and Westport attended another royal party. Thomas was for a time bewitched by the sight of so many famous people who had hitherto been only 'great *ideas*' in his 'childish thoughts', but soon it was only the beauty of the music, coupled with the 'affecting ... spectacle of men and women floating through the mazes of a dance', that saved him from 'so monstrous an indecorum as yawning'. After nearly four hours the boys fled the party, tossing their hats up into the air as they emerged into the open highroad.[47]

The next night – Friday night – was far more exciting, for Westport and Thomas went to the Windsor Theatre. Thomas knew full well that his mother would disapprove of such an entertainment, but before word got back to her, he wrote to explain exactly why he had gone.

> Lord Westport came to me and desired me to go with him to the play. I tried to escape by saying that I had letters to write (which in fact I had); however, as he seemed much disappointed at not going on the last evening of his being near a playhouse, and as he declared he would not go without me, I consented at length to accompany him ... But be assured, my dear mother, I would not have done this for all the world if I could have helped it, had I no other reason for avoiding public amusements than the earnest desire of obliging and obeying you.[48]

Thomas hoped this explanation would pre-empt his mother's pious protests, but he seems also to have offered it with his tongue partially lodged in his cheek. He could not ignore her, but neither was he terribly interested in following her rules. His response in this instance was to do what he wanted, and then pay lip service to her religiosity. His frustration with her expectations was edging its way closer and closer to the surface.

Early Saturday morning, 19 July, Thomas and Westport set off for Ireland to visit Westport's father, Lord Altamont. The first day they travelled one hundred and three miles on their route to Birmingham, passing through Oxford (which Thomas liked '*very much* ... from the *very little* I saw of it') and Stratford (where Thomas 'visited the house in which Shakespeare was born').[49] The next day they went a further seventy miles, crossing in the afternoon from England up into Wales, the road through which 'was much finer than anything I have ever seen or ever expected to see. From Oswestry to Llangollen was the first remarkably beautiful stage.' After spending the night at Corwen, they journeyed on the third day a final seventy miles, reaching Holyhead at ten o'clock on Monday evening, though it was Tuesday before Lord Altamont's servants arrived, and Wednesday at midnight before the two boys boarded the packet for Ireland.[50]

The crossing contained a memorable incident. One of their fellow passengers was 'a woman of rank' named Elizabeth, Marchioness Conyngham, best known later as the last mistress of George IV, but at that time about thirty years old, married with three young children, and very pretty. Thomas met her on Thursday morning. She was in her travelling coach, which had been 'unslung from the "carriage" (by which is technically meant the wheels and the perch), and placed upon deck. This she used as a place of retreat from the sun during the day, and as a resting-place at night.' Lady Conyngham saw Thomas sitting on the deck reading and called him over to her window, 'where she talked with me for about five minutes, and then made me come into the coach, and stay the remainder of the day with her. She conversed with me for above eight hours', and 'seemed a very sensible woman'. That night was 'very sultry' and Thomas and Westport, 'suffering from the oppression of the cabin', decided to sleep on deck. Both were just at the point of falling asleep when they were awoken by 'a stealthy tread' nearby. A man was stealing towards Lady Conyngham's coach. Their first thought was 'to raise an alarm, scarcely doubting' that his purpose was robbery. 'But, to our astonishment, we saw the coach-door silently swing open under a touch from *within*. All was as silent as a dream; the figure entered, the door closed, and we were left to interpret the case as we might.' The two lovers had no idea that their secret tryst had been observed, and the next morning Thomas saw 'the lovely lady ... looking as beautiful, and hardly less innocent, than an angel'.[51] The contrast between how she looked in the day and what she had done at night shocked him. Up to this point, he had led a fairly sheltered existence, but on the deck that evening Thomas got a glimpse of a side of adult life that he had not seen before, and he was old enough now to understand what it all meant. As he neared his fifteenth birthday, he was leaving his boyhood behind.

[iv]

The packet dropped anchor in 'the famous bay of Dublin' some time near six in the morning, and after a boat was manned to put the passengers on shore at Dunleary (now Dún Laoghaire), the boys travelled directly to the city, where at 'nine o'clock precisely' they entered the breakfast room at No. 9 Sackville Street, the townhouse of Lord Altamont. Father and son, who had not seen each other in three years, paid one half-minute down 'as a tribute to the sanctities of the case', before Altamont turned to Thomas with a 'courteous welcome' that removed any unpleasant sense of him as 'an intruder'.[52]

The boys quickly fell into a routine, though Thomas's description of it clearly owes a great deal to the fact that he is writing to his mother.

> I and Westport rise at various times between ½ past 4 and 6. I read the Bible before Breakfast and Lord Westport writes Copies and ciphers. We breakfast with Lord Altamont, then read again, then ride and bathe till about 2 or 3 o'clock, when we dine ... In the afternoon I read and write, and Westport plays with his Cousins. At about 7 o'clock we sup on Bread and Milk and Fruit, (which is also our Breakfast) and at 9 go to bed.[53]

During the periods of writing and reading, Thomas was working on his Greek, teaching Latin to Westport, and speaking French with one of Westport's tutors, so that 'I am considerably improved, I think, in that Language, and am able to speak it with great ease'. His favourite books of the time revealed his wide-ranging intellectual tastes, and included Mungo Park's *Travels into the Interior Districts of Africa* (1799), Jacques Mallet du Pan's *History of the Destruction of the Helvetic Union and Liberty* (1799), and Samuel Johnson's *Rasselas* (1759), which 'has been my bosom-friend ever since I left Bath'. 'I am very well *indeed*', he wrote in closing, 'owing principally, I suppose, to the Change of Air, Sea-bathing, and drinking Tea.'[54]

One week after their arrival – on 1 August 1800 – the boys went with Altamont to the House of Lords to witness the historic passage of the Act of Union. Two years earlier, Irish Roman Catholics seeking parliamentary reform and complete Catholic emancipation had been brutally put down by British troops, first at a critical battle on Vinegar Hill in County Wexford, and then at Ballinamuck in County Longford, where a French landing had arrived too late to assist the insurgents and was defeated within a week. The Prime Minister, William Pitt, responded to the unrest by uniting the parliaments of Great Britain and Ireland, which he also hoped would strengthen British security against the French. Altamont was a staunch supporter of the Union, though Thomas often suspected that he harboured a rebelliousness that would not have been 'displeased' had 'some great popular violence' compelled the two Houses 'to perpetuate themselves'. When the Union Act was read out that day in the House of Lords, however, Thomas remembered distinctly that 'no audible expression, no buzz, nor murmur, nor *susurrus* even, testified the feelings which, doubtless, lay rankling in many bosoms'. The next day Thomas returned to the House of Lords to witness the election of twenty-eight Irish peers – 'Lord Altamont is one of them' – to the British House of Lords. How could Pitt have managed it, he later wondered; how could he have 'prevailed on all these hereditary legislators and heads of patrician houses to renounce so easily, with nothing worth the name of a struggle ... the very brightest jewel in their coronets'?[55]

Altamont had been made a Knight of the Order of the Blue Ribbon 'as a reward for his parliamentary votes', and on 11 August he and five others were honoured at an installation ceremony in St Patrick's Cathedral. 'The day was suffocatingly hot', Thomas reported, but the spectacle was splendid. Westport and Thomas sat with Lord Castlereagh, the Lord Lieutenant of Ireland, and future British foreign secretary. 'Each of the 6 Knights were arrayed (besides their usual Clothes) in 37 yards of *blue* Sattin lined with as many of *white*!! Every Knight had 3 Esquires who were dressed like himself, except that their Robes were *white* lined with *blue*.' 'God Save the King' was performed 'by the Band *within*, accompanied by the Soldiers *without*, in the finest and most *hair-making-to-stand-erect* manner I ever heard'. The ceremony concluded at three o'clock, and was followed by 'a grand dinner at the Castle'. Thomas, however, had 'no Inclination to see half a hundred Lords stuffing and getting drunk', and gave his dinner ticket away. After returning to Sackville Street, he retired to bed about ten o'clock, but was kept awake for 'a couple of hours' by 'very loud Huzzaings'. He was told the next morning that it was a 'Mob who had collected' in the street and 'made Bon-fires to congratulate' Altamont on 'having been made a Knight'.[56]

After nearly three weeks in Dublin, Altamont, Westport, and Thomas travelled to Westport House in County Mayo. The first stage of their journey took them to Tullamore via canal boat, and was marked by a second adventure involving Thomas and a woman. One of their fellow passengers was a snobbish bluestocking who was delighted to meet Westport, but openly contemptuous of Thomas, whom she berated as defective 'in all those advantages of title, fortune, and expectation which so brilliantly distinguished my friend'. For two hours Thomas 'stood the worst of this bright lady's feud', before two women emerged from below deck, and joined in the conversation. One was the widowed Elizabeth Jemima Hay, the Countess of Errol, and the other one of her sisters, most probably the youngest, Margaret Blake, who quickly discerned what was going on, and used her rank and beauty to shield Thomas. With his replies 'no longer stifled in noise and laughter', he was able to display his 'immense reading' and 'vast command of words', which he 'threw out, as from a cornucopia ... trivial enough, perhaps, as I might now think, but the more intelligible to my present circle'. Soon the offensive woman retreated and Thomas and Westport were left to converse with Margaret, whom Thomas stared at so intently that he made her blush. Previously, he had known women only 'in their infirmities and their unamiable aspects, or else in those sterner relations which made them objects of ungenial and uncompanionable feelings'. Now first it struck him 'that life might owe half its attractions and all its graces to female companionship'. What Lady Conyngham had roused, Margaret Blake confirmed. Thereafter Thomas was 'an altered creature'.[57]

They reached Tullamore at eight o'clock in the evening, and determined to spend the night with Lord Tullamore at nearby Charleville, which they journeyed to in a chaise that was 'almost breaking down, full of holes, and so small that I was obliged to sit on Lord Altamont's knee'.[58] Back on the road by six the following morning, the party travelled by chaise and phaeton, and while an accident with one of the phaeton wheels forced them into a blacksmith's shop for repairs, they had by nine that evening reached Tuam, where they stayed for two nights with the archbishop.

Altamont had by this time clearly grown proud of Thomas. On the road he 'had often urged me to translate' another Horatian ode, and 'we had amused ourselves in drawing up a pompous dedication to the Marquis himself with which I was to publish it'. In addition, on their second evening with the archbishop, Altamont desired Thomas to show his translation from the *Monthly Preceptor* to an assembled company, so Thomas wrote it out from memory and handed it to a Mr Murray, who read it aloud. The following morning Altamont and his party left very early 'to avoid being pressed by the Arch-Bishop to stay another day', and after a breakfast on the road at Ballinrobe, they reached Westport House at three o'clock in the afternoon on Saturday, 16 August.[59] The entire journey had been, for Thomas, a trip towards County Mayo, but also back in time. 'Here were old libraries, old butlers, and old customs, that seemed all alike to belong to the era of Cromwell, or even an earlier era than his; whilst the ancient names, to one who had some acquaintance with the great events of Irish history, often strengthened the illusion.'[60]

Thomas enjoyed his new surroundings immensely, from the 'very large and handsome' house to the 'fine Deer Park . . . containing nearly 300 Acres'. His schedule was busy, if aristocratic, and consisted of 'Reading, Hunting, Riding, Shooting, bathing, and Sea excursions', with the daily rides of sixteen or seventeen miles enabling him to see 'almost everything worth seeing in this most romantic Country'. One week after his arrival he climbed 'the famous Croagh Patrick . . . from which may be seen a great part of Connaught. When I was at the Summit I thought of the lines about Shakespeare looking abroad from some high Cliff and enjoying the elemental War. Beneath us indeed was a most tremendous War of the Elements, whilst we were as calm and serene as possible. To our left we saw Clew Bay and the vast Atlantic.'[61]

It was the Irish Rebellion of 1798, however, that most fully captured Thomas's imagination. As far as he could tell, the English had used '*the amplifying*, and the Irish *the diminishing hyperbole*' in their discussions of the conflict, for while the former broadcast 'horrid Accounts of Murders and Battles and Robberies', the latter spoke of 'merely straggling Banditti' who 'unroofed a few Cabbins, and took away some Cattle'.[62] Spurred on by his love of history and his fascination with secret societies, Thomas tried to piece together his own version of events, as he was in a neighbourhood which only two years earlier had been 'the very centre of the final military operations', and he had the opportunity to speak to many people 'who had personally participated' in the 'tragic incidents of the era'. No doubt the trouble was brought closest to him when he learned that 'the *French* and the *Rebels*' had 'twice been in possession' of Westport House, where they had 'made off with the best Books' and left 'memorials even in our bedrooms'. One Westport family friend also swore to it that several of the current workers on the estate were 'active boys from Vinegar Hill'.[63]

In his reminiscences, Thomas remembered staying at Westport House for three or four months. In fact, he was there for just over three weeks.[64] Setting out on Monday, 8 September, he and Westport made their way back to Dublin, and then took the packet across to Parkgate in Cheshire, where they caught the coach to Birmingham and said goodbye. Westport was for Eton. Thomas had been expecting to return to Bath, but had been 'directed, in Dublin, to inquire at the Birmingham Post-Office for a letter' which would guide his motions, and from which he learned that he should continue on to Laxton in Northamptonshire to join his sister Mary, who was visiting at the home of an old family friend. There was, however, no Northamptonshire coach until the following day, and so Thomas resigned himself to several hours in 'gloomy, noisy, and, at that time, dirty Birmingham'. He checked in at the Hen and Chickens and spent a restless night, kept awake until two or three in the morning by those who were retiring to bed, and then about three by those who were being rounded up for early-morning travel by the porters, one of whom accidentally blundered into Thomas's room 'with that appalling, "Now, sir, the horses are coming out"'.[65]

[v]

As he boarded the coach, Thomas was full of emotion. Miss Watson, now Lady Carbery, was the old family friend expecting him in Northamptonshire. Thomas had known her for most of his life, as she used to visit often at The Farm and Greenhay in the company of her guardian, Mrs Schreiber. In 1792, she had married George Evans, Lord Carbery, and in early 1800 the couple lived for a time in Milsom Street, Bath, where they saw a good deal of Mrs Quincey, under whose tutelage Lady Carbery became a zealous convert to 'Evangelical Christianity'. It is perhaps for this reason that, when Lady Carbery returned to the family estate at Laxton, Mrs Quincey followed her, taking up residence with Mrs Schreiber, who lived at nearby Tixover, and whose health was now failing.[66] Beautiful, wealthy, and intellectual, Lady Carbery had always taken an interest in Thomas, and he was anxious to see her again.

At the same time, his spirits were weighed down by a pressing question regarding his future: where was he going to go to school? Mother and son had been debating the question across his weeks in Ireland. Winkfield, he insisted, was too small and too easy, an argument Mrs Quincey seems to have been content to accept. Eton, where she wanted to send him, seems genuinely to have frightened him, and he attempted to turn her from this scheme with accounts that were clearly exaggerated, but that played directly to her religious preoccupations. 'Westport, I remember at Bath to have possessed one of the most amicable Dispositions I ever knew. It is now in ruins.' Yet with all his 'Debauchery, Intemperance, and swearing, I hear with Astonishment' that he is 'reckoned quite *virtuous* at Eton'. Worse still, Thomas had heard tales of a vicious pack mentality. 'You may judge of the Discipline of the School when I tell you that a week ago they beat an old Porter (in the defiance of the Masters, some of whom were standing by and hardly trying to prevent them) with such brutality that his life I hear, is despaired of. – My situation, as a Boy on the foundation would be still more miserable.' Why not a return to Bath Grammar School? Mrs Quincey had concerns about the way the school was conducted, but Thomas had been happy there, and he urged her to agree to this option. The 'Plan' at Bath 'every one allows to be incomparable. It is a very great Improvement, I think, on the Eton Method ... In short every thing you desire me I will do and only ask for this one thing, to go to the Grammar School.'[67]

Yet even as he wrote these words, Thomas recognized that the bigger issue was not which school he would attend, but the revulsion he felt at going to school at all. 'For more than a year, everything connected with schools and the business of schools had been growing more and more hateful to me.' During his recent holiday he had been 'in the midst of glittering saloons, at times also in the midst of society the most fascinating', talking, and drinking, and sightseeing with aristocrats from London to Dublin and beyond, and this was not to mention the time he had spent in the society of beautiful women. 'My whole mind was rushing in like a cataract, forcing channels for itself and for the new tastes which it intro-duced.' He simply could not go back to the petty, puerile society of school-boys. It was a joke, an injustice, a degradation. 'I ... felt very much as in the middle ages must have felt some victim of evil destiny, inheritor of a false fleeting prosperity, that suddenly in a moment of time, by signs blazing out past all concealment on his forehead, was detected as a leper.'[68]

Thomas's mind swam with these gloomy thoughts as he wound his way 'by some intolerable old coach' to Stamford, and then took a chaise down to Laxton. He reached the house just as the dinner bell was ringing for the first time, and was greeted in the portico by his sister Mary, who told him that Lady Carbery wished to see him as soon as he arrived. Hastening to her rooms, Thomas learned from her that she had two other guests, Lord and Lady Massey, a young and happily married Irish couple who were 'domesticated at Laxton' because of 'pecuniary embarrassments' in Ireland. As Lord Carbery was absent at his Limerick estate, might Thomas take upon himself the task of entertaining Lord Massey, as the time hung heavily upon him 'during the long couple of hours through which the custom of those times bound a man to the dinner-table after the dis-appearance of the ladies'. Delighted to have the opportunity of obliging Lady Carbery, and of continuing to socialize amongst adults, Thomas dashed to his rooms, took a hot bath, and 'at the second summons of the dinner-bell ... descended a new creature to the drawing-room', ready to fulfil his role as deputy host.[69]

He did so admirably. Aided by 'three or four glasses of wine, to call back the golden spirits which were now so often deserting me', Thomas talked to Lord Massey of hunting, horses and stables, Ireland, and Laxton, before moving on to Lord Carbery's superb library, where 'on rainy days, and often enough one had occasion to say through rainy weeks', it provided a 'delightful resource ... to both of us'. On evenings, however, when Lady Carbery and Lady Massey chose to go visiting among the neighbouring aristocrats, Lord Massey always remained at home, while Thomas was given the task of chaperoning the two women. His delight in this role may well be imagined, and in the after-dinner hours he had the additional pleasure of listening to the assembled company of men praising the two women. 'Lady Massey universally carried off the palm of unlimited homage. Lady Carbery was a regular beauty, and publicly known for such; both were fine figures, and apparently not older than 26; but in her Irish friend people felt something more thoroughly artless and feminine – for the masculine understanding of Lady Carbery in some way communicated its commanding expression to her deportment.'[70]

During his many morning and evening calls with Lady Carbery, Thomas was particularly struck by two very different local nobles. One was John Henry Manners, fifth Duke of Rutland, who conducted himself like someone 'fitted to uphold the honour of his ancient house', and whose magnificent home at Belvoir Castle inspired Thomas with 'respect for the English nobility'. The other was Henry Cecil, first Marquess of Exeter. Thomas had been eager to meet him, before Lady Carbery drily offered him advice: 'moderate your anxiety ... I believe you will find his splendour approachable'. It turned out that Thomas found no splendour at all. 'In this Lord Exeter I saw repeated instances of blank superciliousness ... unmitigated by courtesy.' His 'after-dinner conversation' was 'exquisite' in its 'imbecility', while his 'talk was not of oxen, but of an animal not greatly superior in interest – viz., himself'.[71]

At some point that autumn, on the suggestion of Mrs Quincey, Lady Carbery sent for the renowned Manchester physician White in the hope that he might be able to bring some relief to Mrs Schreiber, as her health was not improving. Thomas of course already knew White as the family doctor who had looked after him as a child, and who – more meaningfully – had performed the postmortem operation on Elizabeth's skull. White attended Mrs Schreiber at Tixover, but resided during his visit at Laxton, where he and Thomas rode together, and met daily at breakfast and dinner. 'Greatly I profited by this intimacy,' declared Thomas, his polish and erudition once more gaining him entry into the adult world.[72] No degree of intimacy, however, seems likely to have prevailed upon him to broach the subject that must often have been in his mind: White's familiarity with Elizabeth's life and death.

Lady Carbery appears to have been intent on turning Thomas into a country gentleman, and ensuring that he attained 'such accomplishments as were usually possessed by the men of her circle'. For two hours every day he took riding lessons from one of her principal grooms, and for many weeks he accompanied her zealous gamekeeper into the Laxton woods, and did his best to become a good shot.[73] Yet while he delighted to oblige her, Thomas was also very keen to help her. Lady Carbery was moving deeper and deeper into an evangelical enthusiasm of a 'gloomy ... Calvinistic' cast, and she sought his guidance in the cultivation of 'religious knowledge in an intellectual way'. Thomas was not widely read in theology, but he applied himself to the area with great aplomb, and soon claimed to be making discoveries that were 'profoundly just', while his thorough knowledge of Greek gave him insights into the New Testament that convinced Lady Carbery that she too needed to learn that language. After persuading Lady Massey and Mary to join them in their studies, the four rode over to Stamford one morning, and 'astounded the bookseller's apprentice by ordering four copies of the Clarendon Press Greek Testament' to be sent down 'by the mail-coach without delay'. Mary and Lady Massey quickly lost interest in the project, but Lady Carbery 'became expert in the original language of the New Testament', and Thomas encouraged her to read Herodotus as a supplementary pursuit. At this juncture, however, Lord Carbery suddenly returned from Ireland, and his patronizing attitude towards his wife's intellectual endeavours led to the defeat of Thomas's plans to broaden their studies in Greek.[74]

For several weeks Mrs Quincey and Thomas had met at Tixover, where they had doubtless pursued the question of his education. By early November, she had discussed the issue at length with his guardians and reached a decision: Thomas would be sent to Manchester Grammar School. He probably pleaded for Bath right to the end, but three central factors sold his mother on Manchester. One, Thomas would once again be near the most energetic of his guardians, Hall, who already had three of his own children at the school. Two, he would be close to Kelsall, who still managed part of the Quincey estate, and whose household had provided such a happy interlude for Thomas four years earlier. And three, students who attended Manchester Grammar School for three consecutive years were eligible for a bursary at Brasenose College, Oxford, totalling £50 a year. This money, coupled with his £150 patrimony, would enable Thomas to raise his allowance near to the sum thought reasonable for a student to lead a comfortable life at Oxford.[75]

No amount of explanation or rationalizing, however, removed the 'sickening oppression' Thomas felt when his mother announced her decision. He knew she was not one to change her mind, and while he had no doubt hoped that Lady Carbery's affection for him would lead her to intercede on his behalf, her deep religious ties to his mother carried the day and she urged him to submit. Thomas's fate 'in the worst shape' he had anticipated was thus 'solemnly and definitively settled'. He looked on his seven weeks at Laxton as 'the happiest of my childish life', but when the time came, he bid a sad goodbye to Lady Carbery, and passed through the Laxton gates on his way to Manchester. 'Misgivingly I went forwards', he recalled, 'feeling for ever that, through clouds of thick darkness, I was continually nearing a danger, or was myself perhaps wilfully provoking a trial, before which my constitutional despondency would cause me to lie down without a struggle.'[76] Thomas's concerns were only partially justified. A trial was coming, but he would not lie down before it. Rebellion was in his heart.

THREE

Down and Out in Manchester and London

[i]

There was little chance of Thomas liking his new school, but his transition back into the classroom seems to have been as bad as he had feared. 'From the glittering halls of the English nobility, I was transferred in one day to the cheerless ... and rude benches of an antique school-room.'[1] The headmaster of Manchester Grammar School, Charles Lawson, possessed a certain flamboyance, dressed as he was in 'a complete suit of black velvet ... lace ruffles at his wrists, black silk stockings, and diamond buckles on his shoes', with a well-powdered peruke 'projecting like a cauliflower, from behind'. But having spent fifty-one of his seventy-two years at the school, Lawson was out of enthusiasm and 'apparently on the extreme verge of life'. Under his supervision, the curriculum revolved around Latin, Greek, and the Bible. The first class of the day began at seven in the morning and sometimes went on for over two hours, though the boys were expected to be finished breakfast and back at their lessons by half past nine. At noon, classes recessed for three hours, and then the boys returned to the oaken benches to work until five.[2]

Escorted by Hall, Thomas entered the school on Sunday, 9 November 1800, and was registered as 'Thomas, son of the late Thomas de Quincey, merchant, Bath'.[3] From the beginning, he disliked the upper schoolroom where he would be taught, for it was cavernous and presented a 'dreary expanse' of whitewash.[4] Thomas and Hall arrived at the room and paced solemnly up to the front desk, where Thomas presented himself to Lawson, who handed him a volume of *The Spectator* and asked him to translate a section of one of Richard Steele's essays. No task could have been more suited to his skills as a Latinist, and he dispatched it with great proficiency. Duly impressed, Lawson allowed himself the one and only compliment he ever paid Thomas, before enrolling him in his highest class.[5]

Like many other students in the school, Thomas was to stay as a boarder in Lawson's home in Long Millgate, and shortly after his examination –

indeed perhaps later that same Sunday – he was dropped off at his new lodgings. Years later he recalled 'the horrors of my first night in that cave of despair', but in other recollections he makes it clear that his first evening contained some pleasures. Guided by 'a homely servant up dilapidated staircases', he stumbled along 'old worm-eaten passages' until at length he was shown into a dimly lit room in which sat a company of about sixteen boys, two or three of whom came forward to welcome him. 'Heavens!' he recollected with some embarrassment, 'how shocking to my too cultivated ears and too fastidious taste' were their dialects. Yet he immediately noticed 'the grave kindness and the absolute sincerity of their manner'. The students at Bath had more 'graceful self-possession', but the 'best of them suffered by comparison with these Manchester boys in the qualities of visible self-restraint and of self-respect'.[6]

Homework that evening was a translation from Hugo Grotius's *De Veritate Religionis Christianae* (1627). Thomas was impressed by the boys' discussion of it, and especially so by the contribution of the fourteen-year-old Ashurst Turner Gilbert, the future bishop of Chichester, who stood up against the prevailing tenor of the conversation, and 'revolutionized the whole logic' of it. Thomas, however, could not entirely dissemble his 'state of dejection', and in an attempt to cheer him up, one of his new schoolmates brought out some brandy. It was the first time that Thomas had tried it, and he was astonished at the effect it had on him, for it worked a 'rapid change' in his 'state of feeling', and 'at once reinstalled' him in his 'natural advantages for conversation'.[7] Brandy, on many future evenings, was similarly to animate and soothe him.

Classes were soon under way, and it took only a short time for Thomas to discern that Lawson was no longer up to his job. Indeed, the two schoolfellows who joined him in the first form also sailed far beyond the headmaster, who inevitably became the butt of the trio's merriment. Lawson would sit at his desk furiously cramming for a lesson on Sophocles, while '*we* never condescended to open our books, until the moment of going up, and were generally employed in writing epigrams upon his wig, or some such important matter'. Lawson was not about to give up, however. Through 'pure zealotry of conscientiousness', he still insisted on discharging all of his duties 'to the last inch', so that his pupils were confined in the classroom for much of the day, typically short-changed on the time supposed to be allotted for their meals, and given no opportunity for exercise or open air.[8] It was a grinding routine that was harder on Lawson than it was on his students, but it soon began to take a toll on Thomas.

Yet apart from these strains, there were encouraging signs in the first months that he might reconcile himself to Manchester. His mother was trying to make it as appealing as possible. She paid for an 'airy and cheerful' private room that served him for both study and sleep. She sent 'five guineas *extra*, for the purchase of an admission to the Manchester Library'. She bought him a piano, in order that he might indulge his 'voluptuous enjoyment of music' (though he soon decided that he would rather listen to a proficient than learn to play himself). What is more, he was benefiting from the school. His fellow students continued to inspire in him 'a deep respect'. 'My intercourse with those amongst them who had any conversational talents, greatly stimulated my intellect.' On the annual speech day in December, he was asked to recite a Latin exercise on a topic remarkably well suited to his talents, and upon which he no doubt excelled: 'Dolor ipse disertum fecerat', a line from Ovid's *Metamorphoses* which translates as 'For grief inspired me then with eloquence.'[9] It is a theme that underscores much of his finest writing.

Thomas also at this time developed a firm friendship with an old family friend, the Reverend John Clowes, a Church of England clergyman who had published several translations of the famous Christian mystic Emanuel Swedenborg. It was Thomas's first close connection with a published author. Clowes was fifty-seven years old at the time, but to Thomas he seemed much nearer to eighty, 'a sublimated spirit dwelling already more than half in some purer world'. Their friendship was based on a shared enthusiasm for 'literature – more especially the Greek and Roman literature' – and Thomas took great pleasure in the fact that Clowes treated him as an equal. He called often at the clergyman's home, an oasis of beauty and quiet in the centre of the city, and would typically be led by one of the ancient servants into the library, which featured marvellous stained-glass windows and a 'sweet-toned organ', and where Clowes would sit writing, reading, singing, and playing music. On perhaps the most memorable of their meetings, Clowes gave Thomas an edition of Homer's *Odyssey*, and then 'sat down to the organ, sang a hymn or two ... chanted part of the liturgy, and finally, at my request, performed the anthem so well known in the English Church service – the collect for the seventh Sunday after Trinity – (*Lord of all power and might*)'. Thomas benefited enormously from the inspiration and solemnity of these performances, though he did not develop an admiration for Swedenborg, and Clowes never tried to bias him in that direction.[10] His enduring interest in subjectivity, redemption, and spiritual insight, however, almost certainly owe a debt to these hours in Clowes's company.

The schedule at Manchester Grammar School kept Thomas occupied for much of the day, and alone in his room in the evenings he spent most of his time reading. As regarded the classics, Euripides was his favourite Greek dramatist, while he preferred Livy, 'both for style and matter, to any other of the Roman historians'. In English history, he was making himself 'critically familiar' with the period of the Civil War, 'having been attracted by the moral grandeur of some who figured in that day'. And 'already, at fifteen', he had a thorough knowledge of 'the great English poets', including Thomas Chatterton, who had achieved notoriety in the 1760s by forging a series of poems supposedly written by a fifteenth-century parish priest named Thomas Rowley, and who had died in 1770 at just seventeen years old, an apparent suicide.[11] Chatterton's idealism, iconoclasm, and artfulness held immense appeal for Thomas, while the potent myth of Chatterton as the sensitive genius driven to an early grave by a callous society began to shape his own thoughts on self-representation.

None of the opportunities offered by the school, however, removed the sting of being sent there in the first place, and within six months he was irritable and dull. He outlined his distress in a letter to Altamont, who was sympathetic, if surprised. 'The disorder you complain of is certainly of very recent acquirement, and therefore may the more easily be got the better of, as I sincerely hope it will, and speedily,' he wrote on 5 May 1801. 'When we were more acquainted you had no disposition to idleness at all.'[12] Thomas had been more industrious in recent weeks than he cared to acknowledge to Altamont; nevertheless, Manchester Grammar School was turning out just as he had feared, or perhaps as he had decreed. He felt ill. He felt trapped. He felt angry.

The gloom was temporarily broken up by the summer holidays. Thomas, Pink, and Henry were to spend them with their mother, who was renting a cottage in Everton, at that time a 'distinct' and 'well-known village upon the heights immediately above Liverpool'. Pink and Henry were to journey from their school at Horwich Moor down into Manchester, where Thomas was to meet them, and take them on to Everton.[13] Unhelpfully, Mrs Quincey gave him this task even though she clearly doubted his ability to perform it: 'I must repeat, do not let Henry go from you a moment, and let Pink mind the luggage.' For all that, the trip seems to have passed without incident, as the boys wound their way from Manchester through to Liverpool, and then up the hill to Mr and Mrs Best's cottage, 9 Middle Lane (now Everton Terrace). The cottage was so small that you could 'reach the chimneys with your hat', Mrs Quincey had told Thomas, but it had 'a delightful view of the water', and she was 'persuaded' that he would 'like this place'.[14]

Across the street lived William Clarke, a banker, who called on Mrs

Quincey 'merely in the general view of offering neighbourly attentions to a family of strangers', and who lent them books and brought them vegetables. With his knack for befriending adults, Thomas was soon on intimate terms with Clarke, and in one of his favourite roles: mentor. Every morning at dawn he crossed the street to Clarke's house and read the Greek dramatist Aeschylus with him.[15] It was also at Clarke's that Thomas met a number of Liverpool's most prominent Whig intellectuals, including the poet and historian William Roscoe, the physician and editor James Currie, and the minister and politician William Shepherd. In a later reminiscence, he maintained that these meetings gave him little pleasure: Roscoe was 'a mere belle-lettrist', Currie was 'constitutionally phlegmatic', and Shepherd was 'a buffoon'.[16]

Yet even in the reminiscence, it is clear that Thomas had a good deal in common with these men, and that his interaction with them forced him to think more deeply about the composite nature of his own political sympathies. Shepherd was a vigorous critic of 'the pious Hannah More', and Thomas's own dislike of her undoubtedly intensified as he sat and listened to these diatribes. Roscoe deplored the slave trade, as did Thomas, who admired the 'boldness' with which he wrote on the 'popular side' of the political spectrum, and the 'great moral courage' with which he defended his liberal views. Currie had recently produced his landmark edition of the works of Robert Burns, and Thomas talked 'with and against' him as his own knowledge of the poet steadily expanded.[17] Mrs Quincey and Thomas were both reading from the Burns edition, but their reactions to it were very different. She thought Currie had erred by playing up Burns's Jacobinism. Thomas thought the opposite, that Currie had gone out of his way to suppress the poet's radical views. To some extent, in taking such a contrary position, Thomas may simply have been trying to bait his mother. But he seems also to have realized that the difference in their positions could be traced back to a fundamental contradiction in Currie, who embraced 'the essential spirit of aristocracy' even as he aligned himself with 'partisan democrats'.[18]

Roscoe and Currie had one additional role to play that summer. Samuel Taylor Coleridge had been their guest as recently as June 1800, when he visited Liverpool on his way north to take up residence at Greta Hall in Keswick in order that he might live and work near Wordsworth, who resided thirteen miles away at Town End, Grasmere. Coleridge saw 'a great deal' of Roscoe and Currie during his stay, and undoubtedly spoke to them of his many intellectual projects, including his work on the second edition of the *Lyrical Ballads*, which had been called for in response to the steady sale of the first edition, and which appeared in January 1801 in two volumes, the first of which reprinted the 1798 poems in a revised order, and the second of which contained a wealth of new material by Wordsworth.[19] Yet for Thomas, perhaps the most exciting part of the new edition was the title page, as it was here that he learned for the first time that these poems had been written 'by W. Wordsworth', though in his famous 'Preface' to the collection Wordsworth also announced that four of the poems – including 'The Ancyent Marinere' – had in fact been 'furnished' by a 'Friend'. Five months later, when Thomas arrived in Everton, he had still not been able to determine the identity of that 'Friend'. It was almost certainly Roscoe and Currie who informed him that it was Coleridge.[20]

As grateful as he was for the information, Thomas quarrelled with one of the men who gave it to him – in all probability Roscoe, who valued Coleridge as a political writer, but was much less impressed with him as a poet. The *Lyrical Ballads*, Thomas knew, constituted 'a grand renovation of poetic power . . . interesting not so much to England as to the human mind'. Roscoe and Currie, however, continued to believe in both the quality of their own verses, 'and the general standard which they set up in poetry'. Thomas probably held his tongue for a while as he listened to the Liverpool men debate the relative merits of different poets, but at some point he must have told them flatly that they were labouring at a level risibly below Coleridge's – 'the difference being pretty much as between an American lake . . . and a carp pond' – and he evidently caused great offence when he did so. To Thomas, Roscoe and Currie did not deserve to be as close to Coleridge as they were. He did. He understood Coleridge's genius. They did not. They were 'timid . . . imitators' of outmoded poetic devices. He was a kindred spirit. Thereafter, he seems to have seen nothing of the two Liverpool men, but he acted promptly on the knowledge he gained from them, searching 'east and west, north and south, for all known works or fragments' by Coleridge and Wordsworth.[21]

[ii]

And so passed away the summer of 1801, together with 'the wine and the roses, and the sea-breezes of . . . Everton'. In August, Thomas was undoubtedly chafing at the thought of returning to Manchester Grammar School, but when he arrived back at Lawson's house in Long Millgate, or just shortly thereafter, he received some wonderful news: Lady Carbery was coming to live in Manchester! Mrs Schreiber was still in poor health, and White had suggested that they relocate to the city as a much cheaper alternative to him travelling out to them. Thomas was delighted. Every night Lawson gave him leave 'to adjourn for four or five hours to the drawing-room of Lady Carbery. Her anxiety about Mrs Schreiber would not allow of her going abroad into society, unless upon the rarest occasions. And I, on my part, was too happy in her conversation – so bold, so novel, and so earnest – voluntarily to have missed any one hour of it.'[22]

Lady Carbery and Thomas occupied themselves in a number of different ways. White invited them to tour his personal museum, which Thomas had visited as a boy. This time he was not shown the clock-case which housed the mummified old lady, but he and Lady Carbery did see another of the museum's great prizes, for White drew them into a corner and showed them a skeleton. 'That', he said, 'is a cast from the celebrated Lancashire highwayman' Edward Higgins, and he proceeded to regale them with a remarkable story. At the time of Higgins's execution for robbery, White was a student of the anatomist William Cumberland Cruikshank, who regarded Higgins as 'so uncommonly fine' a specimen of the male physique that he wanted the privilege of dissecting him, and so spared 'no money or exertion ... to get into possession of him with the least possible delay'. But not everything went according to plan. By 'some special indulgences from one of the under-sheriffs beyond what the law would strictly have warranted', the hanged man was 'cut down considerably within the appointed time, was instantly placed in a chaise-and-four, and was thus brought so prematurely into the private rooms' of Cruikshank, that life was not 'as yet entirely extinct'. White was among the three or four students present at the time, and to one of them Cruikshank observed quietly: '"I think the subject is not quite dead: pray put your knife in (Mr X. Y.) at this point." That was done; a solemn *finis* was placed to the labours of the robber, and perhaps a solemn inauguration to the labours of the student.' This anecdote – in its combination of the ludicrous and the grotesque – 'struck' Thomas 'a good deal', as it 'seemed to imply that all the gentlemen in the dissecting-room were amateurs' in the business of producing corpses.[23] It was one of his first insights into an enduring preoccupation: murder as a fine art.

He and Lady Carbery were also involved in other more edifying activities. Under the tutelage of the noted Manchester evangelical clergyman Cornelius Bayley, Lady Carbery was learning Hebrew, and she agreed to teach Thomas the language (as he had previously taught her Greek), though the project failed to gain much momentum and was soon dropped. More memorably, one day Thomas decided 'with a beating heart' to read Lady Carbery 'The Ancyent Marinere'. He did not dare seek 'sympathy from her or from anybody else upon that part' of the *Lyrical Ballads* which 'belonged to

Wordsworth'. Those poems were sacred. But the 'wildness' of the mariner's adventures convinced him that he might hazard Lady Carbery's approval of Coleridge. Initially, 'she listened with gravity and deep attention'. Yet the poem did not maintain its hold on her, for when they reviewed it, she 'laughed at the finest parts, and shocked me by calling the mariner himself "an old quiz"'. A measure of redemption came later when Lady Carbery 'suddenly repeated by heart', to Dr Bayley, 'the beautiful passage: – "It ceased, yet still the sails made on"'. Bayley 'seemed petrified: and at last, with a deep sigh, as if recovering from the spasms of a new birth, said – "I never heard anything so beautiful in my whole life"'.[24]

With the Christmas holidays approaching, Thomas was once again called upon to deliver a speech at the annual school assembly. His family was in the audience, as was Lady Carbery, who 'made a point of bringing in her party every creature whom she could influence', including Lord Massey 'with his brother and his lovely wife', Lord Grey de Wilton, and Lord Belgrave. When his name was announced, Thomas rose and declaimed Latin verses (presumably that he himself had written) on the recent British subjection of Malta. 'Furious . . . was the applause which greeted me: furious was my own disgust.' Thomas wanted praise – but not for excelling amongst schoolboys. Anyone with a quarter of his talent could do that. It was a school assembly. The audience would have clapped for anything, no matter whether his verses had been twice as bad or four times as good. And why was he in the position of having to collude in his own humiliation anyway? It was all so irritating, so childish. After he finished, he went and sat down right beside Lady Carbery, rather than returning to his 'official place as one of the trinity who composed the head class'. It was a gesture intended to make his dissatisfaction public. He did not want to be in that room and with those boys. He wanted to be with adults. He wanted to be away. That night Lady Carbery told him 'that she had never witnessed an expression of such settled misery and also (so she fancied) of misanthropy, as that which darkened my countenance in those moments of apparent public triumph'.[25] Thomas was reaching the end of his rope.

Meanwhile, for reasons that were not entirely clear to him, his mother had decided against living in Bath, and had embarked on an extensive tour of England in search of another place to live. She had a number of requirements, including 'good medical advice', 'elegant (or, what most people might think aristocratic) society', and a local clergyman who adhered faithfully to the articles of the English Church as 'interpreted by Evangelical divinity', for her views were now 'precisely those of her friend Mrs Hannah More, of Wilberforce, of Henry Thornton, of Zachary Macaulay (father of the historian), and generally of those who were then known amongst sneerers as "the Clapham saints"'.[26]

When at last Mrs Quincey made a decision, however, she was guided primarily by price, which overturned her other conditions, and which led her to purchase 'the Priory', 'an ancient house ... on a miniature scale' attached to St John's Church in Chester, for the 'unintelligibly low' sum of £500. Internally, 'the glory of the house ... lay in the monastic kitchen', while 'the little hall of entrance, the dining-room, and principal bedroom, were in a modest style of elegance'. Externally, a 'miniature pleasure-ground' contained 'a pile of ruined archways' surmounted 'by the exquisite beauty of the shrubs, wild flowers, and ferns'.[27] Buying the property, and then arranging for major renovations, took a great deal of Mrs Quincey's time, as was plain when she wrote to Thomas. 'I have two letters of yours in my desk, but not easy to find, and I cannot answer,' she informed him. '... I remember you mentioned something about cravats, which I never answered, nor can I now.'[28]

It was February before she found time to pay him a visit. Eight weeks had passed since the Christmas assembly debacle, and it is clear that his frustration had only grown worse. It is also clear that his mother had no inkling of it. Finally, on the morning of Tuesday, 16 February 1802, they had an argument in which Mrs Quincey's angry teenage son gave her an earful. Filled with 'amazement and anguish', she returned to Chester, from where she wrote to him two days later. He had proposed leaving the school and spending two years at home before enrolling at Oxford. 'Surely', she countered, 'Mr Lawson's school may afford you better opportunities for study than you could have in any other family!' He seems to have suggested that he would not lower himself by competing for an Oxford scholarship. 'What to say to you on the subject of pecuniary advantages I scarcely know,' she declared, 'since you are so unhappy as to think £100 a year added to your own fortune despicable, and that the honourable competition with your equals for the reward of literary superiority is a degradation.' He touted what he believed to be his noble lineage. 'Were you to stir up doubtful and remote pretensions to a line of ancestry', she cautioned him, 'you would become truly ridiculous.' He told her he was destined for pre-eminence. She was not so sure. 'I cannot think you believe a total revolt from our rule will make you in any sense great if you have not the constituents of greatness in you, or that waiting the common course of time and expediency will at all hinder the maturity of your powers, if you have them.' He argued vociferously in favour of his liberty. She insisted on his obedience. 'I would urge you to consider that the language you use when you say "I must" or

"I will" is absolute disobedience to your father's last and most solemn act, which appoints you to submit to the direction of your guardians, to Mr Hall and myself in particular, in what regards your education.'[29]

Mrs Quincey sent the letter and waited two weeks. No reply. So she wrote again. She was not going to back down, but he had made his point and she was genuinely worried about him. 'Now that I see you threatened with uncommon danger I must endeavour to help you,' she asserted, 'though I may err in the means, or you may defeat them; my tenderness shall follow you through every change and period of life; if the world forsakes you (a probable thing, though not in the catalogue of your present expectations), I cannot.' But having sounded a fairly conciliatory note in her opening, she went on to push her piety at him in a way that seems likely to have goaded the defiance she was trying to subdue. 'At some period of your life you must be convinced, either to your dismay or advantage, that every human being is brought upon this stage of existence for the great purposes of glorifying God above all, and of doing good, and preparing for his own permanent happiness.' Thomas's problem was that he was pursuing 'self glory', and its 'monstrous adjuncts ... independence and pride'. He set far too high a value on 'the most dangerous faculty of the mind, the imagination', which will 'desolate' his life and hopes 'if it be not restrained and brought under religious government'. He was embracing the wrong books: 'Let your daily reading be the works of men who were neither infidels nor Jacobins', a directive she issued without naming specific authors, though she no doubt had Currie in mind, and perhaps even Wordsworth and Coleridge. Thomas needed to change course, and that meant embracing the right book: 'I command you, in the name of that God whom you must serve or lose, that you do conscientiously read every day at least a chapter in the Gospels or Epistles.'[30]

Thomas did respond to this letter, but he did so in a manner that was unlikely to ease the tensions between them, as he undoubtedly recognized. He began pointedly by addressing his mother as 'Mrs de Quincey', perhaps as a way of signalling right from the start that he intended to defy her even as to her preference in her own surname, and perhaps also to remind her that, in flip-flopping from 'Quincey' to 'de Quincey' and back again, she too had shown signs of pride and uncertainty.[31] He then proceeded to list his grievances, which broke down into three main categories. One, he was lonely. 'Naturally, I am fond of solitude; but every one has times when he wishes for company.' Two, he detested Manchester. 'In this place trade is the religion, and money is the god. Every object I see reminds me of those occupations which run counter to the bent of my nature ... I cannot stir out of doors but I am nosed by a factory, a cotton-bag, a cotton-dealer, or something else allied to that most detestable commerce.' And three, his health was in steep decline. A number of factors were involved, including most prominently the 'want of exercise', 'the badness of the air', 'the short time one has to eat one's dinner in', and the atrocious medical attention he was receiving, for he was now under the care of an aged quack who had prescribed an unvarying consumption of 'one horrid mixture, that must have suggested itself to him when prescribing for a tiger', and that Thomas was convinced was doing him far more harm than good. 'To fight simultaneously with such a malady and such a medicine, seemed really too much.' 'Gradually the liver became affected: and connected with that affection arose, what often accompanies such ailments, profound melancholy.'[32]

There may also have been yet another reason why Thomas wished to leave Manchester. In a report issued only a few years after this time, school officials lamented that 'the resorting to taverns and intercourse with women of the town' had become 'a fashion amongst the Boys in the higher classes of the school, which no vigilance of the masters can suppress'. Thomas seems to anticipate these concerns when he explains to his mother that at 'Lawson's ... there is a form of restraint kept up', but 'any person may elude' it. 'I could prove this to you from many instances of the most unbridled licentiousness – which have fallen under my own observation ... *Here* I have no motive for resisting the temptation to enjoy that unrestrained liberty which is continually offered to me; – at *home*, whilst I retained any shame, I should have at least one motive for curbing my passions.'[33] Thomas's taste for prostitutes developed at around this time, and it seems probable that in this letter he is alluding to his first sexual encounters with 'women of the town'. The experience had confused him, for while he had 'no motive for resisting the temptation', he clearly felt distressed at his inability to curb his passions. He was safer at home. In Manchester, he was fast losing his sense of shame.

Mrs Quincey had a mixed reaction to Thomas's long roll call of complaints. In the main, she was annoyed. 'Must you govern me or must I govern you?' she asked him sharply. 'I see no use in repeating the same things, or all the new ones in the world, if you only say the old one, that you are miserable.' She understood that he wanted to leave Lawson's, but *where* was he going to go, and *how* was he going to employ his time 'to *better* advantage'?[34] She wanted answers on these issues, and Thomas was not addressing them. Further, one section of his letter must really have made her blood boil. Where on earth did he find the gall to sneer at the

Manchester cotton trade? His father had been 'allied to that most detestable commerce', and it had brought him both honour and wealth, as she no doubt forcefully reminded him. Thomas, however, was not in a mood for listening, and he scoffed at his father's legacy even as he prepared to make requests to enjoy more of the fruits of it.

Yet his letter did have some effect. By late April, Mrs Quincey had consented to his appeal to be allowed to leave school well before the end of term, though she did not invite him to live at the Priory: 'it is sufficient to say that the necessity for this affair being settled before you come home is more than ever apparent'. Instead, she paid for him to return to Mr and Mrs Best's cottage at Everton, where she no doubt hoped that he would be restored by relaxation and the fresh sea air. She also agreed to 'produce the £100 a year' that he seems to have been requesting as a kind of allowance, but first she needed more details from him. Would he please write to her by 26 May to inform her of his plans 'within the compass of the £100 a year?'[35]

His answer arrived a week after the deadline his mother had specified, and once again seems to have been designed to provoke rather than to propitiate. Mrs Quincey should probably have taken a deep breath, and responded when she felt calmer. But she let her frustration get the better of her, and in a heated letter she berated her son and drove them both much nearer to the breaking point. 'These opinions of yours at sixteen', she snapped, 'have probably been suggested, certainly swelled into importance, by the advocates for early emancipation and other preposterous theories.' She sincerely lamented his illness, 'and with tenfold concern because it is produced by your sick mind, which no earthly physician can cure'. She was tired of his deliberately confrontational stance: 'you tell me that my warm desire for a thing has strengthened your hatred to it'. She brought in Hall to try and broker a deal, and she was happy to sign any agreement Thomas reached with him. But negotiating with Hall, Thomas shot back, was like negotiating with an 'impassive granite block', and the two failed to find any common ground. Mrs Quincey even agreed to an early removal to Oxford, though Thomas now spoke 'doubtfully' about even wanting 'to go to college'. By late June, after months of bickering and wrong-headedness on both sides, mother and son reached deadlock, for he refused to 'unfold' himself about his future plans, and she would not grant the £100 allowance until she knew what he intended to do.[36] Exasperated and clinging to the last vestiges of her authority, she pulled the financial plug on the Everton cottage, and in July Thomas was back as a student at Manchester Grammar School.

[iii]

Mrs Quincey may have won the battle, but she was about to lose the war. Within only a few weeks of returning to the school, Thomas was suffering from all the old symptoms of ill-health and unhappiness, in addition to the humiliation of being forced to return. He made a decision: he was leaving. Lawson would not like it. Neither would Hall. Neither would his mother. But he could see no other way out of this misery. If no amount of effort on his part solved his problems, why not simply run away from them? His mother was not listening to him when he wrote as a schoolboy. Perhaps he would make a stronger impression when he wrote from a position of liberty. She wanted him to stay at the school. She insisted that he stay. However she could not *make* him stay. 'Under the whirl of tumultuous indignation and of new-born hope' which 'suddenly transfigured' his 'whole being', Thomas committed himself to bolting.[37]

From his guardians' point of view, as he later conceded, his decision was incomprehensible. He had already been at the school for nineteen months. All he had to do was to hold on for another year and a half and he would be eligible for the £50 bursary, a crucial supplement that would enable him to top up his patrimonial allowance, and that would place him at Oxford at around the time of his eighteenth birthday on an 'adequate income' of £200 a year.[38] Surely that was reasonable? Surely he could reconcile himself to that?

He could not. Thomas remembered his resolution as 'the sole capital error' of his boyhood, and he wished that he had been wise enough to listen to whispers of 'monitorial wisdom' that had warned him against 'the evil choice'. At one point he blamed his decision on his own 'wilful despair' and 'resolute abjuration' of hope. Yet at another he denied that it was his fault, and claimed that he was right to fight back against his mother and his guardians. 'The steady rebellion upon my part in one-half, was a mere human reaction of justifiable indignation; but in the other half it was the struggle of a conscientious nature ... feeling it as the noblest of duties to resist ... those that would have enslaved me.' The leading factor in his decision to flee, however, seems to have been his conviction that a 'mere excess of bodily suffering and mental disappointments' left him no choice.[39]

He quickly began to prepare a course of action. Money was needed, and with only two pounds in his pocket, he wrote to Lady Carbery and requested a loan of five guineas. Her response was a letter enclosing twice that amount. Then, he took Ashurst Turner Gilbert into his confidence. He wanted to tip three of Lawson's servants one guinea each, as it was the proper, gentlemanly thing to do for those whose 'daily labours' had been increased by his residence in the house. Since he could not pay them without prematurely disclosing his plans, however, he gave Gilbert the three guineas and asked him to distribute them after he had made his escape. His mother had drummed politeness into him so thoroughly that he made it a priority even when he was running away! Finally, he advanced a small sum to a groom. His plan was to pack up a parcel of books and clothes for himself, and then put everything else – including his growing library – into a large trunk. On the appointed morning, the groom was to steal up to his room, help him to remove the trunk, and then take it off to the carrier, who would forward it on to the Priory. Nothing was to be left behind. Thomas wanted to make it clear that he was gone for good. With these stratagems all in place, he found himself with roughly nine guineas remaining. It was enough, he calculated, to allow him to live for about three weeks at the cheapest inns.[40]

Now, where to go? Not unexpectedly, his initial choice was to travel north to the English Lakes. They had long held for him 'a secret fascination, subtle, sweet, fantastic, and even from [his] seventh or eighth year, spiritually strong' because of their close proximity to his native county of Lancashire, but more significantly, because 'this lovely region' was the home of Wordsworth, whom he longed to meet, and with whom he already dreamt of forming a close friendship. The more he thought about it, though, the more he realized that he needed to wait. The principle of 'veneration' was 'by many degrees too strong' in him for any face-to-face meeting at this point, while the thought of appearing before the poet as a 'homeless vagrant' horrified him. As a result, he quietly put it around that he was planning to run away to the Lakes 'in the hope of thus giving a false direction to any pursuit that might be attempted', and then set his sights on a walking tour through Wales, where the landscape had so impressed him two years earlier when he and Westport had travelled to Holyhead. Adding to the attractiveness of this plan was the thought that his route to Wales would take him through Chester, where he could make a clandestine stop at the Priory, and speak to his sister Mary.[41] Their mother would by that point know of his flight, and while Mary would probably not be able to stop her from fuming, she could at least assure her that Thomas was safe.

Naturally, in the midst of these well-laid plans, there was a hitch. On Monday, 19 July, less than twenty-four hours before he was set to leave, Thomas unexpectedly received a strange letter, postmarked from Hamburgh, and addressed in a foreign hand to '*A Monsieur Monsieur de Quincy, Chester*'. Hastily he tore it open. Out dropped a bank draft for 'about forty guineas'. At first he thought it was some kind of gift from Providence designed to aid him at this most critical moment, but as he read through, he was able to piece together that it was dated from some place in Normandy, and addressed to a poor emigrant, who was a relative of the French sculptor and archaeologist Quatremère de Quincy, and who now in the summer of 1802 had a chance to return to France because of the recent Peace of Amiens. 'Such an obscure person', however, was 'naturally unknown to any English post-office', and thus the letter had been forwarded to Thomas, 'as the oldest male member of a family at that time necessarily well known in Chester'. His initial plan was to carry the letter to the Manchester post office at some point that day, as he was very anxious not to be thought a thief. But he was 'unable to carve out any opportunity' amidst the burdens of Lawson's schedule, and 'without a distinct explanation in my own person, exonerating myself, on the written acknowledgement of the post-office, from all farther responsibility, I was most reluctant to give up the letter'.[42] So he tucked it away with a promise to himself that he would deal with it as soon as he had secured his freedom.

At five o'clock the boys finished their classes and adjourned for the 'solemn evening service of the English Church – read by Mr Lawson', after which the school 'dissolved itself'. Thomas distinctly recalled the light of that summer evening, 'broad and gaudy', as the sun lingered above the horizon, and the clock passed from six to seven to eight, at which time the 'students were all mustered; and the names of all were challenged according to the order of precedency. My name, as usual, came first. Stepping forward, I passed Mr Lawson, and bowed to him, looking earnestly in his face, and saying to myself, "He is old and infirm, and in this world I shall not see him again."' Thomas was right: he never did see Lawson again, but he remembered him with generosity. 'Very sincerely I respected him as a conscientious man', and as a 'sound and accurate (though not brilliant) scholar. Personally I owed him much gratitude; for he had been uniformly kind to me, and ... I grieved at the thought of the mortification I should inflict upon him.'[43]

Thomas left the ceremony, climbed the stairs to his room, and retired to bed. It was a difficult night, and by half past three he was up, resolved though full of conflicting emotion. 'I lingered ... as under some sense of dim perplexity, or even of relenting love for the very captivity itself which I was making so violent an effort to abjure.' He went to his window and gazed out 'with deep emotion at the ancient collegiate church' of St Mary (now Manchester Cathedral), and watched as it began to 'crimson with the deep lustre of a cloudless July morning'. How peaceful the dawn was. How agitated he felt. He turned from the window, dressed himself and, with hat and gloves in hand, prepared to leave. But again he lingered. 'Here I had read and studied through all the hours of night; and, though true it was, that, for the latter part of this time, I had lost my gaiety and peace of mind', yet 'as a boy passionately fond of books . . . I could not fail to have enjoyed many happy hours in the midst of general dejection.'[44]

His final moments in the room were later framed in a way that clearly suggests a parallel to his experiences in the bedchamber of his dead sister Elizabeth.[45] 'Suddenly a sort of trance, a frost as of some death-like revelation', wrapped round him, and he was taken back to the incident almost exactly two years earlier when he and Westport visited the Whispering Gallery, and Thomas was convinced that he heard the softest of sounds seized upon and returned as volleying thunders. What if the words he was now whispering to himself were heard throughout the world? What if the decision he was making to leave Manchester came back to haunt him in huge and menacing shapes? These fantasies staggered him. And then, just as had been the case in Elizabeth's bedchamber, 'a sudden step upon the stairs' broke up his dream, and recalled him to himself. The groom was coming to assist him with his trunk. Thomas surveyed 'the chair, hearth, writing-table, and other familiar objects', before turning to face a portrait of the seventeenth-century Duchess of Somerset 'which hung over the mantelpiece; the eyes and mouth of which were so beautiful, and the whole countenance so radiant with divine tranquillity, that I had a thousand times laid down my pen, or my book, to gather consolation from it'. As an idealized representation of female beauty that is at once celestial and maternal, the duchess seems to have both invoked and displaced Elizabeth.[46] Thomas stared at her picture as the old church clock chimed that it was now six in the morning. He leaned forward, kissed the portrait, and left the room.

The groom was waiting. He retrieved Thomas's massive trunk, hoisted it up on to his shoulders, and began a slow and steady descent, while Thomas took his much smaller package and glided down before him to the foot of the stairs. When, however, the groom neared Lawson's quarters, his nerve faltered, his foot slipped, and the trunk falling from his shoulders, careened down the stairs, and slammed into Lawson's bedroom door 'with the noise of twenty devils'. Both Thomas and the groom thought that all was lost, but the ludicrousness of the situation soon took over, and when the groom 'sang out a long, loud, and canorous peal of laughter', Thomas joined in. As a matter of course they expected the headmaster to appear, but no sound issued from his room. 'Mr Lawson', Thomas concluded, 'had a painful complaint, which oftentimes keeping him awake, made his sleep, when it *did* come, peculiarly deep.'[47]

Gathering courage from the silence, the groom picked up the trunk again, reached the bottom of the stairs without further incident, and passed with Thomas out into Long Millgate, where he placed the trunk in a wheelbarrow and departed for the carrier's. Thomas stood for a few moments watching him as he made his way down the street, and then set off himself on a 'south-western route', a volume of Euripides in one pocket, and a volume of Wordsworth in the other. Looking back on this morning from a distance of more than half a century, he characterized his decision to flee as 'a ruin' which reached him 'even at this day by its shadows'.[48] He had crossed the Rubicon. And fiercer trials lay immediately in wait. He was not yet seventeen years old.

[iv]

What to do with the 'odious responsibility' of the letter? It weighed heavily on him as, two hours after he left Manchester, he made his way into the 'cheerful little town of Altrincham'. He had his breakfast here and rested for about an hour, before regaining the road to Chester. During the remainder of that eventful day, he covered an additional twenty-two miles, exulting already in the enormously beneficial influence of the air and the exercise, and stopping in the evening at a roadside inn to enjoy a 'safe and profound night's rest'. Chester was still eighteen miles away and, towards the close of the following day, he enjoyed the 'matchless spectacle' of an 'elaborate and pompous sunset hanging over the mountains of North Wales'. Lines from Wordsworth's 'exquisite poem' 'Ruth' came to his mind, and Thomas recited them as he neared the town, where he found an inn and spent the night.[49]

The next morning, he set himself the task of getting rid of the letter. He felt certain that, in the fifty hours that had elapsed since his flight from Manchester, two separate parties – one from the school, the other from the post office – must be in pursuit of him, and he worried too that if he walked through the Chester streets he might be recognized by one of his mother's servants. Unable to think in the cramped quarters of his room, he slipped quietly from the inn, shaped a course along the medieval city walls, and then descended into an obscure lane which gradually brought him to the banks of the River Dee. Here he found himself all alone, with the exception of a woman who was distant about a quarter of a mile and walking towards him. Suddenly Thomas heard the roaring of water, and was amazed to see what looked like a small tidal wave surging up the river from behind her.

Both he and the woman 'ran like hares' for a short distance, and then stood together as the wave rushed by 'with the ferocious uproar of a hurricane', and a 'salute of waters' that touched their feet. That, the woman explained, was 'the *Bore*', a natural phenomenon on the Dee that occurs when high sea tides form a wave that travels up the river. As the two discussed the event, it occurred to Thomas that this woman might be just the person he needed to help him solve the problem of the letter. He explained his situation to her, begged to put his thanks 'into the shape of half-a-crown', and was no doubt immensely relieved when she agreed to assist him. Two hours later she was back from the post office with the very welcome news that the letter had been safely returned and all was well.[50]

That left the problem of the Priory, where he needed to get word to Mary about his plans without arousing the suspicions of his mother. At dusk, he reconnoitred the house, hoping in some way to attract his sister's attention, but instead his interest was immediately arrested by the unexpected sight of beautiful Arab and Persian horses in the grounds, as well as a host of extra servants, all of which signalled to him that his uncle Penson was on temporary leave from India and residing there. Thomas went away, returned in an hour with a note for Mary, and gave it to one of his uncle's servants, with a request that he would convey it to 'the young lady whose address it bore'. Not more than a minute later, who glided in amongst the miniature ruins of the Priory 'but my bronzed Bengal uncle! A Bengal tiger would not more have startled me'.[51] The runaway was taken inside and arraigned.

Did he have any idea what he had put them through? As soon as the school officials discovered he was gone, they had sent a letter to Mrs Quincey on a 'well mounted' express, which must have galloped by Thomas at around noon on the first day of his flight, and which arrived at the Priory about three o'clock. More distressingly, that same day, and less than an hour later, a second communication arrived, this time from the post office, 'explaining the nature and value of the letter that had been so vexatiously thrust' into his hands. What were they to think? Mary alone was certain that he was innocent. As soon as she heard the news, she arranged for a male escort and a female servant to accompany her in a carriage-and-four to the Lake District, as the rumour was that Thomas had headed in that direction, and she was determined to speak with him before anyone else did. And now here he was skulking around the Priory while his sister was off on some wild-goose chase! Had he given any thought at all to the kind of example he was setting as the oldest son? Granted, the issue of the letter had now been resolved, but what were his two brothers to make of his example of 'wilful insubordination' at school? Thomas's 'conscience smote' him. He had not thought of his brothers, and his mother's 'sorrowful suggestion' that they might follow his example 'thrilled' him with 'remorse'.[52]

If he could have explained the depth and corrosiveness of his misery, he felt that his mother would instantly have sympathized with him, but his heart was freighted with what he called the 'insupportable ... *burden of the Incommunicable*'. 'At this moment, sitting in the same room of the Priory with my mother, knowing how reasonable she was – how patient of explanations – how candid – how open to pity – not the less I sank away in a hopelessness that was immeasurable from all effort at explanation.' It was just as in that distressing dream of his childhood when, from 'languishing impotence to face ... the difficulty' in front of him, he lay down 'without a struggle before some all-conquering lion'. They were too different. His mother was 'predisposed to think ill of all causes that required many words', while he was 'predisposed to subtleties of all sorts and degrees'.[53]

In his uncle, he found an unexpected ally, and through his intercession two different alternatives were discussed: Thomas was granted permission to stay at the Priory; or he could pursue his original intention of walking amongst the Welsh mountains, provided that he agreed to do so 'upon the slender allowance of a guinea a-week'. It was an easy choice. He knew that his mother was 'ready to extend ... her wonted kindness; but not that sort of kindness which could make me forget that I stood under the deepest shadows of her displeasure'. Every hour in the house increased his agitation. He could not even wait for Mary's return.[54] As soon as it was possible, he lit out for Wales.

His first stop seems to have been at the request of his mother, who had old friends – a Mrs Warrington and a Mrs Parry – residing in the Flintshire vale of Gresford. Thomas's stay with them was short. They 'forced' him into society rather more than he wanted, and he was put off by their highly manicured pleasure gardens: 'even the little brooks were trained to "behave themselves"'. He travelled next to 'the fine vale of Llangollen', where he visited Eleanor Butler and Sarah Ponsonby. Better known as the 'Ladies of Llangollen', these two aristocratic women had retired to Wales over twenty years earlier to devote themselves to literature, gardening, and seclusion. Thomas discussed Wordsworth with them, but they were unimpressed, a response that he almost invariably took as a kind of personal insult. 'They must have felt a very slight interest in myself,' he asserted, and 'I grieve to say that my own feelings were not more ardent towards *them*.'[55]

He pushed on to Bangor, where for some weeks he rented 'a very miniature suite of rooms', and where he probably was on 15 August when he marked his seventeenth birthday. His landlady was a loquacious woman who took great pride in the fact that she had once served in the family of the Bishop of Bangor, Dr William Cleaver. One evening during Thomas's stay she dined with Cleaver, and happened to mention that she had taken in a lodger. Cleaver reminded her that they lived on the highroad to Holyhead, so that a multitude of English and Irish swindlers were likely to find themselves travelling through Bangor. 'O my lord, I really don't think that this young gentleman is a swindler,' she replied, before returning home and tactlessly repeating her remarks to Thomas. 'You don't *think* me a swindler?' he exploded. 'For the future, I shall spare you the trouble of thinking about it.'[56] And with that he packed up and left. Such a reaction suggests more than just his gentlemanly sense of honour or his teenage touchiness. The rumours or the guilt surrounding his possession of the '*Monsieur Monsieur de Quincy*' letter had clearly followed him to Bangor, in his conscience and maybe beyond. Thomas was already very adept at inflating his own anxiety, and it was often the case that 'the crime which might have been, was in [his] eyes the crime which had been'. Or perhaps his tidy account of how the letter was returned by the woman he met on the banks of the Dee conceals a much murkier set of circumstances?[57]

Two and a half hours of walking out of Bangor brought him to Caernarfon, but here he found no lodgings that suited him, 'and for some time, therefore, having a small reserve of guineas, I lived very much at inns'. Indeed, he found comfortable places to stay at 'intermitting distances of twelve to sixteen miles' everywhere from Shrewsbury, Llangollen, Llanrwst, and Conway, through Dolgellau, Tan-y-Bwlch, Harlech, and Barmouth, to 'the sweet solitudes of Cardiganshire' and 'the gorgeous wood scenery of Montgomeryshire'. As summer gradually passed into autumn, Thomas could not imagine a 'happier life ... than this vagrancy'. In the days, he embraced the freedom, the fresh air, and the vigorous walking, all of which were steadily restoring his physical and mental health. In the evenings, he enjoyed the music of the Welsh harp, read when books were available, and honed his skills as a conversationalist, where he prided himself on two essential qualities: 'first, an inexhaustible fertility of topics, and ... secondly, a prematurely awakened sense of *art* applied to conversation'.[58]

He made several new friends in these perambulations, including two lawyers, both of whom he bumped into often as they made their rounds 'on market-days through all the principal towns in their districts'. He also met an accomplished young German named De Haren, who introduced him to the German language, which he picked up with his usual precocity, and which he began to study in the works of such writers as Jean Paul Richter, Theodor Gottlieb von Hippel, and Johann Georg Hamann.[59]

Further, it was probably in late September or early October that Thomas stayed for three pleasant days with a family of young Welsh Methodists, who – it has been plausibly suggested – lived in a large house that has since been demolished, but which used to stand on the farm now known as Glanllynnau, which lies on the main road between Afonwen and Criccieth. When Thomas arrived, the parents were away at a Methodist meeting, but a number of the sons and daughters were on hand, and he soon made himself useful to them. 'Here I wrote ... a letter about prize-money for one of the brothers, who had served on board an English man-of-war; and, more privately, two letters to sweethearts for two of the sisters.' However, when the parents returned, their 'churlish faces' told Thomas that he was no longer welcome, and he set out again.[60]

Cost often shaped his movements. Sometimes he encountered 'preposterously low prices', such as when he lived with cottagers and could spend as little as one guinea in every three weeks. But in other places, accommodations – including the 'expense of a bed and the chambermaid' – totalled as much as half-a-guinea a day, which was three times more than he could afford. Part of his solution was to carry a canvas tent, which he himself manufactured, and which he used roughly nine nights in every two weeks to avoid paying for lodgings. Such ingenuity created its own set of problems, though: 'This tent, as may be imagined, was miserably small; both to make it more portable, and also on account of the tent-pole, which, to avoid notice and trouble, was no more than a common walking cane.' Moreover, sleeping in the fields disturbed the cattle, and Thomas lay awake 'in constant anxiety' lest one of them 'should break into my preserve, and poach her heavy foot into my face'. It was also getting much colder now. Barring rain and wind, it was possible to sleep in the tent until the end of October, but 'as winter drew near, this bivouacking system became too dangerous to attempt'. Indeed, one night Thomas got caught in a storm for six hours wandering about Mount Snowdon, and it was midnight before – 'cold and perishing' – he received assistance and was given a bed.[61]

No longer able to save money by camping, Thomas was forced to look for lodgings well off the beaten track, where prices were much lower, and his dwindling resources could be stretched much further. But there was one 'deadly drawback' in such a scheme: the 'utter want of access to books, or (generally speaking) to any intellectual intercourse. I languished all the day through, and all the week through – with nothing whatever, not so much as the county newspaper once in seven days to relieve my mortal ennui.' In addition, hunger was becoming a real issue. Long walks in the fresh mountain air had done a great deal to restore his health, but they had also given him a large appetite that he was finding it increasingly difficult to satisfy on only one guinea a week, even with his various other cost-cutting measures. Gradually, he was compelled to reduce himself to a single meal a day of only tea or coffee, and at length this too was withdrawn, after which 'so long as I remained in Wales, I subsisted either on blackberries, hips, haws, &c. or on the casual hospitalities which I now and then received'.[62]

In early November, Thomas was back in Bangor or its vicinity, from where he wrote to Lord Sligo, whose former title of Altamont had now passed to his son. Thomas apparently told him nothing of his present troubles, but he was undoubtedly pleased with Sligo's warm and prompt response. 'I derived great pleasure from the note you so kindly addressed to me,' he told him, and 'I shall ... always feel a sincere interest in all which concerns you.' Yet it was also at this time that Thomas began to acknowledge that he could no longer rely on his adolescent connections to keep up a close relationship with an aristocrat such as Sligo. 'Every way, I saw that my own dignity ... required that I should no longer go into any circles where I did not stand on my own native footing ... What had been abundantly right for me as a boy, ceased to be right for me when I ceased to be a boy.'[63] Perched on the edge of adulthood, he needed to make his own way, to build his own successes, to command attention for his own achievements. The thought made him both miserable and reckless.

He came suddenly to a resolution: he was going to live in London. And he was going without telling his mother or his guardians. It meant that he would forfeit his current weekly allowance of one guinea. But he had devised a much better plan that would give him roughly the same amount of money, and far more independence. He would borrow £200 from a moneylender, subdivide that sum into yearly allotments of £50, and then live anonymously in London for four years until he turned twenty-one and came into possession of his inheritance. Rent in the city would cost him 'say £25' a year, which would leave him that sum again for his other annual expenses. Such a plan was more than sufficient for his needs, he reasoned, and unquestionably preferable to eking out an existence from week to week in Wales based on hand-outs from his mother that were no longer even covering his basic necessities. Yes, on this scheme he would miss out on university. But he convinced himself that he was not likely to gain much from a place like Oxford in any case. Far better to live freely in London, enjoy the many riches of the city, and get an education that way. In November he set the wheels in motion, writing to a London moneylender and discussing his plans with various Welsh friends, who pitched in to give him £12, enough he hoped to enable him to travel to London and live there for a few weeks until his loan came through.[64]

As he prepared to leave, 'mere accident' carried him to Oswestry, where he met 'the very warmest amongst my Welsh friends', a lawyer who, 'as it turned out, resided there'. Coerced by his kindness, Thomas stayed with him for several days, enjoying his large library, 'youthful frankness', and 'kindling intellect'. However, when he realized that his presence was interfering with his friend's business obligations, he announced his departure. It was the close of November, but the weather had temporarily turned sunny, and Thomas decided to walk to Shrewsbury, and then catch the coach down into London. He and his friend set off one morning and covered most of the first five miles together, before bidding each other goodbye. The remaining thirteen miles Thomas travelled alone, the beauty of the day, the passing of the season, and the uncertainties that lay ahead all combining to put him in a melancholy mood. 'So sweet, so ghostly, in its soft, golden smiles silent as a dream, and quiet as the dying trance of a saint, faded through all its stages this departing day, along the whole length of which I bade farewell for many a year to Wales, and farewell to summer.'[65]

He arrived in Shrewsbury at least two hours after nightfall, and checked into what was probably the Lion Inn. Four servants with wax-lights guided him into a large ballroom, the only space available to him because of renovations at the hotel. Thomas took a seat and gazed around him. The room, noble and sumptuous, had 'three gorgeous chandeliers' hung from a ceiling of nineteen or twenty feet, and enough space for two orchestras, while its emptiness on this November night invoked within him a contrary vision of those many hours when it must have been full of bustling crowds, and laughter, and music. Outside, meanwhile, a fierce storm had been brewing, and he listened as it raved in 'one vast laboratory of hostile movements in all directions'. Over the course of the past day, Thomas's thoughts had been divided between Wales and London. But now as he sat in the Shrewsbury ballroom, Wales fell away from him, as the towering dimensions of the room and the raging strength of the storm 'brought up continually and obstinately, through natural links of associated feelings or images, the mighty vision of London'. 'Sole, dark, infinite', it brooded 'over the whole capacities' of his heart until he had worked himself up into 'the deadliest condition of nervous emotion'.[66]

On one level, it hardly made sense. Why cut himself off from fifty-two guineas a year in Wales to live on fifty pounds a year in London? Did he fear that if he returned to the Priory his mother or Hall would force him back to Manchester Grammar School? Did he simply want freedom on his own terms at any cost? Or did he imagine himself as a kind of Chattertonian figure, travelling to London – like Chatterton – at seventeen years old, brilliantly gifted and ready to make his mark? Or were there still other factors involved that he simply never divulged – that his many reminiscences disguise rather than reveal?

He was besieged by second thoughts, but his pride would not let him reverse a decision that he already half-regretted. In retrospect, he presented it as a kind of fate, dreadful but irresistible, that drew him down to London, some 'hidden persecution' that bade him 'fly when no man pursued'. But looking back he also felt compelled to embrace the decision, for it defined him even as it damaged him, set him apart even as it set him back. At two in the morning, Thomas heard the sound of wheels, followed a few moments later by the announcement that the London Mail had been given a fresh team of horses and was now ready for departure. He left the hotel and boarded the coach. Twenty-eight long hours later, many of them undoubtedly passed in the dejection of his own thoughts, he arrived, a teenage runaway, at the General Post Office in Lombard Street.[67]

[v]

By ten that morning, Thomas was in the office of a Jewish moneylender named Mr Dell. He had arrived thinking that the process of obtaining a loan was quite straightforward. It was not long before he learned that he was wrong. Dell's first rule of business was that he 'never granted a personal interview to any man'. In order to prosecute the negotiations, Thomas needed to engage an attorney. Dell's office recommended a man named Brunell, who for shady purposes of business also went by the name of Brown, and who lived at 38 Greek Street, a corner house that stood partly in Soho Square, and that has long since been demolished.[68] Thomas headed immediately to the house, which he found to be 'not . . . at all disrespectable', though it had been neglected for many years, and was invested with a 'deep silence' from the 'absence of all visiters'. 'Mr Brown-Brunell' was a 'big, hulking' man who came to the front door, inspected Thomas through a narrow side window, admitted him cheerfully, and conducted him to an office at the back of the house. 'From the expression of his face, but much more from the contradictory and self-counteracting play of his features, you gathered in a moment that he was a man who had much to conceal, and much, perhaps, that he would gladly forget.' He had, however, in Thomas's eyes one central redeeming feature: an 'unaffected love of knowledge, but, above all, of that specific knowledge which we call literature'.[69]

Thomas outlined his situation for Brunell and then left the matter in his hands, while he checked himself into very sparse lodgings, and waited over the next several weeks for his loan to come through. But his loan did not come through. Brunell was 'continually refreshing my hopes with new delusions, whiling me on with pretended preparation of deeds, and extorting from me ... as much as possible for the purchase of imaginary stamps'.[70] At Christmas a year earlier Thomas had stood in front of his peers at Manchester Grammar School and recited Latin verses before going to sit down beside Lady Carbery. This Christmas he sat, alone in London, cut off from family and friends, in penurious circumstances, and treading perilously close to the kinds of bodily suffering that he had already endured in Wales. More than two years ago, in Ireland, and at Eton and Laxton, he had greatly enjoyed fashionable life and fashionable society. But churning just below the surface was his deep sense of loss and alienation. For many years he had felt like a pariah. Now he seems to have determined to become one.

Shortly after Christmas, he was desperate enough to put himself in touch with Hall – almost certainly in a letter sent via Mr Best in Everton – in an attempt to find some grounds for reconciliation. Hall's response to him was cold. 'Sir,' he began curtly,

As you have thought proper to revolt from your duty on a point of the utmost importance to your present interest and future welfare – as you have hitherto persisted in rejecting the wishes of your guardians, who could be governed by no motives but those of promoting your real benefit, you cannot be surprised to hear that they have no new proposition to make. But, notwithstanding all that has passed, if you have any plans in agitation that seem entitled to notice, they are willing to pay them every degree of consideration.

They trust that by this time you are convinced that it was (to speak the least of it) a rash step for a young man of seventeen to throw himself out of the protection of his friends and relations into the wide world, and to have nothing to trust to but the charity or compassion of strangers; and they still cherish the hope that you will renounce your errors, and endeavour to remove the impression of former misconduct by correct and proper behaviour for the future. – I am, Sir, your very humble servant,

Samuel Hall.[71]

Such a letter seems unlikely to have encouraged Thomas to reconsider his behaviour. He appears not to have replied to it, and thereafter communication between the two camps ceased.

By the end of January his circumstances were dire beyond anything he had known in Wales. He was down to his last half-guinea, which he needed to put towards the 'urgent interest of finding daily food', and which meant there was no money left for lodgings. One day, in desperation, he asked Brunell if he could 'make use of his large house as a nightly asylum from the open air', a request that Brunell granted so readily that Thomas was filled with remorse that 'at a much earlier period' he had not applied 'for this liberty; since I might thus have saved a considerable fund of guineas'. At nightfall on that same day, Thomas arrived in Greek Street to take possession of his new rooms, only to discover that the house 'already contained one single inmate, a poor, friendless' ten-year-old girl who was overjoyed to learn that he was to be her companion, as she had for some time been waging a solitary battle against the 'echoing loneliness' of the house, the 'prodigious uproar' of rats on the staircase, the 'real fleshly ills of cold and hunger', and – worst of all – the 'self-created' terror of ghosts. She 'was neither pretty, nor quick in understanding, nor remarkably pleasing in manners', and Thomas was unsure if she was an illegitimate daughter of Brunell's, or simply a 'menial servant'.[72] But he felt great affection for her, and undoubtedly her plight reminded him of Sarah and Mary Hall's desperate life of servitude.

Brunell, he soon learned, did not actually reside in Greek Street. His unscrupulous practices as an attorney drove him each night to seek lodgings in different quarters of London. Some mornings he arrived back at Greek Street very early, some mornings not until ten, and some mornings not at all. When he entered the house, the young girl went below stairs to brush his shoes and coat, while he retired to his office, where he breakfasted on a roll or a few biscuits. Thomas generally contrived a reason for drifting in at this time, and 'with an air of as much indifference' as he could assume, took up such fragments of food 'as might chance to remain'.[73] On many days, a half-eaten roll from Brunell's breakfast table seems to have been his only meal.

Thereafter, he left the house, and filled the time as best he could. He sat in parks. He roamed the streets. He dozed. In one instance, he recalled standing in front of a baker's shop, and surveying some rolls 'with an eagerness of desire which it was humiliating to recollect'. For hours on end, Wordsworth filled his thoughts, and he ruminated intently on the power of his writings and, more tantalizingly, the possibility of his friendship. 'My consolation was . . . to gaze from Oxford Street up every avenue in succession which pierces northwards through the heart of Marylebone to the fields and the woods; for *that*, said I, travelling with my eyes up the long vistas which lay part in light and part in shade – "*that* is the road to the north, and therefore"' to the poet's home at Grasmere. Each day Thomas stayed out in the city until the approach of twilight, at which point he began his walk back to Greek Street, where his welcome knock on the front door brought the girl's 'little trembling footsteps' up to greet him.[74]

The days were long but the nights were even more difficult. Thomas and the girl had assembled what comforts they could to protect themselves from the nightly invasions of damp and cold. They made a bed upon the floor with a bundle of law papers for a pillow, and a horseman's cloak, a large sofa cover, a small piece of rug, and 'some fragments of other articles' for blankets. As the night closed in, the girl huddled close to him, both for warmth 'and for security against her ghostly enemies', and when he was not more than usually ill, he took her in his arms, so that she was tolerably comfortable and often went off to sleep.[75]

Thomas was not so fortunate. He lay awake on many nights, and when he did finally fall asleep, tumultuous dreams ensured that he only received 'what is called *dog-sleep*; so that I could hear myself moaning; and very often I was awakened suddenly by my own voice'. About this time, too, 'a hideous sensation began to haunt me as soon as I fell into a slumber, which has since returned upon me, at different periods of my life – viz., a sort of twitching (I knew not where, but apparently about the region of the stomach), which compelled me violently to throw out my feet for the sake of relieving it'. As the weeks wore into February Thomas was caught in a cruel cycle of physical misery. 'A more killing curse there does not exist for man or woman, than that bitter combat between the weariness that prompts sleep, and the keen, searching cold that forces you from the first access of sleep to start up horror-stricken, and to seek warmth vainly in renewed exercise, though long since fainting under fatigue.' Of all the terrors that human flesh is called upon to face, 'not one – not even hunger' – was in his experience comparable to the ravages of cold. He had learned something of this 'on the wild hill-sides in Wales'.[76] But in London the horrors of the winter air cut even more deeply into him.

The young waif of Greek Street was Thomas's 'partner in wretchedness', but she was not his closest companion during these weeks of deprivation. There was another, older girl – Ann of Oxford Street, 'O noble-minded Ann' – whose hold on Thomas was far stronger. Ann was a prostitute, 'one of that unhappy class who belong to the outcasts and pariahs of our female population'. Thomas felt 'no shame' in avowing that he was 'then on familiar and friendly terms with many women in that unfortunate condition', for he liked to claim – in defiance of some of his own deep-seated bigotries – that at no time in his life had he ever been a person who thought himself 'polluted by the touch or approach of any creature that wore a human shape'. He had many reasons to be grateful to these women. Some of them took his part against watchmen who wished to drive him off the steps of houses, while others protected him 'against more serious aggressions'. But to Ann he owed an even greater debt. In her 'bounty and compassion', she ministered to his 'necessities when all the world stood aloof' from him. For many weeks he walked with her up and down Oxford Street, resting with her 'under the shelter of porticos', and deriving solace with her from 'airs played on a common street-organ'. Just fifteen years old, Ann was 'timid and dejected to a degree which showed how deeply sorrow had taken hold of her young heart'. She had been victimized by a 'brutal ruffian' who had 'plundered her little property'. Thomas was sure that he could help her. He would accompany her to a magistrate, and plead her case for her. English justice, he assured her, did not care if she was poor, and would 'speedily and amply avenge her' for the wrongs she had suffered.[77] He would see to it.

Before the two had a chance to visit a court, however, an incident occurred which haunted Thomas for the rest of his life. He and Ann were pacing slowly along 'the great Mediterranean of Oxford Street' at the end of a day on which he felt 'unusually ill and faint'. At his request, they turned off into Soho Square, where they sat down on the steps of one of the houses. Suddenly, as they rested, Thomas grew much worse.

I had been leaning my head against her bosom, and all at once I sank from her arms, and fell backwards on the steps. From the sensations I then had, I felt an inner conviction of the liveliest kind, that, without some powerful and reviving stimulus, I should either have died on the spot, or should, at least, have sunk to a point of exhaustion from which all re-ascent, under my friendless circumstances, would soon have become hopeless. Then it was, at this crisis of my fate, that my poor orphan companion, who had herself met with little but injuries in this world, stretched out a saving hand to me. Uttering a cry of terror, but without a moment's delay, she ran off into Oxford Street, and in less time than could be imagined, returned to me with a glass of port-wine and spices, that acted upon my empty stomach (which at that time would have rejected all solid food) with an instantaneous power of restoration; and for this glass the generous girl, without a murmur, paid out of her own humble purse, at a time, be it remembered, when she had scarcely wherewithal to purchase the bare necessaries of life, and when she could have no reason to expect that I should ever be able to reimburse her.[78]

Thomas never ceased to believe that Ann had saved his life.

Soon after his collapse in Soho Square, he met in Albemarle Street 'a gentleman of his late Majesty's household. This gentleman had received hospitalities, on different occasions, from my family; and he challenged me upon the strength of my family likeness.' Thomas did not attempt to disguise his identity, and when the gentleman promised to keep his secret from his guardians, he gave him his address in Greek Street, where the next morning a letter arrived. Brunell suspected it contained money, but he turned it over 'honourably, and without demur'. Inside Thomas found a ten-pound bank note.[79]

The windfall seems to have prompted him to renew his efforts to secure the loan that had brought him to London in the first place. To his undoubted relief, he learned that matters were moving. Dell, and 'other advertising money-lenders' to whom he had introduced himself, had determined that the second son of Thomas Quincey did indeed 'have all the claims (or more than all)' that Thomas had described to them. But one question remained: was Thomas the second son of Thomas Quincey? 'This doubt had never occurred to me as a possible one,' he declared; 'I had rather feared ... that I might be too well known to be that person, and that some scheme might be passing in their minds for entrapping me and selling me to my guardians.'[80]

Anxious 'to satisfy their scruples', he pulled from his pocket a series of letters that he had received whilst in Wales, most of which were from the Marquis of Sligo, and his son, the Earl of Altamont. That got Dell's attention, for the Earl's 'great expectations were well known to him', and after reading the letters he agreed to loan Thomas two or three hundred pounds, provided that Altamont guaranteed the payment. Delighted, Thomas immediately made plans to visit Eton, where Altamont was still a student. From his ten pounds, he turned over three guineas to Dell, and a smaller sum to Brunell. A further fifteen shillings went on 're-establishing (though in a very humble way)' his dress. Of the remaining four guineas, he gave one to Ann, and kept three for his travel expenses, on the understanding that when he returned he would divide with her whatever sum remained.[81]

On the dark winter evening of his departure, he and Ann set off towards Piccadilly in plenty of time to catch the coach at the Gloucester Coffee-house. When they reached Golden Square, they sat down and discussed their plans. Thomas was full of hope, but Ann was cheerless and racked by a violent cough. He told her that he expected to return within a week, and they agreed that five nights from that night, and every night thereafter, she would wait for him at six o'clock near the bottom of Great Titchfield Street. He kissed her. She put her arms about his neck, 'and wept, without speaking a word'. Near eight o'clock they parted, and Thomas walked towards the 'tumult and blaze' of Piccadilly, where at quarter past eight he mounted the outside of the Bristol Mail and rode out of London.[82]

Within the first four or five miles of leaving the city, the 'fine fluent motion' of the mail-coach put him to sleep, with the result that he began to annoy a fellow-passenger 'by occasionally falling against him when the coach gave a lurch'. The man complained heavily of the inconvenience. Thomas apologized, and briefly explained something of his recent sufferings. The man's demeanour changed in an instant, and when Thomas unavoidably fell asleep again, he awoke to find that the man had put his arm around him to prevent him from falling off. Further, 'upon the sudden pulling up' of the mail-coach, Thomas discovered that he had slept so soundly that he had travelled six or seven miles beyond his intended stop. As he alighted, his 'friendly companion' entreated him 'to go to bed without delay'. Later Thomas reflected on 'how easily a man, who has never been in any great distress, may pass through life without knowing in his own person ... the possible goodness of the human heart, or, as unwillingly I add, its possible churlishness'.[83]

It was already within an hour of midnight when he began backtracking towards Eton. His route took him across Hounslow Heath, and as he walked slowly along he remembered that a murder had recently been committed there. If he had been Altamont, and heir to a reputed fortune of £30,000, 'what a panic' he should have been under at that moment for his throat! But as it was, 'being little better than an outcast', he reassured himself that he was too poor to be of interest to a murderer. Finally, at about four o'clock, he succumbed to weariness and the cold air, and fell asleep on the road between Slough and Eton, where he was roused at dawn by the voice of a man standing over him. Thomas was unable to determine what the man wanted, but he was glad of the disturbance, for it enabled him to slip through Eton 'before people were generally astir', and to take refuge in a little pub in Windsor, where he washed himself, and as far as was possible, adjusted his dress.[84]

At eight in the morning, roughly twelve hours after he had left London, Thomas went down towards the precincts of Eton to seek Lord Altamont.

On the way he met some junior boys, who gave him very bad news. Altamont was no longer at Eton. He had left to go to Jesus College, Cambridge. This was a disaster: all that effort and money thrown away! Thomas calmed himself down by bringing to mind the fact that he had other aristocratic friends at Eton. What about John Otway Cuffe, Viscount Castle-Cuffe? He and Altamont were cousins, and Thomas had met him some years earlier, perhaps at Bath, or when he had first visited Eton, or during his holiday in Ireland. Yes, he was told, Castle-Cuffe was still at Eton. Thomas called on him, was received kindly, and asked to breakfast. But when the 'luxuries' of the table were placed in front of him, he could not eat them.[85] It had been so long since he had enjoyed a proper meal that he had lost his appetite.

Briefly he explained his troubles to Castle-Cuffe, and then made a request. Might he have some wine? He had 'at all times a craving for wine'. Castle-Cuffe expressed 'deep sympathy' with him, and duly granted his request. 'This gave me instantaneous relief and immoderate pleasure; and on all occasions, when I had an opportunity, I never failed to drink wine.' Thomas's thoughts then turned to the reason for his visit to Eton. He was conscious that his claims on Castle-Cuffe were not really sufficient for the request he was about to make, but unwilling to lose his journey, and no doubt a little flushed by the drink, he asked his question. Castle-Cuffe faltered a little, and 'acknowledged that he did not like to have any dealings with money-lenders', though eventually 'he promised, under certain conditions ... to give his security'.[86]

Thomas stayed another two days – 'I hope that it was not from this love of wine that I lingered in the neighbourhood of my Eton friends' – and then returned in a Windsor coach to London. He took Castle-Cuffe's conditions to Dell, who promptly rejected them, sending him back virtually to square one. Time passed on. There were more delays. Thomas's remaining money disappeared, and he began to relapse towards his 'former state of wretchedness'. 'Suddenly, however, at this crisis, an opening was made, almost by accident', for reconciliation with his guardians.[87]

Details of the negotiations are not known, but clearly the two parties found some common ground. During his time in London, Thomas had become convinced that if he was reclaimed by his guardians, they would force him to return to Manchester Grammar School.[88] Plainly they promised him that they would not do so (if, indeed, that had ever been their intention, for they had been happy enough eight months earlier to let him wander through Wales). His guardians must also have agreed to let him spend the spring and summer at Everton, away from his mother and with a sufficient allowance. Finally, and less contentiously, when he turned eighteen, Thomas was to be allowed to go to Oxford, though the details of his annual allowance had yet to be worked out.

'Meantime, what had become of Ann?' Thomas went each night to the rendezvous point in Great Titchfield Street, but she was not there. He did not know, 'or (as a matter of no great interest)', had forgotten her surname, which he realized now was 'the surest means of tracing her'. The road where she lodged he knew, but not the house, and in any event he remembered that recent ill-treatment by her landlord 'made it probable that she had quitted those lodgings' before they parted. Several more nights passed. Thomas felt certain that she must in some way have been prevented from keeping their engagement, or worse, that they were 'sometimes in search of each other, at the very same moment, through the mighty labyrinths of London'. He 'put into activity every means of tracing her' that his knowledge of the city suggested, and the limited extent of his power made possible. But most people thought that the earnestness of his enquiries 'arose from motives which moved their laughter or their slight regard'. At length, as a 'despairing resource' on his last day in London, he put his address at the Priory 'into the hands of the only person who (I was sure) must know Ann by sight'. It was all in vain. 'To this hour I have never heard a syllable about her,' he wrote more than fifty years later. 'This, amongst such troubles as most men meet with in this life, has been my heaviest affliction.'[89]

How plausible is Thomas's account of his relationship with Ann? Certainly in his wanderings up and down Oxford Street he could have fallen into walking and talking with prostitutes, as the area was well known for soliciting. Some of these women – even women that were younger than him – may well have taken him under their wing: he liked female company, he had very little experience of London, and he would undoubtedly have welcomed their guidance or protection. It is even possible that he developed an especially close relationship with one of them, and that on a particularly bad night, he passed out from fatigue and she, or one of her friends, came quickly to his assistance.

Yet he left no contemporary record of his relationship with her. All his accounts of Ann – in fact, the only accounts of her at all – come in his reminiscences, the first of which was not written until nearly two decades after they met. Genuine experience no doubt played a role, but his portrayal of her seems decisively shaped by a number of other factors. He patterns her on the biblical figure of Mary Magdalen, a sinful but repentant prostitute, as well as on more recent portrayals of the suffering and nobility of the poor from the *Lyrical Ballads*, though he transposes Wordsworth's rural scenes into vivid accounts of urban despair.[90] He also idealizes her as a 'benefactress' and 'saviour' with whom he has a strictly platonic relationship, in part because he has no money, but also because of his strong desire to shield and comfort her, as several years earlier he had hoped to shield and comfort Elizabeth. Indeed, he loves Ann 'as affectionately as if she had been my sister', for at some level in talking about her, he is talking about Elizabeth. She shaped his affection for Ann, as Ann provided a way for him to relive his affection for Elizabeth.[91] In his imagination, the two became conflated as intimate companions, suffering innocents, youthful victims.

Yet at the same time as he was fantasizing about saving Ann, Thomas may also have been having sex with her. In the long and plaintive letter he wrote to his mother just prior to his flight from Manchester Grammar School, he hinted broadly that he had already called on 'women of the town', and certainly a year later he was indulging in visits to Liverpool brothels. In between these two dates he was frequently in the company of London prostitutes, and at different points it seems probable that he was able to find the money to gratify his appetite for them. These sharply differing attitudes towards Ann – one brotherly, the other carnal – go a long way towards explaining the deep feelings of anxiety and remorse that he so clearly associates with her.[92]

Perhaps he did leave his Priory address with one of her friends, but he can hardly have expected that his mother would have been pleased to meet Ann if she had suddenly turned up on the Priory doorstep. Despite his London vagrancy, Thomas had very good social connections and he was on his way to Oxford. Powerfully drawn as he was to both aristocrats and exiles, he of course recognized that his friendships in these two very different worlds were utterly incompatible. He may have been unable to find Ann in the London streets, but he may also have given her the slip, for where he was going, she was not welcome. His representation of her is most probably a composite of different prostitutes and situations. More compellingly, she represents the collision of experience, sentimentality, literary antecedent, and sexual guilt in ways that at once fascinated and tormented him. After sixteen weeks living rough in London, he left the city in haste, passed up through Oxford, and returned to the Priory, deeply scarred by the miseries of the last four months.[93] Though he claims he never saw Ann again, neither did he escape her. As intimate, outcast, saviour, and sibling, she haunted him far into the future.

FOUR

Letters of a Young Man

[i]

'What shall be my character?' Thomas asked himself. 'I have been thinking this afternoon – wild – impetuous – *splendidly* sublime? dignified – melancholy – *gloomily* sublime? or shrouded in mystery – supernatural – like the "ancient mariner" – *awfully* sublime.'[1] These musings, recorded in a diary that he kept from April through June of 1803, place Samuel Taylor Coleridge at the centre of his thoughts in the months immediately following his London ordeal, and show Thomas already patterning his self – or, more especially, his potential self – on Coleridge.[2] At the time of these speculations, Thomas was living at Mrs Best's cottage in Everton, where he had been shunted after returning to the Priory, for his mother had once again decided that she was not prepared to live in the same house with her truant son. Three weeks later, Thomas was out socializing when he met a Mrs Barcroft and a Mr Bree, both of whom lived in the Lake District near Coleridge. She told him that '*Coleridge* is very absent – frequently walks half a mile (to her *uncle's*, I think she said) without being sensible that he has no hat on ... Mr Bree surprises me by telling me that *Coleridge* intends to astonish the world with a *Metaphysical* work ... on which he intends to found his fame.' Thomas listened with great excitement to these gossipy neighbours, and then walked home 'thinking of *Coleridge*; – am in transports of love and admiration for him ... I begin to think him the greatest man that has ever appeared and go to sleep'.[3]

Dreams of Coleridge profoundly engaged him, but they were one of the few bright spots during a time in which he was often dispirited and remote. As had been the case both one and two years earlier, he had gone to Everton in search of rejuvenation, and to some extent he found it. Thomas spent a good deal of his time walking, to the circulating libraries, the bookstores, the new botanical gardens, the concert-rooms, and the theatre, where one evening he saw Charles Mayne Young in *Hamlet*.[4] He lounged on the pier, went to tea-parties, stopped at Everton's famous toffee house, and on

Sundays attended church, though he was not always impressed by the quality of the sermon: 'went to St Ann's; – heard an ass preach'.[5]

On several of his rambles he talked to strangers: a poor woman, a lass who wanted money for some sweets, a man who took shelter with him under a hedge during a downpour. His most striking encounter, however, was with 'a fellow' he met in 'the lanes ... who counterfeited drunkenness or lunacy or idiocy; – I say *counterfeited*, because I am well convinced he was some vile outcast of society – a pest and disgrace to humanity. I was just on point of hitting him a dab on his disgusting face when a gentleman (coming up) alarmed him and saved me trouble.'[6] So much for Thomas's oft-proclaimed sympathy for outsiders! His virulent condemnation of this 'vile outcast' serves as a salutary reminder that there is an often stark difference between the highly crafted accounts of his experience that he produced for public consumption, and the heated outbursts of anger and disgust that he confided to his private letters and diaries. Thomas wrote passionately on behalf of the vulnerable and the abused, and he often acted in their interests, but his concern for them was not as steadfast or as inclusive as he liked to claim.

Over the course of these weeks, he spent a good deal of time with two Everton men: Mr Cragg, a merchant and apparently an old family friend; and James Wright, a partner in the Liverpool publishing and bookselling firm of Merritt and Wright.[7] Thomas dined often at Cragg's, and afterwards played whist, or engaged in conversation with Wright and Cragg, their wives and friends, and any chance visitors. On one occasion the company talked 'of free-will', the 'origin of evil', the 'association of ideas', and the 'incompatibility of eternal punishment – first with God's *justice* and secondly with his mercy'. On another, Thomas assented to John Merritt's opinion that there was 'no harm in sexual intercourse between a brother and sister (commonly termed *incest*)'.[8] Thomas drank at several of these gatherings. On 10 May he 'got tipsy (or rather *elevated*)'. Nine days later he had two glasses of madeira at dinner, 'and five or six after it'. Most memorably, in early June he took part in a 'debauch' before falling asleep on the sofa in Wright's parlour.[9]

These weeks were also marked by an enormous amount of reading. Thomas ranged from Richard Brinsley Sheridan's *The Critic*, Mary Robinson's *Memoirs*, and Thomas Holcroft's *Caroline of Litchfield*, through the Bible and a series of German writers in translation, to a host of contemporary poets, including William Cowper, Thomas Moore, Walter Scott, and Charlotte Smith, whose 'Ode to the Poppy' he found 'particularly' notable, perhaps for its descriptions of the miraculous and 'soul-soothing' powers of opium.[10] At the same time, he was devouring Gothic fiction, especially by women writers such as Mary Pilkington, Ann Radcliffe, Clara Reeve, and Anne Bannerman, whose *Tales of Superstition and Chivalry* he much preferred to Matthew ('Monk') Lewis's *Tales of Wonder.* Sophia Lee's *The Recess* made him cry. Jane West's *Infidel Father* contained descriptions of opium hallucinations that may well have heightened his curiosity about the drug.[11] Thomas also read to others on several occasions. At the Wrights' on 6 May, he entertained their guest Mrs Edmunds in the pre-dinner hour by reading her Burns's 'Ode to Despondency' and Robert Southey's 'Lord William'. A week and a half later, again at the Wrights', he began to read Shakespeare's *The Winter's Tale* to the ladies, and over the course of the next two evenings they listened to him as he completed the entire play aloud.[12] For Thomas, reading was both a private pleasure and a social practice.

Politics, too, deepened their hold on him. In the middle of May, the Peace of Amiens was broken and France returned to war with Britain. On the French side of the equation, Thomas's attitude was straightforwardly aggressive. He loathed Napoleon. 'Of that gilded fly of Corsica ... I said just now ... "May he be thirsty to all eternity – and have nothing but cups of damnation to drink."' On the British side, his attitude was far more mixed. On 23 May, Cragg asked him which 'character of the present day (in *public* life)' he most admired. 'As a *moral* one', Thomas replied, Charles James Fox, the Whig leader of the opposition and a famous champion of liberty. Cragg objected to Fox's '*gaming* and *adultery*', neither of which, Thomas observed, at all lessened his opinion of him. In a letter to his mother only a week later, however, Thomas also spoke up in favour of Fox's arch-adversary, the former Conservative prime minister William Pitt, who had led Britain during its previous battles with Napoleon, and who had recently 'awakened from his long slumber like a giant refreshed with sleep and (no doubt) with wine'.[13]

Thomas's experience of politics and the war effort went beyond talk, though. Liverpool was a hub of military activity, and he could see evidence of the hostilities all around him, from warships in the Liverpool harbour to the French prison in Great Howard Street, which he passed on his walks, and which housed French prisoners of war in terrible circumstances.[14] More dramatically, one day on returning from Bootle, he witnessed first-hand the horrors of a British press gang as it made its way back to the docks after a successful sweep through the Liverpool streets. Among the men the 'pressers' had captured was one who 'hid his face to conceal his emotions: his two sisters stood on the pier among the crowd – weeping and telling his story to the spectators'.

Immediately a general exclamation ran along – 'Ay, that's poor Jack – the boatman' – Who is he? I said. 'Ay! bless him! he's neither father nor mother; – he's quite desolate.' On this general tribute of sympathy and affection, the poor fellow, who had hitherto hid his face to stifle or conceal his grief, could bear it no longer; but, sobbing aloud, lifted up his eyes and fixed them with such mingling expressions of agony – gratitude – mournful remembrance on his friends – relations – and his dear coun-trymen (whom very likely he was now gazing at for the last time) as roused indignation against the pressers and pity for the pressed in every bosom.[15]

Thomas felt an enduring enthusiasm for the war against Napoleon, but at this moment he came face to face with the human cost of the conflict.

He now had a kind of sex life. On seven different occasions, and in a sort of Latin and Greek code, he confided to his diary that he was masturbating. Fascinated by the workings of his body, and a meticulous analyst of his own guilt and excitement, Thomas kept strict track of these episodes, but in a form that could not be deciphered by the servants, his mother, Mrs Best, and so on. 'Effusio ante ωραυ 7th' ('orgasm before the 7th hour') he writes on Monday, 9 May. A week later, he records an 'Εφ. ante ωραυ octodecateen' ('orgasm before the eighteenth hour'). On 30 May, he notes simply 'εφ. σπ.' ('orgasm').[16] He was also visiting prostitutes. After masturbating on the morning of 10 May, he got a little boozy at lunch, and then whored in the afternoon, though his record of the encounter is disjointed and clearly censored: 'seized with the delicious thought the of the girl give her 2 shillings'. After church on Sunday, 22 May: 'enjoy a girl in the fields for 1s and 6d'. After a shopping excursion with the ladies on 26 May: 'go home with a whore to Everton I give all the change I have; 1s 2d'. After a wander through the churchyard on 4 June: 'go to the same fat whore's as I was at the last time; – give her 1s and a cambrick pocket hand-kerchief; – go home miserable'.[17] Thomas's energetic, if furtive, pursuit of these liaisons was driven by his sexually 'delicious thought'. Yet he paid a steep price afterwards, for his strict Evangelical upbringing no doubt exacerbated the shame he felt at these encounters, a shame that is evident in his account of the 'women of the town' in Manchester, that suffuses his relationship with Ann of Oxford Street, and that now brings him home 'miserable' in Everton.

He was by this time committed to becoming a writer, and planned to work in a number of different genres. 'I have besides always intended of course that *poems* should form the corner-stones of my fame,' he declared confidently, though the few excerpts of his original verse in the diary are remarkably undistinguished:

> The moon in her delightful some diviner mood was shining
> And pouring radiance on the ocean's breast . . .
> Her course the while in gentle roll inclining
> Towards the northern *where are placed the* chambers of her rest,
> – I make her sweetly-swelling breast
> My one dear refuge in adversity.

As a playwright, he had three dramas in mind, including one entitled *Yermak the Rebel.* In prose, he planned to write lives of Cataline and Julius Caesar; essays on poetry, character, pathos, and the French and English character; two pathetic tales, one of which featured a 'black man' as the hero; and a novel in which the heroine expires 'on an island of a lake, her chamber-windows (opening on a lawn) set wide open – and the sweet blooming roses breathing their odours on her dying senses'.[18]

On 28 April, Thomas listed the 'sources of Happiness' as '1. Poetry; – 2. Pathos; – 3. Glory; – 4. Love; – 5. Benevolence; – 6. Music', but no combination of these factors relieved his melancholy. He was quick to sense slights, and 'piqued at . . . apparent indifference'. Sometimes he dined with Cragg and uttered 'not above a sentence or two', or sat in company and said not '*one* word to anybody'.[19] On other occasions, he spoke out with a haughtiness that approached contempt. One evening, Cragg asked him if he liked 'the *Odyssey* which he himself thought mightily entertaining'. Thomas replied that he 'could not bear it; and, as a reason, observed that, independent of the insipidity of the story, there was no character in it: "What? not Telemachus?", said C. "No", said I coolly.' On another evening, Wright said he thought that seeing a play well performed was the greatest pleasure human nature was susceptible of. 'Do you think so, Sir?' Thomas asked snidely. 'Yes, Sir, indeed,' Wright rejoined. Thomas 'made no farther remarks', but walked home near midnight 'in a state of exquisite misery'.[20]

Certainly aware of his intellectual advantage, the men seem to have put up with him rather than to have retaliated against him. But he was also in the company of the ladies a good deal, and they chose to handle him in two very different ways. One of their strategies was simply to shun him, either directly – 'neither of the ladies asks me to accompany them' – or indirectly, such as when they sent down a servant to tell him that they had gone into the country, when in fact he discovered later that same day that they had been at home. Their other main tactic was to make his moroseness an object of their fun. 'I amuse the ladies by saying that I wish there was some road down to hell by which I might descend for a short time.' Two weeks later, he made them smile when he told them that it was not 'misery' that stalked him, but 'apathy and dulness'. 'I wish I could look into your mind,' said Mrs Wright, but when Thomas proudly replied that he wanted to keep his thoughts 'shrouded from any penetration', she archly asked him 'why? ... is it because you look down on us with contempt as inferior beings?' Her questions clearly caught him off guard, for he interrupted her and 'wondered that she should impute' his 'concealment to self-elevation'.[21] To them, Thomas was an oddity, intellectual but arrogant. To him, they were company, but not companionship. He did not understand their irritation. They could not fathom his despondency.

Chatterton served him as a model once again. In early April, his 'Chattertonian' melancholia 'returned for the 1st time this ... two years'. Later, and much more vividly, he closed his eyes and imagined 'Chatterton in the exceeding pain of death! in the exhausted slumber of agony I see his arm weak as a child's – languid and faint in the extreme ... stretched out and raised at midnight – calling and pulling (faintly indeed, but yet convulsively) some human breast to console him whom he had seen in the dreams of his fever'd soul.'[22] Thomas is undoubtedly reading himself into these lines, and fantasizing about his own suicide. His despair and ennui, however, were not pushing him in that direction. As was so often the case even in the middle of much deeper miseries, he was determined to shape the course of his own life.

[ii]

It was 13 May. He sat before his diary and summoned all his courage. 'Sir,' he began, 'I take this method of requesting ...' No. Too formal. Too dull. He crossed the words out and started again. This time he did much better. The words were warmer, more arresting. 'What I am going to say, I know, would seem strange to most men; and to most men therefore I would *not* say it; but to you I will, because your feelings do not follow the current of the world.' He paused, read this over with pleasure, and then began his second paragraph. 'From the time when I first saw the "Lyrical Ballads" I made a resolution to obtain (if I could) the friendship of their author.'[23] Thomas was drafting a letter to William Wordsworth. It was something he had been thinking about for nearly four years.

Wordsworth's poetry, as always, had been on his mind. In the opening instalment of the diary, Thomas quoted from 'Lines written near Richmond, upon the Thames, at Evening'. On 12 April, he compiled a list of his twelve favourite poets, beginning with Spenser, Shakespeare, and Milton, passing up through Thomson, Collins, Chatterton, Beattie, Burns, and Penrose, and climaxing with 'Robert Southey; S. T. Coleridge; William Wordsworth!!!' In early May, when brooding on the nature of poetry and drama, he affirmed that there was 'no good pastoral in the world but Wordsworth's *"Brothers"*; and that enchanting composition has more pathos (ah! *what* pathos!) than poetry in it'. And now, these various references coming to a head, Thomas turned from thinking of Wordsworth to writing to him. He finished his second paragraph, and added a third one, cancelling and recasting several more lines as he went, before signing himself 'Your's for ever and ever, Thomas de Quincey'.[24]

He may have copied this letter out of his diary and on to separate sheets, but he did not send it off to Wordsworth. Caution was required. Better to let it sit for a few weeks and then see how it sounded. Thomas did not want to be too forward, too laborious, too humble, too revealing. Over the course of the ensuing days, he no doubt went back to the letter on numerous occasions, and with increasing dissatisfaction. It needed to be more elaborate, more confident. Gradually, he rewrote it, and finally, on the afternoon of 31 May, he completed an augmented and, in parts, thoroughly revised version. Copied and sealed by twenty minutes before 4 o'clock, Thomas took it straight to the post office and mailed it to Wordsworth care of his publisher Longman in Paternoster Row, London.[25]

In its final form, the letter is a remarkable document that dramatically altered the course of Thomas's life. Its main objective – as had been the case from the first draft onward – is to try and obtain Wordsworth's friendship, and Thomas expresses himself with an earnestness that approaches desperation. Young and unknown as he is, he recognizes that Wordsworth can hardly be moved by applause as 'feeble and insignificant' as his. Yet he needs this friendship, and he works hard to prove to Wordsworth that his devotion and his insight make him worthy of it. In the midst of the 'many many bitter recollections' that have shadowed him over the past two years, the possibility of the poet's regard has been his 'only refuge'. He does not want to live with the thought that a lack of effort on his part meant that he missed out on a gift, 'without which what good can my life do me?'[26]

Like Wordsworth, he is a poet. 'What claim then can I urge to a fellowship with a society such as yours ... beaming (as it does) with genius so wild and so magnificent? I dare not say that I too have some spark of that heavenly fire which blazes there.' Yet at the same time Thomas recognizes that he is very different from Wordsworth. His own poetic genius 'has not yet kindled and shone out', while the 1800 *Lyrical Ballads* are a matchless achievement. 'I may say in general, without the smallest exaggeration, that the whole aggregate of pleasure I have received from some eight or nine other poets that I have been able to find since the world began ... falls infinitely short of what those two enchanting volumes have singly afforded me.' Indeed, how could anyone study Wordsworth and not long to know him? Thomas must share his wish with 'every man, who has read and felt the "Lyrical Ballads"'.[27]

Having presented his motives for contacting the poet over the first two-thirds of the letter, Thomas then moves to a series of 'negative reasons why you may suffer me, if but at a distance, to buoy myself up with the idea that I am not wholly disregarded in your sight'. One, 'my life has been passed chiefly in the contemplation and altogether in the worship of nature' (not strictly true of someone who had spent a good deal of time in the city, and who was at least as interested in Gothic fiction as he was in nature). Two, 'I am but a boy and have therefore formed no connections which could draw you one step farther from the sweet retreats of poetry to the detested haunts of men' (again, not strictly true of a seventeen-and-a-half-year-old who seems to have formed at least a few unsavoury connections during his recent months in London). Three, 'no one should ever dare, in confidence of any acquaintance he might have with me, to intrude on your hallowed solitude'. Four, 'you would at any rate have an opportunity of offering to God the pleasant and grateful incense of a good deed ... by blessing the existence of a fellow-creature'. And five, 'as to all external points, I believe that there is nothing in them which would disgrace you' (Thomas was as sensitive as ever about his height).[28]

The letter concludes with a passionate plea for recognition. Wordsworth, Thomas hopes and believes, is the creative and supportive adult who has so long been missing in his life. Deferential in the extreme, he 'bends the knee' before the poet, and promises to 'sacrifice even his life ... whenever it could have a chance of promoting your interest and happiness'. At the same time, Thomas is very proud: 'I will add that, to no man on earth except yourself and *one* other (a friend of your's), would I thus lowly and suppliantly prostrate myself' – the 'friend' of course being Coleridge. And with that, he closes: 'Dear Sir! Your's forever, Thomas de Quincey'.[29]

It was a letter that he needed to write, and it is unquestionably an expression of deep and genuine admiration. Yet at its heart is a very dangerous assumption. In his approach to Wordsworth, Thomas seems to imagine that there is no substantial difference between the man and the poet, that what Wordsworth is and what Wordsworth writes are one and the same. Thus the moral enthusiasm he feels for the poems leads him to praise Wordsworth's 'moral character', and the poetic descriptions of genial feelings that he finds in the *Lyrical Ballads* compel him to assume that Wordsworth will display those same genial feelings in his private friendships.[30] The conviction is understandable in a boy as imaginatively astute and as emotionally starved as Thomas. And, after all, it is not entirely unreasonable of him to assume that in the *Lyrical Ballads* Wordsworth means what he says. But Thomas had very high expectations of the poet right from the start, and they never ceased to burden his relationship with him.

Two long months passed without a response. Thomas began to despair. And then, on 2 August 1803, the day before he was to leave Everton, a letter from Wordsworth arrived. Thomas's excitement must have been almost overwhelming. What the poet said to him was kind and wise.[31] Longman had been very remiss in forwarding Thomas's letter, and Wordsworth had not even received it until 27 July. 'I am much concerned at this as ... my silence must needs have caused you some uneasiness,' he wrote just two days later, mindful of how long Thomas had already been waiting. Wordsworth, it is clear, had been impressed by Thomas's letter. 'The main end which you proposed to yourself in writing to me is answered,' he assured him, 'viz. that I am already kindly disposed towards you', though he added a caveat: 'My friendship it is not in my power to give: this is a gift which no man can make.' The letter then moves on to a series of other topics. Wordsworth is concerned that Thomas has set too great a value on the *Lyrical Ballads*, at the risk of undervaluing 'the proper influence of other writers'. He describes himself as 'the most lazy and impatient Letter writer in the world'. In a few days he will set off on a tour into Scotland for six weeks or two months with his friend Coleridge and his sister Dorothy. Finally, he would derive 'great pleasure' from seeing Thomas in Grasmere should he 'ever come this way'. Then, worried that his invitation sounded too perfunctory, he appended a postscript in which he reissued it in friendlier language: 'I shall indeed be very happy to see you at Grasmere ... I should, I repeat it, be very happy to see you.'[32]

Thomas did not sleep that night. The honour of 'a long answer from Wordsworth' kept him awake 'from mere excess of pleasure'.[33] On the following day he travelled from Everton back to his mother's home at the Priory, where he sat down on the morning of 6 August and wrote his response. To obtain an answer after he had almost 'ceased to expect it' was a 'happiness which falls to the lot of few men'. Wordsworth's letter has afforded him 'great and lasting pleasure', and perhaps even more significantly for the lonely teenager, it has made him 'rise' in his 'own estimation'. The poet's caveat about his friendship not being in his power to give, however, has clearly caused Thomas some concern, for he now backs quickly – and not very convincingly – away from the very reason he had written to Wordsworth in the first place. 'What foolish thing I said of friendship I cannot now recollect,' he claims: 'but, if (as I gather from your remarks on it) I asked for *your* friendship, I must have written without consulting my understanding.' He responds to Wordsworth's concern about the due influence of other poets by assuring him that from his youth onwards he has revered 'Spenser – Shakespeare – Milton – Thomson (partially) – and Collins'. But, he adds, 'it would be mere hypocrisy in me to say' that the works of any of these writers 'are so "twisted with my heart-strings" as the *Lyrical Ballads*'. He expresses joy at Wordsworth's kind invitation to him to visit the Lakes – 'I believe that the bowers of paradise could hold out no such allurement' – and states that he plans to travel to Grasmere next summer. Emboldened by Wordsworth's mention of Coleridge and Dorothy, he closes by wondering if he might please take a liberty, and ask Wordsworth to convey to both of them his 'most sincere and respectful good wishes'.[34] His initial fan letter had done the trick. Thomas was inching closer and closer to his idols.

[iii]

The end of the Peace of Amiens had created a great stir at the Priory. Thomas's uncle Penson, still on leave from India, was a man of formidable energies and, using the Priory as his headquarters, he worked together with three other men to raise a volunteer cavalry in Chester, fuelled by the belief that Napoleon's 'very existence depended upon war', and that every conceivable measure must be adopted in order to stop him.[35] Thomas, meanwhile, lolled about the house with no fixed plans for the future. His mother had agreed to let him stay, but she and her brother still regarded him as a 'boy, nay, a child ... in disgrace', while he treated them with the same intellectual disdain that had irritated Wright and Cragg in Everton only a few months earlier. The simmering tensions between them boiled over one day when Thomas was reading Daniel Defoe's *Memoirs of a Cavalier* to his uncle, who had been laid up by a riding accident. Thomas disliked the book. Penson 'had an old craze in behalf' of it. Thomas dismissed its accounts of the Parliamentary War as 'unfair' and 'most superficial'. Penson opposed him with asperity. The argument escalated. Penson asked Thomas, 'in a way which I felt to be taunting, how I could consent to waste my time as I did'. 'I explained that my guardians, having quarrelled with me, would not grant for my use anything beyond my school allowance of £100 per annum.' Was it possible to live as a student in Oxford on that sum? 'From what I had heard, very probably it was. Would I undertake an Oxford life upon such terms? Most gladly, I said.'[36] Penson spoke to Mrs. Quincey and an agreement was soon struck. Seven days later, Thomas was on his way to Oxford.

He arrived late one December evening in the middle of a snowstorm, winding 'through the long northern suburb' of the town on a slow Birmingham coach that finally pulled into the Corn Market in front of a shabby inn called the Golden Cross.[37] 'Business was out of the question at that hour,' but the next day Thomas assembled the acquaintances he had in the university, most of whom were presumably former students from Bath, Winkfield, or Manchester Grammar School. He wanted their advice on the two crucial questions facing any student seeking admittance to the university. Should he enter as a 'gentleman' or a 'gentleman commoner'? And which college should he go to? Money quickly settled his first question. Gentleman commoners paid much higher fees than he could afford. He would enter simply as a gentleman. As to a college, he wanted one with both a large population (because of the anonymity it would offer), and a 'full cathedral service' (because of the daily opportunities it would provide him for listening to beautiful music). Christ Church, he was told, best fulfilled both of these conditions: its student body was the 'most splendid ... in numbers, rank, wealth, and influence', while its chapel was the cathedral of the diocese. Thomas immediately prepared to call on the Dean of Christ Church, the redoubtable Cyril Jackson.[38]

Arriving at the college, he was shown into a 'spacious library or study, elegantly, if not luxuriously furnished', and was 'really surprised' when Jackson rose graciously at his entrance. The two began a 'very long conversation of a general nature upon the course' of Thomas's studies, before coming at length to the particular purpose of his visit, at which point Jackson 'assumed a little more of his official stateliness', and 'condescended to say, that it would have given him pleasure' to reckon Thomas 'amongst his flock'. 'But, sir,' he said, with some sharpness, 'your guardians have acted improperly. It was their duty to have given me at least one year's notice of their intention to place you at Christ Church. At present I have not a dog-kennel in my college untenanted.' Thomas hastily acquitted his guardians of any fault, 'they being no parties' to his 'present scheme', and apologized for having taken up so much of Jackson's time. The dean seemed about to bend his own rule in Thomas's favour and allow him a place at the college, when their meeting was interrupted by the 'thundering heralds of ... some man of high rank'. Apparently 'distressed for a moment', Jackson then recollected himself and bowed in a manner that indicated to Thomas that he was dismissed. 'And thus it happened that I did not become a member of Christ Church.'[39]

The next few days were passed in what Thomas described as 'thoughtless indecision'. He had brought about fifty guineas with him to Oxford, but he was paying for his rooms at the Golden Cross, and he was also providing 'almost daily entertainments to young friends', which presumably means that he was picking up many of the bills when they went out seeking fun in Oxford. Soon he had cut so deeply into his funds that he worried that he would not be able to afford the payment for 'caution money'; that is, the 'small sum ... demanded of every student' entering the university, 'as a pledge for meeting any loss from unsettled arrears'. In most colleges this fee amounted to £25, but at Worcester College, he learned, it was considerably less. In addition, Worcester was of interest to him because it had a reputation for relaxed discipline, leading him to hope that if he entered the college he could spend his time pretty much as he wanted. True, there was no organ at Worcester, and no musical service, but having assured his mother and his uncle that he could live in Oxford on £100 a year, he 'could not find nerves to face' writing to them to ask for more money. He had only left home a week or so earlier! Worcester it was. He matriculated on 17 December 1803.[40]

The routines of Oxford were soon familiar. Students began their day with attendance at chapel and then breakfast, followed by a study period that commenced about ten and ran for three hours. The classics were at the heart of the curriculum, along with mathematics and divinity. In the afternoon students devoted themselves to leisure, and then congregated in the college hall for dinner, a ceremonial occasion at which they were required to dress formally, and arrange themselves at table according to their year and status. A second chapel service took place in the early evening, after which tea and supper were served. Students could then study, or go out into the town, though there were strict rules about when they had to be back within the college gates. Gambling, boating, riding, and walking were popular, as were private parties, coffee-houses, and the taverns. Prostitution – in both Oxford and the surrounding villages – was common.[41]

Thomas's first set of rooms were charged at the very cheap rate of four guineas a year, but they were 'small and ill-lighted, as part of an old Gothic building', and before long he exchanged them 'for others a little better'. These were almost certainly his rooms 'on Staircase no. 10 in the front quad, up one pair of stairs to the right'. This is where he lived for most of his Oxford career, at a cost of six guineas a year.[42] His other expenses in the first year included 'furniture and the fittings up of these rooms' (£25), the cost of a tutor (£10.10s.), the cost of servants (Thomas overpaid at £5.5s.), 'meals, excepting only tea, sugar, milk, and wine' (just over £1 a week), washing (£6.6s.), candles (£2.5s.), coals (£5.5s.), and groceries (£10.10s.). As these figures make clear, on the strictest economy, it was possible to live in Oxford for under £100 a year, and in Thomas's case the possibility was even greater because Worcester allowed for what were called 'short terms', which meant that he only had to be in Oxford for thirteen weeks a year.[43] Records in the college archives show that during the first three months of 1804 Thomas's expenses were average for an undergraduate.[44]

Yet – characteristically – while he was at first able to keep his college expenditures roughly on budget, he was incurring other, extracurricular costs that were steadily pushing him into deficit. The most prominent of these was book buying, which he now began in earnest.[45] Shortly after moving into Worcester, he went out one morning and bought a copy of Charles Lamb's play *John Woodvil* (1802) and Walter Savage Landor's jacobinical poem *Gebir* (1798), which astonished him 'by the splendour of its descriptions'. Thomas brought the 'two most unpopular of books' back to his Worcester rooms and placed them 'on the same shelf with the other far holier idols of my heart, the joint poems of Wordsworth and Coleridge as then associated in the "Lyrical Ballads" . . . I could not but smile internally at the fair prospect I had of congregating a library which no man had read but myself.'[46] In the months that followed, his servant, Joe Preston, recollected how Thomas was 'always buying fresh books and was sometimes at a loss how to find money for them. In those days men dressed for Hall: and [Thomas] having one day parted with his one waistcoat in order to purchase some book or other went into Hall hiding his loss of clothing as best he could', but the concealment was detected, and Thomas was fined for the breach of etiquette, though this did not change his habits. He was entirely indisposed to 'spend upon a tailor', what he had 'destined for a bookseller'.[47] It was a trend that continued for the rest of his life.

Thomas liked to portray himself as a solitary, and at Oxford he contended that he kept very much to himself. The chief reason for this decision was unhappiness. 'Suppose the case of a man suspended by some colossal arm over an unfathomed abyss – suspended, but finally and slowly withdrawn – it is probable that he would not smile for years. That was my case' at Oxford.[48] Heightening the sorrows of his past were distresses in the present, the most urgent of which concerned his younger brother Pink, who had recently run away from school after being repeatedly flogged by his headmaster. His mother and his uncle Penson sent him letters trying to convince him to return home. But he 'absolutely' rejected all of their offers, and after several weeks of failed negotiations, he signed on as a cabin boy in a South Sea whaler, and left England. Was this not precisely what Mrs Quincey had worried about? The eldest son raised 'the standard of revolt', and the second son emulated his actions. Thomas believed that his brother had 'the soul of a hero', and was right to reject the 'unjust pretensions of authority', but he also felt terrible guilt at the thought that his example had put Pink in harm's way. What if he was killed at sea? What if he never returned? The incident poisoned 'the tranquillity of a whole family' for several years.[49]

Thomas listed the poor intellectual climate at Oxford as another reason why he chose to spend so much time alone. There were 'no very good tutors', and the students were 'generally low in point of attainment', especially when it came to a knowledge of modern literature, where their ignorance was so 'intolerable and incomprehensible' that Thomas 'felt it to be impossible' that he should 'familiarly associate' with them. Indeed, he 'could not even bring himself to mention' Wordsworth by name 'for fear of having to encounter ridiculous observations, or jeering abuse of his favourite (who was laughed at by most of the Oxonians)'.[50]

A final reason for his solitude, remarkably enough, was his poor eyesight. Thomas suffered from myopia, which by the time he went to Oxford was so marked that he was rumoured to be 'a bit of a Jacobin because he failed to "cap" the Master', Dr Whittington Landon, from his 'sheer inability to recognize him by sight'. Later, Thomas computed that during the first two years of his residence at Worcester, he 'did not utter one hundred words'.[51]

Such a claim is, to say the least, an exaggeration. Thomas had private reasons for sorrow, and he may well have remained awkward or scornful in company. But there were gregarious and libidinous sides to him as well, and he seems far more likely to have picked up in Oxford where he left off six months earlier in Everton, rather than to have retreated into isolation and almost total silence. He declared at one point that during his time at Worcester he 'allowed for *no* wine parties'.[52] In another, contradictory account, however, he acknowledged that when he first moved into college 'he was invited by many of the men of his own standing to their parties, which he joined – but he found them to be a drinking, rattling set, whose conversation was juvenile, commonplace, & quite unintellectual. He ... invited them once or twice in return, & then dropped the intercourse', though not the wine-drinking.[53] Preston, his servant, used to say that

Thomas 'did not mix much with the other men, who in their turn resented some of his peculiarities'. Richard Lynch Cotton, the future provost of Worcester, heard that Thomas 'did not frequent wine parties, though he did not abstain from wine', and went on to praise him 'for his rare conversational powers, and for his extraordinary stock of information upon every subject'. Thomas himself recorded making occasional 'appointments to drink a glass of wine' with a former Manchester Grammar School classmate. 'I, whose disease it was to meditate too much and to observe too little, and who, upon my first entrance at college, was nearly falling into a deep melancholy ... was sufficiently aware of these tendencies in my own thoughts to do all I could to counteract them ... and the remedies I sought were to force myself into society.'[54]

The most notable diversion during Thomas's first term at Oxford was the trial, in March, of Rachel Lee, the 'female infidel' who had visited Greenhay nine years earlier and stunned Mrs Quincey and Hall with her frank professions of atheism. Time had not made her more cautious, and she had ended up embroiled in a case of abduction involving two brothers, Loudon and Lockhart Gordon, both of whom were Oxford graduates. Her version was that the brothers had kidnapped her. Theirs was that she had consented to an elopement. Thomas, fascinated as always by crime and secret guilt, determined to attend her trial. Dressed in his academic gown and at the courthouse by eight in the morning, he joined a throng of students who were besieging 'the doors for some time before the moment of admission'. At nine the crowd was allowed in and the trial began. Lee's servants were examined and then, around eleven, Lee herself was called, though she 'was not long exposed to the searching gaze of the court', for when the judge asked her if she 'believed in the Christian religion', she replied '*No*', with the result that the trial was called to a halt, and the brothers 'instantly acquitted'. Thomas went to her lodgings that afternoon, but was told she would see no one until the evening. He returned at dusk to find a mob assembled, and a lady issuing from the front door, 'muffled up, and in some measure disguised'. It was Lee. A post-chaise was waiting in the adjacent street, and she was making her way steadily towards it. 'Before she could reach it, however, she was detected', and 'a rush made to seize her'. Fortunately, a body of students formed a ring around her, 'put her rapidly into the carriage', and 'then, joining the mob in their hootings, sent off the horses at a gallop'.[55]

At the end of his first term, Thomas vacated his Worcester rooms and took up residence about two and a half miles south-east of Oxford in the village of Littlemore, where he stayed with an honest but dull farmer and his five daughters, who 'said more in an hour than their father in a month'. Far from being a recluse, Thomas was 'in those days' a 'giddy thing' who would often laugh with them through a whole morning, 'whilst the mild unmurmuring lord of the premises sate neglected by us all!'[56] One of the chief tasks he had set himself on this holiday was to write again to Wordsworth, as over seven months had passed since he had last contacted him, and – worryingly – he had not yet received a reply. On 14 March, Thomas pulled himself away from all the female attention of Littlemore to compose the letter, transforming himself in the process from excitable teenager to reverent admirer.

After explaining at the outset that he had been prevented from writing until now by the 'painful employments' and 'little . . . unknown cares' which attend leaving home and starting at university, Thomas moves to a much more central concern that has clearly been gnawing at him as a possible explanation of the poet's silence. Had his 'hyperbolical tributes of admiration' roused Wordsworth's suspicions? Had they offended him?[57] Thomas sincerely hopes not. There has been, he promises the poet, no exaggeration in his accounts of the impact the *Lyrical Ballads* have had upon him, as he goes on to detail in a remarkable narrative in which he figures himself as a lost soul who is saved by the redemptive nature of Wordsworth's writing. In 1799, he read 'We are Seven', but 'a long time intervened' before he discovered that the poem was part of a collection called the *Lyrical Ballads*. During this interval he fell under a Gothic spell, and

> from frequent meditation on some characters of our own, & some of ancient story, & afterwards on some of the German Drama, I began to model my conduct & my aims on theirs: by degrees, being dazzled by the glory thrown on such objects by the voice of the people, & miserably deluding myself with the thought that I was led on by high aims, & such as were most worthy of my nature I daily intoxicated myself more & more with that delirious & lawless pleasure which I drew from the hope of elevating my name in authority & kingly splendour above every name that is named upon earth.

In the midst of this 'temporary frenzy' of sensualism and vanity, however, 'it was not possible' that Thomas, maintained from his infancy 'in the Love of Nature, should not, at times relent & resign' himself to a 'confused feeling of purer & more permanent pleasure flowing from other sources'. Gradually, as he weaned himself from these 'feverish & turbulent dreams', he looked around 'for some guide who might assist to develope & to tutor' his new feelings. Then it was that he recollected Wordsworth's poetry, and knew that he needed to seek direction from him.[58]

Thomas's account here is not strictly in line with his other versions of these same events. Wordsworth, for example, seems never to have been crowded from his thoughts in the way that he describes in this letter. On the one hand, there can be no question that Thomas viewed Wordsworth's poetry as embodying new and authentic forms of conduct and feeling, and that he regarded his experience of it as salvational.[59] Yet on the other, Thomas was already highly adept at tailoring his experience in order to please his audience. In his famous 'Preface' to the *Lyrical Ballads*, Wordsworth declared that he hoped his poems would counteract the degrading influence of 'stupid German Tragedies, and deluges of idle and extravagant stories in verse'.[60] In the letter, Thomas presents himself to the poet as living proof that he has succeeded in his aim. After succumbing to the 'undue influence' of 'ancient story' and 'the German Drama', the *Lyrical Ballads* have restored him to his better self, with 'every principle of good' within him 'purified & uplifted'.[61]

Before leaving Worcester, Thomas had given directions that all his mail was to be forwarded on to him at Littlemore. But when some weeks passed without receiving anything, he sent in a servant to check on the situation.[62] Waiting for him there were two letters from Wordsworth. In the first, dated 6 March 1804, the poet is warm and candid. He allays Thomas's fears about his silence by assuring him that his own procrastination has been to blame, and that he has thought of Thomas 'very often'. He speaks as the father figure Thomas clearly wants him to be: 'I need not say to you that there is no true dignity but in virtue and temperance, and, let me add, chastity; and that the best safeguard of all these is the cultivation of pure pleasures, namely, those of the intellect and affections.' At present, Wordsworth explains, he is hard at work on 'a Poem on my own earlier life' (which, over the next several months, grew to become his autobiographical masterwork, *The Prelude*). He has just finished Book III, which concerns his own undergraduate years at Cambridge. 'It would give me great pleasure to read this work to you at this time,' he tells Thomas. 'As I am sure, from the interest you have taken' in the *Lyrical Ballads* that 'it would please you, and might also be of service to you.' Finally, having cautioned Thomas in his first letter that his friendship was not in his power to give, Wordsworth concludes his second by signing himself 'your very affectionate Friend'.[63]

The other Wordsworth letter waiting at Worcester was dated 19 March, and was much shorter. In it, the poet expressed concern that Thomas had not yet responded to his letter of 6 March. Wordsworth had, however, by this time received Thomas's letter of 14 March, and he replied with genuine gratitude. Public perception of his work had been heavily influenced by the tarring he had received at the hands of the *Edinburgh Review* in its infamous October 1802 attack on the 'Lake School of Poetry', and the 'splenetic and idle discontent with the existing institutions of society' that 'seems to be at the bottom of all' Wordsworth's verse.[64] But here in Thomas De Quincey was someone who understood, someone young and ingenuous who could see far beyond the fatuousness and belligerence of the critics. 'I cannot express to You how much pleasure it gave me to learn that my Poems had been of such eminent service to you as you describe,' Wordsworth confided to him. 'May God grant that you may persevere in all good habits, desires, and resolutions.'[65]

Sounding a good deal more self-assured, Thomas composed a long reply to both Wordsworth's letters on Saturday, 31 March, and then concluded with a kind of postscript on Sunday morning. He is thrilled that Wordsworth has told him about his autobiographical poem, and he will wait 'with great expectation for the advent of that day, on which I may hear you read it'. He deplores the assaults of the Edinburgh reviewers, and is Wordsworth's staunch ally in his battle against them. 'I have always felt any momentary indignation at their arrogance overbalanced by compassion for the delusions they are putting upon themselves.' Worcester College is not to his liking. It is 'singularly barren ... of either virtue or talents or knowledge', and he plans to pass no more of his time there than is necessary. On several occasions over the past few years, Thomas concedes that he has actively pursued licentious pleasures, but he is now at pains to assure Wordsworth that he guards vigilantly against them (though his typically drawn-out assurances partially conjure the guilt he is intent on suppressing). 'I have been through life so much restrained from dissolute conduct by the ever-waking love of my mother,' he declares rather surprisingly, '– and of late years so purified from dissolute propensities by the new order of pleasures which I have been led to cultivate that I feel a degree of confidence (not arrogant, I hope) that, even with greater temptations, I should not by my *conduct* at any rate make you repent the notice you have taken of me.' Once again he extends his 'warmest wishes' to Coleridge and to Dorothy, and then, following the poet's lead, signs himself 'Your grateful and affectionate friend'.[66]

In April, he was back in Oxford, and it was probably at some point during his second term that – for the first and last time – he had a conversation with his tutor, a man he identifies only as 'Jones'. 'On a fine morning, he met me in the Quadrangle, and having then no guess of the nature of my pretensions, he determined (I suppose) to probe them.

Accordingly, he asked me, "What I had been lately reading?" Now, the fact was, that I, at that time immersed in metaphysics, had really been reading' Plato's dialogue, the *Parmenides*. But certain that Jones would not know the work, and with no wish to embarrass him, Thomas lied and said William Paley, the Anglican priest and Utilitarian philosopher. 'Ah!' Jones exclaimed. 'An excellent author; excellent for his matter; only you must be on your guard as to his style; he is very vicious *there*.' Tutor and student then bowed and parted. The brief exchange was enough to confirm for Thomas that Jones was a dunce, as his estimation of Paley was exactly backwards. As a philosopher, he 'is a jest, the disgrace of the age', Thomas snorted with the hauteur that so often defined his attitude towards his elders. '... But, on the other hand, for style, Paley is a master.'[67]

By this point, Thomas was studying hard as he both built on past interests and explored new ones. He 'devoted himself principally to the society of a German named Schwartzburg, who is said to have taught him Hebrew', and who also helped him to develop his skills in German. According to Cotton, Thomas's 'university studies were directed almost wholly to the ancient philosophy, varied by occasional excursions into German literature and metaphysics, which he loved to compare with those of Greece and Rome'. Thomas himself recalled that in 1804 he began consciously to read 'in the same track as Coleridge, – that track in which few of any age will ever follow us, such as German metaphysicians, Latin schoolmen, thaumaturgic Platonists, religious Mystics'. His mother cautiously approved of his programme of reading, at least based on what he had told her. 'Your studies under the name of Moral Philosophy cannot be objected to,' she wrote to him on 5 June; 'and as you have spoken only in general terms of your object, I conclude as I hope, that there is nothing objectionable either in the plan you are forming or the end you aim at.'[68]

Had she known of the debts he was running up as he pursued these studies, however, Mrs Quincey would have been seriously agitated. Within seven months of arriving in Oxford, Thomas had become 'embarrassed'. Looking back, he believed that he should have candidly avowed his situation to his mother, 'or to some one of the guardians, more than one of whom would have advanced me the £250 wanted (not in his legal character of guardian, but as a private friend)'. At the time, though, Thomas allowed a 'movement of impatience' to lead him in a 'foolish' direction, and he contacted Dell, the Jewish moneylender he had dealt with in London eighteen months earlier. 'I applied again' and now, as a member of a 'respectable college, I was fortunate enough to win his serious attention to my proposals'. Voluminous negotiations followed, and ultimately Dell advanced him £250 on the outrageous but 'regular' terms of 'paying seventeen and a-half per cent'.[69] The steady erosion of Thomas's patrimony was under way two years before he was even eligible to receive it.

He spent the summer term in Oxford, and then travelled north to Hinckley in south-west Leicestershire, where his mother had moved after selling the Priory, and where presumably he celebrated his nineteenth birthday.[70] By early September, however, he was back down south in London, and in mid-October he returned to Worcester College to commence Michaelmas term.[71] His initial months at Oxford had left him with profoundly mixed emotions. 'From my boyish days', he declared, '. . . I was engaged in duels of fierce continual struggle, with some person or body of persons, that sought . . . to throw a net of deadly coercion or constraint over the undoubted rights of my natural freedom.' But by going to Oxford, practically he became his own master, and no doubt he exulted in being able to borrow substantial sums of money, spend his time as he saw fit, and deal with his mother and Hall on a much more equal footing. Yet Thomas also knew that his status as an undergraduate meant that his boyhood was over, and that the independence he had long sought came at the cost of 'many duties and responsibilities', in Oxford and far beyond. Badly fractured by his past, and living amongst the competing demands of the present, he was deeply unsure of the course ahead, but equally convinced that he possessed the intellectual gifts necessary to enable him to become 'an object of notice to a large society'. No longer 'absorbed into the general unit of a family, I felt myself . . . burthened with the anxieties of a man, and a member of the world'.[72]

PART TWO

THE MAGIC FIX

1804–19

FIVE

High Culture

[i]

Bodily torment, he said, drove him to it. Down in London in the autumn of 1804, almost certainly in an attempt to finalize his £250 loan from Dell, De Quincey was suddenly seized with a toothache, which he tried to alleviate one night by jumping out of bed and plunging his head into a basin of cold water. 'The next morning, as I need hardly say, I awoke with excruciating rheumatic pains of the head and face, from which I had hardly any respite for about twenty days.'[1] On the twenty-first day, a rainy Sunday in early October, he tried to take his mind off the agony by roaming the London streets, where he accidentally met a Worcester College acquaintance who recommended opium. On his way home, De Quincey dropped into a druggist's shop in Oxford Street, bought a tincture of opium, and returned with it to his lodgings.

One dose changed everything. 'I took it', he recalled:

and in an hour, oh! Heavens! what a revulsion! what an upheaving, from its lowest depths, of the inner spirit! what an apocalypse of the world within me! That my pains had vanished, was now a trifle in my eyes: – this negative effect was swallowed up in the immensity of those positive effects which had opened before me – in the abyss of divine enjoyment thus suddenly revealed. Here was a panacea . . . for all human woes: here was the secret of happiness, about which philosophers had disputed for so many ages, at once discovered: happiness might now be bought for a penny, and carried in the waistcoat pocket.[2]

De Quincey had many pleasurable experiences on opium, but no high seems ever to have matched this first one. In a marked degree, he was hooked from the start.

Opium is perhaps the oldest drug known to humankind, and is derived from the milky sap found within the unripe seedpod of the poppy plant,

Papaver somniferum.[3] In Britain at the beginning of the nineteenth century, it was an unremarkable part of daily life. Highly prized by doctors as an analgesic, it was also used ubiquitously by people of every class and age for self-medication in much the same way as aspirin is used today. It was cheap: people who could not afford ale or spirits could afford the drug. It was legal: there was no effort to restrict its sale until the Pharmacy Act of 1868. It could be purchased in a vast range of commercial cure-alls: Batley's Sedative Solution, Collis Browne's Chlorodyne, Dalby's Carminative, Godfrey's Cordial, the Kendal Black Drop, McMunn's Elixir, and Mother Bailey's Quieting Syrup, to name only a few. It was used to treat all manner of major and minor ailments: bronchitis, cancer, cholera, depression, diabetes, gout, malaria, pneumonia, sciatica, tetanus, ulcers, and much else. It was available everywhere: chemists and pharmacists sold it, as did bakers, grocers, publicans, tailors, rent collectors, and street vendors. Laudanum – De Quincey's drug of choice – was a tincture prepared by dissolving opium in alcohol (making De Quincey, technically speaking, a 'laudanum drinker' rather than an 'opium eater'). In De Quincey's day, Britain imported almost all of its opium from Turkey.[4] Morphine, which is the principal active agent in opium, was isolated in 1803, and commercially available by the early 1820s. With the introduction of the hypodermic syringe in the mid-1850s, the 'morphia solution' became widely known for its unparalleled efficacy in dealing with severe pain.[5] Since the beginning of the twentieth century, the drug has been better known in the form of one of its chief derivatives: heroin.

At the time of his first explosive encounter with opium, De Quincey claimed that he had heard of it 'as I had of manna or of Ambrosia, but no further'.[6] This seems unlikely. He was almost certainly given the drug as a young child suffering from ague. He had read several descriptions of its powers in works such as Charlotte Smith's 'Ode to the Poppy' and Jane West's *Infidel Father.*[7] The drug may well have come up as a topic of conversation between him and Lady Carbery, whose father, Henry Watson, successfully smuggled vast quantities of Bengal opium into China, and whose entire fortune of £300,000 went directly to Lady Carbery at his death in 1786.[8] Further, opium was undoubtedly a matter of debate between De Quincey and his uncle Penson, for he was an officer in the military service of the East India Company, whose key commercial interest was opium. Penson was ready to agree with his sister that Britain should abandon its imperialist agenda in India. De Quincey thought otherwise, and rigorously attacked their position.[9] In such a context, the lucrative opium trade must frequently have been a focal point of discussion.

Yet while De Quincey probably came to the drug with more knowledge than he cared to admit, he was almost wholly unprepared for its various and profound impact upon him. Throughout the age, there was a heated debate in the medical community about whether opium should be classified as a sedative or a stimulant. For De Quincey – and for millions of others – it was both. As a sedative, the drug helped him to cope with recurrent bouts of physical suffering, and his ongoing worries about family, money, past griefs, and the future.[10] Most users report that the action of an opiate is oddly paradoxical: once under its influence, their pain is still present, but they feel more comfortable.[11] So it was with De Quincey. Opium made his persistent problems seem lighter and smaller. It drained anxiety. It provided insulation. Amidst the demands of Oxford, and the stresses of modern life, the time and solitude that might have healed him were hard to find. Opium, however, was everywhere, and once he had dosed himself with it, he stood 'aloof from the uproar of life; as if the tumult, the fever, and the strife, were suspended'.[12]

More strikingly, De Quincey was convinced that the drug was his best protection against tuberculosis. 'At the commencement' of his 'opium career', he was 'pronounced repeatedly a martyr elect to pulmonary consumption'. Out of eight children, he was 'the one who most closely inherited the bodily conformation of a father who had died of consumption at the early age of thirty-nine'. Further, he exhibited at a glance 'every symptom … broadly and conspicuously developed', including 'the hectic colours on the face, the nocturnal perspirations, the growing embarrassment of the respiration, and other expressions of gathering feebleness under any attempts at taking exercise'. And finally, the physicians who examined him 'were thoroughly experienced in diagnosing the disease'.[13] More than half a century later, De Quincey remained convinced that laudanum staved off tuberculosis, and had saved him from an early grave.

Of course De Quincey did not consume the drug for medical reasons alone; there were other, more exciting, benefits as well. Once ingested, opium brought about not only a surcease of pain and anxiety, but an increase in intellectual activity, and an overwhelming sense of euphoria. It was a decisive answer to the ennui that had plagued him: 'the primary effects of opium are always, and in the highest degree, to excite and stimulate the system', he declared. When he first began to take the drug, its pleasurable action 'always lasted … for upwards of eight hours' as 'a steady and equable glow', while in later years it often sustained him through twenty-four consecutive hours of 'extraordinary exertion'. The common perception was that – like wine – opium produced intoxication, but this was not the case.

Wine volatilizes and disperses 'the intellectual energies'. Opium introduces 'amongst them the most exquisite order, legislation, and harmony'. Wine 'robs a man of his self-possession: opium greatly invigorates it'. Wine 'calls up into supremacy the merely human, too often the brutal', part of our nature, whereas opium is transcendent. When taken properly, it elevates the 'moral affections' to a 'state of cloudless serenity; and over all is the great light of the majestic intellect'.[14]

He began to experiment. About once every three weeks he left the grind of studying at college and slipped down to London, where he treated himself to 'a debauch of opium'.[15] His various recollections of these experiences have had an enormous influence on literature and art from his time to our own. In knitting together drugs, intellectualism, unconventionality, and the city, he maps in the countercultural figure of the bohemian. Decades before Edgar Allan Poe and Charles Baudelaire, he emerges as the first *flâneur*, high and anonymous, graceful and detached, strolling through crowded urban sprawls trying to decipher the spectacles, faces, and memories that reside there. As 'the Pope' of 'the true church on the subject of opium', he initiates the tradition of the literature of intoxication, and crafts a portrait of himself as the first modern artist, at once saint and exile.[16]

The opera house was a favourite resort on Tuesday and Saturday nights. Sitting amongst the wealthy and civilized, and saturated with laudanum, De Quincey listened in raptures as the Italian contralto Josephina Grassini 'poured forth her passionate soul'. He had always loved music, but 'now opium, by greatly increasing the activity of the mind generally', increased of necessity its ability 'to construct out of the raw material of organic sound an elaborate intellectual pleasure'. In such a state, 'a chorus ... of elaborate harmony' turned his thoughts inward, where he saw displayed, 'as in a piece of arras work, the whole of [his] past life – not, as if recalled by an act of memory, but as if present and incarnated in the music: no longer painful to dwell upon: but the detail of its incidents removed, or blended in some hazy abstraction; and its passions exalted, spiritualized, and sublimed'.[17]

As agreeable as these opera evenings were, De Quincey had another prized diversion that 'could be had only on a Saturday night', and that caused him to struggle with his love of the opera. 'I used often ... after I had taken opium, to wander forth, without much regarding the direction or the distance, to all the markets, and other parts of London, to which the poor resort on a Saturday night, for laying out their wages.' At this point in his life, De Quincey had a good deal more money than these working-class Londoners, but he seems to have enjoyed pretending to be like them. 'Whenever I saw occasion, or could do it without appearing to be intrusive,

I joined their parties; and gave my opinion upon the matter in discussion.' If wages were a little higher, or the price of food was a little lower, De Quincey was glad on their behalf. Yet if the opposite was true, he fell back – rather disingenuously – on opium as a means of solace, for it had the power to 'overrule all feelings into a compliance' with a serene master key.[18] On these long, rambling nights amongst London's working class, De Quincey enjoyed the drugged bliss of both sympathy and separation.

He could, however, go even higher in his enjoyment of opium. The markets and theatres were exhilarating, but he candidly acknowledged that after a while the crowds became 'an oppression', and the music 'too sensual and gross'. For De Quincey, opium was ultimately a drug of private realms, and the opium-eater naturally sought 'solitude and silence', for only under these 'indispensable conditions' could he enter into 'those trances, or pro-foundest reveries' which are the 'divinest state' of opium experience, and 'the crown and consummation' of what it 'can do for human nature'. De Quincey fell often into reveries of this kind. Most famously, during summer nights when he was staying again at Mrs Best's cottage in Everton, he dosed himself with laudanum, and then secluded himself away in a quiet room by an open window, where he sat motionless through the night gazing out at the sea and 'the great town' of Liverpool. 'I shall be charged with mysticism,' he declared, but 'it has often struck me that the scene itself was somewhat typical of what took place' in these reveries. Liverpool 'represented the earth, with its sorrows and its graves left behind, yet not out of sight, nor wholly forgotten. The ocean, in everlasting but gentle agitation, and brooded over by a dove-like calm, might not unfitly typify the mind and the mood which then swayed it.' Tensions, angers, and opposites persisted, but opium transfigured them all into a harmony that was both dynamic and tranquil: 'infinite activities, infinite repose'.[19]

De Quincey was awed by the power of the drug. To 'the proud man', it provided 'a brief oblivion' for 'insults unavenged'. To 'the guilty man, for one night' it gave back 'the hopes of his youth'. To 'the hearts of poor and rich alike, for the wounds that will never heal', it brought 'an assuaging balm'. Opium stole away 'the purposes of wrath', and reversed 'the sentences of unrighteous judges'. It burnished De Quincey. It convinced him that he could cope. Above all, it brought Elizabeth back before him, as it called 'into sunny light the faces of long-buried beauties, and the blessed household countenances, cleansed from the "dishonours of the grave"'. During the opening years of his opium career, De Quincey managed to place a strict limit on the number of times he resorted to the drug. Nevertheless, its manifold attractions must often have impressed themselves upon him.

'Thou only givest these gifts to man,' he exclaimed; 'and thou hast the keys of Paradise, oh, just, subtle, and mighty opium!'[20]

The honeymoon lasted for eight years. Yet not all of De Quincey's early experiences with the drug produced pleasure. Opium also played insidious tricks on him. As soon as he tampered with it, he began to have nightmares, as the agitations of his childhood 'reopened in strength', and 'swept in upon the brain with power, and the grandeur of recovered life'. One of his most distressing 'dream-echoes' concerned the rumours of violence that surrounded the death of his sister Jane. 'The nursery of my childhood expanded before me: my sister was moaning in bed; and I was beginning to be restless with fears not intelligible to myself. Once again the elder nurse, but now dilated to colossal proportions, stood as upon some Grecian stage with her uplifted hand, and ... smote me senseless to the ground.' Then, the scene shifted, and De Quincey was forced to relive again the horror of Elizabeth's death, only now the entire experience from bedchamber to graveside was 'bound up into unity; the first state and the last were melted into each other as in some sunny, glorifying haze'.[21]

At Oxford, too, De Quincey had opium-induced nightmares of a Roman goddess named 'Levana', who is in charge of childhood education, and who operates, not by 'the poor machinery' of 'spelling-books and grammars', but by 'that mighty system of central forces hidden in the deep bosom of human life'. Levana has three chief ministers, 'The Sorrows', each of whom presides over a different kingdom of grief. Two of these ministers De Quincey does not meet for several years, but the eldest of the three, '*Mater Lachrymarum*, Our Lady of Tears', he sees often in his Oxford dreams, and she torments him with talk of seduction and betrayal. 'Through me did he become idolatrous,' she reports; 'and through me it was, by languishing desires, that he worshipped the worm, and prayed to the wormy grave.'[22]

To a certain extent, nightmares such as these would probably have beset De Quincey whether or not he ever took opium. He had what he once characterized as 'a constitutional determination to reverie'. In childhood and adolescence, intense visions or hallucinations fell upon him often in moments of grief and trauma. A great deal of his dream imagery came from wide reading, and his inveterate habit of brooding on his own experience: of 'Levana' and her 'Ladies of Sorrow', he noted that 'there is no great wonder that a vision, which occupied my waking thoughts in those years, should re-appear in my dreams'. Opium is a powerful substance, but it cannot make a dullard interesting. 'If a man "whose talk is of oxen", should become an Opium-eater,' he insists, 'the probability is, that (if he is not too dull to dream at all) – he will dream about oxen.'[23]

Yet despite his wish to credit the powers of his own mind for the splendour of his nightmares, De Quincey did not hold consistently to the claim that opium played no role in enhancing his dreaming faculty. Without the drug he would still have been an extraordinary dreamer, but with it the raw materials in his mind were profoundly altered, as he himself often conceded. 'Some merely physical agencies can and do assist the faculty of dreaming almost preternaturally,' he declared, and 'beyond all others is opium, which indeed seems to possess a *specific* power in that direction; not merely for exalting the colours of dream-scenery, but for deepening its shadows; and, above all, for strengthening the sense of its fearful *realities*.' Traumatic childhood recollection alone did not produce his Oxford nightmares: opium 'co-operated' with his 'nursery experience' to create that 'tremendous result'. 'Eloquent' and heroic, it 'buildest upon the bosom of darkness, out of the fantastic imagery of the brain', drawing De Quincey down into a divine abyss, where his spectacular pleasures and bitter memories played out in nightmare and reverie.[24] For several years, the pleasures of opium outweighed the pains. But all the while the drug was tightening its hold on him.

[ii]

At nineteen years old, De Quincey enjoyed days of 'radiant happiness' in Oxford.[25] He worked hard with Schwartzburg on his German pronunciation, though he insisted on learning everything else related to the language himself, a brave and prescient decision carried out in that 'spirit of fierce (perhaps foolish) independence' which governed most of his actions 'at that time of life'.[26] By the start of his second year he read the language with ease, and embarked on an extended study of authors such as Gotthold Ephraim Lessing, Jean Paul Richter, Friedrich Schiller, and Augustus and Friedrich Schlegel. Yet as significant as these authors were in shaping his views on irony, aesthetics, and literary theory, they were not the central object of his pursuit. For De Quincey, 'the very tree of knowledge in the midst of this Eden' was 'the new or transcendental philosophy of Immanuel Kant' as articulated in his revolutionary *Critique of Pure Reason*.[27]

Initially, De Quincey was awe-inspired by Kant's argument that the traditional way of viewing cognition needed to be reversed, so that instead of assuming that all our knowledge conformed to objects, we thought of objects as conforming to our knowledge, to our ways of knowing. Six weeks' study, however, was sufficient to close De Quincey's 'hopes in that quarter for ever'. By insisting that we can only know an object through its appearance, and not as a 'thing in itself', Kant seemed to De Quincey to destroy the possibility of objective knowledge, for our perception of the world lay 'ultimately in ourselves', rather than in 'any external or alien tenure', as De Quincey himself put it. Yet he admitted that Kant's ideas remained 'painfully irritating to the curiosity', and he came back to him over and over again throughout the course of his career, grappling with him especially when it came to theological issues. 'Neither can I think that any man, though he may make himself a marvellously clever disputant, ever could tower upwards into a very great philosopher, unless he should begin or should end with Christianity. Kant is a dubious exception.'[28]

De Quincey's fascination with Kantian and post-Kantian metaphysics was matched by his ongoing preoccupation with Coleridge, whose deep engagement with German philosophy galvanized his own interest in the subject. Shortly after Christmas in 1804, De Quincey angled for a meeting with Coleridge when he 'obtained from a literary friend a letter of intro- duction' to Charles Lamb, a twenty-nine-year-old clerk at India House, and one of Coleridge's closest personal friends. Lamb was a generous man and brilliant wit with a genius for friendship, but he had also suffered acutely from personal misfortune. In 1795 he battled a six-week bout of madness, and a year later his beloved sister Mary fatally stabbed their mother in a fit of insanity. Lamb had published poetry with Coleridge, as well as *A Tale of Rosamund Gray* and a tragedy, *John Woodvil,* which De Quincey had pur- chased shortly after arriving in Oxford. The letter of introduction represented him to Lamb 'in the light of an admirer', but De Quincey later acknowledged with some embarrassment that he had sought Lamb's acquaintance because of 'the reflex honour he had enjoyed of being known as Coleridge's friend', rather 'than for any which he yet held directly and separately in his own person'.[29]

Their initial meeting was auspicious. Presenting himself at India House, De Quincey was shown into a room with 'a very lofty writing-desk, separated by a still higher railing', within which sat 'six quill-driving gentlemen ... all too profoundly immersed in their oriental studies to have any sense of my presence'. With no servants nearby to announce him, De Quincey walked 'into one of the two open doorways of the railing', touched the arm of the clerk closest to him, and presented his letter himself. 'The gentleman smiled; it was a smile not to be forgotten. This was Lamb.'[30] He clambered amicably down from his perch, shook De Quincey's hand, and invited him that evening to dine with him at 16 Mitre Court Buildings, Inner Temple, where he lived with Mary.

De Quincey arrived shortly after seven, and almost immediately betrayed the real reason for his visit, as he turned 'the conversation, upon the first opening which offered, to the subject of Coleridge'. Mary answered all his questions 'satisfactorily, because seriously', but Charles was provoked. Sensing both the disingenuousness of the visit, and the faintly ludicrous intensity of De Quincey's devotion to the poet, he could not resist the pleasure of goading him by 'throwing ridicule' upon Coleridge. Before long De Quincey was perspiring, and when Lamb began to berate 'The Ancyent Marinere', he could hold his tongue no longer. 'But, Mr Lamb, good heavens! how is it possible you can allow yourself in such opinions? What instance could you bring from the poem that would bear you out in these insinuations?' 'Instances!' snapped Lamb: 'oh, I'll instance you, if you come to that. Instance, indeed! Pray, what do you say to this – "The many men so beautiful, / And they all dead did lie"? *So beautiful* indeed! Beautiful! Just think of such a gang of Wapping vagabonds, all covered with pitch, and chewing tobacco.' Lamb had no doubt a good deal more to say in this vein, but before he could go further De Quincey, 'in a perfect rapture of horror', raised his 'hands – both hands – to both ears' in order to shut out 'Lamb's impieties', though when the diatribe ended and he lowered his hands, Lamb allowed himself one final salvo: 'If you please, sir, we'll say grace before we begin.' De Quincey was unable to determine whether his host was 'really piqued' or just shamming, and he felt 'greatly ashamed' at his 'boyish failure' to resist the bait Lamb had set for him. Yet at the same time, the evening convinced him that Lamb was a 'traitor' to Coleridge, and De Quincey did not call on him again for some years.[31] He had not yet learned to appreciate the wisdom in Lamb's humour.

Weekend opium debauches and the opportunity to meet Lamb were not the only reasons drawing him from Oxford down to London. His book-buying continued unabated as he built up his library in a number of specific areas, including British history, German philosophy, Protestant theology, and 'everything related' to the poet Milton.[32] He went often to the theatre, where he particularly enjoyed watching 'the ever memorable and most excellent' Dorothy Jordan, whose 'laugh itself thrilled the heart with pleasure', and the 'immortal' Sarah Siddons, 'queen of the tragic stage'.[33] De Quincey also insisted that he remained in unsuccessful pursuit of Ann. 'During some years I hoped that she *did* live; and I suppose that, in the literal and unrhetorical use of the word *myriad*, I must, on my different visits to London, have looked into many myriads of female faces', in the hope of meeting her. These searches no doubt assuaged his feelings of loss and guilt. But he 'paid a heavy price' for them 'in distant years, when the human face tyrannised over my dreams, and the perplexities of my steps in London came back and haunted my sleep'.[34]

In the spring of 1805, De Quincey went to visit his mother in her new home at No. 8, Dowry Parade, Clifton, a village near Bristol which Mrs Quincey had chosen in large measure because it was only fourteen miles from Wrington, in Somersetshire, where her dear friend Hannah More resided at Barley Wood with her four sisters. De Quincey apparently liked the house very much, and seems also to have been finding it easier to get along with his mother, for over the next few years he described himself as 'continually resident' in Clifton.[35] Yet mother and son still disagreed over a good deal, including 'Holy Hannah', whom De Quincey condemned as 'eaten up' with the 'cant' of evangelicalism, and far too inclined to sit in luxurious saloons lecturing her 'poor, hard-working fellow-countrymen upon the enormity of the blessings which they enjoy'.[36] More undoubtedly sensed his disapproval, but conceded that he was a 'clever young man', and certainly delighted him in the early autumn when she introduced him to Joseph Cottle, the Bristol publisher of the 1798 *Lyrical Ballads*.[37] Several interviews between the two men followed, as De Quincey plied Cottle for information about Coleridge and Wordsworth, and exhibited 'talents' in their conversations which convinced Cottle that 'young Mr De Quincey' would 'shine' in the future. De Quincey, for his part, called upon Cottle whenever he 'passed through Bristol, simply as a man of letters; and I thought him a very agreeable companion'.[38]

He appears to have spent most of the next six months in Clifton, with perhaps intermittent visits to London or Everton to enjoy an opium debauch. Certainly he seems not to have returned to Oxford, for he is only batteled for one penny each week during the autumn and winter terms in order to keep his name on the books.[39] It had now been several months since he had last communicated with Wordsworth, and in the spring of 1806 he decided to pay the visit that he had so long been contemplating.[40] But after journeying all the way to 'the Lake of Coniston, which is about eight miles from the church of Grasmere', his nerves failed him and he retreated back down to Everton, where on 6 April he wrote to the poet seeking reassurance and detailing the reasons for his long silence: for the past two years he has been 'struggling with an unconfirmed pulmonary consumption' which he inherited from his father, and 'which the sedentariness of a college life greatly aided'; and he has also had to deal with the 'primal affliction' of losing his brother Pink, 'a boy of great promise who, in disdain of the tyranny exercised over him at school, went to sea'.[41] It took some time for De Quincey's letter to reach Wordsworth, who was in London, but on 5 May he responded with concerns over De Quincey's health and kind promises that he remained as anxious as ever that they should meet.⁴² A month later, De Quincey was still in Everton, and wrote back to Wordsworth with the news that he was 'in daily expectation of hearing some final account' of Pink's ship, the *Cambridge*, and that he could not commit to a visit to the Lakes until he heard 'something' which liberated him from his 'present indecision of purpose'.⁴³ In the event, no news of the *Cambridge* arrived, and by the time this was clear, the opportunity to visit Wordsworth had slipped away.

Remarkably divided as always between determination and procrastination, De Quincey journeyed back up to Coniston again in August, and once more set his sights on calling at Dove Cottage. This time he advanced 'to the very gorge of Hammerscar' from where he could actually see Wordsworth's 'little white cottage gleaming from the midst of trees'. But his courage failed him again. De Quincey later remarked that he was prevented from advancing by both a 'laughable excess' of 'modesty' at his own pretensions, and an admiration for Wordsworth that was 'literally in no respect short of a religious feeling'. After only a few short moments gazing down at 'this loveliest of landscapes', he turned and 'retreated like a guilty thing'.⁴⁴

De Quincey was in or near Coniston on 15 August, his twenty-first birthday, and a date he had long anticipated, for he was now legally free from his mother and guardians, and entitled to spend his patrimony as he wished. Perhaps as a way of commemorating the occasion, he sat down three days later at Coniston's Black Bull Inn and wrote out what he called his 'Constituents of Happiness', a list of twelve items that was clearly shaped by the piety and introspection of his mother's evangelicalism, his proximity to both Grasmere and Wordsworth, and a somewhat unexpected ethical idealism that may well be indebted to his reading of William Godwin's radical *Enquiry Concerning Political Justice*.⁴⁵

Not surprisingly, number one on De Quincey's list is 'a capacity of thinking – i.e. of abstraction and reverie', though this is countered by 'the cultivation of an interest in all that concerns human life and human nature'. Next follow 'a fixed and not merely temporary residence in some spot of eminent beauty', and 'such an interchange of solitude and interesting society as that each may give to each an intense glow of pleasure'. Number five is '*Books*' (he underlines it), number six 'some great intellectual project', and number seven 'health and vigour'. Then, 'the consciousness of a supreme mastery over all unworthy passions', 'a vast predominance of *contemplation*', an 'emancipation from worldly cares', and 'the education of a child'. Finally, and perhaps most revealingly, De Quincey lists 'a personal appearance' that is 'tolerably *respectable*'. Now fully grown, he remained under five feet tall, a circumstance that never ceased to bother and embarrass him. Perhaps unconsciously, he notes later in this section that one of the best compensations for a small stature is to acquire 'a high literary name'.⁴⁶

He spent the next two months in Everton before travelling south to Oxford to begin his fourth year of studies.⁴⁷ It was at about this time that some occasion demanded that 'a declamation should be written & delivered in Latin by some one of his college – and it fell to him to do it'. Accordingly, De Quincey 'composed & delivered the oration, and as he had written it with some care & was a tolerable master of the language, it excited considerable attention'. After he finished, 'many persons high in the University came up, shook him by the hand, & congratulated him', while in the days that followed 'he found himself noticed by the head of the College & several of the Students'. De Quincey had not originally been impressed by the intellectual calibre of Oxford undergraduates, but following the triumph of his declamation, 'he received invitations, & soon discovered that *all* the University men were not of the same description as those with whom he had at first associated'.⁴⁸

Christmas holidays arrived, and his mother hoped that he would be at home in Clifton, as he had been last year. Instead, flushed as he was by his inheritance, De Quincey decided to take up lodgings in London at 5 Northumberland Street, Marylebone, in order that he might indulge in urban pleasures.⁴⁹ At this point he could afford such a decision, though he had recently learned that the £2600 he inherited had already been reduced by £600 in order to cover his various debts. At least £250 went immediately to Dell. His mother and guardians saw to it that another £150 was deducted to cover all the expenses incurred by his sister Mary four years earlier when she went in pursuit of him in the Lakes after receiving word that he had absconded from Manchester Grammar School.⁵⁰ The remaining £200 was probably comprised in the main of his debts to booksellers.

Fatally, De Quincey surveyed these losses with 'philosophic indifference'. He was in better spirits than he had been in a long time, as 'a Young Man of Fortune, and no common portion of Originality', in Cottle's crisp summary. In February he returned to Oxford, and established himself in a new set of rooms.⁵¹ A month later he rejoiced as the British Parliament passed the 'great' Act for the Abolition of the Slave Trade, and 'absolutely extinguished' the 'wicked commerce'. When term ended, he headed back to London, where he received a letter from his mother announcing that his uncle Penson had sent him a gift of £50, which she hoped he could enjoy while he was 'among the Booksellers'.⁵²

Yet not all was as De Quincey could have wished. Other letters from his mother and sister Jane confirmed that the family was still no closer to determining what exactly had happened to Pink, for their attempts to trace him were 'perplexed and disappointed by a hundred different and contradictory accounts, given by a hundred different people'.[53] Perhaps even more pointedly, both Coleridge and Wordsworth were in London in late April, and though Wordsworth wrote expressly to tell him that he would be 'most happy' to see him, De Quincey did not respond to his letter, and by the time he did venture down to London, both poets had left town. In the weeks that followed, Wordsworth no doubt began to wonder exactly what sort of person his young admirer was, while De Quincey felt a deepening sense of 'self-contempt' at his own 'want of courage to face' him.[54] Committed as he was to their friendship, he was pinioned between two very different conceptions of the role he wished to play, for he was a humble admirer who hoped to be treated as an equal, and a disciple who wanted to be regarded as a champion.[55] To date he had been able to convince himself that no opening had been just the right opening for their first face-to-face encounter. But impatience was growing on both sides: De Quincey needed to step forward before Wordsworth stepped back.

SIX

Lives of the Poets

[i]

De Quincey loved to travel on the mail-coaches. They fired his imagination in at least five different ways: 'first, through velocity, at that time unprecedented'; 'secondly, through grand effects for the eye between lamp-light and the darkness upon solitary roads'; 'thirdly, through animal beauty and power so often displayed in the class of horses selected for this mail service'; 'fourthly, through the conscious presence of a central intellect, that, in the midst of vast distances, of storms, of darkness, of night, overruled all obstacles into one steady co-operation in a national result'; and finally, through the 'awful political mission' which they 'at that time ... fulfilled', for the 'mail-coaches it was that distributed over the face of the land ... the heart-shaking news of Trafalgar, of Salamanca, of Vittoria, of Waterloo'.[1]

When he boarded these mail-coaches, De Quincey was much more than a passive observer. For many years, people had assumed that the genteel place to ride was inside the carriage. The Oxford sparks of De Quincey's day, however, effected a revolution when they announced their preference for riding on the outside, where they could enjoy 'the air, the freedom of prospect, the proximity to the horses, the elevation of seat', and 'above all, the certain anticipation of purchasing occasional opportunities of driving'. De Quincey himself relished such opportunities, for at no other time did he feel more intimately connected to the grandeur of Britain's social machinery. Yet these mail-coaches also filled him with 'an under-sense, not unpleasurable, of possible though indefinite danger', for their fixed schedules and powerful horses meant they sometimes caused accidents on the road which they had no time to pause and remedy.[2]

De Quincey enjoyed riding the mail-coaches for one final reason: journeying from London down the Bath Road to Clifton, he met Fanny, 'the loveliest young woman for face and person that perhaps in my whole life I have beheld'. Fanny lived at a mile's distance from the Bath Road, 'but came so continually to meet the mail, that I on my frequent transits rarely missed her'. At her stop, De Quincey had only about 'four hundred seconds' to speak with her before the coach moved off again, but he used these moments to flirt and admire. 'Most truly I loved this beautiful and ingenuous girl.'[3] Fanny also had a grandfather, who made an even more indelible impression. He was a coachman on the mail, and reminded De Quincey of a crocodile, as his broad back and stiffening legs meant that he had a 'monstrous inaptitude' for turning round. No single image tortured De Quincey like the crocodile. It brought out his worst fears of self-division and otherness. Fanny filled his dreams. Then her grandfather. Then the crocodile, which in turn awakened 'a dreadful host of wild semi-legendary animals' that swarmed and reviled him. As was so frequently the case, De Quincey in his nightmares found terror residing at the very heart of beauty and pleasure, as the intensely associative qualities of his dreaming mind forced 'horrid inoculation' upon opposite natures.[4] Dreams of this kind tormented him for decades.

[ii]

He was in Clifton in the summer of 1807 when thrilling news arrived. Coleridge was staying with his close friend Thomas Poole not more than a day's journey away in Nether Stowey. De Quincey immediately contacted Cottle in the hope of obtaining from him a letter of introduction to Poole, and on 26 July Cottle happily complied with his request. 'The bearer, Mr De Quincey,' he explained to Poole, 'a Gentleman of Oxford, a Scholar and a man of Genius, feels a high admiration for Coleridge's character, and understanding that he was either with you or in the neighbourhood, Mr De Quincey felt disposed to pay him a passing visit.'[5] Earlier in the year, the thought of presenting himself to Wordsworth and Coleridge in London had paralysed De Quincey, but Coleridge on his own was a possibility. Wordsworth was a father figure. Coleridge was like a favoured older brother, and De Quincey already sensed he had much more in common with him.

That same day, he bent his way south on horseback, crossed the River Bridgwater on a ferry, and presented himself at Poole's 'rustic old-fashioned house' in the evening, only to find that Coleridge, his wife Sara, and their three children were no longer staying with Poole, but had moved on to another friend's house in the area, and may even at that point have been 'on the wing' to a third friend's home in Bridgwater. De Quincey was disappointed but determined, and he eagerly accepted Poole's kind offer to stay with him until they could locate Coleridge. Over the next few days, as they sent out enquiries into the neighbourhood, De Quincey greatly enjoyed the company of this 'polished and liberal' farmer, whose library was 'superbly mounted in all departments bearing at all upon political philosophy', and who was more than happy to share his extensive knowledge of Wordsworth and Coleridge, and their time in and around Nether Stowey.[6]

On or about the fourth morning, De Quincey and Poole received word that Coleridge was almost certainly in Bridgwater staying with the magistrate and merchant John Chubb and his family. Armed with directions on how to find the house, De Quincey quickly rode the eight miles to Bridgwater, where he passed down one of the main streets until he noticed 'a gateway corresponding to the description' he had been given at Poole's. Under it was standing a man who seemed to be about five feet eight; 'his person was broad and full'; 'his complexion was fair'; his hair was black; 'his eyes were large and soft in their expression; and it was from the peculiar appearance of haze or dreaminess ... that I recognized my object'. De Quincey dismounted, steadied himself by making 'two or three trifling arrangements' to his dress, and then advanced. 'This was Coleridge.'[7]

He introduced himself. Coleridge started. Lost in a 'deep reverie', he had not seen De Quincey approach, but he soon awoke to himself and received his young admirer 'with a kindness of manner so marked that it might be called gracious'. The two went inside the Chubb house, where Coleridge evidently felt very much at ease, as he 'rang the bell for refreshments', and extended to De Quincey an invitation to a 'very large dinner party' at the house that evening, which De Quincey quickly accepted. Then, summoning his courage, De Quincey gave Coleridge a gift which he had carried with him from Clifton: 'a scarce Latin pamphlet, *De Ideis*', written by the physician and philosopher David Hartley. In return, De Quincey undoubtedly hoped that Coleridge would be inspired to deliver one of his famous monologues. He was. 'Coleridge, like some great river ... that had been checked and fretted by rocks or thwarting islands, and suddenly recovers its volume of waters, and its mighty music, – swept at once, as if returning to his natural business, into a continuous strain of eloquent dissertation, certainly the most novel, the most finely illustrated, and traversing the most spacious fields of thought, by transitions the most just and logical, that it was possible to conceive.' De Quincey 'seldom sought to interrupt' him during this remarkable, three-hour demonstration, but Coleridge did pause at one point when the door opened and a woman entered. 'Mrs Coleridge,' he said frigidly. De Quincey bowed and 'the lady almost immediately retired'. From this 'ungenial scene', De Quincey surmised what he soon came to know: 'Coleridge's marriage had not been a very happy one.'[8]

That evening, Coleridge 'knew that he was expected to talk, and exerted himself to meet the expectation', but De Quincey could see plainly that he was labouring under 'the weight of dejection', and that the 'restless activity' of his mind 'in chasing abstract truths' was 'in a great measure, an attempt to escape out of his own personal wretchedness'. After a few hours Coleridge and De Quincey left the party to take a walk, during which De Quincey was astonished at the number of people who interrupted them 'to make personal inquiries' after Coleridge's health. At one point, De Quincey mentioned that he had taken laudanum to relieve the pains of a toothache. Coleridge, he claimed, immediately confessed that he was 'under the full dominion of opium', and expressed 'horror at the hideous bondage'. De Quincey already knew as much. He had learned of Coleridge's drug problem from Poole – if he had not heard of it earlier from Cottle – and he may even have introduced the topic of laudanum as a way of eliciting some comment from Coleridge.[9] Whether Coleridge would have taken De Quincey so quickly into his confidence may be doubted, but if he did not confide in him on their first meeting, it was not long before he did.

The two parted at about ten o'clock, and De Quincey rode out of Bridgwater. After the excitement of the day, he knew he would not sleep, and so he determined to travel the forty miles back to Bristol 'through the coolness of the night'. The roads were 'quiet as garden-walks', and De Quincey seemed to himself 'in solitary possession of the whole sleeping country'. Coleridge filled his imagination – his words, his appearance, his 'powers so majestic already besieged by decay' – and De Quincey planned what he might do next to consolidate their acquaintance and assist this 'extraordinary person'.[10]

In August he travelled to Everton for a holiday, but he was back in Clifton by early September, and soon learned that Sara Coleridge and the children – Hartley (aged ten), Derwent (aged six), and Sara (aged four) – had moved into Bristol, while Coleridge himself was back in Nether Stowey with Poole.[11] De Quincey called often on Sara, and spent a great deal of time playing and walking with the children. 'Hartley Coleridge dined with me a few days ago; and I gained his special favour, I believe, by taking him ... through every dell and tangled path of Leighwood,' De Quincey wrote to his sister on 15 September. 'However, Derwent still continues my favourite.'[12] De Quincey undoubtedly talked to both boys about Wordsworth and Coleridge, and in at least one instance his high expectations ended in bathos. On learning that Hartley 'had recently been travelling with his father and Mr Wordsworth', De Quincey asked whether he could recollect any of Wordsworth's remarks. 'Yes,' the boy replied, after a long pause. What did Wordsworth say? 'Why, when we came to Uxbridge,' Hartley answered,

'Mr Wordsworth observed, that what they had the presumption to call buttered toast, was in fact dry toast dipped in hot water.'[13]

Coleridge joined his family in Bristol some time late in September. Earlier in the month he had accepted an invitation from his old friend, the chemist Humphry Davy, to give a winter course of lectures for the Royal Institution in London on the 'Principles of Poetry', and he was increasingly consumed with the preparations. De Quincey visited him often, and the two undoubtedly discussed the lecture series at length, as well as other shared interests, including classical scholarship and Kantian metaphysics. Opium, too, appears to have formed a topic of discussion, or perhaps Coleridge simply noticed in De Quincey the telltale signs of laudanum consumption. Certainly an October entry in his *Notebooks* suggests that De Quincey was using the drug during these weeks, and that Coleridge already recognized the unnerving extent to which his young devotee was also his *doppelgänger*. 'Two faces, each of a confused countenance ... in the eyes of the one muddiness and lustre were blended, and the eyes of the other were the same.'[14]

De Quincey was a guest in the Coleridge home often enough to recognize how serious a problem laudanum was. And he soon realized that debt was also causing a great deal of tension, as Cottle confirmed when he made tactful enquiries. Might Coleridge accept a loan from De Quincey? Cottle agreed to sound him out, and in early October he wrote to Coleridge to tell him that 'an opulent friend' wished to make him 'an offer of three hundred pounds', though upon the stipulation that 'his name should be concealed'. When Cottle put the idea to Coleridge in person a short time later, Coleridge 'appeared much oppressed ... and, after a short silence, he ... said, "Cottle I will write to you. We will change the subject"'.[15] In a letter of 13 October, Coleridge told Cottle that he would accept the money 'as an unconditional Loan', provided that his 'unknown Benefactor is in such circumstances, that in doing what he offers to do, he transgresses no duty, of morals or of moral prudence'.[16]

Cottle communicated the news to De Quincey, who promptly offered to increase the amount to five hundred pounds, or one quarter of his remaining patrimony. 'Can you afford it?' Cottle asked. 'I can,' replied De Quincey. Cottle gently remonstrated. 'A spirit of equity compels me to recommend you, in the first instance, to present Mr C. with a smaller sum, and which, if you see it right, you can at any time, augment.' De Quincey then replied, 'Three hundred pounds, I *will* give him, and you will oblige me by making this offer of mine to Mr Coleridge.' He then contacted John Kelsall, his father's former clerk who was still managing parts of the Quincey estate from Manchester, requesting that he advance him three hundred pounds from his patrimony. The money duly arrived, and was soon in the hands of Coleridge, who on 12 November 1807 sent a receipt: 'Received from Mr Joseph Cottle, the sum of Three Hundred Pounds presented to me through him by an unknown Friend.'[17]

Cottle had done his best to keep the financial arrangements a secret, but within a few months he informed De Quincey that he was satisfied Coleridge entertained '*no doubt* of the source whence the money was derived'.[18] De Quincey probably greeted this news with both pleasure and embarrassment, for he was keen that Coleridge realized how much he admired him, but he did not want a sense of gratitude to strain their friendship. The offer was of course far more than De Quincey could afford, and it provides a telling example of his humility and generosity. Perhaps more than any other contemporary, De Quincey appreciated what Coleridge had already achieved, especially as a poet and metaphysician, and when he learned of his difficulties, he did all he could to make it possible for him to write and think.

The gift – or 'loan' as De Quincey was later forced to insist – was not the only way in which he supported Coleridge during this autumn. For several weeks the poet had been planning to send his family north to the Lakes, where they were to resume living at Greta Hall in Keswick, which they now shared with the family of the historian, essayist, and future poet laureate Robert Southey, whose wife was Sara Coleridge's younger sister. De Quincey volunteered to serve as an escort, for he instantly saw his opportunity to meet Wordsworth, not as a teenage fugitive, or a Lakeland sightseer, but as the trusted companion of the Coleridge family. His offer was readily accepted, and the party set off at the end of October. Four days later they arrived in Liverpool, where De Quincey took up quarters in the Liverpool Arms Hotel, and Coleridge, Sara, and the children stayed with John Theodore Koster, a 'gold merchant of celebrity', and a good friend of Southey's.[19] On the first day Coleridge wrote to tell De Quincey to expect a call from Koster, and on the second to ask if he would like 'to go to the Concert' that evening. Shortly thereafter, De Quincey dined at the Koster house, where he met the Italian soprano Angelica Catalini, whom he had heard repeatedly in London, as well as Koster's daughters, who displayed remarkable abilities in several different languages, and who did not 'shrink, even in the presence of the mighty enchantress and syren, from exhibiting their musical skill'.[20]

At the end of four days in Liverpool, Coleridge returned to Bristol to work on his lecture series, while De Quincey, Sara, and the children headed

north to Grasmere, 'travelling all the way in Chaises, and under the pro-
tecting wing of kind Mr de Q', as Sara put it.[21] He continued to get on
marvellously well with the children. Many years later Derwent recollected
how at one point on the trip De Quincey had to climb out by the front
window of the chaise 'to take the place of a tipsy driver', while Sara recalled
that on this same journey De Quincey 'jested with me ... and declared
I was to be his wife, which I partly believed. I thought he behaved faithlessly
in not claiming my hand.'[22]

The five travellers spent the night at Lancaster, and pushed on the
following day through Kendal to Ambleside and then further towards Town
End, the small hamlet on the southern edge of Grasmere where Dove
Cottage is located. As they followed the road up the hill to White Moss
Common, the 'weariness of moving so slowly' caused De Quincey and the
two Coleridge boys to alight. They gained the summit on foot, and then
ran down the steep slope on the other side, where near the bottom they
followed an abrupt turn in the road and came 'in sight of a white cottage,
with two solemn yew-trees breaking the glare of its white walls'. De Quincey
stopped. A 'sudden shock' seized him.[23] He was now standing just a few
yards away from Dove Cottage.

His 'old panic' returned. But before he could reconsider or retreat, Hartley
bounded in through the garden gate, and the chaise carrying the two Saras

Figure 2: Amos Green's picture of Dove Cottage, 1806

came rattling furiously down the descent and pulled into view. De Quincey was literally trembling. 'This little cottage was tenanted by that man whom, of all the men from the beginning of time, I most fervently desired to see.' His duty was to wait for the 'coming up of the chaise, that I might be ready to hand Mrs Coleridge out'. Yet given the intensity with which he had anticipated this meeting, it is not surprising that he forgot. For had 'Charlemagne and all his Peerage been behind me, or Caesar and his equipage, or Death on his pale horse, I should have forgotten them at that moment of intense expectation'. Following Hartley from the road through the gate and towards the cottage, De Quincey was 'no longer clearly conscious' of his own feelings. And then, 'I heard a step, a voice, and, like a flash of lightning, I saw the figure emerge of a tallish man, who held out his hand, and saluted me with . . . the warmest expression of friendly welcome that it is possible to imagine.' De Quincey had done it. He had introduced himself to Wordsworth. He had shaken his hand. Stunned, he 'mechanically went forward into the house'.[24]

Two women greeted him. The first was Mary Wordsworth, the poet's wife of five years, and now the mother of three young children: John, Dora, and Thomas. Curtseying slightly when De Quincey entered, she advanced towards him with an extended hand and 'so frank an air' that all his 'embarrassment . . . fled in a moment'. She was 'neither handsome nor even comely', but she exercised 'all the practical power and fascination of beauty, through the mere compensatory charms of sweetness all but angelic, of simplicity the most entire, womanly self-respect, and purity of heart'.[25] The other woman in the room was the poet's thirty-five-year-old sister Dorothy, who was less at ease than her sister-in-law, but who clearly surpassed her in vitality and intelligence. 'Rarely, in a woman of English birth, had I seen a more determinate gipsy tan,' De Quincey recalled.

> Her eyes . . . were wild and startling . . . Her manner was warm and even ardent; her sensibility seemed constitutionally deep; and some subtle fire of impassioned intellect apparently burned within her, which, being alternately pushed forward into a conspicuous expression by the irrepressible instincts of her temperament, and then immediately checked, in obedience to the decorum of her sex and age, and her maidenly condition . . . gave to her whole demeanour and to her conversation, an air of embarrassment and even of self-conflict.

De Quincey was used to celebrating the pale and aristocratic beauty of Lady Carbery, or the varied accomplishments of Mr Koster's daughters. Dorothy

was altogether different. 'She did not cultivate the graces which preside over
the person and its carriage,' he candidly acknowledged. 'But, on the other
hand, she was a person of very remarkable endowments intellectually.' He
had not arrived at Dove Cottage prepared to encounter her. She intrigued
him from the start, though, and he soon came 'heartily' to admire her.[26]

Wordsworth and the two Saras entered the cottage a few moments later,
and De Quincey got his first good look at the poet. Given his concerns
about his own physical appearance, he was undoubtedly relieved to discover
that Wordsworth's physique was nowhere near as impressive as his poetry.
Granted, he was 'of a good height, just under five feet ten', but upon the
whole he was 'not a well-made man'. His legs were a problem: they were
serviceable, but the contour was bad and they had been 'pointedly condemned by all the female connoisseurs in legs'. Worse was the bust: 'there
was a narrowness and a droop about the shoulders which ... had an effect
of meanness'. De Quincey conceded, however, that Wordsworth's face 'made
amends' for these defects, for it was 'certainly the noblest for intellectual
effects' that he had ever seen: the mouth firm; the nose 'a little arched, and
large'; the eyes exhibiting 'a light radiating from some far spiritual world';
and the forehead notable for its 'breadth and expansive development'.[27]

At half past five that afternoon everyone gathered upstairs about the tea-
table for the principal meal of the day 'under the simple rustic system of
habits' which the Wordsworths cherished. De Quincey was far too shy to
speak, but he listened with delight to the conversation, 'superior by much,
in its tone and subject, to any which I had ever heard before – one exception
only being made, in favour of Coleridge'. At around eleven o'clock the party
broke up, and De Quincey was shown into a pretty bedroom that he feared
'might turn out the best room in the house; and it illustrates the hospitality
of my new friends to mention that it was'.[28]

Early the next morning, Thursday, 5 November 1807, he was awoken by
a small voice issuing 'from a little cottage bed in an opposite quarter' of the
room. It was Wordsworth's oldest son, four-and-a-half-year-old Johnny,
'soliloquizing' in a low tone: 'Suffered under Pontius Pilate; was crucified,
dead, and buried.' De Quincey listened quietly while the boy finished
reciting his creed, and then got up and dressed. As the son of a merchant,
and as someone who had grown up 'in the midst of luxurious ... display',
he was used to the morning meal as a rather grand affair, but as he made
his way into the sitting room he was once again struck by the rural simplicity
of the Wordsworths' lifestyle, for here was Dorothy preparing breakfast with
no servant, 'no urn', and 'no glittering breakfast service'. Far from turning
up his nose, however, De Quincey thought immediately of Wordsworth,

and 'contrasting the dignity of the man with this honourable poverty, and this courageous avowal of it . . . I felt my admiration increase to the uttermost by all I saw'.[29] Later that day, Sara Coleridge and the children set off in the rain for their thirteen-mile journey north to Keswick, but not before inviting De Quincey to visit them there.

On his third morning at Town End, De Quincey was in for yet more surprises. Wordsworth had proposed that they pay a visit to Keswick in order that De Quincey might meet Southey. The plan, however, was not to travel by a direct route, but 'by way of Ulleswater', for Wordsworth needed to attend to some business in Penrith. Dorothy would accompany them as far as Ambleside, and Mary as far as Eusemere.[30] De Quincey, having heard nothing of horses, assumed that they were going to walk the circuit of forty-three miles, but as they prepared to leave, a common farmer's cart driven by 'a bonny young woman' made its appearance in front of Dove Cottage. Never in his life had De Quincey seen such a vehicle used to transport people. But, as he boldly put it, 'what was good enough for the Wordsworths was good enough for me'. All four passengers climbed aboard, and as they trundled south towards Ambleside, De Quincey was much relieved to discover that their 'style of travelling occasioned no astonishment'. Dorothy often exchanged 'flying colloquies . . . with stragglers on the road', while De Quincey himself found his attention riveted by 'the liberal manner of our fair driver, who made no scruple of . . . seating herself dexterously upon the shafts . . . of the cart'.[31]

At Ambleside, they turned northward and began to ascend the famous Kirkstone Pass, but it soon grew so steep that they had to climb down from the cart and walk to the top. From here they descended rapidly to Brothers' Water, and then travelled into the vale of Patterdale, where they left their cart at an inn, and set off on horses. Riding 'through those most romantic woods and rocks', they saw 'alternately . . . the most grotesque and the most awful spectacles . . . whilst, at every angle of the road, broad gleams came upwards of Ulleswater'. After four miles in this beautiful and solemn landscape, they reached the foot of the lake and 'a house called Ewsmere', where they passed the night.[32]

The next day, Wordsworth and De Quincey departed for Penrith, walking and talking and getting to know one another as they made their way through the woods. At some point during the journey, they paused and Wordsworth read to De Quincey his new poem, *The White Doe of Rylstone*.[33] Towards evening they dined at Eamont Bridge, and then walked into Penrith, where Wordsworth left De Quincey in the house of his cousin, Captain John Wordsworth. The business that had brought him to the town occupied him that night and throughout the following day, leaving De Quincey to make his way to Keswick by himself. With his head no doubt whirling from the Wordsworths' conversation and generosity, he walked the road to Keswick at a leisurely pace, stopping to dine at a little public house in Threlkeld, and not completing his journey until two hours after dark. Greta Hall stood a few hundred yards out of the town, and it was about seven in the evening before 'the arrival of a stranger occasioned a little sensation in the house'.[34]

Sara Coleridge came to the door to greet him, as did a gentleman De Quincey knew instantly to be Southey. In person, he was 'somewhat taller than Wordsworth ... and, partly from having slenderer limbs, partly from being more symmetrically formed about the shoulders than Wordsworth, he struck one as a better and lighter figure ... he wore pretty constantly a short jacket and pantaloons, and had much the air of a Tyrolese mountaineer'. De Quincey spent the night at Greta Hall, and Wordsworth arrived the following day. He and Southey, De Quincey realized at once, 'were not on particularly friendly, or rather, I should say, confidential terms', though he added that a 'mutual esteem' prevented them from quarrelling.[35]

On the following morning the three men breakfasted together and then retired to Southey's beloved library to talk politics. De Quincey had been surprised by much of what he had seen and heard over the past few days. This conversation proved no less unsettling. He was still far too diffident to speak up himself, but his aristocratic attachments were hit hard when the two poets launched an attack on the 'monarchical form of government', and agreed that 'no good was to be hoped for, as respected England, until the royal family should be expatriated'. De Quincey responded to their radicalism with 'an emotion of sorrow, but a sorrow that instantly gave way to a conviction that it was myself who lay under a delusion'. In De Quincey's eyes, Wordsworth was 'a person charmed and consecrated from error'. If he despised the reigning family, perhaps De Quincey should too? After this rousing discussion, Wordsworth and De Quincey set off, Southey walking with them as far as the 'sweet solitary vale of Legberthwaite', and then leaving them to complete their journey back to Grasmere.[36]

On a wet gloomy evening shortly thereafter, De Quincey and Dorothy took a walk to Esthwaite Water, and were returning to Town End through the blinding rain when suddenly Dorothy said, 'Pray, let us call for a few minutes at this house.' They walked through a gate and into a little shrubbery, from where De Quincey gazed up a narrow gravel road towards Low Brathay, the large home of the poet and author Charles Lloyd, whose epistolary novel *Edmund Oliver* (1798) contained a remarkable portrait of Coleridge quaffing laudanum. A few minutes later De Quincey and Dorothy found themselves seated in a small comfortable drawing-room, where Lloyd and his wife Sophia joined them for some hours of pleasant conversation, before Dorothy and De Quincey bade them good night and walked back to Dove Cottage. On this first visit, De Quincey saw enough to interest him in both Charles and Sophia. Later he came to regard Lloyd himself as 'amongst the most interesting men I have known', in part perhaps because of Lloyd's opium habit.[37]

On 12 November, after a week with the Wordsworths, De Quincey prepared to return to Oxford in time to keep the winter term. On the evening of his departure, William and Dorothy kept a longstanding arrangement to dine at the house of a 'literary lady' who seems most probably to have been their Ambleside neighbour Mrs Green.[38] De Quincey too needed to travel to Ambleside, and so Dorothy proposed that, rather than have him wait at an inn by himself, he should join them at the dinner party, after which they would walk him to his chaise. De Quincey agreed to the idea, but when they arrived at Mrs Green's, it was clear that she looked upon him 'as an intruder'. It was an awkward start to an extraordinary evening. With De Quincey, the party consisted of six people, including a stranger and 'a pretty timid young woman'. The dinner was 'the very humblest' he had ever seen, 'but also ... flagrantly insufficient in quantity'. One of the courses was 'a solitary pheasant'. The guests (with the exception of the young woman) were offered a portion, but were too polite to take one, whereupon Mrs Green served herself and happily ate the whole bird! Afterwards Dorothy laughed 'with undissembled glee; but Wordsworth thought it too grave a matter for laughing ... and said repeatedly, a person cannot be honest, positively not honest, who is capable of such an act'.[39]

Brother and sister put him into an Ambleside chaise at around ten that evening, and then returned to Dove Cottage. De Quincey, it is clear, had made a very favourable impression upon Dorothy. 'He is a remarkable and very interesting young man,' she assured her correspondent; 'very diminutive in person, which, to strangers, makes him appear insignificant; and so modest, and so very shy that even now I wonder how he ever had the courage to address himself to my Brother by letter. I think of this young man with extraordinary pleasure, as he is a remarkable instance of the power of my Brother's poems, over a lonely and contemplative mind.'[40]

De Quincey, meanwhile, wound his way out of Ambleside listening with delight to the beautiful whistling of his driver, who during 'the whole of the long ascent up Orrest Head ... made the woods of Windermere ring with the canorous sweetness of his half flute half clarionet music'. A dim presentiment fell upon him. Perhaps he was now travelling on roads that at some point he would travel daily. Perhaps he might 'traverse them in company with faces' that he had not even seen, but that in future years would be dearer to him than any that he yet had known.[41] Perhaps he might live here someday, near Wordsworth and his sister, near the Coleridges and Southeys and Lloyds, near these woods and towns and lakes? Perhaps he even belonged here. De Quincey arrived in Kendal well before midnight and climbed aboard the mail-coach heading south, his mind still ringing with possibilities.[42]

[iii]

His tutor Jones and a friend named John Millar had been putting considerable pressure on him to read for Honours, which in De Quincey's day meant a wide-ranging public examination based essentially on the classics, and including questions on religion, philosophy, mathematics, logic, and algebra.[43] De Quincey did not respond to their requests with much enthusiasm, for he looked upon the examinations as 'so much a farce, & so unfair a standard to try a person's general ability & proficiency, that he had determined not to attempt to gain distinction or even to take a degree'. But Jones and Millar persevered and ultimately De Quincey consented, in part because of 'his wish to serve his tutor', and also because the university had recently given an order that 'the answers in the Greek examinations should be given in Greek', a decision that delighted De Quincey, for it gave him a genuine opportunity for intellectual display, and turned the Honours degree into a prize worth winning.[44]

Students sitting these exams were expected to submit in advance a list of the classical books on which they were prepared to be examined, and usually offered about fifteen in total, with the entire work of an author counting as a single 'book'. De Quincey decided that he could do much better than simply what was expected, though, and 'instead of giving in any particular books', he later claimed he offered up 'Greek literature generally'. It was a reckless decision that gave him only until May to plough through an enormous amount of work, but he felt conscious of going through triumphantly.[45]

When he arrived back in Oxford on 13 November 1807, however, his plans for study hit a road block, as he fell seriously ill with what he called 'a determination of blood to the head', a condition that had bothered him before he left for Grasmere, and that was no doubt aggravated by – if not a description of – the pressure he felt over exams.[46] He got through term as best he could and then returned to 5 Northumberland Street in London, where he consulted an 'able surgeon' – almost certainly the famed John Abernethy – who made two recommendations: drink no wine, and do not bend the head downward. Over the course of the next two months, De Quincey followed these instructions and steadily recovered.[47] Staying away from Oxford undoubtedly helped, as did the chance to spend time with Coleridge, who had now installed himself at 348 Strand (above the offices of *The Courier* newspaper) in preparation for his lecture series. Before leaving Grasmere, De Quincey had promised Dorothy that he would 'take down the heads of the whole course of Lectures'. He missed Coleridge's first performance on 15 January, but met up with him shortly thereafter.[48]

Coleridge was sinking. The first lecture had been a disaster. He was taking 'more than ordinary doses of opium'. His health was so bad that he was frequently unable to rise from his bed. He was finding it difficult to concentrate in rooms that were small and noisy. And his only attendant was a woman memorably named Mrs Brainbridge, who lived in the basement of the building. De Quincey visited daily, and often saw Coleridge 'picturesquely enveloped in night caps, surmounted by handkerchiefs endorsed upon handkerchiefs, shouting from the attics . . . down three or four flights of stairs . . . "Mrs Brainbridge! I say, Mrs Brainbridge!"' On 5 February, Coleridge delivered his second lecture under considerable duress. 'His appearance was generally that of a person struggling with pain and over-mastering illness,' De Quincey reported; '. . . and in spite of the water which he continued drinking through the whole course of his lecture, he often seemed to labour under an almost paralytic inability to raise the upper jaw from the lower.'[49]

In such circumstances, De Quincey served Coleridge as an invaluable aid. He recommended medical help, assisted him with the lectures, and on at least one occasion took him out for a walk through his favourite 'Book Haunts'.[50] Coleridge talked to him at great length. It was probably during these weeks that De Quincey looked into Giovanni Piranesi's *Antiquities of Rome*, while Coleridge, who was standing nearby, described to him another 'set of plates by that artist, called his *Dreams*', which record 'the scenery of his own visions during the delirium of a fever'. The two men also undoubtedly discussed key questions in theology, though not always to De Quincey's satisfaction. 'Frightfully perplexed I am . . . as to what constitutes the so-called *appropriation* of the benefits of Christ's death. Never could I get any one to clear it up to me. Coleridge . . . talked all about it and about it, but never talked it out, that I could discover.'[51] On his side, Coleridge came quickly to value De Quincey's opinion. 'I do therefore earnestly ask of you as a proof of Friendship, that you will so far get over your natural modesty &

timidity, as without reserve or withholding to tell me exactly what you think and feel on the perusal of any thing, I may submit to you.' More disturbingly, Coleridge seems also during these weeks to have grown convinced that De Quincey's use of opium had already turned to abuse. 'I pleaded with flowing tears, and with an agony of forewarning,' he recalled. De Quincey 'utterly denied it, but I fear that I had even then to *deter* perhaps not to forewarn'.[52]

In late February, Wordsworth came down to London after receiving alarming reports that Coleridge was near death. His fears were soon mollified. Coleridge suffered from 'no appearance of disease which could not be cured, or at least prevented, by himself', was Wordsworth's pithy diagnosis.[53] Nevertheless, he loyally stayed in London for a month to try and buoy Coleridge's spirits. De Quincey saw Wordsworth regularly, and had the pleasure once again of hearing him read *The White Doe*. On 3 March, there was a tea party in Coleridge's rooms which brought together Wordsworth, De Quincey, Southey, Lamb, William Godwin, and Daniel Stuart (the editor of *The Courier*). But between illness, indisposition, fatigue, and reverence, there was very little talk, and entertainment for the evening fell to Lamb, whose wit and candour began to win De Quincey over after the friction of their first meeting three years earlier.[54]

Two days later De Quincey returned to Oxford. He had not been able to study during his months in London, and his exams were now only eight weeks away. Yet the more the pressure mounted to study, the more surely he descended into 'a state of palsy as to any power of exertion', a state that reminded him very much of those terrible dreams from his childhood, when he was 'chaced by a lion and spellbound from even attempting to escape'. His mother helped him enormously when she sent him a reading stand 'very ingeniously constructed' to enable him to read and write 'with advantage to my head from the necessity of looking up'. On 25 March he wrote to Dorothy and outlined a highly demanding schedule that included reading thirty-three Greek tragedies in one week. Yet at the same time he was finding 'the motives to all this labour ... inadequate; for the difference between success and non-success are the being placarded on all the college walls as the *Illustrious* Mr A.B.C. or 2ndly. as the *Praiseworthy* Mr A.B.C. or 3rdly. the not being placarded at all'.[55]

Five weeks passed and he remained similarly divided, at least according to the gaps between a contemporary account and a later recollection. On the one hand, he told Dorothy in a letter written just six days before his first exam that he was working extraordinarily hard: 'I am now reading every day for 18 hours out of the 24 – and never go at all to bed but only fall asleep on a sofa when I can keep awake no longer.' On the other hand, he told a friend several years later that an unexpected change in exam policy meant that he virtually stopped studying during the week before his exams began: he had been expecting to answer the Greek questions in Greek, but the university rescinded its decision and directed that the Greek questions were to be answered in English, a reversal that 'completely destroyed all stimulus' in his mind. 'He no longer cared to go through an examination which would only shew that he in common with others had acquired knowledge of a particular description, but would not leave him room to shew his general proficiency. He thought of declining to go up, & it was only the earnest wishes of his friend (Millar) & his tutor that induced him so to do.'[56]

During these weeks, opium almost certainly heightened both his desire to perform well, and his aversion to the entire process. The recent example of Coleridge at the lecture podium, feverish and disorganized, might have been expected to act as a caution, and perhaps it did prevent him from ingesting to excess. But at some level De Quincey also associated the drug with imaginative insight and vast intellectual exertion, and he probably resorted to it more frequently at this time to ease the stresses of high expectations, and to rejuvenate himself for study. What is more, the knowledge that Coleridge needed the drug, and that he had written and spoken great things while on it, undoubtedly made it more attractive, and De Quincey may even have increased his dosages in an effort to bring himself closer to Coleridge, to make himself more like his idol. Opium had been with him for most of his Oxford career, but perhaps it now began its insidious ascent from recreational device to daily necessity. 'So early even as his Oxford days,' wrote Cotton, 'De Quincey, we are told, was incapable of steady application without large doses of opium.'[57]

His exam was in two parts: Latin on Saturday, 14 May; Greek two days later. The first exam went extremely well. De Quincey was asked 'to translate Latin into English, & afterwards to render English, at sight, into Latin. And he could perceive from the whispers, the silence & various other indications, that he was ... likely to pass a splendid examination.' That evening one of his examiners, Edmund Goodenough of Christ Church, went down to Worcester, where he said to a gentleman well acquainted with De Quincey, 'You have sent us to-day the cleverest man I ever met with; if his *vivâ voce* examination to-morrow correspond with what he has done in writing he will carry everything before him.' Disconcertingly, the gentleman replied that 'he feared De Quincey's *vivâ voce* would be comparatively imperfect, even if he presented himself for examination, which he rather doubted'.[58]

So it proved. At some point late on the Saturday, or early on the Sunday, De Quincey bolted. He was already in a fragile state from weeks of study and poor health. Then, 'his contempt for his examiners, the thought of the possibility of failing from the unfair mode of examination', and his frustration over changes 'in the Greek Examination ... came upon him'.[59] Perhaps, too, as he brooded over his performance, he decided that he had not done as well as he had hoped. Or perhaps it was just the opposite. Having shown himself to be 'the cleverest man' in Oxford, he may well have felt overwhelmed at the thought of having to live up to such a reputation. In any event, some or all of these factors badly shook his resolve, and when the examiners summoned him on Monday, he was nowhere to be found. His name was not removed from the Worcester books until 20 December 1810, and he could presumably have returned at any point up until that time to re-sit the exams.[60] But once again he made a rash decision and stuck with it. His Oxford career was over.

[iv]

He headed back to his Northumberland Street bolt-hole, and over the next several weeks took solace in opium, socializing, and book-buying. By now his library contained three or four thousand volumes, and he was taking requests from his family, and from Wordsworth and Coleridge, to look out for specific books.[61] On 8 June, he was in the audience as Coleridge delivered his final lecture of the Royal Institution series.[62] At around this same time he met the Scottish poet and essayist Anne Grant, who recalled she spent 'an idle half day talking with him'. De Quincey, too, recollected their meeting, for Grant was kind to him and her notice 'particularly flattering', though when she learned of his 'profound veneration' for Wordsworth, she put a question to him which he failed to answer to his own satisfaction (or, he felt, to hers).[63] De Quincey also tracked down the eccentric philosopher John 'Walking' Stewart, whom he had first seen in Bath a decade earlier, and whom he now visited repeatedly in his Sherrard Street lodgings.[64]

To the Wordsworths De Quincey appears to have reported that he was too ill to complete his Oxford exams, for in early July Dorothy wrote of their 'sorrow for your illness', and their thankfulness that he had now recovered. Two months earlier the entire family had moved from Dove Cottage to nearby Allan Bank, and Dorothy now invited De Quincey to visit at any time.[65] But he could not yet pull himself away from London, and when at last he did, it was to travel to Mrs Best's for some weeks among 'the fair cottagers at Everton'.[66] Finally, in late

October, De Quincey confirmed his plans to revisit Grasmere, though by this time Allan Bank had become so crowded that Wordsworth wrote to say that, while they would be very happy to see him, they could not accommodate him with a bed. When he arrived a few days later, however, the family kindly made room, apparently by letting him share a bed with young Johnny.[67]

Allan Bank, De Quincey reported, was 'a modern house ... standing under a low screen of woody rocks which descend from the hill of Silver How' on the western side of Grasmere Lake. It had a 'breakfasting-room' on the ground floor which commanded 'a sublime view of the three mountains, Fairfield – Arthur's Chair – and Seat Sandal'. Yet it also had some 'capital defects – it was cold, damp, and, to all appearance, incurably smoky'.[68] The Wordsworths had moved in to give themselves more room, and currently their bustling household was made up of at least a dozen people, including servants and guests. Mary had recently given birth to a fourth child, a girl named Catharine. Coleridge was there, hoping to rescue his fortunes by launching a weekly newspaper to be called *The Friend.* Sara Hutchinson, Mary's sister and Coleridge's longstanding love interest, was assisting him as goad and amanuensis. Sara Coleridge often came over from Keswick, fetching the three children back and forth on visits to their father.

Meanwhile, Wordsworth had immersed himself in contemporary politics. Napoleon's intervention in Portugal and Spain had recently touched off the Peninsular War. British forces under Sir Arthur Wellesley (the future Duke of Wellington) landed in Portugal in early August 1808, and three weeks later defeated the French at Vimeiro. But before Wellesley could pursue his advantage, Sir Harry Burrard and Sir Hew Dalrymple arrived to take over the army from him, and they preferred to negotiate with the French. The result was the Convention of Cintra, the terms of which allowed the French troops and their loot to be transported back to France in British ships. News of the treaty reached Britain in mid-September, and was widely denounced as a cravenly betrayal of the Portuguese and the Spanish. 'We are all here cut to the heart by the conduct of Sir Hew,' Wordsworth wrote on 27 September.[69] A month later he began to channel his indignation into a long essay on *The Convention of Cintra.*

De Quincey did his best to fit in around the projects and tensions of Allan Bank. He bonded quickly with the children, and spent hours playing with them. He enthusiastically embraced *The Friend,* and set himself the task of recruiting as many subscribers as possible, taking five copies for himself, persuading his mother to take another two, and eventually recruiting friends such as the Kelsalls in Manchester and John

Millar at Oxford.[70] He also addressed himself to solving one of Coleridge's bigger problems: where was *The Friend* to be printed? There was no press in the immediate area, and going as far afield as Penrith or Kendal was bound to cause problems in terms of meeting deadlines and checking proofs. De Quincey's solution? He would establish 'the Grasmere Press' which, in addition to producing *The Friend*, would print 'immaculate Editions' of English and Greek classics, as Coleridge happily explained it to Stuart.[71] It sounded like an ideal answer, for Coleridge did not yet understand that De Quincey was as capable as he was of projecting big and impractical schemes. Before long the idea was dropped, and Coleridge came to terms with a printer in Penrith.

De Quincey became equally involved in Wordsworth's project, discussing the *Cintra* essay with him at length, and at one point agreeing to produce a note for it. Wordsworth, obsessed with the topic and anxious for news, would sometimes walk out of Grasmere and up Dunmail Raise towards Keswick at around midnight in the hope of meeting the carrier who brought with him Southey's copy of the *Courier*. De Quincey usually accompanied him on these walks of three or four miles, for it was a chance to speak to Wordsworth without interruptions, to absorb his views on politics and poetry, and perhaps to move beyond the poet's habitual reserve. On one particularly memorable night, Wordsworth and De Quincey sat for at least an hour on a huge block of stone waiting for the carrier to appear, with Wordsworth at intervals stretching himself upon the road, and 'applying his ear to the ground, so as to catch any sound of wheels that might be groaning along at a distance'. Once, when he was

> slowly rising from this effort, his eye caught a bright star that was glittering between the brow of Seat Sandal and of the mighty Helvellyn. He gazed upon it for a minute or so; and then, upon turning away to descend into Grasmere, he made the following explanation: 'I have remarked, from my earliest days, that, if ... the attention is energetically braced up to an act of steady observation, or of steady expectation, then, if this intense condition of vigilance should suddenly relax, at that moment any beautiful, any impressive visual object ... falling upon the eye, is carried to the heart with a power not known under other circumstances. Just now ... at the very instant when I raised my head from the ground ... the bright star hanging in the air above those outlines of massy blackness fell suddenly upon my eye, and penetrated my capacity of apprehension with a pathos and a sense of the infinite, that would not have arrested me under other circumstances.'[72]

For almost ten years, De Quincey had been fascinated by the sources of insight in Wordsworth's poetry. Now, as he walked back down the hill with him into Grasmere, he had those insights brought to life – he had them literally spoken into his own life.

About three weeks after his arrival at Allan Bank, De Quincey walked one evening into Coleridge's ground-floor study to discover Wordsworth in conversation with a young man 'in a sailor's dress, manifestly in robust health ... and wearing upon his countenance a powerful expression of ardour and animated intelligence, mixed with much good nature'.[73] This was John Wilson, a neighbour who lived above the town of Bowness on the beautiful estate of Elleray. De Quincey liked him immediately. The two young men had a good deal in common: both their fathers were prosperous merchants; in 1802, Wilson wrote a fan letter to Wordsworth that was equally discerning – and less reverential – than the one De Quincey sent a year later; both attended Oxford; both had literary ambitions, Wilson initially as a poet; and both were drawn to the Lake District by what De Quincey called 'the deep deep magnet ... of William Wordsworth'.[74] Yet the differences between them were perhaps even more pronounced. Wilson was proudly Scottish. He was about six feet high.[75] He was athletic, exuberant, and instinctual – a far cry from bookish, introverted, and elegant De Quincey. But in this instance opposites attracted. De Quincey later told different – and much less idealized – stories about how they first became acquainted, including one version in which they met in Wales after Wilson had flirted with 'a country girl' at a theatre, and was then 'waylaid ... & most ignominiously mauled' by her 'lover & his friends'.[76] Whatever the circumstances, certainly they were in each other's company by the end of November, when Wordsworth and De Quincey accepted Wilson's invitation to dine at Elleray.[77] Many years later De Quincey movingly described Wilson as 'the only very intimate male friend I have had'.[78]

During his stay at Allan Bank, De Quincey struck different members of the Wordsworth circle in strikingly different ways. His harshest critic was Joanna Hutchinson, Sara's sister, who wrote him off as 'helpless' and 'dissipid'. Sara herself disagreed. To be sure, De Quincey was 'very shy', but she found him a 'good tempered amiable creature & uncommonly clever'.[79] Southey, who hosted him on at least one occasion at Greta Hall, complained of De Quincey's size as though it were his fault. 'I wish he was not so little, and I wish he would not leave his great coat always behind upon the road.' But he was also quick to acknowledge that De Quincey had 'a head brimful of information'.[80] Perhaps not surprisingly, Dorothy was the most positive about him, though even she shared Southey's reservation. 'Mr De Quincey, whom you would love dearly, as I am sure I do, is beside me, quietly turning over the leaves of a Greek book,' she wrote to Catherine Clarkson on 8 December. '. . . We feel often as if he were one of the Family – he is loving, gentle, and happy – a very good scholar, and an acute Logician – so much for his mind and manners. His person is *unfortunately* diminutive.'[81]

By the middle of December, Wordsworth had made good progress on his *Cintra* essay. He published the first section of it in the *Courier* on 27 December, and the second on 13 January, before deciding that the better approach was to move as quickly as possible to issue the entire piece as a pamphlet, as it was too large for regular insertion in the *Courier,* and the story of the Convention was already starting to go cold.[82] With the assistance of Stuart, Wordsworth soon came to terms with a printer (Baldwin) and a publisher (Longman). That left only the issue of who would shepherd the pamphlet through the press. De Quincey was the obvious choice. He had been discussing the subject with Wordsworth for weeks, and he was only too happy to relocate to London for a few months in order to be on the spot for the supervising and proofreading – or, as he put it rather more grandly – for the 'editing' of Wordsworth's pamphlet.[83]

De Quincey was also well suited to the task because he was a much better prose writer than Wordsworth, as Wordsworth himself confessed. 'As the subject of punctuation in prose was one to which I had never attended and had of course settled no scheme of it in my own mind', he wrote to Poole, 'I deputed that office to Mr De Quincey', who assured Wordsworth that he had given the subject a great deal of thought, and who believed that punctuation should serve as 'a representation of the logical divisions – and a gamut of the proportions and symmetry of the different members – of each sentence'.[84]

Coleridge was sceptical from the start. 'I believe, you have seen Mr De Quincy at the Courier office with me,' he wrote to Stuart on 8 February. 'Ho! – He was the very short & boyish-looking modest man, whom I intro- duced to you in Cuthell's Shop . . . Besides his erudition, he has a great turn for manual operations, and is even to something of old batchelor preciseness accurate, and regular in all, he does.' That 'Ho!' has a very unfriendly sound to it.[85] Coleridge clearly thought De Quincey was too fastidious to do a good job of proofing the *Cintra* pamphlet, and his size made it even easier to mock him as unsuitable for the task. Coleridge was also jealous. De Quincey had been stepping on his toes within the Wordsworth circle, especially with William and Dorothy, while with the children – even with Coleridge's own children – he was a runaway favourite. What is more, Coleridge was finding it increasingly difficult to be grateful to De Quincey;

the £300 loan made it hard enough, but De Quincey was still working industriously to find subscribers for *The Friend*, and this after he had put himself down for five copies. *Five* copies! It all felt irritatingly like charity, and Coleridge shot back.

Before De Quincey left Allan Bank for London, Dorothy volunteered to lease Dove Cottage for him, and to organize the furnishings. De Quincey eagerly accepted her offer, and took the house on a six-year lease. He had by this time decided that he would settle somewhere in the area. He liked the appearance of Dove Cottage – 'lovely' rather than 'picturesque', as he put it – and it suited him in terms of cost, location, and size. But of course the primary reason he wanted to move in was because its rooms had been 'hallowed' by Wordsworth, and he saw it as yet another way of interweaving his life with the poet's.[86] On around 20 February, he left Allan Bank for the south, stopping in Liverpool, and then setting off again on 23 February.[87] He was anxious to get to London, and to execute his commission for Wordsworth. But soon he would be back in the north, and Grasmere would be home.

[v]

Flames were consuming the famous Drury Lane theatre when De Quincey arrived in London on the evening of Saturday, 25 February 1809. He went first to Northumberland Street, where he learned that his former lodgings were occupied, and then to Old Hummums, a hotel in Covent Garden, which was also full, but from where he ventured out to watch the 'very fine spectacle' of the fire as it reduced the theatre to what looked like an ancient ruin. That evening he slept in 'a truly Cimmerian hole' at Charing Cross, before moving shortly thereafter into lodgings at 82 Great Titchfield Street, Cavendish Square, near where he had agreed to meet Ann on that ill-fated evening six years earlier.[88]

De Quincey's work on the *Cintra* pamphlet got off to a reasonably good start, and by the end of his second week in London he could not 'detect a single error' in the ninety-six pages that had been 'finally struck off'. Yet even at this early stage there were worrying signs. The printers were often occupied with other business, and seemed to have a habit of getting drunk.[89] Perhaps more disconcerting, however, was the barrage of letters – seven in one week – that Wordsworth was firing off from Grasmere. 'You know he never likes to trust anything away fresh from the Brain,' Dorothy wrote. 'He is now engaged in making an addition to one Paragraph, which is to be transcribed on the other side of this sheet.' But a few hours later

Wordsworth announced that he could not make the transcription in time for the Keswick post, and requested that De Quincey 'Stop the Press' until the addition arrived. 'I hope,' Dorothy closed somewhat sheepishly on 7 March, 'your troubles and perplexities in this affair will end with this.'[90]

They did not. Indeed, they were just beginning. In mid-March a new compositor was assigned to the project, and his work was 'filled with such monstrous errors' that De Quincey was obliged to insist on 'a second proof', and then 'a 3rd proof', and 'I believe, the compositor thinks that I shall soon after want a dozen'. De Quincey also grew anxious about the timeliness of the project, so that when news reached London of France's victory at the Battle of Saragossa, De Quincey wrote and inserted a lengthy footnote to bring the pamphlet up to date. By the end of the month Wordsworth himself was concerned about the 'vexation that has accompanied this business', but he could not help bombarding De Quincey with four more letters filled with requests for clarification and information.[91] There was a 'great body of additions' that needed to be inserted after 'some expression' that Wordsworth could neither quite recollect nor find in his manuscript. If De Quincey deemed it advisable, would he 'add any remarks in the Appendix upon the ... infernal Bulletin of the French'. Was Norway still an independent country, or had it fallen to Denmark? Sir John Moore, one of Wellesley's successors as Commander-in-Chief of the British army in Portugal, had been killed in January: would De Quincey write a review of his recently published letters? If any of the quotations from the Board of Inquiry 'should be grossly inaccurate ... pray correct'. De Quincey's footnote on the Battle of Saragossa was unnecessary, as Wordsworth did not agree with his assessment, and had in any event already updated the pamphlet with additions and revisions of his own. And so on. 'This Letter is a miserable jumble, and my head a perfect chaos,' Wordsworth rightly observed on 26 March. However, that still left De Quincey with the onerous task of trying to sort it all out.[92]

He began to protest. Wordsworth's vague and sometimes contradictory instructions were making it very difficult to ensure accuracy, and De Quincey did not want to be blamed for mistakes that he had done all he could to prevent. But it was the cancellation of his note on Saragossa that really irritated him. 'I meant to have written to-day to Mr Wordsworth to complain a little of the very great injustice which he has done me in what relates to Saragossa,' he told Dorothy with unexpected frankness on 1 April. In part he was upset that his labour had been simply – and tactlessly – thrown away, but he was 'a great deal more hurt that it should be thought possible' that his opinion on Saragossa was different from Wordsworth's.

That was not the case at all. Had Wordsworth read what he had written? De Quincey was going to mail the cancelled sheet to Dorothy 'that you may see what I really did say of Saragossa'.[93]

Wordsworth apologized. 'It gives me great concern to find that after all your fatigue, confinement, and vexation, you should have suffered such mortification as you express from such a quarter.' He explained at length why he had cancelled the note, and assured De Quincey that he was certain their opinions on Saragossa were 'coincident'. That said, he 'quit the subject', as his penmanship was very bad, and his head ached miserably. Dorothy, too, responded to De Quincey, but with a good deal more warmth. 'You have indeed been a Treasure to us . . . We are very grateful for your kindness.'[94] De Quincey was mollified and continued to work hard on the pamphlet. On 5 April he agreed to Wordsworth's request to write a review of Sir John Moore's letters, though by this time he may well have recognized that the assignment furnished 'new matter for misconception on both sides'.[95]

Fortunately, he had other interests which at least partially took his mind off the troubles of the *Cintra* pamphlet. De Quincey spent a good deal of time reading contemporary literature, including Byron's *English Bards and Scotch Reviewers* and More's *Coelebs in Search of a Wife*, as well as poring over the most popular magazines and reviews, such as Leigh Hunt's *Examiner*, William Cobbett's *Political Register*, the *Edinburgh Review*, and the first number of the *Quarterly Review*.[96] He ate and socialized regularly with 'coffee-house friends'. On one occasion he dined at the home 'of a London acquaintance'; on another the Wordsworths' friend Robert Jameson spent the whole night visiting in his rooms. The city captivated him with its sights and sounds, from 'a bill advertising "*Artificial Ears*"' to '2 evenings or 3 . . . spent at an Oratorio and a concert', where his enjoyment of the music was no doubt enhanced by his ingestion of opium.[97] 'Walking' Stewart was his favourite companion during these weeks, and the two discussed a wide variety of topics, including 'female prostitution'. Somewhat unexpectedly – perhaps even somewhat guiltily – De Quincey spoke out vehemently against 'the afflicting spectacle . . . for I could not but view it as a greater reproach to human nature than the slave-trade or any sight of wretchedness that the sun looks down upon'.[98] De Quincey told Dorothy that he was spending virtually all of his time 'in utter solitude', but he was out enjoying London much more than he liked to let on.[99]

Production on the pamphlet slowed down dramatically over the Easter break, and then a snap of extremely cold weather brought on all De Quincey's 'old rheumatic pains' about the head and face, which he treated by putting 'cotton soaked in laudanum' into his mouth.[100] On 22 April,

Stuart wrote to De Quincey to say that the press was reporting to him that the publication of the pamphlet had been repeatedly delayed because of De Quincey's insistence upon a 'multitude ... of corrections'. Anxious that Wordsworth would receive reports of this nature without the proper context, De Quincey wrote directly to Dorothy to explain. Yes, it was true that he had troubled the compositors with numerous corrections, but that was because they had troubled him with numerous errors. Last week, for example, 'out of the six days, the man attended *two*; and must then undoubtedly have been drunk from the absurd blunders and omissions which he made: – and they *will* not (they say, *can* not) put any other compositor to the work'.[101] Increasingly exasperated, Wordsworth wrote immediately to Stuart to request that he would call at the printing office, and use his 'exertions to procure the immediate finishing of the work, which has been most shamefully and injuriously delayed by a drunken compositor whom Mr De Quincey cannot get changed'.[102]

Coleridge – now residing for a time with his wife and children at Greta Hall – heard of these difficulties from Stuart, and could not resist a certain 'I told you so' tone when he replied, though his assessment of the situation, and his insights into both De Quincey and Wordsworth, are characteristically illuminating. 'I both respect and have an affection for Mr De Quincey', he wrote on 2 May;

> but saw too much of his turn of mind, anxious yet dilatory, confused from over-accuracy, & at once systematic and labyrinthine, not fully to understand how great a plague he might easily be to a London Printer, his natural Tediousness made yet greater by his zeal & fear of not discharging his Trust, & superadded to Wordsworth's own Sybill's Leaves blown about by the changeful winds of an anxious Author's Second-thoughts.

To some extent, Coleridge was seeking in this account to justify his own circumstances, for he was encountering many obstacles in trying to launch *The Friend*, and it was gratifying to him to learn that Wordsworth and De Quincey were struggling to get *Cintra* into print. But more than this, he sensed deceit in De Quincey's replies. Could a well known and successful printer like Baldwin really afford such low production standards, and such drunkards on his staff? It seemed much more probable that De Quincey was simply in over his head: 'I can never retract my expressions of vexation & surprise, that *W.* should have entrusted any thing to him beyond the mere correction of the Proofs.'[103] Comments such as these seriously undermined

De Quincey's position with both Wordsworth and Stuart, and placed his movements and explanations under a darkening cloud of suspicion.

Despite all the delays, the printing of the *Cintra* pamphlet was nearing completion when, in early May, Wordsworth suddenly threw a brand-new spanner in the works. What if parts of the pamphlet were libellous? In particular, he was concerned about his statement that Wellesley and the other Convention generals had 'brought upon themselves the *unremovable contempt and hatred* of their countrymen'.[104] Stuart and De Quincey consulted with Baldwin and discovered that the passage could easily be cancelled, but now Wordsworth decided that the entire pamphlet needed to be reviewed for potentially libellous statements. Sara Hutchinson thought the matter laughable: 'We Females shall be very sorry to find that the pamphlet is not published for we have not the least fear of Newgate,' she told De Quincey. Wordsworth, however, was not laughing, and on 10 May he wrote again to request that De Quincey 'procure an interview with Mr Stuart immediately in order, that by your joint efforts every thing may be done which is necessary'. Ironically, after three months of urging the work on, Wordsworth now found that his 'anxiety to have it out' was 'much abated'![105]

It was De Quincey's turn to be exasperated. But he did what he was asked. On Saturday, 13 May he 'read through the whole pamphlet – marking every passage' about which there could be a doubt concerning libel. Then, on Monday morning, he and Stuart met to compare notes. Stuart was sure one section on the Army was actionable, but De Quincey convinced him that it did not pose a serious risk, and the passage was allowed to stand without alteration. Two days later at noon De Quincey went to the press, made the final few corrections to the last set of proofs, and then extorted a promise that four copies of the pamphlet would be struck off that evening. He left in 'a paroxysm of joy', returned after five o'clock to find four unstitched copies waiting for him, and promptly posted them off to Grasmere.[106]

Predictably, Wordsworth was dissatisfied with the result, and when he tried to thank De Quincey, the best he could do was to give praise with one hand and instantly take it back with the other. 'Last night we received the pamphlet,' he began in a letter of 24 May;

> I have not read the whole, but Miss Hutchinson will transcribe, on the opposite leaf, the most material errors which I have noticed ... I am quite satisfied with your note upon Moore, which is very well done; but had I seen his last Letter before I entreated you to be so gentle with him, I should not have been so earnest upon that point ... As to the pa ssage

about the army I hope and believe it is no libel, but certainly Mr Stuart's opinion ... it would have been safe to abide by.

Wordsworth managed to give De Quincey 'sincere thanks for all the trouble' he had undergone, but on the following day he wrote to Stuart to vent his frustration, especially on the question of the libel: 'I learned with great concern from Mr De Quincey that a passage you deemed libellous was not cancelled; this was in direct opposition to my earnest request conveyed in a Letter which I desired him to read to you; in which Letter I expressly said that ... I referred *to you entirely* to decide upon what was libellous, and what was not.'[107]

The coldness of Wordsworth's reply undoubtedly aggravated – or rather reaggravated – De Quincey, but he had a somewhat unexpected ally in Mary Wordsworth, who read her husband's first letter and scolded him for not being more enthusiastic. So on 26 May Wordsworth wrote to De Quincey again, determined this time to 'use stronger language of approbation'. But even on this second occasion he fell back into the same pattern of approval and censure. Certainly De Quincey was a 'master of the subject', but 'I wish you could have contrived to say something handsome of Frier ... I am glad that you treated Moore with so much gentleness and respect – I could not have done so myself ... The punctuation pleases me much; though there are here and there trifling errors in it.' Most damningly, the pamphlet was 'very correctly printed', but he was 'sadly grieved about that error ... in the Mottoe', and he regretted that the work had not been sent to him in proof so that he could have reviewed it himself before publication – the very reason that De Quincey had gone to London in the first place![108]

With publication now so near, Wordsworth must have thought that the worst was over. But more bad news was already on its way to Grasmere. In a letter of 24 May, De Quincey informed Dorothy that two days after he sent the four unstitched copies to Allan Bank, Baldwin agreed to give Stuart notice before printing the final version of the text, in order that he might have one last 'opportunity of seeing whether there was anything libellous in it'. The following morning, however, Baldwin contented himself with simply notifying Stuart that the printing was going ahead, and then promptly striking off 'the whole 500 copies', so that there was no opening for Stuart to make a final check.[109] If anything in the pamphlet was in fact libellous, it was too late now to stop it from appearing. De Quincey took a deep breath and wrote to Wordsworth. He was furious. 'It is an act of great disrespect to you, and may prove of most serious injury to me,' he stormed to Stuart on 28 May. '... I have kept my temper till last night, but I must say that Mr De Quincey's letter ... ruffled me not a little.' Further, when ten copies of the published pamphlet reached Allan Bank in early June, Wordsworth discovered yet another reason for distress, as two of the ten copies contained the passage on the Convention generals deserving 'the *unremovable contempt and hatred* of their countrymen' that he was certain was libellous, and that De Quincey had assured him had been cancelled. How on earth could that passage have made its way into the published work? And how many copies that had already been sold contained it? 'This is a most culpable inattention on the part of some one,' and 'it has mortified me more than I can express,' Wordsworth snapped.[110]

Given all the hold-ups and second guesses, it is perhaps not surprising that *Cintra* did not sell well. The odds were against it from the start, for De Quincey had been told at Longmans that only one in twenty political pamphlets made money – and at a final total of 216 pages, *Cintra* was much closer to a small book.[111] Wordsworth, however, was not interested in these numbers. As far as he was concerned, De Quincey was the primary reason for the troubles that attended *Cintra*'s publication. 'That he has failed is too clear,' he sighed to Stuart, 'and not without great blame on his own part (being a man of great abilities and the best feelings, but as I have found, not fitted for smooth and speedy progress in business).' Wordsworth now cited De Quincey's insistence on his own system of punctuation as a major reason for the delays. 'He had been so scrupulous with the Compositor, in having his own plan rigorously followed to an iota, that the Man took the Pet, and whole weeks elapsed without the Book's advancing a step,' he explained to Poole.[112] Coleridge heard similar reports and was only too happy to agree, though he went a step further and claimed that De Quincey's 'strange & most mistaken System of punctuation' had also damaged *Cintra*'s readability. 'Never was a stranger whim than the notion that , ; : and . could be made logical symbols expressing all the diversities of logical connection,' he tut-tutted. Southey, too, joined the chorus of disapproval. Wordsworth's 'long and involved' sentences had been rendered 'more obscure' by De Quincey's 'unusual system of punctuation', he reported to Walter Scott.[113]

De Quincey may not have heard any of these criticisms directly, but he definitely sensed that his efforts were being condemned, and he resented it. There is – it need hardly be said – nothing wrong with the punctuation of the pamphlet, and it is highly unlikely that it did anything to damage the sales. Wordsworth was right to say that De Quincey was not well suited to smooth progress in business, and it is almost certainly the case that his procrastination and over-zealousness caused delays. But Wordsworth had made a difficult job much worse with his arrogance and insensitivity, to say nothing of his eleventh-hour introduction of the question of libel. That De Quincey felt himself in the dock for what had happened is clear: 'about the supposed libel ... I am anxious to be acquitted on this point – on which I really am not at all in fault'.[114] He had worked very hard in the face of refractory printers, an avalanche of directives from Wordsworth, and an unlooked-for partnership with Stuart in which it was never quite clear what their respective roles were meant to be. De Quincey's postscript on Moore's letters is a telling indication of the amount of work he put in to try and give Wordsworth what he wanted, for the ten pages it occupies in the published pamphlet are the result of seventy-four pages of manuscript.[115] De Quincey had hoped his labour in London would consolidate his position as a friend of Wordsworth's. Instead, it only confirmed the poet in his wariness towards him, a wariness that Wordsworth never overcame and that De Quincey finally accepted with both bitterness and despair.

[vi]

The *Cintra* ordeal opened his eyes to some of the less palatable features in the characters of Wordsworth and Coleridge, but it did not change his future plans. Grasmere had been continually in his thoughts over the course of these long London months, and while Wordsworth had grown more and more dissatisfied with him, the women of Allan Bank had done their best to smooth the tensions between the two men, and to advocate on De Quincey's behalf, while the children of the household retained their great affection for him. In late March, De Quincey wrote a long letter to Johnny in which he described the presents he had bought for him ('I have sent you a few pictures ... There is one that is meant for angels or geniuses – I do not know which'), his business routine ('I go very often to talk to a man who lives at a house where they print books'), and the sights of London that he thought would especially interest a young boy ('there is a great park which is called Hyde Park ... and I saw in it hundreds and hundreds of soldiers marching up and down and learning to fight').[116] Dorothy looked forward to the day when De Quincey would renew his long conversations with Johnny, and Johnny himself worked hard throughout the spring to learn the ballad of 'Chevy Chase', so that he would be able to 'say it all when Mr de Quincey comes home'. Of the three younger Wordsworth children, De Quincey was particularly close to baby Catharine. He was to be her teacher: 'this promise Mrs Wordsworth once made me; and therefore I shall think it an act of the highest perfidy, if anybody should attempt to insinuate any learning into Catharine ... to the prejudice of my exclusive privilege'.[117]

The women of Allan Bank also kept De Quincey regularly informed about the work being done on Dove Cottage in preparation for his tenancy. He had left the matter in Dorothy's hands. 'In all parts give directions as you would choose it to be,' he told her. 'There are only 2 things which I have any special affection for in furniture – viz. the colours of *pink or white* in bed-rooms; – and only one which I specially hate – viz. *stuff* in bed-hangings.' Dorothy consulted with Sara and Mary, and by letter with Mrs Kelsall, who in late April 'sent a very pretty carpet for your new home – but we are not at all satisfied with the colour and pattern of the Calico for Bed-curtains, etc.' Five days later, the workmen began 'in good earnest' upon the renovations, though it was nearly two months before Dorothy could report that they were almost finished. 'Your Cottage is painted, and I hope will be ready by the end of the next week or the beginning of the week after ... Ned Wilson has made deal Bookcases.'[118]

Corresponding with Dorothy about the children and the cottage was a welcome distraction for De Quincey, and it brought the two of them closer together. 'You must take it as a proof of my affection that my penmanship is so bad,' she wrote to him in early May, 'for in proportion as my Friends have become more near and dear to me I have always been unable to keep my pen in such order as to make it write decently.'[119] For his part, De Quincey had been speaking of Dorothy to his sister Jane, who referred to her as De Quincey's 'favoured friend', and who added that she should 'much like to know Miss Wordsworth, and to see what sort of a woman you admire'. More intriguingly, Jane wrote in another letter that if De Quincey was 'really going to ... furnish a cottage ... ought not that beautiful and wild-hearted girl to be consulted? She certainly must have taste, and is the best judge of what will please herself.'[120] This may simply be a sister teasing her brother, and there is no indication that De Quincey thought of Dorothy as 'beautiful', but the epithet 'wild-hearted' fits her better than any woman De Quincey is known to have been acquainted with at this period, and Jane's reference to her as 'the best judge of what will please herself' clearly accords with De Quincey's request that Dorothy furnish Dove Cottage as she 'would choose it to be'. There may never have been any romantic feeling between the two of them. But if there was, these weeks when he was away in London seem to have kindled it to life.

De Quincey's attention during this hectic period was occupied by one final matter. On 10 March, his sister Mary had written to say that their brother Pink, it turned out, had joined the Navy, been taken captive by the

Danes, and was now 'on board the *Superb*, lying near Gothenborg' waiting to come home to England as part of a prisoner exchange.[121] De Quincey waited anxiously for updates on when his brother might return, but no new information arrived for more than two months. And then, in the middle of May, as he walked home one evening through the familiar territory of Greek Street, he unexpectedly bumped into John Kelsall. Pink, he now learned, was in England, and Kelsall 'had accordingly immediately come up to London' in order to verify his identity. The sailor soon made it clear, however, that he had no intention of meeting anyone, for he was 'very much broken down' in both body and spirit, and needed time alone to recover. Mrs Quincey promptly convinced herself that there was an impostor at work who was trying to make off with Pink's inheritance, but De Quincey understood his brother's desire for privacy after intense suffering, though the next morning he took the liberty of writing to him via a hotel address, and soon they were exchanging letters almost daily. De Quincey invited Pink to Grasmere, asked for details of his journeys, and told him about his exciting explorations of German literature. 'It is a great satisfaction to me that my Feelings and actions are intelligible to you,' Pink wrote back tenderly.[122]

Marooned by the recent purchase of '2 or 3 hundred books', De Quincey stayed on in his Great Titchfield Street lodgings through the month of June, for he was so miserable at the thought of having to pack up and move everything that he kept 'putting it off from day to day'.[123] Finally, in early July he tore himself away from London and travelled down into the vale of Wrington in Somersetshire, where he joined his mother and sisters at Westhay, the new and elegant family home that Mrs Quincey and her daughters had designed, and that his uncle Penson had paid £12,500 to build on the understanding that he would live there when he retired from service in the East India Company.[124] De Quincey arrived when construction was still far from complete, and for several weeks 'workmen of every class' forced the family to migrate 'successively into a parlour of a neighbouring farm-house; – into a green-house with no floor; – into a room with a floor but no ceiling; – into a closet 6 feet by 6; – and finally ... into our original sitting-room – with the library adjoining – completely finished'.[125]

In moving from Clifton to Wrington, Mrs Quincey had closed the distance between her home and More's from fourteen miles down to within a single mile, a change that appears to have delighted both households.[126] Indeed, when word spread through the neighbourhood that Mrs Quincey's eldest son had arrived at Westhay, More and two of her sisters were his first callers. They had learned of his interest in the 'infidel philosophy' of Kant, and were anxious to speak to him about it. Descending to the drawing-room, De Quincey took his seat upon a sofa by More's side, and his discussion of the great metaphysician seems to have charmed at least one of her sisters, who later referred to him as 'the sweet young man, Dr Kantian'. But More herself would not be moved beyond the bounds of her strident evangelicalism, 'and thus every avenue is shut up against gaining or communicating anything in her company'.[127] Further, on return visits to More – for De Quincey 'seldom suffered a week to pass without calling to pay [his] respects' – he found her equally hidebound on other subjects. When one of her guests cited a poem in support of an argument, More rejoined, '"Poetry! oh! as to poetry, I forswore *that*, and I think everybody else should forswear it, together with pink ribbons"; meaning, I suppose, in youth.' De Quincey managed to hold his temper, but was delighted when a young woman in the company 'put in this unanswerable demurrer: – "Really, Mrs Hannah More, I could never presume so far as to look upon anything in the light of a trifle, which Milton had not disdained to spend his life in cultivating"'.[128]

Politics also put More and De Quincey at loggerheads. As the summer wore on, De Quincey grew increasingly vocal about the ongoing Peninsular War (his many conversations with Wordsworth and Coleridge had – he felt – conferred upon him expert status), and he could not stomach the ladies and gentlemen of More's circle 'battening on' the liberal-minded *Edinburgh Review*, and extolling the military genius of Napoleon as though it were 'a vain and hopeless speculation' even to try and defeat him. 'I have accordingly tormented them to the utmost of my power,' he told Mary Wordsworth, ' – and have the satisfaction of thinking that I have given extreme pain to all the *refined* part of the community here.'[129] On one particularly memorable occasion, De Quincey and Cottle squared off over the imperfect British victory at the recent Battle of Talavera. De Quincey praised the behaviour of the Spanish. Cottle inveighed against 'all who were so "*unchristian*" as to defend throatcutting', but he eventually left the floor to De Quincey, not because he was convinced by his arguments, but because 'really you're so furious, there's no talking with you'.[130]

Pink agreed to come to Westhay on 8 September. He had been away from home for more than seven years. It was an occasion of immense joy, and De Quincey listened in amazement as his brother detailed his capture by pirates, his secret return visits to England, and his incarceration in Denmark, an experience which so fascinated De Quincey that later he successfully taught himself Danish.[131] But as the weeks slipped away, his friends in the Lakes began to press him to return. 'When are we to see you?' Mary Wordsworth asked him on 12 September. 'All has been in readiness for you, and every one of us wishing to see you for a long long time.' He answered her a month later. His eyes had been giving him trouble, and the entire family had been busy chatting to and making calls with Pink, but he confessed to her that the main reason for the delay was his 'own intolerable procrastination'.[132]

Shortly thereafter, however, he gathered his belongings and forced himself north, first to Cottle's for a brief stay, then on the mail-coach up through Birmingham, and finally to Dove Cottage on or about 20 October.[133] For a few days the Wordsworths' servant girl, Sally Green, came over to cook his breakfast, but he soon tired of this arrangement and moved back into Allan Bank, where he stayed until near the end of November, at which point the Wordsworths' former servant, Mary Dawson, came to work for him in Dove Cottage as his permanent housekeeper. If there had been any awkwardness between Wordsworth and De Quincey over the *Cintra* affair, both had clearly decided to put it quietly aside. 'Mr de Quincey ... has been above a month with us', wrote Dorothy on 19 November, 'and is like one of our own Family.'[134]

For weeks cart loads and cart loads of books had been streaming into Town End, confirming neighbourhood rumour that De Quincey was a 'far learn'd' man.[135] 'You will judge that it is a great pleasure to us all to have access to such a library, and will be a solid advantage to my Brother,' Dorothy observed to a correspondent. Coleridge, who had finally launched *The Friend* in June, often stopped in to browse the approximately five thousand volumes that soon came to cram every corner of the cottage, and carried so many of them back with him to Allan Bank 'that sometimes as many as five hundred were absent at once'.[136] At some point during these weeks De Quincey sat down at Elleray with Wilson, and Wilson's good friend Alexander Blair, as they went to work on behalf of *The Friend*, composing 'The Letter of Mathetes', an essay in which a young idealist explores his need for a moral guide like Wordsworth. Blair recollected that De Quincey 'may have given some suggestions' for the article, and that 'we certainly owed to him our signature', which means 'Learner' or 'Disciple'.[137] Coleridge published the 'Letter of Mathetes' in the seventeenth number of *The Friend* for 14 December 1809. The 'Letter' marks the first production in the rich – if often complicated – literary partnership between De Quincey and Wilson. Wordsworth's 'Reply to Mathetes' appeared in *The Friend*'s seventeenth and twentieth issues. *The Friend* itself collapsed after its twenty-eighth number.

The holidays were a time of great happiness. De Quincey spent Christmas at Elleray with the Wordsworths, while on New Year's Day he played host at

Dove Cottage to the Wordsworths and the Lloyds, and most probably to
Wilson and Blair. There was a 'display of fireworks at the Town end' on 2
January at which 'all the Children and middle aged in the Village were assem-
bled. Mr de Quincey's House was like a fair,' Sara Hutchinson reported.[138]
His life at Dove Cottage had begun in laughter and community. For all the
burdens of the past, he must have thought his future looked bright.

[vii]

Over the next few years, De Quincey divided his time among several friends.
He had a cordial relationship with Southey, who in January 1810 described
him as 'singular ... but better informed than any person almost that I ever
met at his age'. The two took a number of walks together, on one occasion
to Buttermere, and on another through 'the sequestered valleys of Cumberland'.[139] In December 1810 De Quincey hosted Southey for two nights
at Dove Cottage. Four months later Southey returned the favour when he
issued a warm invitation for De Quincey to visit him at Greta Hall – 'Your
chamber is not occupied by the boys, & it will be perfectly convenient to
receive you' – though he warned him about his proposed route, as 'the walk
thro Borrodale is a more formidable undertaking than you perhaps are
aware of'.[140] Their shared love of beautiful books was a talking point, though
at times they spoke more frankly, as when Southey told De Quincey 'that
he highly disapproved both' of Wordsworth's poetic 'theories and of his
practice'.[141]

De Quincey saw a good deal of the Lloyds. Some visits were social. Their
home at 'Low Brathay was distinguished above every other house at the
head of Windermere, or within ten miles of that neighbourhood, by the
judicious assortment of its dinner parties, and the gaiety of its *soirées
dansantes*'. Other calls were more personal. Sophia Lloyd and her mother
used to come over 'frequently ... on summer evenings to drink tea' with
him at Dove Cottage, or he would walk 'upon the darkest nights' over to
Brathay, where he and Lloyd would sit talking from about nine o'clock until
one. Often they ventured out together into the Lakes. Several of their
happiest moments were spent 'by the side of the mountain river Brathay
... listening to the ... sound of pealing anthems, as if streaming from the
open portals of some illimitable cathedral'. Yet already the depressive illness
that was stalking Lloyd was beginning to manifest itself: 'And once he said
to me, when we were out upon the hills – "Ay, that landscape below, with
its quiet cottage, looks lovely, I dare say, to you; as for me, I see it, but I feel
it not at all." '[142]

Wilson was a frequent companion. De Quincey did not care for many of his favourite pastimes – including hunting, fishing, sailing, and staging cock-fights – but the improbable pair walked together 'for twenty years amongst our British lakes and mountains'. De Quincey loved to visit Elleray, for he considered the view from the terrace the most magnificent in all of England. He spent hours conversing with Wilson: sometimes they were in strong agreement (the genius of Wordsworth); sometimes they were decidedly at odds (Wilson admired Napoleon).[143] De Quincey enjoyed Wilson's sheer physical energy, as he danced at the Lloyds' under the excitement of 'lights, wine, and ... female company', or mounted on horseback and chased a neighbour's bull with a fourteen-foot spear.[144] Above all, he was fascinated by Wilson's incomparable knowledge of Lake District wildlife, for 'of all companions that a man *could* have had ... in any chase after a natural phenomenon ... none was equal to ... Wilson'.[145] In spending time with him, De Quincey must often have felt as though he was in the company of a much more benevolent version of his bullying older brother William.

Wordsworth called in regularly at Dove Cottage, for these were the years when De Quincey luxuriated in 'daily nay hourly intercourse' with him. In June 1810 he and Wilson became godfathers to the Wordsworths' third son, William junior.[146] Shortly before or thereafter, Wordsworth also allowed De Quincey to read in manuscript his yet unpublished autobiographical masterpiece, *The Prelude*, a privilege which he accorded to very few outside his immediate family circle. De Quincey instantly recognized the poem's importance, and seems to have gone so far as quietly to transcribe it into '*five* manuscript books' in order that he might consult and enjoy it in the future.[147] Further, it was at this time that he came to a much more expansive understanding of Dorothy's role in shaping William's poetry. For 'whereas the intellect of Wordsworth was, by its original tendencies, too stern – too austere – too much enamoured of an ascetic harsh-sublimity, she it was ... that first *couched* his eye to the sense of beauty – humanized him by the gentler charities, and engrafted, with her delicate female touch, those graces upon the ruder growths of his nature'.[148]

In the summer of 1810, De Quincey travelled to London, where he spent several weeks before moving on to Westhay for a holiday with his family.[149] During his absence, he was especially missed by little two-year-old Catharine Wordsworth, who had been ill in the spring and now walked with a limp. She 'still looks sharply round when your name is mentioned', Mary Wordsworth wrote to him on 20 August, 'and every day she is *for a time* kept quiet, while we are rubbing her, when we say that she shall "ride away to London to meet Mr de Quincey"'. He bought gifts for all the Wordsworth children, and delighted to hear news of them.[150] But Catharine most fully reciprocated his affection, and she had become his favourite. She called him 'Kinsey'. He called her 'Kate'.[151]

In the autumn of 1811, Mrs Quincey, Mary, and Jane all came north to stay at Dove Cottage. The visit lasted two months and was a grand success. De Quincey hosted a number of gatherings at Dove Cottage. His mother and sisters made fashion statements that clearly underlined the family's gentility. 'I wish you saw the number of scarlet Cloaks & silk Pelisses assembled in the Church yard,' Sara Hutchinson enthused to a friend: 'the Norths – the Tillmans – de Qus – Crumps – Kings & Miss W'.[152] There were a series of 'enchanting' excursions. 'The Misses De Quincey have just called, and I must walk with them to the Waterfall at Ghyll-side,' wrote Wordsworth in September, with perhaps slightly strained gallantry.[153] A month later, Dorothy, Sara, and the De Quinceys took a trip to Yewdale, with the De Quinceys pushing on for a visit to Coniston, before meeting up with Dorothy and Sara to drink tea. Mary wrote to her brother a month after they had returned to Westhay: 'tell Mary Dawson we continually long for her brown bread and nice mashed potatoes, and that we talk and think and dream of Grasmere without ceasing'.[154]

For all his visiting with friends and family, however, De Quincey chose often simply to be alone in the Lakes. He watched the fallow deer in Gobarrow Park and the red deer in Martindale. He rambled across 'uninhabited ranges of hilly ground', where 'too often nothing is heard, except, occasionally, the wild cry of a bird'. He enjoyed 'ascending Helvellyn; for ... the swelling and heaving of the billowy scene of mountains around it and below it is truly magnificent'. Of all the Lakeland valleys, Easedale was his favourite: if one place 'on this earth could deserve to be sealed up ... against the intrusions of the world ... this it is – this Easedale'.[155]

Yet perhaps because his nearsightedness made him 'universally ... a poor hand at observing', De Quincey was in many ways a different kind of Laker.[156] As absorbed as he was by Wordsworth's poetry, he did not show much of an interest himself in waterfalls or sheepfolds or sunrises or daffodils. Instead, his interest in the area revolved around its people, its history, and its customs. He attended many private auctions, 'whether of cattle, of farming produce, farming stock, wood, or household furniture', for they brought together the people 'of perhaps a dozen valleys', and were highlighted by gossip and excellent ale. He was drawn to the legends of the district, such as those concerning the 'wheat thrown into the river Ken at Kendal which we have heard from Westmorland butter-women when going to market'.[57] He was fascinated by the Lake District dialect, and one day made a startling discovery about its Danish – actually, as it turns out, Old Norse – origins. 'I do not mean simply that it has some affinity to the Danish,' he emphasized. '... What I mean – is that all the *words* peculiar to the Lake district at least, and most of the *names* attached to imperishable objects (as mountains, lakes, tarns, &c.) are pure Danish.'[58] Perhaps most of all, De Quincey loved to set out into the Lakes by himself at dusk, and 'to trace the course of the evening through its household hieroglyphics ... to see the blazing fires shining through the windows of houses, lurking in nooks far apart from neighbours; sometimes in solitudes that seemed abandoned to the owl, to catch the sounds of household mirth; then, some miles further, to perceive the time of going to bed; then the gradual sinking to silence of the house'.[59]

De Quincey's relationship with the Wordsworth women flourished over the course of his first two years in Dove Cottage. In December 1811, however, he dealt a serious blow to their friendship when he decided to make some changes to his garden. 'What do you say,' fumed Sara Hutchinson, 'to de Q's having polled the Ash Tree & cut down the hedge all round the orchard – every Holly, Heckberry, Hazel, & every twig that skreened it – & all for the sake of the Apple trees that he may have a few more Apples.' Under the terms of his lease, De Quincey was entitled to do as he wished in the garden, but Dorothy thought of him as the custodian of Dove Cottage, not the master, and she was 'so hurt and angry' at his alterations that Sara was sure 'that she can never speak to him more'. How could he have done it? 'He knew how much store they set by that orchard.' Moreover, in the same letter, Sara makes it clear that he has also offended other women in the Wordsworth circle. 'Quincey reads the newspapers standing, or rather stooping with Catharine on his back,' she noted, ' – he is very fond of her but yet does not like to be plagued with her ... for he lives only for himself and his Books. He used to talk of escorting Mary into Wales but I do not believe that she will have his company.'[160]

Ultimately, of course, the storm over the orchard passed, but Sara and Mary were now on their guard, and while Dorothy did speak to him again, he was no longer 'one of the family'. If De Quincey knew of their hostility – and he must have done – he said nothing. But his reasons for making changes to the garden almost certainly extended beyond his wish for more apples. De Quincey took great pride in his own intellectual abilities, and after four years in the Wordsworths' company, he was undoubtedly growing tired of his role as a disciple. It seems probable that at some point during that autumn he came to the realization that the family was never likely to accord him the status of either equal or intimate. What is more, as his relationship with his mother and guardians had long since shown, below his mannered surface, he teemed with subversive desires that he was often prepared to act upon. What better way to assert his independence from the Wordsworths than by making his own mark on Dove Cottage?

December 1811 was also the month that news reached Grasmere of shocking crimes in London's East End. Near midnight on Saturday, 7 December, a man entered Timothy Marr's lace and pelisse warehouse at 29 Ratcliffe Highway. Once inside he locked the door, and within a matter of minutes ruthlessly dispatched all four inhabitants, including an infant. The Marrs' servant girl Margaret Jewell was out at the time fetching dinner. When she returned, and her knocking brought only the stealthy approach of unknown footsteps, she sickened with fear and raised the alarm. Twelve days later, and only a few blocks away, the same man struck again, this time at the household of a publican named John Williamson. Three people were murdered. Two escaped. Several suspects were arrested in connection with these atrocities, including a sailor named John Williams, who was detained on 22 December and who was found hanged in his prison cell four days later, an apparent suicide. The court chose to hear the evidence against him, but the circumstances of his death were widely interpreted as a confession of guilt. On New Year's Eve, his body was publicly exhibited in a procession through the Ratcliffe Highway and then driven to the nearest crossroads, where it was forced into a narrow hole and a stake driven through the heart. De Quincey became obsessed with these murders, and in particular with Williams, whom he regarded as both a 'solitary artist' and an 'accursed hound'.[161] In the years ahead, De Quincey returned again and again to these killings, stalking Williams as he had stalked his victims, and exploiting the details of the Ratcliffe Highway crimes in narratives that alternated unsettlingly between terror, pathos, and black humour.

[viii]

'I never was better in my life than in the spring of 1812,' De Quincey proclaimed. Laudanum was still giving him a good deal of happiness. He had been using it now for nearly eight years, but had avoided dependence because he continued to allow 'sufficient intervals between every indulgence'.[162] He had also – as always – been reading voraciously, and on a Saturday night he often combined the pleasures of books and drugs. In the year 1810 he amused himself 'by reading, in their chronological order, the great classical circumnavigations of the earth'. A year later he began 'to look into loads of books and pamphlets on many branches of economy'. But chiefly he had been studying 'German metaphysics, in the writings of Kant, Fichte, Schelling, &c', and inspired by their efforts, he began to formulate plans for a great philosophical opus of his own, to which he 'presumed to give the title' *De emendatione humani intellectûs* (*On the Correction of the Human Intellect*), after an unfinished work by the Dutch-Jewish philosopher Baruch Spinoza. De Quincey may also, at this time, have been gathering notes for a full-scale examination of Christianity, and '*the Relations of Christianity to man*'.[163]

One of the unexpected consequences of this wide course of reading and speculation was his discovery that Coleridge had committed 'a large variety of trivial thefts' from several German authors. De Quincey found the situation inexplicable. Why, 'with the riches of El Dorado lying about him', would Coleridge condescend 'to filch a handful of gold from any man whose purse he fancied'? Later, however, he came across more serious examples of Coleridge's unacknowledged borrowings, including one instance of 'bare-faced plagiarism ... from Schelling', though even these findings did not shake him from his belief that Coleridge was 'as entirely original in all his capital pretensions, as any one man that ever has existed'.[164]

De Quincey's various indulgences in Dove Cottage brought him physical pleasure and intellectual excitement, but they were not enough to block out an increasingly oppressive reality: he was running out of money. Well over half his patrimony was already gone, and it was now evident to him that he needed to earn an income in order to stabilize his situation. With considerable reluctance, he decided to pursue a legal career, and in March he journeyed down to London to make enquiries. Once reinstalled in his Great Titchfield Street rooms, he consulted with the barrister John Stoddart, who practised in Doctors' Commons, and who gave him 'all the information that was necessary' to enable him to decide 'on the Civil Law as a profession'. De Quincey had originally hoped to begin immediately by keeping the Easter term, but in the event he spent at least five weeks away from London – in Oxford, it seems, for at least part of the time – before returning to enter the Middle Temple on 12 June 1812 as 'Thomas De Quincey, eldest son of Thomas De Quincey of Green Hay, Lancashire, Esq. dec'd.'[165]

During his weeks in London, De Quincey was constantly in the company of Coleridge, who now lived with John and Mary Morgan at 71 Berners Street, Soho.[166] In the months following the demise of *The Friend*, Coleridge and Wordsworth had quarrelled as a result of some indiscreet comments by a mutual friend, Basil Montagu, who visited the Lakes with his wife in the autumn of 1810, and who offered to escort Coleridge down to London in order that he might seek medical help. Before their departure, however, Wordsworth took Montagu aside and quietly told him something of Coleridge's habits. When they arrived in London, Montagu and Coleridge argued – about wine, De Quincey claims – and Montagu falsely told Coleridge that 'Wordsworth *has commissioned* me to tell you ... that he has no Hope of you,' and that 'for years past [you] had been an ABSOLUTE NUISANCE in the Family.'[167] Coleridge was devastated by these comments and for months stopped all communications with Wordsworth, who was now in London seeking to patch things up. De Quincey did his best to stay clear of the animosity between the two friends, though his sympathies were almost certainly with Coleridge, and he no doubt heard him speak at length about his side of the sad story.

That De Quincey was smarting from his own relationship with the Wordsworths is plain from the reports of a visit he himself made to the Montagus' at this time. In one version, he 'fancied that something Montagu said was meant at him: And he got up on the Instant, went up to Mrs Montagu, & wished her good evening, & left the room without saying a word to any one else'. In another version, Mrs Montagu reported to Wordsworth that someone at the party mentioned to De Quincey something that Mary Wordsworth had said to him 'about the possession of the house', whereupon De Quincey 'took fire ... and retired from their House in great Indignation'.[168] What Montagu said is unclear, though Mary's comments presumably related to Dove Cottage (and perhaps the orchard?). In any event, De Quincey's response was to stomp out of the Montagus' house, as he had stomped out of his landlady's home in Bangor a decade earlier when she made ill-judged comments about swindlers. 'He is quite mad with pride,' Wordsworth remarked curtly.

The antipathies and misapprehensions steadily eroding the friendship between De Quincey and the Wordsworths were at least temporarily set aside on 11 June when De Quincey received a letter from Dorothy. It was sealed with black wax and contained tragic news. Three-year-old Catharine Wordsworth had died. 'My dear Friend,' Dorothy began, 'I am grieved to the heart when I write to you – but you must bear the sad tidings – Our sweet little Catharine was seized with convulsions on Wednesday night ... The fits continued till $\frac{1}{4}$ after 5 in the morning, when she breathed her last.'[169] De Quincey was staggered by this news. He had parted from her in cheerfulness, and with no misgivings, only a few short months earlier. And now she was gone. Wordsworth, along with the barrister and diarist Henry

Crabb Robinson, called an hour or two after he had received Dorothy's letter. De Quincey 'burst into tears on seeing Wordsworth and seemed to be more affected than the father'.[170]

He poured out his grief to Dorothy. 'Oh that I might have seen my darling's face once again! Oh what a heavy increase of affliction to me and to her parents is this!' A day passed and he wrote again, this time at greater length and with a deepening sense of shock at what he had lost. 'Nobody', he told Dorothy on 13 June,

Figure 3: A watercolour miniature of a child tentatively identified as Catharine Wordsworth

can judge from her manner to me before others what love she shewed to me when we were playing or talking together alone. On the night when she slept with me in the winter, we lay awake all the middle of the night – and talked oh how tenderly together: When we fell asleep, she was lying in my arms; once or twice I awoke from the pressure of her dear body; but I could not find [it] in my heart to disturb her. Many times on that night – when she was murmuring out tender sounds of endearment, she would lock her little arms with such passionateness round my neck – as if she had known that it was to be the last night we were ever to pass together. Ah pretty pretty love, would God I might have seen thy face and kissed thy dear lips again!

De Quincey closed this letter two days later by inserting himself at the very heart of the Wordsworth family. The 'custom of the country', he recognized, would oblige Dorothy 'to let many idle gazers look at our darling's face after she was dead', but how terrible to think that 'her mother, her father, and I should have been allowed to see her face no more!'[171]

De Quincey's mood over the next week is difficult to determine. The famous sale of the Duke of Roxburghe's magnificent library of an estimated 30,000 volumes was ongoing at the time, and would have been of great interest to him. Yet he later recalled that he was 'disabled ... by fever' and unable to attend, though he sent a proxy who purchased for him some of the most cherished books in his collection.[172] On 17 June, however, Crabb

Robinson saw De Quincey, and it is apparent from his account of their meeting that, while weak and emotional, De Quincey was not 'disabled' by grief or fever. Indeed, as they dined together in the Middle Temple, De Quincey was 'very civil to me, and invited me cordially to visit his cottage in Cumberland', Robinson reports. He is,

> like myself, an enthusiast for Wordsworth; his person is small, his complexion fair, and his air and manner those of a sickly, enfeebled man. From which circumstances his sensibility, which I have no doubt is genuine, is in danger of being mistaken for a puling and womanly weakness ... His conversation is sensible, and I *suppose* him to be a man of information on general subjects. His views in studying the law will never, I think, be realized ... A man must be altogether or not at all a lawyer.[173]

Four days later De Quincey drafted a letter to Dorothy, then rewrote it, and then rewrote it again. The three versions do not necessarily vitiate the sincerity of his anguish, but they do suggest an attempt to stylize it. He worried that Catharine might have called out for him when he was not there. Every day his heart grew 'heavier and heavier'. He had recently passed two evenings with Coleridge in an attempt to stave off dejection. 'Oh that I could have died for her or with her! Willingly dear friend I would have done this.'[174]

In late June, De Quincey was back in Grasmere, where he was overwhelmed by a 'fierce ... convulsion of grief', and his behaviour became decidedly odd. For the next eight weeks, he stretched himself every night upon Catharine's grave in the Grasmere churchyard; 'in fact, often passed the night upon her grave ... in mere intensity of sick, frantic yearning after neighbourhood to the darling of my heart'. His eyes became grief-haunted, and often in the afternoons when he was out on the hills, he saw Kate walking towards him, 'always almost' with a 'basket on her head'. De Quincey did not attempt to resist this 'senseless self-surrender to passion', but 'clung to it as a luxury, (which, in the midst of suffering, it really was in part)'. At the end of August he was seized with a 'nervous sensation' that led to a revival of the excruciating stomach pains he had first experienced with Ann and the young waif in Greek Street during his terrible weeks in London, and that 'yielded to no remedies but opium'.[175]

He decided to leave Grasmere and seek medical advice. But after consulting physicians in Liverpool, Birmingham, Bristol, and Bath, he arrived in Clifton without any improvement in his condition. Then, one night in

November, 'a peculiar sensation arose from the knee downwards', which 'went forwards through a space of about five hour', leaving him 'perfectly free from every trace of the awful malady' which had possessed him, though so physically shattered that he left a few days later to recuperate in the hot sea baths at Ilfracombe. Two months later, De Quincey returned to Grasmere. He saw the snow upon Catharine's grave, and the 'pair of her red morocco shoes' that Mary Wordsworth had left for him as a memento. But he felt no grief. Many years later, De Quincey diagnosed his six-month affliction over Catharine as 'nympholepsy' – a demoniac enthusiasm held by the ancients to overtake men who are bewitched by a nymph.[176] It is a whimsical and half-hearted explanation, and one that revealingly turns away from the real sources of his anguish.

Catharine's death hit him hard for a number of reasons. One, it temporarily restored his close relationship with Dorothy, who put her anger over the Dove Cottage garden away and wrote to him with a warmth that he had no doubt missed a good deal. Two, while he himself may not even have realized it, there was clearly a sexual element in De Quincey's feelings for Catharine. There was nothing strange about him sleeping with her – these kinds of arrangements were commonplace in the Wordsworth household when beds were short. Further, De Quincey certainly thought of her as a child, for he would never have written to Dorothy that openly about an affection that he conceived of as in any way improper. De Quincey knew that sexual interest in the young girl was unthinkable, and he 'always viewed her as an impersonation of the dawn and the spirit of infancy'.[177] But at the same time the possessiveness and self-pity he felt at her death were continually exacerbated by his thoughts of her 'passionateness', her 'dear body', and her 'dear lips', to say nothing of the two months he spent sleeping on top of her grave. Three, with Catharine's intense, unquestioning love now gone, De Quincey saw only too plainly the vulnerability of his own position within the Wordsworth circle. Catharine was his strongest tie to the family, and he probably realized that with her death the gathering hostility against him would soon succeed in banishing him altogether. Tellingly, six months after her death, the Wordsworths lost their middle son Thomas to pneumonia. Wordsworth wrote immediately to De Quincey with the news, but he was largely unaffected.[178] He had been fond of Thomas, but it was Catharine who mattered. When she died, so did his dreams of a cherished place within the family. Four, De Quincey resorted to increasingly heavy doses of laudanum to try and deal with the psychological and physical stress of the event. The drug brought him temporary relief, but it soon began to rebound upon him in the dreadful shape of nightmares and debilitating side-effects that laid siege to his health, and eroded his ability to cope. Finally, and most significantly, Catharine's death devastated De Quincey because it was Elizabeth's all over again. When his sister had died, De Quincey was only six years old, and for years he had done his best to keep his grief over her loss in check. When Catharine died, long pent-up despair over Elizabeth flooded out of him, as the adult tried to process what the child had suffered. De Quincey may only have been able to see his grief over Catharine, but losing the two young girls had melded into a single burden, and he buckled under its weight.

SEVEN

The Road of Excess

[i]

Perhaps he was predisposed to an abuse of opiates: 'I confess it, as a besetting infirmity of mine, that I am too much of an Eudaemonist: I hanker too much after a state of happiness, both for myself and others: I cannot face misery, whether my own or not, with an eye of sufficient firmness.' Perhaps eight years of self-medication and recreational use had made him far more reliant on the drug than he realized: commercial medicines containing opium were available everywhere, and 'under such treacherous disguises' many consumers only detected 'the chain of abject slavery' when it had already 'inextricably wound itself about the constitutional system'. Perhaps the afflictions of his childhood made it almost inevitable: certainly recent studies indicate that parental loss in one form or another – death, separation, desertion – is near the norm amongst opiate *habitués*. Or perhaps he just enjoyed the drug too much: 'I am a *Hedonist*; and, if you *must* know why I take opium, that's the reason why.'[1] It is notoriously difficult to determine what causes addiction, but in whatever measure any or all of these factors contributed, there can be little question that his dysphoria and physical misery following the death of Catharine Wordsworth pushed him over the edge, and in 1813 he became 'a regular and confirmed (no longer an intermitting) opium-eater'.[2]

Opiates are now understood very differently than they were two hundred years ago. In the terminology of De Quincey's day, he had an opium 'habit', not an opium 'addiction', for medical professionals did not begin to develop modern ideas of drug addiction until the second half of the nineteenth century.[3] Then, it was a moral issue, a question of character. Today, the moral argument persists, but it is vigorously challenged by those who see addiction as a medical concern, a 'disease of the brain' rather than a 'disease of the will'.[4] At the turn of the nineteenth century, doctors rarely wrote on the habituation of opiates, and when they did, it was as the regrettable but relatively infrequent consequence of the salutary use of a crucially important tranquillizer and analgesic. Indeed, so little was known about opiates that De Quincey was regarded as an 'expert' on the subject down the nineteenth century and beyond, at least by the non-medical public. Now, 'addiction' is widely understood to refer to the psychological, physiological, and social effects associated with the habitual use of certain substances, including opiates.[5]

In many ways De Quincey – like millions of other nineteenth-century addicts – hardly stood a chance. The drug was socially acceptable, the first and last resort for scores of ailments, and administered by the mouth, so that the supervision of medical professionals was unnecessary. When withdrawal symptoms manifested themselves between doses, most consumers naturally interpreted them as a separate illness and quickly returned to opium as the most obvious 'cure', thus silently reinforcing the downward spiral of addiction without even knowing it. De Quincey was criticized by family and friends for his dependence, while he himself often acknowledged a guilty sense that his addiction was driving him to sin against himself and against his family, but these were the only barriers between him and the drug, and they were never enough to keep him from it. There were no rehabilitation centres, no social programmes, no real medical insights, no legal obstacles, and very few financial ones, given the cheapness of the drug.[6] In common with the vast majority of nineteenth-century opium eaters, once De Quincey got addicted, he stayed addicted.

His ingestion levels varied widely over the long course of his opium career. One grain of opium was the equivalent of about twenty-five drops of laudanum, though it is difficult to translate these quantities into actual dosages of opiates, as different chemists used different methods of preparation, and different lots of raw opium differed considerably in their concentrations of constitutive alkaloids.[7] At the depths of his addiction, De Quincey claimed that his daily ration was as much as 480 grains of opium, or twelve thousand drops of laudanum, an astonishing amount, and especially for a man who was slightly built and under five feet tall. More commonly, De Quincey seems to have consumed around 300 drops of laudanum a day, though this total could rise or fall dramatically depending on his circumstances.[8] On the one hand, if he was trying to cope with inordinate amounts of stress, he almost invariably resorted to larger quantities of the drug. Or if he needed to get work done, he often binged, as he believed opium gave him energy and focus. On the other hand, if he had determined to control his intake, or renounce the drug altogether, his consumption levels could fall to zero for a number of days or even weeks. But he always relapsed. On numerous occasions he assured friends and employers that he was free of the drug. He was not. At four points in his career he engaged in particularly fierce attempts to overcome his addiction. All four attempts failed.[9]

Opium battered De Quincey. Once he was habituated to the drug, he no longer experienced anything approaching the euphoria he used to luxuriate in as an occasional user, while at the same time his addiction began to inflict various pains, the most severe of which was chronic constipation, a condition that affects most opiate addicts.[10] When he tried to come off the drug, what he called 'nervous misery' marked the onset of withdrawal.[11] If he attempted to fight through it, he was hit by nausea, vomiting, alternating chills and sweats, increased sensitivity to pain, aggression, irritability, and depression.[12] Sometimes he battled hard against these miseries, but then his resolution faltered, and he returned to opium. His intake levels climbed gradually upward. He determined on temperance. The grim cycle began again. For almost fifty years De Quincey's addiction imposed highly predictable patterns on a life that frequently descended into chaos.

In one crucial respect, however, De Quincey's profile does not match current medical knowledge about opiate addiction. By common consent, the pain of opiate withdrawal usually lasts less than a week, and is like having a very bad flu. It is unpleasant, but not life threatening.[13] This is not the picture De Quincey paints. After an illusionary early triumph over the drug, he emphasizes that his withdrawal miseries were severe and persistent: 'Think of me as of one, even when four months had passed, still agitated, writhing, throbbing, palpitating, shattered; and much, perhaps, in the situation of him who has been racked.' Some twenty-five years later, he cut back on his opium intake and brought on symptoms so terrible that he felt his condition tending towards suicide. 'For six months no results; one dreary uniformity of report – absolute desolation; misery so perfect that too surely I perceived, and no longer disguised from myself, the impossibility of continuing to live under so profound a blight.'[14]

Why is there such a gap between De Quincey's experience of opiate withdrawal and established pharmacology? To some extent, the discrepancy can be explained by the fact that on several occasions De Quincey knowingly exaggerated his pains in order to garner sympathy, or create a diversion, or heighten a literary effect. He also undoubtedly suffered in varying degrees from what is now known as 'protracted withdrawal syndrome', where withdrawal can last for up to six months, though in forms far more muted than the agonies De Quincey recounts.[15] Another possibility – wide ranging in its implications – is that De Quincey was also an alcoholic, so that his withdrawals were repeatedly complicated by the fact that he was fighting, not just opium, but a toxic blend of opium and alcohol.

Although he sometimes denied it, De Quincey was a great lover of wine, which he began drinking as a very young boy, and which he continued to consume throughout his life.[16] On many occasions in his adulthood he drank to excess, and there are months and even years when alcohol – especially brandy – was clearly an established part of his daily routine. These indulgences, however, make up only a small part of De Quincey's vast total consumption, for his primary source of alcohol was of course all the laudanum he was drinking. He himself insisted that opium did not intoxicate, but he acknowledged that laudanum did, as it was composed of proof spirits that contained anywhere from 45 to 60 per cent pure alcohol.[17] Given De Quincey's heavy reliance on laudanum over nearly five decades, a 'poly addiction' – that is, an addiction to both alcohol and opium – seems almost inevitable. Even at the lower percentage of 45 per cent proof spirits, and when he had his habit under some kind of control, his weekly consumption of alcohol was considerable, while during the periods of his worst excesses he drank the equivalent of between one and two pints of whisky per day.[18]

Withdrawal from alcohol is a much more serious matter than withdrawal from opiates, as it is typically more protracted, and potentially life threatening. It begins with vomiting, sweating, anxiety, and nausea, and in acute or chronic cases can escalate into fever, hallucinations, black-outs, and delirium tremens.[19] There is no way of knowing exactly what role it played in De Quincey's addiction – where opium's influence ended and alcohol's began – and certainly neither substance produces the kinds of enduring withdrawal pains that De Quincey describes. But there can be little doubt that alcohol confused and deepened miseries that he almost exclusively conceived of as related to his abuse of opium, and that it was a crucial factor in both his spiritual despair and his physical suffering.

Laudanum dragged De Quincey through hell, forcing him to practise 'habitual and complex dissimulation', and overwhelming him on countless occasions. Yet like many addicts, in the nineteenth century and far beyond, the severity of his addiction did not prevent him from functioning at very high levels for decades.[20] In many instances, he was able to fight through distressing circumstances. In others, vulnerability and collapse bestowed upon him an odd kind of agency that he turned to striking artistic effect. In 1813, De Quincey went from consuming laudanum to being consumed by it. But his addiction was a prison, not a death sentence. Though it often brought out the very worst in him, it never finally defeated his resolve or his creativity.

[ii]

At seventeen years old, Margaret Simpson was – in De Quincey's eyes –
'a beautiful girl'.[21] Her grandfather, William Park, was a Westmorland
'Statesman' (from 'Estateman', meaning a small farmer who owned his
land), and reportedly obstinate, even occasionally violent, in temper. His
son, William junior, was mentally handicapped. His daughter Mary
inherited at least some of her father's wilfulness, and was given to 'seeking
scandal, village rumours, &c'. She married John Simpson, who was well
read in 'the best literature of the country', and 'a rank Jacobin; not from
any delusion of his judgement, but as a pure malignant towards the nobility –
gentry – clergy – magistracy – and institutions of the land'.[22] The couple
had six children. Margaret was their eldest daughter.[23] The entire family
lived at The Nab, a long, low, and handsome farmhouse of 1702 that is set
just back from the road between Rydal and Grasmere, with Rydal Water
and then Loughrigg Fell in view from the front, and Nab Scar lowering
behind. Today it still looks very much as it did in De Quincey's time.

Margaret's family had farmed The Nab since 1332, so she came from
venerable Westmorland stock, but in terms of social rank, she was decidedly
below De Quincey's own standing as a 'gentleman'.[24] De Quincey, it seems,
did not care. Had not Wordsworth in the *Lyrical Ballads* chosen 'low and
rustic life' as his 'principal object'? Had he not enthused about how 'in that
situation the essential passions of the heart find a better soil in which they
can attain their maturity'; how 'in that situation the passions of men are
incorporated with the beautiful and permanent forms of nature'?[25] In falling
in love with Margaret, De Quincey was following good Wordsworthian
lore, for not only had she lived always amidst 'the beautiful and permanent
forms of nature', but in choosing her De Quincey placed genial feeling and
'the essential passions of the heart' far above societal expectation.

Of course several other factors also shaped his desire for her. De Quincey
liked Margaret because he disliked the courtship rituals of the upper classes,
as he was convinced that they promoted 'that vicious condition in which
trifling takes the place of all serious love, when women are viewed only as
dolls, and addressed with an odious leer of affected knowingness as "my
dear", wink, etc.' Further, though smitten with aristocratic women such as
Lady Conyngham and Lady Carbery, De Quincey had always been attracted
to women from a lower social rank, and he may even have found Margaret's
allure heightened by the radicalism in her family, though he claimed that
in his many political discussions with them he tried repeatedly to turn
them towards the 'better feelings' of his own Toryism, for despite his own

rebelliousness, De Quincey was a determined advocate of the status quo.[26]

In terms of education, De Quincey looked down upon Margaret, and was drawn to her for that reason: 'I could not, perhaps, have loved, with a perfect love, any woman whom I had felt to be my own equal intellectually.' Indeed, when he gave her a copy of Oliver Goldsmith's sentimental novel *The Vicar of Wakefield* and she took the entire story as fact, it only deepened his affection for her.[27] Morally and emotionally, however, De Quincey exalted Margaret, for he saw her as in possession of the innate nobility that he frequently associated with the lower classes: 'a beautiful young woman, in the very poorest family ... so long in fact as she stays under her father's roof, is as perfectly her own mistress ... as the daughter of an earl. This personal dignity ... and the feminine gentleness of her voice and manners ... oftentimes combine to make a young cottage beauty as fascinating an object as any woman of any station.'[28] Finally, though, De Quincey chose Margaret because he insisted on the grandeur of a love in which a man and woman regard themselves as equals: 'what an awful elevation arises when each views in the other a creature capable of the same noble duties – she no less than he a creature of lofty aspirations; she by the same right a daughter of God as he a son of God; she bearing her eyes erect to the heavens no less than he!'[29]

In early 1813, De Quincey's relationship with Margaret was in its inchoate stages, but already it was probably his best consolation for his burgeoning dependence on opium, his distressing financial situation, and the decline of his relationship with the Wordsworths. When he returned to Dove Cottage in January following his time in Clifton, he put himself back in touch with the family, and for a few weeks both sides seem to have tried for a continuation of the warmer feeling that had infused their correspondence in the weeks following Catharine's death. But it was no good. He was nowhere near as eager to please them as he had once been, and their faith in him continued to fall. On 1 February, Dorothy wrote with disdain that nine-year-old John Wordsworth 'now goes to Mr de Quincey for a *nominal hour* every day to learn Latin upon a plan of Mr de Quincey's own "by which a Boy of the most moderate abilities may be made a good latin scholar in six weeks!!!" This said nominal hour now generally is included in the space of twenty minutes; either the scholar learns with such uncommon rapidity that more time is unnecessary, or the Master tires.'[30]

Dorothy did not stop there. Having brought out the knife, she went on later in the same letter to make even more derisive comments about De Quincey's relationship with his housekeeper. 'Mary Dawson talks in private to us of leaving Mr de Quincey' as 'she is tired' of his 'meanness and greediness'. Dorothy was being remarkably unfair. De Quincey had failings, but meanness and greediness were not among them – as his many gifts to the Wordsworth children might have reminded her. Three months after she wrote these remarks, De Quincey generously loaned Wilson a large sum of money that pushed him far beyond his financial means. 'Will 200£ be enough?' he asked. 'If you are in immediate want of the money – could you not draw upon me at a short date?' Then, in August, when Charles Lloyd fell ill, De Quincey graciously urged Sophia Lloyd to avail herself of Dove Cottage. 'If Grasmere can be considered a change of scene to Mr Lloyd – I trust that you will not scruple to make use of my house.'[31] Mary Dawson, De Quincey later observed, was an 'ignorant old maid', who prided herself upon her position at Dove Cottage, and who attributed rules to him in his absence which enabled her to act in her own self-interest, including on one occasion when she seems to have told the Wordsworths that her 'Master' had left 'such and such directions' forbidding them from using the cottage, in order that she and her lover might enjoy it for themselves.[32] What hurt most, though, was that Dorothy believed Mary without ever consulting him.

De Quincey spent parts of the spring and summer in London, ostensibly to pursue his study of the law. He and Coleridge were often together. 'I remember one party at which we met Lady Hamilton – Lord Nelson's Lady Hamilton – the beautiful, the accomplished, the enchantress!' On another evening in Berners Street, De Quincey was enjoying tea and toast with Coleridge, while listening to him hold forth on the Roman philosopher Plotinus, when suddenly a cry arose of '*Fire – fire!*' and the two rushed out of the house and into Oxford Street, where a pianoforte maker's shop was ablaze.[33] In the autumn De Quincey visited his family at Westhay, and it was almost certainly during these weeks that he had the chance to observe the French-Swiss novelist and essayist Madame de Staël at a party. She made a vivid impression. 'Her black hair, floating in masses about her temples, her fierce eyes, and her impassioned gestures, gave her, when declaiming, the air of a Pythoness.'[34]

Back in Grasmere by early October, De Quincey received a warm note from Dorothy, apparently written from the Wordsworths' new home at Rydal Mount. 'We are very sorry to hear that you have been so poorly,' she tells him. 'Pray if you are well enough to come tomorrow bring yourself a pair of slippers and stockings that you may not have to sit with wet feet.'[35] De Quincey probably called as invited, for affection still remained between him and the family, and direct intercourse among them was often cordial enough, the recurrent backbiting on both sides notwithstanding. The more pressing news which greeted him upon his return was that Mary Dawson was pregnant, which meant that he needed to hire a new housekeeper. Who he chose for the post is unclear, but it may well have been Margaret Simpson. 'Q. has got a new servant', Mary Wordsworth remarked, ' – but I will not enter into the wonderful events of Grasmere – disgraceful to be sure they are.'³⁶ Part of the disgrace was that Mary Dawson seems to have been unmarried, but perhaps, too, Mary Wordsworth was alluding to the fact that De Quincey had hired a young woman with whom he was thought to be romantically involved. Certainly the gossip in London a few years later was that he had 'married his housekeeper', and more than forty years on the same rumour persisted in the Lakes.³⁷

He spent Christmas at Town End. Wilson had hoped to be at Elleray for the holidays, but he had determined to become a member of the Scottish Bar, and in mid-December he wrote with regret to inform De Quincey that his studies would keep him in Edinburgh until the spring. He then went on to make a rather disconcerting request: 'In about a fortnight it falls upon me to open a debate in the Speculative Society ... on the question: "Has the Peninsular War been glorious to the Spanish nation?"' The problem was, Wilson did not feel himself 'so well able to discuss this question as I ought to be'. Could De Quincey help? Would he mind jotting down his thoughts on the matter, and then allowing Wilson to use them as his own? On the same night, moreover, Wilson had a second essay to deliver 'on some political or philosophical subject', and he again felt himself without the 'ability to write one'.³⁸ If De Quincey had anything on hand that might suit the occasion, would he please mail it to Edinburgh at his earliest convenience? It is not known whether De Quincey complied with either of these requests, but Wilson had a keen sense of his friend's intellectual capabilities, and it was not the last time he called on him for assistance.

By early February, De Quincey had returned to London, and his legal studies at the Middle Temple. Pink was also in town, and the brothers were often in each other's company. Most memorably, they attended 'an exhibition of two large and splendid pictures' by the Italian Baroque painter Salvator Rosa. After several minutes of gazing at the two works, De Quincey noticed Charles and Mary Lamb in the crowd. Lamb, seeing them, came over to shake hands, but paused as he reached them, for he could see that Pink was about to deliver his opinion of Rosa. 'D—— the fellow! I could do better myself,' he cried, and then – good sailor that he was – he spat out a large lump of his chewing tobacco, which firmly attached itself to the frame of the picture. Some in the crowd 'actually turned round in fright', but

Lamb was gleeful, for he 'almost reverenced' an 'honest homely obstinacy' that refused to be 'enslaved by a great name'.[39]

De Quincey was frequently out with other friends as well. The future critic, dramatist, and judge Thomas Noon Talfourd and 'I became acquainted ... in the beautiful hall of the Middle Temple, whence ... after dining together ... we sometimes adjourned to our coffee' in his chambers, 'and enjoyed the luxury of conversation, with the *élite* of the young Templars'. De Quincey visited again with Crabb Robinson, who characterized him as 'a dry, solemn man, whose conversation does not flow readily, though he speaks well enough and like a sensible man'.[40] Coleridge had by this time moved with the Morgans from Berners Street to Ashley in Wiltshire, and De Quincey travelled out to call on him, 'as it eventually proved, for the last time'. He did not, however, manage to visit with 'Walking' Stewart, for though he was in London, De Quincey during these weeks was 'taking a great deal of opium, and never could contrive to issue to the light of day soon enough for a morning call' upon the ageing philosopher.[41]

His annual summer visit to Westhay was highlighted this year by several meetings at More's with the brilliant actress Sarah Siddons, whom De Quincey had often seen on the London stage. When she read Shakespeare, he heartily admired her, but when she read Milton, 'her failure was distressing; almost as distressing as the sycophantic applause of the surrounding company – all lost, of course, in nearly speechless admiration'. Later, at More's request, De Quincey read to her 'some of Lord Byron's most popular works', and got her to acknowledge that 'perhaps the style of Mrs Siddons's reading had been too much determined to the dramatic cast of emphasis'.[42]

That same summer, De Quincey also hoped that the distinguished American painter and poet Washington Allston would pay a visit to Westhay, for he was staying nearby in Bristol, and the two had clearly met earlier in London. 'Mr Walters, the gentleman who will deliver this note to you ... is very desirous of seeing your great picture,' De Quincey wrote to Allston on 21 July 1814: 'I have therefore ventured to assure him, from my own repeated experience of your kindness, that you will readily allow him this gratification.' Added De Quincey: 'it would give us great pleasure to see you here, if your engagements should leave you time to come over'.[43] At Westhay, he enjoyed an elegant and remarkably cultured lifestyle that undoubtedly bolstered his sense of his family's status and his own worth. In the years ahead, these days both sustained him, and marked a sharp contrast to the hell that was already starting to shadow his steps.

On one of his regular mail-coach rides from the south back up to the Lakes, De Quincey was involved in an accident. It took place in August, and seems most probably to belong to 1814, though De Quincey himself was confused about the year.[44] He had already travelled to Manchester earlier in the day, and was now getting ready to complete the final stage of his journey to Westmorland. It was after midnight. He was the only passenger on the coach. After mounting the box, he dosed himself with 'a small quantity of laudanum'.[45] The coachman was known to him as a driver from the south, and as they made their way out of Manchester, he explained to De Quincey that he was temporarily in the north attending to legal business during the day, and driving at night, an exhausting schedule that meant he had not slept in seventy-two hours. During the first few stages of their ride he fought hard against his drowsiness, but finally, at about mile twenty-four, he surrendered himself to sleep, though not before crossing his legs over his hand so that the reins would not slip free. There was only one other person aboard, a guard at the back, and he too had fallen asleep.

That left De Quincey in charge of the mail-coach as it thundered north up the Preston road into the silence of the night. The horses were familiar with the route, and he remained relatively calm, until he noticed that they were travelling on the wrong side of the road. Serious concern, however, did not seize him until he heard, in the distance, the sound of a wheel. 'Who and what could it be? Was it industry in a taxed cart – was it youthful gaiety in a gig?' De Quincey attempted to gain control of the coach, but he could not pull the reins free from the driver's hand. He then tried to reach the guard's horn at the back, but his way was blocked by the mail piled high on the roof. And then suddenly, 'our frantic horses swept round an angle of the road', and De Quincey could see before him, in the earliest light of dawn, an avenue, six hundred yards in length, with umbrageous trees on either side, and at its far end, just discernible, two young lovers sitting in a light gig.[46] Panicked, he yelled out a warning. They did not hear him. He yelled again. The young man raised his head.

'He saw, he heard, he comprehended, the ruin that was coming down.' Rising to his feet, he pulled on the reins and his horse slowly began to move the gig, first so that it stood at a right angle to the oncoming coach, and then gradually over towards the edge of the road. Thirty seconds remained before the two vehicles collided. Then twenty. Then fifteen. 'Oh hurry, hurry, my brave young man! for the cruel hoofs of our horses – *they* also hurry!' The gig reached the side of the road. The mail-coach flew past. There was a thunderous blow. Either with its swingle-bar, or with one of its horses, the coach had struck the off-wheel of the gig. De Quincey spun around, terrified, and saw the young man safe, but 'frozen into rest by horror'. Far more disturbing was the sight of the young woman. 'Will that spectacle ever depart from my dreams, as she rose and sank upon her seat, sank and rose, threw up her arms wildly to heaven, clutched at some visionary object in the air, fainting, praying, raving, despairing!'[47] Soon her image filled his nightmares in horrifying re-enactments of the accident scene. In some versions she is closely associated with Elizabeth. On occasion she escapes her fate. More often she is swallowed up by death.[48]

[iii]

In September 1814, Wordsworth hosted a party at Rydal Mount attended by De Quincey, Lloyd, Wilson, and the Scottish poet and novelist James Hogg, the 'Ettrick Shepherd'. After dinner, an unusually bright meteor passed through the sky, and the group went out on the terrace to see it. Dorothy thought it 'might prove ominous', but Hogg was more optimistic, and – in his thick Scots accent – described it as 'a treeumphal airch, raised in honour of the meeting of the poets'. Wilson thought the remark 'very good', though he would certainly have ranked Wordsworth's poetry ahead of his own, or Lloyd's, or Hogg's. Wordsworth, however, was indignant, and leading De Quincey aside, 'he addressed him in these disdainful and venomous words: – "Poets? Poets? – What does the fellow mean? – Where are they?"'[49] De Quincey's reaction to Wordsworth's comments is revealing. On the one hand, he soon betrayed the poet's confidence by reporting the incident, perhaps to Wilson, or maybe even directly to Hogg, for De Quincey knew all about Wordsworth's tactlessness, and he was now prepared to speak of it openly. On the other hand, he was probably pleased that Wordsworth had chosen to confide in him, and – moreover – he agreed with him. Hogg's egotism was, as De Quincey later put it, 'absolutely insufferable'.[50] Wordsworth no longer commanded De Quincey's unstinting loyalty, but there was still a good deal of common ground between the poet and his former disciple.

Life in the Lakes remained full of interest. De Quincey continued to study the Danish language. He was one of the subscribers to Isabella Lickbarrow's *Poetical Effusions*, as were Southey and Wordsworth. On a number of evenings he called at Calgarth Park, the large Georgian home of the formidable Richard Watson, Bishop of Llandaff, with whom he discussed Kant.[51] John Merritt, his old bookseller friend from Liverpool, came with his wife to stay at Dove Cottage. 'At times in solitary or desolate places of Westmorland and Cumberland', De Quincey bumped into Coleridge's eldest son Hartley, whom he found 'most intellectual' and 'most eccentric'. Pink bought a house in the village of Wetheral, near Carlisle in Cumberland,

and De Quincey went there to visit him.[52] And of course there was Margaret. She and De Quincey had taken to late-night trysts. 'De Quincey was at the *Nab*', Wilson noted on one occasion, 'and when he returned about three o'clock, found me asleep in his bed'. In December, De Quincey planned a party at Dove Cottage that included 'young Mrs Jackson, Miss Huddleston', and 'the family from the Nab'. Wilson was also invited, and De Quincey was particularly anxious that the gathering benefit from his exuberance and social status: 'come to dinner, if you can; but, at any rate, *come*'.[53]

Wordsworth was well aware by this time of De Quincey's opium habit, but it did not prevent the two from working together on various literary projects.[54] Despite the debacle of the *Cintra* pamphlet six years earlier, Wordsworth asked De Quincey for his help in seeing the famous 1815 edition of his *Poems* through the press, and De Quincey duly obliged when he returned to London to keep the winter term at the Middle Temple. More than this, the poet clearly valued De Quincey's opinion. 'I wished you had mentioned *why* you desired the *rough* Copies of the Preface to be kept, as your request has led me to apprehend that something therein might have appeared to you as better or more clearly expressed – than in the after draught; and I should have been glad to reinstate accordingly.'[55]

De Quincey was also at work at this time on a series of letters defending Wordsworth from the vitriolic abuse of Francis Jeffrey and other *Edinburgh* reviewers. Wordsworth was delighted with the scheme, and wrote to Stuart to suggest that a place for the letters might be found in the columns of *The Courier*. 'Mr De Quincey', he explained amicably, '... is a friend of mine whom you will recollect, with no very pleasant feelings, perhaps as having caused you some trouble while my Tract occasioned by the Convention of Cintra was printing.' But, Wordsworth assured him, 'You need not doubt ... that the Letters will be a credit to any Publication, for Mr D. Q. is a *remarkably* able man.' This optimism proved misplaced. By April it was plain that the letters were never going to be published, and De Quincey's credibility dropped even further at Rydal Mount. 'Notwithstanding his learning and his talents', Dorothy observed flatly, he can 'do nothing; he is eaten up by the spirit of procrastination'.[56]

When he returned from London to Grasmere that spring, or perhaps at some point later in the year, De Quincey walked again through Wales, where he no doubt relived both the exhilaration and the distress he had experienced thirteen years earlier following his flight from Manchester Grammar School. In June, Wellington triumphed at Waterloo. De Quincey was jubilant. Napoleon could be defeated, just as he had said all along. 'And thus, it may be imagined ... I had *my* triumph; and ... I also, in another sense, had *my* vengeance, as the champion in so many disputes of our national character.'[57] Two months later, on 15 August 1815, De Quincey turned thirty years old.

He and Wilson walked, and talked, and drank together throughout that autumn. Wilson had recently lost most of his fortune, and while he had managed to hang on to Elleray, he had been forced to relocate to Edinburgh, in order that he might push forward his plan of passing Advocate. De Quincey's opium and alcohol intake had been steadily increasing for months, and had now peaked at around eight thousand drops of laudanum per day, which sunk him into a state of the 'profoundest melancholy'. Sara Hutchinson reported that Wilson was 'tolerably steady', but that 'Quince was often tipsey ... He doses himself with Opium & drinks like a f[ish] – and tries in all other things to be as great a [*paper torn*] legs as Mr Wilson.'[58]

In November, Wilson and De Quincey journeyed together from the Lakes up to Edinburgh, where De Quincey socialized a good deal. He and Wilson went to the playhouse to see Siddons perform for one of the last times as Lady Macbeth. It may have been during these weeks that he visited again with the poet Anne Grant.[59] J. G. Lockhart, the novelist, essayist, and future biographer of Walter Scott, became an acquaintance, though not an admirer. De Quincey was 'most strange', Lockhart recalled. After dinner, 'he set down two snuff-boxes on the table; one, I soon observed, contained opium pills – of these he swallowed one every now and then, while we drank our half-bottle apiece'. Many years later, Lockhart left another, and far more negative, portrait: 'When sober he was a very interesting companion – a good scholar and a sharp critic – arrogant enough already and pompous but not at all so absurdly as afterwards. He usually however was drunk dead drunk at an early hour – for he drank all he could get and between glasses kept munching opium pills ... I soon dropped him as unfit for a decent house with ladies in it.'[60]

Despite these excesses, De Quincey made a much more favourable impression on others, including the philosopher William Hamilton, who became a valued friend, and the author and advocate Robert Pearse Gillies. 'The talk might be of "beeves", and he could grapple with them if expected to do so', reported Gillies.

> But his musical cadences were not in keeping with such work, and in a few minutes (not without some strictly logical sequence) he could escape at will from beeves to butterflies, and thence to the soul's immortality, to Plato, and Kant, and Schelling, and Fichte, to Milton's early years and

Shakespeare's sonnets, to Wordsworth and Coleridge, to Homer and Aeschylus, to St Thomas of Aquin, St Basil, and St Chrysostom.

De Quincey's wide acquaintance with German literature especially impressed Gillies, and confirmed for him that 'great stores' of knowledge 'were contained therein'.[61]

The stimulation and change of pace he enjoyed in Edinburgh appear to have refocused De Quincey, and when he returned to Grasmere in December, he entered upon a period of happiness that he later referred to as his 'year of brilliant water (to speak after the manner of jewellers)', though he was uncertain about the exact dates of this 'year', and it seems clear that he can be speaking of a period that lasted no more than about five months.[62] What brought about the change? De Quincey drastically improved his mental health by bringing Margaret right to the centre of his emotional life. As his housekeeper, or lover, or both, she spent many days and nights with him at Dove Cottage. In addition, he slashed his opium intake 'from 320 grains . . . to forty grains' per day, and somehow managed to do so without provoking fierce withdrawal pains. The gloom that had been suffocating him 'passed off with its murky banners as simultaneously as a ship that has been stranded, and is floated off by a spring tide'.[63]

Finally, De Quincey cut himself off from Wordsworth. He still wanted a relationship with the poet, but at this moment he found the price of it very high, and he appears to have decided that he needed a respite from the stress and sadness that it often provoked within him. He had a long list of grievances, some unfair, others justifiable. Wordsworth, he claimed, was ungenerous. He 'appropriates whatever another says, so entirely, as to be angry if the originator claimed any part of it', De Quincey asserted. In conversing with him one day, De Quincey 'made some remark, which Wordsworth caught up, & amplified, & repeated, next day. De Quincey then observed, "I am glad you adopt that view of mine". "Yours!" said Wordsworth. "Yes, mine"; said De Q. – "No", cried Wordsworth, indignantly, "it is mine."'[64] Wordsworth was also arrogant. One day he, De Quincey, and Southey were out on a walk, and the topic of conversation turned to the condition of Lloyd, whose mental illness was soon to force his removal to a Quaker psychiatric hospital in York. Southey was making 'earnest inquiries' after the sick man. Wordsworth's answer to him was partly lost on De Quincey, who asked him to repeat it. To De Quincey's surprise – 'my wrath internally, but also to my special amusement' – Wordsworth replied 'that, in fact, what he had said was a matter of some delicacy, and not quite proper to be communicated except to *near friends of the family*.

This to me! – O ye Gods! – to me, who knew, by many a hundred conversations, how disagreeable Wordsworth was, both to Charles Lloyd and to his wife.'[65]

Worst of all, Wordsworth was – in De Quincey's eyes – a hypocrite. How could he disapprove of De Quincey's relationship with Margaret? In the first instance, he himself had done something similar many years earlier when he fell in love with Annette Vallon, the Frenchwoman from a slightly lower social class who bore him an illegitimate daughter in 1792. The affair was no secret among the Wordsworth family, and De Quincey may well have known of it, though if he did he showed remarkable restraint in not making his knowledge public.[66] More urgently, the poet of the *Lyrical Ballads* was judging Margaret, not on personal merit, but on social rank. 'He could not see the loveliness' in her 'fair face', De Quincey implies, because he would not now allow himself to see loveliness in any face that came from a class so far below his own. Indeed, having written Margaret off as unsuitable for De Quincey, Wordsworth went so far as to follow him out at night to prevent him from keeping his assignations with her, or at least so De Quincey suggests in a torn fragment in which he rages against the poet. 'I found myself in the same situation almost every night: [*paper torn*] time almost a hatred for Wordsworth as though a malicious purpose had possessed him: [*paper torn*] possible unless he had corresponded with fairies, that he should then know anything [*paper torn*] He could not: it was impossible: I am sure it was: And yet oh Heavens! it makes / it drove me crazy then, it drives me crazy now.'[67]

De Quincey drew the curtains at Dove Cottage, and he and Margaret relished a winter together of pleasure and solitude. 'Paint me ... a room seventeen feet by twelve, and not more than seven and a half feet high', he instructs an imaginary artist in a famous conceit.

... Make it populous with books: and, furthermore, paint me a good fire; and furniture, plain and modest, befitting the unpretending cottage of a scholar. And, near the fire, paint me a tea-table; and (as it is clear that no creature can come to see one [on] such a stormy night,) place only two cups and saucers on the tea-tray ... for I usually drink tea from eight o'clock at night to four o'clock in the morning ... Paint me a lovely young woman, sitting at the table. Paint her arms like Aurora's, and her smiles like Hebe's: – But no, dear M., not even in jest let me insinuate that thy power to illuminate my cottage rests upon a tenure so perishable as mere personal beauty; or that the witchcraft of angelic smiles lies within the empire of any earthly pencil. Pass, then, my good painter, to something more within its power: and the next article brought forward should naturally be myself . . . As to the opium, I have no objection to see a picture of *that* . . . and . . . you may as well paint the real receptacle, which was not of gold, but of glass, and as much like a wine-decanter as possible. Into this you may put a quart of ruby-coloured laudanum: that, and a book of German metaphysics placed by its side, will sufficiently attest my being in the neighbourhood.

So De Quincey lived with Margaret through the dark and happy winter months of 1816. 'Mr De Quincey has taken a fit of Solitude,' Wordsworth wrote to Gillies in April; 'I have scarcely seen him since Mr Wilson left us' in November.[68]

[iv]

The bubble burst in early summer. Margaret was pregnant. A part of De Quincey was undoubtedly pleased at the thought of becoming a father and having a child, but the news also generated huge anxiety within him, and brought to a decisive close the 'year' of brilliant water. What would the Wordsworths say? His mother? His sisters? Her family? He and Margaret would have to marry. When? Right away? After the child was born? His patrimony was exhausted: how would he support his wife and child? Could he apply himself to the law, or did he need to think of something else? Slowly he unravelled under the stress, and while he stood by Margaret, he simultaneously retreated back into his opium.

At some point during these weeks he received – or thought he received – a visit from a Malay, whose unexpected appearance at the door of Dove Cottage unnerved the servant girl, and sent her upstairs to inform De Quincey that there was 'a sort of demon below' dressed in a 'turban and loose trowsers of dingy white'. De Quincey, who was probably asleep when the stranger arrived, eventually made his way downstairs, where he saw his servant and a young boy from the village standing uneasily beside the Malay. Knowing virtually nothing of 'Oriental tongues', and reasoning that 'Greek, in point of longitude, came geographically nearest to an Oriental' language, De Quincey addressed his visitor in some lines from Homer's *Iliad,* which prompted him to respond in what De Quincey presumed was Malay. Their conversation at a close – and De Quincey's reputation for learning 'saved' with his neighbours – the man lay down upon the floor and rested for an hour. At his departure, De Quincey presented him with a piece of opium that was large enough 'to kill three dragoons and their horses', and was startled to see him 'bolt the whole, divided into three pieces, at one mouth-ful': as had been the case in the accident involving the mail-coach and the young woman aboard the gig, De Quincey worried once more that he might be responsible for killing someone, but as 'I never heard of any Malay being found dead, I became convinced that he was used to opium'.[69] De Quincey breathed a sigh of relief – though not for long. Propelled by the guilt and racial anxiety that underwrite De Quincey's representation of their encounter, the Malay soon returned to make fierce incursions into his dreaming mind.

It was also at about this time that De Quincey received another, unex-pected visitor at Dove Cottage, but on this occasion it was a friend who was living in nightmares, rather than a stranger who caused them. 'The first memorial I had of him was a gentleman, with his hair in disorder, rushing into my cottage at Grasmere, throwing his arms about my neck, and bursting into stormy weeping.' It was poor Lloyd. He had escaped from the mental institution at York, and fled to the Lakes. 'Could there be a situation so full of interest or perplexity?' When healthy, Lloyd had usually been 'gentle and remarkably quiet', but now he spoke in 'a tone, savage and ferocious, towards more than one individual', though when he turned round and discovered Margaret seated at the tea-table, he was mortified at the 'depth of emotion which he had betrayed before a stranger', and thereafter 'his whole manner wore the appearance of studied dissimulation'. De Quincey invited him to stay for the night, and promised to buy him at least an additional day and night in Dove Cottage by throwing false information in the way of the asylum men whom he knew must be in pursuit.[70] Lloyd, however, would stay only for a quick cup of tea, before asking De Quincey to accompany him to his home at Brathay.

The two friends covered the first mile of the route without incident, but as they reached 'an open plain on the margin of Rydalmere', Lloyd suddenly stopped and addressed De Quincey. In one account of their conversation, related by De Quincey just a few years later, Lloyd is firmly in the grip of madness. 'I dare say ... you think you know me,' he asserted: 'but you do not and you cannot. I am the Author of all Evil. Sir, I am the Devil.' De Quincey declared that he 'certainly had thought differently', but Lloyd continued: 'I know also who you are: You are nobody. A non entity. You have no being.' Lloyd then 'entered into a variety of arguments to convince me he was what he pretended ... He reasoned & reasoned, and became more himself, and more cheerful, and the fancy wore away by degrees.' In another description of the same conversation, however, published by De Quincey nearly twenty-five years later, Lloyd is consumed, not by questions of identity, but by the brutal behaviour of his medical attendants. 'At the side of that quiet lake he stood for nearly an hour, repeating his wrongs, his eyes glaring continually ... and again and again threatening ... those vile keepers who had so abused any just purposes of authority. He would talk of little else.' De Quincey's two versions of the conversation are not necessarily mutually exclusive, and over the course of the evening both may well have taken place. However this may have been, as night descended, De Quincey pressed his friend to return with him to Town End, and to take refuge there, but Lloyd would not, and he 'did not wish for company any further' than Rydalmere. They parted, and Lloyd was soon recaptured. The two men did not see each other again, though in later years De Quincey walked often over to Brathay, where he sat by the river and thought in sadness of his friend.[71]

In the early autumn, De Quincey received a letter from his mother. She began with amiable chit-chat about general family business, but then turned to what was undoubtedly her real motive in contacting him.

I ... at last resolve to say a word of the report which we now suppose had no truth in it. It seemed to come from high authority that you were about to marry, and nothing short of an oracular Voice could have made us listen to the tale, considering your want of means to meet the demands of a family ... I cannot help begging you to let me know your designs, and also to consider well before you trust the mere impulse of feeling, if, as I have but just now heard, the sober judgment of your Friends cannot approve the step.

De Quincey must have been appalled. Wordsworth – surely the 'oracular Voice' – had either directly or indirectly seen to it that Mrs Quincey learned of her son's reckless attachment. She was understandably concerned, for Wordsworth would no doubt have stressed Margaret's slender means and lack of education. Mrs Quincey was keeping an open mind. 'I can abate much of what the world demands in marriage,' she told her son. But, she added, 'I know there are congruities which are indispensable to *you*.'[72] With his background, connections, and intellect, could he really be happy with an ignorant farm girl from a jacobinical family?

Crabb Robinson called in at Dove Cottage on 5 September. De Quincey was in a bad way, 'an invalid ... very dirty and even squalid ... He seemed embarrassed when he saw me, and did not ask me to walk upstairs' – perhaps because Margaret was staying over? Later on that same day De Quincey visited Robinson at the Salutation Inn at Ambleside. 'He was in much better spirits than when I saw him in the morning,' Robinson reported, no doubt because he had by this time revived himself with laudanum. Robinson mentioned to 'Wordsworth and the ladies' that he had seen De Quincey, and they all kindly encouraged him to accept his offer to take a walk together. Yet at this point Wordsworth himself would not even talk to De Quincey, nor De Quincey to him. On 24 September, the poet walked with Robinson from Rydal Mount to near De Quincey's house, and then left him. On the return trip, De Quincey escorted Robinson to the gate of Wordsworth's garden-terrace, but no further. That evening, Wordsworth returned with Robinson to Town End, but did not meet De Quincey.[73]

The following morning, De Quincey and Robinson took a long walk together over the hills to 'Dungeon Gill Force', and then 'by Tilberthwaite to Coniston Water Head'. Neither enjoyed the experience. De Quincey displeased Robinson when he asked him 'an abrupt & unhandsome question': had Mr and Mrs Wordsworth been speaking about his relationship with Margaret? Robinson lied and said '*No*', not wishing to fan the flames of De Quincey's resentment any further. After a walk that lasted seven hours, the two men returned to Dove Cottage heartily tired of one another. Yet Robinson was impressed by De Quincey, at least as an intellect. 'He is very arrogant, but I believe he has something to be vain of.'[74]

Gossip-mongering about Margaret's pregnancy was probably quite widespread, and at about this time she and De Quincey seem to have made the decision to leave Dove Cottage, and to travel twenty-four miles south to take up residence 'at the house of Quarrelflat' near Holker on the Cartmel Peninsula, where for several weeks they enjoyed what amounted to a holiday. De Quincey had plenty of laudanum with him, they took a servant girl or two to wait on them, and they 'used to bathe on the sea shore in front of the house'. As Margaret's due date approached, however, it is not clear whether they stayed on at Quarrelflat by design, or returned either to Dove Cottage or The Nab. Be this as it may, on 9 November 1816, their son – William Penson De Quincey – was born.[75]

Wordsworth and De Quincey were never further apart than in their response to the event. The poet took a malicious delight in it. 'You will recollect ... that a little Friend of our's was profuse in praises of the "more than beauty" – "the angelic sweetness" – that pervaded the features of a fair young Cottager dwelling upon the banks of Rydal mere,' he chortled to Lamb. 'To be brief, Love and opportunity have wrought so much upon the tender frame of this terrestrial angel, that, to the surprise of Gods, Men, and Matrons, she has lately brought forth a Man child.' To De Quincey, however, William's birth was a moment of joy. 'The loveliest sight that a woman's eye opens upon in this world is her first-born child; and the holiest sight upon which the eyes of God settle in Almighty sanction and perfect blessing is the love which soon kindles between the mother and her infant.'[76]

Three months later, on 15 February 1817, De Quincey married Margaret in Grasmere Church. The evidence is contradictory, but the Wordsworths appear not to have attended.[77] Certainly the family view of the matter had not changed. 'Mr de Quincey is married; and I fear I may add he is ruined,' Dorothy wrote with disdain, and probably a little jealousy.

> By degrees he withdrew himself from all society except that of the Sympsons of the *Nab* ... At the up-rousing of the Bats and the Owls he regularly went thither – and the consequence was that Peggy Simpson ... presented him with a son ten weeks ago ... He utter'd in raptures of the beauty, the good sense, the simplicity, the "angelic sweetness" of Miss Sympson, who to all other judgments appeared to be a stupid, heavy girl, and was reckoned a Dunce at Grasmere school ... As for him I am very sorry for him – he is utterly changed – in appearance, and takes largely of opium.[78]

Lamb was less vitriolic, but hardly less sparing. 'Is Mr *** really married?' he asked Dorothy with a snicker, 'and has he found a gargle to his mind? O how funny he did talk to me about her, in terms of such mild quiet whispering speculative profligacy.'[79]

De Quincey was badly wounded by this criticism. He felt deserted. He felt betrayed. Even after his marriage the Wordsworth women refused to visit Margaret. 'I was a mere football of reproach,' as he memorably put it.[80] Yet in his choice of her as his partner De Quincey was fully vindicated, for contrary to the expectations of many, his marriage was a successful one, though the support she gave him was outstripped by the stress he visited upon her. 'Ah! happy, happy years!' he later exclaimed of his time with Margaret in Dove Cottage, '... in which every wind and sounding hurricane of wrath or contempt flew by like chasing enemies past some defying gates of adamant, and left me too blessed in thy smiles – angel of life! – to heed the curses or the mocking which sometimes I heard raving outside of our impregnable Eden.'[81]

Wonderful though it was, Margaret's love did not seal De Quincey off from the outside world as wholly as he liked to claim. Dove Cottage was their sanctuary, but he could still hear 'the curses' and 'the mocking' that raved both without its walls and within himself. Up until the middle of 1817 – he once claimed – he had been a happy man, but then 'farewell – a long farewell to happiness'. Money was in very short supply, and he was forced to borrow £40 from his sister Jane.[82] Far more seriously, his dependence on laudanum now spiralled out of control, and for weeks on end he anaesthetized himself, leaving Margaret largely alone to face new debts and the responsibilities for baby William. Then, committing himself to sharp reductions, he provoked the pains of severe withdrawal. If for many years laudanum had composed De Quincey, he now watched helplessly as it multiplied and dissolved him. Sometimes, when he felt well enough, he read Milton or Wordsworth aloud to Margaret. More often she read tracts on political economy to him. His great work of philosophy, *De emendatione humani intellectûs*, lay 'locked up, as by frost'. But for misery and suffering, he remarked, 'I might, indeed, be said to have existed in a dormant state'.[83]

Four factors began to shape his nightmares: his daydreams were transmuted into the dreams of sleep; he felt suicidal despondency; space and time expanded infinitely; and the minutest incidents from his past were revived. The subject matter of these dreams ranged from the literary, to the personal, to the apocalyptic. Their initial splendours were 'chiefly architectural'. In London several years earlier, Coleridge had described Piranesi's *Dreams* to De Quincey, who now found that they mirrored – or perhaps incited – the 'power of endless growth and self-reproduction' which haunted him in his sleep. Amidst a vast Gothic hall, De Quincey saw a staircase, and 'upon it, groping his way upwards, was Piranesi himself':

follow the stairs a little further, and you perceive it come to a sudden abrupt termination, without any balustrade, and allowing no step onwards to him who had reached the extremity, except into the depths below. Whatever is to become of poor Piranesi, you suppose, at least, that his labours must in some way terminate here. But raise your eyes, and behold a second flight of stairs still higher: on which again Piranesi is perceived, but this time standing on the very brink of the abyss. Again elevate your eye, and a still more aerial flight of stairs is beheld: and again is poor Piranesi busy on his aspiring labours: and so on, until the unfinished stairs and Piranesi both are lost in the upper gloom of the hall.

What is more, to these sublime architectural dreams 'succeeded dreams of lakes – and silvery expanses of water', which in turn blended with the anxieties he felt as a teenager roving through the London streets, and searching in vain for Ann. 'Upon the rocking waters of the ocean the human face began to appear: the sea appeared paved with innumerable faces, upturned to the heavens: faces, imploring, wrathful, despairing, surged upwards by thousands, by myriads, by generations, by centuries: – my agitation was infinite, – my mind tossed – and surged with the ocean.'[84]

[v]

De Quincey's age witnessed the creation of a mass media, and the most dynamic of its early voices was *Blackwood's Edinburgh Magazine*, which stunned the literary world when it first appeared in October 1817. Its editor, William Blackwood, was 'a short, "stubbed" man, of about five feet six ... with a plain, straightforward business air, – like that of a substantial tradesman'.[85] Already a successful publisher, his immediate objective in joining the periodical press was to challenge the *Scots Magazine*, an ailing miscellany published by his Edinburgh rival, Archibald Constable; less directly, he hoped to establish a spirited Tory monthly that would challenge the influence of the Whiggish *Edinburgh Review* and complement the ponderous Toryism of the *Quarterly Review*. Further, Blackwood seems to have realized that the magazine format itself, which had remained essentially unaltered since Edward Cave introduced his *Gentleman's Magazine* in 1731, was now ripe for change, and in *Blackwood's* he established a new pattern for magazines by removing all the formal departments, mixing together fiction, reviews, correspondence and essays, and infusing exuberance throughout. Before long *Blackwood's* was convincingly proclaiming itself 'a Real magazine of mirth, misanthropy, wit, wisdom, folly, fiction, fun, festivity, theology, bruising and thingumbob.'[86] It was able to blend authority and elitism with frankness and bravado, claiming the approval of the aristocracy while repeatedly championing the breadth of its own popular appeal.

In the early years, Blackwood took editorial advice from his two leading contributors, J. G. Lockhart and John Wilson, De Quincey's closest friend, but by 1820 he had firmly established himself as the magazine's sole editor. 'He has only one great fault,' wrote James Hogg, another important contributor; '*he never will confess that he has been in the wrong*'.[87] Under Blackwood, 'Maga', as he himself referred to it, was especially well known for its truculent High Toryism, which informed its infamous reviews of the so-called 'Cockney School', a term the magazine coined to describe a group of London-based writers whom it smeared as liberal-minded mediocrities of low birth, inferior education, and loose morals, and whose members included the essayist William Hazlitt and the poet John Keats. In addition, *Blackwood's* published groundbreaking fiction, and some remarkably insightful literary criticism, especially on Wordsworth and – unexpectedly –

the radical poet Percy Bysshe Shelley. The first issue alone contained Wilson's notorious review of Coleridge's recently published *Biographia Literaria*, Lockhart's scabrous attack on Leigh Hunt as the King of the Cockneys, and the celebrated 'Chaldee Manuscript', an allegory in mock-biblical language, in which Whig enemies and Tory friends appear in the fictional guise of birds and beasts. Outrage was widespread, but within a matter of months, *Blackwood's* was the pre-eminent magazine of the day. A host of imitators followed, including the *New Monthly Magazine* and the *London Magazine*, but none could keep pace with its energy and appeal.

De Quincey was thoroughly undisposed to sell his knowledge for money, and to 'commence trading author' with the periodical press. He had aimed much, much higher. 'My ambition was, that by long and painful labour, combining with such faculties as God had given me, I might become the intellectual benefactor of my species', as both 'the first founder of true Philosophy', and 'the re-establisher in England (with great accessions) of Mathematics'.[88] But with the possibility of practising law as remote as ever, and his grander intellectual aspirations frozen by opium and anxiety, he desperately needed to find more immediate ways of making money, and following Wilson in writing for *Blackwood's* undoubtedly seemed the most practical and lucrative option. Southey made a good living – around £275 a year – writing for the *Quarterly* and other periodical publications.[89] At least temporarily, De Quincey must have told himself, he might do the same.

His contributions to *Blackwood's* may have begun as early as the first number, for Wilson's review of Coleridge is prefaced by a striking rhetorical *bravura* that may well belong to De Quincey.[90] A few months later Wilson sent De Quincey a copy of Shelley's new poem, *The Revolt of Islam*, with a request that he write a review of it for *Blackwood's*. De Quincey read the poem and was surprised to find in it 'more ability of a particular sort than he expected, or indeed than he had conceived Shelley ... to possess'. He did not formally review the poem, but he did state his judgement of it in a letter to Wilson, which he and Lockhart then used as the basis of a January 1819 article which praised *The Revolt* 'very highly', the magazine's virulent Toryism notwithstanding.[91] Shortly thereafter, Wilson sent a second book – David Ricardo's *Principles of Political Economy and Taxation* – to De Quincey, again in the hope that he would produce a *Blackwood's* review. De Quincey was immensely impressed, despite the fact that most Tories vilified Ricardo, and his close alignment with prominent philosophical radicals such as James Mill. 'Thou art the man!' De Quincey cried of Ricardo. 'Wonder and curiosity were emotions that had long been dead in me. Yet

I wondered once more.' Indeed, so inspired was he by Ricardo's ability to introduce 'a ray of light into the unwieldy chaos' of previous discussions that he drew up his own *Prolegomena to all Future Systems of Political Economy*, a title he modelled on Kant's *Prolegomena to all Future Metaphysics*. In the opiated torpor of these days, however, neither the book nor the review ever appeared.[92]

John Murray, publisher of the *Quarterly Review*, was also interested in De Quincey's services, almost certainly on the recommendation of Southey. In the early autumn of 1818 he and De Quincey met, most probably at Dove Cottage, where Murray offered De Quincey '100 guineas for a good Classical article', and soon sent him 'for reviewal ... the entire works' of Friedrich Schiller in twenty-six volumes. No classical article was forthcoming, though, and after four months the Schiller edition was 'still lying here, I am sorry to say, untouched'.[93] In May 1819, Wordsworth hoped to have De Quincey write a *Quarterly* article 'upon the Bullion question', but Southey told him that the journal would not be interested, as De Quincey's arguments against the resumption of cash payments were in direct conflict with the *Quarterly's* established position on the subject. 'This I am sorry for,' declared Southey, 'because if De Quincey could bring his reasonings before the public through a favourable channel I think he would go far towards exploding a mischievous error.'[94]

Westmorland politics provided him with yet another opportunity for employment. In early 1818, Henry Brougham, reformer, *Edinburgh* reviewer, and future Whig Lord Chancellor, was named as the candidate who planned to contest one of the two Westmorland seats in the forthcoming general election. Both seats had long been in the possession of the local Tory landowners, the Lowthers. De Quincey threw himself into the campaign with vigour, not only because his political sympathies were powerfully engaged by the Lowther cause, but because he saw it as an opportunity to reconnect with Wordsworth, who was also busily involved on behalf of the Lowthers, and whose connections in the area De Quincey rightly thought might be useful to him in securing a steady income.

On 23 March, Brougham championed the forces of reform in a heady address to a Kendal crowd. De Quincey immediately drafted a response, and two days later tentatively approached Wordsworth, first 'with a view to your revisal of what I have written', and then with a request that Wordsworth use his influence with the Lowther election committee to help him find a publisher. The poet was encouraging, and a week later De Quincey sent him the completed essay, which Wordsworth read with Lord Lowther in Kendal, augmented by interweaving a passage of his own 'related to facts', and then praised in a note to De Quincey, whose response was swift and rather fawning: 'It was the very highest gratification to my wife and myself, that we could reap from it, to find that what I had then sent was honoured by your approbation.' Witty, concise, and effectively partisan, *Close Comments Upon a Straggling Speech* appeared as a pamphlet a few weeks later.[95] It was De Quincey's first stand-alone publication.

He then sent out a feeler. The Lowther interest in Westmorland was planning to establish a Tory newspaper in Kendal, but had not yet done so. Rumour had it that '*one* cause at least of the delay was the want of an Editor'. De Quincey heard that the post had been offered to Wordsworth, and that he had refused it. 'Now, – if this be so', De Quincey wrote to him, 'and if the post be still undisposed of, – do you know of any reasons which should make it imprudent or unbecoming in me to apply for it? If you do not … I feel confident that you will do me the kindness to assist me in obtaining it with your recommendation.' It was a bold step, especially as De Quincey acknowledged in the same letter that Wordsworth probably felt some doubt about him as regards 'punctuality … and power of steady perseverance'. He did his best to reassure him on that score. 'I have suffered too much in conscience … ever to offend in that way again,' he declared confidently.[96]

How Wordsworth responded is not known, but De Quincey did not get the editorship, which went instead to a London journalist named C. J. Fisher. Yet despite his disappointment, De Quincey showed himself willing to stay involved in the Tory campaign. On Saturday, 23 May 1818, the new weekly paper, the *Westmorland Gazette*, appeared for the first time, and in its second number for 30 May, De Quincey published his 'Philadelphus, on Mr Clarkson's Letter', a detailed response to the tireless anti-slavery campaigner Thomas Clarkson, who had recently published a letter in the rival *Kendal Chronicle* in which he detailed his decision to assist Brougham in his Westmorland canvass. 'Though he has written on other subjects with great credit, both to his head and heart', De Quincey argued, Clarkson 'may be fairly pronounced, in the present case, a … most perplexed and vacillating politician'.[97]

De Quincey's productivity on behalf of the Lowthers throughout the spring suggests, perhaps, that he had temporarily been able to bring his laudanum intake under control. These months, however, were not generally ones of stability. He was bitten three times by a dog, placing him for many weeks 'under fear of *Hydrophobia*', and he was plagued by some of the most horrendous nightmares of his career.[98] In particular, the tired Malay who had visited Dove Cottage two years earlier was transformed, by the 'fierce chemistry' of his dreaming mind, into a 'fearful enemy' who generated within De Quincey a vicious xenophobia, and who brought to the surface his deepest fears about persecution, self-division, and alterity. Asleep in his English cottage, De Quincey was transported every night into 'Asiatic scenes', where he was

> stared at, hooted at, grinned at, chattered at, by monkeys, by paroquets, by cockatoos. I ran into pagodas: and was fixed, for centuries, at the summit, or in secret rooms; I was the idol; I was the priest; I was worshipped; I was sacrificed. I fled from the wrath of Brama through all the forests of Asia: Vishnu hated me: Seeva laid wait for me. I came suddenly upon Isis and Osiris: I had done a deed, they said, which the ibis and the crocodile trembled at. I was buried, for a thousand years, in stone coffins, with mummies and sphynxes, in narrow chambers at the heart of eternal pyramids. I was kissed, with cancerous kisses, by crocodiles; and laid, confounded with all unutterable slimy things, amongst reeds and Nilotic mud.

At the beginning of the dream, De Quincey describes himself as cut off from the Orient by a 'barrier of utter abhorrence'. At its close, his identity is disintegrating 'amongst reeds and Nilotic mud'.[99] Like opium, the Malay is both without and within him, an almost unlocatable figure who reveals to De Quincey the terrifyingly permeable boundary between waking and sleeping, West and East, self and other, external and internal.

[vi]

Margaret Thomasiana De Quincey was born on 5 June 1818.[100] Her arrival was an occasion of great happiness at Dove Cottage, but it also meant an additional mouth to feed, and further bills to pay. De Quincey again turned to his family for financial assistance. His uncle Penson sent £84, and his mother later topped this sum up to £100 by adding De Quincey's share of the rent on a Manchester warehouse. Both made it clear to him, moreover, that he could now expect to receive this sum as an annual family remittance.[101]

More good financial news arrived in early July. Fisher, the editor of the *Gazette*, had been fired after only seven issues. The proprietors of the paper wanted someone who could passionately articulate Tory values in the face of a torrent of liberal-minded criticism from the *Chronicle*, and Fisher had disgusted them with his timidity and impartiality. De Quincey was the obvious choice to replace him, and – perhaps with a good word from Wordsworth – the proprietors offered him £160 per year to assume the editorship. In the first instance, De Quincey turned them down, as they insisted he move to Kendal. In a second round of negotiations, however, a deal was struck. Out of the £160 yearly salary, De Quincey would pay a clerk of the press named John Kilner two guineas a week to be on the spot to perform all the mechanical tasks related to the production of the *Gazette*. That left roughly £50 a year for De Quincey, which the proprietors rounded up to a salary of one guinea a week. Under this arrangement, De Quincey would continue to live in Grasmere, with regular visits to Kendal to supervise Kilner. Sometimes he would select and revise articles for publication, but his 'proper duty' as editor was 'simply to write a political essay on some subject' of his own choosing.[102]

De Quincey embraced his new role with gusto. After years of reading and thinking, the *Gazette* provided him with his first sustained opportunity to craft a public voice that was distinct and marketable. The appointment pleased Wordsworth, though he was not without misgivings: 'the new Kendal Paper has passed into the hands of a most able man', he informed Lord Lonsdale; 'one of my particular Friends: but whether he is fit, (I mean on the score of punctuality) for such a service, remains to be proved'. De Quincey's first issue of the *Gazette* appeared on 11 July. Nearly three weeks later he wrote from Kendal to his 'sweet wife': 'I have found nothing but trouble here', yet 'I hope ... that I shall soon get the Paper into a right train.'[103] He did. For several months De Quincey defied his critics, and kept to the grind of the demanding weekly schedule.

Politics were the lifeblood of the *Gazette*, and De Quincey wrote as an anxious, sometimes semi-hysterical, High Tory who viewed 'the signs of the times' as 'unusually impressive', and who stood staunchly behind a conservative agenda that was essentially imperialistic, defensive, and intolerant, though the internecine war between the two Kendal-based newspapers no doubt led him on occasion to exaggerate his own views in an attempt to surpass or pre-empt the *Chronicle*. Combativeness, De Quincey believed, was necessary in order to rally Tory support in Westmorland. Perhaps even more importantly, it was also at the heart of his conception of how to sell newspapers: 'If the *Chronicle* knocks the *Gazette* down one week, the *Gazette* must get up and knock the *Chronicle* down the next ... There is no unpardonable crime but tediousness; and no sin, past benefit of clergy but dulness.'[104]

De Quincey, however, had a fine line to walk. When he attacked the *Chronicle* as 'atrociously jacobinical', or published too many vengeful letters from *Gazette* readers, he ran the risk of being labelled ungentlemanly or desperate. Parts of the *Gazette* were 'most low scurrilous & abusive', Lord Lowther complained in one instance. '... Do not let us face the enemy on the advantage ground of good breeding.' But when, on the other hand, De Quincey was too polite, or ignored the *Chronicle* assaults altogether, he left himself open to the charge that he was not defending the good old Tory cause. 'It is no longer political to meet them mildly,' Lord Lowther wrote on another occasion, in direct contradiction to his earlier view. 'If they recommense attacks, we must stand up to them.'[105] De Quincey moved briskly, if uneasily, between these two extremes, and managed for the most part to keep his readers content with the direction of the paper. In terms of explicit confrontation between the two editors, De Quincey did not know that the *Chronicle* was edited by a man named Richard Lough, but Lough knew of 'De Quizzy', and regularly flailed him for his 'patrician·pen' and – more personally – for his 'midnight rambles through and around this town (as your august personage is rare seen anywhere between sun-rise and sun-set)'.[106]

The *Gazette* covered all the major political debates of the day, including those on the Corn Laws, the Poor Laws, the Game Laws, the National Debt, taxation, colonial policy, and education reform. As an unyielding anti-bullionist, De Quincey wrote at length on the question of the resumption of cash payments by the Bank of England. He championed emigration as a means of removing the 'redundant', and potentially rebellious, portions of the British population. He railed against the need for Catholic Emancipation. Catholics in Britain were not allowed to hold a seat in Parliament, purchase land, or inherit property. 'We deny that we persecute the Catholics by denying them certain privileges,' he retorted; 'and we deny that there is any "bigotry" in refusing political power to the Catholics'.[107] De Quincey also attacked liberal-minded leaders: Brougham is 'an object of just fear'; the utilitarian philosopher and economist Jeremy Bentham is an impostor and a charlatan; and the pioneer socialist Robert Owen – who so long ago had bought Greenhay from Mrs Quincey – is an 'imbecile' whose plans for utopian co-operatives provoke laughter from knowledgeable economists like Ricardo.[108]

The biggest political event of these months took place in August 1819. Radicals, led by the orator Henry Hunt, rallied on St Peter's Fields in Manchester to protest high food prices, and push for parliamentary reform. The local magistrates, alarmed by the size of the gathering, ordered it dispersed by the yeomanry, who seized Hunt, and then turned their sabres on the close-packed crowd. Within ten minutes, eleven people were dead, and around four hundred were injured. The massacre (likened to Waterloo) infuriated radicals across Britain and beyond, and became known as 'Peterloo'. The *Chronicle* issued declarations of solidarity with those seeking reform, opened a fund for the victims of the violence, and excoriated both the magistrates and the yeomanry. At the *Gazette*, De Quincey saw it very differently. 'The magistrates have in our judgment taken no step but such as sound discretion warranted. The meeting, both from it's size and it's composition, was dangerous to the peace and property of the neighbourhood ... The magistrates were therefore justified in dissolving it. It was their duty to do so.'[109] In the overheated political atmosphere of England in 1819, De Quincey used the *Gazette* as a platform from which to survey the ills that beset the country. In virtually every instance, his remedy was an unrepentant version of Toryism that bludgeoned down the cries for reform, and insisted defiantly on the status quo.

As vital as his political belligerence was to the success of the paper, De Quincey also published articles in a variety of other areas. British literature was a central feature. He championed *Blackwood's* as a literary journal of 'distinguished ability', and reprinted Wilson's 'Letters from the Lakes' after their initial appearance in the magazine.[110] He praised the seventeenth-century poet John Donne, published the poetry of Wordsworth and Shelley, and described Walter Savage Landor as 'a man of transcendent genius'.[111] When the famous Gothic novelist Matthew 'Monk' Lewis died in May 1818, De Quincey wrote a brief biography describing him as a 'great genius ... addicted ... to the demonology of belles lettres'.[112] Under De Quincey the *Gazette* also gave a prominent place to European books and writers. Not unexpectedly, he attacked French literature as 'decidedly the feeblest ... which the human mind has created'. In all branches of philosophy, however, 'not England only but all Europe ought to yield the precedency to the Germans', and in particular he lauded Kant, who was often attacked in the *Chronicle*. 'Since the time of Luther', De Quincey shot back, 'no one man has had so extensive ... an influence upon the course of human thought ... Great indeed is the strength of Kant.'[113]

Sensationalism was the other key component in De Quincey's mind when he put together an issue of the *Gazette*. Assize reports, especially of murders, were a staple: '*First*, Because to all ranks alike they possess a powerful and commanding interest; *Secondly*, Because to the more uneducated classes they yield a singular benefit, by teaching them their social duties in the most impressive shape ... *Thirdly*, Because they present the best indications of the moral condition of society.' Elsewhere De Quincey made the case for publishing these reports rather more bluntly: 'As to old women, and the mob of newspaper readers, they are pleased with anything, provided it is bloody enough.'[114] Other articles chosen for the *Gazette* concerned suicides, rapes, laudanum, freak accidents, and the bizarre. Perhaps most strikingly, only a few months after Mary Shelley published *Frankenstein*, De Quincey ran a feature called 'Galvanic Experiment on the Dead Body of a Murderer', which gave his readers details of the experiments of a Dr Ure, who used electric rods to contract muscles on the corpse of a murderer. 'On moving the second rod from the hip to the heel ... every muscle in his countenance was simultaneously thrown into fearful action; rage, horror, despair, anguish, and ghastly smiles, united their hideous expression in the murderer's face.'[115]

During the first nine months of his editorship, De Quincey turned the *Gazette* into an effective Tory flagship that entertained and instructed its expanding readership. Yet there were problems almost from the start. In the early months, he had to contend with Wordsworth, who was as anxious as ever to use De Quincey's talents, but who could not resist giving him directions on how he thought the paper should be run. On several occasions, Wordsworth spoke to him about how to handle personal calumny in the *Gazette*. 'I have had a conference with the Editor,' he reported to Lord Lowther in September 1818, '... about a rascally Letter to you which appeared in the last ... *Chronicle*, and still more rascally notice of it by the Editor of that Journal. We have agreed upon the mode of noticing both.' Wordsworth also called a number of times to ask De Quincey to terminate long-winded political discussions in the paper. 'He acknowledges the propriety of it; but he has no firmness. – I shall be at him again upon the subject.'[116] In response to Wordsworth's meddling, De Quincey sometimes simply did as he wished and then scapegoated Kilner, whom he claimed had misunderstood or failed to follow his instructions for cancelling or altering contentious material.[117] More commonly, though, De Quincey just turned a deaf ear, for of course he had plenty of 'firmness', especially when it came to defying authority, and he was not about to let Wordsworth dictate how he edited the paper. Later, De Quincey boasted to friends that, although the *Gazette* was established 'with a view of supporting the Lowther Interest ... I so managed it as to preserve my Independence'.[118]

A more formidable problem was the eighteen miles between Grasmere and Kendal. Bad weather or bad planning sometimes meant that De Quincey did not get his manuscripts to the *Gazette* offices on time, leaving Kilner to cobble the paper together at the last minute with whatever material came to hand. Illness – often opium-related – also frequently undermined De Quincey's efforts: 'I had during the week compelled myself to make up the Paper; nearly the whole was of my selection: I had even written some articles which would, I trust, have bothered the Broughamites . . . But, when it came to correcting and transcribing these articles on Tuesday night, I was so overcome by pain that I could not do it.' On 28 January 1819, De Quincey had even to battle fire. It was a Thursday night and he was up late trying to finish his share of the *Gazette* in time for Friday's post. 'In a single moment a volume of smoke passed between him and his paper so suddenly as to darken it in one instant as much as if the candles had been extinguished. On looking round to the fire, nothing was at first seen; but in half a minute a great fork of flames . . . sprung out from a crevice on one side of the grate.' De Quincey roused Margaret and the servants, and the blaze was put out in time for him to send an account of it to Kilner a few hours later in the Friday-morning manuscript bundle. The story duly appeared in the *Gazette* for Saturday, 30 January.[119]

His money woes continued to worsen, despite his *Gazette* salary, and the offers from *Blackwood's* and the *Quarterly*. In a long letter to his mother, he reviewed his past life, informed her for the first time of his marriage, and – in a staggering blend of self-pity and arrogance – castigated the women in his family for thinking of him as 'ruined – a lost creature'.

You would scarcely have addressed me, if I had been a member of Parliament or a distinguished Barrister or a judge or Chancellor of the exchequer, in the tone which you hold in your last letter which addresses me sometimes as a baby and sometimes as a poor crazy nervous decayed gentleman boarded out by his friends in a retired situation . . . If I, instead of labouring for years to mature a great scheme of philosophy and education, had pushed myself forward in the path of common vulgar ambition . . . I am sensible that I should have experienced a very different treatment from all my female relations.[120]

He then came to the point of his letter: could he borrow £150 to clear all his debts? Mrs Quincey was at her finest when she responded: ignoring all his bluster, she sent him £160, before going on to align the Westhay household with him in his choice of Margaret: 'Let me at once assure you we all think there can be but one reasonable view taken of the condition in life which you have described your Wife's to be, and that view is the same as yours, that it is a happy and respectable one, and we are greatly rejoiced to find that she has dignified it by her conduct.'[121] De Quincey was often impatient with or dismissive of his mother, but in many tight situations she met him far more than halfway.

In the spring of 1819, new dreams descended upon him. It was Easter Sunday morning. He was standing at the door of Dove Cottage. Right before him lay 'the very scene which could really be commanded from that situation, but exalted, as was usual, and solemnized by the power of dreams'. No living creature was to be seen, except that in the Grasmere churchyard the cattle were reposing around the grave of Catharine Wordsworth. De Quincey determined to walk abroad, and to try for a day to forget old griefs. He turned, as if to open his garden gate, and suddenly upon the left he saw an Oriental landscape, very different from the scene around Dove Cottage, and yet harmonized with it by the power of the dream. More significantly, in this Eastern setting, De Quincey finds, not the avenging terrors of the Malay, but the possibilities of salvation, while at the same time Catharine is transformed into the figure of another, older love, who is once again portrayed as both sexual and innocent. At a vast distance De Quincey sees the 'domes and cupolas of a great city'. And then,

> not a bow-shot from me, upon a stone, and shaded by Judean palms, there sat a woman; and I looked; and it was – Ann! She fixed her eyes upon me earnestly; and I said to her at length: 'So then I have found you at last' . . . Seventeen years ago, when the lamp-light fell upon her face, as for the last time I kissed her lips (lips, Ann, that to me were not polluted), her eyes were streaming with tears: the tears were now wiped away . . . Suddenly her countenance grew dim, and, turning to the mountains, I perceived vapours rolling between us; in a moment, all had vanished; thick darkness came on; and, in the twinkling of an eye, I was far away from mountains, and by lamp-light in Oxford-street, walking again with Ann – just as we walked seventeen years before, when we were both children.[122]

The intensity of De Quincey's inner life was simultaneously an escape from, and an escalation of, his external predicaments, and opium deepened this paradox, as it both consoled him for past sorrows and – particularly in the throes of withdrawal – redoubled their fury.

As he neared the end of his first year as editor of the *Gazette*, its proprietors met to insist upon some changes. His distance from the press had begun to cause serious problems, and they resolved that 'a notification be made to the Editor expressing their sentiments of the great importance of a regular communication between the Editor and the Printer of the Westmorland Gazette by want of which it appears that great inconvenience has frequently arisen from the exclusion of the latest London news'. They suggested that he move to Kendal to be closer to the office, and warned him also to refrain from 'direct remarks on any products or observations which may appear in the Kendal Chronicle'. De Quincey must have given them satisfactory assurances that the situation would improve, for he retained the editorship, and over the course of the next few months he published some of his most impressive work for the paper, including essays on 'Immanuel Kant, and John Gottfried Herder', 'Immanuel Kant & Dr Herschel', 'The Planet Mars', and a four-part series on 'The Danish Origins of the Lake Country Dialect'. By October, however, he was writing very little for the paper, and on 5 November 1819 the *Gazette* Committee Minutes record that 'Mr De Quincey be respectfully informed that his Resignation is accepted'. Eight days later, the proprietors announced that Kilner was the paper's new editor.[123]

During his sixteen months at the helm, De Quincey accomplished a good deal. His management of the paper was sometimes slipshod or disingenuous, but he sharpened its political agenda, broadened its appeal, and raised its sales. After his departure, shareholders did not see another dividend for at least seven years.[124] The *Gazette* also gave De Quincey a good deal, for it acquainted him with the opportunities and demands of the periodical press, and enabled him to map the literary guises and central themes that would preoccupy him over the course of his career. Just after De Quincey took over the *Gazette*, he promised to exalt it into a 'philosophical Journal'. He did not reach this goal, but 'writing in The Gazette ... 1st taught me ... my real power,' he declared.[125] More to the point, bigger things lay just ahead.

PART THREE
THE MAGIC PREFIX
1819–41

EIGHT

Famous

[i]

He lived on credit. Throughout the winter, De Quincey drew so many bills on Wilson that by March 1820 the total had reached £90. 'I scarcely see how I can avoid bankruptcy,' Wilson cried in protest.[1] Unsure of where to turn, De Quincey hunkered down in Dove Cottage, where he divided his time between opium, scholarship, and fatherhood. Three-year-old William liked to wander into his library, stack up the largest books he could lift, and then fire away at the 'mighty structure' with a bow and arrows until it crashed to the floor. Sometimes De Quincey would join in and shoot at piles of philosophy books, to the 'frantic joy' of William, and perhaps as an indication of his own intellectual frustrations. In June, the family welcomed a third child, Horatio.[2]

With books and babies vying for space, De Quincey made a remarkable decision. He would leave his library and his papers in Dove Cottage and rent a second house for his growing family. Fox Ghyll, a handsome cottage situated about one mile north-west of Ambleside, was owned by Robert Blakeney of Whitehaven, and currently for rent at 60 guineas a year for the house and furniture.[3] The De Quinceys liked the cottage, agreed to Blakeney's terms, and were settled in their new home by the late summer, while still of course paying rent on Dove Cottage. 'Mr de Quinceys Books have literally turned their master & his whole family out of doors,' Sara Hutchinson observed with amused contempt. The Fox Ghyll lease was only for six months but, predicted Sara, there the De Quinceys 'will remain unless unsettled by an earth-quake or a second accumulation of Books'.[4]

De Quincey was trying hard to bring his laudanum addiction under control. His consumption at this time had stabilized at around 175 drops per day, though he sometimes went as high as 500 or even 700, and on other occasions dropped as low as 100, a reduction that within four days brought on the agonies of withdrawal. 'Unceasing restlessness night and day: sleep – I scarcely knew what it was ... lower jaw constantly swelling:

mouth ulcerated ... violent sternutation: ... impatience and hideous irritability.' Relief came only with the consumption of more opium. De Quincey
was wedged between 'the collision of both evils – that from the laudanum,
and that from the want of laudanum'.⁵

Margaret attended him through these dreadful sieges of physical and
spiritual despair. His sufferings frightened her, and when she witnessed the
horror of his attempts to reduce his opium dosages, she was the 'first to beg
me to desist'.⁶ At length De Quincey 'grew afraid to sleep'. One solution
was simply to stay up the whole night and the following day. Another was
to ask Margaret and the children 'to sit around me and to talk: hoping thus
to derive an influence from what affected me externally into my internal
world of shadows'. But the plan backfired, and rather than the external
relieving the internal, the internal 'infected and stained as it were the whole
of my waking experience'. 'Oh ... what do you see? dear ... what is it that
you see?' was Margaret's 'constant exclamation'. The answer was nightmare
worlds of apocalypse and desolation in which his dreaming mind echoed
and reimagined some of the most traumatic moments from his childhood
and teenage sufferings. In the midst of his other distresses, these new terrors
pushed him towards thoughts of suicide.⁷

[ii]

Blackwood's seemed his best alternative. He had already produced copy for
the magazine, its popularity and influence continued unabated, and both
Wilson and Blackwood were anxious to have him on board. De Quincey
'solemnly promised' a contribution for the March 1820 number, and Blackwood delayed the printing of the magazine for several days, but nothing
arrived. Five months later, De Quincey committed to producing a review
of the economist Robert Malthus. Again there was nothing. Wilson simply
had to laugh. 'I tried to convince Blackwood that you never *had engaged to*
write for the Magazine, and his face was worth ten pounds – for it was pale
as a sheet. – I told him, however, that now you *were* engaged.'⁸

Wilson was also pressing De Quincey at this time for another reason. In
the spring he had decided to let his name stand for the Professorship of
Moral Philosophy at the University of Edinburgh. Merit was supposed to
decide the outcome, but politics did, and Wilson's Toryism carried the day.
His excitement at being elected to the Chair, however, was tempered by the
absurdity of his situation, for he now had to deliver 120 lectures on a subject
about which he knew virtually nothing. Unsurprisingly, and as he had done
in the past, he turned to De Quincey, who was of course deeply read in the

area. 'I intend giving half-a-dozen lectures on the Greek philosophy – Socrates, Plato, Aristotle, &c.', Wilson wrote with a candour that is almost risible. 'Have you any books about them and their system; or can you write me some long letters about either, or their philosophy? ... What does, in your belief, constitute moral obligation? – and what ought to be my own doctrine on that subject?' De Quincey's response to Wilson was partial and reluctant, and it is unclear how much, if any, material Wilson was able to extract from him on this occasion.[9]

Illness plagued De Quincey throughout the autumn as he drifted on at Fox Ghyll. Six weeks of 'indescribable suffering' left him convinced that he had 'no hope of recovery', while Margaret fought on bravely, managing the house, caring for the children, and stretching the money as far as it would go.[10] Something had to be done, and in December De Quincey finally determined to journey to Edinburgh, and to write fulltime for *Blackwood's*. He travelled first to the King's Arms Inn at Keswick, and then procured a 'loan of about 6 guineas' from Southey to take him the rest of the way. The friends he had made on his 1815 visit to the Scottish capital were, he told his 'dear Peggy', 'more kind' than he could express, and he was soon installed in lodgings at 30 Northumberland Street in the New Town.[11] His health, too, seems to have benefited, both from the change of scene and from the advice of Dr George Bell, an eminent Edinburgh surgeon, who listened to his sad tale of physical suffering and prescribed 'ammoniated tincture of Valerian'.[12]

Blackwood and De Quincey were soon in touch, and on 9 December they reached an agreement regarding the timeline for submissions. But within three days they were at odds, for Blackwood ran his magazine with a firm hand, while De Quincey – confident that he could make a dramatic difference to the magazine – seems to have thought that he would be able to set his own terms. 'I *do* "keep my word" – not "once" merely, but always – when I am aware that it is pledged,' he snapped to Blackwood at the opening of a long letter of explanation and justification. Blackwood fired back a short note urging him to get on with his work.[13] De Quincey responded with a second long letter, detailing the reasons for the first one, and explaining the major cause of his many delays. 'Opium has reduced me for the 6 last years to one general discourtesy of utter silence. But this I shall think of with not so much pain, if this same Opium enables me (as I think it will) to send you an article not unserviceable to your Magazine.' A week later De Quincey's 'Opium article' was 'very far advanced', and he was writing it 'with pleasure' to himself.[14]

At this same time, De Quincey also completed his first solo article for the magazine. 'The Sport of Fortune', translated from Schiller's 'Das Spiel des Schicksals', is a short tale of terror and abjection rooted in historical fact, and centring on one of De Quincey's favourite themes: revenge.[5] He almost certainly took the story from the twenty-six-volume edition of Schiller's works sent to him for review by Murray over two years earlier, and at last realized some small return on this asset. The story was standard Gothic fare, but Blackwood was ebullient. 'I am so happy to receive anything from you that your two pages appear like the 24 of any one else,' he exclaimed. 'It was the knowing what you *could do* if you were once *resolved to do* which made my repeated disappointments so very mortifying.'[6] De Quincey's translation duly appeared in *Blackwood's* for January 1821.

Blackwood's mortifications were not yet at an end. Early in the New Year De Quincey was promising to sell himself 'soul and body to the service of the Magazine for two years', but simultaneously alienating Blackwood with irritating requests for more money, paper, deadline information, and so on.[7] De Quincey's provoking explanations of his tardiness hardly helped matters: 'I move slowly whenever I am uncommonly witty,' he assured Blackwood of an article he was preparing on the Lake District.[8] The situation boiled over on 8 January when De Quincey sent Blackwood a remarkable letter:

> If Wilson and Lockhart do not put themselves forward for the Magazine I foresee that the entire weight of supporting it must rest on my shoulders: I see clearly that I must be its Atlas ... A more dreary collection of dulness and royal stupidity never did the world see gathered together than the December No. exhibits ... I am hard at work, being determined to save the Magazine from the fate which its stupidity merits.[9]

It is difficult to know where De Quincey was aiming with such a letter. Blackwood did not find it funny.

> I can only excuse your letter ... by supposing that you were hardly awake when you wrote it. When I apply to you to be the Atlas of my Magazine it will be time enough for you to undertake the burthen. And in the meantime I must beg leave to say that if you cannot send me anything better than the 'English Lakes', it will be quite unnecessary for you to give yourself any further trouble about the Magazine.[20]

De Quincey replied with a half-hearted apology, and the promise of more copy, but he had burned his bridge. By the end of January the relationship between the two men had broken down completely. De Quincey retreated to Fox Ghyll, and spent the month of February indoors, consuming laudanum and battling 'a rheumatic affection' of his face.[21]

Running counterpoint to De Quincey's attempts to launch his career in Edinburgh is a disturbing tale of violence and deception which divided his loyalties and consolidated his retreat from *Blackwood's*. In January 1820 the *London Magazine* was founded as a direct challenger to *Blackwood's*. In format the two magazines closely resembled one another. Both were devoted primarily to a combination of independent critical opinion and original literary material, but the *London* was more polished, dispassionate, and liberal in tone, and it promised to convey 'the very "image, form, and pressure"' of London, as opposed to those 'popular Journals' that were based in the 'secondary towns of the Kingdom', like Edinburgh.[22] The *London* actively disapproved of *Blackwood's* habit of malicious reviewing and rancorous personal abuse.

John Scott – handsome, sensitive, and hot-tempered – was the *London's* first editor. He gathered and then led a remarkable group of writers, including Charles Lamb, William Hazlitt, John Clare, Mary Russell Mitford, and John Hamilton Reynolds. His initial plan as regarded *Blackwood's* was to try to avoid open conflict, and in May 1820 he went so far as to praise the 'ability, energy, and effect' with which the magazine had 'vindicated ... several neglected and calumniated, but highly deserving poetical reputations'.[23] Within a few months, however, the situation had degenerated into pomposity and insult. Wilson warned the *London* not to compete too closely with *Blackwood's*. Scott immediately replied that Wilson and Lockhart wrote for a magazine in which 'the most licentious personal abuse was to be the lure for one class of readers, and the veriest hypocritical whine, on matters of religion and politics, the bait for another'.[24]

De Quincey's loyalties in the dispute were all in *Blackwood's* corner, and in an extraordinary outburst of indignation and juvenile savagery, he urged Wilson to 'make an example' of Scott.

I do so loathe the vile whining canting hypocrisy of the fellow ... Lampoon him in songs – in prose – by night and by day – in prosperous and adverse fortune. Make him date his ruin from Nov. 1st 1820 – Lash him into lunacy ... My abhorrence of this beast is deep – serious – and morally grounded. He himself ... insults his sovereign in the basest way upon his *private* concerns and ... carries the bestialities of Radicalism into literature ... oh! slave – oh! bugger![25]

Wilson did not take De Quincey's advice, but tensions between the two magazines continued to escalate nonetheless. In February, Scott challenged *Blackwood's* ally Jonathan Christie to a duel, and was wounded by a bullet to the stomach. He hung in a fever for eleven days and then, on 27 February 1821, he died.

De Quincey's reaction to the tragedy was very different from what might have been expected. After championing the *Blackwood's* cause for several months, he now changed sides and 'sincerely regretted' Scott's loss. In part he was motivated by guilt. Scott had died because of violence he himself had helped to foment. De Quincey also changed his mind because – like Scott – he disapproved of *Blackwood's* habit of personal calumny, especially when it was directed against the 'Cockney School' poet John Keats. 'To speak conscientiously, I cannot wholly approve of every thing you have done,' De Quincey told Wilson: 'what I should most condemn ... is the harsh (and latterly to my feeling more painful than anything simply harsh – *good naturedly contemptuous*) treatment of Keats'. Finally, De Quincey transferred his sympathies because he had come to believe that Blackwood was largely responsible for the tragedy of Scott's death. Scott had often demanded to know who edited the rival magazine. Blackwood had refused to reveal himself, and then launched elaborate campaigns of misinformation that left Scott flailing in the dark until the situation was out of control. Scott had been stubborn and rash in pursuing his various charges, but Blackwood bore a heavier responsibility for failing to answer them.[26] During his weeks in Edinburgh, De Quincey had not gotten along with Blackwood. Now, with the news of Scott's death, he decided he wanted nothing more to do with *Blackwood's*.

De Quincey's recoil from the Edinburgh magazine involved one more complicating factor. Envy and resentment appear at this time to have seriously undermined his friendship with Wilson. It is not hard to see why. De Quincey felt himself to be possessed of far greater talent than his friend, and he knew intimately of Wilson's parasitism and charlatanry. Yet while his own circumstances continued to decline, Wilson was thriving as the lead writer for *Blackwood's*, and enjoying his lucrative new status as Professor of Moral Philosophy. In mid-February, Wilson complained of the 'indignities and degradations' he suffered in paying the bills that De Quincey continued to draw on him. But at the same time he asked De Quincey for more help with his philosophical lectures without any reference to compensation or acknowledgement, and he requested further that De Quincey take various steps to ensure that the fraud went undetected. Speak of the lectures 'as chapters in a work of your own, if you please, when you write to me,' Wilson directed him. And 'could you contrive to give your letters a less mysterious outward appearance?'[27] Such requests must have galled De Quincey. His simmering anger with his closest friend soon surged to the surface.

[iii]

De Quincey spent the spring at Fox Ghyll. His neighbour Edward Quillinan, who later became Wordsworth's son-in-law, reported that De Quincey 'remained in bed, I understood, all day, and only took the air at night, and then was more shy than an Owl'. Mary Wordsworth hoped that the De Quinceys would give up Fox Ghyll by the summer so that it could be rented to her cousin, Thomas Monkhouse.[28] The cottage, however, clearly suited the family, and they no doubt hoped to hang on to it as long as they could.

That meant money. Dire necessity had forced De Quincey north in December and that same necessity now forced him south. In June he travelled to 'London avowedly for the purpose of exercising my pen, as the one sole source then open to me for extricating myself from a special embarrassment'. At De Quincey's request, Wordsworth kindly supplied him with a letter of introduction to Thomas Noon Talfourd, whom De Quincey knew from his visits to London as a law student, but whom he now felt he had 'no right to trespass upon ... without some stronger warrant than any I could plead in my own person'.[29]

Talfourd gave De Quincey a warm reception, and soon introduced him to John Taylor and James Hessey, the men who had purchased the *London* following the death of Scott. According to John Clare, Taylor was 'a man of very pleasant address' who worked himself 'into the good opinions of people in a moment', though the effect was 'not lasting'.[30] His partner – nicknamed 'Mistessy' by Keats – was thin, dressed principally in black, and had a 'readiness of droll quotation'. De Quincey found both men 'hospitable and friendly'.[31]

As a publishing house, Taylor and Hessey had the high distinction of issuing books by Carlyle, Clare, Coleridge, Hazlitt, Keats, Lamb, and Landor. Both also served as editors of the *London*. Taylor took the lead role, and was centrally concerned with the content of each issue. Hessey performed various editorial functions, but was much more occupied with the financial side of the business. Under Scott, the *London* had established a reputation for London-bias and liberal idealism. Both remained hallmarks under Taylor and Hessey. De Quincey had a great deal to offer such an agenda, particularly as an admirer of Shelley and Keats, an enthusiast for

London, and a keen popularizer of Ricardian economics. Taylor and Hessey offered financial terms to contributors that were 'ultra munificent'.[32] De Quincey took note and committed himself to the magazine, though he realized with some unease that if the animosity between *Blackwood's* and the *London* flared up again, his status as a former *Blackwood's* contributor made him an easy mark for reprisals.

He took lodgings at 4 York Street (now 36 Tavistock Street), Covent Garden. The premises was owned by the well-known German bookseller Johann Heinrich Bohte. De Quincey's portion of the house was a small, two-storeyed section at the back, for which he paid twelve shillings a week.[33] The only access to his rooms was from York Street. He walked through the front part of the house, passed under a roofed-in section, and then climbed a few steps to his door. Beneath the ground floor was a vaulted passage given over to darkness and rats. On the first floor were two small rooms, the larger of which he used for writing. During his stay De Quincey took full advantage of Bohte's large selection of German books, and later claimed to have 'read "a matter" of three thousand tales, long and short'.[34]

Yet his immersion in Bohte's book collection would not have blinded him to one of the most bizarrely ironic twists of his career: John Scott had been the previous tenant of the rooms. After he was wounded in the duel, the surgeon gave 'directions that Mr Scott's apartments, at Mr Botte's [*sic*], in York-street, should be prepared for his reception'. Scott, however, was too badly wounded and could not be moved, though after his death he was returned briefly to Bohte's, from where on 9 March a hearse and four carried his body to St Martin-in-the-Fields for burial.[35] Scott's family vacated the rooms some time shortly thereafter, and in the summer De Quincey moved in. Seven months earlier he had urged Wilson to 'ruin' Scott. Now he was living in his rooms, meeting his friends, and writing for his magazine. He must often have felt as though he was living a double life, with *Blackwood's* just behind and the *London* right in front of him.

De Quincey was anxious to get to work for Taylor and Hessey, but relocating to London came at a high cost. He missed Margaret: 'Oh, that I had the wings of a dove,' he thought as he wandered in the evening and looked northward towards Westmorland, 'And *that* way I would fly for comfort.' He missed his children: 'I was obliged to relinquish my daily walks in Hyde Park and Kensington Gardens, from the misery of seeing children in multitudes, that too forcibly recalled my own.' Soon 'I began to view my unhappy London life – a life of literary toils, odious to my heart – as a permanent state of exile from my Westmorland home.'[36]

His deep affection for his family, however, may not have prevented him from indulging in old habits. De Quincey usually walked in the evening 'from 6 o'clock till ½ after 9 or 10'. To some extent, he was motivated by his belief that exercise was essential 'to keep up any degree of health'. He also ventured out to buy opium, and had lately purchased small quantities from 'three respectable ... druggists, in widely remote quarters of London'. In part, too, De Quincey sought to extend his 'studies of the working poor' with 'solitary walks at night' through Drury Lane, St Giles, and Clare Market.[37] But De Quincey was an addictive personality, and while there is no hard evidence, it seems at least possible that he also used these long nightly excursions to gratify his penchant for prostitutes. His teenage relationship with Ann was vividly before him during these weeks, and his evening walks took him back through their old haunts, which remained notorious for prostitution, as he well knew: 'I am again in London: and again I pace the terraces of Oxford-street by night.' When he visited prostitutes in Liverpool as a teenager, he came home ashamed. If he was again in the company of London prostitutes, thoughts of Margaret probably brought on guilt in larger and more complicated shapes, not least because each encounter would have cost him money and introduced the possibility of disease.[38]

Residence in London was intended to solve his debt problems, but they continued to pile up around him, in large measure because he was paying rent on Dove Cottage, Fox Ghyll, and 4 York Street. He solicited a £35 loan from Cottle, 'having no friend after my mother excepting Southey ... in whose kindness I had so much confidence as I had in yours'. De Quincey wrote to Coleridge as well, and pleaded with him to repay the £300 'loan' he had given to him in late 1807. But his fellow opium addict had not a shilling, and his circumstances were as perilous as De Quincey's own. 'I feel that I am lingering on the brink – and what to say, my dear Sir! I know not!' Coleridge cried.[39] In mid-November De Quincey wrote to Taylor: 'I do not know whether I am doing wrong ... when I ask you – Whether it would be convenient to you and Mr Hessey to let me have ... the sum of twenty or twenty-five pounds in any sort of bill that you please.'[40]

Sickness too pressed down on him, as he faced both 'my infernal persecution, the Rheumatism' and 'a sore throat which ... increased into a return of fever'. In December, he was 'very unwell in the Evening, with the Cramp in his Stomach, owing to an omission for 2 days to take some medicine prescribed by Dr Darling', the well-known Scottish physician who attended him throughout these months. Four weeks later De Quincey wrote to Hessey, 'I am in great distress (bodily I mean) every evening – and all the night through.'[41]

As these various troubles and distractions swirled around him, De Quincey armed himself with opium and prepared himself for the task of writing.[42] Earlier that year in Edinburgh, he had begun to weave together various notes and memoranda – some of which may have been composed months earlier – into an 'Opium Article'.[43] He now set his sights on finishing it, for the work had been welling up in him for a long time. De Quincey claimed that he wrote the 'introductory part ... with singular rapidity', and the manuscript evidence bears him out: there are interlineations, changes in pagination, breaks in mid-sentence, and anxious notes to compositors.[44] He seems to have delivered the manuscript to Taylor in eight separate batches. Typically, he worked frantically on each section while Taylor complained that 'his Copy comes in so very slow'.[45]

On 9 August De Quincey availed himself of Taylor's 'kind permission to delay the conclusion for a day (or two), because I shall thus be able to execute some parts of it in perhaps a more satisfactory manner'. Later that same day, however, the threat of arrest for debt drove him out of his lodgings, and into 'the tumult of coffee houses', where he found it 'difficult to write at all'.[46] Fear and sickness kept him away from York Street for a week. When he returned, proofs of the opening pages of the article were waiting for him. He worked hard over the course of the following few days, and by 22 August the narrative had evidently grown long enough to be divided into two parts.[47] Shortly thereafter, the opening instalment of his *Confessions of an English Opium-Eater* appeared in the September issue of the *London* in an unremarkable position two-thirds of the way through the magazine. It was published anonymously, as was the convention at the time.

He set to work on the second part on 7 September. Its two major sections – 'The Pleasures' and 'The Pains' of opium – took shape over the next ten days, and by 20 September he much wished 'to see the whole lying under my eye finished all but final corrections'. De Quincey adopted a curiously inconsistent attitude towards the article's final presentation. On the one hand, he fretted over the wording of a single phrase ('visions as ugly, and phantoms as ghastly'), and wrote to Taylor and Hessey to ensure that they directed the printer's eye 'to the right arrangement': 'it seems a trifle but it sounds to my ear an inartificiality'. On the other hand, he was surprisingly blasé about which material was included in or excluded from the final version. 'Some passages can easily be left out of what I send. I have kept back several sheets, convinced that you will have too much. Yet one is about the best dream.'[48]

In the end, very little is known about what De Quincey held back.[49] But what he sent was superb, and Taylor and Hessey manoeuvred ably between his finickiness and his nonchalance. The second part of the *Confessions* was given pride of place in the October issue. 'The Lion's Head', an editorial column which introduced each number of the *London*, announced that 'we are not often in the habit of eulogizing our own work, – but we cannot neglect ... calling the attention of our readers to the deep, eloquent, and masterly paper which stands first in our present Number'.[50]

De Quincey's *Confessions* are one of the most innovative and influential autobiographies of the nineteenth century. In them, he invents recreational drug taking, not because he is the first to consume opiates or alcohol for non-medical purposes (he is hardly that), but because he is the first to memorialize his experience in a compelling narrative that is aimed at a broad commercial audience. His *Confessions* are an intimate, if highly selective, exploration of his past life, in which boyhood episodes and engaging conversational banter gradually give way to distorted worlds of personal tragedy and psychic anguish played out with horrifying repetitiveness in the tortured mind of the dreamer. The work, subtitled 'An Extract from the Life of a Scholar', opens with a brief, rhetorical address to the reader, before moving to a 'preliminary' confession in which De Quincey attempts to answer one of the key questions of his addiction: 'How came any reasonable being to subject himself to such a yoke of misery, voluntarily to incur a captivity so servile, and knowingly to fetter himself with such a seven-fold chain?'[51] His response is to detail the decisive emotional and imaginative moments from his past that he now believes led him down into the trap of drug dependence, beginning with his childhood and early education, and then passing on to his sorrows as a teenage runaway in Wales and especially London, where his narrative centres on his experiences with Ann. For many years he had searched for her in the London streets, but now he thinks of her, 'more gladly, as one long since laid in the grave; in the grave, I would hope, of a Magdalen; taken away, before injuries and cruelty had blotted out and transfigured her ingenuous nature, or the brutalities of ruffians had completed the ruin they had begun'.[52]

The second half of the *Confessions* is divided into two parts. 'The Pleasures of Opium' highlights the euphoria of his early experiments with laudanum: 'portable ecstasies might be had corked up in a pint bottle: and peace of mind could be sent down in gallons by the mail coach'.[53] 'The Pains of Opium' is devoted to an unprecedented exploration of the bodily and mental deprivations of addiction, and climaxes with a section in which De Quincey exploits an explicitly poetic prose to capture the spectacular energy and gloom of his recent nightmares, including ones in which his various historical readings infuse his own anxieties about violence, women, and death.

> And I heard it said, or I said to myself, 'these are English ladies from the unhappy times of Charles I. These are the wives and the daughters of those who met in peace, and sate at the same tables, and were allied by marriage or by blood; and yet, after a certain day in August, 1642, never smiled upon each other again, nor met but in the field of battle; and at Marston Moor, at Newbury, or at Naseby, cut asunder all ties of love by the cruel sabre, and washed away in blood the memory of ancient friendship'. – The ladies danced, and looked as lovely as the court of George IV. Yet I knew, even in my dream, that they had been in the grave for nearly two centuries. – This pageant would suddenly dissolve: and, at a clapping of hands, would be heard the heart-quaking sound of *Consul Romanus* – and immediately came 'sweeping by', in gorgeous paludaments, Paulus or Marius, girt round by a company of centurions, with the crimson tunic hoisted on a spear, and followed by the *alalagmos* of the Roman legions.[54]

At the close of his narrative, De Quincey declares that if his account of opium has taught the reader 'to fear and tremble, enough has been effected'. The *Confessions*, however, are not a cautionary tale. Opium is the 'true hero', and De Quincey figures as a noble explorer of the self, whose account of the highs make them seem almost irresistible, and whose Gothic renderings of the lows make them seem even more so.[55]

De Quincey's title harkens back to the confessions of St Augustine and Jean-Jacques Rousseau, but he regarded these two key predecessors as passionless, and reconceived the confessional genre as a vehicle for the exploration of those moments of intense emotional insight that shape the mind of the writer.[56] He taps also into the strong contemporary interest in the confessional mode, which was at the centre of legal and religious power, and which was intimately associated with a privileged access to private truths.[57] The most significant contemporary precedents include *The Confessions of J. Lackington* (1804), *The Confessions of William Henry Ireland* (1805), Charles Lamb's 'Confessions of a Drunkard' (1813), and a host of Gothic novels, including Ann Radcliffe's *The Italian; or the Confessional of the Black Penitents* (1797), Charlotte Dacre's *Confessions of the Nun of St Omer* (1805), and Robert Pearse Gillies's *Confessions of Sir Henry Longueville* (1814).[58]

There had been previous accounts of opium smoking and opium eating in works such as Samuel Purchas's *Hakluytus Posthumus or Purchas his Pilgrimes* (1625), Sir John Chardin's *Travels in Persia* (1711), and Baron de Tott's *Mémoires . . . sur les Turcs et les Tartares* (1784–5), but the consumption of the drug for non-medical reasons was supposed to be an exclusively Oriental practice, and one that led directly to oblivion. De Quincey dramatically changed that view.[59] Mounting his argument along racial lines, he sneeringly remarked that Turks who took opium usually sat 'like so many equestrian statues, on logs of wood as stupid as themselves'. De Quincey, on the other hand, is emphatically an *English* opium-eater, which means that the drug produces a very different effect on his refined faculties and profound sensibilities. 'I question whether any Turk, of all that ever entered the Paradise of opium-eaters, can have had half the pleasure I had. But, indeed, I honour the Barbarians too much by supposing them capable of any pleasures approaching to the intellectual ones of an Englishman.'[60] Yet by ingesting vast quantities of an Eastern drug, De Quincey undermines the very Englishness he is bent on extolling. In his accounts of his opium experience, he emerges as an uneasy hybrid, at once domestic and foreign, familiar and exotic, contaminated and clean.

Politically, the *Confessions* are equally paradoxical. De Quincey enjoys an elitist education, quotes the arch-conservative Burke, and comments rather glibly on the pleasures of narcotic wanderings among London's working classes. He knows several men of 'eminent station' who are opium-eaters, including 'the late dean of ——; Lord ——', and 'a late under-secretary of state', while his dreams contain lurid fantasies of racial superiority.[61] Yet at the same time he rejects educational and parental authority and lives outside traditional social structures. He is an exile, a solitary, a sinner. He draws on the work of anti-slavery campaigners such as William Roscoe. He alludes to the poetry of Keats. Shelley's *Revolt of Islam* is cited three times. Hazlitt is the third finest analytic thinker in England, behind Coleridge and Ricardo, whose liberal economic doctrines are lauded as revolutionary.[62] In the *Confessions*, De Quincey both endorses and rejects the status quo, while his enthusiasm for privilege is confounded by his embrace of Cockneys, Whigs, abolitionists, and rebels.

De Quincey modelled himself on Coleridge, whose public persona was closely associated with opium dependence, unfulfilled potential, Gothic imaginings, the poetry of Wordsworth, and the philosophy of Kant. Wordsworth was also central, for his autobiographical epic *The Prelude* shaped De Quincey's discussions of the growth of his dreaming mind. The painter John Martin may be an additional source. His *Belshazzar's Feast* was on display at the British Institution in London in the summer of 1821, and drew huge crowds. It depicted the celebrated moment from the Old Testament when Daniel interprets the writing on the wall which spells Belshazzar's doom. Its stupendous colonnades, panicked multitudes, vast distances, and apocalyptic subject matter are deeply congruent with De Quincey's dream finale. Even more striking is the fact that one of De Quincey's rare attempts at poetry concerns Belshazzar's Feast, and seems most likely to date from this period.

> Depths behind depths were there – dim, labyrinthine apartments ...
>   spaces abysmal
> Where golden galleries ran high overhead through an endless
> Mass of stair cases climbing; till sight grew dizzy with effort
> Of chacing the corridors up to their whispering gloomy recesses.[63]

[iv]

The impact of the *Confessions* was immense. 'Everybody who noticed magazines at all is interested in the Fate of the Opium Eater,' wrote Taylor. Charles Knight had 'never read anything more deeply interesting' than the first instalment. James Mackintosh 'read the second part ... with more delight than I know how to express'. Nearly twenty-five years later, George Gilfillan noted that the *Confessions* 'took the public by storm. Its popularity was immediate and boundless; nor, even yet, has it declined.'[64]

There were over a dozen reviews. De Quincey was faulted for disorganization, vanity, and moral laxity. 'The work is written throughout in the tone of apology for a secret, selfish, suicidal debauchery,' declared the *Eclectic Review*: 'it is the physical suffering consequent upon it, that alone excites in the Writer a moment's regret.'[65] Most reviewers, however, were enthusiastic. The *Imperial Magazine* described the *Confessions* as produced by a 'mind gifted with first-rate talents'. For the *Medical Intelligencer*, De Quincey's 'confessions are a valuable addition to our stock of medical information'. The *United States Literary Gazette* found that De Quincey's language was 'always exquisitely felicitous ... and sometimes powerful and magnificent in the extreme'. 'We thought it one of the most interesting, and certainly the very most extraordinary, production that we had ever seen,' declared the *Album*.[66]

The anonymous appearance of the work generated a good deal of debate about its authorship. Lamb and Coleridge were leading suspects.[67] Edgar Allan Poe insisted that the *Confessions* were 'composed by my pet baboon,

Juniper, over a rummer of Hollands and water'. Several others were less entertaining, but more in the know. Crabb Robinson had read only the first instalment when he stated that the work 'must be by De Quincey. It is ... a fragment of autobiography in emulation of Coleridge's diseased egotism.' Shelley's publisher Charles Ollier complimented Taylor 'upon having "the best prose writer in England" for a contributor', and 'mentioned the name of the Author'. Anne Grant also knew. She and De Quincey had met twice several years earlier, and apparently De Quincey rehearsed for her the story he would eventually tell in his *Confessions*, for when Grant read the work she 'directly recognized' him through the 'thin disguise'.[68]

For some, the *Confessions* were an admonition. 'Better, a thousand times better, *die* than have anything to do with such a Devil's own drug!' Carlyle exclaimed after reading the work.[69] But for scores of other readers, De Quincey's account of his experience was almost as seductive as the drug itself, and his *Confessions* were embraced as an invitation to experimentation.[70] In 1823, one doctor reported an alarming increase in the number of people dying from an overdose of opium, 'in consequence of a little book that has been published by a man of literature'. That same year, the anonymous author of *Advice to Opium Eaters* noted that 'many persons had greatly injured themselves by taking Opium experimentally, which trial they had been enticed to make by the fascinating description of the exquisite pleasure attendant on the taking of that drug, given in a recent publication on the subject'.[71] The 1824 edition of the *Family Oracle of Health* announced that the

> use of opium has been recently much increased by a wild, absurd, and romancing production, called the *Confessions of an English Opium-Eater*. We observe, that at some late inquests this wicked book has been severely censured, as the source of misery and torment, and even of suicide itself, to those who have been seduced to take opium by its lying stories about celestial dreams, and similar nonsense.[72]

Southey cited 'one who had never taken a dose of opium before', but 'took so large a one for the sake of experiencing the sensation which had made De Quincey a slave to it, that a very little addition to the dose might have proved fatal'. Coleridge read the *Confessions* with 'unutterable sorrow ... The writer with morbid vanity, makes a boast of what was my misfortune.' The painter and poet William Bell Scott recalled the time when he and a fellow student took opium in 'imitation' of De Quincey, 'till my friend went into a comatose state, out of which he could not be roused. All night long I sat by him, and into the next day, when he came to himself.'[73]

The *Confessions* created great interest in De Quincey's past, but many questioned the veracity of the narrative. 'Do you suppose it is to be considered as a *true* history?' Lloyd asked Talfourd. 'Is it not very singular that we should have associated with him for several years pretty confidentially, & should never have heard him allude to one of these adventures?' Doubts about the authenticity of his narrative soon reached De Quincey, who was quick to acknowledge that he had not told 'the *whole* truth': 'delicacy towards some who are yet living, and of just tenderness to the memory of others who are dead', made that impossible. He insisted, however, that he had told 'nothing *but* the truth', for he had spoken 'fearlessly, and as if writing private memoirs for my own dearest friends'.[74] One evening Lamb began 'a sort of playful attack' upon him about the *Confessions*, and 'added something in a jeering but good humoured way about Oxford Street'. De Quincey did not laugh.

> 'There are', said he, 'certain places & events & circumstances, which have been mixed up or connected with parts of my life which have been very unfortunate, and these, from constant meditation & reflection upon them, have obtained with me a sort of sacredness, & become associated with solemn feelings so that I cannot bear without the greatest mental agony to advert to the subject, or to hear it adverted to by others in any tone of levity or witticism.'[75]

The *Confessions* were a commercial endeavour in which De Quincey drew on a broad series of cultural, political, and literary sources, and successfully exploited his experience in order to engage a mass magazine audience. At the same time, they were also a sincere if partial record of his past, and they powerfully commemorate his deep personal hurt over his losses and his addiction.

[v]

He claimed he 'lived in the most austere retirement' during his months in London, yet as in Edinburgh the previous December, many sought his company, and he was very often happy to oblige.[76] Taylor and Hessey held regular dinner parties for their contributors on their premises at 93 Fleet Street. Wine and venison were in liberal supply, as were camaraderie, humour, and eccentricity. The poet and *London* essayist Bryan Waller

Procter remembered how the 'hearts of the contributors were opened, and with the expansion of heart the intellect widened also. If there had been any shades of jealousy amongst them, they faded away before the light of the friendly carousal.'⁷⁷ De Quincey consented to attend one of these gatherings soon after the publication of the *Confessions*, though his health was bad. Dinner was 'fixed at "*half-past five, for six*"; and ... as an invalid, or, as the hero of the day, I was planted inexorably, without retreat, in the place of honour by the fireside'.⁷⁸

On several evenings, Taylor and De Quincey talked long into the night, on the identity of Junius, political economy, philosophy, the management of the magazine, and much else.⁷⁹ 'Mr Taylor professed himself a religious dissenter,' De Quincey recalled, 'and ... he manifested an illiberal spirit ... in the temper which he held habitually towards the Church of England.' De Quincey was shocked to meet with 'so much levity of rash judgment' in Taylor, and seems to have guided their conversations towards more abstract theological concerns. 'From a Conversation last Evening with Mr De Quincey,' Taylor remarked, 'I learn that the old Disputers about the Existence of God are likely to have a third Claimant of the Honour of Philosophy in this Department, in the Person of a German, who asserts that God neither *is* nor *was* ... but is *about to be*.'⁸⁰ Taylor greatly enjoyed these discussions, though on at least one occasion De Quincey outstayed his welcome. 'I am so much and often taken up with Conferences, etc., with Contributors, and about the Magazine that my Time is never at my own Disposal. It is now ½ past 12 and the Opium Eater has only just left me.'⁸¹

De Quincey also became friendly with several star contributors to the *London*, including John Hamilton Reynolds, Thomas Hood, Allan Cunningham, and Thomas Griffiths Wainewright, painter and art critic, who was one of the mainstays of the magazine, and who later almost certainly murdered three members of his family. De Quincey dined with Wainewright on 6 December at Taylor and Hessey's, and vividly recollected their evening together.

> Amongst the company, all literary men, sate a murderer, and a murderer of a freezing class; cool, calculating, wholesale in his operations, and moving all along under the advantages of unsuspecting domestic confidence and domestic opportunities ... He was a contributor to a journal in which I also had written several papers. This formed a shadowy link between us; and, ill as I was, I looked more attentively at *him* than at anybody else.

A few days later Wainewright sent De Quincey an 'invitation to a dinner party, expressed in terms that were obligingly earnest ... From an accident I was unable to attend, and I greatly regretted it.'[82]

The toast of the *London* circle was Charles Lamb, whom De Quincey had of course known for many years, and whose famous *Essays of Elia* were currently the most popular feature in the magazine. When flushed with wine, Lamb was 'joyous, radiant with wit and frolic, mounting with the sudden motion of a rocket into the highest heaven of outrageous fun and absurdity; then bursting into a fiery shower of puns, chasing syllables with the agility of a squirrel bounding amongst the trees'. He lived now with Mary at No. 20 Great Russell Street, not far from De Quincey's York Street door, and on many evenings De Quincey went over to dine, for the brother and sister 'absolutely persecuted' him 'with hospitalities'.[83]

On one occasion he and Lamb argued about Hazlitt. De Quincey rated him lower than Lamb felt was just. De Quincey cited Hazlitt's cynicism. Lamb countered that 'it was for the intellectual Hazlitt, not the moral Hazlitt, that he professed so much admiration'. De Quincey retreated enough to 'admit the splendid originality of much that Hazlitt has done' in the hope that he might 'effect a compromise with my opponent'. Lamb, however, pushed on and 'chose to insinuate (whether sincerely and deliberately I cannot say) that Hazlitt was another Coleridge'. This was too much. 'I, whose studies had been chiefly in the field of philosophy, could judge of *that*,' De Quincey returned with pique. 'Lamb felt, or counterfeited a warmth, that for the moment looked like anger.' Doubtless there were fine thinkers in Westmorland. 'But you must allow for us poor Londoners. Hazlitt serves for *our* purposes. And in this poor, little, inconsiderable place of London, he is one of our very prime thinkers.' Lamb continued until it was hard to tell whether he was in jest or earnest, though if he 'felt any vexation, it was gone in a moment; and he shewed his perfect freedom from any relic of irritation, by reading to me one or two of his own beautiful compositions'.[84]

Richard Woodhouse, barrister and occasional writer, is best remembered now as the close friend of Keats, and the most important transcriber and collector of 'Keatsiana' in the years following the poet's death. What is not as well known is that during the autumn of 1821, he was also a close companion of De Quincey, whose conversations he recorded with Boswellian fullness. Here is the closest we come to the pleasure of listening to De Quincey talk.

'The word Patron is a favourite word with me, from its association with those high & noble instances of patronage, about the age of Elizabeth; when great men took a pride & pleasure in fostering ability, and lending their names & protection to Authors. This patronage was without humiliation or servility – each party felt that he was receiving as well as conferring a benefit. The Poet, in return for present countenance & favours had it in his power to transmit his patron's name down with honour to posterity. He made a sort of glory of this mutual obligation – and the praise that he gave, though somewhat excessive, was the Poetic garb in which he decked the expression of his own excited feelings. It was the illumination which genius & enthusiasm always throw round their subject. At the same time that they thus made their offerings or expressed their gratitude to their noble friends, they did not scruple to tell them that those offerings & those thanks would be the means by which their names & Characters would be handed down to future times.'

Woodhouse set down this anecdote, and a good deal more, 'in the first person, because, tho' not the very language of the narrator, it contains the substance of what he said, and is given somewhat in his manner, & in the order in which he gave it; and it will afford some idea of the general tenor of his conversation, & of the richness of his mind'.[85]

De Quincey gossiped to Woodhouse about his life in the Lake District, and 'mentioned several stories, entirely groundless, & carrying in their very horror an assurance of their falsehood & absurdity'. One such rumour was that De Quincey himself was the father of Catharine Wordsworth. Another 'unnatural tale current, & which the Opium-Eater had heard even in London', was that Wordsworth had been 'intimate with his own sister'. De Quincey condemned the story as an 'abominable accusation bruited about' to Wordsworth's prejudice by 'his coarse-minded neighbours'.[86]

The contemporary literary scene was a frequent topic of conversation. De Quincey read more of Keats's poetry, almost certainly at the instigation of either Woodhouse or Reynolds, and while he found *Endymion* 'the very midsummer madness of affectation', he was enormously impressed by *Hyperion*, which presented 'the majesty, the austere beauty, and the simplicity of Grecian temples enriched with Grecian sculpture'.[87] In December, the *Literary Gazette* attacked Keats in its review of Shelley's *Adonais: An Elegy on the Death of John Keats*. De Quincey 'expressed in the strongest terms his execration, at such a rascally & villainous assault upon the memory of anyone scarcely yet cold in his tomb'. On another occasion, he wondered why anyone would think of comparing the poetry of Wordsworth and

George Crabbe, 'who had not one thing in Common in their writings. Wordsworth sought to hallow & ennoble every subject on which he touched', while Crabbe did all he could to make his subjects 'flat, prosaic & commonplace'.[88]

Socializing brought him pleasure and relief, but not everyone enjoyed his company. 'I did not like him,' Procter declared. He was 'certainly an able man; and he was, I believe, liked and admired by those to whom he uncovered his more amiable qualities. But this exposition did not take place in London, where his attractions were not manifested.' Crabb Robinson called on De Quincey as 'a visit of duty'. 'He is in ill-health, is querulous, very strongly impressed with his own excellence, and prone to despise others.' On another visit, however, he took a more tolerant view. De Quincey was 'less offensively arrogant than he was, and is fully sensible of every intended kindness. Talfourd came and sat with him.'[89]

At some point during these months, Wilson showed up in London. De Quincey welcomed his friend, and spent a good deal of time with him, but the appearance of *Blackwood's* lead writer in the midst of the *London* circle foisted upon him exactly those anxieties he had fretted about when he first signed on with Taylor and Hessey. On the one hand, he did not want the *London* circle to learn that he had exhorted Wilson and Blackwood to humiliate John Scott, and that he had been in Edinburgh working for *Blackwood's* the month before Scott was slain. On the other hand, he did not want Wilson to think that he had betrayed *Blackwood's* by publishing with its arch rival, the spectacular *London* appearance of the opium article he had initially promised to *Blackwood's* notwithstanding. Wilson knew all the intimate details of De Quincey's marriage, finances, drug addiction, and Lake District experience. He was a good friend, but he was also erratic and spiteful. If the magazine wars resumed, De Quincey was convinced that Wilson would use his private knowledge to flail him in the pages of *Blackwood's*.

De Quincey's tactic was to strike back – at least privately – before Wilson could assail him publicly, and he launched a vicious personal assault on his oldest friend. Wilson wrote 'the most objectionable of the articles' in *Blackwood's*, De Quincey assured his *London* friends. He will 'domineer over those authors who have as yet no reputation in the world, he will grudge them their fair degree of credit, he will abuse them, & strive to keep them back, & even to crush them'.[90] Wilson was also – as De Quincey well knew – an intellectual impostor. He had a 'happy knack at catching & making use of the thoughts of other people', but that was about the extent of his ability. He had 'no opinions of his own on any subject'; he 'never had any originality'; he had 'no principles at all, and no judgment'.[91]

Berating Wilson in this way may have shored up De Quincey's credentials as a loyal *London* supporter, and exposing him as a fraud no doubt enabled De Quincey to vent anger that had been building inside him for a long while. But smiling to his face, and then stabbing him in the back, was a task that wore badly on De Quincey's nerves, and before long guilt and fear reduced him to something approaching paranoia. He 'had a sort of feeling or ominous anticipation, that possibly there was some being in the world who was fated to do him at some time a great & unexpiable injury – and this thought often weighed upon him', Taylor reported. 'He was not superstitious, but he could not get rid of this impression. Many circumstances seemed to make it not improbable that Wilson might be that man.' De Quincey was even more forthcoming when he discussed his dread with Woodhouse. He and Wilson had already crossed one another 'in respect of the two Magazines. These things Wilson can never forgive: they will rankle in his mind: and at some time or other I am sure he will do what he can to injure me. I care not for myself, but there are quarters through which he can wound me.'[92] Wilson had already published ferocious character assassinations of writers like Coleridge, another scholar, author, Lake District neighbour, *Blackwood's* colleague, and opium-eater. In the weeks following the publication of his *Confessions*, De Quincey convinced himself that he was next.

[vi]

He stayed committed to writing for the *London*. The December 1821 issue opened with a letter from the Opium-Eater promising 'a Third Part of my Confessions'. For the same number he also produced an introduction to his favourite German writer, Jean Paul Richter, complete with two translations from his novel *Flegeljahre*. The 'perilous gas of wit in John Paul' is so exuberant that he may 'blow up', De Quincey joked. Yet 'from every sort of vice and infirmity he drew nutriment for his philosophic mind. It is to the honour of John Paul, that in this, as in other respects, he constantly reminds me of Shakespeare.'[93] De Quincey's assessment constitutes, by broad agreement, the first important critical article on Jean Paul in English. Carlyle remembered the essay 'first put me upon trying to be orthodox and admire. I dimly felt poor De Quincey ... to have exaggerated', but he 'then passed for a mighty seer in such things'.[94] De Quincey began the year by publishing a translation of Schiller in *Blackwood's*. He ended it by publishing a translation of Richter in the *London*. A good deal had happened in between.

And he had big plans for the future. Woodhouse reported that he was 'to write, for the *London Magazine*, an introduction to some English Hexameters which he has composed', as well as articles 'on the mode of reading Latin – on Kant's philosophy – on Coleridge's literary Character', and 'on Political Economy'. The 'Lion's Head' for December also contained a list of his future contributions, which included a number of 'LETTERS to a YOUNG MAN of TALENT whose Education had been neglected', and several 'TRANSLATIONS in Prose and Verse from the most eminent of the FINE WRITERS OF MODERN GERMANY'.[95] De Quincey's literary ambitions extended at this time to novel writing as well. Taylor and Hessey, convinced of the selling power of their star contributor, advanced him 150 guineas to produce the work.[96]

The large lump payment made it possible for De Quincey to plan his return to the Lakes. After seven months away, he was anxious to be home: 'The picture of Fox-ghyll . . . was for ever before my eyes.' He seems to have thought of a Christmas visit to his mother, but gave up these plans. 'My anxiety is now so great, that I could not endure such a delay.'[97] His time in London had been a success. Through illness and anxiety, he had launched himself to fame with the *Confessions*, and established his place within the *London* circle. Further, there had been no assault upon him in *Blackwood's*, nor would there be. Yet De Quincey's fears turned out to be fully justified. He would be attacked with an animus and intimate knowledge that thoroughly humiliated him, and from a quarter closely allied to Wilson – but that was to come.

De Quincey's departure from London was set for 29 December. In the afternoon he went to Fleet Street, where he met Taylor, Hessey, and Woodhouse, and where he lingered almost too long. 'If Hessey had not almost pushed him off he would not have got to the Place in Time,' Taylor wrote. 'I never saw an Instance in which much Reflection so completely deprived a Man of active Energy as in De Quincey.'[98] At last he bid Taylor goodbye, and then walked with Hessey and Woodhouse to his lodgings in York Street, where he went inside to collect his travelling box, while his friends waited outside, Hessey with his watch in his hand. Before he could re-emerge, however, De Quincey was stopped by Bohte, who wanted payment for four books of German philosophy that De Quincey had recently purchased on credit. De Quincey 'compromised the matter by promising a bill at 3 months from Westmorland', and then hastened through the darkened London streets with Woodhouse and Hessey, who saw him 'into the mail'. Another *London* contributor, Allan Cunningham, had departed 'by another Coach for the north the same Evening. It was a subject of regret to both that they had not travelled together.' The journey was dreadful, but De Quincey was home 'in $21\frac{1}{2}$ hours', arriving in time to greet the New Year with Margaret and their children at Fox Ghyll.[99]

NINE

En Route

[i]

De Quincey seems to have asked the Wordsworths if he could borrow their ass, only to find that the animal insisted on bolting from its confinement at Fox Ghyll and running away to Ambleside. 'I meant, if the rain had not been so heavy, to have come over this morning to Rydal Mount to concert something about the poor foolish creature,' he wrote to Dorothy in a friendly and engaging letter. 'For all agree that he is a most excellent creature if he had but more *conduct* – in fact, if he were not the most "outward" ass in existence.'[1] De Quincey was also being called upon to deal with the high-spirits of his children. He had agreed to allow Thomas Monkhouse to use the Fox Ghyll coach-house when Monkhouse visited the Wordsworths in the spring of 1822, but there was no lock on the door, and one of the De Quincey children, together with some friends, stole into the building and began playing on Monkhouse's carriage. De Quincey spoke to the servants and then wrote to assure Monkhouse that 'no further intrusion of that sort will occur'.[2]

He took pleasure in these domestic concerns, but if he had hoped for peace on his return to the Lakes, he was not to find it. Money remained a pressing problem. In the dizzying cross-purpose of his finance, he had created a '*new London debt ... in the very act of extinguishing the old Westmorland debt*'. Within weeks of returning to Fox Ghyll he was 'harassed by Duns' and 'almost out of his mind'. 'I have been employed – morning, noon, and night ... in beating off creditors,' he wrote to Hessey on 29 April.[3] One large sum was owed to Margaret's family. Another was due to Mr Blakeney for the rent on Fox Ghyll. 'I do not understand Mr De Quincey,' Blakeney complained to Wordsworth; 'he has promised by two different Letters to pay his rent, but the Bill is not yet come to hand.'[4]

De Quincey pursued a variety of options in an attempt to alleviate his financial distress. He planned to sell his furniture, 'my house here being a furnished one'. He prepared to sell a part of his library, 'as a desperate remedy for a desperate case'.[5] He wrote once again to his mother, who had of course recently learned – from the pages of a public journal no less! – that he had for nearly two decades been secretly consuming large quantities of laudanum. The shock must have been terrible, and she gave him a fulsome account of her unhappiness. She was not going to be gulled this time by 'all the flattering accounts' he gave her of his 'literary expectations'. She had less money than he supposed. The sale of his library would bring 'nothing like the amount' he expected. His troubles were in several instances self-inflicted: 'I can easily believe, and cannot but believe, that your stomach is miserably injured by the Opium you have swallowed.' If De Quincey imagined, however, that she did not wish to offer him comfort, he did her little justice. 'I am, in truth, always your affectionate Mother.'[6] Enclosed was a bill for fifty-four pounds.

The money, if not the censure, was undoubtedly welcome, but it was nowhere near enough. De Quincey pushed forward with his book sale. 'On Monday May 13 will commence at the Kings Arms Inn in Kendal the sale of a Library in the principle languages of modern Europe, together with a collection of Ancient Classics &c.' De Quincey had hoped the sale would raise from £400 to £650, but it was as his mother prophesied. He made only £170, of which £32 went in fees and most of the rest 'to purchasers of books who happened to have bills against me'.[7]

Endlessly compounding these troubles was of course his laudanum habit, which he chronicled with an almost obsessive interest. Rarely could he face the thought – in modern parlance – of going 'cold turkey', so he resolved on gradually weaning himself from the drug. During the writing of the *Confessions* he had relied heavily on laudanum to combat the pressures of deadlines and homesickness. When he returned to Fox Ghyll, his intake levels ranged between 160 and 300 drops per day. Then, on 24 June, he began his most well-documented attempt to break free from the drug. 'I went off under easy sail – 130 drops a day for 3 days,' he reported; 'on the 4th I plunged at once to 80: the misery which I now suffered "took the conceit" out of me at once: and for about a month I continued off and on about this mark: then I sunk to 60: and the next day to – none at all'. This was the first time in nearly ten years that De Quincey had existed without opium, and he persevered in his abstinence for upwards of half a week.[8]

It proved too much. He could not sleep. He could not sit still. Excessive perspiration obliged him to use a bath five or six times a day, and he was racked by sneezing, 'a sudden distention of the stomach; violent biliousness; rheumatic pains; then pains resembling internal rheumatism –

and many other evils'. These griefs, however, he considered 'all trifles compared with the unspeakable, overwhelming, unutterable misery of mind which came on in one couple of days', and continued almost unabatedly into September. He endured both terrible gloom and a whirling excess of ideas. On the fortieth day of his experiment he was 'in higher spirits ... than for many years back', but at other times he felt 'the wretchedness of a lunatic'.[9]

The experiment ended in defeat. Withdrawal agonies eroded his resolution and drove him to swallow a huge dose. 'It was solely by the tortures connected with the attempt to abjure it, that it kept its hold.'[10] By the middle of the autumn he was an unresisting addict once again, and back up at his usual levels of ingestion. The truce brought a measure of stability, but choosing addiction over withdrawal hardly marked a step forward. Hessey reported on 7 October that De Quincey was 'very ill'. Dorothy Wordsworth walked by Fox Ghyll, where De Quincey was 'shut up as usual – the house always blinded – or left with but one eye to peep out of – *he* probably in bed – We hear nothing of him.' At the end of November, Mary Wordsworth noted drily, 'the Seer continues in close retirement'.[11]

[ii]

De Quincey was in regular touch with Taylor and Hessey, and continued to tantalize them with promises of exciting articles. One night 'in high summer, when I lay tossing and sleepless for want of opium, – I amused myself with composing the imaginary *Confessions of a Murderer*', he wrote to Hessey in October. But the article did not arrive, nor did any of the other work he had promised them. 'The opium eater crossed us once with a dazzling path, and hath as suddenly left us darkling,' Lamb wrote to Wordsworth.[12] Disappointed but undaunted, Taylor and Hessey kept their much-celebrated contributor before the public by issuing the magazine text of the *Confessions* as a book in a print run of 1000 copies. Sales were brisk. A second edition of 1000 copies was published before the end of the year, and a third edition of another 1000 copies appeared on 24 December 1823.[13]

De Quincey's failure to produce more for the *London* did not push his stock down. 'In 1822', he later declared, 'I had 3 offers made to me which promised to be very favourable.'[14] Despite earlier friction between him and Blackwood, one of these offers almost certainly came from *Blackwood's*, which was being friendly to the point of flattering him in its pages. In March 1822, the magazine began to publish the *Noctes Ambrosianae*, a raucous and wide-ranging series of dialogues that presented the people and places of the *Blackwood's* circle in a fictionalized form. Wilson, the lead author of the series, appeared as 'Christopher North', and in the second number for April he praised 'the English Opium-Eater' as 'an invaluable contributor to any periodical'.[15] De Quincey was content at this point to stay with the *London*, but from the corner of his eye he could no doubt see the admiring interest of Wilson and *Blackwood's*.

In the late autumn he was once again animated with big plans. A number of articles were 'in a very forward state', he assured Hessey, and he would soon be down in London to complete his work on them, for he had convinced himself that he could not finish them in the isolation of Fox Ghyll.[16] Hessey had by this time learned to take De Quincey's promises with a grain of salt, but in November De Quincey made the necessary arrangements for another prolonged stay in London, and on 9 December he bid his family goodbye and headed south. Originally he had considered returning to lodge with the Bohtes, but a breach had opened up between the two parties over money and his late hours, and he took rooms instead with the Newbon family at 5 Racquet Court, Fleet Street, nearly opposite the premises of Taylor and Hessey.[17]

De Quincey arrived in London believing that he was within £100 of being free from the 'intolerable bondage of debt', but within only a few weeks it was clear that his situation was in fact growing increasingly bleak.[18] He claimed that he had extinguished the rent due on Fox Ghyll, but in early January Blakeney's agent John White was after him for arrears. Opium continued its treachery, as it 'indirectly aggravated the misery which for the moment it relieved'. One Saturday the entire Newbon household was up all night in the room directly over his head as his landlady went into childbirth.[19] 'Why am I now in London?' he burst out to Hessey in late January, ignoring his own earlier rationalizations that it would be easier for him to get his work done there, and claiming now that he was on site as a service to his publishers. 'Are you aware', he asked Hessey sharply in a long and distraught letter, '... 1. of the enormous sacrifice which I am making in *personal happiness* by staying at a distance of 300 miles from my own family in London? 2. Are you aware of the *price in money* at which I am doing this? 3. Have you ever asked – *whose interests* this residence in London was meant to serve?'[20] The questions were unfair. Hessey simply wanted the material: he did not mind whether De Quincey was in the Lakes or London when he wrote it. De Quincey, however, was overwhelmed.

Yet even as these various distresses coiled round him, he backed away from 'the brink of a precipice', and began to write. He was now committed to the periodical press for his livelihood, and he had not lost confidence that he could profitably exploit what the *New European Magazine* called 'the magic prefix of "*by the Opium eater*"'.[21] In January 1823, the first of his five 'Letters to a Young Man whose Education has been Neglected' was published in the *London*. An extended series of observations on authorship, literature, language, memory, translation, and philosophy, the 'Letters' contain a suggestive comparison between De Quincey and Coleridge, who has 'great and various powers', but 'unfortunately too little talent for teaching or communicating any sort of knowledge'. He might produce 'another *Ancient Mariner*', argues De Quincey, but 'I wish he would leave transcendentalism to me'. Such gibes are designed to tempt Coleridge to 'sally out of his hiding-place in a philosophic passion, and to attack me'. 'Two transcendentalists' who are also two opium-eaters 'can hardly ever before have stripped in any ring'.[22]

The 'Letters' also feature a famous definition which De Quincey owed 'to many years' conversation with Mr Wordsworth'.[23] What do we mean by literature? he asks. Traditionally, works that provide instruction are classified as the 'literature of knowledge', while works that provide amusement are called the 'literature of pleasure'. The dichotomy is a false one, though, for 'the true antithesis to knowledge ... is not *pleasure*, but *power*'. And 'if it be asked what is meant by communicating power, I in my turn would ask by what name a man would designate the case in which I should be made to feel vividly, and with a vital consciousness, emotions which ordinary life rarely or never supplies occasions for exciting'. De Quincey then embodies the literature of power in describing a Shakespearean example of it:

When in King Lear, the height, and depth, and breadth of human passion is revealed to us – and for the purposes of a sublime antagonism is revealed in the weakness of an old man's nature, and in one night two worlds of storm are brought face to face – the human world, and the world of physical nature – mirrors of each other, semichoral antiphonies, strophe and antistrophe heaving with rival convulsions, and with the double darkness of night and madness, – when I am thus suddenly startled into a feeling of the infinity of the world within me, is this power? or what may I call it?[24]

Like much of his finest criticism, De Quincey formulated the idea of the 'literature of power' in dialogue with Wordsworth, though his popularization of it in the 'Letters' adds an immediacy and a range that are uniquely his own.

He stayed productive throughout the spring. In March, he reviewed

Letitia Matilda Hawkins's *Anecdotes, Biographical Sketches, and Memoirs*, and the following month he produced the most important early critical account in English of Johann Gottfried Herder, whom he had already discussed briefly in the *Westmorland Gazette*.²⁵ He also translated several tales by the prolific German storyteller Friedrich Augustus Schulze, who wrote under the pen name 'Friedrich Laun'. 'Mr Schnackenberger; or, Two Masters for One Dog', is a rollicking tale of ill-fated amours and mistaken identities. 'The Dice' is a much darker narrative of satanic pacts, broken promises, and addictive behaviours.

After the distresses of his first few months in London, De Quincey was out and about a good deal. 'He was with me again last Night,' Hessey told Taylor on 14 March, with a trace of irritation. In early April, he and De Quincey went 'to see Figaro at the Opera House – we were much entertained, but dreadfully hot'.²⁶ De Quincey reconnected with several *London* contributors, including Thomas Hood, who described him as 'almost boyish ... from a peculiar delicacy of complexion and smallness of features'. As sub-editor of the magazine, it was Hood's 'frequent and agreeable duty' to pick up copy from De Quincey at his Racquet Court lodgings, where he found him 'in the midst of a German Ocean of *Literature*, in a storm, – flooding all the floor, the table and the chairs, – billows of books tossing, tumbling, surging open'. Hood often stayed far into the night listening to De Quincey, and watching as gradually his cheeks grew pale and his eyes 'a degree dimmer'. These signs, according to Hood, marked the 'waning influence' of laudanum.²⁷

De Quincey met a number of new people as well. William Hazlitt, like De Quincey, was a distinguished contributor to the *London*, a close friend of the Lambs, and a penetrating critic of Wordsworth and Coleridge. His unswerving radicalism and incessant flailing of the Tories, however, placed him on a political collision course with De Quincey. Procter testified that the two 'thought poorly of each other. Hazlitt pronounced verbally that the other would be good only "whilst the opium was trickling from his mouth" ... De Quincey, on the other hand, seems to have forced opportunities for sneering at Hazlitt'.²⁸ Two or three times the unlikely pair 'walked for a few miles together: it was in London, late at night, and after leaving a party'. De Quincey was 'depressed by the spectacle of a mind always in agitation from the gloomier passions', but amused by the pertinacity with which Hazlitt clung, 'through bad reasons or no reasons, to any public slander floating against men in power'.²⁹

Hazlitt related a story which highlights the stark difference between the two writers. One day he happened to see the Duke of Cumberland walking down Pall Mall. Men took off their hats when they saw him, and the Duke bowed in return. As he passed into Cockspur Street, however, he encountered a 'Negro sweep'. 'What was to be done?' Could the Duke from his 'majestic pedestal' descend to 'gild with the rays of his condescension such a grub'? Forced to make a decision, the Duke kept his hat on and gave the black man half-a-crown. Hazlitt was outraged. 'I insist upon it, that he was entitled to the bow, since all Pall Mall had it before him.' De Quincey disagreed. 'The bow would not be so useful to the black as the half-crown', and 'this bow, so useless to the sweep ... would react upon the other bows distributed along the line of Pall Mall, so as to neutralize them one and all'. De Quincey then sketched a little scene which he had once witnessed on the occasion of a visit to Drury Lane by George IV when regent. Hazlitt listened 'fretfully to me when praising the deportment and beautiful gestures of one conservative leader; though he had compelled *me* to hear the most disadvantageous comments on another'.[30]

Yet the radical and the royalist were not always at odds. In May 1823, the middle-aged Hazlitt published *Liber Amoris*, the obsessional tale of his disastrous love for Sarah Walker, the teenaged daughter of his landlord. The book was a gift to Tory assassins, who read it as confirmation of the degradation and moral confusion bound to result from a commitment to left-wing politics. Crabb Robinson was one of many who found it 'nauseous and revolting'. De Quincey, however, did not see it that way. 'I must reverence a man, be he what he may otherwise, who shews himself capable of profound love,' he declared. 'Pity was no demand' of Hazlitt's; 'laughter was no wrong: the sole necessity for *him* was – to empty his over-burdened spirit'.[31] Hazlitt sent De Quincey a copy of the book as a token of appreciation for his support. Indeed, he may have conceived the intense autobiographical introspection of *Liber Amoris* as a kind of counter-example to De Quincey's *Confessions*.[32]

De Quincey was also introduced to the Scottish preacher Edward Irving, who was then at the height of his fame, and who was regarded· by De Quincey as 'unquestionably, by many, many degrees, the greatest orator of our times'. The two met at a dinner party, where an exuberant Irving 'strode about the drawing-room ... with the air of one who looked upon himself as clothed with the functions of Jonah sent to Ninevah'. Nobody would have been surprised, De Quincey recalled, 'if he had dined on locusts and wild honey'. Irving talked at length of phrenology and went so far as to examine De Quincey's skull, where he detected 'conscientiousness' and 'veneration' in great strength (or so De Quincey claimed). The two walked homeward together and found themselves united in their dislike of 'common literary society'.[33]

There was, however, a moment of unpleasantness. As they neared Charing Cross, a female beggar came up to them and asked for charity. De Quincey of course had no money to spare, though the woman immediately engaged his sympathies, for he knew all about the desperation of London's street-walkers. But Irving showed no compassion, and 'shook off the poor shivering supplicant, whose manner was timid and dejected, with a roughness that would have better become a parish beadle towards a stout masterful beggar'. De Quincey put Irving's behaviour down to an 'untameable fervour' in his manner rather than a deficiency of kindness, but the incident clearly bothered him.[34]

Occupied as he was with the *London* and its circle, De Quincey also found time during these months to start moonlighting. His former landlord Bohte was one of three publishers involved in a three-volume collection of German supernatural stories entitled *Popular Tales and Romances of the Northern Nations*, and it was most probably in response to a request from him that De Quincey produced 'The Fatal Marksman', a translation of a tale by Johann August Apel that had already been adapted in Friedrich Kind's libretto to Carl Maria von Weber's immensely successful opera, *Der Freischütz* (1821).

Similarly, De Quincey began to publish in *Knight's Quarterly Magazine*, and almost certainly a year earlier than has commonly been thought. Charles Knight, a liberal editor and publisher, founded his *Quarterly Magazine* in June 1823, and listed Allan Cunningham, William Mackworth Praed, Coleridge's second son Derwent, Edward Bulwer, and Thomas Babington Macaulay among his most important contributors.[35] De Quincey is known to have produced two translations for *Knight's* in the autumn of 1824, by which time he and Knight had become good friends, but the fullest index of authors' contributions to the magazine lists two articles by De Quincey that were first published in 1823. De Quincey knew the magazine's early numbers, for he was familiar with Henry Nelson Coleridge's 'Scibile', which was published in the first issue, and which De Quincey regarded as 'truly admirable'. More striking testimony comes from Henry Malden, a prolific contributor to *Knight's*, who knew that De Quincey was busy on behalf of the new magazine. 'If De Quincey is within reach, pray extract something from him,' he wrote to Knight on 15 September 1823. 'His last article was much liked.'[36]

Reference to this 'last article' raises the possibility that De Quincey contributed to *Knight's* as early as its first number, but he does not feature in the contributors' index for June, and none of the articles in the issue seems clearly to belong to him. Malden's desire to have material from De Quincey, however, appears to have produced results, as two pieces by him are listed in the contributors' index for the second issue of October. Both are signed 'Archibald Fraser'. The first, a poem entitled 'The Raven, a Greek Tale', is in the manner of Theocritus, and describes an argument between Learchus and his lover Peroe. The work does not seem especially De Quinceyan, and he wrote poetry infrequently, but Peroe's final speech certainly suggests the presence of the Opium-Eater. She has taken a lover who is 'far more beautiful' than Learchus, and is now 'Lost in th' intoxicating dream'. Learchus frowns sternly, but Peroe explains: 'I yielded to his flatteries and his prayers, / And sunk into his arms – nay, start not – hear, / They were the arms of poppy-crowned sleep.'[37]

The second piece, 'The Black Chamber', seems very likely to be De Quincey's. It is another translation of a German tale of terror by Apel, very much in the style of 'The Fatal Marksman', and just the sort of work he was producing at this moment. De Quincey enlarges the opening by playing up the animosity between two rival magazines, and he slightly reworks the closing commentary on the history of ghosts, but elsewhere he adheres closely to his source. 'The Black Chamber' features obligatory moments of terror, and apparently supernatural occurrences which are explained away as the result of a hidden door in a wall between two bedrooms. Yet at least one character, Wermuth, retains a partial faith in spectres. 'It is not till the period when ghosts are banished, that men begin to tell their histories.'[38]

The strong output of these months brought De Quincey a steady income, but did not relieve his sorrows. He had not yet seen his fourth child, Francis John, who was born at Fox Ghyll on 26 November 1822, and baptized on 28 February 1823. He fretted that his letters to Margaret were being 'pried into by such good but curious people as sometimes volunteer' to carry them from Ambleside to Fox Ghyll. His health was a constant concern, as was his opium habit. In late May or June, the demand for copy especially pressing, he wore himself out 'sitting up and taking laudanum for 3 days in succession'.[39] And to top off these anxieties, Mrs Newbon was demanding her rent, and 'adding servant, washerwoman, medicines, and a few other &c.' De Quincey did not see how he would be 'able to leave this place ... under £16.10'. Shortly thereafter he simply fled without paying the rent, and in July took refuge in the Swan Inn – most probably the one at Holborn Bridge. He assumed an alias to keep the Newbons and his many other creditors from tracking him down. '"Mr M – in the Swan" – or simply "The Gent. in the Swan" is enough by way of direction.' His circumstances partook of both farce and deep distress. 'If you ask the man at what coffee-house I am,' he solemnly instructed Hessey, ' – I must request of you, *not as an act of friendship* but as an act of mere honour under some circumstances which I shall mention to you when I see you, not to communicate my address to any body.'[40]

The situation was untenable, even by De Quincey's standards, and he determined upon escape to Westmorland. The journey was expensive at eight guineas, but he somehow managed to raise the funds and avoid his creditors. On the evening of Monday, 4 August, after eight months in London and the production of at least a dozen articles, he slipped quietly away, travelling first to Manchester and then – his enthusiasm for the outside of the coach undiminished – 'on the box of the Mail the whole way to Preston'.[41] He arrived at Fox Ghyll just before eight on Wednesday morning. The trip was exhausting, and many of his London problems would follow him north, but he was undoubtedly delighted to be home. Dorothy Wordsworth saw him soon after his arrival, and noted a marked change. 'The opium eater must have left off his opium,' she declared optimistically (if inaccurately): 'he is returned quite well, and looks younger than he did seven [years] ago. He drank tea with us lately.'[42]

[iii]

De Quincey's fame was spreading. There had been 'scarcely one day's interval since my return without callers from amongst the lakers, bringing letters of Introduction to me *as* the Opium Eater', he told Hessey in September.[43] The travel writer John Carne 'passionately wished to see' De Quincey, whose '*Confessions of an English Opium-Eater* ... has made so much noise in the world'. He called one morning at Fox Ghyll but De Quincey 'was not visible, and I concluded was not risen'. He had better luck that evening when he returned to find De Quincey and his eldest son William – now six years old, 'with a beautiful countenance and flaxen hair' – just back from a mountain walk. De Quincey was 'one of the smallest men you ever saw, with very fine features, and eyes beaming with intellect and opium', Carne reported. 'He is an uncommonly clever man, and his interesting con-versation, his faded countenance, on which the sense of his past miseries seemed still to rest, and the sweet tone of his voice, made me feel almost attached to him.'[44]

Wilson and De Quincey saw each other often that autumn. The intense animosity De Quincey had felt towards him in the weeks following the publication of the *Confessions* had apparently been resolved or forgotten.

Wilson remained intent on bringing De Quincey back to *Blackwood's*, and De Quincey seems to have been increasingly willing to listen to these plans. In September, Wilson wrote robustly to Blackwood that De Quincey is 'disgusted with all the Cockneys and intends to get rid of them in half a year ... [He] is very friendly to Maga & us all'.⁴⁵ Wilson also made these sentiments public. Some of De Quincey's *London* articles were signed '*by the late Opium-eater*'. Wilson provokingly misread this tag in *Blackwood's* as a means of suggesting that De Quincey was meant for better things. 'Mercy on us!' he exclaimed in the September issue. 'Is the English opium-eater dead? ... The air of Cockaigne must have killed him ... May we meet in another and a better Magazine.'⁴⁶

Such a meeting promptly took place – in a manner of speaking. Unable literally to reinstate De Quincey with *Blackwood's*, Wilson did the next best thing when he fictionalized him as 'The Opium-Eater' in the October instalment of the *Noctes Ambrosianae*, and then had him walk into Ambrose's Tavern in Edinburgh and spend an evening talking, drinking, and eating with the *Blackwood's* crew. Over the course of the dialogue, the Opium-Eater answers questions about Wordsworth, castigates Francis Jeffrey, and praises *Blackwood's* for its criticism of Shelley, which 'did you immortal honour'. At one point Christopher North asks, 'Pray, is it true, my dear Laudanum, that your "Confessions" have caused about fifty unintentional suicides?' 'I should think not,' replies the Opium-Eater defensively. 'I have read of six only; and they rested on no solid foundation.' Near the end of the conversation, the Opium-Eater drops a bombshell when he announces that Coleridge is 'not only a plagiary, but, sir, a thief, a *bonâ fide* most unconscientious thief' who 'has stolen from a whole host of his fellow-creatures'.⁴⁷ It was the first time that Coleridge had been accused of plagiarism in print. Wilson undoubtedly drew much of the dialogue – especially the comments concerning Shelley and Coleridge – from actual conversations with De Quincey, and over the course of the instalment he brought the Opium-Eater vividly to life.

Taylor and Hessey cannot have been pleased. They did not 'like the appearance, even, of losing an Author', and *Blackwood's* inveterate habit of blurring the line between fact and fiction made it seem as though one of their prized contributors had a place in the inner circle of their chief competitor.⁴⁸ Their concerns in this regard would only have been heightened by a new tone in De Quincey's letters that was goading and critical. The September number of the *London* was 'thought a good one', he reported to Hessey from the Lakes, though he added woundingly that this 'rather surprises me'. He complained of 'many ... defects of due *energy*' in the management of the magazine, and wondered if Taylor and Hessey might not be suffering from 'dyspepsy'. As he prepared 'an Abstract of all the minor and miscellaneous Essays of Kant', he told Hessey to 'beware how you think cheaply of these'. In case Hessey failed to take the hint, De Quincey spelled it out in a follow-up letter: 'Wilson appears sure that Blackwood is most anxious to obtain a good account of Kant for his Magazine.'[49]

Perhaps De Quincey could sense that the situation at the *London* was deteriorating, as it fell further and further behind its Edinburgh rival in terms of sales and prestige. Taylor and Hessey still recruited and published some of the finest writers of the day, and they had both been kind and generous to De Quincey. But Taylor's vagueness and reserve was an increasing source of concern to his contributors, and the magazine as a whole began gradually to lose that spirit of camaraderie and liberal intellectualism that had been such distinguishing features under John Scott. When comparing the two magazines, even key *London* contributors found *Blackwood's* superior. 'The London Magazine wants the personal note too much,' Lamb complained to Hessey. 'Blackwood owes everything to it. Think on it.'[50] Another *London* contributor, Mary Russell Mitford, had a confession to make: 'in my secret soul (don't tell Mr Talfourd), though he and I both write in the *London* along with the Proctors, the Reynoldses, and the Charles Lambs, I like *Blackwood's* better'. It has a 'fine, swaggering, bold-faced impudence – a perfection of lying and of carrying it off – which is delightfully amusing'.[51]

Yet while the tide was clearly running in *Blackwood's* favour, De Quincey's complaints about the *London* appear to have been designed, not to signal an imminent defection back to the Edinburgh magazine, but to win more gratitude and money from Taylor and Hessey. He had worked hard for them in London throughout the first half of the year, and once he settled back into Fox Ghyll he found himself able to maintain this same high rate of productivity, a marked change from a year earlier, when he had lived in the cottage and been unable to complete a single article. In the *London* for September, De Quincey commemorated the recent death of his friend 'Walking' Stewart, 'a sublime visionary' whose 'mind was a mirror of the sentient universe'. Stewart and Percy Shelley had died within a few months of each other, and De Quincey revealingly compared the two. Both had 'a fine vague enthusiasm and lofty aspirations in connexion with human nature generally and its hopes', though 'in maintaining their own system they both found themselves painfully entangled at times with tenets pernicious and degrading to human nature'.[52]

'On the Knocking at the Gate in Macbeth' appeared in the *London* for

October, in the same issue as Hazlitt's 'Pictures at Wilton', Lamb's 'Letter of Elia to Robert Southey', and the first instalment of Carlyle's biography of Schiller. It is one of De Quincey's most celebrated pieces of literary criticism, and marks the first time in his writings that he imaginatively revisits the bloody scenes of December 1811, when John Williams savagely murdered seven people in London's East End. Guided by the injunction 'never to pay any attention to his understanding when it stands in opposition to any other faculty of his mind', De Quincey approaches Williams from two starkly different angles. Famously, he introduces the satiric aesthetic that enables him to see Williams's performance 'on the stage of Ratcliffe Highway' as 'making the connoisseur in murder very fastidious in his taste, and dissatisfied with any thing that has been since done in that line'.[53] At the same time Williams's extreme brutality leads De Quincey to reflections on the psychology of violence, as well as to an absorbing interrogation of the moment in Shakespeare's play when Macbeth and Lady Macbeth return fresh from the slaying of Duncan, and are unexpectedly interrupted. During the scene, 'the world of devils' is revealed, De Quincey remarks.

> But how shall this be conveyed and made palpable? In order that a new world may step in, this world must for a time disappear. The murderers, and the murder, must be insulated – cut off by an immeasurable gulph from the ordinary tide and succession of human affairs – locked up and sequestered in some deep recess: we must be made sensible that the world of ordinary life is suddenly arrested – laid asleep – tranced – racked into a dread armistice: time must be annihilated; relation to things without abolished; and all must pass self-withdrawn into a deep syncope and suspension of earthly passion. Hence it is that when the deed is done – when the work of darkness is perfect, then the world of darkness passes away like a pageantry in the clouds: the knocking at the gate is heard; and it makes known audibly that the reaction has commenced: the human has made its reflux upon the fiendish: the pulses of life are beginning to beat again.

After reading the essay, Lamb observed that De Quincey had 'written a thing about Macbeth better than anything I could write; – no – not better than anything I could write, but I could not write anything better'.[54]

German literature remained a central preoccupation throughout these months. De Quincey translated three essays from Kant, including 'On National Character, in Relation to the Sense of the Sublime and Beautiful'. In the fifth number of a series entitled 'Notes from the Pocket-Book of a Late

Opium-Eater', he provided what seems to be the first English translation of any part of Schiller's key treatise *On the Aesthetic Education of Man*.[55] His translation of Jean Paul Richter's 'Dream Upon the Universe' is a superb exploration of time, apocalypse, alienation, and God's mysterious presence, in which he both follows Richter and charts his own psychology. 'At length the human heart within me was overburthened and weary, and yearned after some narrow cell or quiet oratory in this metropolitan cathedral of the universe. And I said to the Form at my side – "Oh! Spirit! Has then this universe no end?" And the Form answered and said – "Lo! it has no beginning."'[56]

Economics were another key concern. De Quincey's brief essay on Malthus opened the *London* for October 1823, and is notable chiefly for provoking Hazlitt to the charge of plagiarism. An embarrassed De Quincey responded in the 'Lion's Head' of the December issue, acknowledging that he had seen Hazlitt's work, and that there was indeed a good deal of overlap, though intentional plagiarism seems unlikely. De Quincey can hardly have wanted to put information he knew was stolen from Hazlitt where Hazlitt himself was almost certain to read it. Less consciously, De Quincey had by this time assimilated so much economic information that he was probably no longer able to distinguish between what originally belonged to him, and what belonged to Hazlitt, to Ricardo, to Malthus, and to several others.[57] In any event, he did far greater justice to his abilities in 'Dialogues of the Three Templars on Political Economy, Chiefly in Relation to the Principles of Mr Ricardo', published in the *London* for April and May 1824, and described by De Quincey himself as 'the best' two articles he had ever written. At the core of the inquiry is Ricardo's theory of value, and its far-reaching implications for economic thought. 'Grant me this one principle, with a few square feet of the sea-shore to draw my diagrams upon, and I will undertake to demonstrate every other truth in the science.'[58]

Reviews of the 'Dialogues' were generally positive. Philosophical radicals like John Ramsay McCulloch characterized them as 'unequalled, perhaps, for brevity, pungency and force', while Samuel Bailey found De Quincey traced Ricardo's doctrines 'fearlessly to their legitimate consequences'.[59] Other readers, however, found him simply dull. De Quincey had initially taken the *London* by storm with the extremity and intense subjectivity of his *Confessions*. Now he was publishing long, arid treatises on economics. 'Taylor has lately refused a paper of Procter's & one of Reynolds's, & kept back Darley's reply to Terentius Secundus,' fumed the poet Thomas Lovell Beddoes, 'for the purpose of introducing that thrice-double demoniac the aeconomical opium-eater.' Pithily and prophetically he concluded, 'Exit London.'[60]

[iv]

Wherever he was, was wrong. Living at Fox Ghyll cut him off from books, ready money, urban anonymity, and the enlivening conversation of the *London* circle. Eventually the pull of London would become strong enough and he would set off, full of ideas and optimism. Once settled in the south, however, he would almost immediately begin to have second thoughts. His expenses would be far higher than he projected. His lodgings were noisy and cramped. He missed Margaret and their children. Fox Ghyll would come to seem a haven of support and understanding where he could be happier and equally productive. Gradually he would extricate himself from London and travel to the north, brimming with ideas and optimism, and where within weeks he would think it necessary to return to London. Within this broad cycle of dislocation and perplexity spiralled De Quincey's day-to-day existence of walking, reading, visiting, parenting, paying bills, consuming laudanum, and writing through long solitary hours for the *London*.

The pressures on him had been mounting for weeks. 'That beautiful residence near the Lakes, Fox Ghyll, Loughrigg, Grasmere, is announced for sale': so ran an advertisement in the Westmorland and Cumberland papers. Blakeney had recently died, and his widow had decided to put the property on the market, perhaps in response to De Quincey's habitual inability to pay the rent. Prospective buyers were soon knocking at his door. De Quincey was reluctant to let them in. Farcical scenes ensued, including a particularly disagreeable encounter with a violent would-be owner.[61]

Creditors were also pressing him: John Newby, miller; John Green, butcher; George Pearson, grocer; Mr Newton, wine merchant; Mrs Robert Fleming, dressmaker; Miss Preston, haberdasher; and so on.[62] Matters came to a head near Christmas when an Ambleside bill was unexpectedly returned. De Quincey briefly considered flight as his best option, but 'in what direction – I hardly know; for I have not half a crown disposable for travelling ... I am scarcely able to crawl ... I will never give another bill as long as I live.' Wordsworth called at the peak of these distresses. De Quincey lied and said he was not at home. Almost immediately he wrote to apologize. 'I feel so much pain at not having been able to express my sense of the favour you did me in calling,' he assured the poet, ' – that I think it right to explain that the load of labour, under which I groan, has continued to make it impossible for me to get out for one half hour even.' Wordsworth seems to have been prepared to accept explanations such as this one, for De Quincey later recalled several conversations with him at this time 'partially connected with political economy', and especially with the doctrine of rent.[63]

He spent the first six weeks of 1824 in bed, battling an addiction that had him completely surrounded. 'If I take no laudanum, I am in a state of semi-distraction', but 'if I take even 12 or 15 drops' there is a 'return of bilious symptoms which often put me *hors d'état* for any sort of labour'. He believed 'some affection of the liver' was pushing him towards madness. An unnamed doctor prescribed 'very large doses of the blue pill', but these only made him sicker.[64] In the spring his mother gave him the £84 annually remitted to him by his uncle Penson. Clamouring creditors took most of it, though De Quincey was certain that he had been 'grossly swindled' by his Ambleside grocer Pearson, and turned the matter over to a lawyer. Throughout April he walked the three miles from Fox Ghyll to Dove Cottage, where he rummaged through mountains of old letters and bills in order to produce a long legal document that would explain his financial situation, and prevent 'a series of nearly a dozen arrests' that would have forced him to flee the country in order to avoid prison.[65]

De Quincey's stress in the Lakes added greatly to Hessey's in London. For two and a half years, the publisher had managed to remain reasonably calm as he waited for De Quincey to deliver his copy, but he no longer had that luxury: the *London* was now losing around £500 a year; several contributors were up in arms about various editorial decisions; and Taylor was slipping towards a nervous breakdown.[66] In March, Hessey lost his patience with De Quincey, and itemized his debts to the firm in a letter 'couched in terms of most unprovoked ill-temper and violence'. De Quincey responded in kind. Hessey undoubtedly had a right to insist upon 'the most minute accuracy' when it came to the financial transactions of the magazine. But 'Good God!' cried De Quincey. 'If you had let me know beforehand that you would detain anything I sent in order to repay yourself, – I would, on learning the amount, have instantly set about some steps for meeting your demand as soon as possible.'[67] The situation was soon resolved, but it flared up again in late April, when Hessey complained bitterly of De Quincey's 'cruel delay' in sending material. De Quincey wondered why Hessey was not more generous. 'Messrs. Hazlitt, Reynolds, &c. have put you to a thousand times more inconvenience in a single month than I in a year.' His excuse was unparalleled suffering. 'Theirs – that they got drunk, – went to the play, – had a cold, – gave a party.'[68] Hessey seems not to have responded to De Quincey's assessment of the *London* circle, though he can hardly have found it either helpful or accurate. Both editor and contributor were becoming fed-up, with the situation and with each other.

De Quincey resolved to travel back to London, undoubtedly in an effort to speed up the exchange of material, and ease the frustrations that were undermining his relationship with Hessey. His departure, of course, meant a return of all the old strains that beset him when he and Margaret were separated. On 6 May he had 'no money', but soon he managed to scrape enough together for the coach fare, and by the middle of the month he was in Liverpool, where his health – and probably his resolve – broke down, and he ended up staying for a month with his friend Merritt.[69] De Quincey set out for London again in mid-June, but this time got caught in a downpour while travelling on the outside of the coach, and ended up at the George Inn in Litchfield 'in a shivering fit, with very high pulse'.[70] It was two additional weeks before he set out for a third time. Had he known the nasty shock that was waiting for him, he may well have turned around and retreated to Fox Ghyll.

[v]

On Saturday, 3 July 1824, at around six in the morning, De Quincey reached London aboard one of the northern mails. The coach delivered its bags in Lombard Street, and then drove him down 'to a great city hotel'. After indulging in the 'luxurious refreshment' of a hot bath, he seated himself at the breakfast table around eight, where the waiter brought him the morning edition of *The Times*. His eye passed indolently over the paper until it fell on a list of new publications. His heart immediately misgave him. A satirical journal – *The John Bull Magazine* – had just published its inaugural issue, and he was singled out as one of the 'Humbugs of the Age'.[71] Fearing the worst, De Quincey headed straight for Smithfield, where the publisher kept a shop. He entered, bought a copy of the magazine, and went out into the street. In the weeks immediately following the publication of his *Confessions*, De Quincey had become semi-hysterical in the conviction that Wilson was about to smear him in the pages of *Blackwood's* in retaliation for switching his allegiances to the *London*. The attack had not come then. But it did come now.[72]

William Maginn delivered the blow. A clever and recklessly malicious satirist, he had risen to great prominence in *Blackwood's*, both in his own right and as the fictive Ensign O'Doherty in the *Noctes* sketches. He did not know De Quincey, but he did know Wilson, who almost certainly provided the details for the attack, though perhaps in unguarded moments of merriment, rather than as part of a deliberate plot. However this may have been, Maginn rounded on De Quincey from several different fronts.

He lashed him for the 'wretched infirmity' of his drug addiction, his 'hanger-on' status with 'the lake school' of Wordsworth and Coleridge, and his 'nauseating succession of idle boasts' about his learning and language skills. His physical appearance was even more laughable. 'Conceive an animal about five feet high, propped on two trapsticks, which have the size but not the delicate proportions of rolling-pins, with a comical sort of indescribable body, and a head of most portentous magnitude ... As for the face, its utter grotesqueness and inanity is totally beyond the reach of the pen to describe.' Maginn then turned on Margaret. She was De Quincey's 'servant-maid long before he married her'. More grievously, 'we should request Quincy to give us an extract from his parish-register, dating the birth of his first child, and also his marriage ... It would be an important addition to the chronology of the county.'[73]

Blood was his first thought: he would trace his assailant and challenge him to a duel. But he soon thought better of it. Doubtless he remembered the recent killing of John Scott. Wilson at least came immediately to his defence. 'You would disapprove, I suppose, of the attack on De Quincey in the John Bull Magazine?' Ensign O'Doherty asks Christopher North in the August number of the *Noctes*. 'Disapprove?' North retorts, ' – I utterly despised it, and so, no doubt, did he.'[74] Wilson's public display of friendship, however, could not stop the slander from spreading, and De Quincey underwent the further humiliation of discovering that his old Westmorland nemesis, the *Kendal Chronicle*, had cheerfully reprinted large excerpts from the assault as the lead article in its 14 August number. De Quincey seems eventually to have discovered that Maginn was responsible for the calumny, but at the time he could only submit in impotent rage as he was – in Carlyle's summary – fried 'to cinders on the gridiron of the *John Bull*'.[75] Wilson had not sanctioned the article, but De Quincey had been right to worry. Indirectly and at last, *Blackwood's* punished his disloyalty with the kind of ferocious character assassination that he had worried all along would break suddenly upon him, 'like a bull-dog at the throat'.[76]

Consolation, for these and other troubles, came most often in the form of friendships. One was with Matthew Davenport Hill, an educationalist and legal reformer, who leaned well to the left politically, and who was closely connected with figures such as Bentham and Brougham. Hill had recently published his *Plans for the Government and Liberal Instruction of Boys in Large Numbers*, which De Quincey had enthusiastically reviewed in the *London* for April and May 1824. Clearly linked to utilitarian philosophy, Hill's educational system contemplated 'the whole man with a reference to his total means of usefulness and happiness in life'. De Quincey was especially impressed with the humanity of Hill's plan. The boys were to be self-governed, and responsible for their own discipline and administration. Corporal punishment was to be entirely abolished in order to avoid not only the physical pain that was inflicted on the student, but the psychic trauma of shame and embarrassment that went with it. De Quincey – the miseries of his own and Pink's school experience-undoubtedly before him – found such measures 'very wise'.[77]

Hill was delighted with the review and sought to make De Quincey's acquaintance. He and his wife Margaret lived in a cottage near the parish church at Chelsea, and discovered that De Quincey was lodged nearby at 4 Eccleston Street, Pimlico. Hill invited De Quincey to a family dinner, and before long he was a regular visitor. The Hills were astonished at 'the wealth of his conversation, and his felicity of expression'. De Quincey came occasionally to their Sunday morning breakfast table, where he met a wide range of liberal writers, including Macaulay. Fond as always of the society of women, he charmed 'Mrs Hill with his conversation in the long evenings when she sat up for her husband'. One morning the Hills discovered De Quincey at their door 'wet and shivering' from 'having slept under a hayrick in the Hampstead fields', undoubtedly to escape angry creditors.[78]

De Quincey also became closely associated with one of Hill's good friends, Charles Knight. As we have seen, De Quincey probably became a contributor to *Knight's Quarterly Magazine* in 1823, but it was the summer of 1824 before he knew Knight personally, and had 'naturally' fallen into company 'with the whole band' of his contributors. Knight recorded that De Quincey's health was bad and that he was swallowing large doses of opium, but he added that he and his wife Sally were captivated – like the Hills – by his aristocratic manners, eccentric appearance, and inspired conversation. 'One hour of De Quincey – better, three hours from nine till midnight – for a rapt listener to be "under the wand of a magician."'[79]

Two of De Quincey's tales, 'The Incognito' and 'The Somnambulist', were published in *Knight's* for August, and the same issue took a page from *Blackwood's* when it featured a fictional account of a dinner for contributors at which the 'Opium-Eater' makes an unexpected but welcome appearance. 'Even now do I feel the gnawings of that poison with which I have drugged my veins,' he tells the company.

We all looked at each other with surprise. 'Can it be?' was on every tongue. 'May I venture to ask, Sir, whom I have the honour of seeing amongst us?' ... 'My name, Sir, is ——; but you may have heard of me as a too celebrated Opium Eater.' We all involuntarily bowed; and in two

ABOVE LEFT: De Quincey's father Thomas Quincey, a successful Manchester linen merchant whose *Short Tour in the Midland Counties of England* was published in 1775.

ABOVE: De Quincey's mother Elizabeth Penson Quincey, a woman whose faults arose 'from austerity, too hard perhaps, and gloomy'.

LEFT: De Quincey when he was two years old, and living just outside Manchester at The Farm. He claimed his earliest memories dated from this age.

Greenhay, where the Quinceys moved when Thomas was six years old, and where both his father and sister Elizabeth died.

De Quincey, aged seventeen, when he was a student at Manchester Grammar School.

The home of Charles Lawson, headmaster of Manchester Grammar School. It was from here that De Quincey bolted in the summer of 1802.

Mrs Best's cottage in Everton, where De Quincey experienced some of his most intense opium reveries.

Henry Edridge's pencil drawing of
William Wordsworth, 1806.

Washington Allston's portrait of
Samuel Taylor Coleridge, 1814.

Thomas Lawrence's sketch of the suspected
murderer John Williams, drawn in the prison
cell, 1811.

Fox Ghyll, where the De Quinceys lived from 1820 until 1825.

The Nab was the family home of De Quincey's wife Margaret, and was owned by De Quincey himself from 1829 until 1833.

Thomas Hood's sketch of De Quincey at around the time he wrote the 1821 version of his *Confessions of an English Opium-Eater.*

John Harden's pen and ink sketch of John Wilson at Brathay, 1809. De Quincey described Wilson as 'the only very intimate male friend I have had'.

Sir William Allan's portrait of William Blackwood, c. 1830. As editor of the immensely successful *Blackwood's Edinburgh Magazine*, Blackwood published some of De Quincey's finest work.

John Taylor (left) and James
Hessey, who co-edited the
London Magazine, and who
first published De Quincey's
*Confessions of an English
Opium-Eater.*

ABOVE: Mavis Bush Cottage, which the De Quincey children rented in 1841, and where De Quincey himself lived often in the 1840s and 1850s.

RIGHT: De Quincey spent most of his final six years in the left half-flat on the second floor at 42 Lothian Street, where he died in December 1859, and which is marked in this picture with a plaque outside his window.

BELOW: De Quincey's daughters Margaret, Florence and Emily.

A daguerreotype of De Quincey, 1850.

minutes Haller and our illustrious friend were deep in a discussion on political economy, while Murray and Tristram appealed to him in the intervals of the debate upon their contrary views of the knowledge of Greek in Europe, at the time of Dante.[80]

Knight's portrait – like Wilson's – is rooted in actual observation, and neatly captures the way in which drugs, erudition, and eloquence defined De Quincey's public persona.

He socialized in the *London* circle as well, where for the first time he met fellow contributor John Clare, whose depressed spirits drew his sympathy, and whose poetry he much admired. 'He had studied for himself in the fields, and in the woods, and by the side of brooks. I very much doubt if there could be found, in his poems, a single commonplace image.' Clare was fascinated with 'the French style of beauty as he saw it amongst the French actresses in Tottenham Court Road' (De Quincey's polite way of referring to Clare's taste for prostitutes), but he retained in the midst of the tumult and glare of London the 'most hearty and almost rapturous spirit of admiration' for Wordsworth. To De Quincey he undoubtedly seemed a kindred spirit. Clare, for his part, had been greatly impressed by the *Confessions*, and left a vivid vignette of De Quincey: 'A little artless simple seeming body something of a child over grown in a blue coat and black neckerchief for his dress is singular with his hat in his hand steals gently among the company with a smile turning timidly round the room – it is De Quincey the Opium Eater.'[81]

The *London* for August and September featured De Quincey's notoriously unsympathetic review of Carlyle's translation of Johann Wolfgang von Goethe's *Wilhelm Meister's Apprenticeship*. Of the author: 'not the baseness of Egyptian superstition, not Titania under enchantment, not Caliban in drunkenness, ever shaped to themselves an idol more weak or hollow than modern Germany has set up for its worship in the person of Goethe'. Of *Wilhelm Meister*: 'in German novels such things may be tolerated, as also in English brothels'. Of Carlyle as translator: 'the Scotticism of "open *up*" is perfectly insufferable ... No man in these volumes opens a book; he opens it "up": no man opens a door; he opens it "up": no man opens a letter; he opens it "up"'.[82] Carlyle read the review and condemned De Quincey as 'a man who writes of things which he does not rightly understand'. In fact, De Quincey's review seems to have gone right to the heart of Carlyle's own misgivings about his translation. A year earlier he himself had complained about the novel's indecency: 'when I read of players and libidinous actresses and their sorry pasteboard apparatus for beautifying and enlivening the "moral world", I render it into grammatical English – with a feeling mild and charitable as that of a starving hyaena'. What is more, he later conceded that De Quincey 'was quite right in his animadversions on some of the Scotticisms in the first edition'.[83]

Strikingly, after dismissing Carlyle's translation of a German novel, De Quincey himself took on a similar task. In the spring of 1824, Bohte attended the annual Book Fair in Leipzig, and was surprised to discover that a new novel by Walter Scott had just been translated into German. In this there was nothing unusual: Scott was a very popular author in Germany, and rival booksellers produced translations of his novels almost as fast as they appeared. What was unusual, though, was that this new title, *Walladmor*, had not yet reached the bookshops of London. His curiosity piqued, Bohte purchased the novel and brought it back to York Street, where his suspicions were soon confirmed: *Walladmor* was a fake. It was written by Georg Wilhelm Heinrich Häring, who produced dozens of novels under the pseudonym 'Willibald Alexis', and who had already translated some of Scott's poetry.[84] When Alexis realized that Scott had not produced a new *Waverley* novel for the 1824 Fair, he enterprisingly produced his 'translation' to fill the gap in the market, and meet the insatiable public demand for Scott's work.

'We must have *Walladmor* . . . if Heaven or Earth can get it,' De Quincey wrote eagerly to Hessey in September. A review would be of 'universal interest'. Bohte's copy 'was bespoke for Sir Walter Scott', but De Quincey could borrow it on two conditions: one, it had to be returned in thirty-two hours; and two, it had to be in mint condition, which meant that no more than one-sixth of the uncut leaves could be opened. De Quincey complied, and read the 883 pages of *Walladmor* in the stipulated time, gazing up the pristine folds like someone 'in the uneasy position of looking up a chimney'.[85] In a lengthy October review, De Quincey labelled the novel 'the boldest hoax of our times', and proceeded to sketch the whole of the plot through a combination of hastily chosen set-pieces and facetious badinage. He was impressed, though: 'there is great life and stir in the movement of the story; much dramatic skill in devising situations; and an interest given to some of the characters, beyond the mere interest of the action, by the passions which move them'.[86]

Such enthusiasm had an unexpected result. The public was anxious to know more of the pseudo-*Waverley* novel, and Taylor and Hessey seized the moment by commissioning De Quincey to produce a full translation 'on the conditions of dividing profits and risk'. De Quincey, his various debts to the firm still hanging over his head, quickly agreed. He would generate forty-eight pages of copy a day. One week would bring him to the end of the first volume, three weeks to the end of the project. Once he began to read the novel carefully, however, he made a depressing discovery. It was 'trash ... absolutely beyond hope', and it needed to be thoroughly rewritten if it was to become coherent, let alone marketable. Scrambling to supply the press with eight pages a day, De Quincey forged, altered, and dramatically pruned, eventually collapsing the 'three corpulent German volumes ... into two English ones, of rather consumptive appearance'. The novel was advertised in *The Times* for 1 and 20 October, and 1, 9, and 24 November. It finally appeared on 20 December, though the volumes themselves were dated 1825.[87]

Walladmor is a Welsh tale of pirates, prisons, lovers, madness, and mistaken identity. It tells the improbable story of Bertram and Nicholas Walladmor, twin brothers who are kidnapped from their ancestral castle as babies and then brought together again in a shipwreck over twenty years later. Bertram has been raised in northern Germany and returns to Wales in search of the picturesque. Nicholas, bred up by brigands, is deeply in love with his cousin, Genevieve Walladmor, and has recently become involved in the key political episode of the novel, the Cato Street Conspiracy of February 1820, when a number of radicals plotted to assassinate all members of the British Cabinet. Revenge drives the plot. Half-crazed Gillie Godber lost her young son twenty-four years earlier when he was sentenced to death for his role in the killing of two revenue officers who were trying to stop a group of smugglers. Gillie frantically tried to save her son, but the novel's patriarch, Sir Morgan Walladmor, refused to intervene and the boy was executed. Later it is revealed that he played a part in the smuggling operation, but was not involved in the killings. After his death, Gillie curses the House of Walladmor and arranges for the kidnapping of the twins. Lady Walladmor is soon dead. Sir Morgan's life is blighted by grief.

De Quincey worked within the broad outlines of the plot, but changed a good deal.[88] Alexis's blunders in geography and chronology are repaired. One character is added, another removed, and several renamed. The St David's day celebrations are rewritten. Loads of 'rubbish – political, astrological, "and diabolical"' – are excised, as are any hints of vulgarity. Miss Walladmor is cured of her 'hysterical affection' and becomes much more dignified. The prose style is sharpened, and on several occasions De Quincey cannot resist introducing passages of conspicuous rhetorical display, as when Bertram has a dream vision of mysterious vengeance. Most notably, De Quincey recasts the entire ending of the novel, which now climaxes with the death of Miss Walladmor in the arms of Nicholas, who flees to South

America, where he dies as a soldier. Bertram is now the sole heir, and Sir Morgan approaches death in the hope that 'Grief shall be o'er at Walladmor'.[89] Public interest in the German hoax and English counter-hoax did not last long, but De Quincey's book – his second in three years – found admirers. *Walladmor* was 'well worth reading', wrote Sara Hutchinson, ' – as the style & descriptions are far very far beyond anything in merit that you meet with in such publications – seldom indeed any where – for every thing that he does must be clever'.[90]

[vi]

Margaret gave birth to a boy named Paul Frederick at Fox Ghyll on 25 November 1824.[91] He was named after De Quincey's favourite German author, Jean Paul Friedrich Richter, and was the couple's fifth child in eight years. At the same time Letitia Luff, a longstanding friend of the Wordsworths, had purchased Fox Ghyll, and taken upon herself the trouble of 'ousting the de Quinceys'. On one occasion she sent labourers into the garden in an apparent attempt to drive Margaret and the children from the cottage, though they could not be legally '*forced* to quit' for almost a year.[92] Margaret hung on, but her already battered ability to cope could not easily take these additional strains. She began slipping towards collapse.

Her husband could offer little assistance. He was chained to London, and in as much difficulty as ever. Creditors were in constant pursuit, and he told at least one of them that he had been in Boulogne, 'whither I had been compelled to go for the purpose of meeting an English friend on business'. The French port was a well-known retreat for English debtors, but De Quincey was probably just making excuses. It is doubtful that he could have found either the time or money to make such a trip, and local records in Boulogne have so far revealed no trace of him. Illness laid him low for much of October, and a broken tooth compounded his suffering.[93] He tried to produce material at a faster rate, but relentless demands for money rarely overcame his own exacting literary standards, and he chose most often to discard or withhold inferior material, rather than try to sell what did not satisfy his own judgement. It was a policy that ensured the quality of his published work and that garnered him a good deal of respect, but it all came at a heavy price.

By this stage De Quincey was dividing his loyalties between the *London* and *Knight's*. The final instalment of his 'Notes from the Pocket-Book of a Late Opium-Eater' series appeared in the *London* for December, and a rather laboured satire of Thomas Frognall Dibdin's *Library Companion*, promised to Hessey in September, was duly published in January 1825. At the same time, De Quincey assured Knight that he was anxious to assist 'your journal' in 'whatever way I can', and after three years of giving top priority to the *London*, he marked a decided shift in his allegiances when he told Knight that he considered his 'first service as always due to you'.[94]

Such a balancing act was familiar to him, and unlikely to endear him to either publication. In the event, he did not have to sustain it for long. On 4 December, Taylor reported that Henry Southern, co-editor of the *Westminster Review*, had offered to take a share in the *London*, and within weeks Taylor and Hessey had turned their magazine over to him.[95] De Quincey undoubtedly recognized that Southern's strongly utilitarian views would cramp his ability to write for the *London*, and he published nothing further in it. Remarkably, 4 December was also the day that De Quincey called on Knight and 'was concerned to find that your Journal was at an end'. He expected that Knight's friends would rally round to promote some new undertaking, and he unrealistically promised 'that you may count upon me as *one* of your men for any extent of labours'. But it was too late. The magazine was 'a loss and a trouble', Knight declared, and 'with the sixth number I determined to announce that its career was ended'.[96]

With his two main sources of income gone, De Quincey turned once again to his mother for help. Her reply was a frank financial update. His uncle Penson had recently returned from India to live with her. His income had dropped from £4000 a year to £700, and he shared her passion for home improvement. Major works were in progress at Westhay, including the construction of a new dining-room and a separate suite of apartments for Penson. Mrs Quincey's own income amounted to £600 a year, out of which £250 went to Westhay and £150 to miscellaneous expenses. She told De Quincey she was prepared to divide what remained and remit £100 a year to him: £20 could be sent now, and the rest would follow in March and May. Generous and well-meaning as she often was, though, she closed her letter with the kind of cold censoriousness that had caused so many problems in the first place. De Quincey had sent her a copy of *Walladmor*. She was unimpressed: 'I cannot expect that your literary productions either as a Translator or an Author will rise in moral tone to my point, for I suppose you must please your Readers, and unfortunately little is required.'[97]

With no obvious source of income, and his mother unable to advance the bulk of the new remittance until the spring, De Quincey cast about for employment. Taylor and Hessey still owned their publishing house, and he wrote to them about his financial difficulties, but they appear not to have offered him any work.[98] *Blackwood's* crossed De Quincey's mind as a possibility, and he put himself in touch with Wilson. 'I am quite free from opium,' he assured him disingenuously, but the drug had badly damaged his liver, and he painted a vivid picture of his distress. To fence with illness 'with the one hand, and with the other to maintain the war with the wretched business of hack author, with all its horrible degradations, – is more than I am able to bear'. Yet stepping back from his grief, De Quincey was able to acknowledge a way out. 'With a good publisher and leisure to premeditate what I write, I might yet liberate myself: after which, having paid everybody, I would sink into some dark corner, educate my children – and show my face in the world no more.'[99] Was he suggesting that William Blackwood was the 'good publisher' he needed to put himself in the clear?

Wilson may well have responded positively, but at this point De Quincey was in such dire straits that any agreement the two reached would probably have come to naught. Soon after losing his position with the *London* and *Knight's*, De Quincey had abandoned his lodgings in Pimlico and been forced into the winter streets, a no doubt harrowing reminder of his life over twenty years earlier when he had lived in the capital as a runaway. 'At this moment I have not a place to hide my head in', he reported on 24 February. He was 'lying out in the suburban fields, or sleeping in retired doorways, or upon bulkheads'.[100]

Eventually Knight tracked him down and kindly took him back to his lodgings at 7 Pall Mall East, where he gave him a room. De Quincey's ragged clothes and dirty shirt worried Sally Knight, and she asked her husband to raise the issue. 'Why, to tell you the truth,' De Quincey responded solemnly, '. . . I have, at this precise moment, no other shirt in the world. I left my last but one in a poor lodging-house in the Hampstead Road, because I could not pay for my night's lodging.' The Knights apparently saw to it that De Quincey got more shirts, but he was – to say the least – an idiosyncratic house guest, and more shirts did not necessarily solve the problem. 'His sensitiveness was so extreme,' recalled Knight, 'in combination with the almost ultra-courtesy of a gentleman, that he hesitated to trouble a servant with any personal requests without a long prefatory apology.' On one occasion, Sally Knight and the children were in the country, and Knight invited a few friends over to meet De Quincey. When the evening concluded, he tapped on De Quincey's door to bid him good night, only to find him 'sitting at the open window, habited as a prize-fighter when he enters the ring. "You will take cold," I exclaimed. "Where is your shirt?" "I have not a shirt – my shirts are unwashed." "But why not tell the servant to send them to the laundress?" "Ah! how could I presume to do that in Mrs Knight's absence?"'[101]

The Knights harboured De Quincey throughout the spring as he waited for money from his mother and apparently wrote for no one. 'It was a pleasant time of intellectual intercourse for me,' wrote Knight. '. . . I was associated with Hill, and St Leger, and De Quincey, who each thoroughly relished the conversation of the others.'[102] In the north, however, the situation had come badly unravelled. Carlyle reported that De Quincey's wife and children were 'living or starving on the scanty produce of his scribble, far off in Westmorland'. Margaret had held on to Fox Ghyll as long as she could, but in the early spring she and the children had moved out of the cottage, and into her parents' home at The Nab.[103] It is not clear whether the Simpsons were away, or whether they simply did not want her living with them, but Margaret was 'thrown entirely upon herself, with no soul (unless her eldest sister) to speak a word of comfort to her'. In July, harkening back to a time of much greater intimacy, De Quincey wrote to Dorothy Wordsworth and implored her to call on Margaret. Had he not sympathized with Dorothy thirteen years ago when Catharine had died? 'Now, when I am prostrate for a moment – and the hand of a friend would enable me to rise before I am crushed, do not refuse me this service.' He beseeched Dorothy to go and drink tea with Margaret. Talk over her distress. She must not 'lie down too much', but 'walk in the fields when it is cool', and 'take some *solid* food'.[104]

De Quincey's anxiety over Margaret was genuine, but undoubtedly exacerbated by his guilty awareness of the disparity between their respective situations. He was living in very agreeable circumstances with the Knights and waiting for money from his mother, while she took care of five young children and fought a losing battle against poverty and isolation. He was not above making excuses for failing to do all he could. 'Repeated interruptions from the Press', he assured Dorothy, had not allowed him to finish a long letter to Margaret.[105] Yet it is virtually certain that he was not at this moment writing anything for publication. He had time to finish his letter. He just did not.

The money from his mother seems finally to have arrived in late July or early August. What is more, there had been an exciting change of plan. She had promised him £100 in total, but been able to send £300![106] De Quincey's relief must have been inexpressible. Gathering his few belongings, he told Knight's servant that he was leaving to rejoin his family at Grasmere. Yet two or three days later he was still in London. Knight traced him to 'a miserable lodging on the Surrey side of Waterloo bridge', where De Quincey explained that his mother's draft was on 'a London banker at twenty-one days' sight', and that when he had tried to cash it, he had been told that he would have to wait until the three weeks had passed. He could not face apologizing to Knight's servant for the inconvenience of his unexpected return, and so he had taken lodgings and prepared to wait. Knight of course immediately explained that an advance was possible. 'Come to me tomorrow morning, and I will give you the cash,' he instructed De Quincey. 'What? how? ... Can the amount be got before the draft is due?' 'Never fear – come you – and then get home as fast as you can.' De Quincey duly appeared at Knight's, cashed the draft, and 'went away home', probably somewhere around 15 August, his fortieth birthday. He reached The Nab on 13 October. At some point he was well off his usual route north and passed through York, where he saw the famous American grammarian Lindley Murray.[107]

Why, especially given Margaret's despair, did it take De Quincey so long to get to The Nab? His perplexity about his mother's remittance is hard to understand. He had long been familiar with bank drafts, and it is highly unlikely that he was unaware of a fast method of raising money on them. Similarly, the trip to Grasmere could be made in under twenty-four hours, but on this occasion it took De Quincey two months. Illness may have waylaid him on the road, as it had on his way down to London, but at some level it seems clear that he was stalling. With £300 to pay his debts, and no publisher demanding work, De Quincey quite suddenly found himself tasting freedom for the first time in several years. He was apparently disinclined to give it up quickly. Margaret and the children gave him a great deal, but they also required a great deal, and it took De Quincey a while to muster the strength necessary to return. 'Wife and children', he once observed, '... being a man's chief blessings, create also for him the deadliest of his anxieties.' How was he as a writer to 'win his inspiration for poetry or romance from the prelusive cries of infants clamouring for daily bread'?[108]

De Quincey's reappearance at The Nab was undoubtedly an enormous relief to Margaret, and a joy for the children, particularly William and Margaret, who knew him much better than the three younger boys, Horace, Francis, and Fred. For all his reservations, De Quincey too seems to have settled in well, and he was soon caught up in the rounds of domestic life.[109] The Wordsworth women were aware of his return, and maintained a catty interest in him. 'How I should have enjoyed seeing you personate the Opium Eater,' Wordsworth's daughter Dora wrote to Edward Quillinan on 17 October. 'By the way, the poor little man is returned – he reached the Nab Thursday last.' De Quincey's drug habit was a leading source of conversation. Sara Hutchinson had little time for his pretence. 'He tells Miss W. that he had entirely left off opium before he came hither, but has been obliged to have recourse to it again; "as he has *no Shoes* to walk in & without exercise he is obliged to take it" – I suppose it is *easier* to send to the Druggists than to the Shoe Maker.'[110]

Wilson was holidaying at Elleray, and soon in touch. He and Lockhart had recently founded a literary annual called *Janus*. Would De Quincey be willing to write something for them? Wilson had also agreed to write a *Quarterly Review* article on the lectures of the Edinburgh philosopher Thomas Brown. Would De Quincey confide his views of Brown to Wilson, who did not 'despair of being able to interweave them with my own in a way not unsatisfactory to your mind'.[111] De Quincey promised to supply material for both ventures, but he resented these requests as much as ever, and he sent nothing for either one.

He was hardly in a position to be turning down work. Astonishingly, the £300 from his mother was nowhere near enough to clear his debts, and shortly after arriving at The Nab he suffered 'the miserable consequences of an Arrest for £90'. He uncharitably blamed his own bad financial decisions on others, for 'a little knowledge of business in those about me would have saved me from all these disgusting exertions and expenses'. He does not comment on life at The Nab, but the seven De Quinceys in the house – with or without Margaret's parents – could not have been easy, and in December 1825 he notified the owner of Dove Cottage, Mrs Benson, that he wanted to renew his lease 'for *five* years from next May day'.[112]

As he entered the New Year, De Quincey was hit by 'heart-withering depression'. Only three or four times in as many months could he bear 'going into the smallest company – such for instance as that of Rydal Mount'. Spring brought modest improvements in his condition. On or around 1 March he received £100 from his mother, though it disappeared almost upon arrival. At some point De Quincey held a 'general conflagration' of his papers, undoubtedly in an effort to streamline the move from The Nab back into Dove Cottage, which had stood empty – or, more accurately, jammed with his books and papers – for nearly six years.[113] The family moved in early June, and were soon re-established in their old home.

De Quincey had not sold an article in eighteen months, and already he was skidding back into serious debt, despite large lump sums from his mother, a liberal annuity, and only one rent to pay. He claimed, as he often did, that he had 'totally weaned' himself from opium, but these were fictions that he told himself in desperate or in optimistic moments. When he ingested the drug in 1804, an 'abyss of divine enjoyment' suddenly revealed itself. Now, laudanum had 'so much diminished' the sensibility 'of my stomach … that … nothing ever stimulates my animal system into any pleasure. Suffer I do not any longer: but my condition is pretty uniformly = 0'.[114] He concentrated on finding a way forward.

Writing for *Blackwood's* was again his best opportunity. Indeed, returning to it had always lurked in the background as a possibility. De Quincey had badly offended Blackwood five and a half years earlier, but surely Wilson might help to bring about a reconciliation, particularly when he pointed to the popularity and diversity of De Quincey's *London* output. Wilson caught immediately at the proposal, for having De Quincey in Edinburgh would be of immense help to him in terms of both his university lectures and his magazine writings. But De Quincey too would benefit: Edinburgh was closer and cheaper than London; Wilson took a sincere interest in him; and *Blackwood's* would pay him well.

He signalled his change of attitude in a remarkable letter to Wilson of 10 June 1826. Seven months earlier Wilson had proposed that they collaborate on a *Quarterly* review of Thomas Brown. De Quincey had shirked the obligation then, but he was now anxious to compose the article 'in partnership'. After years of pressing for just such an arrangement, Wilson must have been elated. De Quincey had one other request. Could Wilson 'find time to enquire and let me know whether there is anything in which I could assist Mr Blackwood at this moment'? Wilson's response was apparently in the affirmative. On 12 September the poet Samuel Rogers reported that 'the opium-eater ... lives in the house where we first found Wordsworth and dines with him to-day'.[115] But within a few days De Quincey had packed his box and travelled north. His London life was over. His future lay in Scotland.

TEN

Urban Intellectual

[i]

Where was all his money going? De Quincey received an allowance from his mother that totalled around £200 a year; his work for the periodical press yielded an additional £150 in a good year; and there were also the 'contributions' which he was 'not ashamed to raise among his too generous friends'. 'I judge he has actually a better income than many tolerably endowed Clergymen, Rectors too, and Gentlemen, with large families,' wrote Mrs Quincey.[1] Part of the problem was simply De Quincey's mismanagement of debt. Part of it was the various demands of a growing family. Part of it was his inveterate book-buying. And part of it was his disastrous habit of renting two, three, or even four lodgings simultaneously. There was, however, another major expenditure that clearly undermined his finances, and that he typically only hinted at: the expense of all the laudanum.

How much did the drug cost him a year? Wilson stated candidly that De Quincey's 'chief expense is opium on which he spends £150 a year'. It is notoriously difficult to determine how accurate such an estimate might be. But, to take a low figure, 25 drops of laudanum could be had for a penny (on the old currency system of 240 pennies in a pound). De Quincey's daily consumption rose as high as 12,000 drops, but usually hovered somewhere around 300 drops.[2] The higher dosage would have cost him a staggering £14 per week, though it is doubtful that he could have sustained these levels of ingestion for any length of time. The lower dosage would have cost him about 85 pence per week. Even on the assumption that De Quincey would probably have been at the lower end most of the time, it is possible to see that Wilson's calculation is not an unreasonable one, especially as De Quincey was probably spending more than the assumed price for individual doses.[3] What the exact numbers were we will never know, but De Quincey's drug habit was plainly a large and ongoing expense for someone with his commitments. It is hardly surprising that he plunged from crisis to crisis, with brief and probably opium-inspired spikes of confidence in between. Unless he could find a way to bring his expenses down drastically, it was simply not possible for him to get his head above water, no matter how hard he worked, how much he borrowed, or how much he published.

Drugs and debt crippled De Quincey in much the same way. Both relationships were rooted in denial, fabrication, and guilt. Both shared a common psychology. De Quincey invariably found that the closer he came to breaking his dependence on laudanum, the fiercer his struggles became. Similarly, he felt 'unusual happiness' when he believed himself close to deliverance from debt, and yet he trembled in the knowledge that he would be 'more furiously persecuted' for the amount that remained 'than ever I had been when my debts were heaviest'.[4] As opium was the solution to opium, so borrowing was his best answer to debt, and the two central afflictions of his life reinforced and extended one another in seamless circles of misjudgement, despondency, and alienation.

[ii]

'To our great astonishment', wrote Blackwood on 18 September 1826, De Quincey suddenly appeared from nowhere 'expressly to write articles for the Magazine'.[5] Both men undoubtedly remembered the fractiousness that had led to the breakdown of their relationship nearly six years earlier, but both were also ready to move on. De Quincey's timing was fortuitous. Lockhart had recently left Blackwood to become the editor of the *Quarterly Review*, and Maginn was proving too erratic for Blackwood to rely on with confidence. De Quincey had 'faults and failings', as Blackwood realized, 'but I know ... that he is a man of first rate abilities'. Others agreed. Next to Coleridge, said veteran *Blackwood's* contributor David Macbeth Moir, De Quincey is 'the most splendid of the mystics'.[6]

Determined on this occasion to please, De Quincey delivered a 'very elegant article of 16 pages' to Blackwood when he went to dinner at his house on 17 October. 'Gallery of the German Prose Classics. By the English Opium-Eater. No. I. – Lessing' appeared in the magazine for November and January, and featured key extracts from Gotthold Ephraim Lessing's *Laocoön* (1766), one of the most important works of German Romantic aesthetics. Maginn described it as a 'very valuable' contribution, but warned Blackwood that he 'may wait a year for such another – & by that time you will have wished [De Quincey] at the bottom of the Forth'.[7] The third and final instalment of the 'Gallery' appeared in February as a translation of E. A. C. Wasianski's *Immanuel Kant in Seinen letzten Lebensjahren* (*Last Days of Immanuel Kant*; 1804). By stating that his translation drew from several different biographical sources, when in fact he had followed almost exclusively in Wasianski's footsteps, De Quincey made it sound as though he had done more work than he actually had. At the same time, in 'The Last Days' he produces his most suggestive exploration of Kant by revealing his highly ambivalent attitude towards the philosopher, and the ways in which Kant's rationality and hypochondria invoked within him a complicated fascination.[8]

His work on the 'Gallery' series made De Quincey the natural choice to review his friend Robert Pearse Gillies's *German Stories* (1826), an anthology of tales published by Blackwood, and including the work of E. T. A. Hoffmann, Caroline Pichler, Laurids Kruse, Caroline de la Motte Fouqué, and others. Several of the tales in Gillies's collection turn upon the 'appalling interest of secret and mysterious murder', though De Quincey is not always deadly serious: 'Pleasant it is, no doubt, to drink tea with your sweetheart, but most disagreeable to find her bubbling in the tea-urn.' The review demonstrated how quickly and thoroughly he was able to reproduce *Blackwood's* characteristic blend of erudition, irony, and audacity, for it possessed 'all the mirth and Magic of the Magazine', noted Moir.[9]

Meanwhile, alone again with the children, Margaret was bearing up. Dorothy Wordsworth called in at Dove Cottage on 15 November, and sent De Quincey a 'letter of good tidings'. Her visit coincided with William's tenth birthday. She had recently seen him 'at the head of the school-boys; as it might seem a leader of their noontide games'. Horace was also 'among the tribe', and both boys were 'as healthy-looking as the best'. Yet all was not well. Margaret's manner had 'something of sadness' in it as she told Dorothy how De Quincey was 'not likely very soon to be at home'. Dorothy delicately suggested to both wife and husband that perhaps a change of plan was necessary. There were 'many impediments to literary employments to be regularly carried on in limited time, at a distance from the press, in a small house, and in perfect solitude'. If De Quincey had some kind of 'permanent engagement' in Edinburgh, 'why not settle there for the time ... Lodgings are cheap ... and provisions and coals not dear'.[10] Margaret was reluctant to discuss the idea with her husband, but bade Dorothy write to him about it. Both women undoubtedly hoped that he would see the wisdom in at least temporarily moving his entire family to Edinburgh.

Throughout these months De Quincey lived in Wilson's new home at 6 Gloucester Place, where he kept mostly to his room, and survived on coffee, boiled rice and milk, and a piece of mutton 'from the loin'. Betty, Wilson's cook, received her daily dietary instructions from him 'in silent awe ... for, had he been addressing a duchess, he could scarcely have spoken with more deference':

> Owing to dyspepsia afflicting my system, and the possibility of any additional disarrangement of the stomach taking place, consequences incalculably distressing would arise, so much so indeed as to increase nervous irritation, and prevent me from attending to matters of overwhelming importance, if you do not remember to cut the mutton in a diagonal rather than in a longitudinal form.

Betty reverenced De Quincey, but these interviews 'pretty well exhausted' her patience. 'Weel, I never heard the like o' that in a' my days,' she exclaimed; '. . . a' this claver aboot a bit of mutton nae bigger than a prin.'[11]

His opium addiction turned day into night. 'An ounce of laudanum per diem prostrated animal life in the early part of the day,' Wilson's daughter Mary recollected. 'It was no unfrequent sight to find him in his room lying upon the rug in front of the fire, his head resting upon a book, with his arms crossed over his breast, plunged in profound slumber.'[12] At night, however, De Quincey came to life, working from eight in the evening until dawn (with a break towards midnight for a walk), or entertaining the company until three or four in the morning at one of Wilson's dinner parties, where he was invariably accompanied by his laudanum bottle. 'He could do nothing without this stimulant,' recalled one guest. Wilson indulged De Quincey in his nocturnal routine. 'Now and then as I went down-stairs at seven in the morning', he remembered, 'I would meet De Quincey coming up to bed with a candle in his hand.' But Wilson also found his friend's opium habit a frustration. 'Hang you, De Quincey!' he would cry. 'Can't you take your whisky toddy like a Christian man, and leave your d——d opium slops to infidel Turks, Persians, and Chinamen?'[13]

The two friends periodically ventured out together. One day they decided to take a trip to the seashore at Portobello, just east of Edinburgh, to test for themselves the theory 'that every *tenth* wave was conspicuously larger than the other nine'. Unfortunately, when they arrived 'the Yeomanry (of Mid-Lothian, I think)' were executing with some difficulty a charge on the small beach. The sight of the men dampened Wilson's spirits by reminding him too keenly of the years when he himself had served in the ranks of military volunteers. De Quincey, however, seems to have enjoyed the outing, and he and Wilson undertook subsequent expeditions to the beaches and countryside around Edinburgh. Not so pleasant were De Quincey's infrequent trips to the university, where Wilson in his capacity as Professor of

Moral Philosophy appeared to De Quincey as a figure of fun. 'All dignity and impressiveness as a lecturer were destroyed by his drawing his forefinger down the side of his nose at the end of almost every paragraph ... The hearer began to anticipate it whenever he saw Wilson coming to a pause, and the fulfilment of the expectation raised a sense of the ridiculous even in Wilson's grandest passages.'[14]

In February 1827, De Quincey published one of his most famous essays in *Blackwood's*. 'On Murder Considered as One of the Fine Arts' seizes on the satiric and artistic approach to murder that he introduced four years earlier in his *London* article 'On the Knocking at the Gate in Macbeth'. John Williams is again the focal point of his ruminations, though De Quincey quickly broadens his discussion to explore the history of murder, as well as the practice and theory that stand behind any art form, from a good painting to a good assassination. 'People begin to see that something more goes to the composition of a fine murder than two blockheads to kill and be killed – a knife – a purse – and a dark lane,' he remarks with the deadpan aplomb that gives the essay such energy.

> Design, gentlemen, grouping, light and shade, poetry, sentiment, are now deemed indispensable to attempts of this nature. Mr Williams has exalted the ideal of murder to all of us ... Like Aeschylus or Milton in poetry, like Michael Angelo in painting, he has carried his art to a point of colossal sublimity; and, as Mr Wordsworth observes, has in a manner 'created the taste by which he is to be enjoyed'.[15]

De Quincey's breezy and ironized attitude towards violence helped to transform it into intellectual entertainment that could be marketed in a variety of fictive, impassioned, and comic guises, and that was rapidly consumed by a reading public insatiably interested in palatable versions of murder.

Several influences shaped De Quincey's approach, from the accounts of criminals in the Newgate Calendar to Kant's discussion of the sublime.[16] Yet perhaps his most important source was Wilson, who in his April 1824 instalment of the *Noctes* mapped in several of the specific features of 'On Murder'. Like De Quincey, Wilson evaluates disasters aesthetically: 'I call this a very passable fire ... I fear the blockheads will be throwing water upon [it], and destroying the effect.' He is preoccupied with criminality: 'a set of amusing articles might ... be occasionally compiled from the recorded trials of our best British murderers'. He blends brutality and intellectualism: 'one meets with the most puzzling malefactors, who perpetrate atrocious deeds upon such recondite principles, that they elude the scrutiny of the most perspicacious philosophers'. Wilson even mentions John Williams – 'the Midnight Malletteer', as he calls him – and details some of the more gruesome aspects of his crimes, such as the way in which he 'tidily and tenderly' covered up the Marr infant 'when he knew that he had pierced its gullet like a quill'. In 'On Murder', Moir asserted, De Quincey sometimes approaches Wilson 'so closely that I can scarcely persuade myself of there not being a little intermingling'.[17]

Yet while indebted to Wilson, De Quincey moves far beyond him in his brilliant conflation of ethics and aesthetics. On the one hand, the victim of a murder 'ought to be a good man', he insists. Indeed, 'severe good taste' demands that 'the subject chosen ought also to have a family of young children wholly dependent on his exertions'. On the other hand, analysing the artistry of the murderer produces the liberation and fun that come from a temporary release from social values. 'Everything in this world has two handles,' he declares. 'Murder, for instance, may be laid hold of by its moral handle ... and *that*, I confess, is its weak side; or it may also be treated *aesthetically* ... that is, in relation to good taste.'[18]

Such an approach opens the floodgates to a treatment of violence that is both disturbing and seductive. De Quincey's remark that 'every philosopher of eminence for the two last centuries has either been murdered, or, at the least, been very near it' initiates a hilarious survey in which he observes that Descartes was almost murdered by 'professional men'; Hobbes 'was not murdered' but 'was three times very near being murdered'; Malebranche was in fact murdered by Berkeley; and Kant 'had a narrower escape from a murderer than any man we read of', except Descartes. In a discussion of artistic preconception, De Quincey bemoans the fact that 'people will not submit to have their throats cut quietly; they will run, they will kick, they will bite; and, whilst the portrait painter often has to complain of too much torpor in his subject, the artist, in our line, is generally embarrassed by too much animation'.[19] These poker-faced lamentations run riot through the essay. In 'On Murder', De Quincey made violent crime a subject which could be detached from social circumstance and then exploited, intellectualized, and avidly enjoyed.

He stayed at Wilson's until the early spring, when he made at least a brief return to Grasmere, for on 6 November 1827 Margaret gave birth to their sixth child and second daughter, Florence Elizabeth. De Quincey was back in the Lakes again in July, when a tourist who watched a rush-bearing ceremony at Grasmere church observed 'the "Opium Eater" ... Mr and Mrs Wordsworth, Miss Wordsworth and Miss Dora Wordsworth'.[20] Perhaps they were all of the same party? De Quincey no doubt cherished these times in the Lakes with his family, but unremitting financial pressure meant that he could never afford to stay for long. Soon he was back in Edinburgh, though not with *Blackwood's*. A new scheme was under way.

[iii]

The *Edinburgh Saturday Post* was a small, eight-page newspaper that espoused hardline conservative views. It was against freedom for Catholics, minorities, and the working class, while it stickled for 'church and state' and 'the ascendancy of the aristocracy'. Established in May 1827, it was owned by the Edinburgh lawyer David Blackie, and written primarily by three opinionated and humourless Scottish Presbyterian ministers: Thomas Nelson, George Milligan, and Alexander Peterkin, who served as editor. It had a small circulation: 400 or 500 at the most.[21]

That summer the English Opium-Eater joined the three Scottish ministers on the *Post*, perhaps because of another falling-out with Blackwood, perhaps because he thought it might provide a more substantial income, or perhaps because he liked the idea of returning to the kind of work he had done during his days as editor of the *Westmorland Gazette*. Writing for the *Post* made some sense in terms of politics, for De Quincey knew how to produce the kind of inflated Toryism that pleased his readers and fellow contributors. Yet he was clearly the odd man out. His Englishness bristled at their Scottishness; his notoriety challenged their piety; and his irony chafed at their matter-of-factness. At *Blackwood's*, his close friendship with Wilson made him an insider. At the *Post*, his broader perspective and delight in ambiguity made him an outsider. It is difficult to say which role he enjoyed more.

If De Quincey had hoped that the new position would prove more lucrative, he was to be disappointed. The *Post* paid only small sums for an individual article, and while many of these needed to be only a couple of hundred words long, he was forced to produce scores of them in order to generate a reasonable income. What is more, the weekly schedule of the newspaper – as opposed to the monthly timetable of a magazine like *Blackwood's* – put him under incessant pressure. He wrote on a broad range of topics, from diet, drunkenness, phrenology, and religious controversy to the letters of Junius, the Bank of England, and the teaching of languages. De Quincey was the *Post*'s music critic, and reviewed several concerts, including four by the Italian Opera Company, which visited Edinburgh during the winter of 1827–8. After attending a performance of Rossini's

Barber of Seville at the Theatre Royal, De Quincey memorably described 'Miss Fanny Ayton' as sometimes forcing 'her voice beyond its physical capacities, – occasioning thus, what approximates to a scream'.[22] In a series of literary reviews he singled out Burke for possessing 'the finest and subtlest understanding that appeared in the eighteenth century'; Southey as 'a man of high moral feelings'; Wilson for his ability to generate 'the very sublime of fun'; and Macaulay for writing 'in a style stamped with the characters of youth, levity, inexperience and audacity'.[23]

Contemporary politics, including emigration, slavery, the elective franchise, free trade, and the activities of the great Irish liberator Daniel O'Connell, all came in for consideration. De Quincey shuddered at the thought of plans to repeal the Test and Corporation Acts, which 'would leave the Protestant establishment ... defenceless', and pave the way for Catholic emancipation. He used Ricardo to condemn Brougham, Malthus, and Owen, though his combination of strict political conservatism and liberal economic thought was highly anomalous, and soon made him a mark. The *Post* 'is a clever paper', wrote the rival *Standard*, 'notwithstanding that it aims to be that most incomprehensible, and preposterous of all things – a Tory political economist'. De Quincey's greatest concern during these months was the revolving door in the Prime Minister's office, where George Canning and then Lord Goderich led coalition governments in 1827, before the appointment in January 1828 of the Duke of Wellington, to whom De Quincey looked for 'nothing but uncompromising firmness', even as he detected the same reprehensible 'spirit of *trimming*' that had been a hallmark of recent Tory administrations.[24]

In addition to providing all manner of copy for the *Post*, De Quincey replaced Peterkin as its editor for September and October 1827. The paper immediately became more literary and more English, while its review section increased seven-fold to almost two full pages a week. De Quincey's most demanding task involved writing the lead political article. The *Post* was the only Edinburgh newspaper to appear on Saturday evening, which meant that it contained London news from Thursday. All other Edinburgh newspapers came out on Saturday morning, so their English news was only as recent as Wednesday. In order to obtain this advantage, the *Post* hired someone in London to buy all the London newspapers every Thursday, bundle them up by six o'clock in the evening, and place them on the express mail-coach to Edinburgh. All being well, the mail-coach would pull into the Princes Street post office around six o'clock on Saturday evening. One of De Quincey's clerks would then pick up the bundle and race back to Register Street where the *Post* offices were located. De Quincey then had under an hour to read the London news and write the *Post's* leader, which was quickly set and printed along with the rest of the newspaper. He grew greatly proficient at these short bursts of high-stress productivity, though by November either he or the *Post's* proprietor Blackie had grown dissatisfied with the arrangement, and Peterkin was reinstated as editor.[25]

Edinburgh was gradually becoming home. De Quincey probably stayed at Wilson's as he settled into fulltime work on the *Post*. Depressed, however, 'by this entire separation from my family', and recollecting besides that the education of my two eldest children was now urgently calling for my attention', he resolved to take his own lodgings, relieve some of the pressure on Margaret, and bring ten-year-old William and nine-year-old Margaret to the Scottish capital. De Quincey remembered travelling down to Carlisle to meet the two children on 3 October, but a letter of 22 September reveals that at least 'Willy' was already in Edinburgh by that date.[26] It is not known where the three lodged, but it was probably '*19 Pitt Street, 3rd flat – right hand door*', where they were certainly staying the following year. Dora Wordsworth believed that De Quincey was 'coming home every month, & then every week', and undoubtedly Margaret hoped for such a schedule, but time and money would have made it very difficult for De Quincey to leave Edinburgh.[27] It seems more likely that he and Margaret endured further months of painful separation.

Friendships were as necessary to him as ever. He saw a good deal of William Hamilton, whom he had first met on his visit to Edinburgh in late 1815, and whose 'pancyclopaedic acquaintance with every section of knowledge that could furnish keys for unlocking man's inner nature' animated and challenged De Quincey. The two discussed 'schemes literary and philosophic', as well as the deep attractions of animal magnetism. 'If you are not better engaged this evening would you come over to Coffee – with the Children?' Hamilton wrote in an undated but typically kind invitation.[28]

Wilson remained a close companion. One day he called on De Quincey and found him wrapped in a 'sort of grey watchman's coat, evidently made for a man four times his size, and bought probably at a pawnbroker's shop'. De Quincey launched into a discussion of transcendental philosophy, during which he became so vehement that his coat fell open, and revealed that he had 'nothing else on of any description whatever'. 'You may see I am not dressed,' De Quincey said. 'I did see it,' replied Wilson. De Quincey 'thought it not of any consequence'. Wilson agreed. De Quincey folded the coat 'round him and went on as before'.[29]

Thomas and Jane Welsh Carlyle became new and unexpected friends. After mauling Carlyle's translation of *Wilhelm Meister* in the *London* three years earlier, De Quincey in the *Post* spoke slightingly of Carlyle's *Edinburgh Review* article on Richter, which contained 'the greatest oversight, on the part both of editor and reviewer that I remember throughout my whole acquaintance with periodical literature'. Yet despite these negative reviews, Carlyle 'wished to know' De Quincey, and in November the two men met 'half accidentally' at the house of Carlyle's close friend John Gordon. De Quincey 'grew pale as ashes at my entrance', Carlyle observed; 'but we soon recovered him again'.[30]

He is essentially a gentle and genial little soul; only that the Liver is diseased, and the '*I-ety*' is strong and both together sometimes overset his balance. Poor soul! One of the most perfect *gentlemen* I have ever seen; and yet here he is living in *lodgings*, with two of his little children (writing for bread in the paltriest of all newspapers) while his wife with other two [*sic*] resides in Westmorland, – as a kind of 'hostage' to his creditors!

Carlyle lent De Quincey Richter's *Autobiography* and suggested that he translate it for *Blackwood's*, so that 'he might raise a few pounds and "fence off" the Genius of Hunger yet a little while ... He is an innocent man; and ... extremely *washable* away'.[31]

The following week De Quincey visited the Carlyles at their Comely Bank home and sat till midnight. He is 'one of the smallest man-figures I ever saw', Carlyle remarked; 'shaped like a pair of tongs ... When he sat, you would have taken him, by candlelight, for the beautifullest little Child; blue-eyed, blonde-haired, sparkling face, – had there not been a something too, which said, "*Eccovi*, this Child has been in Hell!"' His conversation captivated Jane: 'What wouldn't one give to have him in a Box, and take him out to talk!' she declared. Writing to John Taylor in late December, Carlyle confirmed that 'Mr De Quincey is here', and what 'may seem still stranger, he and I, the Reviewer and the Reviewed, ar[e] very good friends!'[32]

The feeling was mutual. De Quincey found Carlyle's conversation 'spiced with paradox and tending to extravagance', but 'brilliant in the extreme'. Commenting in the *Post* only days after they had met, he described Carlyle's *Edinburgh Review* assessment of 'The State of German Literature' as revealing 'a young and hopeful enthusiast, reverencing the aspirations and the destiny of human nature'. It was Jane, however, who most fully engaged De Quincey, for he experienced a severe illness at this time and she nursed him back to health, possibly even at Comely Bank. De Quincey 'retained the most profound feeling of gratitude for her motherly kindness, combined with the highest possible opinion of her character and intellectual power ... "She was, indeed, the most angelic woman I ever met upon this – God's earth!"[33]

His health did not improve for long. On an otherwise convivial evening at Hamilton's in March 1828 De Quincey looked 'rather care-stricken', and when Carlyle called round at his lodgings shortly thereafter, he found him 'invisible in bed' at two in the afternoon. 'His landlady, a dirty very wicked looking woman, said if he rose at all it was usually about five o'clock!' Just over a month later De Quincey was '"in a manner living upon opium"; and ... very low'.[34]

Action was necessary and he found the strength to effect some change. Dove Cottage 'I directed to be shut up, servants all but one dismissed, and that one sent' with the three youngest boys to live with their grandparents at The Nab, 'a paradise to *them* from the mighty barns and spacious pastures which they thus obtained for playrooms'. Horace and Francis were old enough now to go to school in Rydal.[35] Margaret, probably with Fred and her new baby Florence, then journeyed to Edinburgh to join De Quincey and their two oldest children, 'so that for three-quarters of a year we had a larger establishment in Edinburgh than in Westmorland'. De Quincey had plans to teach William Greek, but the boy told Jane Carlyle that 'his father wished him to learn it through the medium of Latin and he was not entered in Latin yet because his father wished to teach him from a grammar of his own which he had not yet begun to write'.[36]

Nothing from De Quincey had appeared in *Blackwood's* for over a year, but the March issue featured his 'Toilette of the Hebrew Lady', a translation from Anton Theodor Hartmann's *Die Hebräerin am Putztische und als Braut* (1809–10) that Moir aptly characterized as 'full of learning and most curious research'. A sequel to 'On Murder' soon followed, but it lacked the excoriating wit of the original and Blackwood rejected it.[37]

Undoubtedly stung – De Quincey could never afford to work on an article and then not sell it – he redoubled his efforts for the *Post*. In May the paper changed its name to the *Edinburgh Evening Post and Scottish Literary Gazette*, and took an even more contentiously conservative view. De Quincey was again promoted to the editor's chair, though this time he shared it with a newer recruit, the Reverend Andrew Crichton. Catholic emancipation was a focal point throughout these months, and De Quincey stepped up his attacks on the 'systematic outrageousness' of the Irish and the 'abject timidity' of the English.[38]

In the summer, Margaret and the children may have returned to The Nab, or possibly even to Dove Cottage. Perhaps De Quincey accompanied them for part of the time, but the weekly demands of his co-editorship were heavy, and he may not have been able to get away. Certainly he was in Edinburgh in September, when his old friend Matthew Davenport Hill called to learn that De Quincey had 'for the tenth time renounced opium, which he said he had not tasted for one hundred and eighty days'.[39] Before his friends, and in certain frames of mind, De Quincey may well have convinced himself of the accuracy of such a claim. In his more realistic moments, however, he knew that he was speaking false – as Hill probably suspected. His stress was too high and his dependence too deep. Opium remained a daily necessity.

At some point he returned briefly to live at Wilson's, where one evening the future novelist and terror fiction writer Samuel Warren came to dinner. De Quincey – 'dressed in black, pale, care-worn, and with a very high forehead' – spoke languidly at first, but as the evening progressed he consumed laudanum and grew more animated. 'Is such a thing as *forgetting* possible to the human mind?' he asked the company. 'Is not every impression it has once received, reproducible?' Warren 'was so absorbed with watching and listening to the conversation' that he left 'almost supperless, in spite of the kindly pressure of Mrs Wilson'.[40]

De Quincey, Margaret, and – almost certainly – the four children were back in Pitt Street by December. That month *Blackwood's* featured his essay on 'Rhetoric', which he memorably defined as the ability 'to hang upon one's own thoughts as an object of conscious interest, to play with them, to watch and pursue them through a maze of inversions, evolutions, and Harlequin changes'.[41] For Wordsworth, the article demonstrated that 'whatever [De Quincey] writes is worth reading', though he added mildly that it contained 'some things from my Conversation – which the Writer does not seem aware of'. More remarkably, 'Rhetoric' led an anonymous essayist in the popular London *Athenaeum* to urge De Quincey to put his name forward for the Professorship of Logic at the recently founded University of London. 'We adjure him, by the spirits of Aristotle and of opium ... to consider deeply before he declines offering himself as a candidate.'[42]

As Christmas neared, the Carlyles were in touch. They had recently moved to Craigenputtock in Dumfriesshire, and word had reached them that De Quincey had been enquiring after Jane. Would he come and visit? ' *Then* indeed we had made a fair beginning, and the "Bog School" might snap its fingers at the "Lake School" itself,' Carlyle wrote facetiously. But De Quincey was in no position to make such a visit, as perhaps the Carlyles realized. His 'health and spirits were much broken', and his resources soon to be 'closed up'.[43] By 27 December he had moved his family from Pitt

Street to Porteous's Lodgings, 18 Duncan Street, almost certainly in an attempt to save money and evade creditors. Margaret's health was so bad that De Quincey's mother and uncle began to discuss 'the means of giving help in case your poor Children should be left without the care of a Mother'.[44] William, now twelve years old, fell seriously ill for a few weeks in early spring, while ten-year-old Margaret was sent for more than a year to the houses of old friends, 'partly as a visitor at Professor Wilson's, but chiefly, as a visitor, almost as an adopted child', in the Darnaway Street home of Captain Thomas Hamilton, the younger brother of William Hamilton. 'Never mind her dress,' he told De Quincey gently on one occasion, as the young girl probably lacked an appropriate outfit for visiting. On another, he and his wife hoped to see the De Quinceys at dinner as soon as Margaret 'feels equal to such an exertion'.[45]

In the spring of 1829, De Quincey was hard at work for three different Edinburgh periodicals. As radicals and reformers successfully pushed forward an agenda that sought to extend the franchise and circumscribe the power of the aristocracy, De Quincey wrote *Evening Post* essays denouncing 'the sweeping hand of *liberalism*', and his first explicitly political article for *Blackwood's* on the duplicity of 'The Duke of Wellington and Mr Peel' over the Catholic Emancipation Act, which had gone forward as De Quincey feared, and which he was convinced struck a ruinous blow to the Established Church by allowing Catholics in Britain to participate fully in political and public life.[46] Yet politics were not all that preoccupied De Quincey, for at this same time he also contributed a review of the writings of the Italian poet Alessandro Manzoni to a new sixteen-page Saturday magazine, the *Edinburgh Literary Gazette*, which a few weeks later featured his three-part 'Sketch of Professor Wilson'. Cast in the form of a letter to an American tourist, the essay is most notable for the almost risible lengths De Quincey goes to in order to avoid discussing Wilson as an intellectual. After the first instalment was published, Wilson wrote directly to De Quincey to ask that the 'Sketch' be more scholarly and substantial: 'I wish you would praise me as a lecturer on Moral Philosophy ... Am I a good critic?' De Quincey promised a fourth essay devoted to Wilson's 'particular position ... in relation to modern literature', but no such essay appeared.[47] For all the kindness he had received from Wilson over the past few years, he could not bring himself to praise him as a writer and thinker.

The De Quincey family began winding up their 'Scotch affairs' in May, but it was the middle of June before they finally mounted a mail-coach – 'which mail we had wholly to ourselves' – and set off 'under a heavenly summer morning' for The Nab, which they reached early the following day.[48]

Wordsworth called shortly thereafter, but was not admitted 'on account of illness which confines [De Quincey] in a great measure to his bed'. 'This grieves me much,' Wordsworth declared kindly, 'as he is a delightful Companion and for weightier reasons, he has a large family of young Children with but a slender provision for them.' Wordsworth and his son John (De Quincey's former pupil, now an ordained clergyman) made other stops at the cottage over the next few weeks, as did the poet's daughter Dora and her friend, the author Maria Jane Jewsbury. De Quincey promised to return these compliments, but on 17 July Dora snidely observed that his '"tomorrow" for calling at Rydal Mount [has] not yet arrived'.[49]

A full explanation came two days later. 'My illness was a fever,' De Quincey told Wordsworth, 'caught, I believe from a fellow passenger on the Edinburgh Mail upon the 12th of June.' For eighteen days he had been 'utterly prostrated', existing on only a little lemonade or ginger beer, and 'scarcely able for a fortnight to crawl from room to room'. Even now, five weeks later, he was 'not ... strong enough ... to go more than a few yards into the field behind the house', though in other respects he felt 'perfectly well and in good spirits'. In the 'course of this week I shall certainly be able to come over' to Rydal Mount for a visit.[50]

At least part of this account was a fib. De Quincey may well have been sick, but there was no passenger on the Edinburgh mail, as he himself made clear when he declared that he and his family had the coach 'wholly' to themselves. Why did he tell Wordsworth otherwise? The answer seems obvious enough. Opium, not fever, had caused his illness. In order to gird himself for the departure from Edinburgh, De Quincey had probably increased his dosage. Once back in the Lakes the drug took its revenge. De Quincey wanted none of this known to the poet, who had sufficient experience of Coleridge and De Quincey to spot the telltale signs of drug abuse. When Wordsworth called, De Quincey kept out of sight. When politeness finally demanded he contact him directly, he falsified the reasons for his ill-health. De Quincey did not want an open breach, and he may even have been gratified by Wordsworth's neighbourliness, but it came too late to make much of a difference. When it had mattered, the poet had been both interfering and aloof. Now his calls seemed mainly an intrusion. For De Quincey, it was bad enough that he was still an addict; he did not need to be judged for it, especially by the Wordsworths.[51]

The return to the Lakes brought the entire De Quincey family together again, and must have occasioned enormous relief in grandparents, parents, and children. What is more, before them all lay a brief respite. Improbable though it was, De Quincey had just become an estate owner.

[iv]

Storm clouds had been gathering over The Nab for many months. When Margaret's grandfather William Park died in 1825, he left the estate to Margaret's mother Mary, though it was at the time so badly encumbered with debt that by 1828 she and her husband faced the possibility of having to sell. In desperation, they turned to De Quincey. He of course had no money, but he did have a great deal of experience with moneylenders, and he soon concocted an ingenious plan.

John Simpson urgently needed £900 to pay off a series of debts. He valued The Nab at £3000. De Quincey offered to raise a second mortgage in order to purchase the estate from him. Simpson agreed to sell to De Quincey for £2500, and in the winter and spring of 1829 letters – and then De Quincey himself – shuttled back and forth between Edinburgh, the Lake District, and Manchester as a deal gradually came together. A Mr Gerard Pendlebury was willing to advance money on The Nab, and a mortgage was finally fixed at £1400. Simpson would get the £900 he needed. The remaining £500 would go to De Quincey. Each was answerable for the interest on his share. De Quincey would eventually be responsible for discharging the £1400 principal of the mortgage. In addition, he agreed to pay interest of $3\frac{1}{2}$ per cent on the equity of £1100, on the understanding that when Margaret's parents (and her mentally impaired uncle William) died, that sum would be paid to the parties stipulated in John Simpson's will. Finally, at his death, Simpson wanted his favourite grandchild, De Quincey's eldest son William, to receive £500, and De Quincey undertook to guarantee this sum as well. In total, then, he would eventually pay out £3000 – his father-in-law's estimate for the value of the property – and become owner of The Nab. The deal hit various snags along the way, but came together in May, and by the middle of June the De Quinceys were installed at their estate.[52]

In the long term, the plan was madness. Given De Quincey's financial history, there was not the remotest possibility that he was going to be able to keep up with even the interest payments. But, as he rather disarmingly put it, 'You know there is such a thing as buying a thing and yet not paying for it,' and in the short term, everybody won.[53] Simpson paid his debts. De Quincey put £500 in his pocket. And poor Mr Gerard Pendlebury remained blissfully unaware of the frustrations in store for him.

Liberated from his most pressing anxieties, De Quincey wanted to share his good fortune, and he wrote ebulliently to the Knights to ask them to come and visit:

Think what a glorious El-Dorado of milk and butter and cream cheeses and all other dairy products, supposing that you like those things, I can offer you, morning, noon, and night. You may absolutely bathe in new milk, or even in cream, and you *shall* bathe if you like it. I know that you care not much about luxuries for the dinner-table, else, though our luxuries are few and simple, I could offer you some temptations: mountain lamb, equal to Welsh; char, famous to the Antipodes; trout and pike from the very lake within twenty-five feet of our door; bread, such as you never presumed to dream of, made of our own wheat.

The Knights were unable to take up De Quincey's invitation, but in October the Hills accepted what was probably a very similar offer.[54]

De Quincey enjoyed extolling the rural virtues of his new home, but it was soon clear that The Nab was not the haven he had hoped it would be. Space was at a premium. The house was much larger than where the De Quinceys had been living in Edinburgh, but at least sixteen people were squeezing into it: the De Quinceys and their six children; Margaret's parents and uncle and possibly some of her sisters; and several servants. The bustle it occasioned was too much for Margaret, who was pregnant again, and so De Quincey planned to take her, two children, and two servants, and remove to Dove Cottage, which of course he was still renting. Some time that autumn a boy, Julius, was born, though it is unclear whether he arrived at The Nab or Dove Cottage.[55]

Blackwood's was missing him, though he had little inclination to write, and there was not much time or quiet had he wanted to. 'When he wons in Westmorland', Wilson wrote in the *Noctes* for December 1829, 'he forgets Maga, and a' the rest o' the civileezed warld.'[56] It was – it need hardly be said – a lifestyle he could not afford, and by the New Year deep cracks were visible in the financial dyke he had constructed around The Nab. De Quincey needed work, and he did not much mind who gave it to him. He wrote to liberal-minded friends. Did Knight know how 'a man might make his way to a professorship in the London University'? Hill was one of the founding members of the Society for the Diffusion of Useful Knowledge, which sought to make good books available at low prices to the working class. Did he know of 'any literary work, tolerably lucrative'? De Quincey also tapped Tory contacts. To Blackie, he promised 'continued and effectual help'.[57] Lockhart was one of the advisers on John Murray's new Family Library series, and in reply to De Quincey's 'application' he suggested works on either the Lake District or Oxford, to which De Quincey responded with an offer to produce '*A History of the Crusades*' or a 'Digest ... of the *Corpus Historiae Byzantinae*'.[58]

Wisely, De Quincey contacted Blackwood as well, and placed before him a host of new proposals. Might he be interested in a collection of *New Canterbury Tales*, a book patterned on both the Chaucerian precedent and the Gothic *Canterbury Tales* (1797–1805) of the sisters Harriet and Sophia Lee? 'I am perfectly willing', Blackwood answered, 'to give you Two Hundred Guineas for the entire copyright of your work should it extend to two volumes of 400 pages.' De Quincey also assured Blackwood he had 'several papers in a state of forwardness' for the magazine, including one on the Italian philosopher Giordano Bruno, another on the history of logic, and a third 'on the flight of the Calmuck Tartars from Russia to the frontiers of China'.[59]

Wordsworth called in mid-February and saw De Quincey (perhaps for the last time) looking very well, and busy on his *Canterbury Tales*. But shortly thereafter Margaret was 'at the point of death from jaundice', and one of the children contracted erysipelas. More bizarrely, in March 'a servant woman of mine went mad, and threatened and continually plotted destruction to herself and several persons of my family ... For a fortnight and a little more, were we obliged to keep a howling – yelling maniac in our house.' In the midst of this chaos De Quincey tried to write and seems to have produced a reasonable amount, though he informed Blackie that what he had attempted for him was 'so poor and so unsuitable, and run out to such a length, that I have burned it'.[60]

He had to get away. London was a possibility, but it was soon supplanted by Edinburgh. It could not have been an easy decision, especially given Margaret's poor health and their newest baby. At the end of March, De Quincey missed 'meeting the interest on a large mortgage', and was soon harassed by 'disagreeable business' undoubtedly related to The Nab. On 'Monday afternoon May 24' he returned alone to Edinburgh, less than a year after he had packed up his family and moved back to the Lakes.[61] Wilson once again provided him with a room at his house in Gloucester Place. De Quincey never ceased to fantasize about living in the Lake District as a gentleman scholar, but he spent most of his career in the city as a deadline-driven intellectual.

Returning to the routine he had established four years earlier when he had first moved into Gloucester Place, De Quincey worked long hours and wrote often in consultation with Wilson. His health was as precarious as ever, and at one point 'an accidental blunder' of Wilson's cook inflicted upon him a dreadful colic. Peaks in his opium ingestion brought both stamina and 'continued ... suffering from Diarrhoea'.[62] He remained reclusive. The University of Edinburgh student and future historian John Hill Burton called at Wilson's in the hope of seeing him, but 'the Opium-Eater ... chose neither to appear in the drawing-room nor the dining-room'. On another evening, however, Blackwood's eldest son Alexander called on some matter of business and did De Quincey 'the favour of sitting a half hour with me'.[63]

Wilson brought his house guest alive in the pages of *Blackwood's* when he gave 'The Opium-Eater' a large speaking part in the *Noctes* for April, May, June, and August 1830. The portrait contains caricature, but it is rooted in Wilson's many years of intimacy with De Quincey, and communicates a lively sense of what it was like to watch and listen to him as he discoursed on Wordsworth, Ricardo, Kant, Coleridge, sublimity, education, periodical literature, and much else. The Opium-Eater is seen '*filling up drops of laudanum in the minimeter to 120*', and boasting that he has reduced his daily dose of laudanum to five hundred drops.[64] His hours are erratic: he lies 'in bed till sax o'clock o' the afternoon'. His digestion is delicate: 'Edinburgh beef and mutton, however long kept, are difficult of mastication.' His manners are impeccable: 'were I ask't to gie a notion o' your mainners to them that had never seen you, I shou'd just use twa words, Urbanity and Amenity'.[65] His writings are highly prized. 'Will you accept from me ... an essay, to be entitled, "Comparative Estimate of the English and Scotch Character?"' the Opium-Eater asks Christopher North. 'My dear sir,' North responds, 'when did I ever decline an article of yours?'[66]

In August, De Quincey began a period of great productivity for *Blackwood's* with the publication of 'Kant in his Miscellaneous Essays', which he addressed to Christopher North, and which he revised after Wilson read the conclusion and suggested that it should be extended. Confrontational to the point of character assassination, De Quincey describes Kant as 'something of a brute' who 'never read any thing at all'.[67] Yet in the essay he follows Kant in identifying God, freedom, and immortality as the three major concerns of philosophy; successfully outlines the key difference between the categories of Aristotle and Kant; and comments incisively on a number of minor works, including *Toward Perpetual Peace* (1795).[68]

Politics, too, fixed De Quincey's attention, and from September through February he produced five jeremiads in direct response to the ominous events of the day. On the Continent, the second French Revolution took place in late July 1830. The Bourbons were finally overthrown, and the Duc d'Orléans proclaimed king. Revolution spread across Europe. In Britain, there was mounting pressure on the government to address such issues as the enormous national debt and the abolition of slavery. William IV had succeeded to the throne following the death of George IV in late June, and Tories feared that he would prove more sympathetic to reform and the Whigs. In the autumn there were disturbances throughout rural southern England, as protesters destroyed machinery and demanded higher wages. Wellington's government collapsed in November, and the Whigs, under Lord Grey, came to power for the first time in a generation. Lord John Russell introduced a Reform Bill in March 1831.

Stunned by these incidents, De Quincey in the five essays ranges across British history in order to demonstrate the disastrous consequences of reform. He draws extensively on the anecdotes and statistics that filled the mass media, as well as on the rhetoric and ideas of Milton, Wordsworth, and especially Burke. 'REVOLUTION! – French Revolution! – Dread watchword of mystery and fear! – Augury of sorrow to come! ... Is it then indeed true that another French Revolution has dawned?'[69] Expansive and overheated, the series constitutes De Quincey's reflections on the second Revolution in France, and the momentous events that followed in its wake.

These articles give voice to genuine political anxiety, but they were also written to order. Gone were the days when De Quincey mocked Blackwood over the dullness of his magazine, or gave notice that he was willing to become its Atlas. From the late 1820s onward Blackwood commissioned specific political articles, and De Quincey complied with his directions to the point of obsequiousness. 'I shall of course immediately attend to your wishes,' he wrote to Blackwood in August. And 'with respect to the sug-gestion as to the higher grounds of religious principle', he told him a month later, ' – I assure you that I have of late years most sincerely held such views myself.'[70]

Alongside his political work, De Quincey in September and October published his lengthy review of James Henry Monk's recent biography of the great eighteenth-century Cambridge classicist Richard Bentley. De Quincey devised the review in collaboration with Wilson, and is heavily indebted to Monk throughout, but he also uses his extensive classical knowledge to point to errors in Monk, who duly corrected them when a second edition was called for.[71] The Bentley articles were generally credited to De Quincey's old nemesis William Maginn. 'They are not written by me,' he rejoined, 'but by a much cleverer fellow, and a much better scholar, Thomas De Quincey.' Moir compared 'what the other periodicals have said on Monk's book', and was confident that 'the eloquence and learning of Maga's critiques will shine more distinctly preeminent. Scholastic literature is evidently De Quincey's forte, and within that magic circle not one of his contemporaries ... is fit to try a fall with him.'[72]

If *Blackwood's* featured classical studies as a kind of alternative to its political agenda, it also used classicism to serve that agenda, as is clear in De Quincey's January, February, May, and June 1831 review of a series of new books on Samuel Parr, the Whig scholar and polemist. The Parr articles display the same voluminous classical erudition that is so much in evidence in the Bentley review, but De Quincey's assessment is blatantly political. Sydney Smith called Parr 'by far the most learned man of the day', and Macaulay referred to him as 'the greatest scholar of the age'. For De Quincey, however, a first-rate liberal makes a third-rate classicist, and after aligning Parr with the new Whig government, he dismisses him as vain and vulgar.[73]

Blackwood continued to pay for De Quincey's contributions at the rate of ten guineas a sheet (sixteen printed pages), and he added to this total when articles were delivered in a timely way. Yet De Quincey frequently sent promised material late, and rarely did he send an essay in its entirety, so that Blackwood grudgingly found himself doling out money in a convoluted series of instalments, advances, credits, and loans. When De Quincey complained of poor treatment or became befuddled by arrangements he himself had requested, Blackwood brought him firmly into line. 'I simply adhered to a written agreement, which I concluded you should have been as much aware of as I was,' he informed De Quincey in one testy exchange. '... I do not expect blame to be thrown upon me if I adhere to my ordinary rules of business.'[74]

But Blackwood was not all business. In November he responded generously when De Quincey turned to him in crisis. It was Margaret. She had now been without her husband for six months, and she was again coming undone. Burgeoning personal and financial strains appear to have forced her to leave The Nab shortly after he departed for Edinburgh. She and the seven children took lodgings either with or near Margaret's sister Anne, most likely at Lingstubbs, a farmhouse lying just west of Penrith. Living in lodgings, however, soon produced its own set of problems, and Margaret was now 'threatening suicide', a 'condition of spirits' De Quincey took seriously, as 'at a very early period of her life she really did make an attempt of the kind she now threatens'. He sent her long letters addressing 'each particular grievance' and 'endeavouring to tranquillize her mind', but money was what was needed. At five in the morning on 20 November, an exhausted De Quincey wrote a desperate letter to Blackwood asking him for yet another advance. Under the circumstances, Blackwood could hardly have refused him, but he replied in a 'very liberal manner' with 'over-pay' for De Quincey's 'exertions'.[75]

Something had to be done. The November crisis passed, but living apart had never worked well for either husband or wife, and Margaret was now worn to the breaking point. De Quincey's solution – long ago suggested by Dorothy Wordsworth and perhaps at the heart of Margaret's most recent cries for help – was to move his entire family to Edinburgh. Initially, he wondered if Blackwood might do him the favour of obtaining some information about the furnished houses in Portobello, but in the event he moved from Wilson's to 7 Great King Street, an expensive address in Edinburgh's New Town. Margaret and the children travelled to Edinburgh in late December, and the family was installed in their new home by early in the New Year.[76]

De Quincey and Margaret never again lived apart. Her mental and physical health remained fragile, as indeed did his, but they both tried hard to support each other, and to care for their children. 'Even during the long night-watches . . . my mother was with him much of the time,' their daughter Florence remembered. De Quincey needed 'a certain amount of perfect quiet, though not necessarily of solitude . . . for the shaping of his work', and Margaret carefully trained the children 'to respect his busy times'. Husband and wife superintended 'the behaviour of the children at the dinner-table, examining each little scaramouch to see that it had not effected an entrance with unwashed hands'. Florence especially recalled her father's tenderness on those occasions when her 'small ill-regulated uproar' in the middle of the night brought his 'kind, careful arms', which rescued her 'from a weariful bed' and carried her 'to the bright warm room', where she enjoyed the 'dignity and delight of "sitting up with papa"'.[77]

Yet in spite of the consolations it brought, Great King Street created as many problems as it solved. De Quincey claimed that he took such a large house with the intention of keeping boarders, but it is difficult to believe that he seriously pursued this scheme. The rent was approximately £200 a year, and when he fell into arrears he 'dipped into a new term' in order to defer payment.[78] At some level De Quincey seems to have felt that he deserved to live in a beautiful home such as Greenhay or Westhay or Great King Street – that as an adult he deserved the luxury that had surrounded him as a child – and he repeatedly convinced himself that 'his own powers of work' would enable him to meet his heavy financial responsibilities. Yet within months he conceded that renting Great King Street brought new 'misfortunes', and that he was 'not wholly without reasons for self-blame'.[79] Later, in a much less generous moment, he criticized Margaret, who 'brought me into heavy difficulties ... Not that she had any expensive habits in her own person, but that she was incapacitated by temper from controlling a household of vicious servants such as we found requisite in Great King Street and she was preyed upon openly and secretly by grasping relatives.'[80]

Creditors soon descended. Thomas Benson sent a representative to call on De Quincey to enquire about payments due on Dove Cottage. De Quincey bought himself some time by paying part of what was owed, but Benson's representative soon returned to demand 'payment of a sum considerably larger', which De Quincey could not find. Wednesday, 11 May 1831 marked a new low, as he came for the first time into contact with the Scottish legal system. John Carfrae, a bookseller, entered a 'Protest' (the formal declaration in writing that a bill has been presented and payment refused) against him for £37.16s.6d.[81] No other court action followed, so De Quincey must have been able to pay or placate the bookseller.

Prostrated by influenza in early July, he suspended work on 'several articles in preparation' and turned his thoughts back to politics, almost certainly on instructions from Blackwood.[82] 'On the Approaching Revolution in Great Britain' was published in August, and in the article De Quincey ratcheted up his rhetoric from previous assaults on Reform by writing in the guise of an elderly English gentleman who feels not only betrayed by the new Whig government, but certain that he faces the 'absolute ruin' of his property and investments. 'At a time of life when energy languishes ... I am consumed with a burning – a just – I will presume to say, a righteous indignation at the atrocious scenes now passing in this country.' No matter how far he himself sunk into poverty, De Quincey always wrote for *Blackwood's* as a champion of aristocratic privilege. Yet that summer his private life must also have seemed a touchstone of British public life, for in both he saw deepening unease and widespread instability.[83]

Beset by 'illness or nervousness' throughout the autumn, De Quincey wrote nothing for *Blackwood's*.[84] With no money coming in, his situation grew critical, especially at The Nab, where payments on the property were badly in arrears, and Pendlebury was threatening to sell. In December or early January, De Quincey travelled first to London, most probably to speak with moneylenders, and then on to visit his mother, from whom he also hoped to raise funds. 'From the love we all bear to the place', Margaret wrote to the solicitors representing Pendlebury, 'there need be no doubt that we will all of us make any sacrifice rather than endanger its loss.'[85]

De Quincey returned to Edinburgh on the afternoon of 31 January. His trip had not been wholly successful. Mrs Quincey came to his aid once again by agreeing to pay the £180 owing on The Nab, but she stipulated that the money was a loan to be recouped out of his annual £200 allowance, which would now be reduced to £100 for two years. The consequences of such a bargain were immediately apparent: in the enervating see-saws of his existence, the situation at The Nab temporarily improved, while in Edinburgh his circumstances further declined. Less than a day after his return, he wrote distractedly to John Wilson's brother Robert, a banker, to explain that he was facing 'utter ruin' if he could not 'turn aside' a bill for £30. Wilson apparently sent the money, for De Quincey did not suffer prosecution. At around this time he also obtained £110 from his sister Jane, though that sum too quickly disappeared – to Dove Cottage, to The Nab, to Great King Street, to the necessities involved in raising a family of seven.[86]

In an effort to retrench, De Quincey sold some of his books (a sure sign of desperation), and on 15 May he moved his family from Great King Street to 1 Forres Street, a less expensive address but still in the New Town.[87] His children seem to have borne up fairly well under these strains. It was almost certainly at this address that two of his younger sons played one day with the future author Francis Espinasse, who described them as 'flaxen-haired, fair-complexioned, with angelic looks and English accents'. Their 'name was De Quincey', they said proudly, and 'their papa ... was "an author"'. On 23 July, even De Quincey himself had reason to be pleased. 'My debts ... are now under *two* hundred,' he assured Blackwood, ' – whereas 3 months ago they were little under *three*.'[88]

Overall, however, his situation continued to worsen. 'Dunned at times furiously: and at times ... at my wits' end', De Quincey only a day later could not pay 'for Water Duty ... and *there* the penalty is of course to lose this sine-qua-non of life'.[89] On 2 August he faced a 'small debt case', and twelve days later he was forced to leave home 'suddenly in expectation of a process of arrest'. Then, some time after 2 September, he was again forced into hiding. 'It would be dangerous to me, that any servant should know where I am,' he reported to Blackwood; but his son Horace would bring 'any communication ... left at Forres Street, in 15 or 18 minutes at farthest'.[90]

With so many creditors at his heels, De Quincey inevitably faced a curious procedure in Scottish law known as being 'put to the horn'. In Scotland, a debtor could not technically be imprisoned, so a legal fiction developed in which the Crown demanded that a debtor satisfy his creditors. If the debtor failed to do so, he was held to be in violation of a royal command, and his offence was publicly announced by a messenger-at-arms, who blew three blasts on a horn at the market-place in Edinburgh, and then denounced the 'rebel' by name. De Quincey suffered this very public humiliation on a number of occasions, the first of which was 20 September 1832 for a debt of £10 owing to his former Duncan Street landlord John Cathcart Porteous.[91]

The legal progression was simple: from 'protest', to 'horning', to prison. De Quincey gave Porteous £5 at the time of the horning, but he still owed him £5, and when it was not paid as promised, Porteous took the next step. On 2 October he had De Quincey imprisoned in the Canongate Tolbooth, a spired, dark-mouthed building near the foot of the Royal Mile. De Quincey's mortification must have been acute, and within hours he had negotiated his release on the grounds of ill-health. 'The usual pressure upon myself ... is just now at high pressure mark,' he told Blackwood, ' – a furnace 7 times heated.' Three weeks later De Quincey was again arrested, but was able to purchase his release with the money raised 'by a composition'. In mid-December he returned to the prison according to the conditions of the bail bond, but was liberated the same day, probably due to the forbearance of Porteous.[92]

In the middle of these miseries, tragedy struck. 'We have had the misfortune, which to us is a very heavy one, of losing our youngest child – a boy of rather more than 3 years old,' De Quincey wrote to William Hamilton. Julius 'died in his mother's arms'. Margaret's shock was aggravated by the fact that she had not 'been informed of his danger by the Surgeons', and that when she rose 'at midnight to resume her charge of him, she mistook the extreme tranquillity of his death for sure indications of his recovery; and was not undeceived until within one half minute before he expired'. De Quincey went on to make a peculiar request. Margaret wanted the child buried in Grasmere, and De Quincey had been 'informed that the proper course – is to ask permission of some friend, who may happen to have a vault or a piece of burying ground in Edinburgh: for depositing the coffin there during the next 9 or *at the utmost* 12 months'. Did Hamilton have a vault in Edinburgh? 'Would it be possible or convenient for you to grant us the permission we are seeking?'[93]

It is not known how Hamilton responded, but Julius was buried in Edinburgh, and the straitened circumstances of the family make it highly unlikely that he was ever moved. During preparations for the funeral, De Quincey was forced to flee when one of his creditors somehow ascertained that he was at home, and sent an officer around to arrest him. He could not even grieve in peace. He later wrote mournfully of Julius: 'With respect to a little child of my own, whom we lost at three years old, I made a discovery –

which but for the merest accident I never *should* have made – that *his* happiness had been greatly disturbed in a way that afflicted me much.' Five months after Julius's death, on 27 February 1833, De Quincey and Margaret's eighth and last child, Emily Jane, was born.[94]

[v]

'I myself, though much debilitated ... have never wholly given up writing,' De Quincey declared in the summer of 1832. Indeed, though there were occasional periods of dormancy, he continued to deliver copy at a remarkable rate given the turmoil that constantly threatened to engulf him. Two and a half years earlier he had asked Hill about the possibility of writing for the Society for the Diffusion of Useful Knowledge. Nothing came of his enquiries then, but De Quincey had been back in touch with Knight, who was currently publishing a 'Gallery of Literary Portraits' under the Society's auspices, and who was pleased to receive from De Quincey a 'spirited memoir of Milton', which he published that summer.[95]

De Quincey continued to write only about a third of what he promised to Blackwood, but that still meant a good deal of material. His 1832 novel *Klosterheim: or the Masque* was published in a single volume, and appeared under the signature of 'THE ENGLISH OPIUM-EATER'. De Quincey's attitude towards the project was workmanlike, to say the least. Do you 'wish to have Klosterheim lengthened'? he asked Blackwood. '... I can throw in a chapter of 8–10, or 12 pp ... if you think this of importance.'[96] Blackwood evidently did think it 'of importance', and De Quincey duly supplied an extra chapter.

Set at the midway point of the Thirty Years' War (1618–48), *Klosterheim* concerns Maximilian, an avenging Catholic hero whose rightful place as Landgrave has been usurped by a duplicitous tyrant in league with the Protestant forces of Sweden. Dressed as a mysterious masque, Maximilian perpetrates a series of murders and abductions that are finally shown to be fabrications, the product of special effects and 'victims' who go willingly. In the sublimely operatic conclusion, the Landgrave unveils the body of a dead woman. He believes her to be Maximilian's lover Paulina, but she is in fact his own daughter Adeline, whose execution he has unwittingly commissioned. The Landgrave dies, and Maximilian is restored to his rightful place as ruler of Klosterheim.

On one level the novel is a highly conventional example of the kind of Gothic romance made famous by Ann Radcliffe in the 1790s. On another it is De Quincey's most ambitious exploration of intrigue and betrayal, and reveals the perplexed nature of his own political sympathies, for in *Klosterheim* the Protestant De Quincey gives the Catholics the victory, and confounds his attraction to power with his affinity for the outcast. On still another level, the novel is redolent of De Quincey's private experience. Like the mind of the opium-eater, the city of Klosterheim is strangely cut off from its surroundings. In the day various authority figures attempt to maintain order, while at night chaos reasserts itself in ways that are both inspired and frightening.[97] Crabb Robinson declared that *Klosterheim* 'made no noise – perhaps because of its lumbering style and forming one small volume only', but Coleridge asserted that 'in purity of style and idiom' the novel reached 'an excellence' to which Walter Scott 'appears never to have aspired'.[98]

De Quincey was also hard at work for *Blackwood's*. His 'Prospects of Britain', published in April 1832, takes as its subject a pamphlet by James Douglas of Caver, and communicates the pervasive sense of crisis in the Tory ranks as the government prepares to enact the Great Reform Bill. Exactly one year later, his review of Thomas Gordon's *History of the Greek Revolution* charts the 'exceedingly romantic and scenical character of the leading incidents' in the War of Greek Independence, but is perhaps most memorable for its spiteful attack on Lord Byron's 'intense vanity'.[99] Finally, in October 1832, De Quincey launched his six-part series on 'The Caesars', his most detailed historical study and his first collection of biographical essays. Drawing extensively on Suetonius's *Lives of the Caesars* and the *Historia Augusta*, he weaves together his preoccupation with political intrigue, classical scholarship, black humour, the moral efficacy of Christianity, the expansion and decay of empires, and the 'hideous excesses of the Roman Imperator'.[100]

Yet despite these strong levels of productivity, the relationship between De Quincey and Blackwood had become increasingly overshadowed by irritation and unpredictability. It took three months of haggling before Blackwood was able to extract De Quincey's review of Gordon, and in the end he published only one of the three instalments that De Quincey sent to him, a decision that the proud and penurious De Quincey found very difficult to endure. In March 1833, De Quincey accepted a dinner invitation from Blackwood with 'great pleasure', but shortly thereafter the relationship between the two men appears to have soured, and nothing from De Quincey appeared in the magazine over the course of the following fourteen months, after which time Blackwood printed the final three instalments of 'The Caesars' for June, July, and August 1834.[101] The following month Blackwood died, and his magazine passed into the hands of his sons, Alexander and

Robert. In the meantime, De Quincey had embarked on a long-term relationship with a radical Edinburgh magazine that was established in direct opposition to *Blackwood's*, and that pushed his career in new and controversial directions.

ELEVEN

Tales of Terror

[i]

He liked to feel the noose tighten around his neck. He enjoyed panic. He sought alienation. He courted anxiety. These emotions brought intensity to his experience. They allowed him to develop an image of himself as the focus of great attention, as a person whose actions mattered, as someone fighting heroically against odds that would have defeated others. 'Under these difficulties, that to most men would be overwhelming when combined into one simultaneous storm, I . . . have continued . . . to fight my way right and left,' he declared to Alexander Blackwood. Earlier, after battling through a list of ailments that included despondency, hunger, and acute physical pain, he assured Robert Blackwood that, in similar circumstances, 'I do really think that not many men could have struggled at all.'[1]

Playing the victim enabled De Quincey to indulge his passion for the sublime. Trapped 'on the deck of a burning ship', or at his 'last gasp', or 'tied to a stake to be baited by my creditors', he transformed himself into the central figure in a Gothic drama of flight and pursuit. 'Ever since I knew you', he once told Hessey, 'I have had to struggle with difficulties more like the cases of romance than real life.'[2] And if he was not actually being pursued, his imagination conjured demons. 'He was constantly beset by idle fears and vain imaginings,' reported Knight. 'Various trivial obstacles', Hill observed, '. . . were continually acting as lions in his path.'[3] De Quincey 'was haunted by an idea that he was being pursued by his various and no doubt much-tried landladies,' said Eliza Priestley. John Hill Burton recounted how De Quincey once pled the 'absolute necessity' of borrowing seven shillings and sixpence, only to find that he had a fifty-pound banknote in his pocket.[4] De Quincey mismanaged his time and money because to a considerable degree he wanted to be hounded. The pursuit was incessant because there are 'people that he *won't allow* himself to be released permanently from', as his daughter Margaret emphasized. He had a taste for suffering, a craze for being despised. 'I am sure it is not in my character to exaggerate,' he told Wordsworth.⁵ The opposite was true.

Victimization brought De Quincey comfort and camouflage. It enabled him to dodge his responsibilities. He was ill. It was not his fault. Physical pain left him unable to function. He 'would lay down his life if he might but get up and walk; but he [was] powerless as an infant, and [could not] even attempt to rise'. On one level laudanum shackled him, but as a ready and inexhaustible pretext for missing deadlines and evading agreements, it released him on another. 'Perfect weakness is often secure,' he stated: 'it is by imperfect power, turned against its master, that men are snared and decoyed.' Letters in which he portrayed himself as 'in the slough of despond' were 'like the cuttle fish', his daughter Florence remarked. Their main purpose was 'to throw ink in the eyes of the enemy, and himself' for failing to deliver some manuscript.⁶

Opium played a vital – and typically paradoxical – role in this economy. On the one hand, it rounded off the sharpest edges of his anxiety. Without opium 'life would have been intolerable to him; and certainly he would never have been able else to write what he had written'. Yet on the other, the drug deepened his unease, and he welcomed it for that reason. Under the 'parching effects of opium', he acknowledged, '... mole-hills are inevitably exaggerated by the feelings into mountains'. Recalled Florence: 'It was an accepted fact among us that he was able when saturated with opium to persuade himself and delighted to persuade himself (the excitement of terror was a real delight to him) that he was dogged by dark and mysterious foes.'⁷ Opium terrorized De Quincey, but that was part of the attraction. In his world, the line between the conscious and the unconscious frequently gave way. His dreams were invaded by a figure he called the 'Dark Interpreter', 'a mere reflex of my inner nature'. The Interpreter, however, 'will not always be found sitting inside my dreams', warns De Quincey. At times the internal becomes the external, and the Interpreter lives 'outside, and in open daylight'.⁸

The fierce pressures that he allowed to build around him had a practical side. They forced him to produce. Writing was 'always an extreme labour and difficulty to him', and the more addled he was by poverty, debt, and addiction, the more pressure he was under to deliver, with the result that he usually did. The chaos that seemed to be keeping him from writing was actually driving him to it. 'Failing ... dire necessity', he affirmed, 'I believe that I should never have written a line for the press.' Further, these pressures often shaped his subject matter. He was a keen observer at the spectacle of his own distress, and he actively re-lived past trauma and brought on new anguish as a means of generating copy and amplifying emotion.⁹ 'Long disappointment – hope for ever baffled, (and why should it be less painful because *self*-baffled?) – vexation and self-blame, almost self-contempt ... these feelings had impressed upon my nervous sensibilities a character of irritation – agitation – restlessness – eternal self-dissatisfaction.' Drugs greatly facilitated his quest for his own degradation. De Quincey claimed that the pains of withdrawal invariably forced him back under the tyrannies of laudanum, but there was a part of him that revelled in the loss of power brought about by addiction, and that derived a masochistic pleasure from his repeated acts of self-annihilation.[10] In De Quincey, an arrogantly high opinion of his own intellectual abilities was confounded by an implacable streak of self-laceration.

Yet De Quincey's complicated pursuit of his own mortification did not always provide the pleasures he sought. When the drugs wore off, or his fantasies wore out, he seems often to have been genuinely surprised to find himself – and on many occasions his family – in seas of trouble, and he worked frantically to get everyone ashore. 'Anxiety from fear, is bad: from hope delayed, is bad: but worst of all is anxiety from responsibility, in cases where disease or weakness makes a man feel that he is unequal to the burden.'[11] Legal officers and creditors pursued De Quincey in droves, as the brutal black and white of the court records demonstrate, and he hid, fled, and holed up in an exhausting effort to stay one step ahead of them. Often without enough money for food, clothing, or warmth, De Quincey and his family lived in the certain knowledge that, if he was imprisoned again, their already grim circumstances would steeply decline. 'All weakness is suffering and humiliation,' he asserted, 'no matter for its mode or its subject.'[12]

William Muir, a solicitor in the Scottish Supreme Court, was one of those actively hunting De Quincey, and in a document addressed to Alexander Wilkie, an Edinburgh messenger-at-arms, he details the activities of his various officers and assistants. De Quincey's house was watched 'this day for nearly 4 hours', Muir reported, 'but could not find him'. A day later assistants were 'again watching in the neighbourhood' and 'searching over the walks', but could 'obtain no trace of him'. Weeks passed without success. There was 'no certain intelligence', 'some persons asserting' that De Quincey was 'at the Lakes, and others that he was in the environs of Edinburgh'. Eventually, 'continuing ... enquiries ... on repeated occasions' produced the report that De Quincey had been 'seen lately in the Meadows'. Officers staked out the area 'at different times of the day & upon different days, but did not fall in with him'.[13]

At last, a break. An assistant waited a 'whole day in the Meadows where in the Twilight he discovered a person corresponding to the marks given him of Mr De Quincey'. He 'followed & watched through many turns & windings & finally lost sight of him about the South end of Clerk Street'. Undaunted, officers spent their time 'going round the Meadows and neighbouring Lanes repeatedly and also watching the South end of Clerk Street & neighbourhood', until they heard that De Quincey and 'some of his family had been seen ... near the top of Montague Street', where after 'searching ... several lodgings' they 'found & apprehended the debtor'. There was some delay, and then De Quincey and the officers proceeded towards the gaol. De Quincey wooed paranoia, but that did not mean no one was after him. It seems a miracle that he kept writing in the midst of these relentless pressures from both without and within. Such was what he once called 'the complex misery of my condition'.[14]

[ii]

'I have not seen him this winter,' Carlyle told John Stuart Mill on 18 April 1833; 'and no man, except Bailiffs, it appears, has for the last eighteen months.'[15] Thomas Hamilton made several unsuccessful attempts to see De Quincey, but heard tales of him ranging from the distressing to the ludicrous. On one occasion he indiscreetly discussed De Quincey's hardships with Dora Wordsworth, whose longstanding antipathy now approached callousness. 'The Opium eater ... has discovered a new mode of procuring a cheap dinner for his family,' she gossiped to Quillinan, ' – he buys game which is too bad for other folks & thus dines them all for one shilling.' On another occasion, Hamilton heard that two sheriff's officers had arrived at De Quincey's lodgings, and one of them 'presenting a writ said: "I arrest you, Sir."' De Quincey looked coolly at the documentation and replied: '"Oh, you are mistaken, Sir. This writ is against my brother. My name is Charles, not Thomas." The men said he was called Thomas by every one, but De Q. was confident. So one of them stept out into the kitchen to the servant. "What's your master's name, Betty?" "Charles, Sir", with a curtsey.' One of De Quincey's daughters had 'slipped out of the room & told her to say so if she should be asked by either of the men'.[16]

With 'a family of 12 persons' (including Margaret, the children, and the servants) 'absolutely dependant' on him for the 'mere daily necessities of warmth – light – food &c.', De Quincey resorted once again to selling his books 'at the rate of about 30s. for 1s.' Now forty-eight years old, his health had been badly undermined over the winter by an 'attack of Ague, and immediately afterwards of Erysipelas, accompanied by a nervous illness'.[17] That spring De Quincey was liable 'to arrest from various quarters', a fact brought home forcefully when on 23 May both he and Margaret were put to the horn for unpaid rent at Forres Street. Scrambling, De Quincey moved his family to Caroline Cottage, which was located just outside Edinburgh, near the village of Duddingston, and under the lee of Arthur's Seat.[18] The cottage was owned by Lady Caroline Nairne, the Scottish songwriter and laureate of Jacobinism, though she was living in Ireland at the time and her agent made the bad mistake of renting to a couple who had been 'horned' only forty-eight hours earlier. The country surroundings were undoubtedly welcome after the pollution and confinement of Edinburgh, and perhaps reminded the De Quinceys a little of their time at The Nab. Margaret's sister Betty came to stay that summer.[19]

There was, however, no relief in the financial pressure, and De Quincey filed for his *Cessio Bonorum* (literally, 'a cession of goods'), a provision under Scottish law which secured a debtor from personal arrest. The process required him to compile a list of his assets and debts. The assets were then voluntarily surrendered to his creditors, who sold them and applied the proceeds to their claims. The debts were not cleared away unless the assets ceded were sufficient for that purpose. Any property De Quincey might later acquire could also be claimed by his creditors, though at no point could either he or his family be deprived of the bare necessities. Carlyle put the matter in a nutshell: De Quincey is 'busy *getting a Bankruptcy transacted*'.[20]

He listed his assets at £762.9s., but the calculation was hardly realistic, as most of the money was actually in the form of debt, and at the top of De Quincey's list was 'Samuel Taylor Coleridge, Poet, Hampstead', who was cited as owing De Quincey £315 for 'cash lent in November 1807' and an additional £393.15s. in 'interest at 5 per Cent from 1 December 1807 till 1 December 1832 25 years'. Nor was De Quincey's calculation entirely honest, as he listed his 'Books manuscripts &c' in Dove Cottage at a value of only £5.10s., while the thousands of volumes squirrelled away there – including several of the rare books that he had purchased at the Duke of Roxburghe's sale – would undoubtedly have fetched a far higher sum.[21]

He registered his debts at £617.16s. Fifty-one creditors – from Edinburgh, Westmorland, Cumberland, Lancashire, and London – staked a claim, and the list of their names and occupations throws remarkable light on De Quincey's professional, legal, social, and domestic concerns: 'William Newton Wine Merchant', 'Thomas Troughton Stationer', 'James McLaren Boot & Shoe maker', 'Mrs Agnes Muirhead Lodging Letter Great King Street', 'David Hunter Tinplate Worker', 'Agnes Wilson Dressmaker', 'James Trotter Writing Master', 'Paul Baxter Collector of Police Duties', 'Archibald

Haddow Cowfeeder', 'William Green Butcher', 'Thomas Wilson Carpenter', 'Cornelius Nicholson Bookseller', 'Christopher Gardner Brazier', 'John Thomson Grocer and Spirit Merchant', 'Miss Margaret Preston Haberdasher', and 'William Sproat Schoolmaster', to name fewer than a third of those to whom De Quincey owed money. The document, signed on 9 July 1833, was witnessed by De Quincey's solicitor, William Duguid, and his eldest son William, now sixteen.[22]

Such an extensive, legal declaration might have been expected to give De Quincey a fresh start, or at least some breathing room. But as he had few, if any, assets to turn over to his old creditors, and as he was already accumulating debts to a series of new ones, there was in fact very little change in his situation. Benson was again pressing him for the Dove Cottage rent, and was by this point angry enough to threaten to reclaim the property without allowing time even for the removal of personal effects. De Quincey consulted two lawyers and wrote back confident that he had the legal upper hand. 'The consequences ... are serious', he advised, if 'a landlord ... should take any false step, and the dangers so heavy – that I am satisfied no man of sense would act hastily.'[23] Out-manoeuvred, Benson retreated to plot a more effective course, while De Quincey – or rather his manuscripts and books – remained the tenant of Dove Cottage.

The Nab was a different story. Having received no money since De Quincey's mother had forwarded him £180 in April 1832, Pendlebury foreclosed on the mortgage. Margaret's blacksmith brother William wrote De Quincey 'a letter of ruffian brutality', abusing him 'as a swindler' and objecting that he himself had been forced to pay Pendlebury £100, a sum he intended to recover either by selling his father's 'stock and crops' or De Quincey's 'property and books'. De Quincey seems not to have responded directly to William, but he fired back a letter to his father-in-law. William could not 'hold the language which he does to us, if you had done justice to our conduct', he protested. For seventeen months, Margaret had 'denied herself and her children every comfort of life' in order to enable De Quincey to make up the £180 he had borrowed from his mother. Yes, he had 'delayed a few months in paying this year's interest', but was 'that any reason for doubting that I should pay it soon'? Pendlebury would get his money, and in the meantime, Simpson should not suffer himself 'to be sent off like a parcel directed to me'.[24]

Some of these comments seem to have made their way back to William, who stepped forward at the last moment and offered to pay both the principal and the interest on the property. But it was no use. Pendlebury had had enough. The Nab was advertised for sale in late September at the

Salutation Inn, Ambleside. After generations in Margaret's family, it passed into other hands. Her mother seems to have died soon after the sale, while her father and mentally handicapped uncle Park travelled to Edinburgh to live at Caroline Cottage.[25] The rumour mill claimed that De Quincey had 'made his father-in-law sell his little estate for his benefit & father & family were brought literally to the parish'.[26] In fact, De Quincey spent a great deal of his own money on The Nab with nothing to show for it, and then provided a home for Simpson and Park.

Domestic life remained a bizarre combination of tenderness and severe anxiety. Simpson, quiet, upright, and no doubt devastated by recent events, became a source of comfort to the De Quincey children, who listened in delight as he expressed himself 'by words from the Bible, Milton, Shakespeare, Pope's "Homer", and sometimes a whole "Spectator", humorous or grave, as the exciting subject might have been, and all in the homely, kindly Westmorland dialect'.[27] Such tranquillity was shattered, however, when the pressures that raged around De Quincey forced themselves inside his family circle, and at no moment more dramatically than when one of his creditors seems to have resorted to kidnapping. 'I have had a little child detained from me by violence at Portobello,' De Quincey wrote to one of his publishers. 'Which I mention because it has interrupted my writing, having involved me in applications to the Sheriff &c. for 4 days – and in other measures. I am driven hard by the rewards &c. necessarily promised in this case. I trust you will let me have 30 shillings.'[28] Nothing more is known of the situation.

The final resort of Edinburgh debtors was the Holyrood sanctuary, and in late November De Quincey left his family in Caroline Cottage and moved into Mr Brotherstone's Lodgings, Prospect Buildings, near Holyrood House.[29] His decision was probably precipitated by a third horning on 13 November, this time for £17 owing to 'Henry Gibson Duguid, Teacher of Music'.[30] Formerly an Augustinian Abbey, Holyrood was now governed by a Bailie, whose chief duties included registering residents at a cost of two guineas, conducting the local court, and overseeing the prison. The sanctuary encompassed an area between six and seven miles in circumference, and included Holyrood Palace and the surrounding cluster of old lodgings, shops, and taverns, as well as Arthur's Seat, Salisbury Crags, and about half of Duddingston Lake. Within these boundaries debtors could move with impunity, and on Sunday they enjoyed the additional right of wandering anywhere they pleased, provided they were back within the sanctuary before midnight, a stipulation that often involved them in a race towards the boundary line at the foot of Canongate with their creditors in hot pursuit.[31] For De Quincey, and for many others, the sanctuary made an acceptable alternative to prison, and indeed De Quincey may have taken Caroline Cottage with one eye on its close proximity to Holyrood.

The move into Brotherstone's Lodgings brought 'a total cessation of direct intercourse' between De Quincey and Caroline Cottage 'for the purpose of misleading a knave who held some acceptances of mine fraudulently obtained (in fact stolen)'. But as the weeks passed De Quincey began shuttling between the two residences, the combined rent costing him 'from 10 guineas to 12 pounds' per month, and his stay at either place probably dependent on whether or not he was facing the imminent threat of arrest.[32] The arrangement provided him with a good deal of flexibility, but it was of course far more than he could afford. By 4 February 1834, he did not have the money to buy ink, paper, or laudanum, and he could not leave the sanctuary 'without very urgent danger ... emissaries are on the watch in all directions'.[33] 'We heard of De Quincey being located within the debtor's sanctuary of Holyrood,' William Bell Scott declared. 'He was to be seen like the ghost of one whose body had not received the clod of earth to entitle it to rest in peace, and his growing son, it was reported, was getting well into his teens like an uncared-for dog.'[34]

The rent on Caroline Cottage had been in arrears almost from the start, and when Lady Nairne's representatives instituted a 'system of menaces ... perfectly uncalled for', De Quincey quit the cottage and moved his entire family into the sanctuary, where they took 'miserable' lodgings at Mrs Miller's, Holyrood Gardens, Palace Yard, and where – as Margaret later recalled – they avoided 'and were avoided by all of their former friends'.[35] At the same time, De Quincey gave up his own lodgings at Brotherstone's and took a single room in the Holyrood household of Miss Margaret Craig. Cost probably prompted the relocation, but both the Brotherstone and Craig lodgings seem to have served him in the same way: they were offices – sanctuaries within the sanctuary – where he could escape the demands of parenthood and concentrate on his writing. Not even in Holyrood, however, could he avoid persecution for debt. Beyond its boundaries, the bookseller Carfrae put him to the horn for the fourth time.[36] Within its boundaries, paying 'enormously' at Mrs Miller's, and not wishing to 'drive any hard bargain' at Miss Craig's, meant that he soon found himself in the Holyrood court facing at least four prosecutions, though in each instance he seems to have escaped the lowest rung for an Edinburgh debtor: imprisonment *within* the sanctuary.[37]

The move to Holyrood coincided with a damaging new direction for De Quincey. 'Ever since ... coming to the Abbey ... I have taken spirits,' he reported: 'first about 2 or 3 glasses; and often for some months milk and rum.' Of this time, Florence remembered that her father's 'best chance of accomplishing anything was from about nine or ten o'clock in the evening till about four to six o'clock in the morning. And his most deadly certainty of failure was the touching of anything in the nature of wine or spirits.'[38]

[iii]

William Tait was 'a big, jolly-looking man, with a broad black ribbon attached to a watch or glass hanging down his vest'. A politician of 'the Radical school', he founded *Tait's Edinburgh Magazine* in April 1832 'by way of rival to mine', as William Blackwood put it, 'and of course it is as much Radical as we are Tory'.[39] Of Tait, De Quincey declared: 'I have not known any man in the course of my life who has so much impressed me with the feeling of his being largely – unaffectedly – and deeply interested in whatever can be supposed likely ... to exalt the standard of human nature'.[40] In the first issue of his magazine, Tait wrote that 'we are upon the confines of a new era ... Mighty questions have been stirred; deep interests have been created; old things are passing away.' Two months later the 1832 Reform Bill – which served primarily to remove the glaring inequalities in representation by transferring voting privileges from the 'pocket' and 'rotten' boroughs controlled by the aristocracy to the heavily populated industrial towns – passed into law, and by April 1833 Tait could justly claim that 'during the arduous contest between the people in conjunction with Earl Grey's administration and the Whig party, on one side, with the enemies of all Reform on the other, we have not ceased to advocate the just cause'.[41]

Despite the magazine's strong start, Tait made two major changes in 1834. First, he dropped the price from half-a-crown to a shilling, a move that made his magazine more affordable for artisans and the working class, and that for a time pushed his sales at least as high as *Blackwood's*. Second, he absorbed *Johnstone's Edinburgh Magazine* into *Tait's*, and made its editor Christian Isobel Johnstone his new co-proprietor and primary editor. Johnstone instituted a number of changes, from a larger, double-columned format to a focus that was broader and more literary. She was the 'working genius' of the magazine, recalled the miscellaneous author James Glass Bertram, and she 'generally passed judgment on the articles offered'.[42] During this period, *Tait's* featured work by leading radicals such as Richard Cobden, John Bright, John Stuart Mill, and Leigh Hunt, as well as by a host of women writers, including Catherine Gore, Harriet Martineau, Amelia Opie, and Mary Russell Mitford. It was a magazine 'dedicated to purposes of political change such as many people thought revolutionary', De Quincey observed. His mother agreed: 'You will not write where you might with honour & no compromise of your professed principles; money being spent, and no choice left, you take up with Mr Tait.'[43]

At least one reader was curious to know how the 'Tory . . . and Orthodox' De Quincey could become 'a writer in one of the most radical periodicals of the day'.[44] There were a number of reasons. Tait's offices were conveniently located in Princes Street, close to Blackwood's, and within easy walking distance of Holyrood. Tait also paid better than Blackwood, usually 'at the rate of fourteen guineas per sheet of sixteen pages', and even 'more liberally' to 'two or three writers . . . such as Mr De Quincey'. Further, Tait was keen to accept De Quincey's work at a time when Blackwood was not. 'Hannah More, I have seen, is dying,' De Quincey wrote to Blackwood in a mood of ghoulish opportunism. 'I can furnish a sketch of her daily habits.'[45] And a few months later he wished to write a review of J. C. Colquhoun's *Animal Magnetism*, 'with regard to which I have some curious details'.[46] Neither of these articles, however, appears to have interested Blackwood, and so De Quincey took them down the street to Tait, who was happy to publish both.

There was yet another reason why De Quincey signed on with the new magazine. *Blackwood's* typically demanded that he stifle the liberal element in his politics, whereas in *Tait's* – even more than in the *London* – he was free to exploit it. To be sure, De Quincey did not always seize the opportunity. He was 'a Tory of the purest strain', remarked Tait, who on more than one occasion went so far as to insert editorial footnotes into De Quincey's essays in an attempt to puncture their inflated conservatism. But De Quincey's politics were not as inflexible as Tait initially believed, and vice versa. 'Gradually I became astonished at the large amount also of our agreements,' De Quincey told him, '. . . and I remember . . . some twelve or fourteen great themes, relating to colonial – penal – financial – or educational legislation, upon which we were in perfect harmony.'[47] Though sometimes tarred as a furious right-winger, De Quincey's sympathies extended to both sides of the political spectrum. He was 'a Tory from the spiritual and ideal side of Toryism', concluded the *Quarterly Review*, but he was also 'in many respects a "Liberal" in the truest sense of the word. He was ready to challenge all comers, to investigate all problems, to hold every truth up to the light.'[48]

A more informal and tolerant De Quincey began to emerge. In *Blackwood's* he damned 'the incendiary press' for spreading 'poisonous and corrupting doctrines', while in *Tait's* he applauded the press's 'energy', 'vigilance', and 'sagacity'.[49] In *Blackwood's* he attacked 'petty shopkeepers' who lived 'near to the base of society' as an 'order of men ... purely Jacobinical'; but in *Tait's* he acknowledged that while 'Jacobinism' is 'the seminal principle of all political evil', it is 'natural to the heart of man ... A good man, a high-minded man, in certain circumstances, *must* be a Jacobin.'[50] In *Blackwood's* he denounced Reform as a ruinous measure that would bring about 'a prodigious expansion of democratic strength'. In *Tait's* he argued that 'in every great and enlightened nation ... there is, and must be, a tendency widely diffused to the principles of sane reform'.[51] In *Blackwood's* he condemned the French Revolution as a 'Record of an Iliad of woes!' In *Tait's* he praised it as an 'awakening era' and 'grand explosion of pure democracy'.[52] De Quincey was often bellicose in the articulation of his conservative views, but he was also a canny writer who needed to sell his work, and who possessed a remarkable ability to tailor his views to suit different – and in some cases oppositional – magazine contexts.

His career with *Tait's* began in November 1833 with an engaging translation of Kant's essay on 'The Age of the Earth', but his first major impact on the magazine came three months later when he launched his highly popular 'Sketches of Life and Manners; from the Autobiography of an English Opium-Eater', a series that eventually grew to twenty-five instalments before concluding in 1841. Wandering 'backwards and forwards' from his earliest years, through key experiences from his adolescence not covered by the *Confessions*, to his days with the *London*, De Quincey mined his memory for moments of beauty and despair, and delivered the whole in a prose style that was, by turns, rapt, ironic, anecdotal, and forthright.[53] The series encompasses favourite topics such as secret societies, German metaphysics, the art of prose composition, and the idea of sin. He comments on a number of major contemporaries: William Blake is 'that fine mystic', Mary Wollstonecraft is 'the sole rival in this country of the noblest of her sex – Madame Roland', and Byron is a 'plagiarist'.[54] Personal moments of isolation and fear are set against a broad series of social engagements and professional relationships, while De Quincey's preoccupation with classical literature is juxtaposed to several pressing contemporary interests, including the 'gorgeous empire' of the British and 'the benefit of railroads'.[55]

Closely related to the 'Sketches', and eventually folded within them, are the group of essays commonly known as the 'Lake Reminiscences'. The first of these, 'Samuel Taylor Coleridge', was prompted by 'the unexpected news of this great man's death' in late July 1834, and appeared in *Tait's* in four instalments from September through January.[56] De Quincey's motives were typically mixed, for the articles were written partly to relieve his 'deep sentiments of reverential affection' for Coleridge's memory, and 'partly, in however imperfect a way, to meet the public feeling of interest or curiosity'. De Quincey was fulsome in his praise, describing Coleridge as 'the largest and most spacious intellect ... that has yet existed amongst men', and highlighting his accomplishments in poetry, psychology, philosophy, biblical scholarship, and German literature.[57] Yet De Quincey also moved with disarming frankness over the crucial areas that still haunt Coleridgean biography: his opium addiction, his political apostasy, his decline as a poet, and – as Wilson had ventriloquized through 'The Opium-Eater' a dozen years earlier in the *Noctes* – his plagiarisms. 'Coleridge loses by Dequincey,' wrote Ralph Waldo Emerson, 'but more by his own concealing uncandid acknowledgement of debt to Schelling.' De Quincey's four articles constitute the first important critical biography of Coleridge, and reveal him with unmatched immediacy.[58]

The articles were highly controversial. 'All the persons I have met with who have read them, have risen from them with the same disgust,' declared Julius Hare. Crabb Robinson thought it 'deplorable that men of talent like De Quincey, under the pressure of want, should seize on the reputation of a deceased friend as a prey, turning his personal acquaintance with them to profit'.[59] Coleridge's nephew Henry Nelson Coleridge condemned De Quincey's 'vile heap of personalities', and 'the incredible meannesses of thought, allusion, or language perpetrated in these papers'. Southey was even angrier: 'I have told Hartley Coleridge ... that he ought to take a strong cudgel, proceed straight to Edinburgh, and give De Quincey, publicly on the streets there, a sound beating!'[60]

Others, however, took a more balanced view. Carlyle contended that De Quincey wrote 'merely for sake of the highly needful trifle of money, poor soul, and with no wish to be untrue (I could believe) or to hurt anybody, though not without his own bits of splenetic conviction also'. Wordsworth damned the articles as 'obnoxious', but conceded that it was 'not to be doubted' that De Quincey was 'honoured' by Coleridge's confidence, and that he had extolled Coleridge's 'intellectual powers as much as the most ardent of his Admirers, if discreet and judicious, would do'.[61] Most revealingly, Coleridge's daughter Sara objected that De Quincey had seen Coleridge's mind '*too* much in the mirror of his own'. Yet 'of all the censors' of her father, she added, De Quincey 'is the one whose remarks are the most worthy of attention', for he had 'sufficient inward sympathy with the subject of his criticism to be capable in some degree of beholding his mind, as it actually existed, in all the intermingling shades of individual reality; and in few minds have these shades been more subtly intermingled than in my Father's'.[62] De Quincey's essays caused a good deal of controversy, but even some of his detractors recognized their immense value.

[iv]

'Listen for a moment,' De Quincey wrote tremblingly to Tait in November 1834, ' – and then judge what it was possible for me to have done.'[63] William, De Quincey's eldest son, was ill. For several months he had been battling deafness and then headaches, which in the last few weeks had grown increasingly severe. With a view to easing the pain and facilitating sleep, he had begun to use laudanum in considerable doses. On 4 October Dr J. H. Balfour was called in. William appeared to be suffering from 'some deep-seated disease of the head', Balfour reported. 'The patient was tall and emaciated, his eyes were large, his countenance had a pallid hue, and he appeared to be of a strumous habit.' Balfour immediately ordered a number of measures, including 'a blister ... to the back part of the head and the nape of the neck', and the prescription of purgative pills, savine ointment, 'two grains of calomel, and half a grain of opium, to be taken twice a day'. But there was little improvement. William's throat was 'scarified, in order to afford relief from the feeling of suffocation'. His eyes 'at this time became very prominent'.[64]

William's parents kept a constant vigil, reducing Margaret to 'the fiercest despair' and De Quincey to 'the very lowest state of physical dejection'. Gradually over each of William's eyes a 'film of darkness' spread until he was 'totally blind'. There was no chance of him recovering either his hearing or his sight. 'Good God!' cried De Quincey, ' – what a destiny of horror!'[65] On 9 November William turned eighteen. Shortly thereafter, 'he was in a very restless and agitated state, being frequently troubled with horrible dreams, and throwing off the bed-clothes, as if in great agony. The recollection of some family distresses seemed to prey upon his mind, and he frequently alluded to them in a very striking manner.' He was slipping away, and De Quincey's grief was undoubtedly deepened by the guilty knowledge that his own actions had produced many of the 'family distresses' now haunting his son. William 'could still answer questions rationally', but the 'paleness of his complexion, and the prominence of his eyes, combined as they were with blindness and deafness, contributed to give his countenance a peculiar ghastly and cadaverous appearance'. On 25 November at half-past nine in the morning he 'expired without a struggle'.[66]

An autopsy took place '*28 hours after death*'. Under the scalp was 'a large mass of olive-green coloured matter', and under the skull-cap were 'thin layers of similar green-coloured matter, interspersed with some bloody spots'.[67] More than four decades earlier De Quincey seems to have imagined – and possibly even to have witnessed – the disfigurement caused by the doctors when they examined the brain of his dead sister Elizabeth. This time he was spared that trauma. He surveyed William 'one hour *after* the surgeons had laid the skull in ruins', but 'the dishonours of this scrutiny were hidden by bandages, and had not disturbed the repose of the countenance'. Balfour concluded that the 'disease in this case appears to be of a very uncommon nature', and was 'unable to suggest any remedy'.[68] De Quincey believed that both his eldest sister and his eldest son had died of hydrocephalus. Today, William's disease would almost certainly be diagnosed as acute leukaemia.

It was a cruel blow. De Quincey and Margaret had lost two sons in just over two years. William was 'the crown and glory of my life', De Quincey later declared, and 'upon him I had exhausted all that care [and] hourly companionship could do for the culture of an intellect in all stages of his life somewhat premature'.[69] Mrs Quincey expostulated with her son 'against the expense of putting his family (7 persons) into mourning dresses for poor William, knowing that either the tradesman who furnished them must go unpaid, or the Father must prefer the alternative of taxing his generous Friends for the payment'. De Quincey responded indignantly to his mother's pleas, and then turned to his friends, who paid for his family's mourning clothes.[70]

From Mrs Quincey's perspective, her son was out of control. No amount of money seemed to move him any closer to solvency. In a letter of 13 December she poured out her distress to Dorothy Wordsworth, whom she had met when she visited De Quincey in the Lakes in 1811, and with whom she had clearly stayed in touch. 'My daughter has often assisted her brother, to her own heavy loss,' Mrs Quincey reported, and 'to pay off the last arrears' of De Quincey's debts, she herself had cut into her own 'very limited income by the reduction of principle'. In the space of eighteen months she had advanced him the enormous sum of £620, and this total was 'over and above the yearly £200'. Yet De Quincey's requests for money kept coming, and at present he was already in advance £35 upon his quarterly payments of £50.[71]

Severe financial pressures, however, may not even have been the worst of it, as Mrs Quincey hinted three months later in another, much darker letter to Dorothy. '*My Son is not the Ruler* of his family,' she insisted: 'this thought certainly brings to my remembrance, a long by-gone history of violence, which I'm afraid to look back upon in another quarter, as it would lead me only to fear more misery and greater perils in the path of handsome Daughters, so poor and so expensive.' Mrs Quincey's comments recall the reports that Margaret's grandfather William Park was sometimes given to violence, and seem to point directly at Margaret and her management of the family, though Mrs Quincey may also intend Margaret's father, or her uncle Park, both of whom were still members of the De Quincey household. It is impossible to say what truth – if any – is involved in her various claims. Certainly she was deeply and genuinely disturbed at what she saw as her son's 'sad lack of moral discipline'. But she was also anxious – perhaps especially in a letter to a former Grasmere neighbour like Dorothy – to make it plain that the situation was not all De Quincey's fault. Indeed, the problems on the Simpson side of the marriage made her feel 'compassion' for her son. If Dorothy responded to Mrs Quincey, her letter has been lost. There are no other suggestions that there was violence within the De Quincey family.[72]

[v]

Work was De Quincey's best remedy for the wounds of William's death, wounds 'applied as if with premeditating skill exactly to those points in which chiefly I was most vulnerable'. 'I believe that in the course of any one month since that unhappy day,' De Quincey avowed, 'I have put forth more effort in the way of thought – of research – and of composition than in any five months together selected from my previous life.'[73] In fact, his productivity did not increase dramatically following William's death, though to write at all must have cost him a great deal, no matter how unyielding the pressure to sell articles.

Other distractions kept him from focusing too sharply on his grief. Less than a month after William's death, De Quincey was back in the Holyrood court, this time for £12.1s.8d. owing to David Nicolson, merchant. His drinking continued: it was now 'water and spirits', he confessed; 'often, I fear, bad spirits'.[74] Tait provided some companionship: 'On Sunday or Monday, I *will walk* in any direction you please,' De Quincey told him in March. Smallpox raged in Edinburgh during the spring and all six De Quincey children 'were attacked … though all had been vaccinated'. In June, De Quincey faced yet another sudden and unexplained demand for money. Another remittance from his mother seems to have alleviated the distress.[75]

Meanwhile, in the Lake District, Benson had finally found a way to force De Quincey out of Dove Cottage. De Quincey countered the notice with an unrealistic proposal to rent the house for two or three more years, but Benson brushed this notion aside. Confronted then with the task of removing his property after renting the cottage for twenty-six years, De Quincey proposed sending a Mrs Garcia and one of his children to Grasmere.[76] But this plan too collapsed, and in the event De Quincey himself travelled to the Lakes, where in six days and seven nights he transferred his possessions – including thousands of books – from Dove Cottage to Lingstubbs, the farmhouse near Penrith where Margaret and the children had stayed in 1830. Physically, it was a demanding task.[77] Emotionally, it may have been even worse. 'Cottage, immortal in my remembrance!' he apostrophized. 'From the beginning of the century to 1835 ... was it either mine or Wordsworth's.' Yet when De Quincey finally completed the move, 'the weight of a world' passed from him. 'I am now a changed man,' he assured Tait in July. 'I now possess my mind: heretofore I was under a possession.'[78]

Back in Edinburgh, De Quincey received word that his uncle Penson had died. He of course hoped that provisions in the will would help to lighten his financial burden. It was not to be. Penson bequeathed De Quincey an annuity of £100, which he had already been sending him for several years, as well as his wardrobe, plate, and household linen. De Quincey's mother wrote to apprise him of different arrangements concerning the will, and to admonish him not to pawn the items devised to him, as 'it would add to my bitter regrets, both to think of my folly and your scorn, of our goodwill in the surrender of our rights and your disrespect to your Uncle's memory'.[79]

Having voiced one anxiety, she could not rest until she had voiced two others. One, 'I have heard and noticed before, though you replied not, that you are still an Opium-Eater, and this dreadful Drug ... acts on you ... to the full extent which the more common forms of intoxication effect!' And two, 'I reject as quite incredible' a report 'that your Children's education is neglected'. In a recent letter from her granddaughter Margaret 'no less than seven false spellings of very common words appear. I blame not the poor Child but you and you only my son ... A Parent with your means, who does thus, is utterly unworthy of Children.' Mrs Quincey offered to pay for tutors, but De Quincey 'would not consent'.[80]

Such censoriousness, coming just eight months after William's death, was hardly helpful. The children *were highly educated*, he insisted in reply, a claim supported by their accomplishments as adults, as well as by a list of his debts, which included a writing master, a teacher of dancing, a teacher of music, and a schoolmaster. At the same time Mrs Quincey was right to worry. Chaos swirled constantly around her grandchildren, and she would not have been surprised when Emily later complained 'rather bitterly of her own ignorance and lack of training'. Looking back, Margaret acknowledged that there were problems. 'Papa left us to nature', and 'behaved very badly by some of us for our spelling and all ordinary branches of education'. Yet she also insisted that he fostered among them a strong sense of intellectual independence. 'I always feel grateful' to him 'for never having arbitrarily withheld *any* book from us – he guided our tastes in forming judgments of them.' In this regard, she concluded, 'Papa ... did for us ... something better than the most careful Fathers do according to the notion of this world on these matters'.[81]

Part of the problem, at least from De Quincey's point of view, was that his mother was missing a key irony: now well over eighty years old, she stood resolutely in the way of the inheritance that would have enabled him to address some of the difficulties that had prompted her criticisms in the first place. 'Not only has she absorbed $\frac{2}{3}$rds of my father's fortune, but has intercepted the whole of a second, and almost the whole of a 3rd (my uncle's),' he remarked gloomily, though the humour of the situation was not lost on him. '... If all men had mothers living to ages so excessive and mothers by strange coincidence of accident absorbing one estate after another, who would escape embarrassment?' A short time later, he pawned his uncle's plate and linen, and then opened negotiations to obtain a loan on the annuity.[82]

Throughout these months De Quincey worked on a political article that he told Tait required more 'writing cancelling rewriting' than anything of equal length that he had ever produced, though such claims may have been designed to put pressure on Tait to accept an article that in many ways ran counter to the agenda of his magazine. In 'A Tory's Account of Toryism, Whiggism, and Radicalism', published in *Tait's* for December 1835 and January 1836, De Quincey propounded the doctrine, not that Whiggism is wrong and Toryism right, but that 'Whig principles and Tory principles are both and equally true'. They are the 'two great forces at work in the British constitution; and the constitution is sustained, in its integrity, by their equilibrium'.[83]

Such theorizations were intriguing and abstract enough to appeal to *Tait's* readers, but – unusually for De Quincey – much of the rest of his argument did not suit the specific periodical context he had in view, as he descended into a shrill and tenuous promotion of conservatism that was clearly going to rile both Tait and his readers. Rather than send the two essays back, however, Tait accepted them as they stood, and then inserted over two dozen editorial footnotes, in which he heckled, dismissed, and belittled De

Quincey's Tory dogma. 'Mr De Quincey greatly underrates the *real* power of Parliament.' His distinctions are 'wire-drawn'. He contradicts himself. His theories are 'delectable': there 'cannot be a half dozen . . . Tories in Great Britain' who believe them.[84] These editorial interventions naturally irritated De Quincey, who responded with a third instalment of 'A Tory's Account' in which he chided Tait for his errors and oversights. Tait brought the exchange to a close by rejecting the article outright. De Quincey got the message.[85] In his many future dealings with Tait, he did not again allow his Toryism to get the better of him. Turning from political polemic to the richer and more varied ground of his 'Life and Manners' sketches, he published the tenth instalment of the series in June 1836.

That same month complicated negotiations involving the Penson annuity came to a close when De Quincey's solicitor J. J. Smith secured for him a loan of £950 from the Caledonian Insurance Company. 'The time occupied in the affair from first to last . . . amounted to six calendar months,' De Quincey recalled, adding that the enquiries of the insurance office passed from 'levity and carelessness' in the first two months to 'mere torture' in the final two.[86] At around this same time, Margaret appeared before the Lord Provost in Edinburgh to sign various deeds. Details of the meeting are not known, but it may well have concerned unfinished business at The Nab. The transaction generated a further sum of money, and enabled the De Quinceys to treat their thirteen-year-old son Francis, who was staying for a time at Lingstubbs. 'Order your clothes after your own fancy,' his father instructed him: 'only, do not get any long coat – but a *jacket* of any form you like . . . Your Mama sends you a thousand kisses.'[87]

The influx of money, coupled with the fact that he was no longer paying on either The Nab or Dove Cottage, brought a measure of stability to De Quincey's finances that had been unknown for several years. Indeed, after weathering nearly a dozen court actions for debt in the years 1832 through 1834, not a single action was brought against him in 1835 or 1836.[88] The relief for him and for his family was no doubt immeasurable. It was most probably in 'the bright summer mornings' of 1836 that Florence remembered her father capturing baby Emily 'fresh from her bath . . . and dancing her about the garden; the child, with its scanty white raiment and golden head, looking like a butterfly glowing among the trees'. Some time during the autumn De Quincey must have been away from Holyrood for more than fourteen consecutive days, for his benefit of protection lapsed and he had to register for a second time when he returned on 24 November.[89]

As had been the case with various financial boons in the past, De Quincey relaxed from writing and published nothing during these months. He got very little exercise and drank a good deal, 'often taking 4 to 5 wine glasses of spirit' and 'seldom less than $3\frac{1}{2}$'. He ate little: a typical dinner was two cupfuls of 'mutton broth thickened with rice', followed by 'a few spoonfuls of minced collups ... with a little potatoes'. Yet his health was remarkably good. He had cut back on 'the multitude of pills' he took for the constipation caused by opium, and he had also made a 'great discovery': omitting supper before going to bed greatly improved his health. On 5 March 1837 he noted 'an excessive degree of what ... I have remarked for many months ... namely of healthy power'.[90]

[vi]

It was the calm before his bitterest storm. In February and March he returned to his *Tait's* 'Life and Manners' sketches with an uncharitable account of his time as a teenager in the Liverpool circle of William Roscoe, James Currie, and William Shepherd, all of whom he painted as decidedly minor figures: 'Mr Roscoe is dead, and has found time since then to be half forgotten; Dr Currie, the physician, has been found "unable to heal himself"; Mr Shepherd ... is a name and a shadow.' De Quincey took a certain glee in turning on these men, and he probably felt confident that enough time had passed for him to do so without direct rebuttal. He was mistaken. Roscoe and Currie were indeed dead, but Shepherd was alive and well and living in Gateacre, and he responded with a letter to the editor of *Tait's* in which he vindicated his friends and pointedly dismissed De Quincey, whose slavery to a 'deleterious drug' had inflamed his brain and impaired his memory. De Quincey took the criticism in his stride, while his editor Johnstone defended him in the May issue.[91] As both no doubt recognized, controversy of this kind was good for business.

More strikingly, in July – after an absence of nearly three years – De Quincey returned to *Blackwood's* with an essay he had originally proposed to William Blackwood in 1830.[92] 'Revolt of the Tartars' is an elaborate piece of Oriental fantasy in which De Quincey describes the 1770–71 migration of a tartar tribe from the eastern border of Russia to the western fringe of the Chinese empire. Invoking both a series of famous military expeditions and the biblical exodus, the tale describes how the tartars are persecuted by their Russian pursuers, and how both sides suffer the ravages of hunger, disease, and exhaustion, as well as the extremes of cold and heat. At the climax, the tartars reach Lake Tengiz and the benevolent protection of the Chinese emperor Kien Long just as their Russian enemies chase them down in a frenzy of thirst and slaughter. 'Wheresoever the lake was shallow enough to allow of men raising their heads above the water, there, for scores of acres, were to be seen all forms of ghastly fear, of agonizing struggle, of spasm, of convulsion, of mortal conflict, death, and the fear of death – revenge, and the lunacy of revenge.'[93] De Quincey's account is neither historically nor geographically accurate, but his impassioned prose vividly captures the despair and courage of the tartar journey.

The sale of two articles to *Tait's* and one to *Blackwood's* demonstrated again De Quincey's marketability and range, but the money it generated did little to stem a fierce new tide of financial distress. The £950 he had raised on his uncle's annuity had clearly run out by the early weeks of 1837. Soon he was hard pressed for the payment of bills he had recklessly guaranteed on behalf of a Holyrood friend named Major William Miller, and he now revealed that he still owed a 'very considerable sum' to his father-in-law.[94] Between April and December creditors swarmed. De Quincey was sued at least ten times, and twice put to the horn. In June, he wrote despondently to his lawyer Smith seeking 'to raise another loan from the Insurance Office upon my reversionary interest in the other parts of my uncle's property'.[95] Smith strongly advised him not to borrow, to which an indignant De Quincey replied that his application 'never was for advice … but for your practical aid in effecting the loan'. A month later the money had still not come through, and De Quincey was 'hunted in every direction by writs and diligences'.[96]

Then, the unthinkable. Margaret, whose fragile health had been a cause of concern for several years, became seriously ill towards the end of June. By the middle of July the sickness was 'making ravages … such as I do not wish to speak of or to think of'.[97] On 7 August, at the age of forty-one, she died from typhus fever. Perhaps there was talk of returning her body to Grasmere, but Margaret was buried at the west end of Princes Street in St Cuthbert's churchyard. Coming hard on the deaths of Julius and William, this third grief hit De Quincey with an intensity that was almost unbearable. He and Margaret had marked their twentieth wedding anniversary only six months earlier, and stretching back even before the time of their marriage she had been his partner and his closest friend. Their need for each other had been most clearly evident in the pain they both endured when they were separated. 'Looking back to that time, when I was a mere child,' Florence wrote, 'I yet seem to see that his mind was unhinged by these sorrows.' James Glass Bertram found De Quincey in the sanctuary looking 'pale and fragile … Shortly before my visit Mrs De Quincey had died, and his bereavement was, as I heard him say to Mr Tait, "a source of ever-present grief to him."'[98]

De Quincey explored the anguish of Margaret's death through writing, a kind of salvational act for him, as it had been with other sorrows in his past. He plunged into and idealized their life together, especially their early years in Grasmere. 'When the gate moved upon its golden hinges that opened to me the paradise of her society – when her young, melodious laughter sounded in my too agitated ear – did I think of any claims that *I* could have? Too happy if I might be permitted to lay all things at her feet.' This paradise slipped away, for the years came 'in which circumstances made me an Opium-Eater; years through which a shadow as of sad eclipse sate and rested upon my faculties'. Yet even these years now seem bliss by comparison, for at least they were years together; 'years through which I was careless of all but those who lived ... within "my hearts of hearts"; years – ah! heavenly years! – through which I lived, beloved, *with* thee, *to* thee, *for* thee, *by* thee! Ah! happy, happy years!'[99]

Like Elizabeth Quincey, Ann of Oxford Street, and Catharine Wordsworth before her, Margaret now became a symbol of suffering innocence who returned to him in vivid dreams. At one point, she appears 'in the sweet sunny morning of June', and almost immediately invokes 'my sister's coffin in the month of June'. 'Are the dusky and distant stages of life – thus dimly connected?' De Quincey asks. In another instance, she emerges before him in a dream set five years before they actually met, beckoning him towards and then warning him away from Dove Cottage. 'All was peace and the deep silence of untroubled solitude – only in the lovely lady was a sign of horror that had slept under deep ages of frost in her heart.' Not all De Quincey's dreams of Margaret, however, conjured fear and death, for 'sometimes, after days of intellectual toil ... I wrap my head in the bed-clothes ... and then through blinding tears I see again that golden gate; again I stand waiting at the entrance; until dreams come that carry me once more to the Paradise beyond'.[100]

De Quincey felt guilt over Margaret's death. He was undoubtedly thinking of Julius, William, and her when he wrote of the 'two or three' afflictions which have been 'most hard to bear, because not unmingled with pangs of remorse for the share which I myself may have had in causing them'. He felt resignation. His daughters had seen 'the silence and tranquillity with which I have supported losses the heaviest by which I could have been assailed'.[101] He felt renewed and bitter anger, especially at the Lake District neighbours who had snubbed Margaret. He remembered how, after his marriage, he ceased to see, and ceased to hear of, the Southeys and the Coleridges, though their transgressions were nothing to those of the Wordsworths: 'the hour is passed irrevocably, and by many a year, in which an act of friendship so natural, and costing so little, (in both senses so priceless), could have been availing. The ear is deaf that should have been solaced by the sound of welcome.' Most searingly, De Quincey recalled Wordsworth's inability to see 'the loveliness of a fair face now laid low in the dust', a face 'which struck my own eyes with awe as well as love. I may say that I perfectly hated him for his blindness.'[102]

The most potent and sustained expression of his grief, however, came in one of his finest tales of terror. 'The Household Wreck' was published in *Blackwood's* in January 1838, less than five months after Margaret's death. De Quincey grounds the tale in a well-known case of shoplifting that almost certainly came to his attention many years earlier when he was a teenager in Bath.[103] But his primary concern in the tale is with the terrible fragility of human hope, and those 'cases ... in which a single week – a day – an hour sweeps away all vestiges and landmarks of a memorable felicity'. The unnamed narrator, clearly modelled on a younger version of De Quincey, is healthy and prosperous, but also haunted by 'an over-mastering and brooding sense ... of some great calamity' travelling towards him. He lives in domestic bliss with his beautiful wife Agnes, a 'daughter of the hills' whose character and history invoke Margaret at almost every turn.[104]

One morning Agnes ventures into town on errands, but fails to return at the appointed time. The narrator, soon frantic, is consulting with servants when a policeman knocks on the door with news that Agnes has been arrested for shoplifting. The narrator goes immediately to the police station, where he learns that she has already been incarcerated, and that a new law makes it impossible for him to see her 'during the progress of the official examinations'. The next day he haunts the area around the prison in the company of a mob of vagrants, from whom he contracts a fever that consigns him to his bed for several weeks, leaving Agnes to face the terrors of her trial alone. When he finally revives, it is to discover that Agnes has been found guilty and sentenced to ten years of hard labour. The narrator gains surreptitious access to the prison and effects Agnes's escape, taking her to lodgings which, though squalid, are still 'a sanctuary ... from treachery'. The entire ordeal, however, has been too much for her, and she dies two months later. The narrator's wrath 'rises, like a towering flame, against all the earthly instruments of this ruin', but when an angry mob beats the shopkeeper who falsely accused Agnes, and he confesses his perfidy towards her in his dying moments, the narrator's revenge is perfect.[105] 'The Household Wreck' exalts and compresses many of the circumstances of De Quincey's relationship with Margaret, from their early happiness in Grasmere to the persecution, criminality, and anguish of their years in Edinburgh. The tale indulges in wish-fulfilment, and rages against fate and the malevolence of others. Yet washing over all is the paradoxical sense that, while the narrator loves his wife, he is able to do so little to protect her.[106] With the atmosphere and inevitability of nightmare, De Quincey charts the complex trauma of losing Margaret.

His other troubles continued. On the day Margaret died, David Nicolson sued him again for £12.1s.8½d., a sum that had been owing for at least three years. Within two days of her death De Quincey's good friend Major Miller also died, leading to two more suits against De Quincey for bills he had guaranteed for Miller. Miss Craig was after him for rent, driving him back into the city of Edinburgh, where he lost the protection of the sanctuary, but found it easier to hide from creditors.[107] In November he took up residence in the house of Frances and Christian Wilson at 42 Lothian Street.[108] At around this same time the publisher Adam Black 'found the little man one day in the hands of the sheriff's officers conveying him to Calton gaol. He stopped the melancholy procession and finding the debt for which De Quincey was seized to be under £30, he became responsible for it on condition of De Quincey's furnishing the articles on Shakespeare and Pope' for the *Encyclopaedia Britannica*, an arrangement to which De Quincey readily agreed.[109]

Meanwhile, nineteen-year-old Margaret had assumed the central place in the sanctuary household. Indeed, according to one friend, her father would 'undoubtedly have sunk ... had it not been for the high character, the energy, decision, and premature business capacity' which she manifested at the crisis of her mother's death.[110] De Quincey – hidden away in Lothian Street, and unable to leave without the possibility of incurring arrest – was reduced to seeing his children only once a week from 5 p.m. to dinner on a Sunday, when he could walk the city and visit the sanctuary with impunity. To some extent, such an arrangement was necessary in order for him to make money. 'You young children was noisy and he could not study,' one of De Quincey's Lothian Street landladies told Emily years later.[111] De Quincey, however, was also looking for an escape. The sudden and unexpected demands of single parenthood were overpowering him. 'I felt resting upon me always too deep and gloomy a sense of obscure duties, that I never *should* be able to fulfil,' he conceded, ' – a burthen which I could not carry, and which yet I did not know how to throw off.' To Florence at least, his actions amounted to 'deserting his family'. He had 'the terrible burden' of six children 'that he literally didn't know what to do with', and he ran away 'for his own enjoyment'.[112]

De Quincey returned to fulltime writing eight months after Margaret's

death, but he found it very difficult to manage without her, and he soon
came to rely heavily on his children. William Watson, a bookseller-con-
noisseur, related how 'Mr De Quincey's young, fair-haired English laddies'
were sent to him to borrow money.[113] Thirteen-year-old Fred and ten-
year-old Florence acted for their father as go-betweens, delivering copy to
publishers, picking up money, relaying messages, and waiting for hours at
appointed meeting places. To Black: 'One of my children was last night
instructed to call for your answer this morning.'[114] To Tait: 'Would you by
Fred let me have 25s.'[115] To Blackwood: 'My little daughter, who carries this,
will bring anything safely.'[116] The children may well have recognized the
importance of the tasks they were performing, but they could not always
cope with the adult world their father had thrust them into. 'Three separate
times, in three separate lodgings,' De Quincey snapped unkindly, 'I had
been traced by the emissaries of my creditors; and always through the
carelessness of my children, who suffered themselves to be followed unconsciously.' He seems not to have realized the terrible strain he was inflicting
on them. 'I know the north and southbacks of the Canongate, George the
Fourths Bridge the cross causeway &c as hideous dreams,' Florence recalled,
'my heart rushing into my mouth with the natural terrors of footsteps
approaching and rushing down again into my shoes when left to quiet and
the ghosts.'[117]

Others too found themselves drawn into De Quincey's business affairs.
Policemen, messenger boys, landladies, servants, and friends all delivered
manuscripts and messages for him when he could not get out of the
sanctuary or be seen in the streets of Edinburgh. In one instance a cabman
arrived at Tait's shop with a manuscript from 'a little gentleman, as polite
as a prince, although he wasn't dressed like one'. On other mornings 'a
young woman would enter the shop . . . and throwing down a roll of paper,
with an exclamation of "There!" would rush off as abruptly as she had
entered'. Upon examination, the manuscript would be found 'addressed in
the neatest of handwriting to, "William Tait, Esquire"'.[118]

Tait's shop boys were sometimes instructed to carry money to De
Quincey. 'Once, when a cheque for a very moderate sum was sent to him,
a messenger brought it back to Mr Tait with the intimation that at the
moment "so large an amount was not required by him, two pounds being
all he wanted."' Bertram recalled delivering both proofs and money to De
Quincey, who in at least one instance sent him on a further errand. 'Might
I request you – there is a place of entertainment, a public-house, almost at
the door – to have the kindness to go there and ask the lady who keeps it
to give you money of lesser amounts for this note . . . and, if at the same

time you will be good enough to ask the servant of the establishment to send me a small supply of the excellent brandy which is kept there, you will still further oblige me.'[119]

De Quincey was an often erratic witness of his own condition. Sometimes he felt he had enough money for conscientiousness and generosity. 'I am now in far more affluent circumstances than last year,' he told a creditor confidently on 21 February 1838; 'and am paying off all debts of every description at the rate of £15 a week.' In early March he settled accounts with his landlady Miss Craig by guaranteeing *her* rent for the next fifteen months. And for several weeks he sent money to 'a certain Peggy Brown', a 'char-woman, a washerwoman' in Holyrood who 'had been discharged from the Infirmary as cured of a fever', but who was 'weak and incapable of work'.[120]

During these same months, however, De Quincey also wrote at length of his own persecution and sorrow. He began the New Year under arrest, and pleading for help from Wilson, Blackwood, and Tait.[121] In March, Nicolson again threatened him with '*instant* persecution', and a particularly tenacious creditor, the Albion Clothing Company, made 'renewed applications'.[122] He could not even afford money for the coal needed to heat his room: 'My hand is so cold I cannot guide a pen,' he told Tait plaintively.[123] The tailor John Craig put him to the horn in April, as did his sanctuary landlady Jane Miller a month later. 'Will you be so good as to let me have one pound?' he implored Blackwood on 6 June. 'I am utterly aground without even paper or pens ... If I fail, and once get into prison, I am booked for utter perplexity for a year and more.'[124]

A measure of relief came that spring when De Quincey left Lothian Street and took up residence at 31 Windsor Street with the daughters of his deceased Holyrood friend, Major Miller. 'Better or more excellent creatures than these three sisters never existed,' he declared. His days in the house were quiet, and in the evening he enjoyed dinner, tea, music, polished conversation, and the 'luxuries of elegant female society'. But the respite, as De Quincey himself put it, 'was *too* happy to last'. Peggy Brown, the charwoman he had assisted, betrayed him when she followed 'Little Fred, by night and more than once', until she discovered where De Quincey was hiding. Convinced that she would turn him over to his creditors, De Quincey took 'sorrowful leave of my three fair young friends', and moved to accommodations they located for him. Shortly thereafter the sisters themselves moved from Windsor Street to 18 Duncan Street, where De Quincey looked forward to visiting them. 'I will take my chance of finding you at home,' he wrote to them on 26 May, before going on to make a request: 'give me no whiskey'. On a previous occasion in Windsor Street he seems to have 'annoyed ladies in the drawing room by my potations'.[125]

In June, trouble erupted at Lingstubbs. The farmer (probably a Mr Carr) who had rented De Quincey space to house the books he had formerly stored at Dove Cottage had grown tired of waiting for payment, and had evidently decided to recoup his losses by advertising about '2 thousand volumes' from De Quincey's library 'for public sale'. On 'the Coronation Day' – Queen Victoria officially received the crown on 28 June 1838 – a distraught De Quincey 'left town by the mail for Penrith', where he found the book sale already in progress, and a 'drunken ruffian' in charge.[126] Digging through 'heaps of dust and rubbish', he was able to rescue 'the jewels of my library ... books, for which I would not take a thousand guineas', but he could not stop a Mr Lawrence Harrison, who 'in the space of one minute ... completed a contract for ransoming the books: he offered 20 guineas on the spot; and ... in 3 or 4 hours the books were all carted away into his care'. De Quincey was devastated. Not only had he lost a sizeable portion of a library that he had jealously guarded for years, but would 'you believe it, all my papers – letters even to my wife, hers to me in early days – were all open to the public? Oh my God! ... The agitation of my dreams, always tumultuous at intervals, has been fearful since this accursed affair began.'[127]

On 7 July, De Quincey left Penrith and the Lakes for perhaps the last time. The hunt for him in Edinburgh was 'hot' throughout the rest of the summer.[128] A small hotel called the Guildford Arms, in Register Street, was one of the places in which he was 'occasionally pleased to hide himself'. The Miller sisters helped to keep creditors off his trail. William Wilson, an unidentified friend, lived at 1 Montague Street, and De Quincey also took refuge there.[129] In early August his luck appeared to run out when catchpolls arrested him for his debt to the tailor Craig, but Black came once more to the rescue and De Quincey was 'liberated' almost immediately. The pressure of 'finding the *daily* expenditure' for his children was relieved when De Quincey managed to obtain credit at a Mr Thompson's in Duncan Street, but the arrangement collapsed in late September and De Quincey was forced back on the necessity of raising ready cash – as he emphasized to Black – '*each separate morning*'.[130]

While creditors dogged him, he pursued his solicitor J. J. Smith, whose handling of the Penson annuity had aroused his suspicions. In October Smith seems to have agreed to 'paying over the £120 which he admits having of mine'. This money may be part of the original £950 loan from the Caledonian Insurance Company that Smith had found some excuse to withhold from De Quincey. Or it may be money that Smith had stolen from him, for at some point during these weeks De Quincey discovered that Smith had guaranteed bills for De Quincey's friend Major Miller in the amount of £100, and then silently reimbursed himself out of De Quincey's loan. In any event, Smith later absconded to America, and De Quincey simply lost the money.[131] The option of raising a second loan on the annuity was similarly ill-fated. De Quincey claimed that '9 or 10 different Insurance Offices' had offered him a loan of £2000, but each had ultimately turned him down 'upon putting the question to me if I were not the Opium-Eater'. Habitual brandy drinkers could get insurance, De Quincey later protested, but not laudanum addicts.[132]

As the year drew to a close, he and his family sunk to the point of deprivation. For the past three months 'my household, now of 9 persons, had been reduced to a single meal a day – usually at night', he explained to Wilson. 'Even then my youngest daughter, 5 years old, besieged the ears of all about her with clamours for something to eat from morning to night.' For the past three weeks the stress had been 'worse than ever: no article of dress, no household utensil belonging to me, no plate received under my uncle's will, but has long disappeared (you may be sure) at the pawnbroker's ... I need not pursue the odious recital. The story is humiliating enough.'[133]

[vii]

Though the turmoil of his life constantly intervened, De Quincey wrote furiously across these months of flight and grief. Black had originally hired him to produce two entries for the *Encyclopaedia Britannica*, seventh edition (1830–42), but he eventually increased that total to four. De Quincey wrote on Goethe, a poor choice, as his disparaging attitude had changed little since he attacked Carlyle's translation of *Wilhelm Meister* fourteen years earlier. His entry on Schiller was much more enthusiastic, for De Quincey regarded him as 'the representative of the German intellect in its highest form'. A third article on Alexander Pope praised him as 'the most brilliant of all wits who have at any period applied themselves to the poetic treatment of human manners'.[134] Finally, 'no paper' ever cost De Quincey 'so much labour' as his essay on Shakespeare; the result, enthused *Fraser's Magazine*, was an 'admirable and ingenious memoir' in which De Quincey was 'alert and vigorous'.[135]

At the same time, De Quincey asserted that he wrote 'exactly 200 days without intermission' for Tait: 'what could I do? To stop for a single day ... was to endanger my children's daily support.' De Quincey claimed that he produced the articles 'in a coffee room of a mail coach inn; with a sheriff's officer lurking near; in hurry too extreme to allow of reading them over even *once*; and with no after revision'.[136] Tait, however, saw these articles as De Quincey delivered them, and he told a very different story. 'Every piece of manuscript belonging to the Autobiography which he put into my hands bore many, very many proofs of having been carefully read over and corrected,' he declared. 'As to *hurry*, or rapidity of writing, I ... can only say that he has always told me that he composes *very slowly*; that his language costs him a great deal of attention; that he studies the connection of every sentence with its neighbours.' Further, 'I know that the quantities of manuscript he brought me, at times when I knew he was anxious to write as much as he could, shewed that he did not compose with rapidity or hurry; for they were small as compared to the time he took to produce them.' In a more candid mood, De Quincey himself admitted as much: 'instead of being any compliment it is the most profound insult, the idea one can write something rapidly. It is no homage to the writer; it is villainous insensibility to the written.'[137]

Tait's featured four instalments of the 'Life and Manners' series in 1838, including a three-part essay on Lamb for April, June, and September. In late autumn, on a bitterly cold day of snow and sleet, Bertram saw De Quincey at his Holyrood Gardens address, 'wrapped in an old camlet cloak, cowering over the remains of what ... had been originally a good fire', his 'strikingly beautiful face' overcast by a 'sad and pre-occupied' look.[138] Bertram carried to him the proofs of an article entitled 'A Brief Appraisal of the Greek Literature', which appeared in *Tait's* for December 1838 and June 1839.

The New Year saw De Quincey commence perhaps his best-known biographical study. Written in the early months of 1838 but published from January through August 1839, De Quincey's five-part examination of the life and writings of Wordsworth serves as a companion piece to his earlier four-part series on Coleridge. The essays move broadly and digressively to incorporate accounts of Southey and Coleridge, as well as a moving tribute to Dorothy: 'I have not seen you for many a day – shall never see you again perhaps; but shall attend your steps with tender thoughts, so long as I hear of you living.' Word had reached De Quincey that a 'nervous depression' was now clouding Dorothy's days. His response is highly revealing. 'It is too much to expect of any woman (or man either) that her mind should support itself in a pleasurable activity, under the drooping energies of life, by resting on the past or on the present: some interest in reversion, some subject of hope from day to day, must be called in to reinforce the animal fountains of good spirits. Had that been opened for Miss Wordsworth, I am satisfied that she would have passed a more cheerful middle-age.' With typical incisiveness, De Quincey points to Dorothy's denial of her own literary and intellectual gifts as the reason for her mental collapse.[139]

Yet over the course of the five essays, it is the poet who holds centre stage. De Quincey sketches his biography, including his early days in the Lakes ('I do not conceive that Wordsworth could have been an amiable boy'), his time at Cambridge ('he felt – to use his own words – that his hour was not come'), and his commitment to the French Revolution ('mighty was the transformation which it wrought in the whole economy of his thoughts').[140] Throughout De Quincey summarizes and quotes from Wordsworth's as yet unpublished poem *The Prelude*, possibly from memory but more probably from a transcription that he seems to have produced in 1810 or 1811 when Wordsworth allowed him to read the poem in manuscript.[141]

As was the case in the Coleridge series, De Quincey's attitude towards his subject matter is highly ambivalent, placing him in what he once described as 'a strange sort of contradictory life'.[142] Wordsworth is 'the most original and most meditative man of his own age', a man 'of unimpeached, unimpeachable integrity' who is 'not simply destined to be had in everlasting remembrance by every generation of men, but ... to be had in that *sort* of remembrance which has for its shrine the heart of man'. Yet Wordsworth has also failed De Quincey many times in 'friendship and kindness': 'I acknowledge myself to have been long alienated' from him for reasons 'too deep and too personal for a transient notice'. 'Sometimes even I feel a rising emotion of hostility – nay, something, I fear, too nearly akin to vindictive hatred.' In retrospect, the failure of their relationship was partly 'Wordsworth's in doing too little' and partly 'mine in expecting too much'.[143]

The articles make it clear that the poet could be a trying companion. One day during tea he took down a volume of Burke from De Quincey's bookshelf and proceeded to open its uncut leaves with a butter knife 'that left its greasy honours behind it upon every page: and are they not there to this day?' The experience, De Quincey remarks with equanimity, 'just brought me acquainted with Wordsworth's habits, and that particular, especially, with his intense impatience for one minute's delay which would have brought a remedy'.[144]

Other observations were woundingly indiscreet. Both William and Dorothy had aged prematurely, as 'strangers invariably supposed them fifteen to twenty years older than they were'. Mary Wordsworth had a squint. 'It *ought* to have been displeasing or repulsive' but, De Quincey assures us, 'in fact it was not'. Wordsworth himself was poorly put together.

His 'walk had a wry or twisted appearance; and not appearance only – for I have known it, by slow degrees, gradually to edge off his companion from the middle to the side of the highroad'. More invidiously, one summer morning Dorothy and De Quincey were following the poet and a Westmorland clergyman at a little distance, when Dorothy became 'positively mortified' at what she saw. Next to the 'fine towering figure' of the clergyman, Wordsworth looked narrow and bowed. 'Is it possible?' she asked De Quincey 'in a tone of vexation'. 'Can that be William? How very mean he looks!'[145]

With recollections such as these De Quincey knew that he had crossed the line, and on occasion he fought to keep them out of *Tait's*: 'For God's sake do not send the paper to the press as it is.' In at least two instances he was successful, and Tait reluctantly agreed to remove passages that would have done 'very great injury' to De Quincey, 'besides giving very great pain' to the Wordsworths.[146] Yet at the same time De Quincey had more than enough bile in him to relish the publication of material that revealed Wordsworth in a bad or embarrassing light, though he did not necessarily want to take responsibility for it. His strategy was to send Tait sensational material and then claim that it had been printed before he had been given the chance to edit it. 'If ... you ever look into my Autobiographical Sketches,' he instructed his old friend Talfourd, '... bear in mind that I disown them.'[147] Such disclaimers, according to Tait, were a ruse. De Quincey was telling the story that he wanted to tell, and Tait was doing all he could to accommodate him in terms of time and space. What is more, while they squabbled over different aspects of the series, author and editor were driven by the same objective: selling magazines. And as they both undoubtedly recognized, the juicier the gossip the better.

Reaction to the series was predictably divided. For some, it had the effect Tait most ardently desired. After reading the fifth instalment, the poet and translator Edward FitzGerald concluded that *Tait's* 'seems to be very well worth a shilling a month'.[148] For others, De Quincey's tactlessness was unforgivable. 'The fellow cannot even let Mrs Wordsworth's squint alone!' stormed Hartley Coleridge. Harriet Martineau was philosophical. De Quincey has 'perpetuated an act of treachery scarcely paralleled, we hope, in the history of Literature', especially in his unauthorized use of *The Prelude*. But as she cuttingly put it, 'nobody's name and fame could be really injured by anything De Quincey could say'. Wordsworth himself did not read the articles, but he seethed at what he heard of them: 'A Man who can set such an example, I hold to be ... one of the most worthless of mankind.'[149] Even he was partially mollified, however, when Crabb Robinson told him that De Quincey had described Mary as 'a better wife than you deserve. "Did he say that?" W. exclaimed in a tone of unusual vehemence. "Did he say that? That is *so* true that I can forgive him almost anything else he says."' Robinson himself aptly summed up the series: 'scandalous, but painfully interesting'.[150]

De Quincey concluded his account of Wordsworth in August, but in the 'Life and Manners' sketches that appeared over the next several months, the poet was never far from his thoughts. De Quincey complains rather pathetically that Wordsworth has never honoured 'Professor Wilson or myself . . . with one line, one allusion, from his pen; but many a person, of particular feebleness, has received that honour'. He memorably derides the poet for his 'inhuman' egotism: 'never describe Wordsworth as equal in pride to Lucifer; no, but if you have occasion to write a life of Lucifer, set down that, by possibility, in respect to pride, he might be some type of Wordsworth'. Again he broods on Dove Cottage, invoking both the ghost of Margaret and the memory of Wordsworth. That house, writes De Quincey, 'by ties personal and indestructible', has been 'endeared . . . to my heart so unspeakably beyond all other houses, that even now I rarely dream through four nights running, that I do not find myself (and others beside) in some one of those rooms'.[151]

Working for *Tait's* clearly liberated De Quincey to write searchingly and prolifically of his own past. Yet as his 'Sketches' wound their way to a close, he and Tait found the friction between them growing steadily worse. Matters came to a head in November 1840 when an angry De Quincey pointedly informed Tait that he 'considered himself not well used in the 3 following points': one, the press repeatedly lost proofs that he had corrected; two, the press took no care, or most insufficient care, to adopt the corrections he made to the proofs; and three, the press harassed him about correcting proofs when very often proofs already corrected had not yet been printed.[152] Tait, who had been forbearing in the face of such outbursts, was apparently no longer prepared to put up with them. In February 1841, he published the last of the 'Life and Manners' sketches, and De Quincey disappeared from the pages of the magazine.

[viii]

Remarkably, during this same period, De Quincey also published extensively with *Blackwood's*. Indeed, sometimes there was overlap, and both *Blackwood's* and *Tait's* featured an essay from him in the same month. When it came to being difficult, however, De Quincey did not play favourites. To

Blackwood – as to Tait – there were the incessant requests for money, and the usual delays: 'my manuscripts have become so injured by acid medicines, port wine, and ink thrown upon them – that I am obliged to patch them, piece them, and in some instances rewrite them'.[153] When articles were submitted, De Quincey grumbled that Blackwood inflicted 'castrations' on them, or misplaced parts of them, leading him to protest that he would 'sooner sacrifice the money' than lose work that had cost him so much time and effort.[154] In a particularly testy exchange, De Quincey told Blackwood that he believed him 'incapable of countenancing any unprincipled act', a provocative expression that moved Blackwood to 'indignation and scorn'.[155] Blackwood later declared in exasperation that he could no longer become mixed up in De Quincey's private affairs, to which De Quincey mildly replied that he was 'not aware of ever having done anything of the kind'.[156]

These frustrations notwithstanding, Blackwood typically exercised towards De Quincey an 'accommodating spirit', and the two men managed to keep their relationship on track much of the time.[157] In June 1838 De Quincey presented Blackwood with 'a German Tale (*scene laid in Germany*, I mean, but entirely my own invention), turning upon secret murder'. Blackwood rejected it as too long, but when De Quincey agreed to allow 'friends' of Blackwood to cut it 'to about half its present length', the tale was transformed into his most successful foray into terror fiction. Published in the August number, 'The Avenger' is a story of vigilantism and retribution in which De Quincey offers a 'moral lesson' that 'deserves the deep attention of coming generations', though the corrupt and bloody world of the tale make it difficult to determine what exactly that moral lesson is.[158]

Maximilian Wyndham is an idealized hero who returns from the Napoleonic Wars to settle in a quiet town in north-eastern Germany. Before long a series of brutal murders take place, all of which involve a killer who plants himself within a house and then exterminates the occupants. Footsteps in the chapel promise to 'furnish a clue to the discovery of one at least among the murderous band', while the terrified townspeople grapple with 'the mystery of the *how*, and the profounder mystery of the *why*'. Eventually the murderer is revealed to be Maximilian himself, who is Jewish, and whose mother was publicly flogged to death in the town when he was a boy. Maximilian swears vengeance at her death, and then grows into a quiet but murderously angry adult who knows that the seemingly innocent inhabitants of the town are actually sadists and extremists who executed others for the crime of their race. As he pursues his homicidal career, however, Maximilian comes to seem at least as cruel as his victims, though he insists that their wrongs create his rights. When his reprisals careen so far out of control that he accidentally takes the life of his wife Margaret, he regards her death not as a confirmation of the dead-end futility of violence, but as a final sacrifice that affirms the divinity of his mission. In a closing confessional letter, Maximilian anticipates the rise of crime and detective fiction as he explains the inspired ways in which he committed his acts of murderous vengeance, and marks 'the solution of that mystery which caused such perplexity'.[159]

That autumn De Quincey stumbled when he submitted an article to Blackwood that was thrown back upon his hands. 'I do not perceive the law or principle on which Blackwood rejects or receives,' he cried to Wilson, clearly a serious matter for him, and one that in the past had rarely been a problem.[160] But if he had temporarily lost his bearings, he soon recovered them, for in January 1839, as he worked on his Schiller article for the *Encyclopaedia*, and published the first of his five Wordsworth articles for *Tait's*, De Quincey began his most prolific period as a writer for *Blackwood's*, producing twenty-five articles in twenty-five months, and doing so across a strikingly wide range of topics.[161] 'Generally ... you cannot doubt that for many reasons I should prefer writing for your Journal,' De Quincey assured Blackwood that same January, for he was always adept at telling individual publishers what they wanted to hear.[162] Yet the statement also signals a genuine change in direction. For the past five years, he had concentrated on producing for *Tait's*. Now, as that relationship dwindled into acrimony, *Blackwood's* once again became his primary concern.

De Quincey wrote at length on theology, philosophy, and classical scholarship. His reply to David Hume's argument 'against miracles' was published in July 1839, and centres on a discussion of 'constituent miracles', two of which are 'absolutely indispensable to Christianity, and cannot be separated from it even in thought, viz. the miraculous birth of our Saviour, and his miraculous resurrection'. 'The Essenes', a three-part article for January, April, and May 1840, makes a convoluted case for the incorporation of the Jewish brotherhood of the Essenes within the Christian fold, and is grounded in his conviction that Christianity is superior to all other religions, and Protestantism to all other forms of Christianity. In 'Modern Superstitions', published in April 1840, De Quincey argues that 'superstition, indeed, or the sympathy with the invisible, is the great test of man's nature ... In superstition lies the possibility of religion.'[163] Several of these theophilosophical articles were thoroughly revised before they were published, for De Quincey had exacting standards and Blackwood pushed him hard to ensure that he reached them. What is more, though De Quincey may not always have been aware of it, he was still writing *Blackwood's* articles in collaboration with Wilson, who corrected his response to Hume 'with the utmost accuracy', and who helped to prune 'The Essenes' in order to render it 'suitable to the Magazine'.[164]

Literary criticism also preoccupied De Quincey. His article on the 'Theory of Greek Tragedy' explores the essential difference between the ancient and the English drama. The Greek tragedy is, by 'comparison with the life of Shakespeare, what the inner life of the mimetic play in Hamlet is to the outer life of the Hamlet itself. It is a life below a life.' In 'Milton', he details both how the 'mighty poet' was able to introduce 'the Pagan pantheon into Christian groups', and why he used 'words of art' such as '*architrave*' and '*amphitheatre*' in his descriptions of the 'primitive simplicities of Paradise'. Wordsworth is lauded in a four-part article on 'Style' for 'by far the weightiest thing we ever heard on the subject of style; and it was this – that it is in the highest degree unphilosophic to call language or diction "the *dress* of thoughts"; and what was it then that he would substitute? Why this: he would call it "the *incarnation* of thoughts". Never, in one word, was so profound a truth conveyed.'[165]

Politics retained their grip, as De Quincey once again donned the robes of a 'furious Conservative' who taxed 'even the bigots' of his party 'with being too frigid'.[166] His haughty nationalism frequently passes off British imperial interests as the civilizing mission of Christianity. In 'Foreign Politics', he examines the first 'Anglo-Afghan War' of 1839–42, while in 'The Opium and the China Question' he vigorously defends Britain's role in the first 'Opium War', a three-year battle fought between Britain and China over Britain's illegal smuggling of opium from India into China, and which takes as its unspoken premise De Quincey's vested interest in ensuring that opium continues to flow from the East back to the West. Britain's domestic agenda also brings out the John Bull in him. 'Hints for the Hustings' is his most provocative consideration of a series of key contemporary issues, including the so-called 'bedchamber crisis', when the Conservative leader Robert Peel insisted that the Whig ladies of Queen Victoria's bedchamber be removed, and the Queen imperiously refused; the Irish Catholic secret society of Ribbonmen, who wore green ribbons as badges, and were notorious for their sectarian outrages; the intractable problem of the Corn Laws, controversial measures of agricultural protection that benefited large landowners and punished the working class by keeping the cost of domestic grains artificially high; and Chartism, a working-class movement for parliamentary reform that De Quincey dismisses as 'nothing more than ancient Jacobinism'.[167]

Perhaps the most memorable article from these months is his November

1839 sequel to 'On Murder Considered as One of the Fine Arts'. The essay opens with a bantering address to Wilson as Christopher North before moving to the description of a raucous dinner at which murder connoisseurs celebrate the achievements of a long line of practitioners, from Indian Thugs and Jewish Sicarii to more recent adepts such as the infamous Edinburgh killers William Burke and William Hare. De Quincey introduces a curmudgeon known as 'Toad-in-the-hole', who has grown despondent of late at the paucity of really fine murders, but who is given new life when he learns of Williams's sensational 1811 debut on the Ratcliffe Highway. In both the original and the sequel De Quincey exploits the same satiric topsy-turviness that enables him to graze the brink between comedy and horror, though in the sequel morality is not so much suspended as inverted. Artistic and ethical standards must be maintained, insists the narrator. 'For if once a man indulges himself in murder, very soon he comes to think little of robbing; and from robbing he comes next to drinking and Sabbath-breaking, and from that to incivility and procrastination. Once begin upon this downward path, you never know where you are to stop.'[168]

[ix]

Months of immense productivity for Black, Tait, and Blackwood had no immediate effect on De Quincey's finances. He seems to have been both so inured to desperation that he could not see beyond it, and so in need of it that he did not want to. His money problems were genuine, but almost entirely avoidable. A bewildered Florence later attributed these terrible financial pressures to 'some strange failure of intellect – they were so purposeless, and brought such unspeakable pain to his own higher nature and to those he loved'. Added Emily: 'I think no one will make much out of my father who does not take in the extreme mixture of childish folly joined to a great intellect.'[169]

'Snowed up'. That was De Quincey's term for a room that he had so stuffed with books and papers that 'there was not a square inch ... on the table to set a cup upon', 'no possibility of making his bed', 'no chair which could be used for its legitimate purpose', and no track 'from the door to the fireplace'. When the confusion grew to the point where he could no longer work, De Quincey often simply locked the door and turned elsewhere, 'leaving his landlady, if ... honest, fearfully impressed with the mysterious sin of meddling with his papers, but, if dishonest, with such a handle for playing upon his morbid anxieties, as was a source of livelihood'. De

Quincey's habit of renting multiple rooms seems only to have grown worse as time went on.[170]

In the autumn of 1838, he was sued twice by his solicitor Thomas McIndoe, who had recently added his name to the long list of those who had provided De Quincey with legal advice. Two of De Quincey's sons had stayed with McIndoe at 113 Princes Street earlier in the year and the suits probably involved arrears on the rent. At around this same time De Quincey himself went one evening to consult with McIndoe, whose wife noticed that 'some essential part' of his 'outgoing raiment was wanting', and asked him to stay until the next morning in order that she might have time to mend it. De Quincey accepted the kind invitation and was before long himself the regular occupant of McIndoe's 'bedroom by the side of the dining-room'. The Scottish preacher William B. Robertson, a kinsman of McIndoe's, visited De Quincey often, and vividly recalled his 'low-toned, weird, musical speech – to which I would, alone with him, night after night, listen for hours together'. Many years later, Robertson's younger sister remembered being in awe of 'that door and the mysterious man behind it, who put forth his hand to receive his meals'. One day she and De Quincey's daughter Emily were playing in the lobby when 'the door of the dreaded room was opened softly' and De Quincey asked if he might speak to her. The young girl ran screaming into the kitchen, but Emily dragged her back to the door, and pushed her in. 'De Quincey spoke kindly, and said, "I do not wish to frighten you, my dear, but only to ask you whether your name is Rober*t*son, Rob*i*son, or Rob*in*son."'[171]

Other company gathered round. Hill Burton, who had sought an introduction years earlier, met him now and offered his aid 'in borrowing a few books'. The publisher Robert Chambers declined De Quincey's offer to become a contributor to *Chambers's Edinburgh Journal*, but the two men became friends. 'He used to spend many Sundays at my father's house', recalled Chambers's daughter, 'and had to rush back to get into Sanctuary before twelve o'clock, after which hour he could be arrested. For the sake of convenience he left a pair of his Wellington boots in my mother's keeping.'[172] The preacher and biographer George Gilfillan was introduced to De Quincey and 'spent two nights with him. He is the most extraordinary specimen of humanity I ever met with.' The newspaper editor and writer Robert Carruthers visited with De Quincey in Tait's shop, and the next evening enjoyed an oyster supper with him, 'when I listened with intense pleasure and surprise to his musical voice and eloquent periods for at least six mortal hours'.[173] An anonymous recollection, most probably by the writer and clergyman Robert Aris Willmott, described passing a night with De

Quincey at around this time. 'The winds, keen and cutting as a scythe, swept the North Bridge of Edinburgh; but snugly seated in the Rainbow, we bade defiance to its blast. When fully kindled up and warmed in his subject, his whole talk is poetry.' John Pringle Nichol, Professor of Astronomy at the University of Glasgow, met De Quincey at a dinner party hosted by the novelist Catherine Crowe, 'in whose house in Darnaway Street' De Quincey spent 'many a pleasant evening'. 'The little man came very late, dressed in a rusty suit of black. In the drawing-room, after dinner, he and Dr Nichol stood together in a corner, engaged in talk, when, in a slow, measured tone, De Quincey said to his new acquaintance, "Dr Nichol, can you lend me twopence?" He borrowed money ... to lay out on opium, and always asked for very small sums, knowing that they would not be refused.'[174] In May 1840 De Quincey lamented 'the utter solitude I have suffered for more than 2 years'. Seven months later he told Blackwood that, 'except Mrs McIndoe once in 6 or 7 weeks, and my son Fred, I have seen no human being, for 15 months'.[175] Such claims were clearly intended to convince his publishers that he was focused solely on work, but as had often been the case in the past, De Quincey was socializing far more than he liked to let on.

Getting out was probably very good for him. He was often in poor health, 'condemned to a watery diet of slops', or plagued by 'obstinate sleeplessness', or simply 'too ill to write'.[176] In July 1840 his eyes gave way as he worked through the night by a gas light that had no glass and burned 'with a fierce flickering sort of roar'. For a month back 'I have had but a feeble glimmer of sight', while for 'the last three days large spots of colour obscure everything'.[177] Deplorable living conditions further undermined his health, but there was no money to improve the situation. His 'hereditary funds' were locked up by past debt.[178] Black, Tait, and Blackwood were all garnishing large portions of his wage to pay bills they had guaranteed.[179] And the vast majority of the money that did come to him went immediately to support his six children, as well as Margaret's father and possibly her uncle Park. Between January 1839 and July 1840 De Quincey was sued seven times, including once by McIndoe, and twice by his sanctuary landlady Jane Miller, who submitted a petition to seize his books and papers for sale.[180] In May 1840, as various ills closed down upon him, De Quincey produced one of the most harrowing letters he ever wrote:

Having in a moment of pinching difficulty for my children about 10 months since pawned every article of my dress which would produce a shilling, I have since that time had no stockings, no shoes, no neck handkerchief, coat, waistcoat, or hat. I have sate constantly barefoot; and, being constitutionally or from the use of opium unusually sensible of cold, I should really have been unable to sit up and write but for a counterpane which I wrap round my shoulders ... Such hardships ... I could support with some chearfulness, – were they of any use to others. But the painful result from the whole is – that, after paying little to any creditor but one, as regards that one I am about £100 worse than I was when I began. This is terrific.[181]

On 15 August 1840 De Quincey turned fifty-five years old. He had managed to fight on for three years without Margaret, but not to pull himself free of deprivation.

For all its severity and persistence, however, there is an aspect of De Quincey's grief that cannot be taken at face value. De Quincey sought often to hide or excuse broken promises, late-night visitings, book collecting, and especially his drug addiction, which he mentioned only sporadically in his correspondence with his employers, but which fundamentally shaped his daily existence. His favourite tactic was to draw attention away from these indulgences by creating a diversion, most often in the form of a barrage of cries for more time, more money, and more support. In January 1839 he faced 'the severe pressure of legal hunters'. In February he was 'writing (as often I am compelled to do) in the street'. May: 'I have been driven to dire extremities'. July: 'I am in the very centre of a fierce struggle'. December: 'Already I have been aground for half a week'.[182] January 1840: 'I shall never extricate myself to the end of time'. March: 'I am driven to the last gasp'. May: 'the persecutions I suffer allow me no choice'. October: 'I am a done man'. December: 'I am overwhelmed by a most perplexing affair'.[183] February 1841: 'I am in the greatest difficulty for money'.[184]

Yet throughout all these struggles, De Quincey harboured in his McIndoe lodgings 'about 8 separate works' of the sixteenth-century Italian philosopher Giordano Bruno, along 'with one or two' other volumes 'almost equally rare'. These were the volumes for which he declared that he 'would not take a thousand guineas'.[185] While hunger, cold, and despair bit deeper into him and into his family, and while he protested loudly and frequently against his fate, he refused to pawn or auction these precious jewels from his library. His need for them appears to have been almost as strong as his need for opium. The books were in his possession when he died.[186] De Quincey lived amidst grim realities, and often he fought bravely against them. But on other occasions he manufactured or exploited his distress in order to front his quiet pursuit of opium, and books, and freedom.

He tried to take care of his children. From their grandmother they received what paid 'for clothes, schooling, house, up to the 12th of each month', but 'on the 13th' they fell upon him, and 'their total weight' was often more than he could bear. At an especially low ebb he appealed to Blackwood for the 'punctual payment of "trifling" balances' in order to save one of his daughters from 'a 14 hours' starvation'.[187] Yet in periods of relative calm he was generous with his children far beyond his means. One day he bought all his daughters bonnets, and on another evening he escorted one of them to a dance at Robert Chambers's house.[188]

His two eldest sons, meanwhile, were now old enough to leave home. Horace was to enter the military. The cost, including the commission, was over nine hundred pounds, seven hundred of which fell jointly on De Quincey and his mother, and above two hundred more solely on De Quincey. How on earth he raised these funds is not clear, but the money was paid and Horace prepared to join the 26th Regiment.[189] Francis was to go into business. John Kelsall, who decades earlier had been brought into the mercantile trade by De Quincey's father, had a son, Strettel Kelsall, who was now eager to return the favour by bringing one of De Quincey's sons into the trade, and before long Francis had joined Kelsall and moved to Manchester.[190]

In the summer of 1840 De Quincey owed his Holyrood landlady Jane Miller just over £175 for rent and a series of small loans. The family received a formal notice to quit the house in August.[191] De Quincey was 'thoroughly harassed' by these circumstances and 'unable to write a line'. His children, however, took action: first they successfully persuaded him to turn over 'the management of his small fixed income' to them; and then they obtained Mavis Bush Cottage, a 'decent little home' seven miles outside of Edinburgh near the village of Lasswade, where they moved on 14 August. It was a change, Florence declared, 'which rests in my memory as one of the most lively foretastes of Paradise I have had in my life'.[192] The hell of sanctuary was finally over.

De Quincey did not join his children at the cottage, but he too was making plans to leave Edinburgh. McIndoe had become his fiercest persecutor. The situation seems to have broken down in April 1840, when he sent a terse letter to De Quincey, addressed in the third person when they were both living in the same house. Given De Quincey's enormous literary output over the past two years, McIndoe apparently speaks with some justification when he points out that 'Mr De Quincey ... has enjoyed a great deal of care and has been saved from a great deal of vexation' during his time at 113 Princes Street. But McIndoe was no longer prepared to wait for 'Mr De Quincey, because he appears to be indifferent' to any claims made upon him for arrears, 'however pressing these may be'.[193] For three weeks McIndoe made 'the most violent efforts at ejecting' De Quincey, and it was at least another three before the two men effected some sort of truce, and De Quincey was able to return to his writing.[194] Unfortunately, the situation collapsed again in November, when McIndoe renewed his demands that De Quincey either pay the rent or leave the house, though De Quincey insisted that McIndoe's immediate object was retaining his manuscripts: 'personally I was not a prisoner: but by my papers, which would have been held over my head for years to come as a screw for extorting money, I was'.[195] Trapped and intimidated, De Quincey's description of his circumstances typically assumes the cast of terror fiction. Mrs McIndoe has avowed 'openly to me that she has been trying and feeling my letters to ascertain if they contained bank notes ... After this who could doubt tampering with locks, listening, eaves dropping.' He had to get out. 'But I am obliged to proceed cautiously,' he confided to Blackwood: 'and amongst other cautions *I have earnestly to request that you will not leave this letter lying on any table open to strangers ...* A *boy* amongst your servants, or a *porter ...* might chance to make treacherous discoveries.'[196]

It was late February before De Quincey had the 'prospect of liberation from the dire perplexity of my position without sacrificing my manuscripts'. Shortly thereafter, he packed up as much as he could, hired a porter, and somehow stole from McIndoe's without being detected, just as he had stolen from Charles Lawson's house as a Manchester schoolboy nearly four decades earlier. He headed to Glasgow, where by early March he was living with Professor Nichol at the university.[197] McIndoe sued him one final time in April, though at that point he almost certainly had no idea where he was. 'Henceforwards I am a free man,' De Quincey claimed exultantly.[198] It was a rare moment of joy after months of suffering and upheaval. But De Quincey was far from free.

PART FOUR

SUSPIRIA

1841–59

TWELVE

Lasswade

[i]

'What has he done? – From the beginning of his career to this hour, I know of no man who has so uniformly and consistently avoided writing any thing *good*.'¹ So a disgruntled reader condemned De Quincey in an October 1840 letter to William Tait. Yet by the early 1840s the impact of De Quincey's writings, and especially of his *Confessions*, was remarkably extensive. In 1828, the French poet and playwright Alfred de Musset produced *L'Anglais, mangeur d'opium*, a free translation of the *Confessions*. Just eighteen years old when the work was published, Musset followed the broad outline of De Quincey's tale, but omitted several passages, summarized others, and inserted a great deal, including an entire episode in which De Quincey meets Ann again at a ball, fights a duel on her behalf, and then elopes with her.²

Propelled by Musset's adaptation, De Quincey's influence soon spread through France, and well beyond. The composer Hector Berlioz drew on De Quincey's fascination with nightmares, opium, and idealized portraits of young women in the production of his *Symphonie Fantastique* (1830).³ Théophile Gautier's 'La Pipe d'Opium' (1838), as well as Honoré de Balzac's 'L'opium' (1830), 'Les litanies romantiques' (1830), and 'Massimilla Doni' (1839), all rework different aspects of the *Confessions*. The Russian novelist Nikolai Gogol borrowed from Musset's translation for 'The Nevsky Prospect' (1835), particularly in his portrayal of the city, where the shadows, outcasts, drugs, and despair of De Quincey's Oxford Street shape his representations of Saint Petersburg's Nevsky Prospect.⁴

American writers too responded to De Quincey. During his first visit to Britain in 1833, Ralph Waldo Emerson was 'inspired' with the 'wish to see the faces of three or four writers': 'Coleridge, Wordsworth, Landor, De Quincey'.⁵ In 'Turkish Sketches' (1836) the Reverend Walter Colton found his imagination 'so kindled, by the perusal of a little book called the "Opium-Eater", that I resolved to put its pleasing assurances to a practical test. So, sending to an apothecary's shop, I procured two enormous doses of the precious drug.'[6] In 'How to Write a Blackwood Article' (1838), Edgar Allan Poe offers exuberant praise of the *Confessions*: 'fine, very fine! – glorious imagination – deep philosophy – acute speculation – plenty of fire and fury, and a good spicing of the decidedly unintelligible'.[7] Moreover, several of Poe's most famous tales, including 'Ligeia' (1838) and 'The Fall of the House of Usher' (1839), contain opium addicts, while in 'The Masque of the Red Death' (1842), he draws deeply on De Quincey's *Klosterheim*.[8] William Blair consciously modelled his *Opium-Eater in America* (1842) on the *Confessions*. 'Before my entranced sight', writes Blair, 'magnificent halls stretched out in endless succession, with gallery above gallery, while the roof was blazing with gems, like stars whose rays alone illumined the whole building, which was thronged with strange, gigantic figures.'[9]

In Britain, De Quincey's most decisive impact seems to have been on Branwell Brontë, who read the *Confessions* for the first time around 1839. The book captivated him, and he soon followed De Quincey into opium addiction, which 'seized on his nervous system' until he 'underwent the torture of the damned'. In late 1839 Brontë moved to the Lake District, and shortly thereafter paid a visit to Coleridge's eldest son Hartley, who was at that time living at The Nab.[10] In April 1840 Brontë sent De Quincey 'Sir Henry Tunstall', one of his finest poems, as well as translations of five odes from Horace. 'There are doubtless many mistakes of sense and language,' Brontë told De Quincey. '. . . I had not when I translated them, a Horace at hand, so was forced to rely on memory.' De Quincey seems not to have responded to Brontë, but he did manage to avoid the fate that engulfed his young admirer, who died eight years later in the grip of debt, alcohol, and opiates. In procuring the drug, Elizabeth Gaskell remarked, Brontë 'showed all the cunning of the opium-eater'.[11]

[ii]

John Pringle Nichol was a political economist, a radical, and the Regius Professor of Astronomy at the University of Glasgow. A lifelong friend of John Stuart Mill and a notable influence on Poe, Nichol 'looked like a poet, without knowing that he did so'. De Quincey arrived at the Old College in Glasgow to take up an invitation to visit that Nichol had extended a few years earlier when the two had first met in Edinburgh. To De Quincey, Nichol was 'most kind', and especially interesting for his 'intellectual characteristics', which placed the 'deep meditative style of his mind . . . in conflict for ever with the tumultuous necessity in *him* for travelling along the line of revolutionary thought'.[12]

De Quincey had been staying at the college about two weeks when Nichol received a shipment of 'the earliest amongst a series of splendid instruments' that were to be housed in a new Observatory being built in Glasgow's west end, but which in the interim Nichol was forced to store in the confined space of his own rooms.[13] Now obviously in the way, De Quincey transferred himself just a short distance to the Old College lodgings of Edward Law Lushington, a Cambridge 'Apostle', the Professor of Greek at Glasgow, and the future brother-in-law of Alfred Tennyson. De Quincey and Lushington had met for the first time at Nichol's only days earlier, but a friendship quickly developed. De Quincey arrived at Lushington's on 16 March and, on sitting down to dinner that same day, was seized 'with a violent affection, inflammatory and connected with strong delirium, that for many subsequent days prostrated me in an infant state of helplessness', as he explained in a letter to Blackwood, who was waiting for various articles from him.[14]

Illness often prevented De Quincey from delivering manuscripts on time, and in this instance he may well have been sick. But he was not giving Blackwood the whole story. Far from being unable to leave his bed, two days after arriving at Lushington's, De Quincey was back in Edinburgh, where he was arrested 'in the hands of ... Mr William Tait', and 'at the instance of Frances Wilson', his former landlord in Lothian Street. What is more, not only was he charged under his own name, but also under the name of an alias, 'T. E. Manners Ellis', a remarkable indication of the kinds of duplicity he resorted to in order to try and elude his pursuers.[15] On this occasion he seems once again to have avoided prison, but he was clearly not anxious to tell Blackwood that he had been in Edinburgh, at Tait's, and under arrest. So he pleaded sickness, and returned to writing for Blackwood as soon as he could. Blackwood, it seems, was none the wiser.

Staying with Lushington was not intended to be more than a temporary solution, and by 12 April De Quincey had taken lodgings in the High Street 'opposite the gate of the Professor's Court in the old College'. From here he sent Blackwood two translations, one of which featured the letters of the historian Barthold Georg Niebuhr, and the other of which brought together key passages from the autobiography of the poet and historian Ernst Moritz Arndt. Living in these 'strange' lodgings, however, soon reduced De Quincey to a state of 'extreme perplexity'.[16] He was without the support of his family, and he could meet very few of his financial obligations in Glasgow, for virtually all of his income was funnelled by Blackwood to his children at Lasswade or his creditors in Edinburgh.

Within only a few weeks De Quincey was convinced that he would soon be forced out 'into the street'. Compounding these problems was the ongoing deterioration of his health, which collapsed again in early May, leaving him unable 'to rise even to let the bed be arranged'.[17] More than a month passed before he felt well enough to walk. At least, De Quincey claimed, his drinking had been brought under control. 'Were it not for my excessive temperance, I should long since have been dead,' he assured Blackwood, though this may have been another half-truth, for at this same moment he also observed that neither in classical times 'nor in our days is there any just appreciation of the subsidiary benefits which sometimes arise from strong liquors'.[18]

Part of his solution to these troubles was to move again, this time to 79 Renfield Street, where he rented two rooms in the family home of Mr Thomas Youille (or Yuille), a college officer and a 'trust-worthy man' on a salary of £40 a year.[19] Youille was for many months a generous landlord whose wife and daughters were soon involved in assisting De Quincey with money, books, supplies, and the mail. The new and much more supportive surroundings undoubtedly brought De Quincey a degree of relief, and yet his overall situation remained much the same. Gilfillan seems to have visited at around this time, and found De Quincey 'in a mean room, such as students were wont to live in for five or six shillings a week ... I heard of him, either before or after that time, living a while in a friend's house, in a half-torpid condition under opium.'[20]

At some point during these weeks De Quincey also received a visit from his son Horace. The boy was soon to enter the Army and, having travelled through England on 'some farewell visits to family connexions', he returned to Scotland to bid goodbye to his father. His spirits on the occasion, however, were weighed down by a familiar family problem. Horace owed the tailor Buckmaster £116 for '*extra* equipment' purchased after all the initial costs were paid in full, and he was in arrears an additional £60 to a series of 'petty creditors chiefly in England'. Both debts, De Quincey reported, Horace 'relied upon being able to meet himself within a year by means of presents which he anticipated from near relatives in England'.[21]

June brought alarming news from Lasswade. Margaret was ill. She had suffered two 'nearly fatal' haemorrhages, and the local surgeon, Mr Smith, apprehended 'a 3rd which ... would *certainly* be so'. Filled with terrible anxiety, De Quincey had to wait several days before he learned that his daughter was almost out of danger, though his immense relief was coupled with the guilty recognition that the 'illness was caused by her sensibility to the persecution she underwent' from angry creditors who had tracked her down to Lasswade. 'This child will die, I foresee, under the misery of her situation,' De Quincey reported. 'For she has no firmness to face it, – is entirely guiltless of wrong: and I, unless I can do something effectual and sudden, shall feel myself in part the cause.' Like her mother and namesake before her, Margaret lived in the country and fought off creditors while De Quincey buried himself in the city and struggled unsuccessfully to make enough money for both himself and his children. Once again he was filled with the dreadful thought that he might be responsible for someone's death, if only partially in this instance. At one especially difficult moment Margaret and Francis took the risky step of borrowing £250 in their own names in an effort to put an end to the harassment.[22]

Most of his pursuers lost sight of him when he decamped to Glasgow, but De Quincey stayed in touch with Mary Miller, to whom, along with her sister Jane, he still owed rent on his Holyrood Gardens rooms. He made several payments to her, and even revealed how she might contact him through either Nichol or Lushington.[23] Later she called on him at Youille's 'for the purpose ... of raising money'.[24] A second former landlady also wished to speak to De Quincey, but her attentions were far less welcome. Mrs McIndoe had decided to hound him with the same vigour previously shown by her husband. She traced De Quincey to Glasgow, where she tricked one of Nichol's daughters into revealing his whereabouts.[25] De Quincey fled on that occasion, but 'she tracked him from lodging to lodging, and took advantage of the hours when she knew he was not at home, to procure admission to his rooms'. Eventually De Quincey 'represented to Professor Nichol that the woman had conceived a violent but hopeless attachment to him, which he could not reciprocate'. His risible explanation belies the depth of his anxiety. Plagued on the one hand by 'the morbid value he set upon his papers' in her possession, and on the other by her repeated demands for money, De Quincey regarded her as 'his evil genius'.[26]

That summer the Tories under Sir Robert Peel swept back into power with a long-expected general election victory over the Whigs. De Quincey's response, 'Sir Robert Peel's Position on Next Resuming Power', appeared in *Blackwood's* for September 1841, and celebrated a return to conservative values and policies. Britons had been thoroughly disillusioned by the false promises of Whiggery. 'We believe the great Reform mania, which has agitated our public atmosphere in varying strengths through the last eleven years, to be now at length ebbing to its very lees,' De Quincey declared. The defeated Whig Prime Minister Lord Melbourne had stayed in power far too long. 'Chop off his hands, he clings by his feet; chop off his feet, he clings by his teeth. And in reality, even these images do not express the intensity of that last desperate struggle by which [he] has clung to his seat.'[27]

Beyond contemporary politics, De Quincey needed to be as resourceful as ever to keep generating articles. Procrastination, he confessed to Lushington, remained amongst his 'infirmities', but Lushington's classical expertise, together with his willingness to borrow books from the university library, enabled De Quincey to produce a string of *Blackwood's* essays on Greek literature, beginning with 'Plato's Republic' in July, and followed shortly thereafter by a three-part examination of 'Homer and the Homeriade' for October, November, and December. 'Prof. Wilson, I believe, takes an interest in this question', De Quincey informed Blackwood; 'and will be pleased, I flatter myself, with the paper: which is unequalled amongst mine at least for quantity of previous reading.'[28]

December brought word that Horace was 'afloat for China', where he would fight with British forces under Sir Hugh Gough in the 'Opium Wars'.[29] A month earlier, and almost certainly in the knowledge that his son would soon be in the East, the jingo in De Quincey surged to the surface in his *Blackwood's* assessment of the 'Canton Expedition and Convention'. Though Britain was illegally importing opium into China, its aggression in the war was wholly justified, De Quincey argues. In a country like China, 'it happens too often ... that to murder is the one sole safeguard against being murdered ... We did nothing wrong, because nothing that was not essential to self-preservation.' Indeed, despite the bloodshed, De Quincey is brutally confident that Britain's imperial agenda in the East will ultimately be seen as mutually advantageous. 'Many times must the artillery score its dreadful lessons upon their carcasses, before they will be healed of their treachery, or we shall be allowed to live in the diffusion of peaceful benefits.'[30]

The New Year hit him with rounds of debilitating illness. He was racked by purpura, and while Blackwood greeted the news with some scepticism, De Quincey assured him that he had exaggerated neither his despair nor the malignity of the disease. 'Dr Easton ... told me – that ... he expected for some days that mortification would take place in the right leg: and to my landlady he said – that it was the very worst case of *Purpura* which he had seen in his Hospital experience.'[31] After a 'shocking relapse' in February, Dr Easton called in Dr Hanna, who concluded that gout was 'mixed up with *purpura* in this case'.[32] Three months passed without improvement, and opium only made his problems worse. 'The *purpura* is so radicated that upon any use of a stimulant tho' but for an extra effort of one 24 hours, or any sacrifice through this stimulant of a few hours' sleep, – both legs are in one night scorched scarlet and purple, rheumatism on waking seizes the whole frame, I cannot lift either arm, – and other incapacitating effects follow.'[33]

Constipation was one of those effects, and another direct result of his opium addiction. In March his 'condition from danger of inflammation of the bowels had become shocking'. That 'I did not kill myself was owing chiefly I believe to my taking no liquor – and hardly anything else'. His doctors prescribed remedies, but De Quincey could not afford them. 'Even the oranges, which are ordered by Dr Hanna, I cannot buy.'[34] De Quincey beseeched Blackwood to help him relieve the suffering. 'Nothing else than *Seidlitz powders* has, for some years, availed in my case: and 3 separate doses are required to reach the effect. Now, if you would oblige me by sending me 21 of the powders, so as to form 7 distinct days' doses, – this would amply suffice for a fortnight.' Blackwood generously complied and, in the short term, De Quincey was 'very much better indeed', though soon the laxatives began to work so well that he had the opposite problem.[35] 'In the whole system of houses, to which this house is attached, there exists but one *templum Cloacinae*. Now imagine the fiend driving a man thither thro' 8 and 10 hours successively. Such a man becomes himself a public nuisance, and is in some danger of being removed by assassination.'[36]

Poor health, moreover, was not all that plagued De Quincey. Writing supplies were a real problem. In March he rejoiced when he received three new pens, and later he asked Blackwood if the seidlitz powders he was sending could be wrapped in some writing paper, 'such as this on which I write'? Better still, maybe Blackwood could send paper 'a little *more* satiny or glazed', for De Quincey remained as finicky as ever about the presentation of his work, no matter how bad the surrounding circumstances.[37] Mundane tasks filled him with an anxiety amounting to dread. 'This morning I opened a letter which has been in my hands for 4 days, but which from nervous cowardice according to my practice I had not opened.'[38] Expectedly, Mary Miller and the McIndoes were after him again about back rent, and he had fallen badly into arrears with the Youilles.[39] Unexpectedly, 'a fire arose in the shop immediately below' his rooms, and while his 'papers and everything else' were safely removed, the 'vexation' caused 'a total interruption of 7 hours'.[40]

Yet he kept writing. The Conservatives had been in power for seven months when he returned to contemporary politics with his April 1842 assessment of 'Sir Robert Peel's Policy'. 'Not steam power is at this moment more effectually revolutionizing the world' than those agitators who want to repeal the Corn Laws, and who argue in favour of 'what is now called

Manhood Suffrage'. Drastic measures were needed to stave off these reckless demands, and De Quincey saw reason for great optimism when Peel introduced one of the most famous budgets of the nineteenth century on 11 March. 'It was understood at a glance that his measure, in so far as it was burdensome, had been called for by the negligence and errors not of himself, but of his opponents; and that, in so far as it promised to be splendidly effective, it was indebted to his characteristic boldness, and his determination to look the national difficulties in the face.'[41]

De Quincey's confidence in Peel remained high over the course of the summer, but he found himself increasingly unnerved by the actions of the insurrectionists. Though he lived among the poor, and had done so for many years, he regarded them in *Blackwood's*, not with sympathy, but with deep suspicion. 'We, who often talk with poor men ... have rarely found them other than jacobins at heart,' he stated in 'Anti-Corn-Law Deputation to Sir Robert Peel', published in the magazine for August. He was equally to the point a month later in his article on 'The Riots', where he condemned the Chartists and Corn League activists for trying to 'put an end to our whole polity and civil existence'. 'To a man,' he explained to Blackwood, 'I look upon the working poor, Scottish or English, as latent Jacobins – *biding their time.*'[42]

Overheated political assaults were a De Quinceyan speciality in *Blackwood's*, but that autumn he also wrote on Ricardian political economy, which had long inspired radicals, but which De Quincey embraced as an abstract system of power and exchange that brought him both intellectual excitement and aesthetic pleasure. Published in *Blackwood's* for September, October, and December, 'Ricardo Made Easy' lauds Ricardo for revolutionizing the science of economics, particularly in his analysis of value and rent, and offers a series of memorable examples that illuminate key Ricardian ideas. Yet De Quincey does have frank misgivings about Ricardo, especially concerning his opposition to the Corn Laws. 'David, ringleader of the wicked anti-corn-law mutineers', he writes scornfully, 'how is it ... that "very filth and shame" did not check thee in thus calling for aid upon that honest truth which thy whole faction had so deeply foresworn?'[43] The third and final instalment of 'Ricardo Made Easy' was a good deal more digressive than the previous two, but – revealingly – it pleased Alexander Blackwood, who announced to his brother John that De Quincey had 'wound up his Political Economy lectures in capital style'.[44]

Near the end of the year he received terrible news: Horace had died, apparently of a malarious fever, at Chich Choo in China, on 27 August 1842.[45] When notices from foreign newspapers began to reach Britain a few months later, Margaret and her sisters were frantic, and sought confirmation of the death. They wrote first to their father in the hope of 'quickening' him 'in attending to the subject', but he did not respond.[46] They then contacted Robert Blackwood, who wrote to John in London: 'I wish you to make particular enquiry about the following in a Newspaper published at Calcutta and which came home with the *November* Mail. There is a paragraph that Horace De Quincey of the 26th had died at Hong Kong ... His sisters are in real distress and believe him dead.'[47] Wilson seems at this time to have told De Quincey that there was 'some doubt ... about the death of his son', but was obliged soon afterwards to confirm the worst. 'I am sorry,' De Quincey replied, '... but it was against my advice he went to China at all.'[48] Such a callous attitude towards one of his children is highly uncharacteristic, and comes in the midst of a recollection by Wilson that contains several errors of fact. But it may be that after months of illness and sorrow, and following the deaths of Julius, William, and Margaret, De Quincey had simply reached the end of his ability to respond to yet more loss in his family.

Contradictory reports of him emerge over the next several months. According to De Quincey himself, 'excessive illness' plagued him through the winter, and well into the spring. 'The pains of gout ... are the least thing,' he wrote to Blackwood on 19 March 1843: 'the greatest is – the deadly languishing from blood continually growing more torpid.'[49] A month later 'the horny substance, which encrusts my feet, increases continually', and by May he was 'much more sunk and dilapidated here than ever before'.[50] When his old friend Charles Knight called in, however, he found De Quincey looking better than he had done twelve years earlier. He had 'a beard a foot long ... the cultivation of which, he said, was necessary to his health'. These same months saw Professor Nichol's young son John, the future Regius Professor of English Literature at Glasgow, take a series of walks with De Quincey out to the new Observatory. Nichol later described their conversations as among his 'most cherished recollections'.[51]

De Quincey stayed busy recasting and expanding his three articles on 'Ricardo Made Easy' with the intention of turning them into a book. By the end of April the project was nearing completion, but De Quincey was apparently feeling overwhelmed by the size of the task and the clutter of his room. It is unclear whether he asked for help or his daughters sensed that he needed it, but in early May he was joined in Glasgow by his twenty-year-old son Francis, who had recently moved back to Lasswade after deciding against a career with Mr Kelsall in the Manchester mercantile trade. His appearance was a great relief to his father. 'Without his aid', De

Quincey confessed, 'from my dire immobility, I never could have separated' the papers intended for the book from the 'masses of others with which by long lying about they had got confounded'. It took father and son about two weeks to pull the final sections together, and on 16 May they mailed to Blackwood 'the *entire* remainder of the little book on Political Economy'.[52]

Debt, however, continued to undermine De Quincey's own economy.[53] His landlord Youille had been patient for months, but on 22 May he gave De Quincey an ultimatum: 'if on Thursday June 1 ... I could pay up an arrear still standing against my name, – well and good: if not, that on that day I must take my departure'. De Quincey hung on until the evening of 2 June, but he could not find the money, and he was 'obliged to go' after two years with the Youilles.[54] Francis almost certainly assisted him as he gathered together as much as possible from the heaps of books and papers that he had accumulated, and made his way from Glasgow to his children's home at Lasswade.

[iii]

It marked a turning point. Margaret, with great courage and common sense, had used her father's annuity, plus the money he had sent to her from Glasgow, to pay off debts, and to bring what must have seemed previously unimaginable levels of comfort and financial stability to the household. Mavis Bush contained eight rooms, 'one of which (the largest), or what in London is called the *first* floor, is used as a drawing-room, and one about half the size, on the ground floor, a dining-room'. The cottage was home to all five De Quincey children: Francis and Fred were as yet unsettled on careers, while Margaret, Florence, and Emily lived in 'the most absolute harmony', doing chores, reading books, playing music, and visiting when they could.[55] De Quincey himself occupied the small study on the ground floor to the right of the entrance, which he soon crammed full of manuscripts and books, though his daughters kept the confusion in check in order to ensure that his 'papering' did not gradually force them all out of the house.[56] The family kept two female servants, a housemaid and a cook.

'My father's habits were simple, almost to asceticism,' Florence remembered. 'Owing to the neuralgic suffering ... he early lost all his teeth; and, from the extreme delicacy of his system, he could eat nothing less capable of perfect mastication than bread, so that only too often a little soup or coffee was his whole dinner.'[57] The cold bothered him a great deal, and even in the months of July and August, he was forced to sit in the 'closest proximity to a blazing fire', with cloaks, blankets, counterpanes, hearth-rugs, and horse-cloths piled upon his shoulders.[58] Yet his overall condition was much improved, he contended, for he had begun to take 'iron as a medicine', and it had bestowed upon him what he had long lacked: 'some hope of restoration'.[59]

Walking became a central part of his daily routine, for in his eyes working the laudanum out of his system through exercise was one of the best ways of combating his addiction. One circuit around the perimeter of the back garden was forty-four yards, meaning that 'forty rounds were exactly required for one mile'. De Quincey usually began before breakfast, and within ninety days he had walked a thousand miles. Initially he counted his progress by a rosary of blue and white beads, but the plan proved troublesome, and he switched to a system of applying stones to the separate bars of a garden chair.[60] The effect of this routine on his spirits was miraculous: 'for the first time during many years I am able to write both energetically and satisfactorily to myself', he declared to Blackwood on 13 October 1843.[61]

Life at Mavis Bush brought some of the irritations that he had previously experienced at Dove Cottage and Fox Ghyll. Bad roads could make communication a challenge, as could a postal system that relied on domestic servants and 'a boy six years old to all appearance'.[62] Grumbled De Quincey: 'I can communicate more easily with Astrachan or with Mecca than with Lasswade.'[63] Creditors had no trouble getting in touch, though. Like the Millers and McIndoes before him, Youille seized the mass of papers that De Quincey had been unable to carry when he vacated his Glasgow lodgings, and he was now actively uttering threats. The case is one of 'real urgency', De Quincey wrote apprehensively to Blackwood. 'Mr Y's "women-folk", at least his daughters, are particularly kind and obliging: but *he* is a savage.' In October De Quincey was 'furiously pressed' to 'keep ahead of the hot pursuit' of his creditors.[64] Meanwhile, his aged father-in-law, who had been living with the family, was laid low by his final illness. 'His complaint is ossification of the entire intestines,' De Quincey explained in January. Simpson died on 2 February 1844. He had outlived his daughter by six and a half years.[65]

Five letters from the War Office lay on De Quincey's desk, and in the spring he finally forced himself to open them. They all concerned Horace. After his death, his effects had been sold at Hong Kong for £114.13s.5d. In his reply, De Quincey proposed distributing the money between various creditors, and undertook to clear off whatever debts remained. An official at the War Office, clearly unaware of who he was, described the letter as 'obviously written by a Man of taste and talent. The arrangement is highly creditable to him.' Margaret later contacted the War Office in the belief that Horace might be entitled to prize money, but this was not the case.[66]

The fate of their brother notwithstanding, Francis and Fred were considering a career in the army. Blackwood kindly made enquiries on their behalf, although De Quincey was apparently confused as to what end. 'Supposing that you could succeed in the case, is it not a military Cadetship you meant? For a civil one, you know, requires a preliminary course of study at Haileybury.'[67] Margaret, even more anxious than her father about the future of the two boys, went a few unexpected steps further when she wrote directly to Wordsworth, in the knowledge that he had recently become Queen Victoria's poet laureate, and in the hope that he might use his position to help secure places for her brothers. 'I trust that as the daughter of an old friend you will forgive the liberty I take in addressing you,' she began, before going on to explain that 'the Duke of Wellington in answer to a letter from my Aunt (Miss de Quincey) promised my youngest Brother Frederick a commission in the Army ... but we are told that such promises are never attended to unless reminded of them by some influential person'. Margaret was conscious of the 'indelicacy' of her request, but she hoped the 'urgency of the case' would be 'some apology'. In a discreet postscript she added, 'I need hardly say that this letter has been written without the knowledge of my Father, or indeed of the Family but a Sister.' Wordsworth, in response, showed himself still remarkably willing to assist De Quincey. He took a 'kind interest' in the affair, and it was probably through his attention that De Quincey was put in touch with Lord Lonsdale, who within ten days saw to it that Fred was appointed as an 'Ensigncy in the 70th foot'. 'Allow me to offer our united thanks for your kindness in this matter,' a grateful Francis wrote to Wordsworth.[68]

Old and new friends began to call at Mavis Bush, though perhaps not so often as De Quincey would have liked. Blackwood had travelled out the previous December, and was planning to visit again in the spring.[69] Lushington was in Edinburgh in November 1844 and wrote to enquire about the possibility of staying overnight. 'Without any shadow of inconvenience we can offer you a bed,' De Quincey told him. '... The Lasswade coach brings you in so as to reach *us* (I understand) by half-past five.'[70] The parish schoolmaster at Lasswade, William Young, had become a good friend of the family, and promised to visit De Quincey in December.[71] Most notably, Wilson was pledged to dine at Mavis Bush just before the New Year.[72] After years of intimacy in the Lake District and then Edinburgh, the two men had not seen much of each other in recent years, and there may even have been some definite break in the late 1830s or early 1840s. 'It seems to me an illustration of Coleridge's, "Alas, they had been friends in youth,"' Florence asserted, 'each indebted to the other at critical periods of their improvident lives for kindly help, perhaps not admitted as generously as they might have been by Professor Wilson when he was the successful man ... and my father may have been embittered; but we are glad to remember that they met again in our home in Lasswade in the old kindly, joyous spirit.'[73]

De Quincey's various domestic concerns were woven around a writing schedule at Mavis Bush that he established early, and that enabled him to remain characteristically productive. Much of his time that first autumn was devoted to correcting the proofs of the book he had sent to Blackwood just before leaving Glasgow, and which was published in the spring of 1844 as *The Logic of Political Economy*. Not the *Prolegomena to all Future Systems of Political Economy* that he had promised so many years earlier in the *Confessions*, the *Logic* was instead devoted to the rather more modest aim of investigating the doctrine of value.[74] It is a typical De Quinceyan performance, complete with Latin tags, rhetorical flourishes, incisive definitions, autobiographical asides, and references to Wordsworth, Coleridge, and Kant. What Carlyle dubbed the 'dismal science' elicits from De Quincey wry humour and colourful examples, including one which concerns 'the first sale in England of a RHINOCEROS', another about turnips, and a third involving a passenger on a Lake Superior steamboat who is just about to set off into the wilderness, and who is 'vehemently desirous to purchase' a musical snuff-box as his sole hope for amusement 'for a space of ten years to come'. Ricardo, observed De Quincey, possessed a 'powerful and original' mind, but a 'natural inaptitude for the task of simplifying' or '*communicating* knowledge'.[75] In the *Logic*, De Quincey takes this task to himself. Lively, resourceful, and illuminating, the book constitutes his most successful attempt to transmit and develop key aspects of Ricardian doctrine.

Yet for all its readability, the *Logic* is even more distinctly marked by contradiction. On the one hand, De Quincey is fascinated by the permanent and impersonal workings of Ricardo's system, where the great capitalist stands 'in the very centre of the vast money machinery accumulated in London', and observes the 'monetary symptoms ... eternally perceptible in the condition of every trade'. Yet on the other, De Quincey acknowledges the ways in which Ricardian theory has become intertwined with a host of contemporary issues, and deplores the ways in which Socialists, Jacobins, and Chartists have personalized and mutilated Ricardo's 'profound truths'.[76] Mill wrote the most important review of the book, and highlighted the inconsistencies in De Quincey's argument when he came firmly to the defence of the Chartists. 'Mr De Quincey thoroughly understands his master,' he allows, but 'the trade in food ought to be free' as De Quincey himself is 'bound to hold ... by every fair deduction from his own principles'.[77] Mill, however, found enough in the *Logic* to cite it several times in his own *Principles of Political Economy* (1848).[78] More strikingly, De Quincey's discussion of 'the growing substitution of female for male, and above all of childish for adult, labour' in the *Logic* is cited by Karl Marx in his examination of 'Machinery and Large-Scale Industry' in *Capital* (1867).[79]

Preparing the *Logic* for Blackwood coincided with the commencement in *Blackwood's* of De Quincey's last sustained assault on the political, religious, and cultural forces that he believed were irreparably damaging the institutions that constituted Britain's pre-eminence, both as a nation and as a colonizer of other nations. Protestantism is the key concern in these essays. De Quincey claims that it brings 'peace, freedom, security, and a new standard of public morality' to colonized lands, as he puts it in his November 1843 article on 'Ceylon', where 'God will now countersign his other blessings ... by superadding the one blessing of a dovelike religion.' Racial hatred, however, keeps breaking through the religious veneer. Ceylon is full of 'filthy and bloody abominations of creed' that render its inhabitants almost sub-human. Of the two peoples that occupy the island, De Quincey is certain that the 'Cinghalese are soft, inert, passive cowards', while 'your Kandyan is a ferocious little bloody coward, full of mischief ... and never to be trusted for a moment'. Nowhere does he question the British mission. Might is right. 'The nation that *can* win the place of leader, is the nation that ought to do so.'[80] He mobilizes a similar rhetoric in his August 1844 article on 'Affghanistan'.

De Quincey may have been able to convince himself that Protestantism was having a positive influence in Britain's colonies but, ironically enough, he was having to work hard to defend the Established Church from a series of threats at home. In May 1843, a majority of the Church of Scotland's General Assembly walked out in protest over government refusals to grant spiritual independence to the Church. De Quincey, chronicling these events in 'Secession from the Church of Scotland' for February 1844, argued that the blatant rejection of established authority and the subsequent founding of the Free Church of Scotland smacked of jacobinical excess. 'When we hear of ... divinity becoming the handmaid to insurrection,' he stormed, '... we go back in thought to that ominous organization of irreligion, which gave its most fearful aspects to the French Revolution.'[81] Yet as bad as things were in Scotland, in England they were perhaps even worse. John Henry Newman, John Keble, and Edward Pusey were leading members of the Oxford Movement, which sought to revive Catholic practices and thought within the Established Church. 'Puseyism', De Quincey warned in an October 1843 assessment of 'The Last Session of Parliament', was 'a power of more ominous capacities than the gentleness of its motions would lead men to suspect, and is well fitted ... to effect a volcanic explosion – such as may rend the Church of England by schisms more extensive and shattering than those which have recently afflicted the Church of Scotland'.[82]

All of these various anxieties came to a head when De Quincey turned his attention to Ireland. Daniel O'Connell, whose successful campaign for Catholic Emancipation had so angered De Quincey in 1828–29, was now pushing for the repeal of the Act of Union. De Quincey himself had watched the passage of this agreement in the House of Lords when he visited Ireland in 1800, and he was convinced that its repeal would initiate a fatal 'dismemberment' of the British empire. Peel, in response to the burgeoning insurgency, rattled the British sabre while simultaneously pursuing a number of concessions, including a considerable increase to the annual stipend for the Catholic seminary at Maynooth. De Quincey condemned the decision. 'If this Maynooth endowment prospers, Protestantism will receive a deadly wound in the empire which is, and *has* been, and by Providence was appointed to be, its main bulwark.' For De Quincey, the solution was obvious: 'Now is the time for grasping this nettle of domestic danger, and, by crushing it without fear, to crush it for ever.'[83]

Such adamantine support of the British imperial agenda makes unpalatable reading now, but it brought De Quincey great acclaim within *Blackwood's* circles, as he undoubtedly intended. 'We are a horrible John Bull ourselves', he proclaimed during the winter of 1844–5, a period that marked a particularly high point in his relationship with the magazine. In January he attended a 'very nice party' at Blackwood's, where he was 'uncommonly good in his way & told some capital stories'.[84] A few months later he attended a similar gathering, and may have enjoyed himself too much: 'Could the learned have the slightest shade of a suspicion – that I was a trifle "cut" last night?' he asked sheepishly.[85] On at least two other occasions he actually moved in with the Blackwood family in order to finish off an article. 'One paragraph has occupied him for the last three days,' Alexander reported to John, '& yet the body talks away about the facility with which he can now write.'[86]

De Quincey's central role with *Blackwood's* was commemorated when Robert and Alexander commissioned John Watson-Gordon to produce a portrait of him for their saloon. De Quincey was fifty-nine years old at the time, though in the finished product he looks a good deal younger. Seated and solemn, he gazes just off to the right, revealing a full left sideburn. His forehead is wide and steep. He looks both intent and detached. His right index finger is tucked into the leaves of one book, his left arm rests on another. He is dressed in a white shirt and black vest, over which he wears a large brown cloak. For the Blackwoods, the most arresting part of the portrait was 'the infernal size of mouth he has & this John Watson cannot help shewing'. De Quincey, as self-conscious as ever about his appearance, objected: 'if my mouth resembles this I am very much mistaken'. His eyes seem a much more striking aspect of the picture. Countless hours of writing and reading have now strained them to the point of misalignment. 'They sparkle not, they shine not, they are lustreless: can that be a squint which glances over them towards you? No! it is only a slight habit one of them has of occasionally looking in a different direction from the other.'[87]

A prominent position within the *Blackwood's* circle did not prevent De Quincey from socializing among liberal-minded intellectuals not associated with the magazine. The critic and biographer David Masson, who many years later edited De Quincey's work, first met him in a room 'high up in one of the tall houses' in Edinburgh's Old Town, and was struck by 'the peculiar beauty of his head and forehead', his immense erudition, and 'his use of a phrase very beautiful in itself, and which seemed characteristic of his manner of thinking. Describing some visionary scene or other, he spoke of it as consisting of "discs of light and interspaces of gloom"'. Gilfillan also called on De Quincey at this time, and left a memorable portrait of what it was like to spend an evening with him. 'Conceive a small, pale-faced, wo-begone, and attenuated man, with ... no coat, check shirt, and neckcloth twisted like a wisp of straw, opening the door of his room' and 'advancing towards you with hurried movement, and half-recognising glance'. He salutes 'you in low and hesitating tones', and asks you to be seated. Then, taking 'a seat opposite you, but without looking you in the face', he launches into a stream of wisdom and learning, 'out-Kanting Kant, or out-mystifying Coleridge, or demolishing some ricketty literary reputation, or quoting, in his deep and quiet under tone, some of the burning words of Shelley or Wordsworth'. He talks 'as long as you are content to listen', and it is three in the morning before you depart, leaving him at his desk, where he works until dawn.[88]

Figure 4: John Watson-Gordon's portrait of Thomas De Quincey, 1845

[iv]

Boiling just below the routines and relationships of his daily life was his battle with addiction, which continued to mete out terrible mental and bodily anguish. His long walks around the back garden at Mavis Bush were improving his health, but his 'irregular' use of the drug still needed to be 'reformed'. Laudanum, he admitted to Lushington, 'might be the secret key to all this wretchedness'.[89]

He cut sharply back on his dose. For six months, utter despair. 'One dreary uniformity of report – absolute desolation; misery so perfect that too surely I perceived, and no longer disguised from myself, the impossibility of continuing to live under so profound a blight.' He contemplated suicide. 'Too certainly I felt that to this my condition tended; for again enormous irritability was rapidly travelling over the disk of my life, and this, and the consciousness of increasing weakness, added to my desolation of heart.' Then, in late February 1844, a breakthrough: 'One firm system pursued through eight months as to one element, and nearly three as to another' brought in a moment 'such a rectification of the compass as I had not known for years'. This state of clarity 'departed from me within forty-eight hours', but 'that no way alarmed me – I drew hope from the omen'.[90]

Hope, however, proved hard to sustain. In early May De Quincey confided to Blackwood that his struggles with the drug were pushing him 'from purgatory into the shades of a deeper abyss'.[91] He began a private journal in which he chronicled the insidious nature of addiction.

Did you ever read of leprosy as it existed in Judea, or – and that was worse – as it existed in Europe during the dark ages? Did you ever read of that tremendous visitation in the early days of Judaism, when, if the poor patient would have hushed up his misery in silence, the walls of his house whispered of his whereabouts? Horrible! that a man's own chamber – the place of his refuge and retreat – should betray him! . . . Not fear or terror, but inexpressible misery, is the last portion of the opium-eater. [92]

On Christmas Day 1844, De Quincey recorded in his journal an epiphany that betrays just how often he must have lied to himself. His laudanum dependence had for more than three decades imposed a highly defined grid of acquisition and consumption upon the turmoil of his existence, yet he could pretend otherwise to the point that his addiction still caught him by surprise.

This night ... has first solemnly revealed itself to me that I am and have long been under a curse, all the greater for being physically and by effort endurable, and for hiding itself, *i.e.*, playing in and out from all offices of life at every turn of every moment. Oh, dreadful! by degrees infinitely worse than leprosy – than ——. But oh, what signifies the rhetoric of a case so sad! Conquer it I must by exercise unheard of, or it will conquer me.[93]

De Quincey was facing facts. Writing – his impassioned prose – might help him analyse or objectify his drug addiction, but it could not release him from it. He was trapped in endless circles, walking around and around the back garden at Mavis Bush just as over and over again he fought cycles of denial and guilt, excess and restraint, secrecy and candour, despondency and hope.

Coleridge dominated his thoughts. De Quincey almost certainly has him in mind when he describes 'a man called X—— who has often jumped out of bed – bounced like a column of quicksilver – at midnight, fallen on his knees and cried out, while the perspiration ran down his wasted face, and his voice waked all the house, "O Jesus Christ, be merciful to me a sinner!" – so unimaginable had been the horror which sleep opened to his eyes'. De Quincey compared their addictive states, and fathomed Coleridge's chaos by the darkness of his own. 'It is as if ivory carvings and elaborate fretwork and fair enamelling should be found with worms and ashes amongst coffins and the wrecks of some forgotten life or some abolished nature,' he observed.

In parts and fractions eternal creations are carried on, but the nexus is wanting, and life and the central principle which should bind together all the parts at the centre, with all its radiations to the circumference, are wanting. Infinite incoherence, ropes of sand, gloomy incapacity of vital pervasion by some one plastic principle, that is the hideous incubus upon my mind always. For there is no disorganised wreck so absolute, so perfect, as that which is wrought by misery.[94]

On the surface, De Quincey's addiction did not prevent him from carrying on as a writer, a father, and a friend. But within, it fragmented his sense of self to the point of disintegration.

In 'Coleridge and Opium-Eating', published in *Blackwood's* for January 1845, De Quincey surveys his relationship with the drug, and the 'shocking' contradictions that underwrite his experience of it. Opium is a con: it can convince an addict of twenty-five years that he can lay it 'aside easily and for ever within seven days'. Opium is a trade-off: 'it defeats the *steady* habit of exertion, but it creates spasms of irregular exertion'. Opium is irresistible: in that 'ruby-coloured elixir, there lurked a divine power to chase away the genius of ennui'. Opium is a scourge: it withers life 'root and branch'. And finally De Quincey acknowledges what he has often only intimated: opium is a celestial lover. For those 'whose nervous sensibilities vibrate to their profoundest depths under the first touch of the angelic poison, even as a lover's ear thrills on hearing unexpectedly the voice of her whom he loves, opium is the Amreeta cup of beatitude'.[95]

De Quincey's dreams blazed into new splendour, and he found himself forced to confront the shame and fear that he associated with so much of his past. 'On some fatal morning in middle-life', he explained, ' – the far-off consequences' of 'actions done in youth' come back upon you. 'And you say to yourself, "Oh, Heaven, if I had 50 lives – this crime would reappear" ... So was it with my affliction.' 'Some things that had sunk into utter forgetfulness, others that had faded in visionary power – all rise as gory phantoms from the dust.'[96]

Both tortured and inspired, De Quincey grew intent on catching these phantoms as they rushed upwards into his dreaming mind.[97] In the summer of 1844 he decided that he would 'write another *Opium Confession*', and by early January he could report to Blackwood that he had never before 'succeeded so entirely to my own satisfaction. I am a new birth for composition.'[98] Wilson and two others read the opening section and all independently agreed that it was 'very greatly superior' to the original *Confessions*. Indeed, De Quincey considered the new piece 'the *ne plus ultra*, as regards the feelings and the power to express it, which I can ever hope to attain'.[99]

Suspiria de Profundis – literally, 'Sighs from the Depths' – was published in *Blackwood's* for March, April, June and July, and chronicled in some of his most elaborate prose the poignant memories and dreadful nightmares that had gripped him during the opium sieges of the last several months. Described by De Quincey as '*a Sequel to the Confessions of an English Opium-Eater*', *Suspiria* is in fact a 'prequel', for it centres on the childhood death of Elizabeth, which De Quincey did not – or could not – confront in the *Confessions*, but which he now rehearses at length, first in a section entitled 'The Affliction of Childhood', and then in a series of prose poems, including 'The Palimpsest', 'Savannah-La-Mar', and 'The Apparition of Brocken'.

The powerful and often paradoxical relationship between drugs and the human imagination is at the heart of *Suspiria*. In his 'Introductory Notice', De Quincey alternately invokes Carlyle and Wordsworth to describe how opium offers great spiritual benefits. Modern British society is defined by the 'colossal pace' of industrial advance, and 'the continual development of vast physical agencies' such as 'steam in all its applications'. Forced to live too constantly with 'eternal hurry' and 'varied company', people are 'haunted as if by some jealousy of ghostly beings'. Some minds are reduced to lunacy, others to 'a reagency of fleshly torpor'. Counter-forces must be marshalled, forces in the direction of religion, philosophy and, most crucially, 'the power of dreaming', which De Quincey characterizes as 'the one great tube through which man communicates with the shadowy', and which at its noblest 'forces the infinite into the chambers of a human brain'. Opium has a critical role to play in this process, for it 'seems to possess a *specific* power ... not merely for exalting the colours of dream-scenery, but for deepening its shadows; and, above all, for strengthening the sense of its fearful *realities*'.[100]

Yet if the drug helps to foster a private sense of the sublime, it also eviscerates that sense.[101] Twice, De Quincey now claims, he has fought the 'dark idol' of opium, and twice he has emerged victorious, though on both occasions he has relapsed because of his failure to undertake rigorous exercise as 'the one sole resource' for making withdrawal endurable. Then, beginning in the summer of 1843, he fights a third battle, but there is no victory this time, only a further fall. What is worse, whereas on the previous two occasions he has risen again after his clash with the drug, this time he knows almost instinctively that there is no possibility of re-ascent. The 'dreadful symptoms' of his addiction have been 'moving forward for ever, by a pace steadily, solemnly, and equably increasing', and now at last they have run him down. 'Were the ruin conditional, or were it in any point doubtful, it would be natural to utter ejaculations, and to seek sympathy,' De Quincey observes. But 'where the ruin is understood to be absolute', the case is otherwise. 'The voice perishes; the gestures are frozen; and the spirit of man flies back upon its own centre ... One profound sigh ascended from my heart, and I was silent for days.'[102] In *Suspiria*, as in the *Confessions*, opium is revelation and destruction, simultaneously deepening and obliterating the self.

How to cope with these intense pressures? De Quincey's answer in *Suspiria* is that suffering is essential to the full development of the self. Suffering is part of God's plan. 'He works by earthquake ... he works by grief.' It is as vital as joy. 'The rapture of life ... does not arise, unless as perfect music arises – music of Mozart or Beethoven – by the confluence of the mighty and terrific discords with the subtle concords.'[103] Most memorably, it is various and vast enough to be transformed into myth, as De Quincey does in his prose poem 'Levana and Our Ladies of Sorrow'. Levana is the Roman goddess of early childhood. She is assisted by three Ladies. All of us have our spiritual education shaped by at least one of them. De Quincey knows all three. In his early life he lived under the dominion of *Mater Lachrymarum*, who 'night and day raves and moans, calling for vanished faces'. As an adult he came to know *Mater Suspiriorum*, whose meekness 'belongs to the hopeless'. More recently, he has encountered *Mater Tenebrarum*, 'the mother of lunacies, and the suggestress of suicides'. His education is by this point well advanced, yet the Ladies will continue to assail him, tempt him, scorch him: 'So shall he read elder truths, sad truths, grand truths, fearful truths. So shall he rise again *before* he dies. And so shall our commission be accomplished which from God we had – to plague his heart until we had unfolded the capacities of his spirit.' In the face of the desolation of addiction, *Suspiria* argues that grief enriches and reconstitutes the self. 'My heart trembled through from end to end,' wrote De Quincey's fellow opium addict Elizabeth Barrett Browning after reading the work. 'What a poet that man is! how he vivifies words, & deepens them, & gives them profound significance.'[104]

De Quincey would have been delighted to hear such praise, for he had struggled mightily with *Suspiria*, and had been very dissatisfied throughout much of the publication process. So anxious was he about the printing of the work that he decided to leave Lasswade and take lodgings at Miss Carrick's, 71 Clerk Street, Edinburgh, in order to ensure that he was on hand to safeguard against misunderstandings and double-check the proofs for accuracy.[105] The relocation, however, hindered as much as it helped, for word of his whereabouts soon reached the ears of many of his Edinburgh creditors, who promptly began to harry him for payment on debts that in some instances stretched back seven years or more.[106] 'Unideaed wretches!' De Quincey exclaimed late one evening after trying for hours to shake off two determined bailiffs. 'I tried them on every subject under heaven, but they did not seem to have a thought in their minds unconnected with their base and brutal profession!'[107]

The publication of *Suspiria*'s first instalment in March appears to have gone smoothly, but De Quincey was greatly distressed when he read the second instalment for April. Unauthorized changes had been inserted into his text, and he denounced 'some unknown person at the Press' who was 'constantly doing him the most serious injuries'.[108] Further, restrictions on space meant that the instalment had been cut off before the inclusion of

'Levana and Our Ladies of Sorrow', which De Quincey had relied on as the 'main artillery' for the number. 'It will not only *here* – but *hereafter* absolutely ruin the better part of the impression that might else be made, if there is not some dispensation from the general rule of compression' into a space of sixteen pages. After reading the third instalment, however, Blackwood resolved, not that he should make more room for *Suspiria*, but that his readers were in need of a break from it, and he deferred the continuation of the series from the May until the June issue, a decision De Quincey regarded as 'a knock-down blow'.[109] He remained conciliatory: 'if you will tell me what you finally wish for, I on my part will do my best to accomplish it'. But did Blackwood not realize what an elaborate undertaking it was to write and rewrite a work such as *Suspiria*? 'Of all the tasks I ever had in my life,' De Quincey declared pointedly, 'it is – from the aerial and shadowy nature of the composition – the most overwhelming.'[110]

In July the relationship between the two men disintegrated. 'My horror … for inserting' *Suspiria* in *Blackwood's* 'takes this form', De Quincey wrote bitterly, ' – that I am thus made a party – nay, I make myself a party to the ill-treatment, the undervaluation of my own truth.' He still had great hopes for the work, ranging from a third and fourth part, to a series of prose poems with titles that included 'The Dreadful Infant', 'The Princess and the Pomegranate', 'Morning of Execution', and 'The Nursery in Arabian Deserts'.[111] In October, Robert Blackwood turned the editorship of the magazine over to his brother John, who was far less willing to accommodate De Quincey. A month later De Quincey wrote with icy formality to inform 'Mr Blackwood … that, in the course of this present month, he will send the remainder of the *Suspiria* (now nearly finished) – making in all from 72 to 80 pp of the Magazine'.[112] No new material arrived, however.

Following its magazine publication, Alexander Blackwood had thoughts of reissuing *Suspiria* in a book that would also include the 1821 *Confessions*. John Taylor, the former co-editor of the *London Magazine*, owned the copyright, though, and he wanted £100 for it. Blackwood baulked at such a high price – 'the thing is out of the question' – but Taylor retorted that De Quincey still owed him £150 for a novel that he had promised in 1822 and never delivered.[113] Such a debt was 'not improbable', Blackwood rightly acknowledged, but he refused to increase his offer and negotiations collapsed. De Quincey too had hopes of turning the work into a book, which he would preface 'by a Letter of some length' to his three daughters.[114] This plan also failed to materialize, for his conception of *Suspiria* continued to outrun what he was able to accomplish. Yet even in its incomplete form it remains one of his most compelling narratives, in its treatment not only of his childhood afflictions, but in its searching attempts to assess the variable effects of opium, creativity, industrialism, and addiction.

[v]

He reverted to a familiar pattern. His relationship with one magazine in disarray, he went immediately over to its chief rival. William Tait had published nothing by De Quincey since early 1841, but he overlooked the disagreements in their past, and warmly welcomed him back within the *Tait's* fold, as indeed the Blackwoods had done twice in their turn before him. De Quincey set promptly to work, and between September 1845 and September 1846 he published thirteen articles in *Tait's*, including two for March and two for April.

'On Wordsworth's Poetry' constitutes his finest assessment of the poet. For decades, Wordsworth's long philosophical poem *The Excursion* (1814) had been celebrated as his major achievement. To De Quincey, however, *The Excursion* was badly damaged by its '*undulatory* character' and 'colloquial form', whereas works such as 'We Are Seven', 'The Two April Mornings', and 'Ode: Intimations of Immortality' were 'generally scintillating with gems of far profounder truth'.[115] De Quincey's reading explicitly inverts the contemporary view of Wordsworth, and clearly anticipates our own.

More literary and political assessments followed. In a review of Gilfillan's *Gallery of Literary Portraits*, De Quincey discussed a series of liberal figures, from John Keats to the reform-minded Baptist minister John Foster. To be sure, he found little to admire in William Godwin, whose radical treatise on *Political Justice* (1793) carried 'one single shock into the bosom of English society, fearful but momentary', and whose terror novel *Caleb Williams* (1794) contained 'no merit of any kind'. But he was much more just to his old acquaintance William Hazlitt, who 'wilfully placed himself in collision from the first with all the interests that were in the sunshine of this world', but who 'requited his reader for the pain of travelling through so gloomy an atmosphere, by the rich vegetation which his teeming intellect threw up as it moved along'.[116] Most compellingly, in his essay on Percy Shelley, De Quincey justified his longstanding admiration of the radical poet by drawing a line between the sublime poetry and the heinous ideas which motivated it, a tenuous strategy which nevertheless prefigures the approach of several key Victorian critics, including Matthew Arnold. 'Can we imagine the case of an angel touched by lunacy?' De Quincey asks. 'Have we ever seen the spectacle of a human intellect, exquisite by its functions of creation, yet in one chamber of its shadowy house already ruined before the light of manhood had cleansed its darkness? Such an angel, such a man ... was Shelley.'[117]

The same run of *Tait's* essays also contained De Quincey's most optimistic views of the social and political forces transforming Britain, notwithstanding the fact that many of the same forces had recently provoked him to thunderous disapproval in *Blackwood's*. His article on the Whig writer and politician Sir James Mackintosh argues that a great part 'of our political life and struggling is but one vast laboratory for sifting and ascertaining the rights, the interests, the duties, of the unnumbered and increasing parties to our complex form of social life'. In 'On Christianity, as an Organ of Political Movement', the Christian religion appears, not as in lockstep with British imperialism, but as at the heart of four great movements of social reform: Christianity 'first caused the state of *slavery* to be regarded as an evil'; it promoted the rise of '*charitable institutions*'; it allowed for the '*social* influence of woman'; and it led to the foundation of societies seeking 'the extirpation of war'. Finally, in his essays on Wordsworth and Mackintosh, De Quincey champions the legacy of the French Revolution. 'It was the explosion of a prodigious volcano, which scattered its lava over every kingdom of every continent, every where silently manuring them for social struggles,' he avows; 'this lava is gradually fertilizing all; the revolutionary movement is moving onwards at this hour as inexorable as ever ... Man walks with his head erect; – bastilles are no more.'[118]

De Quincey wrote several of these essays in Glasgow, where he had returned after the breakdown of his relationship with *Blackwood's*. He stayed again with Nichol, this time at the new Observatory, which he liked immensely. 'How serene, how quiet, how lifted above the confusion and the roar ... is the solemn Observatory', he remarked. '... And duly, at night, just when the toil of over-wrought Glasgow is mercifully relaxing, then comes the summons to the labouring astronomer.'[119] Nichol invited him to stay for a week, but De Quincey seems to have remained at the Observatory for about five months.[120]

He was not an easy house guest, as Nichol, Knight, Wilson, and several others already knew. In his October 1845 essay 'On the Temperance Movement of Modern Times', De Quincey sought to help others renounce their alcohol or drug habit, and touted himself as someone whose extensive knowledge 'upon the subjects of abstinence' had given him the right to offer hints upon it. Yet it is clear that it was at this same juncture that he sank back down into his own deep dependence on opium. Nichol's son John offered a vignette of him during his stay at the Observatory that Gerard Manley Hopkins recorded in one of his early notebooks: 'De Quincey would wake blue and trembling in the morning and languidly ask the servant "Would you pour out some of that black mixture from the bottle there". The servant would give it him, generally not knowing what it was. After this he would revive.'[121] It was at Nichol's, too, that De Quincey informed the poet Charles Mackay that 'after a course of abstinence, extending over a considerable period of failing health and energy', he had returned to the practice of 'laudanum-drinking' with 'the most beneficial effects both upon his mind and body'. Indeed, after months of consequences 'so dreadful and utterly unconjectured by medical men', he was 'glad to get back under shelter'.[122]

De Quincey seems to have been with Nichol until at least November, at which time he informed an unknown correspondent that his general address was 'Lasswade near Edinburgh', but that 'for the present, and until Christmas, a better address is – To the care of William Tait Esq. Publisher, Princes Street, Edinburgh'.[123] Certainly just after Christmas he was back in Edinburgh, for on 30 December he attended a production of Sophocles' tragedy Antigone, which he then reviewed in Tait's for February and March. Charmed by the performance of Helen Faucit in the title role, De Quincey compared her to Helen of Troy and animatedly described the impact of her entrance: 'Then, suddenly, – oh, heavens! what a revelation of beauty! – forth stepped, walking in brightness, the most faultless of Grecian marbles.' The only blemish in her performance was that in the closing scene 'her voice grew too husky to execute the cadences of the intonations'. Faucit later protested that she had a bad cold on the night De Quincey saw her, and she was 'vexed' to find that his review dwelled 'upon a passing and purely accidental failure' in her voice.[124]

Early in the New Year De Quincey learned of his mother's death.[125] She had for several years been deaf and 'so agitated by any novelty of whatever nature' that medical men and her daughter Jane had done their best to shield her from excitement.[126] Mother and son had never been close, and they had not seen each other in fourteen years, though De Quincey had of course solicited her financial assistance on several occasions over that period. 'She was above 97,' he observed calmly: 'and her death was therefore always a thing to be expected, though not now more than for years past.'[127] Under the terms of the will, Jane received all the personal property and the house, Weston Lea, in Bath, where Mrs Quincey had lived after Westhay, and where she had died. De Quincey received £200 per annum from the estate, but as his mother had already been advancing him this sum for many years, his financial situation was unchanged. The money almost certainly went directly to Margaret, who with her sisters continued to manage both Mavis Bush and, to some extent, the financial affairs of their father.[128]

Back residing in Edinburgh, and probably often at Lasswade, De Quincey became preoccupied with the interests of his two sons. Francis, still living with his sisters, had decided to go into medicine, and now walked the seven miles back and forth each day to attend lectures at the University of Edinburgh. In late January, he was anxious to help secure the appointment of John Goodsir as the new Professor of Anatomy. De Quincey himself took up the cause, and at one point visited Tait to request that he use his influence on behalf of Goodsir, who was duly appointed to the Professorship later in the year, to the delight no doubt of father and son.[129]

Fred, De Quincey's other son, had now been in the military for nine months, and was stationed in India. In a letter 'dated *Umballah* about the 18th of January', he informed his family that 'he was then nearing the head quarters with a party of recruits for his own regiment (the 80th)'.[130] A month later, on 10 February 1846, he saw action in the bloody Battle of Sobraon, the fourth and final conflict of the First Sikh War (1845–46). 'I *have*, in my possession, and will restore, and have read, Fred's letter from the Punjaub,' De Quincey wrote excitedly to Margaret. 'What a godsend!' Fred received a medal for his part in the Sobraon conflict, and 'very soon after got his lieutenancy'.[131]

In May, De Quincey was 'prostrate and utterly prostrate' after having stayed in the house too long 'without air or exercise', but these recurrent bouts of ill health did not prevent him from writing, and in the summer he turned his attention to an article on astronomy, a topic that had absorbed him for much of the previous year.[132] 'Nobody can study the stars without a profound pity or contempt for the ... religious animosities and unchristian hatreds of mankind,' De Quincey had said to Nichol one evening over dinner when he was staying at the Observatory. 'The stars always preach to me that I am a prisoner, that I am condemned, possibly for some sin I have committed in a previous, but now forgotten, state of existence.'[133]

According to Mackay, it was also during this dinner that Nichol received a letter from William Parsons, third Earl of Rosse, who had recently built a powerful new telescope. Nichol had long been a supporter of the so-called 'Nebular Hypothesis', which Rosse now wrote to announce had been undermined by his discovery that the nebulae were individual galaxies, not gaseous masses as Nichol had previously believed. 'A magnificent discovery!' De Quincey exclaimed. Further investigation soon established that sections of the great Orion Nebula could even be resolved into stars, and that the universe was much vaster and more chaotic than had been realized. Nichol was in Edinburgh in April to give a series of lectures, and conveyed the most up-to-date information to De Quincey, who rather graphically comprehended its implications. 'Dr Nichol ... has ... cut the lovely throat of – the *Nebular Hypothesis*.'[134]

Nichol's new book, *Thoughts on Some Important Points relating to the System of the World* (1846), attempted to come to terms with these remarkable new discoveries. De Quincey's review of the volume, published in *Tait's* as 'System of the Heavens as Revealed by Lord Rosse's Telescopes', explores the various and profound impact these same discoveries have made upon him. In the private realm, De Quincey invokes the deep trauma he associates with the autopsies performed upon his son William and his sister Elizabeth when he describes Nichol's reprint of Sir John Herschel's drawing of the Nebula in Orion. Pictured in the stars De Quincey sees a man's head 'thrown back', but it is a head appallingly disfigured, for 'in the very region of his temples, driving itself downwards into his cruel brain ... is a horrid chasm, a ravine, a shaft, that many centuries would not traverse'.[135] As a public statement, De Quincey confronts Victorian conceptions of space, and the scientific debates over the evolution and constitution of the heavens. Rosse 'found God's universe represented for human convenience ... upon a globe or spherical chart having a radius of one hundred and fifty feet', and he 'left it sketched upon a similar chart, keeping exactly the same scale of proportions, but now elongating its radius into one thousand feet'. The new information demolished the best available cosmology, and left astronomers struggling to account for humankind's increasingly obvious insignificance. The Great Nebula, as De Quincey averred, was 'famous for its frightful magnitude and for the frightful depth to which it is sunk in the abysses of the heavenly wilderness'.[136]

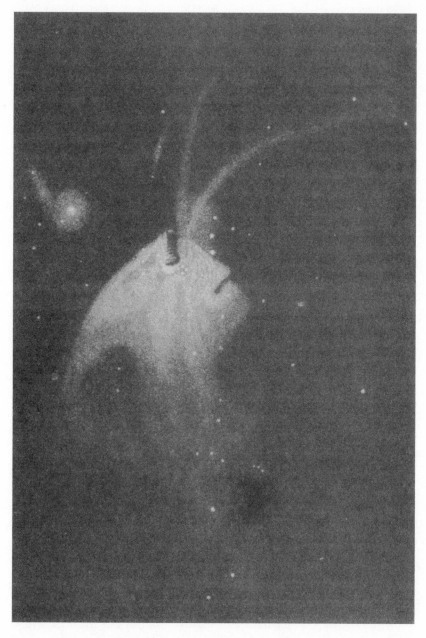

Figure 5: The Nebula in Orion, from Nichol's Thoughts on Some Important Points relating to the System of the World *(1846)*

THIRTEEN

The End of Night

[i]

'A new literary public has arisen', De Quincey announced astutely in 1846. When he began his career, aristocrats still exerted a profound influence on book and periodical publication, but over the course of the last three decades a much larger class of readers had 'formed itself within the commercial orders of our great cities and manufacturing districts', driving 'the interest of literature . . . downwards through a vast compass of descents'. This new reading audience, 'changed in no respect from its former condition of intellect and manners and taste, bringing only the single qualification of ability to read, is now strong enough in numbers to impress a new character upon literature'.[1]

De Quincey watched this process of democratization with a good deal of suspicion. As early as 1822 he had complained of the 'stupidity' of the reading public, and throughout his career his efforts to engage a wide audience put intense pressure on his conception of himself as a scholar and a gentleman. 'A mob is a dreadful audience for chafing and irritating the latent vulgarisms of the human heart,' he sighed. 'Exaggeration and caricature, before such a tribunal, become inevitable, and sometimes almost a duty.' On occasion his frustration with the mass media boiled over. 'My plans far transcend all journalism high or low,' he snapped in 1847. 'And through fifty different channels I will soon make this mob of a public hear on both sides of its deaf head things that it will not like.'[2]

Yet despite his deep misgivings, financial need meant that De Quincey typically wrote with one eye firmly fixed on pleasing the gallery. 'It is treason in a writer . . . to produce hatred or disaffection towards his liege lord who is and must be his reader,' he remarked. And if times changed, the writer was obliged to change with them. 'An attention to the unlearned part of an audience, which 15 years ago might have rested upon pure courtesy, *now* rests upon a basis of absolute justice,' he observed in 1853. 'Formerly . . . the learned reader would have told me that I was not entitled to delay *him* by elucidations that in *his* case must be supposed to be superfluous ... At present, half-way on our pilgrimage through the nineteenth century, I reply to such a learned remonstrant – that ... this infliction of tedium upon *him* is inseparable from what has now become a duty to others.' De Quincey disliked the vulgarity and pandering associated with the magazine press, and he often longed for more elegant and educated audiences. Nevertheless, he spent his entire career shrewdly exploiting the press's cultural and financial power, and he was keen to celebrate its ability to enlighten, transform, and unite. 'So travels the press to victory,' he cried: 'such is the light, and so broad, which it diffuses: such is the strength for action by which it combines the hearts of nations.'³

[ii]

William Tait had decided to retire. After more than twenty-five profitable and productive years in the publishing business, he sold *Tait's* to Alexander Alison, a wealthy and reform-minded ironmaster, who moved the magazine from Edinburgh to Glasgow, and who promptly hired the bright young journalist George Troup as his editor.⁴ Retaining De Quincey was one of Troup's top priorities, and in December 1846 he sent his business manager Colin Rae Brown to Edinburgh to try and 'secure the continued services of De Quincey as a leading contributor, and also to endeavour to get him to reside in Glasgow – for a time – so that he might be closely identified with the "future" of the well-known Whig-Radical organ'. Brown and De Quincey met and soon came to terms, though De Quincey stipulated that his stay in Glasgow was not to exceed six months, and that he needed 'apartments of a modest kind ... secured for him at the *highest altitude* possible in the northern part of the city'. 'I had some painful experiences of life in Glasgow several years ago,' he explained, 'when I was victimized to within an inch of my life by the sulphuretted hydrogen – or some such noxious exhalation – which was then discharged into the atmosphere by the so-called "Secret Works" at the "Townhead."'⁵

Brown found De Quincey lodgings 'on the northern heights of the city' at 112 Rottenrow Street, in the top flat of a 'three-storey building with a grimy front and a white-washed gable'.⁶ Mrs Tosh, De Quincey's new landlady, was 'a quiet, fairly well-educated widow, of some sixty years of age' who kept her house 'in a manner that might be termed scrupulously clean'. De Quincey seems to have moved in around the middle of December, and immediately became to Mrs Tosh 'a source of "muckle wonderment!"'⁷ 'There maun surely be somethin' raaly wrang wi' my lodger,' she remarked.

'He doesna eat as muckle in a week as my wee oo (grandson) eats in a day.'[7]

The new accommodations were 'exactly what he wanted', but De Quincey 'was not destined to remain long under the watchful, motherly care of Mrs Tosh'. In early January 'her little grandson was suddenly struck down by scarlet fever', and Brown 'had to make immediate arrangements for transferring our valued contributor and his few belongings to another domicile'. 'Ah,' De Quincey remarked as he prepared to move again, 'that reminds me that I have been paying the rent of apartments in Renfield Street for a number of years. Many valuable books and papers are or should be there still.' Brown 'stared, almost agape, in downright amazement'. On 15 January De Quincey was staying at the Royal Hotel in George Square, but within three days he had come to some sort of arrangement with Youille, and re-installed himself in the Renfield Street rooms he had vacated three and a half years earlier when he moved to Lasswade.[8]

With his financial affairs in increasingly good order, and duns no longer in hot pursuit, De Quincey moved about with a great deal more freedom than had been the case during his previous stays in Glasgow. Gilfillan saw him 'more than once'.[9] Lushington called often to take a walk, and on at least two occasions De Quincey 'came to dinner', where Mrs Lushington – Tennyson's younger sister Cecilia – played him 'the loveliest of *waltzes*'.[10] To Troup, De Quincey was 'a constant and much-appreciated visitor', and the two soon 'formed an intimate friendship'. After indulgences in laudanum, De Quincey used to wonder 'if he were fit to appear at a dinner party', and was 'generally guided' by Troup's opinion.[11] In February, an unnamed lady escorted him to a concert featuring the child prodigy Louisa Vinning, whose 'middle notes are beautiful and bell-like', and the Tyler family, who played 'lovely German airs ... full of rich festal joyousness', though De Quincey strongly objected to the 'outrageous national vanity' of the Scots for including '*Ah ah the wooing o' it!*' on the same programme.[12] At some point he journeyed to the western coast to visit his friend William Robertson, now a minister at Irvine. But Robertson was not at home, and De Quincey's shabby appearance roused the mistrust of the landlady, who worried that he 'might have felonious intentions with regard to the minister's books'.[13]

Charles Mackay, then editor of the liberal *Glasgow Argus* newspaper, received 'not unfrequent visits' from De Quincey, 'which were generally concluded by the request on his part of the loan of sixpence or a shilling to purchase laudanum – a whole wine-glassful of which he was accustomed to drink with as little compunction as if it had been claret'. On one occasion Mackay bumped into De Quincey on the street. 'I knew I should meet you,' De Quincey told him. Every human being is 'surrounded with a spiritual atmosphere', and 'three streets distant, I was mysteriously aware that you were somewhere in the neighbourhood'.[14]

Brown has left the most vivid impression of De Quincey during this period. The two men met often for a 'mild lunch' at the Rose Tavern in Argyll Street. Like many before him, Brown was particularly struck by the refinement which characterized De Quincey's actions and speech. When he made reference to a fellow journalist, 'Mr John B. St John, pronouncing the surname in a pretty broad, Northernly accent, as "Saint John"', De Quincey put on 'a grave look, and holding up his thin, pale right hand in deprecatory style, said, "Singen, my dear sir, Singen"'. One afternoon the two discussed Robert Burns. 'Ah!' De Quincey remarked, while his eyes visibly dilated, 'the Ayrshire Colossus is still expanding outward and upward, in spite of all his detractors.' On another occasion, De Quincey and Brown dined with Nichol out at the Observatory, and then walked back into town through an 'almost blinding "Scotch mist"', leading De Quincey to a disquisition on the 'damps and fogs of the late autumn', and then to an idea for Winter Gardens in 'all our large manufacturing towns' to provide a place of 'instruction and amusement' for the poor.[15]

Yet while immersed in the intellectual and social attractions of Glasgow, De Quincey kept in close touch with his three daughters, travelling to Lasswade in April 1847 to spend a week with them before they set out on a holiday – almost certainly the first of their lives – to the south of England. De Quincey was filled with apprehension for their safety. 'On *some* railways (and my poor girls never were on *any*), the doors of the carriages are not always securely fastened; and in the dark, or in the dusk, an accident might more easily happen than in full daylight.'[16] Once they had set off, however, he received news of their travels with great delight, and sent playful letters in reply. 'How is Florence?' he asked. 'I heard with anxiety that she was rather what people call *delicate*. I hope by this time, through sea-air, &c., she has become *in*delicate.' Margaret wondered if he was reading their letters promptly. 'It is only letters that make me unhappy which I defer, until by accident, perhaps, they never get read at all,' De Quincey explained. 'Complimentary letters, and letters of amusement from their news or their comments, I read instantly.'[17]

In June the Brontë sisters sent De Quincey a copy of their recently published *Poems by Currer, Ellis, and Acton Bell* in acknowledgement of 'the pleasure and profit we have often and long derived from your works'. Wordsworth, Lockhart, and Tennyson received the same letter. De Quincey 'greatly admired' the poetry of the volume – especially Emily's – and was in 'every way well disposed' towards the authors. The sisters also sent him copies of their novels – Charlotte's *Jane Eyre*, Emily's *Wuthering Heights*, and Anne's *Agnes Grey* were all published before the year was out – but De Quincey was nowhere near as impressed with their prose. 'I fear this lady or gentleman, which ever the author is, is making a mistake,' he remarked after laying down one of the novels: 'young ladies, who are the chief readers of novels, will never stand to be interested in that sort of people: what they like is some heroic person, say a young or successful officer.'[18]

De Quincey's health – surprisingly stable for months – gave way in early August. The summer heat and the 'sometimes *self*-generated' debilitation of a poor diet predisposed him to 'the contagion of fever', which he believed he had contracted as he walked among the poor Irish families who were 'lying out all the summer on the bridges over the Clyde'.[19] His fever broke after a month, but the physical anguish continued. Sometimes it took the form of 'a bar rigid as a poker in the stomach, sometimes a more tormenting one as though the stomach were filled with cotton, sometimes (though more rarely) of an indescribable corrosive acid'. De Quincey fought these afflictions with his usual weapons: exercise ('I walk with a watch in my hand so as to *average* 10 miles a day'), and diet ('I am most abstemious, taking no one thing likely to irritate the stomach – except only coffee').[20] His condition had improved by the middle of October, when – remarkably – his drug of choice was hemlock, 'which once before did me so much good', and which now bestowed at least a 'moment's peace'. Throughout these battles he consumed laudanum, though his attitude towards it remained deeply divided. 'Since leaving off opium', he remarked wryly, 'I take a great deal too much of it for my health.'[21]

Troup and Brown had brought De Quincey to Glasgow to try to ensure that he remained a highly productive contributor to *Tait's*. They would not have been disappointed. He wrote seventeen essays in thirteen months. Walter Savage Landor's recent two-volume edition of his *Works* is the occasion of a four-part review in which De Quincey expresses misgivings about Landor's 'perverseness' and degrading religious notions, but celebrates him as 'a man of great genius', a 'leader in storms, a martyr, a national reformer, an arch-rebel'. Landor himself was delighted with the assessment, and that summer sent De Quincey a 'very prettily bound' copy of his collection of *Poemata et Inscriptiones*. 'There is no author from whom I *could* have been more gratified by such a mark of attention,' wrote De Quincey.[22]

Two historical essays – 'Joan of Arc' and 'The Nautico-Military Nun of Spain' – belong also to these months, and complement one another in intriguing ways. The former drew exalted praise from the *Eclectic Review,* which described De Quincey as, 'since Tacitus, *potentially* the greatest of history writers. He is as eloquent, as epic, as impassioned in his nobler narrative as Carlyle, and he is far more dignified, less melodramatic, and purer in style.' Yet in 'Joan of Arc', De Quincey's fascination with historical events seems less notable than his disturbing attitude towards women. 'You can do one thing as well as the best of us men,' he observes, '... you can die grandly, and as goddesses would die were goddesses mortal', an assertion strikingly anticipated only a year earlier by Poe's declaration in 'The Philosophy of Composition' that 'the death ... of a beautiful woman is, unquestionably, the most poetical topic in the world'.[23] 'The Nautico-Military Nun' is a second historical narrative, and one that again concerns a cross-dressing female soldier, this time the seventeenth-century adventurer Catalina de Erauso, who escaped from a convent at fifteen, fought as a Spanish soldier in South America, and later apparently drowned in the Gulf of Mexico. De Quincey clearly thought of 'Joan of Arc' and 'The Nautico-Military Nun' as two parts of a similar project, and planned to issue them together in a book, though nothing came of the idea. Very often in his writings, the suffocating protection of fathers, brothers, husbands, and sons leads to the death of women. Joan and Catalina are different. Both escape the home, and both die in their own cause.[24] To De Quincey, however, Joan is emphatically more inspiring in death than in life. Only Catalina – or 'Kate' as he suggestively calls her – is allowed a life of independence and achievement that is undiminished by the mysterious circumstances that surround her death.

Finally, during these months De Quincey produced his three-part examination of 'Protestantism', in which he analyses both John Henry Newman's recent conversion from the Church of England to Rome, and his *Essay on the Development of Christian Doctrine* (1845). Provocatively distinguishing between 'Newmannians' and '*Old*mannians', De Quincey explains that 'Rome founds herself upon the idea, that to *her*, by tradition and exclusive privilege, was communicated, once for all, the whole truth from the beginning. Mr Newman lays his corner stone in the very opposite idea of a gradual development given to Christianity by the motion of time, by experience, by expanding occasions, and by the progress of civilization.' Newman expressed marked displeasure with De Quincey's account: 'I wonder if he saw even the outside of my book on doctrinal development,' he growled. 'If he ever saw it, he would have known that the object of it, and the matter of it, was solely and entirely to answer the very objection which he makes.'[25]

Working with De Quincey brought Troup and Brown the usual

frustrations. In one particularly irritating instance, Troup twice sent a messenger to De Quincey's lodgings looking for copy, and twice the messenger returned with the same information: 'the old gentleman has no' got 'oot o' his bedroom yet!' 'Dreadfully put about', Troup sent Brown, who found De Quincey 'either uncommonly sound asleep or in a state of stupor. He lay stretched out on the hearthrug before the parlour fire-grate ... clad in an old dressing-gown, with no stockings on his feet, and merely a pair of thin, loose slippers over his toes. "I'm sure the puir body's deid!" the landlady exclaimed.' Brown searched amidst the chaos of the room and soon found the manuscript he was looking for, 'neatly tied up with red tape, and addressed to the "Editor of *Tait's Magazine*"'. At least, Troup acknowledged, De Quincey became far more responsive once he had an article in press, for all Troup had to do at that point was to send a message explaining that he was 'revising the proof, and would *do his best with the Greek quotations*', to bring De Quincey 'at once ... to the office. The very idea of a wrong accent or a printer's mistake in his Greek was intolerable.'[26]

Yet if the editor was often frustrated, the writer too felt he had cause for grievance. Editorial tampering always infuriated De Quincey, and he strongly objected when Troup made deep and unauthorized cuts to his work. 'People that have practised composition as much, and with as vigilant an eye as myself,' De Quincey insisted, 'know ... by thousands of cases, how infinite is the disturbance caused in the logic of a thought by the mere position of a word.'[27] Like Tait and the Blackwoods before him, Troup may have made the changes because he thought they improved the article, or because of circumstances beyond his control, including delays brought about by De Quincey himself. To De Quincey, that was not the issue. What mattered was the integrity of the writing. 'Who is answerable for the beauty, for the grandeur, for the effect of my papers?' he demanded. Troup holds that 'if he bears the blame, no harm is done ... But where or how does he bear the blame? My name is there: *his* is not.' Over the course of the autumn these tensions apparently ruptured De Quincey's relationship with *Tait's* and Troup, and by November he had left Glasgow and returned to his family at Lasswade.[28]

Here he found Francis hard at work on his Edinburgh MD thesis on a highly topical issue – *The Religious Objections to the Use of Chloroform in Obstetric Medicine*. Only a few weeks earlier, James Young Simpson, the Professor of Obstetrics at Edinburgh, had successfully used chloroform as an anaesthetic agent. Simpson's discovery met with considerable opposition from the clergy, who denounced it based on a literal understanding of Genesis 3:16, in which God curses Eve: 'in sorrow thou shalt bring forth children'. De Quincey – long himself a sufferer of acute physical pain – was squarely on the side of science, as he explained to Francis in a lengthy letter, in which he dismantled the arguments of 'the *religiosity* people', and applauded Simpson, whose 'immortal discovery ... I should think will be found to have done more for human comfort, and for the mitigation of animal suffering, than any other discovery whatever.' Within a matter of months, De Quincey's position was vindicated. 'Here, in Edinburgh', Simpson wrote, '... the religious, like the other forms of opposition to chloroform, have ceased amongst us.'²⁹ Later Francis copied out his father's letter and appended it to his thesis.

[iii]

On 28 December 1847, the Glasgow Athenaeum threw a large party. De Quincey was invited, but an illness 'of a very depressing character' forced him to send his regrets. Had he been able to attend, he would almost certainly have met Charles Dickens, who was the guest of honour, and who described the soirée as one of 'unbounded hospitality and enthoozymoozy ... I have never been more heartily received anywhere, or enjoyed myself more completely'.³⁰ Dickens later listed De Quincey's works as among his 'especial favourites', but De Quincey did not hold him in the same regard. 'Extravagance and want of fidelity to nature and the possibilities of life are what everywhere mar Dickens to me,' he had lamented to Florence a few months earlier; 'and these faults are fatal, because the *modes* of life amongst which these extravagances intrude are always the absolute realities of vulgarised life as it exists in plebeian ranks amongst our countrymen at this moment.'³¹

De Quincey was similarly critical of another major contemporary, Ralph Waldo Emerson. 'He was heard depreciating [him] as the *palimpsest* of a small Thomas Carlyle'. When Emerson came to Edinburgh, however, he and De Quincey met on at least four occasions, and seem to have taken considerable pleasure in each other's company. 'Sir, I never hear the name of your country without being awe-struck at its future!' De Quincey exclaimed when they were introduced on Sunday, 13 February.³² To Emerson, De Quincey was 'a very gentle old man, speaking with the utmost deliberation & softness. & so refined in speech & manners, as to make quite indifferent his extremely plain & poor dress'. That evening De Quincey talked 'of many things easily', from the duties of a guest and the rates of pay on the periodical press, through anecdotes of Wilson and Wordsworth, to an account of two Edinburgh street girls, one of whom took 'eight shillings out of his waist-coat pocket, & the other, his umbrella'.[33]

The following Saturday, De Quincey hosted a dinner for Emerson at Lasswade before travelling back into Edinburgh with him to hear his lecture on 'Eloquence'. Emerson was delighted – 'De Q at lecture!' – but the 'American nasal sing-song in his speech' seems to have put De Quincey to sleep.[34] Two days later, De Quincey saw Emerson off at the train station after writing him a letter of introduction to Coleridge's son Derwent. At some point during the week, Emerson gave De Quincey an inscribed copy of his *Essays: First Series, New Edition*, which De Quincey annotated at some length. 'By Emerson's own confession', he recorded, 'the Opium Eater is ruler of the *Night*.'[35]

De Quincey travelled in a remarkable social circle, as Emerson's visit revealed. He still socialized often at the home of Catherine Crowe, and 'so far got rid of his formality of Mrs or Miss as to speak of her and to her uniformly by her Christian name of Catherine'.[36] De Quincey and Emerson dined with David Scott, the poet and painter, and De Quincey afterwards visited his studio, where he was transfixed by Scott's picture 'of the Resurrection on the Day of the Crucifixion'. 'Is it possible!' cried De Quincey. 'When I met him the other evening, I thought him the dullest of mortals; but now I have been an hour with him among the tombs, I find him quick with thought, and the most interesting of men!'[37] Samuel Brown, the chemist, took a kind and steadying interest in De Quincey. One evening as they travelled together into Edinburgh, De Quincey 'grew very nervous', apparently at the thought that he might encounter his nemesis, Mrs McIndoe. Brown had a thorough knowledge of De Quincey's torments in this regard, and assured him 'that his old enemy . . . had removed to another quarter of the city'. De Quincey is 'serene & happy, among just these friends, with whom I found him', Emerson asserted: 'for, he has suffered in all ways, & lived the life of a wretch, for many years; & Samuel Brown, Mrs Crowe, & one or two more, have saved him from himself, & from the bailiff, & from a fury of . . . his landlady, – & from opium; & he is now clean, clothed, & in his right mind'.[38]

On the outs with both *Blackwood's* and *Tait's*, De Quincey produced an essay on 'War' that Brown helped him to place in the February issue of *MacPhail's Edinburgh Ecclesiastical Journal*, edited by Peter Landreth, and known as the unofficial voice of the established Church of Scotland. In the article, De Quincey argues that military conflict is both a physical and a moral necessity. Kant's essay on *Perpetual Peace* is praised for its 'great sagacity, though otherwise that little work is not free from visionary self-delusions', while Wordsworth's notorious proclamation that 'Carnage is

[God's] daughter' is marshalled in support of De Quincey's contention that the 'cessation of war ... would not be for the welfare of human nature, but would tend to its rapid degradation'.[39]

This same month De Quincey was asked by the Glasgow Athenaeum to contribute to their forthcoming *Album*, and in response produced a self-mocking essay on 'Sortilege', dated 'FEB. 24, 1848'. There is a bathtub in his study at Mavis Bush, he announces, and in it is all manner of paper, from dinner invitations and half-completed essays to unanswered letters and long-forgotten bills. While Margaret, Florence, and Emily look on, De Quincey orders Francis to dip his hand into the reservoir and fish out something that might be suitable for publication in the *Album*. Francis's first four attempts – *'Prepare to dip!'* – are failures. No one would want to read a 'horrid' dun, or a lecture to De Quincey 'by an ultra-moral friend ... on procrastination'. On his fifth and final try, however, Francis pulls forth a blank sheet of paper, which De Quincey then fills with a jocular lecture on astrology.[40]

More deeply engaging was the opportunity to write for the *North British Review*, a quarterly journal edited by the Free Church of Scotland minister and writer William Hanna. Established in 1844, the *North British* sought the middle ground between the avowedly religious magazines that were too exclusively theological and too rigorously sectarian, and those political, literary, and scientific journals that excluded religion altogether, or gave it only minor notice. De Quincey himself described it as a 'liberal' journal.[41] In the May issue, he reviewed John Forster's recent biography of Oliver Goldsmith, and while illuminating on eighteenth-century literature and men of letters, he is most incisive on contemporary politics. 'Mr Forster, in his views upon the *social* rights of literature, is rowing pretty nearly in the same boat as Mr Carlyle in *his* views upon the rights of labour. Each denounces, or by implication denounces, as an oppression and a nuisance, what *we* believe to be a necessity inalienable from the economy and structure of our society.'[42]

A second review, this time of William Roscoe's recently reprinted edition of Alexander Pope, was published in August, and occasioned some of De Quincey's most celebrated thoughts on the definition and role of literature. 'Didactic poetry', he maintains, 'is a contradiction in terms. 'No poetry can have the function of teaching.' Poetry can teach 'only as nature teaches, as forests teach, as the sea teaches, as infancy teaches, viz., by deep impulse, by hieroglyphic suggestion'. De Quincey also returns to his famous distinction between the 'literature of knowledge' and the 'literature of power', which he first introduced in the *London* nearly twenty-five years earlier, and which he now reformulates in a way that shifts the emphasis from the affective to the moral.[43] 'What do you learn from Paradise Lost?' he asks.

> Nothing at all. What do you learn from a cookery-book? Something new, something that you did not know before, in every paragraph. But would you therefore put the wretched cookery-book on a higher level of esti-mation than the divine poem? What you owe to Milton is not any knowledge, of which a million separate items are still but a million of advancing steps on the same earthly level; what you owe – is *power*, that is, exercise and expansion to your own latent capacity of sympathy with the infinite.

The definition provides perhaps the best example of what De Quincey expected of literature, and of what he himself hoped to achieve.[44]

In November, his old friend Thomas Noon Talfourd's *Final Memorials of Charles Lamb* formed the ostensible subject of his third and final *North British* review. Across a survey that covers Lamb's prose style, his friendship with Coleridge, his *Elia* essays, and his religious convictions, De Quincey interweaves his own memories, from his early experiences with Lamb in London, to their evenings together as colleagues on the *London*. 'Both Lamb and myself had a furious love for nonsense,' De Quincey writes. Yet he is also keenly aware that Lamb's life was darkened by the madness which assailed his sister, and which on at least one occasion seriously threatened him. 'Is there peace on earth for the lunatic?' De Quincey wonders solemnly. 'Charles Lamb, thou in thy proper person, shalt enter the skirts of this dreadful hail-storm: even thou shalt taste the secrets of lunacy, and enter as a captive its house of bondage.'[45]

During that autumn De Quincey appears to have left Mavis Bush and moved back into Edinburgh. There had perhaps been some quarrel between father and children, for he saw little of them over the next several months. 'They are young and thoughtless,' he declared tersely. Certainly on occasion their high spirits grated on him. 'Oh my dear girls, I fear you are talking sad nonsense,' he would whisper to himself, before introducing 'a specimen of genuine and first-rate talk' that was designed to bring their 'female' minds up to a 'masculine and philosophic level'. In a less patronizing mood, De Quincey noted that 'we, who see most of each other, nearest relatives united in the same household, see but little of that inner world – that world of secret self-consciousness – in which each of us lives a second life apart and with himself alone'.[46]

Margaret, Florence, and Emily almost invariably treated their father with affection and respect. But they were each spirited, witty, and intelligent 'supporters of the rights of women in the democracy of Mavis Bush', and all three were more than capable of voicing objections both to their father's point of view and to 'his cranky ways'. At dinner one evening, his condescending attitude towards them was so irksome that they were – in Margaret's words – 'quite ready for a "stand-up fight" for our tastes'. In another instance, a friend wrote asking for help in retrieving 'two valuable books' that he had loaned to De Quincey. It was probably Margaret who replied that 'she had done her best, but the truth was her father had for two days been sitting on them and at night took them to his room and put them under his pillow'.[47] Once De Quincey slopped whisky and water on himself, and then cleaned up the mess by reducing a pair of Margaret's 'very pretty lace cuffs' to 'a piece of dirty wet rag'. On another occasion, he trimmed the candles using a tiny pair of scissors belonging to Florence, who 'with a terrific scream precipitated herself' upon him when she discovered what he had done.[48] De Quincey often 'set something on fire, the commonest incident being for some one to look up from work or book to say casually, "Papa, your hair is on fire", of which a calm, "Is it, my love?" and a hand rubbing out the blaze was all the notice taken'. One night a maid reported with alarm that De Quincey's study was on fire. The sisters rushed downstairs, but were told by their father that they could not use water to combat the blaze, 'as it would have ruined the beloved papers'. Instead, De Quincey entered the room, locked the door behind him, and put the flames out with a heavy rug. 'He was not a reassuring man for nervous people to live with,' Florence remarked mildly. Margaret was more to the point: 'for Papa, we are at constant war with him'.[49]

Living again in Edinburgh, De Quincey was 'oppressed' by various 'calls upon my time', though in September he seems to have enjoyed the visit of a young Greek scholar, Neocles Jaspis Mousabines, who shared his enthusiasm for Wordsworth, and who journeyed down to the Lake District to meet the poet with a letter of introduction provided by De Quincey. 'My Dear Sir,' De Quincey began, before outlining to Wordsworth how Mousabines had been 'powerfully and unaffectedly impressed by the study of your works', as De Quincey himself had been half a century earlier when he began his study of the poet. De Quincey signed himself, 'Your faithful friend and servant'.[50] Despite everything that had transpired, he still felt close enough to the poet to address him directly and with a trace of their former intimacy. It was the last time the two men were in contact.

A 'deep-seated nervous derangement' had plagued De Quincey for several months, and in late October he decided once again that only by conquering his addiction could he hope to restore his health. Resolving on abstinence, he cut himself off for eighteen days, during which time he 'descended into utter despair', before sliding even further downward into the 'profoundest suffering and utter hopelessness – (rigid obstruction, throbbing without intermission, and sub-inflammation)'. And then suddenly, 'to my utter surprise', on 23 November 'the misery passed off after breakfast, not fully and consciously until about one or half-past one; so it continued until after cocoa, when for an hour or so a reaction of misery set in, which again passed off; and now, half-past eleven at night, I am almost as well as before cocoa'.[51]

De Quincey had fought hard against the agonies of laudanum withdrawal on several previous occasions, ascending towards the hope of sobriety in some instances, and plunging towards rock bottom in others. But this time he reached a startlingly different conclusion about 'the cause of my misery'. For decades he had been convinced that it was the opium, but now 'it appears more strongly' that it 'must be the alcohol'. He fought on for another three and a half weeks, and felt confident that he could triumph. 'The advance will not, perhaps, be continuous,' he realized, '... but it will burst out more and more at intervals like a fugue, until the restoration shall be perfect.'[52] There was, however, no restoration. A greater understanding of his laudanum habit did not help him to defeat it, and by the spring of 1849 he had relapsed again. Further, at this same moment, one of his most implacable creditors, the tailor Craig, tracked him down and demanded money that had been owing for several years. De Quincey either could not or would not pay, and in the early summer, after avoiding incarceration for almost fifteen years, he went to prison for the second time.[53]

John Blackwood got word of his plight, and bailed him out in exchange for the promise of a series of articles for the magazine. In July, De Quincey submitted 'Conversation and S. T. Coleridge', an article in which he mixes praise with a good deal of censure and biographical summary: 'Treachery there was in [Coleridge's] own nature, and almost by a necessity he yielded to the dark temptations of opium.' Blackwood liked parts of the article, but he rejected it. 'In anything you write there must be fine expressions & thoughts but in this case I do not think you are at all happy in the mode of handling your subject.'[54] It was a setback for both De Quincey and Blackwood, but De Quincey regrouped by focusing his energies on an article that he had begun to compose at around the same time as *Suspiria*, and that he seems at various points to have considered part of it.[55] The result is one of his most remarkable achievements.

[iv]

Too late. Those words haunted De Quincey. It was too late to help Elizabeth, Catharine, Ann, William, Margaret. It was too late to meet his deadlines, to avoid laudanum, to stop the tortures of his dreaming mind. In 'The English Mail-Coach', published in *Blackwood's* for October and December 1849, De Quincey confronts 'the dreadful legend of TOO LATE'.[56] But this time, at least in the powerful mythology of the tale, he is 'in time'.

De Quincey opens the essay with meandering badinage and anecdotal humour that he steadily deepens into impassioned strains of resurrection and grief. At the centre of the tale is his memory of the night when the mail-coach on which he was riding was involved in the near-fatal collision with the gig just outside Preston. Over thirty years have elapsed since the accident, yet it continues to replay itself endlessly in his nightmares, where the gig, the coach, and the young girl have become conflated with both the tragedies of his childhood and his intense commitment to nationhood.

Memories of the mail-coach trigger within De Quincey penetrating insights into time, spirituality, the self, and sudden death. There is, he contends, an abysmal infirmity in the human will that leads us to act against our own better interests. Dreams cannot explain this frailty, but – either consciously or unconsciously – they enact for us that fatal moment when we all guiltily embrace it. The result is a deep division within ourselves that precedes, rather than reflects, our experience of the world, and that creates within each of us an inexhaustible sense of shame and sin. As Adam fell in paradise, so for De Quincey in dreams a bait is offered to the infirm places in our individual wills, and in taking it we complete for ourselves the aboriginal fall.[57]

The bifurcation of the self that haunts all of us is especially severe in De Quincey, as is evident in his ongoing dreams of Fanny, the beautiful girl he used to meet when travelling many years earlier on the Bath Road. In these nightmares, De Quincey conjures up the face of Fanny, which invokes a rose in June, and these two images proliferate until he sees 'roses and Fannies, Fannies and roses, without end'. Then come thoughts of Fanny's grandfather, the coachman, whose inability to turn round reminds De Quincey of a crocodile, an association which immediately calls forth a 'dreadful host of wild semi-legendary animals', including 'griffins, dragons, basilisks, sphinxes'. At length these 'fighting images' crowd together 'into one towering armorial shield', and De Quincey is brought face to face with his deepest fear. 'The dreamer finds housed within himself', he trembles, '... some horrid alien nature.'

What if it were his own nature repeated, – still, if the duality were distinctly perceptible, even *that* – even this mere numerical double of his own consciousness – might be a curse too mighty to be sustained. But how, if the alien nature contradicts his own, fights with it, perplexes, and confounds it? How, again, if not one alien nature, but two, but three, but four, but five, are introduced within what once he thought the inviolable sanctuary of himself?[58]

From one vantage point, this is a terrifying portrayal of a consciousness divided against itself in ways that clearly suggest schizophrenia. But from another it is even more disturbing, for it suggests that there are parts within us that are not human, but 'alien', and that in our worst nightmares aspects of our selves are inoculated upon these alien natures – inoculated upon the vile, the bestial, the unthinkable.[59]

De Quincey's dreams of Fanny 'betray a shocking tendency' to pass from 'lovely floral luxuriations ... into finer maniacal splendours'.[60] Yet if his recollections of the mail-coach propel him downward into the depths of his own consciousness, they also propel him outward into a consideration of Britain in the Victorian age. De Quincey feels an intense nostalgia for the now obsolete mail-coach system of his youth, while he is divided in his opinion of the Industrial Revolution, which is to him a source of both fascination and terror. His account of the accident on the Preston road illustrates what happens when a mail-coach runs out of control, but his entire narrative hints at the infinitely greater trauma that would ensue if the newer steam technologies went similarly out of control. In the same way, De Quincey acknowledges that industrialism has bestowed benefits, but he also believes that something is lost when machines replace people. The mail-coaches promoted 'inter-agencies' between passengers and horses, whereas the railways have 'disconnected man's heart from the ministers of his locomotion'. Trains travel much faster as 'a fact of ... lifeless knowledge', but 'on the old mail-coach ... we heard our speed, we saw it, we felt it as a thrilling'. The 'pot-wallopings of the boiler' are spiritually deadening, while the 'laurelled mail, heart-shaking, when heard screaming on the wind', provided innumerable opportunities for the sublime.[61] In the 'Mail-Coach', De Quincey recognizes the achievements of the Industrial Revolution, but he expresses profound misgivings about its imaginative costs and potential dangers.

He is much more certain about Britain's role in the Napoleonic Wars. The political mission of the mail-coach in distributing news of Britain's military campaigns against Revolutionary France has fused in his imagination with the accident on the Preston road to produce kaleidoscopic nightmares in which Napoleon's defeat at Waterloo is assimilated within a broader myth of Britain as a righteous colonial power charged by God with the task of preserving and extending Christian civilization.[62] In the spectacular 'Dream-Fugue' which closes the piece, a celestial mail-coach carrying the words 'Waterloo and Recovered Christendom' flies headlong down the grand aisle of a cathedral towards a girl who is at once Elizabeth, the goddess Britannia, and the young woman aboard the gig.[63] Death seems inevitable. And yet this time death is cheated. For 'at the last, and with one motion of his victorious arm', God sweeps the girl, 'now grown up to woman's height', far upwards to an altar, where she stands 'sinking, rising, trembling, fainting', but safe. In the fifth and final movement of the fugue, De Quincey and all the 'children of the grave' emerge through the eastern gates of the mighty cathedral, 'rendering thanks to God in the highest – that, having hid his face through one generation behind thick clouds of War, once again was ascending – was ascending from Waterloo – in the visions of Peace'.[64] It is one of the most astonishing moments in all of De Quincey – a mind-boggling amalgamation of Protestantism, patriotism, history, and the self in which innocence is redeemed and God's ways are justified.

'The English Mail-Coach' is De Quincey's last article for *Blackwood's*, and marks a fittingly bittersweet close to his connection with the magazine. On the one hand, his departure left a bad taste in the mouth of Blackwood, who had received nowhere near enough material from De Quincey to reimburse him for the money he had paid to effect his release from prison, and who in response had De Quincey's portrait turned out of the *Blackwood's* saloon.[65] On the other, the 'Mail-Coach' brought *Blackwood's* considerable acclaim, especially for the purple prose of its conclusion, and clearly influenced a number of contemporary authors, including major figures such as Herman Melville in *Moby Dick* (1851) and George Eliot in *Felix Holt* (1866).[66]

[v]

He was not long without a publisher. James Fields, of the Boston firm of Ticknor, Reed, and Fields, had been writing to him for several months with a proposal to produce an American edition of his works. 'Some years ago we published in this city an Edition of "The Confessions of an Opium Eater,"' Fields explained, 'and being about to issue another, we beg to ask if it will be agreeable to you to supply a list of your other articles & where published that we may include in a larger volume of your writings a complete collection of your essays &c.' The notion of a collected edition of his work seems never even to have occurred to De Quincey, and his first reaction was incredulity. 'Sir, the thing is absolutely, insuperably, and for ever impossible. Not the archangel Gabriel, nor his multipotent adversary, durst attempt any such thing!'[67]

Fields, however, was determined to proceed, and loose copyright laws at the time allowed him to do so, though he kept in close contact with De Quincey, and paid him handsomely from profits he was not legally obliged to share with him.[68] In August 1850 he issued *Confessions of an English Opium-Eater* and *Suspiria de Profundis* as volume one, and a collection of *Biographical Essays* as volume two. Five other volumes followed within a year, including *Life and Manners* and the *Literary Reminiscences*. The firm printed 1500 copies of each title, and reprintings started within a few months. William Davis Ticknor declared that the De Quincey edition had 'far exceeded our expectations', and he was particularly gratified by 'the kind expressions that come to us from every quarter in regard to the real value of these writings'. In late 1852 Fields reported that De Quincey was 'still the rage'. By 1853, Ticknor, Reed, and Fields had sold over 45,000 copies of De Quincey.[69]

Meanwhile, in Edinburgh, De Quincey had introduced himself to the publisher James Hogg, and become a contributor to *Hogg's Instructor*, a monthly magazine of humour, information, and reviews that was printed in Edinburgh and London, and that reached a middle-class audience of 5000–6000.[70] De Quincey wrote for the *Instructor* on miscellaneous topics ranging from 'Conversation', 'Logic' and 'French and English Manners', to 'Judas Iscariot', 'California', and 'On the Supposed Scriptural Expression for Eternity'. In his most interesting work for the magazine, however, he surveys the 'revolutionary character' of contemporary British society in ways that are both sympathetic and slightly ominous. The 'Young England' of Benjamin Disraeli has received 'a volume of new life-blood' from the 'evocation of new interests, new questions, new sympathies – and the remarkable concurrence, with this intellectual awakening, of a far cheaper and more stirring literature'. Railways continue to transform social and economic life, for they are 'not only swift in themselves, but the causes of swiftness in everything else; so that very soon, I am convinced, out of pure, blind sympathy with railway trains, men will begin to trot through the streets'. Immense strides have been made in 'the capital interest of Education', which is now 'solemnly recognized as a national *duty*', with measures in progress for bringing it, 'like water or gas, almost to every cottage door'. In summation: 'I cannot but feel a steady persuasion that this age is labouring with a deeper fermentation of thought and self-questioning than has ever before reached the general heart of a nation.'[71]

Productive relations between De Quincey and the *Instructor*, however, did not prevent him from returning briefly to *Tait's*, which was now printed in London and under the editorship of the Cambridge-educated barrister and journalist Horatio Mansfield.[72] In 'Lord Carlisle on Pope', published in April, May, and June 1851, De Quincey conceded that Pope was 'the most brilliant writer of his own class in European literature', but he damned him for his narrowness, false refinement, conventionalism, and dishonesty. After the publication of the second instalment of the article, Thornton Leigh Hunt criticized 'DE QUINCEY's rambling exaggeration on POPE'. Rejoined De Quincey: 'I do not see any actual exaggeration, simply because I do not see that any exaggeration is possible.' Of far more concern to him were the 'press errors' that had appeared in the first instalment, the result of trying to write and revise 'at a distance of 400 miles' from London. De Quincey voiced his dissatisfaction with the arrangement, but Mansfield was apparently unsympathetic, and 'Lord Carlisle on Pope' was De Quincey's last article for *Tait's*.[73] His departure from the magazine brought to a close a relationship that had lasted eighteen years, and that had been the prompt for some of his most progressive and engaging work.

At some point he removed himself from his Edinburgh lodgings and returned to live at Mavis Bush. Margaret, Florence, and Emily were all still at home, though Francis had by this time successfully completed his medical degree at the University of Edinburgh, and emigrated to Brazil.[74] In late March, the person in charge of collecting data in Lasswade for the 1851 census knocked at the door of the cottage, where he discovered that De Quincey had not yet filled in the required form, and was soon flustered at the thought of having to do so. 'Where was he to sign? What was his occupation, etc.? At length he inscribed his own name and entered himself as a "writer to the magazines"'. When the enumerator recorded the information in his book, however, he listed De Quincey as an 'Annuitant'.[75] These two very different responses highlight a paradox that repeatedly shaped De Quincey's conception of himself. From one point of view, he was justly proud of his accomplishments as a professional writer with a burgeoning international reputation. But from another, he resented the ways in which the magazines had forced him to temporize and commodify his knowledge, and he never ceased to think of himself as a moneyed man of leisure who had no real need to write at all.

The enumerator then enquired about the other occupants of the cottage. De Quincey gave the names of his three daughters, but was 'floored' when he was asked to specify their 'occupation'. Eventually he took up his pen, 'put a bracket round the three names, and wrote against them -- "These are like the lilies of the field; they toil not, neither do they spin"'.[76] It was hardly an accurate description. De Quincey may have believed – or even hoped – that his daughters devoted most of their days to leisure, but in addition to the responsibilities of running the household, they spent a considerable portion of their time managing his affairs and correspondence, as well as doing what they could to ensure that he took care of himself. De Quincey was proud and still remarkably self-reliant, but Margaret, Florence, and Emily were much busier – especially when he took up residence at Mavis Bush – than he knew or cared to acknowledge. The census record closes with the information that the De Quincey household also included a thirty-two-year-old cook, Jane Stewart, and a nineteen-year-old maid, Marion Duncan.[77]

De Quincey embraced the pleasantries and routines of Mavis Bush, but they were not enough to stave off the terrible episodes of mental and emotional stress that still waylaid him. An 'undecipherable horror' brooded day and night over his nervous system, and brought on 'whirlwinds of impatience', as he explained in a remarkable letter to the poet and essayist Mary Russell Mitford, who long ago had contributed to the *London Magazine* at the same time as him. 'Whatever I may have been writing is suddenly wrapt, as it were, in one sheet of consuming fire – the very paper is poisoned to my eyes. I cannot endure to look at it, and I sweep it away into vast piles of unfinished letters, or inchoate essays.' De Quincey was 'quite alone' in his study, so no one witnessed these fits, nor 'if they did, would my outward appearance testify to the dreadful transports within'.[78] Yet across these months he continued to labour as hard as ever at his prose. 'This I *do* know', he declared in December 1851, 'that here, as always, I have written my best. That is, given the conditions under which I wrote, which conditions might chance to be very unfavourable; hurry, for example, exhaustion, dissatisfaction with my subject, &c., and latterly overwhelming nervousness; these allowed for, always I have striven to write as well as I could.'[79]

[vi]

Many people saw De Quincey at this time, and left vivid recollections of their encounters with him. A Mr Sinclair claimed that he used to accompany De Quincey 'to the apothecary's in Edinburgh where stands Scott's monument, to see him toss off a wine-glass of laudanum and with a *sang-froid* as if the draught had been mere water'. Bertram and De Quincey met often in Princes Street, where 'he would take a turn or two with me, speaking his beautiful English'.[80]

Thomas Cooper, the Chartist and religious lecturer, visited De Quincey at Mavis Bush and gave him a copy of his *Purgatory of Suicides* (1845), a political epic in Spenserian stanzas that Cooper had composed whilst in prison for sedition. De Quincey 'showed true courtesy in speaking to me on political subjects', Cooper asserted, to the point where either Margaret or Florence 'proudly chid' him for not 'maintaining his sentiments with dignity'. '"My dear," said [De Quincey], whose small slender frame shook with feeling, "do not talk so, I beseech you – you will insult Mr Cooper."' Harriet Martineau, the essayist, novelist, and economist, spent an afternoon at Mavis Bush. De Quincey 'spoke of her with real liking', while Martineau, who suffered from deafness, responded particularly to De Quincey's voice, 'so clear, so soft, so sweet; so delightful a contrast to the way people have of bawling to me"'.[81]

In addition to various exchanges with James Hogg, De Quincey met often with Hogg's son James junior. Once the two were overtaken by a severe thunderstorm and driven into Paxton's Royal Exchange Hotel for shelter. 'While there having a basin of soup, the waiter, after closely scrutinising my companion, gently touched him on the arm, and said, "I think, sir, I have a bundle of papers which you left here some time ago" ... It then turned out that my friend had slept at this hotel some twelve months before, and on that occasion had confided these papers to the waiter, asking him to keep them till he called for them.' On another occasion, De Quincey and Hogg walked together in the country, where De Quincey easily outpaced the much younger man, ascending a steep hill near Lasswade 'like a squirrel' while keeping up 'an unremitting monologue on the Beauties of Herder'.[82]

Hill Burton saw much of De Quincey. 'His costume, in fact, is a boy's duffle great-coat, very threadbare, with a hole in it and buttoned tight to the chin, where it meets the fragments of a parti-coloured belcher handkerchief; on his feet are list-shoes covered with snow, for it is a stormy winter-night; and the trousers – some one suggests that they are inner linen garments blackened with writing-ink.' One night De Quincey stayed over at Burton's, where he 'lugged a considerable heap' of books to his room, including Burton's 'best bound quarto', which he spread 'upon a piece of bedroom furniture, readily at hand, and of sufficient height to let him pore over it' while he lay recumbent on the floor, 'with only one article of attire to separate him' from nakedness. On a different occasion, De Quincey described to Burton his horror at a peacock that had come to live near Mavis Bush, for 'not only the terrific yells of the accursed biped ... pierced him to the soul, but the continued terror of their recurrence kept his nerves in agonizing tension during the intervals of silence'.[83]

In January 1852, Hill Burton walked to Lasswade with John Ritchie Findlay, editor of *The Scotsman* newspaper. It was the beginning of a close friendship between De Quincey and Findlay. 'We talked, among many other things, about Macaulay,' Findlay stated. De Quincey remarked that a 'passion for speaking was usually the sign of a weak and shallow mind, but that Macaulay was a remarkable exception to this rule'. Ten days later Burton and Findlay walked out again, this time for dinner with De Quincey and his daughters. Their conversation concerned 'all the current topics of the day', and a variety of ecclesiastical matters, including 'the great Antichrist controversy'. In the course of the evening, the party heard the sound of children's voices, and went out into the back garden to find a group of young 'guisers' singing. De Quincey evidently misunderstood the reason for their visit, and 'instead of rightly regarding them as village children on an evening frolic, fancied that they were in actual distress, and making a somewhat peculiar and more than usually clamorous appeal for charity. Silence was strikingly broken by his exclaiming, "All that I have ever had enjoyment of in life, the charms of friendship, the smiles of women, and the joys of wine, seem to rise up to reproach me for my happiness when I see such misery, and think there is so much of it in the world."'[84]

Francis Jacox, a clergyman and prolific magazinist, was one of the most enthusiastic of De Quincey's youthful admirers, and in the summer of 1852 he spent the better part of a week at Mavis Bush, where he witnessed firsthand the misery De Quincey endured as a result of his addiction. 'During the days that I was his guest I could not but take note of the vicissitudes of temperament and spirits to which he was subject,' reported Jacox. 'For some time in the morning of each day he appeared to be grievously depressed and prostrate; the drowsy torpor of which he complained so keenly was then in fullest possession of him.' His eyes looked 'heavy', 'filmy', and 'void of life'. Sometimes De Quincey fought this lethargy well into the afternoon, though he was usually able to revive himself earlier with a walk in the fresh air and a cup of good coffee, which acted upon him 'like a charm, bracing up his energies' and 'clearing up his prospects'.[85] Jacox may well have believed that De Quincey effected his recovery in this way, for he makes no mention of laudanum, but the drug was undoubtedly at the root of both De Quincey's stupor and his resurgence.

De Quincey's misery, however, did not diminish his intellectual energy. He talked to Jacox about the music of Pergolesi, Mozart, Beethoven, and Bellini. Activists such as Charles Kingsley and the 'Christian Socialists' 'puzzled' him. A politician like William Gladstone 'had a charm for him: "But what am I to think ... of his sympathies with a party abroad which at home would be identified with extreme democracy?" Not that extreme democracy in politics, any more than abstract atheism as such, was to Mr De Quincey otherwise than philosophically interesting.' Modern literature led him to discuss a wide range of authors, including Coleridge, Lamb, Madame de Staël, Charles Maturin, George Henry Lewes, and William Makepeace Thackeray. 'Referring to Wordsworth's happy immunity from distracting anxieties ... Mr De Quincey exclaimed, "Heavens! had I but ... had his robust strength, and healthy stomach, and sound nerves, with the same glorious freedom from all interruptions and embarrassment!"' On the subject of *Bleak House*, 'then in course of publication', De Quincey objected that Dickens was 'repeating himself ... and a heavier cause of complaint lay in the popular author's dead set against the "upper classes", as such, and his glorification at their expense of the idealised working-man'.[86]

At the end of his visit, Jacox walked with De Quincey into Edinburgh and up the Mound, where he noticed the 'nervous solicitude' with which De Quincey 'refrained from any gesture while passing a cabstand that might seem to warrant any driver in concluding himself summoned and engaged. Some unhappy experience of a mistake of this kind may have been the secret of his disquiet, for evidently he entertained a dread of the "overbearing brutality of these men"'. Passing on to a bookshop window, De Quincey examined a copy of Nathaniel Hawthorne's *Mosses from an Old Manse* (1846), which Jacox went inside and purchased for him. De Quincey began to talk of 'Hawthorne's genius, and to mention a recent visit of Emerson's, – to neither of whom could he accord quite the degree of admiration claimed for them by the more thoroughgoing of their respective admirers'. The two men then proceeded through George Square and into the Meadows, where De Quincey assured Jacox that he need accompany him no further on the way back to Lasswade. 'It was between eight and nine on that lovely July evening that I took leave,' Jacox remembered. '... The last I saw of him, he had opened Hawthorne's book, and went along reading as he walked.'[87]

A month later, De Quincey's American publisher Fields, near the end of an extended stay in Britain, accepted an invitation to visit Mavis Bush. At the time appointed for his arrival, De Quincey stood waiting on the garden porch, and before long Fields's Edinburgh carriage came into view. Stepping forward to the gate, De Quincey prepared to receive his guest, while Fields claimed that he immediately noticed the 'alabaster shine' on De Quincey's face, which he had often observed 'in other opium-eaters', as well as the restlessness of his body, which 'also proclaimed his well-known habit'. With 'exquisite courtesy', De Quincey greeted Fields and escorted him into the cottage, where 'beautiful' Margaret De Quincey – whose poor health often kept her at home – sat reading. 'Soon after came in his other two daughters whom he introduced as "fresh from the Kirk". His second daughter Florence is a great beauty.'[88]

Lunch was served, and then Fields – locked arm in arm with the 'smallest ... looking little man I ever saw' – walked over the hills to nearby Roslin Castle. De Quincey spoke 'very freely about his Opium Life and seemed to consider it no failing that he had destroyed his constitution'. He took a great interest in the countryside. 'You should have seen him listening with his head uncovered to a stock dove that sat cooing over against a cottage wall and you should have heard his indignant railing as he showed me where the Esk had been turned away from its proper channel for some mill-purpose.' At one point De Quincey stopped to dwell on his youth and 'dead companions', before acknowledging with a sigh that these were topics 'too sad for this bright day'.[89]

The conversation turned to books and authors. Conscious as ever of his audience, De Quincey abandoned the qualified enthusiasm for Emerson and Hawthorne that he had displayed in his earlier conversation with Jacox, and he lauded the two American writers to his American publisher. 'Emerson seems to have made a most favourable impression on the whole De Q. family. His visit to their cottage they will always remember & more than once during the day the Opium Eater quoted him with delight. Hawthorne's books De Q. has read himself and always he told me with great interest.' De Quincey also spoke to Fields of British authors he had known as personal friends, referring to Lamb and Southey with 'love and tenderness', and invoking 'those days among the hills of Westmorland when his daily companions' were Coleridge and Wordsworth. Wilson was the subject of a number of humorous anecdotes, yet he was now in very poor health, and when De Quincey mentioned him, 'his eyes filled and his voice trembled'.[90]

That evening, as Fields prepared to leave, he quietly slipped into Margaret's hand a cheque for £50, as the first of several instalments he paid to De Quincey for his share in the profits of the American edition of his works. De Quincey insisted on accompanying Fields back into Edinburgh. 'I feel that at my period of life, and your home being three thousand miles away, the chances are against our ever meeting again.' Fields could not allow him to walk the whole way, but he sent his fly a few miles down the road, and the two men set off. De Quincey spoke of 'his family and his sons, one in India and one in Brazil, and gave me a history of all his joys and sorrows. Evidently a little crazed I should say he was.' When the two finally parted it was 'dark and lowering on the brow of a hill looking towards Edinburgh'. 'God bless you,' said De Quincey, before turning back towards Mavis Bush. Fields watched him, 'vanishing, reappearing, vanishing', until he was lost in the mist.[91]

FOURTEEN

Recollected

[i]

De Quincey consolidated the shift in his reputation from Romantic bohemian to Victorian man of letters when, in 1853, he began to publish *Selections Grave and Gay*, his own revised edition of many of his most important essays. Fields's 'American energy' was at the core of the enterprise, for in collecting De Quincey's widely spread magazine work into a series of handsome and affordable volumes, he provided a service which De Quincey himself candidly admitted he 'could not have accomplished in twenty years'.[1] When the Fields edition began to circulate in Britain, James Hogg and his son persuaded De Quincey to produce his own British selection. The agreement placed De Quincey in an awkward position with Fields, for by using the American edition as a basis for revision he was rendering it obsolete. In the event, however, both publishers benefited. Fields's edition underwrote Hogg's, while De Quincey saw to it that the new material he produced for Hogg was released to Fields, who duly rolled it into the ongoing American project.[2]

The chance to amend, justify, and reimagine what he had written sometimes more than three decades earlier brought out all of De Quincey's fussiness. Typically, he fretted over the spelling of '*porticoes . . . porticos*', or consulted 'three or four different lexicons' to decide whether 'calligraphy' should be spelled with a single or a double 'l'.[3] Scarce wonder that the labour often proceeded very slowly. De Quincey's 'whole constitution and habit of mind were averse from sustained and continuous work of the kind', Hogg sighed. 'He was constantly being caught with new plans, and when I was desirous of pushing on the publication of the works, would entertain me with the most ingenious devices and speculations.' The publisher soon found, however, that it was of no use 'to show impatience – that the causes of delay were for the most part beyond his control: that he did not lack the will to make efforts, but the power, and that the power was most amenable when he was left unharrassed'.[4] Through charm, resolution, and infinite

Figure 6: George D'Almaine's portrait of James Fields, 1849

patience, both Hogg and his son stayed at De Quincey's elbow and gradually cajoled fourteen volumes from him. De Quincey could only work by fits and starts, as illness, opium, and perhaps brandy – 'that dreadful potentate' – continued to ground him: 'pardon me . . . and read in this furious nonsense the restlessness of my shattered nerves'.[5] But he produced in the end a characteristically accomplished body of work.

Volume One of his *Selections* was published on 21 May 1853. De Quincey opened with a 'General Preface' which reads in part like an apologia for his career as a magazinist: the harsh and peremptory deadlines of the mass media often drove him into hurried writing, while producing for specific magazine audiences had the effect at times of narrowing his publicity, especially amongst those classes of 'leisure and wealth'.[6] De Quincey's account hardly does justice to his own popularity and productivity, but in the 'Preface' he slights the magazines in order to re-fashion himself as an author no longer shackled by the demands of time and money, and who now presents his last and best thoughts in the dignity of a selected edition.

His writings, De Quincey goes on to explain, are best thought of as falling into three categories. The first comprises those papers which propose 'primarily to amuse the reader; but which, in doing so, may or may not happen occasionally to reach a higher station, at which the amusement passes into an impassioned interest'. The second encompasses 'those papers which address themselves purely to the understanding as an insulated faculty'. And the third concerns a 'far higher class of compositions', such as the *Confessions* and especially *Suspiria*, for in them De Quincey 'attempts to clothe in words the visionary scenes derived from the world of dreams, where a single false note, a single word in a wrong key, ruins the whole music'.[7]

Volume One contains the first thirteen instalments of his *Autobiographic Sketches*, a series in which De Quincey once again reaches far back into his past, moving in this instance from infancy to 'premature manhood' through a combination of newly written material and revisions to work previously published in *Blackwood's*, *Tait's*, and *The Instructor*.[8] When the volume appeared, De Quincey wrote a flattering letter to George Henry Lewes, co-editor with Thornton Leigh Hunt of the radical weekly newspaper, *The Leader*. Would Thornton's father, the iconic liberal Leigh Hunt, like a copy of the *Sketches*? More to the point, might Lewes review it, though 'you are too generous to suppose that I wish to bespeak any public notice from you beyond the most equitable and enlightened notice which *The Leader*, more by much and more uniformly than any other journal whatever that I have ever seen, accords to all books whatsoever'.[9] Lewes was enthusiastic about the volume, and a two-part review duly appeared in *The Leader* for 11 and 25 June: 'Thomas De Quincey we hold to be the greatest of English prose writers. We are not in the habit of making such assertions lightly, and ... beg the reader to consider that all our remarks are made in reference to the very highest standards, such as the commanding excellence of De Quincey's writing claims from all.' Shortly after Lewes's review appeared George Eliot reported, 'I have De Quincey's Autobiographical Sketches with me, and have now done with them.'[10] Perhaps Lewes passed his copy of the book to her?

The second and concluding volume of the *Sketches* was published on 24 January 1854, and is largely concerned with De Quincey's revisions to his *Tait's* essays on Coleridge and Wordsworth. Retained – indeed augmented – are his allegations regarding Coleridge's plagiarisms, though in other respects De Quincey is more conciliatory in his attitude towards both poets, toning down a number of passages that originally gave offence, and excising others altogether. 'The truth and life of those Lake Sketches is something wonderful,' Mitford declared. 'Of course the blind worshippers of Wordsworth quarrel with him; but there is quite enough left to praise and admire in the bard of *The Excursion*.'[11]

Henry Arthur Bright wrote at length on both volumes in the *Westminster Review*, where he praised De Quincey's essays as 'filled with passages of a power and beauty which have never been surpassed by any other prose writer of the age', before going on to a balanced assessment of De Quincey's strengths and weaknesses.[12] Hawthorne, for whom De Quincey was a 'special favourite', thought the overall tenor of Bright's review inexcusably tepid, and he told him so. 'Your article is calm, wise, well-considered, and, so far as it goes, unquestionably just; but yet you remind me of a connoisseur of wine, sipping a drop or two out a glass, and praising or criticising its flavour, when you ought to swallow it at one gulp, and feel your heart warmed through and through with it.'[13]

Volume Three of the *Selections – Miscellanies, Chiefly Narrative –* appeared on 9 June 1854. It featured revised versions of three articles from *Blackwood's* and another three from *Tait's*, including 'System of the Heavens', which Nichol thought De Quincey should have updated much more thoroughly. 'The Nebula, as now known, is wholly different from what it seemed' in 1846, when De Quincey had first published the article. 'Its form is not the same – thanks to the great telescopes, which have revealed so much more of it.' De Quincey confessed himself perplexed by Nichol's response. 'That a new stage of progress had altered the appearances, as doubtless further stages will alter them, concerns me nothing,' he asserted. '. . . Wordsworth in at least four difference places . . . describes most impressive appearances amongst the clouds . . . Would it have been any just rebuke . . . if some friend had written to him: "I regret most sincerely to say that the dragon and the golden spear had all vanished before nine o'clock?"'[14] Nichol wanted scientific accuracy, but De Quincey was still haunted by that hideously broken skull in the stars.

An initial round of productivity on the new edition came to a close on 16 November 1854 when De Quincey published revised versions of his two *Blackwood's* articles 'On Murder Considered as One of the Fine Arts', as well as a newly written 'Postscript', in which he indulged in his most extensive exploration of the Williams murders. Contemporary descriptions of the crimes in newspapers and pamphlets thoroughly shape his account, yet De Quincey also omits and distorts events in order to intensify the sense of panic. The black humour of the first two essays returns fitfully, as when De Quincey observes that 'it is really wonderful and most interesting to pursue the successive steps of this monster'. But in the main he replaces satire with horror: 'Rapidly the brave man passed onwards to the shop, and there beheld the carnage of the night stretched out on the floor, and the narrow premises so floated with gore, that it was hardly possible to escape the pollution of blood in picking out a path to the front-door.'[15] In its coherence, intensity, and detail, the 'Postscript' is De Quincey's most compelling investigation of violence. Opium, he once declared, had 'killed Coleridge as a poet'.[16] With the publication of Volume Four, De Quincey – now sixty-nine years old – could justly claim that the drug had not had the same effect on him.

[ii]

The philosopher Shadworth Hodgson was a 'cousin' of Margaret, Florence, and Emily, and he visited Mavis Bush on at least two occasions, including once in the summer of 1853. There was a 'precise resemblance' between De Quincey's 'uttered' and his 'written speech', Hodgson recalled, and he used to like to pace up and down with his copy of Bruno's *De Monade, Numero et Figura* in his hand, 'repeating from it and referring to it'. Further, after surveying De Quincey's works, Hodgson observed with some justice that De Quincey's mind 'is stationary; there is no growth, no enlargement, of his intellectual basis, as he advances in life. He speaks in his later essays from the same platform of ideas as in his earlier ones.'[17] Yet De Quincey was also 'a keen, omnivorous reader of the newspapers', and his thought was very often inflected by events in the contemporary world, whether it be 'the great Crystal Palace', the Crimean War, the recent determination of the height of Mount Everest, or the ways in which telegraphs were 'overthrowing Space and Time'.[18] 'It has been said that he had no interest in the passing topics of the day,' Hogg junior asserted. 'No greater mistake than this has ever been committed in the description of the character of Thomas De Quincey."[19]

The young novelist and editor James Payn wished to meet the English Opium-Eater, but unfortunately travelled to Lasswade on a day when he was 'in very bad spirits'. De Quincey had 'a face like death in life', reported Payn, though the instant he began to speak 'it lit up as though by electric light'. At the meal table, Payn went to pour himself some port wine, only to discover that 'it was in fact laudanum'. Life, De Quincey explained, was 'a mere misery to him from nerves', and could only be rendered 'endurable by a semi-inebriation with opium'. As Payn took his leave, he asked if De Quincey ever journeyed to Edinburgh by coach. 'Certainly not,' De Quincey replied with some sharpness, for he had a horror of 'commonplace people and their pointless observations'. 'Some years ago', he declared, ' ... I was standing on the pier at Tarbet, on Loch Lomond, waiting for the steamer. A stout old lady joined me', and 'pointing to the smoke of the steamer ... she said: "La, sir! if you and I had seen that fifty years ago, how wonderful we should have thought it!"' De Quincey shuddered. 'The same thing ... might happen to me any day, and that is why I always avoid a public conveyance.'[20]

He remained deeply interested in the plight of the poor. 'To upper class funerals he never went,' Emily asserted, but he often attended those of the working class. Florence detailed how 'his presence at home was the signal for a crowd of beggars, among whom borrowed babies and drunken old women were sure of the largest share of his sympathy'. Oliver White, an American journalist, visited Mavis Bush and was asked by one of De Quincey's daughters for his opinion of the Scots. Before he could answer, though, De Quincey turned to him and observed 'in a kindly, half-paternal manner' that the servant who 'waits at my table is a Scotch girl. It may be that you have something severe to say about Scotland. I know that I like the English Church, but I never utter anything that might wound my servant. Heaven knows that the lot of a poor serving-girl is hard enough.'[21]

Margaret, now thirty-five years old, had for several years played the primary role in overseeing her father's life at Lasswade. Now she had some big news: she was getting married. Robert Craig, a Lasswade neighbour, was the son of John Craig, a well-known Scottish Whig who had taken an active part in the movement for parliamentary reform. The De Quincey sisters had known Craig 'most intimately' since 1842, and by the time he formally proposed to Margaret, she had loved him 'for nearly ten years'.[22] The couple were married on 13 December 1853 – 'a bright frosty day' – in St Mary's Church, Dalkeith. 'The church was crowded with spectators, chiefly Presbyterians,' Emily noted, 'for which I was very glad, as even episcopalians said they had never seen such a solemn wedding.'[23] Shortly thereafter the newlyweds went to live in Ireland at Pegsborough and then at Lisheen in Tipperary, where they ran two farms, one of which Robert rented from his sister. Nine and a half months after the marriage, on 25 September 1854, Margaret gave birth to a baby girl, Eva Margaret Craig.[24] De Quincey was elated. 'As to the particular name chosen, it is to *my* feeling a very pretty one,' he wrote to Emily, who with Florence had travelled to Ireland to see the new baby. Eva, he added, was the name of the heroine of Edward Bulwer's *A True Story of Light and Darkness* (1842), and of Charles Maturin's *Women; or, Pour et Contre* (1818). Indeed, 'simply through the power of Maturin ... the name of *Eva* has shaped itself to my symbolizing fancy in the image of a white rose'.[25]

With Margaret gone, the running of the household fell chiefly to Florence, who managed with the same competence and cheerfulness as her eldest sister. In June 1854, however, De Quincey decided he needed to be back in Edinburgh. There were a number of reasons for his decision. He wanted a change. He wanted to be nearer the libraries and his publisher Hogg as he laboured on his *Selections*. He wanted 'to be rid of the continual interruptions to which he was liable at home', as Florence explained in a letter to Hawthorne. And there was yet another, more telling, reason: 'a desire which perpetually haunted him to fly from himself'.[26]

He moved back into 42 Lothian Street, where he had first lodged in 1837 following the death of his wife, and where he may have continued to pay rent on rooms for months or even years after he left in the spring of 1838. The house, now demolished, stood originally in 'a dense street of shops' and other rather dingy tenements in the Old Town, close to the university. It was 'entered from the street by an arched passage', from which a 'stone staircase' ascended 'to the several half-flats' into which the whole was divided, 'each with its independent door and door-bell'. There were 'six such half-flats above the ground-floor; and that in which De Quincey had his rooms was the left half-flat on the second floor'.[27]

The house was now run solely by Christian Wilson, whose husband Frances had died. There were several other lodgers staying with her, including 'two gentlemen students' and her unmarried sister, Jane Stark, a tall, stout woman who suffered from deafness, and who from her 'simple and temperate life' was 'particularly healthy'.[28] When De Quincey arrived, he was 'without any preparation in the way of luggage or otherwise', but Mrs Wilson, 'a conscientious and careful woman, had preserved for him a quantity of clothing which he had left on his former sojourn', possibly as much as sixteen years earlier! Lothian Street cost De Quincey 'as nearly as possible twenty shillings a week, washing included', although he admitted that this total did not take into account his expenses for 'laudanum, brandy, and library subscription'.[29]

No doubt De Quincey had sought a place where he felt he would be well looked after, and indeed 'in many things' Miss Stark soon took on the role of waiting upon him 'like a baby'. She arranged his books, sat up with him as he corrected proofs, and delivered countless notes from him to Hogg concerning the production of the *Selections*. More than once she 'put him out' when 'he had fallen asleep with his head on the table, and overturned a candle on his papers. She used to buy his apparel for him piecemeal: now a pair of socks, now a pair of boots, now a coat, now a waistcoat -- never a whole suit.' She even called for him when he was out for the evening, 'lest he should forget to come home at the hour fixed'. In return for her assistance, De Quincey 'used sometimes to hire a carriage and drive her and her niece out to Lasswade to spend the day, and at other times he escorted them to the theatre'.[30]

If De Quincey had in fact hoped that his move to Lothian Street would give him some respite from socializing, he was to be disappointed. Robert and Anne Chambers were in touch, and he wrote to tell them of his 'overwhelming' labours on his *Selections*. Hill Burton may have been responsible for keeping him out so late one evening that he arrived back at his own door – 'or what he believed to be . . . his own door' – to find himself locked out. De Quincey first tried to rouse either Mrs Wilson or Miss Stark with prolonged knocking, but when that failed, he 'scrambled over a wall, and [took] his repose in a furrow'.[31] Gilfillan called, and reported that John Wilson's death in April 1854 'seems to have touched [De Quincey] deeply', though he remained in two minds about his friend, and only a few months later 'ridiculed the sickly, false sentiment' of Wilson's works. After several conversations, Gilfillan drew up a list that reveals the remarkable breadth and complicated nature of De Quincey's intellectual sympathies: he 'did not admire Macaulay, nor Carlyle, nor Brougham, nor Goethe', but 'his love of Burke, Coleridge, Schiller, Jean Paul Richter . . . Wordsworth, Shelley, Hazlitt, and Wilson, was profound'.[32]

Perhaps the most frequent visitor to Lothian Street was Findlay, who discovered De Quincey on one occasion with a 'small glass of laudanum in one hand' and a 'teacup in other'. Findlay recalled his friend's many eccentricities: De Quincey 'rarely laughed'; he still 'seldom rose till four or five' in the afternoon; he wore a large white flannel jacket in bed ('something like a cricketer's coat'); and he sometimes grew a beard because shaving was a 'grand difficulty', and the smell of a barber's fingers was 'intolerable'.[33] One evening, as the two men paced back and forth between Dean Bridge and the west end of Princes Street, De Quincey reflected on the 'stale, flat, and unprofitable' course of his life, and turned away from it 'shuddering and ashamed'. A 'little wine or spirits' was occasionally necessary to raise him up to 'something like the common level of humanity'. Nothing, however, 'but a large dose of laudanum gave him relief'.[34]

After six months in Lothian Street De Quincey could report to Florence that he had not run up even 'a fraction of debt'. Yet former creditors still occasionally harassed him. Apparently he owed rent on the rooms he had guaranteed in 1838 for his Holyrood landlady Miss Craig, and it may have been another Holyrood proprietor, either Jane or Mary Miller, who claimed that he still owed her 'one hundred guineas "and upwards"'. De Quincey appeased Miller with the payment of about ten guineas over the course of three months, and then wrote to Emily in Ireland asking if Margaret could throw any light upon the exact nature of the debt.[35]

More pressing from his point of view was the fact that Miller held '*papers and books* of mine'. And she was not alone. In one instance, a woman in possession of some of his manuscripts simply wanted them delivered into the proper hands, though De Quincey was 'under some hallucination as to indebtedness to her'.[36] This woman may have been his Clerk Street landlady Miss Carrick, with whom he lodged in order to see *Suspiria* through the press; or a 'Mrs Harris', who at one point was 'confidently supposed to be the possessor' of *Suspiria* manuscripts. On another occasion, a person extorted money from De Quincey for one package of papers, and then came to him again 'professing to have found more papers of great value'. De Quincey paid the sum demanded, and was then 'left a worthless packet, mostly of straw neatly done up in many folds of papers'.[37] This trick may have been the work of the McIndoes, who continued their harassment of him. In the autumn of 1854, Mrs McIndoe died after drinking to excess and then falling backward 'on the area steps of a house in George Square'. In order to raise money for the funeral, her son offered to sell De Quincey the last of the papers in his family's possession. De Quincey agreed. Then, in May 1855, Mr McIndoe died, 'entirely broken down by drink'. This time two McIndoe sons descended, and besieged De Quincey 'with applications the most violent' for money to bury their father. De Quincey, however, 'refused to interfere', and the persecution seems at last to have stopped.[38]

Throughout the autumn of 1854, meanwhile, Florence and Emily enjoyed their time in Ireland with Margaret, her husband, and baby Eva. De Quincey missed them all, and was beset by gloomy dreams. In one of them,

> a door opened: it was a door on the *further* side of a spacious chamber, I myself standing on the foreground, i.e. on the *hither* side of that chamber. For a few moments I waited expectingly, but not knowing *what* to expect. At length a voice said audibly and most distinctly, but not loudly, – *Florence and Emily*, with the tone of one announcing an arrival. Soon after but not immediately, entered Florence, but to my great astonishment no Emily ... A shadow fell upon me, and a feeling of sadness – which increased continually as no Emily entered at the door.

De Quincey condemned this dream as 'too monotonous', but it contains in a less impassioned form that combination of the familiar and the menacing that underwrites some of his most famous dream sceneries.[39]

Florence and Emily returned to Lasswade in the New Year, much to the delight of their father, who promised to come and visit them soon, and who sent long letters from Lothian Street, 'a somewhat pathetic sign' – as Florence observed – 'of a struggle between his perfect trust in us and a consciousness that it was not a usual course of action to leave two young women so entirely alone in a solitary country place'. In late February the two sisters travelled into Edinburgh to visit with their father, who emerged 'from the gloomy depths of the street' to greet them 'like some revelation from another world'. Later that same night, De Quincey escorted them to a concert by the 'celestial pianofortist' Marie-Félicité-Denise Pleyel. A few weeks later 'Misses Florence and Emily' were back in Edinburgh, this time to accompany their father to an evening party given by the Findlays.[40]

Spring came and the sisters were off again, this time to visit at Boston in Lincolnshire, from where Florence wrote to her father with some exciting news. She too was getting married. De Quincey, with his gift for spotting ambiguity, originally thought that she had unwisely rejected her suitor, Colonel Richard Baird Smith, but he was not about to play the tyrannical father: 'a woman is not only the best judge, but in the last resort is the *sole* judge of what is likely to promote her own happiness'. In re-reading Florence's letter, however, he was very pleased to discover that he had been in error, and he went on to voice his high approval of his future son-in-law, 'whom we have all so much admired for his strength of character and the unassuming dignity of his manners'.[41]

Florence, 'always remarkable for her pale, statuesque beauty', had probably been engaged to Smith for several years, and it seems likely that they would have married earlier had it not been for her 'duty to Papa'. He is, as she explained to Smith, 'so quaint and eccentric and requires so much arrangement that we have long since agreed that one of us alone is not equal to it'. Yet Florence was ultimately able to overcome these reservations, encouraged no doubt in various ways by her sisters and her fiancé. Within weeks of formally accepting him she was preparing to travel to India, where Smith was stationed. De Quincey shared in her excitement: 'I take for granted that your route will be the usual overland one through Egypt. What a fine thing to see the Pyramids, the Red Sea, &c!'[42]

That autumn Margaret and Eva came to stay at Lasswade, and De Quincey and his granddaughter – 'a little sunny picture, with her golden hair and dark blue eyes' – quickly became 'thick cronies'. Observed De Quincey: 'She is the only baby of twelve months old that ever struck me as *arch*.' The pleasure he took in her company, however, characteristically darkened into anxiety when she and her mother returned to Ireland. 'How many times I am not sure', De Quincey wrote to Margaret, 'more than 3 to a certainty, 5 I should think, – dear little Eva has been seen by me in dreams drinking from the spout of a boiling tea-kettle, or (as once) of a boiling tea-pot.'[43]

In order to prepare herself for the separation from her family, Florence commissioned the famous James Archer portrait in which Margaret and Emily are preoccupied with Eva, while De Quincey leans forward in a chair beside them; his attire formal but scruffy, his body relaxed yet alert, and his blue eyes striking in their intensity amidst the domesticity and informality of the scene. 'Papa ... is capital,' said Emily of the portrait. 'When talking he very often leans forward in that way', with his elbow resting on his leg. Later, Florence added that 'people think that it is the best likeness we have of my Father'.[44]

Figure 7: James Archer's portrait of Thomas De Quincey, with his daughters Emily and Margaret, and his granddaughter Eva, 1855

Plans for Florence's journey were gradually agreed upon. She would travel as far as Calcutta by herself, where she would be met by her fiancé and her brother Fred. 'I have the very heartiest and warmest approval of Papa, and all the friends I care for of my marriage,' she wrote on her birthday, 6 November, 'so that with the exception of the long lonely journey and the great separation from so many that are dear to me, I feel myself to be a very favoured women.' Setting out 'by the middle November mail', her trip to the East seems to have passed without incident, and on 10 January 1856 Florence Elizabeth De Quincey married Richard Baird Smith in the cathedral at Calcutta. Two months later Emily reported that her sister was 'living a very nice life' in India, though before long Florence's circumstances were to change drastically.[45]

[iii]

Since completing work on Volume Four of the *Selections*, De Quincey's health had been only so-so. A 'malady' of 'sudden sickness, fever, and light-headedness' forced him to his bed for days. 'He complained of pain in his left arm which, as he described it, seemed like rheumatism.' After a bout of influenza his eyes gave him a great deal of trouble – 'some days all but blind, and on some nights roused up for hours by the pain'.[46] He was taking various medicines for these ailments, including 'sulphate of zinc' and, on one evening of experimentation, a cocktail from an almost exhausted stock of medicine bottles that he found in the guest room of an Edinburgh friend. Often laudanum relieved his sufferings. Sometimes it had 'no effect'.[47] Walking was still part of his daily routine, but he could no longer manage the distances he had walked with ease for decades. Usually his route took in 'the quietude of the Meadows and Morningside', as well as the Queensferry road. Perhaps too on some evenings he carried on further to the west end of Princes Street and St Cuthbert's churchyard, where he could visit the grave of Margaret. In total he walked for about seven miles. 'Not much certainly,' he confessed; 'but as much as I can find spirits for.'[48]

He had been 'off and on' at Lothian Street for fourteen months (and a total cost of fifty guineas) when he found his strength failing him, and made the decision to return to Mavis Bush.[49] On 15 August 1855 – his seventieth birthday – he told guests who had travelled out to see him that he 'did not feel a day older than when he was seventeen', but in the autumn he was struck down by some unknown ailment that prostrated him for weeks. 'I found De Quincey the other day had not moved out of his house since Xmas day,' Lushington wrote to Tennyson on 3 March 1856, '& his feet were becoming excessively painful, no doubt from this, but he took a walk of 4 or 5 miles with me & seemed rather the better for it.'[50]

De Quincey was gearing up for the completion of his last major project, an expansion of the *Confessions of an English Opium-Eater* as Volume Five of his *Selections*. He had begun work on the revisions as early as 1854, when he made desultory changes in an 1852 Fields edition of the original text. In April 1855 he was convinced that the work needed 'endless alterations and corrections', and seemed 'sorely troubled' about 'how to do it'. A month later, however, he was 'very busily engaged' in the revision process, and over the next year he gradually amassed – through intermitting and 'despairing effort' – a substantial body of amendments and extensions. With the new manuscript largely completed by the end of May, De Quincey moved back into Lothian Street, where he prepared to see the work through the press.[51]

Like the recasting, the printing was to prove an ordeal. 'I have been in constant expectation of hearing that Hogg and Son, his luckless publishers have been conveyed to a lunatic asylum in consequence of Papa's procrastination,' Emily observed drily.[52] And procrastination was only one of several problems. Whitewashers needed access to his room, and reared a scaffold against a set of drawers which contained the manuscript papers he was working on. He had to give up an extra room he was using to make way for a new tenant. Twice in one day he was interrupted by unexpected American visitors. He was sick 'for want of laudanum'. He was 'partially delirious' from 'want of sleep and opium'.[53]

Further, when he could work, the sheer number of proofs, manuscripts, and revises often reduced him to perplexity. Typically, 'I have come upon a layer or stratum of which I was seeking – but written so confusedly and stenographically – that as yet, (11 A.M. on Wednesday) I am in a mist.' Scores of notes passed between him and the Hoggs, for De Quincey was 'in terror of mutual misunderstandings', and as confounded as ever by the paradox that 'to evade misinterpretation ... requires a redundancy of words'.[54] Throughout the autumn the Hoggs patiently encouraged him while he pushed the task forward, and on 13 November, after six months 'of labour and suffering that, if they could be truly stated, would seem incredible', they published the revised version of De Quincey's *Confessions*.[55]

It was now three times its original length. In part, this was De Quincey's decision. The 1821 *Confessions* 'had never received any strict revision', and he seized this opportunity to integrate into the new version 'what had been left imperfect' in the old. In part, however, De Quincey also expanded the work for commercial reasons. Unrevised, the *Confessions* would have run to about 120 pages in the *Selections* format, whereas Volumes One through

Four had already averaged from 320 to 360 pages. 'Such being the case,' he explained, 'no remedy remained but that I should *doctor* the book, and expand it into a portliness that might countenance its price.'[56]

De Quincey made a number of notable additions, from accounts of his youthful experiences in St Paul's Whispering Gallery and along the River Dee, to digressions on insurance companies, 'our great national literature', and the 'self-conflicting' Victorian age.[57] Coleridge comes up a great deal, and while De Quincey might have been expected to opt for charity in this summation, he decides instead to insist on his former friend's shortcomings, perhaps in response to previous criticisms of him by the Coleridge family, perhaps in a final peevish display of anger towards a man who in so many ways had been his rival. As a reader of poetry, Coleridge sounds as though he is 'crying, or at least wailing lugubriously'. As a conversationalist, his 'capital error' was in 'keeping the audience in a state of passiveness'. As an opium addict, he was a self-deluded slave 'not less abject than Caliban to Prospero – his detested and yet despotic master'. De Quincey had originally intended to close the revised *Confessions* with a 'crowning grace' of 'some twenty or twenty-five dreams', but all of these had either been lost or accidentally burned, with the exception of 'The Daughter of Lebanon', an impassioned account of a youthful prostitute, and an apposite conclusion to a narrative 'in which the case of poor Ann the Outcast formed ... the most memorable and the most suggestively pathetic incident'.[58]

Perhaps the most remarkable additions to the narrative, however, are those in which De Quincey reflects on his experience with drugs and addiction. For over forty years he has performed 'manoeuvres the most intricate, dances the most elaborate, receding or approaching, round my great central sun of opium. Sometimes I ran perilously close into my perihelion; sometimes I became frightened, and wheeled off into a vast cometary aphelion, where for six months "opium" was a word unknown. How nature stood all these see-sawings is quite a mystery to me: I must have led a sad life in those days.'[59]

Yet despite the enormous toll the drug has exacted, De Quincey sings its praises more fulsomely in the revised *Confessions* than in any other place in his work. Indeed, in addition to retaining the celebratory sections from the 1821 version, he retracts 'all passages, written at an earlier period under cloudy and uncorrected views of the evil agencies presumable in opium'.[60] The drug, he now contends, is a 'blessing'. It provides 'relief from ... *taedium vitae*' – a weariness or loathing of life. It supports 'preternatural calls for exertion'. It has astonishing powers over the 'shadowy world of dreams'. Beyond all other known agents, it is 'the mightiest for its command,

and for the extent of its command, over pain'. Taken daily, and under steady regulation, it seems to provide the only means of adequately controlling 'nervous irritation', that 'secret desolator of human life'.[61] Finally, it is 'the sole known agent – not for curing *when* formed, but for intercepting whilst likely to be formed – the great English scourge of pulmonary consumption', the disease which had killed his father, and which had seemed so clearly in his youth to be stalking him. But for opium's ability to block tubercular advance, De Quincey swears, 'thirty-five years ago, beyond all doubt, I should have been in my grave'.[62] Expectedly, his letters and table-talk for this period make it clear that the drug continued to ravage him, but before the public, and in his final commentary on the subject, he maintained that opium, and all its many blessings, had given him years of life.[63] For an audience that perhaps saw him first as an opium-eater and second as an author, De Quincey was working hard to rewrite his own history, and to establish himself, not as a slave to the drug, but as a beneficiary of it.

[iv]

William Makepeace Thackeray was in Edinburgh delivering his lectures on *The Four Georges* during the same month that De Quincey published his revised *Confessions*. Findlay hoped to bring the two writers together at a party on 22 November, but at the last minute De Quincey sent a note saying he was too ill to attend. Thackeray regretted that the introduction did not take place, as 'nothing would have pleased him more than to have met a man whose writings he so much admired'. Findlay showed him De Quincey's note, which Thackeray praised for 'the extreme neatness of its style, and penmanship, and antique courtesy of its tone'. A few days later Findlay tried again to effect a meeting between the two men. This time De Quincey seems to have been well enough to attend, but chose instead to remain in Lothian Street correcting proofs with Hogg junior.[64]

His lack of interest in Thackeray belies a broad interest in '*current* literature', which he borrowed often from Mudie's Circulating Library.[65] De Quincey enjoyed Harriet Beecher Stowe's anti-slavery novel *Uncle Tom's Cabin* (1852) 'exceedingly', took 'pleasure' in the works of Elizabeth Barrett Browning, and praised Tennyson's poetry for its 'rich pictorial effects and inwrought elaborate jewellery of phrase', though he desiderated 'dramatic strength, direct human interest, and grandeur of imagination in opposition to mere opulence and vitality of fancy'.[66] Elizabeth Gaskell's controversial *Life of Charlotte Brontë* (1857) also caught his eye. All three Brontë sisters 'had some very *noble* features in their characters', he declared, 'but not many that were *amiable*', and he highlighted in particular Charlotte's 'preternatural timidity, shyness, and shrinking from notice', which he attributed to 'a morbid basis of self-esteem nourished almost into insanity by solitude'. As for the sisters' father and brother, they were 'scamps', especially 'leathery Herr Papa', an 'intolerable monster of selfishness' who turned his daughters 'out of doors to get their own bread in a far worse service ... than that of a housemaid: for surely it is better by much to go down on one's knees to scour the front doorsteps, with the prospect at night of creeping to an undisturbed bed – in humble respectability, than to make *one* in a crowd of most vulgar Belgian girls'.[67]

De Quincey's interest in murder continued unabated, as he pored over newspaper accounts of various crimes in an attempt to track down 'the missing links in the chain of evidence'. In the early summer of 1856, the so-called 'Rugeley Poisoner' William Palmer stood trial in London for murdering John Cook, a racing buddy with whom Palmer was financially entangled. 'Never for one moment have I doubted Palmer's guilt,' De Quincey informed Emily. 'And until he, manifestly desiring to benefit by a quibble, said, "Cooke did not die" (or "was not poisoned") ."by strychnia", I (like all others) held as a matter of certainty that the murderer and the mode of murder were equally manifested. Since Saturday last, however (when in second and third editions of the *Scotsman* and the *Express* I read telegraphic accounts of the execution), I have been shaken in that opinion.'[68]

Just over a year later, De Quincey was wrapped up in the sensation surrounding the case of Madeleine Smith, who was put in the dock in Edinburgh for allegedly poisoning her lover Émile L'Angelier. Public interest ran 'higher by far than in any case' that De Quincey had ever heard of, and while the Lord Advocate was 'confident (almost, I should say, exultingly confident) of winning the game against Miss Smith', De Quincey was deeply suspicious of the Crown's evidence and conduct. 'To me it seems that from the very first Miss Smith has been cruelly treated,' he stated. 'Never in the world was a young woman summoned to face an agony so frightful as that of *hearing* her letters read in an assembly of men and boys – oftentimes coarse, brutal, scoffing – and read for what purpose?'[69] Smith's trial lasted ten days and, on 9 July 1857, the jury returned a majority verdict of not guilty, undoubtedly to De Quincey's delight.

His preoccupation with events at home, however, was often eclipsed by the momentous state of affairs abroad. In late 1856, De Quincey's blood began to boil as China and Britain entered into the so-called Second Opium War. First in the pages of Hogg junior's recently founded *Titan* (a continuation in enlarged form of his father's *Instructor*), and then in a separate pamphlet entitled *China*, De Quincey mounted ferociously racial attacks on the 'arrogant pretensions of the East'.[70] He wants military conflict with the Chinese (indeed they are 'unmanageable' without it), and implores the British commanders to act 'before any trader in "*moderation*" or pacific measures' arrives from England. Gone even is the notion of Christianity as a civilizing force. The Chinese, he now suggests, are beyond redemption, for 'few of us who read this chapter of Chinese spoliation altogether go along with these Missionaries in their proselytising views upon a people so unspiritual as our brutal friends the Chinese'.[71] Old age had mellowed De Quincey in several respects, but his chilling faith in British superiority still made him very volatile.

Worse, his writings on the Second Opium War turned out to be only the first instalment in an extended examination of Eastern affairs, for in June word reached Britain of the outbreak of the Indian Mutiny, a widespread rebellion against British rule by Indian troops (sepoys) that began in Meerut, and quickly spread to Delhi, Agra, Cawnpore, and Lucknow. In the best of circumstances, De Quincey would have been furious at this attack on British imperial interests, but his emotions in this instance were endlessly exacerbated by the fact that he had family in harm's way. Fifteen years earlier he had lost Horace in China. Now 'the *Daily News* ... says that the Mutiny has ... broken out at Ferozepore', De Quincey reported to Emily on 29 June. That is 'Fred's station, is it not?'[72] More urgently, Florence and her husband were living at Roorkee, only one hundred miles north of Delhi. On 18 May, just eight days after the outbreak of the Mutiny, Florence gave birth to a daughter, Florence May Baird Smith, in the fortified workshops of the town.[73]

De Quincey became increasingly hysterical as news of sieges and bloody counter-resistance made its way to Britain over the course of the next several weeks. 'Oh Emily I have no heart *now* for any one thought but what concerns poor insulated Florence and her baby,' he wrote on 9 September. Two months later he was suffering in his nervous system 'to an extent that ... had not experimentally been made known to me as a possibility', 'except once in 1812', when Catharine Wordsworth had died.[74] Night after night he was haunted by the same dream: 'a vision of children, most of them infants, but not all, the *first* rank being girls of five and six years old, who were standing in the air outside, but so as to touch the window; and I heard, or perhaps fancied that I heard, always the same dreadful word, *Delhi*'. This 'fierce shake' to his nerves also 'caused almost from the beginning a new symptom to expose itself ... viz, somnambulism; and now every night, to my great alarm, I wake up to find myself at the window, which is sixteen feet from the nearest side of the bed. The horror was unspeakable.'[75]

As his private anxieties mounted, De Quincey concentrated on producing a series of public pronouncements in the *Titan* in which he brutally denounced the mutineers. 'From the foundations of the earth, no case in human action or suffering has occurred which could less need or less tolerate the aid of artificial rhetoric than that tremendous tragedy which now for three months long has been moving over the plains of Hindostan.'[76] The British had done nothing to provoke the outrage: 'no conquering state was ever yet so mild and beneficent in the spirit of its government'. The 'true originators' of the Mutiny were the 'Indian princes and rajahs', while the sepoys were 'childish', 'base', 'treacherous', 'infatuated savages' who had embarked on 'this most suicidal of revolts' with the same 'defect of plan and coherent purpose as have ever characterized the oriental mind'.[77] Now these Indian soldiers must be hunted down as part of what De Quincey viewed as the inevitable restoration of British rule. Soon 'prisoners will begin to accumulate by thousands; executions will proceed through week after week; and a large variety of cases will yield us a commensurate crop of confessions'. De Quincey's sympathies often extended to the weak and the abused, but rarely when it came to foreign affairs, where he simply believed that Britain was entitled to a colonialist project. 'There is no known spot of earth which has exerted upon the rest of the planet one-thousandth part of the influence which this noble island has exercised over the human race.'[78] The incalculable suffering caused by the forced infliction of that influence did not trouble him.

In addition to his work for the *Titan*, De Quincey published Volumes Six and Seven of his *Selections* during the autumn of 1857. Sales were strong. 'Two at least, but I think three, of the six volumes already published have *silently* gone into second editions,' De Quincey told Emily in November, while 'the London publishers, Messrs. Groombridge, say, that, as the collection advances, the volumes show a tendency to sell more rapidly'.[79] Of even more interest, perhaps, was the fact that De Quincey was now making very good money. On 23 January 1858, he sold all his writings – as they had initially appeared in the magazines, and as they now stood in the *Selections* – to Hogg for just over £808. Combined with the proceeds to come from the seven volumes of the *Selections* not yet published, and the money that continued to accrue from the sale of the American edition, De Quincey may have made as much as £2000 during the last decade of his life.[80] Past creditors still sought him out, but now he seems to have been in the position of loaning them money, rather than owing it to them.[81]

[V]

'For a year or two before he died, Mr De Quincey rarely moved out of doors,' Findlay recalled.[82] Embargoed in the 'anchorage of No. 42 Lothian Street', and surrounded in his room by 'superfluous furniture' and a floor 'covered 2 feet deep with papers', De Quincey sat writing 'at the very extremity of one corner' of his work table in an area not larger than a post-chaise. To at least one guest he looked 'like Cato seated on the ruins of Carthage'.[83] Volume Eight appeared on 30 April 1858. Work on it had kept him tied to his desk for 'many successive months', and created a certain pungency in his rooms. 'He thinks that he has pitched on the cleanest lodgings in Edinburgh but they are even dirty for Scotch lodgings,' Emily later protested. 'It used to be a filial exercise to go and penetrate into the den for it goes sorely against the grain to face a smell or odour or whatever the correct thing is for a lady to say.'[84]

Despite his close confinement, Emily reported that her father was doing 'uncommonly well'. 'In fact he seems to grow better and more interested in things than he used to be when he was thirty years old. He had much more the decay of old age then than he has now.'[85] De Quincey, however, was nowhere near as sanguine, and continued to chronicle the many blights to his health, including lumbago, 'nervous misery', inflammation in his eyes and, most seriously, purpura in his right foot. 'You will ask me – Why I do not consult a surgeon?' he wrote to Lushington. 'The brief answer is – that wishing to be sure of a sound opinion in the first place, and (in the event of any operation being requisite) – secondly of a first-rate operator, I think of going to London.'[86]

It is unlikely he made such a trip, but that summer he did feel well enough to journey to see Margaret and her family in Tipperary, his first visit to Ireland since he had travelled there with Westport nearly six decades earlier. Accompanied by Emily and Fred (who was on leave from India), he enjoyed visiting with his daughter, and especially with his granddaughter and new grandson, John Francis Craig, who had been born on 26 July 1856. 'He sat in his own room here, just as he does at home', Margaret recounted, 'and whenever ... there was a sudden lull in the house' the children were 'discovered discoursing with him'. Yet at nearly seventy-three years old, De Quincey found the upheaval and strain of travelling 'very trying', and by August he was glad to be back quartered in the familiar chaos of Lothian Street. Margaret noticed a marked decline in him, especially as regarded his conversational powers. 'He was only with us a month, and I can't help hoping that during that time he had never got over the fatigue of travelling,' she remarked with some concern.[87]

Hogg continued to call regularly at Lothian Street, where he consulted De Quincey about editorial matters at the *Titan*, and steered him back to the task of revising the *Selections* on innumerable occasions. De Quincey usually drank moderately when they were together. 'As a stimulant', Hogg remembered, 'he preferred a particular preparation of brandy; and his maximum allowance of this during an evening ... was measured in a manner peculiar to himself – *two wine-glasses two-thirds full*.' Laudanum he also 'regularly took largely diluted in water', for as supplied by the chemist the drug now caused 'a very annoying and even painful itching in the nostrils'. When preparing the dosage, De Quincey seldom required a spoon or measure. From long habit, he simply held the wine-glass up to the light and added the required quantity. In at least one instance, however, he accidentally took more in the night than he had intended, and the next morning a Lothian Street attendant found him in 'a state of stupor'.[88]

'I was a good listener,' Hogg declared, and for hours he sat close by as De Quincey ranged freely over his favourite topics. On music: 'Hundreds of times I must have heard him dwell with impassioned force upon the *capacity* of the violin as a musical instrument.' On past friends: '"If ever you meet Carlyle, will you tell him from me – "' and he charged me with a solemn and moving message' that referred 'to Mrs Carlyle'. On contemporary authors: 'on countless occasions, [he] expressed to me his high opinion of Hawthorne'. On delight: 'nothing ... afforded De Quincey such frequent and intense amusement' as the thought of Kant wearing an elaborate contraption to hold up his stockings because he feared garters would hinder 'the circulation of the blood'. On violence: 'Of all the subjects which exercised a permanent fascination over De Quincey, I would place first in order Thuggism in India ... The far-reaching power of this mysterious brotherhood ... exercised an influence on his mind which seemed never to wane.'[89]

The publisher and author spent an enormous amount of time going over manuscripts and proofs. After gazing 'with a sort of anxious, affectionate, almost frightened look upon his manuscript treasures', De Quincey would deliver a 'grave reminder that in order not to delay the press, it was *absolutely* necessary ... that any slip, or note, or matter not yet forwarded to the printer, should be perfectly within reach of his hand at a single moment's notice'. Yet, as Hogg came gradually to recognize, De Quincey was partially performing these anxieties. For however solemnly he expanded upon them, 'he would almost invariably look up with just the faintest smile and twinkle of the eye, as much as to say, "Do you really believe it all?" or, "Will it not be all the same a hundred years hence?"[90]

He remained astonishingly productive. Volume Nine of the *Selections* appeared on 18 October 1858, and was followed by his final burst of productivity: Volume Ten on 10 February, Volume Eleven on 6 May, Volume Twelve less than a week later on 12 May, and Volume Thirteen on 11 July 1859. On 24 May, he wrote a sketch of a typical day. At three forty-five in the morning he is wide awake, but as 'a miserable suffering cripple – not daring to stoop, or to stretch out [his] arm' – it takes him over three and a half hours to dress. At seven thirty he is brought his breakfast, which consists of tea and two or three biscuits. Half an hour later the newspapers arrive – 'villainous compounds, full of malice and of endless misconstructions' – followed at eight thirty by a letter from Margaret. At nine he sets to work on the *Selections*, and it is noon before he pauses for his 'trifle of a dinner'. Shortly thereafter a stranger summons him away and it is ten minutes after three before he returns to Lothian Street, where Hogg's messenger boy Johnny is expected 'every minute to fetch the Proofs', upon which 'no progress is made'. Near four De Quincey falls asleep, but he is up by just after seven, when he returns to work.[91] It is probably well into the evening before he retires again to bed.

Over the summer he toiled on the fourteenth and final volume of the *Selections*, but he was growing steadily weaker, and in the autumn he took to his bed. At first Mrs Wilson and Miss Stark were probably able to attend to him, but in early October Hogg sent for Emily, who immediately cut short a visit to Margaret in Ireland to return to Edinburgh, where she moved into rooms in Lothian Street, as her father was already too ill to be moved out to Lasswade. On Saturday, 22 October, Dr Warburton Begbie called for the first time, and found De Quincey 'in the parlour, sitting on a sofa, but resting his head on a cushion placed on a chair before him; this posture was assumed not from pain, but by reason of feebleness'. De Quincey gave Begbie an account of his symptoms, and 'readily acknowledged the perniciousness of habitual indulgence in opium; though he was equally ready to claim for the potent drug effects eminently beneficial'. Begbie prescribed a series of 'remedies' and soon noted in De Quincey 'a decided and ready power of rallying', though De Quincey wryly rejoined that a 'life that was to be floated on stated doses of beef-tea did not seem . . . worth the struggling for'.[92]

Through the 'days of dull November . . . with all its gloominess and more than ordinary fog', Findlay, Burton, and Hogg stopped in to visit with him. De Quincey was still 'clear enough' to converse 'with fluency about anything in the newspaper that interested him', and 'to the last he was able to read without the help of spectacles'. Yet he was becoming very frail. 'I used to lift him in my arms like a child', and 'he told the doctor I was a "female Hercules"', Emily recalled. 'He did not know how light he was.'[93] What is more, his mind was beginning to wander. One night he complained to Emily that 'his feet were feeling very hot and tired. I pulled off some blankets from them and put them into what I thought would be a more comfortable position. "Is that better Papa?" I asked. "Yes, my love, I think it is. You know my dear girl that these are the feet that Christ washed."'[94] On 19 November, Lushington told Emily Tennyson that he had seen 'poor De Quincey', who was 'somewhat seriously ill with a sort of delirious fever: his daughter told me he was now better, but one cannot quite be sure how much the better means – he was taking rather more opium than the Dr seemed to approve'.[95]

As the end neared, his childhood and his children were constantly before him. He referred to his 'dear dear Mother', and was 'sure a better, kinder, or juster man' than his father 'could never have existed'. He called out loudly for Florence, and spoke often of his sons as if they were his brothers. When Margaret arrived from Tipperary, he soon viewed her as someone who 'had been all along with him, and if she went out of the room' he would say 'Go and call Maggie back.' Once towards evening he sighed, 'They are all leaving me but my *dear* little children.' Eva, his granddaughter, he called 'in some measure the child of my old age'. 'Is that you Horace?' he asked one night. 'No, Papa it is me, Emily.' 'Oh, I see, I thought you were Horace for he was talking to me just now.'[96]

In early December he was suffering from bed sores, and Emily arranged for a water bed to be brought to Lothian Street. 'I feel so much better my dear,' he said after being tucked into his new bed, 'and I shall soon feel a very great deal better.' But by the morning of 7 December it was evident that he was dying. 'His breathing seemed very laborious and there was a great deal of rattling in it.' Begbie assured Margaret and Emily that their father was not in pain, and that he would die without a struggle. In the afternoon De Quincey gazed at those around him and – polite to the last – said 'thank you', before lapsing into a drowsy and then insensible state.[97] His daughters hovered round, convinced he would last only a few more hours, but he lingered on through the night.

When dawn came, Margaret and Emily 'did not like to let in the ... light', and so the room remained illuminated by 'only a candle'. In *Suspiria de Profundis*, written fifteen years earlier, he had declared his belief that his traumatic experience as a young boy in the bedchamber of his dead sister

Elizabeth would rise again before him 'to illuminate the hour of death', and he asked Elizabeth to 'plead for us with God, that we may pass over without much agony'. Perhaps he got his wish. For as death came upon him, he threw up his arms, as if in great surprise, and exclaimed distinctly, 'Sister! sister! sister!'[98] Then his loud breathing slowed to a last few sighs, terrible from their very softness. Thomas De Quincey died at nine thirty in the morning on Thursday, 8 December 1859.

[vi]

'Is what I hear true?' Findlay asked. Mrs Wilson, who opened the door, did not answer, but ushered him 'at once into the chamber of death. On the simple uncurtained pallet ... the tiny frame of this great dreamer lay stretched in his last long dreamless sleep. Attenuated to an extreme degree, the body looked infantile in size – a very slender stem for the shapely and massive head that crowned it.' Said Emily: just before and just after death 'he looked more like a boy of fourteen, and he looked very beautiful'.[99]

Under 'Cause of Death, and how long Disease continued', the Death Certificate reads, 'Catarrh with fever seven weeks.' Begbie wrote that De Quincey died from 'exhaustion of the system' rather than from any 'specific disease'. A postmortem examination was performed, but all that is known of the results is a rumour 'to the effect of De Quincey's organs having received no damage from his prolonged opium eating indeed being exceptionally sound'.[100]

'Like other men, I have particular fancies about the place of my burial,' De Quincey had written in 1822, when he was residing at Fox Ghyll, and exactly halfway through his life of seventy-four years: 'having lived chiefly in a mountainous region, I rather cleave to the conceit that a grave in a green church yard amongst the ancient and solitary hills will be a sublimer and more tranquil place of repose for a philosopher than any in the hideous Golgothas of London.' But as so much of the second half of De Quincey's life was spent in Edinburgh, it is fitting that he is buried there, beside Margaret (and, it is to be hoped, Julius and William), beneath a simple circular-headed gravestone, in St Cuthbert's Churchyard.[101]

The obituaries were mixed. 'Death has brought a close to the sad and almost profitless career of "the English Opium-Eater,"' *The Athenaeum* opined, 'removing from the world an intellect that remained active to the last, but had never at any time been of much service to his fellow-men.' *The Scotsman* took a very different view: 'This announcement will excite a deeply sympathetic interest among all lovers of English literature throughout the world. With his departure almost the very last of a brilliant band of men of letters, who illuminated the literary hemisphere of the first half of our century with starry lustre ... is extinguished.' *The Times* reprinted *The Scotsman* obituary.[102]

There was no will, but on 6 January 1860 an official from the City of Edinburgh took an 'Inventory of the Personal Estate of the deceased Thomas De Quincey'. In Scotland, books and other effects in Lothian Street, plus property he was apparently still storing in Holyrood, and money that was soon to fall due to him from Hogg, came to a total of just over £218. In England, 'Books in the possession of Mr Harrison, Penrith', and dividends and rents that formed part of his mother's estate, comprised nearly £45, making a grand total of £262.13s.9d. In addition, property left to him in trust by his mother now came into the possession of his children.[103] On 26 January, Thomas Nisbet, auctioneer, sold De Quincey's library, which featured over seven hundred volumes, and included writings by Burke, Wordsworth, Coleridge, Shelley, Wilson, Lamb, Mill, Macaulay, Emerson, Dickens, Thackeray, and Tennyson. That same day Hogg published the final volume of the *Selections*.[104]

Margaret wrote to Lushington to ask him if he would like to choose one of her father's books. 'Any one referring to the subjects we used so often to talk about, mental philosophy or the old English writers, would be a highly prized memorial of him,' he informed her, and 'all the more if there happened to be any notes by himself scattered about the pages.' Fields sent a letter to Florence, who had returned to Britain too late to see her father for a final time. 'Dear old man!' he exclaimed. 'Some of the best moments of my life I owe to him, the great Master of English Prose.' Perhaps most memorably, hearing, during the composition of *Les Paradis artificiels*, of De Quincey's death, Baudelaire spoke of him as having 'one of the most original' minds in 'all of England'.[105]

The Aggregate of Human Life

Grasmere Lake. It is a beautiful morning, most probably in the autumn of 1839. Hartley Coleridge and an acquaintance, Charles MacFarlane, are out for a walk. De Quincey comes up as a topic of conversation, as his Lake recollections of Wordsworth, Southey, and Hartley's father are at present appearing in *Tait's Magazine*, and Hartley has been greatly distressed by what he has read. 'I will tell you what De Quincey is,' he says to MacFarlane in a quick, emphatic way; 'he is an anomaly and a contradiction – a contradiction to himself, a contradiction throughout! He steals the aristocratic "de"; he announces for years the most aristocratic tastes, principles, and predilections, and then he goes and marries the uneducated daughter of a very humble, very coarse, and very poor farmer. He continues to be, in profession and in talk, as violent a Tory and anti-reformer as ever, and yet he writes for Tait.' Hartley then stomped his foot on the ground. 'And for that same', he declared, 'I should not be very unwilling to pitch the Opium-Eater into this lake!'

Hartley's exasperation is understandable. Yet in terms of the paradoxes that shape De Quincey's life and writings, he might have produced a list that was considerably longer. Most strikingly, in the key areas of his experience, De Quincey repeatedly chose what he fought hard to overcome. He kept turning to his mother for help, even as he committed himself to throwing off her authority. He desperately wanted a close relationship with Wordsworth, but despised him for his arrogance and tactlessness. He railed against the demands of the periodical press, but published almost everything he wrote in that medium. He struggled mightily against debt, yet rented and bought and loaned and drank in a way that ensured he would not escape it. He loved his wife and children, but placed them under unrelenting stress – including deprivations such as cold and hunger. For over half a century he championed the powers of laudanum, even as he battled again and again to renounce it. These central contradictions frustrated even his admirers. Perhaps they originated in a childhood that seemed to him to end almost before it began. Certainly they were exacerbated by his hedonistic delight in pleasure, and his masochistic embrace of pain, as they were by a drug that he thought of as both a poison and a cure. Sometimes these paradoxes almost shook him apart. But on many other occasions they conferred upon him an energy and an insight that enabled him to comment meaningfully on a vast array of literary, political, philosophical, economic, and cultural concerns, stretching from classical Greece and Rome to many of the issues that defined Britain in the first half of the nineteenth century. After more than twenty years of close observation, Wilson concluded that De Quincey was 'a nature of dreadful passions subdued by reason'.

Since his death, De Quincey's reputation has fluctuated a good deal, but the impact of his writings has been remarkably pervasive, and is now most compellingly seen in three main areas. As a prose stylist, he could reach almost any register – from the bellicose, to the reportorial, to the ironic – but he was at his most penetrating when he turned his attention to the lives of major contemporaries such as Coleridge and Wordsworth, or the darkened channels of his own inner life. In these essays, he extended the range and the possibilities of English prose in nuanced explorations of dream worlds, childhood recollections, drug-altered consciousnesses, and sublime moments of personal revelation. 'He shifted the values of familiar things,' wrote Virginia Woolf. 'And this he did in prose, which makes us wonder whether, then, it is quite so limited as the critics say, and ask further where the prose writer, the novelist, might not capture fuller and finer truths than are now his aim if he ventured into those shadowy regions where De Quincey has been before him.'

Further, his essays 'On Murder Considered as One of the Fine Arts' had a decisive impact on *fin-de-siècle* decadence, and on terror and detective fiction. Their energetic combination of perversity, aesthetics, and humour frequently confound the reader between sympathy and voyeurism, while their enduring appeal taps the world-weariness that regards the spectacle of murder with both cynicism and fascination. De Quincey's most prominent followers in this area stretch from Edgar Allan Poe, Charles Dickens, and Arthur Conan Doyle to George Orwell, Vladimir Nabokov, and Peter Ackroyd. De Quincey is 'the first and most powerful of the decadents', G. K. Chesterton declared. 'If any one still smarting from the pinpricks' of Oscar Wilde or James Whistler 'wants to convict them of plagiarism in their "art for art" epigrams – he will find most of what they said said better in *Murder as One of the Fine Arts*.'

Finally, in interweaving drugs, the city, despair, and genius, De Quincey initiated the literature of addiction, and its portrait of the modern artist on a quest that begins with insidious promises of transcendence, but is soon vitiated by consumerism, disembodiment, and deadening repetition. A host of writers followed in his wake, including Wilkie Collins, Charles Baudelaire, and Robert Louis Stevenson in the nineteenth century, and Aleister Crowley, Jean Cocteau, Aldous Huxley, Malcolm Lowry, Hunter S. Thompson, and Ann Marlowe in the twentieth. 'De Quincey', asserted W. S. Burroughs, '... wrote the first, and still the best, book about drug addiction ... No other author since has given such a completely analytical description of what it is like to be a junky from the first use to the effects of withdrawal.'

De Quincey made laudanum the central fact of his existence, and for nearly forty years he successfully exploited his notoriety as 'the English Opium-Eater', even as he worked hard on many occasions to keep his dependence on the drug hidden away from friends, family, employers, and sometimes himself. The indignities and misfortunes of his life were at times so bizarre as to strain the limits of credulity. 'His image lives on in the memory ... like a character in fiction, rather than a reality,' Jorge Luis Borges once observed of him. Yet De Quincey was also a man who lived very much amidst the tensions and opportunities of his own age, and who fought hard when circumstances or people sought to thwart him. Though oftentimes blown far off-course, he was a man of remarkable determination, especially when it came to his writing, which got the care and attention he seems not to have felt he could bestow upon himself. De Quincey endured the afflictions of his childhood and the blights of opium to write a prose that was partially indebted to those griefs, but which also surmounted them. His representations of himself, and of the complexities of his age, influenced some of the major literary figures of the nineteenth and the twentieth centuries, and continue to inform our understanding of autobiography, subjectivity, violence, and addiction.

Appendix

THE VALUE OF MONEY

Money, and the lack of it, plays an enormous role in De Quincey's story. There are at least five different ways of computing the relative value of the pound. Below is a table based on the retail price index, which measures what goods and services would have cost in De Quincey's lifetime, compared with what we would pay now, and which provides one of the best ways of assessing the vicissitudes of his financial situation. For complete details, see the Economic History Services website: www.eh.net.

Shillings		*Pounds*	
1780	2008	1780	2008
1s	£5.34	£1	£106.71
1790		1790	
1s	£4.84	£1	£97.15
1800		1800	
1s	£2.70	£1	£54.09
1810		1810	
1s	£2.82	£1	£56.49
1820		1820	
1s	£3.37	£1	£67.31
1830		1830	
1s	£3.80	£1	£75.94
1840		1840	
1s	£3.56	£1	£71.17
1850		1850	
1s	£4.28	£1	£85.64

Notes

The standard edition of De Quincey's writings is *The Works of Thomas De Quincey*, gen. ed. Grevel Lindop, 21 volumes (London: Pickering and Chatto, 2000–2003). It is abbreviated below as *Works*. Full details of all other published items are given in the Bibliography.

There is still no complete edition of De Quincey's letters. Wherever possible, reference to his correspondence is made to one of the selected editions, or to a previously published source, checked whenever possible against the original manuscript. In all other instances, reference to De Quincey's letters is taken from manuscript sources, which are abbreviated as follows:

BC MS: Berg Collection, New York Public Library

BLYU MS: Beinecke Library, Yale University

BL MS: British Library

BLO MS: Bodleian Library, Oxford University

BPL MS: Boston Public Library

CUL MS: Cornell University Library

DCL MS: Dove Cottage Library

DWL MS: Dr Williams's Library

ESDL MS: Ella Strong Denison Library, Scripps College

EUL MS: Edinburgh University Library

GROS MS: General Register Office for Scotland

HL MS: Huntington Library, San Marino, California

HLH MS: Houghton Library, Harvard University

HRC MS: Harry Ransom Center, University of Texas at Austin

LKMC MS: Lee Kohns Memorial Collection, New York Public Library

LRO MS: Liverpool Record Office

MPL MS: Manchester Public Libraries

NAS MS: National Archives of Scotland

NLI MS: National Library of Ireland

NLS MS: National Library of Scotland

PC MS: Private Collection

PCSC MS: Pforzheimer Collection of Shelley and his Circle, New York Public Library

PML MS: Pierpont Morgan Library

PUL MS: Princeton University Library

RUL MS: Rochester University Library

TCLC MS: Trinity College Library, Cambridge

TRC MS: Tennyson Research Centre, Lincoln Central Library

UIL MS: University of Iowa Libraries

UKL MS: University of Kentucky Libraries

WCLO MS: Worcester College Library, Oxford

PROLOGUE

James Hogg junior gave two somewhat contradictory accounts of his first meeting with De Quincey: see Hogg (1895), 169–71 and Japp (1890), 314–15. The remaining details are drawn from Hogg (1895), 176–7, 252; Sackville West (1974), 288–9; and *Works*, 17. 14, 20.

CHAPTER ONE: Life is Finished

[1] *Works*, 19. 101; NLS MS: 4051, ff. 159/160.
[2] *Works*, 2. 148–9, 271–4.
[3] Bain (1890), 17–21.
[4] Japp (1890), 2; HLH MS: bMS Eng 1009 (3).
[5] *Works*, 10. 3; Mortimer (1900), 147, 153.
[6] Mortimer (1900), 153–8; Axon (1907), 207.
[7] *Works*, 19. 270–1, 81.
[8] NLS MS: 4055, f. 175; Fairbrother (1915), 274; De Quincey (1937), 44; Procter (1874), 261.
[9] *Works*, 10. 4; Procter (1874), 261; Lindop (1994), 181.
[10] Eaton (1936), 3.
[11] BLYU MS: Osborn Manuscript Files: ACC: 01.1.9; Eaton (1936), 4.
[12] *Works*, 19. 4.
[13] *Works*, 10. 4–5, 6.
[14] Green (1908), vii; Eaton (1936), 9; Lindop (1981), 3.
[15] Anonymous (1879), 244, *Works*, 19. 435.
[16] *Works*, 19. 240, 239; 10. 9.
[17] *Works*, 10. 10; 19. 6.
[18] *Works*, 10. 10; 15. 160.
[19] *Works*, 16. 432–3; 19. 68.
[20] Lindop (1994), 181; *Works*, 19. 271, 4; 10. 12.
[21] Sackville West (1974), 8; *Works*, 17. 82; Axon (1900), 10.
[22] *Works*, 17. 82; 10. 7.
[23] *Works*, 10. 10; 2. 158; 15. 160.
[24] *Works*, 10. 10; 19. 6, 39; McDonagh (1994), 159.
[25] HLH MS: bMS Eng 1009 (3); Eaton (1936), 5–6.
[26] *Works*, 19. 23.
[27] *Works*, 19. 75, 258; Eaton (1936), 8.
[28] *Works*, 10. 7, 9; 19. 17, 75.
[29] *Works*, 10. 8; 1. 58–69.
[30] Quincey (1775), 92–3; *Works*, 10. 9.
[31] BC MS: De Quincey mb; Lindop (1985), 97–111.
[32] *Works*, 15. 175; BC MS: De Quincey mb.
[33] BC MS: De Quincey mb.
[34] BC MS: De Quincey mb; *Works*, 10. 5; 19. 239.
[35] Plotz (2001), 134.
[36] *Works*, 19. 24, 7.
[37] *Works*, 19. 74.
[38] *Works*, 15. 167–8; 19. 72–4; 13. 419; 19. 74–7.
[39] *Works*, 19. 10; 15. 137.
[40] Procter (1874), 261; *Works*, 15. 138.
[41] *Works*, 19. 6–7.
[42] *Works*, 15. 139, 141; 10. 11.
[43] *Works*, 15. 141, 154, 139; Anonymous (1879), 245.
[44] Lindop (1981), 9; *Works*, 15. 141.
[45] *Works*, 15. 142.
[46] *Works*, 15. 143–5.
[47] *Works*, 10. 11; 15. 146; Barrell (1991), 112.
[48] *Works*, 15. 146–7.
[49] *Works*, 15. 158; Miller (1963), 17–23, 76–80.
[50] *Works*, 15. 148–9, 745–6; 19. 3–4.
[51] *Works*, 19. 3–4.
[52] *Works*, 15. 188, 163, 189.
[53] HLH MS: bMS Eng 1009 (3); *Works*, 19. 23.
[54] HLH MS: bMS Eng 1009 (3); Anonymous (1879), 245.
[55] *Works*, 19. 24; Jordan (1963), 270.
[56] *Works*, 15. 136; Axon (1907), 207; HLH MS: bMS Eng 1009 (3).
[57] *Works*, 19. 60; 10. 12.
[58] *Works*, 15. 176, 134; 4. 133; 10. 11.
[59] *Works*, 16. 656; 19. 182, 239–40; 15. 337, 432.
[60] *Works*, 15. 78–81.
[61] *Works*, 10. 9, 7; 19. 260–1, 60.
[62] *Works*, 19. 179–82.
[63] *Works*, 15. 157–9.

[64] *Works*, 15. 163; 10. 111.

[65] *Works*, 15. 163–4.

[66] *Works*, 15. 165–7.

[67] Rzepka (1995), 175–83; McDonagh (2008), 124–5.

[68] *Works*, 19. 27–30.

[69] *Works*, 15. 148; 19. 25–6.

[70] *Works*, 19. 32–4, 37.

[71] *Works*, 19. 38–43, 63.

[72] *Works*, 19. 46.

[73] *Works*, 19. 52–3, 47.

[74] *Works*, 2. 113–15; 19. 80.

[75] *Works*, 2. 115–17.

[76] *Works*, 2. 114; 19. 90.

[77] *Works*, 15. 157; 4. 133.

[78] *Works*, 15. 165.

[79] *Works*, 19. 71–2.

[80] *Works*, 15. 192; MPL MS: q824.81B49; *Works*, 19. 55.

[81] *Works*, 19. 56–7.

[82] *Works*, 15. 191, 665.

[83] *Works*, 19. 63, 66–7.

CHAPTER TWO: The Ray of a New Morning

[1] *Works*, 19. 88.

[2] Eaton (1936), 31; *Works*, 19. 88; Podmore (1968), 54–5.

[3] Austen (1923), 5. 78–9; Burke (1958–78), 9. 73, 83.

[4] *Works*, 19. 88.

[5] *Works*, 2. 117–19.

[6] Morrison (1998), 5; *Works*, 19. 90; 2. 14.

[7] *Works*, 19. 90–2.

[8] Lindop (1981), 21.

[9] *Works*, 19. 64; Plotz (2001), 159.

[10] Woof (1985), 33.

[11] Japp (1890), 267; *Works*, 16. 167–8.

[12] *Works*, 2. 150; 3. 132; 19. 93.

[13] *Works*, 19. 93; 11. 123–4.

[14] *Works*, 4. 233; 16. 85, 147; 3. 69.

[15] Lindop (1981), 357; Bridgwater (2004), 97; *Works*, 16. 152.

[16] Woof (1985), 32–3.

[17] *Works*, 19. 95; Japp (1890), 25–6.

[18] *Works*, 19. 95.

[19] Woof (1985), 33.

[20] Japp (1890), 24–5.

[21] HL MS: 37659; *Works*, 19. 95.

[22] *Works*, 2. 14; Woof (1985), 33.

[23] *Works*, 19. 96; 2. 14; Japp (1890), 40.

[24] Japp (1890), 26–7.

[25] Japp (1890), 26; Morrison (1998), 5; *Works*, 1. 2.

[26] *Works*, 1. 6.

[27] Mancuniensis (1864), 125; *Works*, 19. 119.

[28] *Works*, 10. 287; Jordan (1963), 36.

[29] Wordsworth (1992), 88.

[30] Roberts (2000), 105–6; Coleridge (1983), 2. 7.

[31] Morrison (2008), 65–6.

[32] Plotz (2001), 176–7.

[33] Coleridge (2001), 1. 416; Wordsworth (1992), 119.

[34] *Works*, 1. 38.

[35] Japp (1890), 44.

[36] Roberts (2000), 102–3; Lindop (1985), 103; Eaton (1936), 2.

[37] HL MS: 37659; cf. Japp (1891), 1. 20.

[38] *Works*, 19. 97.

[39] Byron (1973–94), 2. 7.

[40] Woof (1985), 33; Eaton (1936), 41.

[41] NLI MS: 40, 911/3 (10).

[42] NLI MS: 40, 911/3 (11).

[43] Japp (1891), 1. 34.

[44] Japp (1891), 1. 35; PML MS: Misc Ray, MA 4500.

[45] *Works*, 19. 111–12; 2. 156.

[46] *Works*, 19. 118–19.

[47] Japp (1891), 1. 34; *Works*, 19. 124, 121, 126.

[48] Japp (1890), 32.

[49] Japp (1891), 1. 35; PML MS: Misc Ray, MA 4500; Japp (1890), 31.

[50] Japp (1891), 1. 35; Japp (1890), 31.

[51] *Works*, 19. 130–1; Japp (1891), 1. 27; PML MS: Misc Ray, MA 4500.

[52] *Works*, 19. 130–1, 133; Japp (1891), 1. 26–8.

[53] Japp (1891), 1. 28–9.

[54] PML MS: Misc Ray, MA 4500.

[55] *Works*, 19. 137, 140; PML MS: Misc Ray, MA 4500.

56 *Works*, 19. 135; PML MS: Misc Ray, MA 4500.

57 *Works*, 19. 209, 211–12.

58 PML MS: Misc Ray, MA 4500.

59 PML MS: Misc Ray, MA 4500; *Works*, 2. 314.

60 *Works*, 19. 142.

61 PML MS: Misc Ray, MA 4500; NLS MS: 21239, ff. 1/2.

62 PML MS: Misc Ray, MA 4500.

63 *Works*, 19. 143, 159, 223; PML MS: Misc Ray, MA 4500.

64 *Works*, 19. 172; PML MS: Misc Ray, MA 4500.

65 NLS MS: 21239, ff. 1/2; *Works*, 19. 172–4.

66 *Works*, 19. 215; PML MS: Misc Ray, MA 4500.

67 PML MS: Misc Ray, MA 4500.

68 *Works*, 19. 214, 216.

69 *Works*, 19. 221–3.

70 *Works*, 19. 223, 228, 232.

71 DCL MS: 2007.49.1.

72 *Works*, 19. 258.

73 *Works*, 10. 94; 19. 255; 2. 142.

74 *Works*, 19. 215, 246–7, 251–2.

75 *Works*, 2. 120; 19, 256; Lindop (1981), 46.

76 *Works*, 19. 256, 255, 253; 10. 87.

CHAPTER THREE: Down and Out in Manchester and London

1 *Works*, 10. 354.

2 Lindop (1981), 48; Bentley (1990), 45–6.

3 Smith (1866–74), 2. 224.

4 Bentley (1990), 43; *Works*, 2. 120–1.

5 *Works*, 2. 121, 127–8.

6 *Works*, 2. 128–9; 10. 352, 354, 353.

7 *Works*, 2. 129, 131.

8 *Works*, 2. 14, 139–40.

9 *Works*, 2. 136–8; Smith (1866–74), 2. 225.

10 *Works*, 10. 181–5.

11 *Works*, 10. 185, 144; 2, 258.

12 Japp (1891), 1. 48.

13 *Works*, 10. 187; Lindop (1981), 52.

14 Japp (1891), 1. 61–2; *Works*, 1. 9.

15 *Works*, 10. 187, 189; Japp (1891), 1. 61, 63.

16 *Works*, 10. 190–2.

17 *Works*, 10. 191, 190, 195.

18 Japp (1891), 1. 62; *Works*, 10. 193–6.

19 Coleridge (1956–71), 1. 607.

20 Wordsworth (1992), 122; Wordsworth (1974), 1. 118; Roberts (2000), 72–88.

21 *Works*, 10. 288, 191.

22 *Works*, 10. 195; 19. 259.

23 *Works*, 6. 126; 19. 433; Axon (1899), 15–21.

24 *Works*, 19. 265–6.

25 *Works*, 19. 266–7, 430.

26 *Works*, 19. 273; 2. 167.

27 *Works*, 19. 274–5; 2. 167–8.

28 Japp (1891), 1. 67–8.

29 Japp (1891), 1. 70–2; Eaton (1936), 65.

30 Japp (1891), 1. 72–5.

31 PML MS: Misc Ray, MA 4500.

32 Japp (1890), 53–4; *Works*, 2. 140–1.

33 Bentley (1990), 47; PML MS: Misc Ray, MA 4500.

34 Japp (1891), 1. 78, 76.

35 Eaton (1936), 70; Japp (1891), 1. 83, 86–7.

36 Japp (1891), 1. 83–6; *Works*, 2. 142.

37 *Works*, 2. 143.

38 *Works*, 2. 142.

39 *Works*, 2. 110, 139, 143; 19. 431; 15. 189.

40 *Works*, 2. 144–5, 157.

41 *Works*, 2. 146–7, 139, 173, 148.

42 Lindop (1981), 66; *Works*, 2. 148–51.

43 *Works*, 2. 151, 154–5.

44 *Works*, 2. 151, 155, 330.

45 Barrell (1991), 28–9.

46 *Works*, 155–7; Barrell (1991), 29.

47 *Works*, 2. 158.

48 *Works*, 2. 158, 139.

49 *Works*, 2. 160, 158.

50 *Works*, 2. 160–6.

51 *Works*, 2. 166–8.

52 *Works*, 2. 172, 170, 168–9.

53 *Works*, 2. 170.

54 *Works*, 2. 168, 171, 174.

55 *Works*, 2. 174–5.

56 *Works*, 2. 175.

57 *Works*, 15. 148; Sackville West (1974), 48–52; Lindop (1981), 70.

58 *Works*, 2. 178–80, 182.

[59] *Works*, 2. 183.

[60] Hughes (1900), 292–9; *Works*, 2. 185–6.

[61] *Works*, 2. 184–5, 180–1; 10. 209; 4. 248.

[62] *Works*, 2. 187, 20.

[63] Japp (1891), 1. 49; *Works*, 10. 211.

[64] *Works*, 2. 194–5, 187.

[65] *Works*, 2. 187–91.

[66] *Works*, 2. 357, 191–3.

[67] *Works*, 2. 194.

[68] *Works*, 2. 207, 197, 195, 331; Adcock (1929), 135.

[69] *Works*, 2. 195–7.

[70] *Works*, 2. 197–8.

[71] Japp (1891), 1. 90–1.

[72] *Works*, 2. 198–9, 202, 200.

[73] *Works*, 2. 200.

[74] *Works*, 2. 212, 214, 200.

[75] *Works*, 2. 199.

[76] *Works*, 2. 199, 198.

[77] *Works*, 2. 202–4.

[78] *Works*, 2. 208, 203–4.

[79] *Works*, 2. 204–5.

[80] *Works*, 2. 206–7.

[81] *Works*, 2. 206–7.

[82] *Works*, 2. 207–9.

[83] *Works*, 2. 209–10.

[84] *Works*, 2. 210–11.

[85] *Works*, 2. 211–12.

[86] *Works*, 2. 212.

[87] *Works*, 2. 212, 35.

[88] *Works*, 2. 205.

[89] *Works*, 2. 213, 208.

[90] *Works*, 2. 36, 214, 333; Morrison (2008), 65.

[91] *Works*, 2. 204, 208; Rzepka (1995), 148.

[92] Rzepka (1995), 141–9; *Works*, 1. 46; 2. 202.

[93] Rzepka (1995), 147; *Works*, 1. 14, 349.

CHAPTER FOUR: Letters of a Young Man

[1] *Works*, 1. 26.

[2] Baxter (1990), 65.

[3] *Works*, 1. 44–5.

[4] *Works*, 1. 51.

[5] *Works*, 1. 20.

[6] *Works*, 1. 37, 54, 40, 22.

[7] Eaton (1927), 218–19, 228–9.

[8] *Works*, 1. 44, 47, 53.

[9] *Works*, 1. 26, 34, 48–9.

[10] *Works*, 1. 35; Eaton (1927), 235.

[11] *Works*, 1. 54, 45, 14, 349.

[12] *Works*, 1. 24, 33–4.

[13] *Works*, 1. 55, 36, 42.

[14] *Works*, 1. 40, 45, 360.

[15] *Works*, 1. 25–6.

[16] *Works*, 1. 25, 32, 40.

[17] *Works*, 1. 26, 35, 37, 46.

[18] *Works*, 1. 38, 20, 22.

[19] *Works*, 1. 20, 37, 40, 45.

[20] *Works*, 1. 36, 38–9.

[21] *Works*, 1. 52, 34, 39, 49–50.

[22] *Works*, 1. 13, 22.

[23] *Works*, 1. 28–9.

[24] *Works*, 1. 13, 15, 21, 30.

[25] *Works*, 1. 43, 40.

[26] *Works*, 1. 40–1.

[27] *Works*, 1. 40–1.

[28] *Works*, 1. 41–2.

[29] *Works*, 1. 42.

[30] *Works*, 1. 42; Whale (2008), 83–5.

[31] Jordan (1963), 16.

[32] Wordsworth (1967), 400–1.

[33] *Works*, 10. 235.

[34] Jordan (1963), 32–5.

[35] *Works*, 19. 269.

[36] *Works*, 19. 275, 279.

[37] *Works*, 10. 112; Lindop (1981), 110.

[38] *Works*, 10. 112, 139–41, 119.

[39] *Works*, 10. 121–2.

[40] *Works*, 10. 122–3; Hogg (1895), 107–8.

[41] Sutherland and Mitchell (1986), 333, 317, 336–9, 425–9; Brock and Curthoys (1997), 272, 14, 280–1.

[42] *Works*, 10. 123; Japp (1891), 1. 107; Daniel (1893), 14.

[43] *Works*, 10. 123, 136–8; Jordan (1963), 36; Lindop (1981), 117.

[44] Lindop (1981), 120.

[45] *Works*, 2. 238.

[46] *Works*, 10. 235.

[47] Daniel (1893), 14; *Works*, 10. 111–12.

48 *Works*, 10. 142.

49 Japp (1891), 1. 224; *Works*, 19. 193, 202, 187; 10. 215.

50 Morrison (1998), 31, 1; *Works*, 10. 144–5.

51 Hogg (1895), 233; *Works*, 10. 147.

52 *Works*, 10. 138; McDonagh (2008), 135.

53 Morrison (1998), 31.

54 Daniel (1893), 14; Hogg (1895), 108; *Works*, 10. 359; 2. 228.

55 *Works*, 19. 78, 84–7.

56 *Works*, 20. 362.

57 Jordan (1963), 36.

58 Jordan (1963), 36–7.

59 Whale (2008), 83.

60 Wordsworth (1974), 1. 128–9.

61 Jordan (1963), 37.

62 Jordan (1963), 38.

63 Wordsworth (1967), 452–5.

64 Jeffrey (1802), 71.

65 Wordsworth (1967), 458.

66 Jordan (1963), 38–41.

67 *Works*, 10. 147.

68 *Works*, 10. 161, 293; Hogg (1895), 108; Japp (1891), 1. 232.

69 *Works*, 2. 206.

70 Eaton (1936), 116.

71 *Works*, 2. 41; Lindop (1981), 119.

72 *Works*, 15. 189; 10. 109.

CHAPTER FIVE: High Culture

1 *Works*, 2. 42.

2 *Works*, 2. 43.

3 Booth (1996), 1, 15.

4 Milligan (1995), 20, 22, 27; Hayter (1968), 30–1; Foxcroft (2007), 11.

5 Milligan (2005), 542.

6 *Works*, 2. 42.

7 *Works*, 1. 35, 14.

8 Vetch, rev. Bowyer, 'Watson' (2004), 55. 617.

9 *Works*, 19. 277–9.

10 Leask (1992), 175–9; Milligan (2008), 51–8.

11 Hardman and Limbird (1996), 529.

12 Plant (1999), 12; *Works*, 2. 51.

13 *Works*, 2. 248–9.

14 *Works*, 2. 47, 103, 44–5.

15 *Works*, 2. 47, 220.

16 *Works*, 2. 220; Butler (1981), 175.

17 *Works*, 2. 48.

18 *Works*, 2. 49–50; Barrell (1991), 2.

19 *Works*, 2. 50–1.

20 *Works*, 2. 51.

21 *Works*, 19. 17–18.

22 *Works*, 15. 177–9, 181.

23 *Works*, 15. 130, 182; 2. 12.

24 *Works*, 15. 131, 169; 2. 51, 74.

25 *Works*, 15. 198.

26 Wordsworth (1974), 1. 128–9; *Works*, 10. 161.

27 *Works*, 10. 162.

28 *Works*, 10. 163, 174, 173, 298.

29 *Works*, 10. 235, 237.

30 *Works*, 10. 237.

31 *Works*, 10. 239–41.

32 *Works*, 11. 58.

33 *Works*, 11. 193, 243–4; 2. 252.

34 *Works*, 2. 213, 227.

35 Jordan (1963), 175; *Works*, 2. 249.

36 *Works*, 9. 333; 8. 476; Hogg (1895), 153.

37 Cottle (1848), 340; Cottle (2008), 167.

38 Cottle (1848), 340–1; *Works*, 9. 347.

39 WCLO MS: Battels Books.

40 Jordan (1963), 22.

41 *Works*, 11. 45; Jordan (1963), 42–3.

42 Wordsworth (1969), 26.

43 Jordan (1963), 44–6.

44 *Works*, 11. 45–6; 10. 239.

45 *Works*, 1. 364, 70–1.

46 *Works*, 1. 72–4.

47 *Works*, 1. 74, 76.

48 Morrison (1998), 31.

49 Japp (1891), 1. 113–14.

50 *Works*, 2. 173.

51 Japp (1891), 1. 243; Cottle (2008), 161; LKMC MS: Manuscripts and Archives Division.

52 *Works*, 6. 208; Japp (1891), 1. 240.

53 Japp (1891), 1. 242.

54 Wordsworth (1969), 143; *Works*, 11. 110.

55 *Works*, 11. 46; Jordan (1963), 24.

CHAPTER SIX: Lives of the Poets

1 *Works*, 16. 409.

2 *Works*, 16. 411, 409.

3 *Works*, 16. 418–19.

4 *Works*, 16. 419, 421–2.

5 Jordan (1963), 25.

6 *Works*, 10. 288–9.

7 *Works*, 10. 295.

8 *Works*, 10. 295–7, 300.

9 *Works*, 10. 303, 295, 294.

10 *Works*, 10. 304.

11 Eaton (1936), 116.

12 Potter (1934), 7; Japp (1890), 91.

13 *Works*, 5. 93.

14 Coleridge (1957–2002), 2. 3166.

15 Japp (1891), 1. 127–8; Cottle (1848), 341.

16 Coleridge (1956–71), 3. 34.

17 Japp (1891), 1. 132.

18 Japp (1891), 1. 133.

19 Potter (1934), 8; UKL MS: Special Collections and Digital Programs; *Works*, 11. 48.

20 UKL MS: Special Collections and Digital Programs; *Works*, 11. 48.

21 Potter (1934), 7–8.

22 HRC MS: Thomas De Quincey Collection, Letters; Coleridge (1873), 1. 12.

23 *Works*, 11. 49.

24 *Works*, 11. 49–50.

25 *Works*, 11. 50.

26 *Works*, 11. 52–3.

27 *Works*, 11. 56, 55, 58.

28 *Works*, 11. 111–12.

29 *Works*, 11. 112–13.

30 *Works*, 11. 113; Reed (1975), 366–7.

31 *Works*, 11. 113.

32 *Works*, 11. 115–16.

33 Jordan (1963), 89.

34 *Works*, 11. 116.

35 *Works*, 11. 116–17.

36 *Works*, 11. 123–4.

37 *Works*, 11. 193, 192.

38 Reed (1975), 368.

39 *Works*, 11. 168–9.

40 Wordsworth (1969), 180.

41 *Works*, 11. 171–2.

42 Jordan (1963), 86.

43 Brock and Curthoys (1997), 14, 346.

44 Morrison (1998), 31.

45 Lindop (1981), 159; Morrison (1998), 31.

46 Jordan (1963), 86.

47 Coleridge (1956–71), 3. 48, 47; Jordan (1963), 86.

48 Coleridge (1956–71), 3. 46; Wordsworth (1969), 180; Jordan (1963), 88.

49 *Works*, 10. 320.

50 Coleridge (1956–71), 3. 46; *Works*, 10. 321; Coleridge (1957–2002), 2. 3276.

51 *Works*, 2. 68, 258; Reed (1975), 374; Hogg (1895), 232.

52 Coleridge (1956–71), 3. 49; Gillman (1838), 251.

53 Wordsworth (1969), 495.

54 Jordan (1963), 89; *Works*, 10. 205, 247; Reed (1975), 377.

55 Eaton (1936), 145; Jordan (1963), 87–8.

56 Jordan (1963), 90; Morrison (1998), 32.

57 Hogg (1895), 110.

58 Morrison (1998), 32; Hogg (1895), 109–10.

59 Morrison (1998), 32–3.

60 Lindop (1981), 160.

61 Japp (1891), 1. 278; Coleridge (1956–71), 3. 48; Wordsworth (1969), 257.

62 Coleridge (1987), 1. 122.

63 Grant (1844), 3. 14; *Works*, 10. 206.

64 *Works*, 3. 134.

65 Wordsworth (1969), 257.

66 Japp (1891), 1. 277.

67 Wordsworth (1969), 272; Jordan (1963), 55.

68 *Works*, 7. 5; 11. 175.

69 Wordsworth (1969), 267.

70 Coleridge (1969), 2. 424–5, 439, 446.

71 Jordan (1963), 178; Coleridge (1956–71), 3. 177.

72 *Works*, 11. 74.

73 *Works*, 7. 6.

74 *Works*, 2. 147.

75 *Works*, 7. 8.

76 Emerson (1960–82), 10. 536.

77 Reed (1975), 403.

78 *Works*, 11. 173.

[79] Hutchinson (1954), 12.

[80] Warter (1856), 2. 108.

[81] Wordsworth (1969), 283.

[82] Wordsworth (1974), 1. 199–200.

[83] Jordan (1963), 199.

[84] Wordsworth (1969), 351; Jordan (1963), 123.

[85] Coleridge (1956–71), 3. 177; Jordan (1963), 59.

[86] *Works*, 11. 177.

[87] Reed (1975), 409; Jordan (1963), 93.

[88] Jordan (1963), 101–2, 104.

[89] Jordan (1963), 107, 101.

[90] Wordsworth (1969), 292, 294.

[91] Jordan (1963), 117, 119; Wordsworth (1969), 298.

[92] Wordsworth (1969), 298–300, 306–7, 302.

[93] Jordan (1963), 132–3.

[94] Wordsworth (1969), 318, 320.

[95] Wordsworth (1969), 317.

[96] Jordan (1963), 185, 241, 120, 123, 99.

[97] Jordan (1963), 193, 241, 171, 179, 188.

[98] *Works*, 3. 136.

[99] Jordan (1963), 188.

[100] Jordan (1963), 135–6, 144.

[101] Jordan (1963), 145–6.

[102] Wordsworth (1969), 321.

[103] Coleridge (1956–71), 3. 205–6.

[104] Wordsworth (1969), 328–9.

[105] Wordsworth (1969), 330, 340.

[106] Jordan (1963), 162, 164, 167.

[107] Wordsworth (1969), 341–2, 344.

[108] Wordsworth (1969), 347–8.

[109] Jordan (1963), 173.

[110] Wordsworth (1969), 350, 354.

[111] Jordan (1963), 183; *Works*, 1. 80.

[112] Wordsworth (1969), 350–1.

[113] Coleridge (1956–71), 3. 214; Southey (1849–50), 3. 246.

[114] Jordan (1963), 198.

[115] *Works*, 1. 80.

[116] Jordan (1963), 130, 126, 128.

[117] Wordsworth (1969), 324, 348; Jordan (1963), 185.

[118] Jordan (1963), 108; Wordsworth (1969), 327, 330, 360–1.

[119] Wordsworth (1969), 339.

[120] Japp (1891), 2. 1–2; 1. 285.

[121] Japp (1891), 1. 250.

[122] Jordan (1963), 175, 174; Japp (1891), 1. 251–61.

[123] Jordan (1963), 237.

[124] *Works*, 19. 271; Japp (1891), 1. 283; HL MS: 37699; Japp (1891), 2. 5; HL MS: 37698.

[125] Jordan (1963), 244.

[126] Jordan (1963), 240.

[127] *Works*, 9. 335; Japp (1891), 2. 14; Jordan (1963), 251–2.

[128] *Works*, 11. 238; 9. 345–6.

[129] Jordan (1963), 249; *Works*, 9. 338.

[130] Jordan (1963), 250.

[131] *Works*, 3. 82; 6. 308–9.

[132] Jordan (1963), 254–5, 248–9, 243; Wordsworth (1969), 371.

[133] Jordan (1963), 256; Reed (1975), 439.

[134] Wordsworth (1969), 374, 376.

[135] *Works*, 11. 182.

[136] Wordsworth (1969), 376–7; *Works*, 10. 321.

[137] Coleridge (1969), 1. 377.

[138] Reed (1975), 444–6; Hutchinson (1954), 22.

[139] Southey (1849–50), 3. 274; *Works*, 10. 316; 7. 81.

[140] Wordsworth (1969), 457–8; ULK MS: Special Collections and Digital Programs.

[141] *Works*, 10. 311.

[142] *Works*, 11. 200, 197, 193, 206, 201.

[143] Gordon (1863), 45–6; *Works*, 9. 66; 7. 18, 24–5.

[144] *Works*, 11. 200; 7. 10–11.

[145] *Works*, 13. 418–19.

[146] *Works*, 11. 576; Reed (1975), 454.

[147] *Works*, 11. 80–2; Emerson (1960–82), 10. 535.

[148] *Works*, 11. 52–3.

[149] Eaton (1936), 198; Jordan (1963), 256.

[150] Wordsworth (1969), 429; Jordan (1963), 256–60.

[151] Jordan (1963), 269; *Works*, 11. 236.

[152] Hutchinson (1954), 28, 33.

[153] Japp (1891), 2. 23; Wordsworth (1969), 511.

[154] Reed (1975), 484; Japp (1891), 2. 81.

[155] *Works*, 16. 733; 11. 208; 3. 163; 11. 145.

[156] *Works*, 2. 163.

[157] *Works*, 11. 147–8; 13. 343.

[158] *Works*, 1. 294.

[159] *Works*, 11. 126.

[160] Hutchinson (1954), 36–8.

[161] Morrison (2006), *On Murder*, x–xi; *Works*, 20. 40, 53.

[162] *Works*, 2. 53, 231.

[163] *Works*, 10. 291; 2. 64, 52, 63; 20. 410, 435.

[164] *Works*, 10. 292–3.

[165] Jordan (1963), 260, 262; Eaton (1936), 199.

[166] *Works*, 10. 336.

[167] Coleridge (1956–71), 3. 296.

[168] Morrison (1998), 2; William and Dorothy Wordsworth (1993), 63.

[169] Morrison (1998), 20; Wordsworth (1970), 23.

[170] Jordan (1963), 263–4; Robinson (1938), 1. 103.

[171] Jordan (1963), 263, 265, 266–7.

[172] *Works*, 14. 40; Nisbet (1860), 37.

[173] Robinson (1938), 1. 104.

[174] Jordan (1963), 210, 270–1.

[175] *Works*, 11. 237; 2. 13.

[176] *Works*, 11. 238.

[177] *Works*, 11. 238.

[178] Wordsworth (1970), 50–1.

CHAPTER SEVEN: The Road of Excess

[1] *Works*, 2. 54, 103, 251–2; Maddux and Desmond (1981), 57.

[2] *Works*, 2. 231.

[3] Milligan (1995), 23–5.

[4] Dalrymple (2006), 9–59; Hoffman and Froemke (2007), 52–83.

[5] Milligan (2005), 543–6; Milligan (1995), 23; Parssinen (1983), 8.

[6] Milligan (1995), 22–3; Hayter (1968), 28, 37–8; Black (2008), 145.

[7] Milligan (2003), 261.

[8] *Works*, 2. 233, 245.

[9] *Works*, 2. 109.

[10] Hardman and Limbird (1996), 532.

[11] Bonner (1936), 101.

[12] Hardman and Limbird (1996), 536, 567; Milligan (1995), 23.

[13] Dalrymple (2006), 20–7.

[14] *Works*, 2. 75; Japp (1890), 243.

[15] Hardman and Limbird (1996), 569.

[16] *Works*, 2. 220; 15. 245; 19. 181.

[17] Terry and Pellens (1928), 63–4; Abrams (1970), 66–7.

[18] Terry and Pellens (1928), 63–4; Abrams (1970), 66–7.

[19] Hardman and Limbird (1996), 563; Dalrymple (2006), 20–2.

[20] *Works*, 2. 249; DeGrandpre (2006), 103–11.

[21] *Works*, 20. 24.

[22] Armitt (1916), 677–8; *Works*, 20. 403; Japp (1890), 144; Jordan (1963), 306.

[23] Lindop (1981), 206; Wordsworth (1970), 372.

[24] Lindop (1981), 206; Woof (1985), 74.

[25] Wordsworth (1974), 1. 122, 124.

[26] *Works*, 21. 134; Jordan (1963), 306.

[27] *Works*, 11. 94; 20. 24–5.

[28] *Works*, 13. 310.

[29] *Works*, 21. 134.

[30] Wordsworth (1970), 80.

[31] Wordsworth (1970), 81; NLS MS: 21239, f. 4; CUL MS: Wordsworth Collection.

[32] *Works*, 11. 253–4.

[33] *Works*, 10. 336; 6, 114.

[34] *Works*, 9. 335.

[35] William and Dorothy Wordsworth (1993), 142.

[36] Wordsworth (1958), 11.

[37] Morrison (1998), 2; Jordan (1963), 231.

[38] Japp (1891), 2. 35–6.

[39] *Works*, 10. 251–2.

[40] *Works*, 11. 261; Robinson (1938), 1. 137.

[41] *Works*, 10. 335; 3, 135.

[42] *Works*, 11. 242–3; 2. 252.

[43] Musgrove (1954), 16.

[44] *Works*, 16. 404–5.

[45] *Works*, 16. 434.

[46] *Works*, 16. 439.

[47] *Works*, 16. 440–2.

[48] *Works*, 442–9.

[49] Hogg (2003), 68.

[50] *Works*, 11. 282.

[51] Lickbarrow (1994), vii, xi, xii; *Works*, 3. 94; 10, 325.

[52] NLS MS: 21239, f. 5; *Works*, 21. 66; Duckers (1920), 684.

[53] Gordon (1863), 136; Jordan (1963), 226.

[54] Wordsworth (1958), 24–5.

[55] Wordsworth (1970), 195.

[56] Wordsworth (1970), 198–9, 230.

[57] *Works*, 2. 184; 9. 343.

[58] *Works*, 2. 56; Hutchinson (1954), 88.

[59] *Works*, 11. 243; Grant (1844), 3. 14.

[60] Lang (1897), 1. 97–8; Woof (1985), 103.

[61] *Works*, 17. 148; Gillies (1851), 2. 220–1.

[62] *Works*, 2. 55; Rzepka (1995), 215.

[63] *Works*, 2. 58, 56.

[64] Emerson (1960–82), 10. 535.

[65] *Works*, 11. 197.

[66] Jordan (1963), 235.

[67] *Works*, 11. 590; Jordan (1963), 226–7.

[68] *Works*, 2. 60; Wordsworth (1970), 298–9.

[69] *Works*, 2. 57–8.

[70] *Works*, 11. 202–4.

[71] *Works*, 11. 204–6; Morrison (1998), 10–11.

[72] Japp (1891), 2. 109–10.

[73] Robinson (1938), 1. 187–8, 194.

[74] Morley (1927), 1. 90; Robinson (1938), 1. 195–6.

[75] Stockdale (1872), 400–1; Japp (1891), 2. 116.

[76] William and Dorothy Wordsworth (1993), 162; *Works*, 21. 6.

[77] Jordan (1963), 278–9.

[78] Wordsworth (1970), 372.

[79] Lamb (1935), 2. 219.

[80] Robinson (1922), 58; *Works*, 11. 135.

[81] *Works*, 11. 135.

[82] *Works*, 2. 61; Japp (1891), 2. 117.

[83] *Works*, 2. 63–5.

[84] *Works*, 2. 66–70.

[85] Neal (1865), 660; Morrison (2006), 'William Blackwood', 27–8.

[86] Maginn (1822), 106.

[87] Hogg (2004–8), 1. 401.

[88] Japp (1891), 2. 114, 111.

[89] Simmons (1945), 151.

[90] Leask (1992), 181, 252.

[91] Morrison (1992), 36–41; Morrison (1998), 24; *Works*, 20. 196–210.

[92] *Works*, 2. 64–5.

[93] Morrison (1998), 11; Japp (1890), 154.

[94] Wordsworth (1970), 543–4.

[95] Jordan (1963), 306, 310; Wordsworth (1970), 464; *Works*, 1. 94–104.

[96] Jordan (1963), 319.

[97] *Works*, 1. 106, 112–13.

[98] Japp (1891), 2. 117.

[99] *Works*, 2. 66, 70–1.

[100] GROS MS: 13/12/1853 De Quincey, Margaret Thomasiana (O.P.R. Marriages 676/ 0030 0391 Cockpen); Japp (1891), 2. 116.

[101] Japp (1891), 2. 117, 67, 62.

[102] *Works*, 1. 106–7; Japp (1890), 153; Caseby (1985), 123.

[103] Wordsworth (1970), 478; Woof (1985), 86.

[104] *Works*, 1. 246, 156.

[105] *Works*, 1. 315, 143; Caseby (1985), 132.

[106] Caseby (1985), 99; Works, 20. 467; Lindop (1981), 227–8.

[107] *Works*, 20. 149–95; 1. 259–61; Caseby (1985), 141.

[108] *Works*, 1. 210, 248–9.

[109] *Works*, 1. 252–3.

[110] *Works*, 1. 219; Hutchinson (1954), 152.

[111] Works, 1. 276, 189; Morrison (1992), 38.

[112] *Works*, 1. 274.

[113] *Works*, 20. 153; 1. 189, 285–6.

[114] *Works*, 1. 147; 6. 131.

[115] Caseby (1985), 154.

[116] Wordsworth (1970), 489, 488, 512.

[117] *Works*, 1. 108; Caseby (1985), 131, 141–2.

[118] Morrison (1998), 7.

[119] *Works*, 1. 107, 180; Jordan (1963), 324.

[120] CUL MS: Wordsworth Collection.

[121] Japp (1891), 2. 119, 122–3.

[122] *Works*, 2. 72–3.

[123] Lindop (1981), 236; *Works*, 1. 108.

[124] Caseby (1985), 144.

[125] *Works*, 1. 152; 15. 452.

CHAPTER EIGHT: Famous

[1] Japp (1891), 2. 41–2.

[2] *Works*, 2. 327; NLS MS: 4051, f. 124.

[3] Symonds (1994), 140; Wordsworth (1978), 210.

[4] Hutchinson (1954), 209.

[5] *Works*, 2. 82–3; 10. 263.

[6] *Works*, 2. 62.

[7] *Works*, 2. 327, 66.

[8] Japp (1891), 2. 42, 43, 45.

[9] Japp (1891), 2. 44–5; Morrison (1998), 18.

[10] Symonds (1994), 33.

[11] Symonds (1994), 48, 49–50.

[12] Morrison (1999), 47–8.

[13] Symonds (1994), 51, 56.

[14] Symonds (1994), 56, 63.

[15] Bridgwater (2004), 54.

[16] Symonds (1994), 58–9.

[17] Symonds (1994), 63–8.

[18] *Works*, 20. 249–59; Symonds (1994), 66.

[19] Symonds (1994), 68.

[20] Oliphant (1897), 1. 427–8.

[21] Symonds (1994), 70–1, 72.

[22] Scott (1820), 'Preface and Prospectus', iv.

[23] Scott (1820), 'Lord Byron', 496.

[24] Wilson (1820), 105; Scott (1820), '*Blackwood's Magazine*', 513.

[25] Symonds (1994), 34.

[26] Symonds (1994), 72, 33–4, 72–3.

[27] Japp (1891), 2. 46–8.

[28] Jordan (1963), 295; Wordsworth (1958), 76.

[29] *Works*, 11. 261, 262.

[30] *Works*, 11. 262; Robinson and Powell (2002), 131.

[31] Keats (1958), 2. 318; Chilcott (1972), 8; *Works*, 11. 262.

[32] *Works*, 11. 262.

[33] Symonds (1994), 156.

[34] Rayment (1913), 104–5; *Works*, 6. 15.

[35] Reynolds (1973), 27; O'Leary (1983), 162.

[36] *Works*, 2. 41; 10. 262.

[37] Symonds (1994), 86; *Works*, 2. 11; Hogg (1895), 199.

[38] *Works*, 2. 41; Leask (1992), 189.

[39] Symonds (1994), 74–5; Coleridge (1956–71), 5. 162.

[40] Symonds (1994), 127.

[41] Symonds (1994), 87, 89, 135; Morrison (1998), 18.

[42] *Works*, 10. 264–5.

[43] *Works*, 2. 3, 37, 70, 72; 10. 265.

[44] *Works*, 10. 265; Symonds (1998), 138.

[45] *Works*, 2. 280; Chilcott (1972), 137.

[46] Symonds (1994), 79, 83.

[47] Symonds (1994), 85.

[48] Symonds (1994), 92, 101, 103–4.

[49] *Works*, 2. 325–8.

[50] *Works*, 2. 37.

[51] *Works*, 2. 9, 12.

[52] *Works*, 2. 36.

[53] *Works*, 2. 43.

[54] *Works*, 2. 68.

[55] *Works*, 2. 75, 74; Parssinen (1983), 5.

[56] *Works*, 20. 16; Lindop (2003), 7–8; Ford (2007), 232.

[57] Foucault (1990), 57–65.

[58] Black (2008), 145–7; Bridgwater (2004), 85.

[59] Milligan (1995), 20, 25–7.

[60] *Works*, 2. 47–8.

[61] *Works*, 2. 11.

[62] Lindop (1995), 'De Quincey's Wordsworthian Quotations', 58–65; Morrison (2008), 68–77.

[63] *Works*, 20. 337.

[64] Symonds (1994), 97; Knight (1864–5), 1. 271; Japp (1890), 178; Gilfillan (1857), 2. 153.

[65] Anonymous (1823), *Eclectic Review*, 371.

[66] Anonymous (1823), *Imperial Magazine*, 89; Anonymous (1822), *Medical Intelligencer*, 290; Anonymous (1825), 40; Anonymous (1822), *The Album*, 177.

[67] Clare (1985), 441; Anonymous (1825), 38.

[68] Poe (1969–78), 2. 340; Robinson (1938), 1. 267; Morrison (1998), 9; Grant (1844), 3. 14–15.

[69] Wilson (1923), 250.

[70] Dalrymple (2006), 61–89.

[71] Lindop (1981), 248; Anonymous (1823), *Advice to Opium Eaters*, iv.

[72] Woof (1985), 56.

[73] Southey (1965), 2. 450; Gillman (1838), 247–8; Scott (1892), 1. 98–9.

[74] Symonds (1994), 97; *Works*, 2. 78.

[75] Morrison (1998), 22.

[76] *Works*, 11. 261.

[77] Procter (1866), 156.

[78] *Works*, 11. 276.

[79] *Works*, 5. 207; 11. 262; 3. 349–63; Chilcott (1972), 138.

[80] *Works*, 11. 262; Chilcott (1972), 138.

[81] Taylor (1925), 263.

[82] *Works*, 16. 388, 390.

[83] *Works*, 10. 272, 266.

[84] *Works*, 10. 269–70.

[85] Morrison (1998), 12–13.

[86] Morrison (1998), 23.

[87] *Works*, 15. 307.

[88] Morrison (1998), 23, 26.

[89] Procter (1877), 211, 213–14; Robinson (1938), 1. 275–6.

[90] Morrison (1998), 1.

[91] Morrison (1998), 24, 7.

[92] Morrison (1998), 18.

[93] *Works*, 2. 79; 3. 23, 26.

[94] Ashton (1980), 16–17; Clubbe (1974), 58.

[95] Morrison (1998), 9; Hood (1821), 584, 583.

[96] Symonds (1994), 150.

[97] *Works*, 10. 262; Symonds (1994), 134.

[98] Taylor (1925), 265.

[99] Symonds (1994), 145, 135; Morrison (1998), 33.

CHAPTER NINE: En Route

[1] Jordan (1963), 327–8.

[2] CUL MS: Wordsworth Collection.

[3] BL MS: Add. 37215, ff. 10–12; Blunden (1936), 138–9; Symonds (1994), 144.

[4] Armitt (1916), 684.

[5] Symonds (1994), 143; Eaton (1936), 287.

[6] Japp (1891), 2. 125–7.

[7] Symonds (1994), 146, 143, 157.

[8] *Works*, 2. 82.

[9] *Works*, 2. 82–3; Symonds (1994), 152–3.

[10] *Works*, 2. 74.

[11] Rollins (1965), 2. 424; Wordsworth (1978), 168; Jordan (1963), 295.

[12] Symonds (1994), 155; Lamb (1935), 2. 320.

[13] Rollins (1965), 2. 426; St Clair (2004), 596; Advertisement (1823), 4.

[14] Symonds (1994), 248.

[15] Wilson (1822), 487.

[16] Symonds (1994), 153.

[17] Eaton (1936), 292; Symonds (1994), 170–1, 176.

[18] BL MS: Add. 37215, ff. 10–12.

[19] Eaton (1936), 295; Symonds (1994), 180, 176.

[20] Symonds (1994), 182.

[21] Symonds (1994), 179, 237.

[22] *Works*, 3. 48, 95, 49.

[23] *Works*, 3. 70.

[24] *Works*, 3. 70–1.

[25] Stockley (1929), 108.

[26] Rollins (1965), 2. 433, 443.

[27] Hood (1839), 558–9.

[28] Procter (1877), 213.

[29] *Works*, 15. 276.

[30] *Works*, 15. 277–8.

[31] Robinson (1938), 1. 296; *Works*, 10. 268; 15. 276.

[32] *Works*, 10. 268; Butler (1984), 209–25.

[33] *Works*, 11. 249; 5. 136.

[34] *Works*, 11. 250.

[35] Morris (1983), 208–15.

[36] Gray (1881), 261–3; Knight (1864–5), 1. 305; Clowes (1892), 157.

[37] De Quincey [?] (1823), 'The Raven', 352.

[38] De Quincey [?] (1823), 'The Black Chamber', 361.

[39] BL MS: Dep. 10568/1; Armitt (1916), 685; Symonds (1994), 193, 206.

[40] Symonds (1994), 203, 209–10.

[41] Symonds (1994), 211.

42 Wordsworth (1978), 218–19.

43 Symonds (1994), 215.

44 Carne (1885), 132–3.

45 Symonds (1994), 216–17.

46 Wilson (1823), 338.

47 Wilson and Lockhart [?] (1823), 500, 495.

48 Chilcott (1972), 151.

49 Symonds (1994), 215, 211.

50 Lamb (1935), 2. 323.

51 Mitford (1870), 1. 374.

52 *Works*, 3. 141–2.

53 *Works*, 3. 150–1.

54 *Works*, 3. 153; Lucas (1905), 2. 69.

55 Schiller (1967), 338.

56 *Works*, 4. 61.

57 Hazlitt (1823), 459; *Works*, 3. 168–74.

58 Symonds (1994), 244; *Works*, 4. 78.

59 McCulloch (1845), 33; Bailey (1825), xxiv.

60 Beddoes (1894), 24.

61 Symonds (1994), 212.

62 Symonds (1994), 264, 267.

63 Symonds (1994), 241, 239; *Works*, 14. 51.

64 Symonds (1994), 262, 264; *Works*, 3. 181.

65 Symonds (1994), 267, 271.

66 Chilcott (1972), 158, 181; Lamb (1935), 2. 385, 394–5; Robinson (1938), 1. 301.

67 Symonds (1994), 250, 248.

68 Symonds (1994), 270, 274.

69 Symonds (1994), 272, 281.

70 Symonds (1994), 282.

71 *Works*, 11. 291; Advertisement (1824), 4.

72 Forward (1937), 244–60.

73 Maginn (1824), 21–3.

74 Lockhart and Wilson (1824), 242.

75 Symonds (1994), 283; Carlyle (1970–continuing), 3. 233.

76 *Works*, 11. 294.

77 *Works*, 4. 122, 141.

78 Hill (1878), 98, 493, 57; Knight (1864–5), 1. 327.

79 Symonds (1994), 295; Knight (1864–5), 1. 272, 328–9.

80 Knight (1824), 208.

81 *Works*, 11. 273–4; Robinson and Powell (2002), 144.

82 *Works*, 4. 169, 189, 180, 174.

83 Carlyle (1970–continuing), 3. 260; 2. 437; Shepherd (1881), 2. 276.

84 Thomas (1964), 20, 23.

85 Symonds (1994), 285; *Works*, 10. 279; 4. 221.

86 *Works*, 4. 218, 259.

87 *Works*, 10. 284, 280–1; Forward (1937), 247.

88 Bridgwater (2004), 110–27.

89 *Works*, 4. 445, 269, 386, 356.

90 Hutchinson (1954), 354.

91 BL MS: Dep. 10568/1.

92 Wordsworth (1978), 318.

93 Symonds (1994), 289–90, 294, 291.

94 Symonds (1994), 285, 294, 293.

95 Taylor (1925), 265–6.

96 Symonds (1994), 300–1; Knight (1864–5), 1. 334.

97 Japp (1891), 2. 128–32.

98 Symonds (1994), 307.

99 Symonds (1994), 304.

100 Symonds (1994), 304; MacFarlane (1917), 83.

101 MacFarlane (1917), 82–3; Knight (1864–5), 1. 329–30.

102 Knight (1864–5), 1. 339–40.

103 Carlyle (1970–continuing), 3. 233; Symonds (1994), 309.

104 Jordan (1963), 331.

105 Jordan (1963), 331.

106 Symonds (1994), 310.

107 Knight (1864–5), 1. 330–1, 340; *Works*, 6. 121.

108 *Works*, 16. 311.

109 Japp (1890), 194.

110 Wordsworth (1978), 388; Hutchinson (1954), 310.

111 Japp (1890), 193–4.

112 Symonds (1994), 310, 313.

113 Symonds (1994), 310–12.

114 Symonds (1994), 310; *Works*, 2. 43.

115 Symonds (1994), 311; Clayden (1889), 432.

CHAPTER TEN: Urban Intellectual

1 Woof (1985), 97; Japp (1891), 2. 47.

2 Cranbrook (1884), 158; Berridge and Edwards (1981), 29; *Works*, 2. 245.

3 Symonds (1994), 184–5.

4 Symonds (1994), 181.

5 Symonds (1994), 320.

6 Groves (2000), 327; Moir (1955), 1. 302.

7 Symonds (1994), 321; Ashton (1980), 12.

8 Goldman (1965), 68–75; Clark (2003), 270, 262.

9 *Works*, 6. 19, 15–16; Moir (1955), 1. 314.

10 Wordsworth (1978), 492–3.

11 Gordon (1863), 327–8.

12 Gordon (1863), 328.

13 Cranbrook (1884), 158; MacFarlane (1917), 80; Fields (1894), 107.

14 *Works*, 13. 418–20; Hogg (1895), 151–2.

15 *Works*, 6. 113.

16 Morrison (2006), *On Murder*, xiv–xv.

17 Wilson (1824), 382, 377, 379; Moir (1955), 1. 332.

18 *Works*, 6. 131–2, 114.

19 *Works*, 6. 118–19, 121, 124, 127.

20 BL MS: Dep. 10568/1; Jordan (1963), 298.

21 *Works*, 5. 1–2; Groves (1998), 126–31.

22 *Works*, 5. 178.

23 *Works*, 5. 144, 170, 95, 14.

24 *Works*, 5. 278, 315; Tave (1966), 119–20.

25 Groves (1998), 127–30.

26 Symonds (1994), 339; PML MS: Misc English, MA 3007.

27 *Works*, 6. 302; Jordan (1963), 299.

28 *Works*, 17. 153; Japp (1891), 2. 57.

29 Cranbrook (1884), 158.

30 *Works*, 5. 9; Carlyle (2000), 303; Carlyle (1970–continuing), 4. 291.

31 Carlyle (1970–continuing), 4. 282–3, 291.

32 Carlyle (1970–continuing), 4. 291, 300; Carlyle (2000), 303.

33 Japp (1890), 427; *Works*, 5. 136; Hogg (1895), 187–8.

34 Carlyle (1970–continuing), 4. 341–2, 363.

35 Symonds (1994), 340; Armitt (1916), 698.

36 Symonds (1994), 339–40; Eaton (1936), 363.

37 Moir (1955), 1. 405; *Works*, 6. 279–301.

38 Groves (1998), 128–9; *Works*, 6. 219, 221.

39 Groves (1992), 42; Hill (1878), 85.

40 Warren (1854–5), 5. 497–8.

41 PC MS: Charles Agvent Collection; *Works*, 6. 163.

42 Wordsworth (1979), 17; Anonymous (1828), 969.

43 Carlyle (1970–continuing), 4. 433; Japp (1891), 2. 166.

44 PC MS: Charles Agvent Collection; Japp (1891), 2. 167–8.

45 Symonds (1994), 339; BL MS: Dep. 10568/2; Silverman (2009), [32]; Japp (1891), 2. 55, 57.

46 *Works*, 6. 260.

47 Gordon (1963), 326; *Works*, 7. 26–7.

48 Symonds (1994), 341.

49 Wordsworth (1979), 89; Wordsworth (1944), 57.

50 Symonds (1994), 337.

51 Jordan (1963), 298–301.

52 Armitt (1916), 689–92; Eaton (1936), 320–2; Lindop (1981), 290–1.

53 Symonds (1994), 340.

54 Symonds (1994), 341; Knight (1864–5), 1. 340.

55 Symonds (1994), 342; Armitt (1916), 686.

56 Wilson (1829), 861.

57 Symonds (1994), 356, 353, 382.

58 Symonds (1994), 370, 373, 372.

59 Symonds (1994), 361, 358–9.

60 Wordsworth (1979), 206; Symonds (1994), 357, 381, 380.

61 Symonds (1994), 381, 384.

62 Symonds (1994), 401, 406.

63 Gordon (1863), 234; NLS MS: 4717, ff. 26/27.

64 Wilson (1830), 'Noctes Ambrosianae. No. XLVIII', 682; Wilson (1830), 'Noctes Ambrosianae. No. XLIX', 812.

65 Wilson (1830), 'Noctes Ambrosianae. No. XLIX', 812; Wilson (1830), 'Noctes Ambrosianae. No. XLVIII', 667, 661.

66 Wilson (1830), 'Noctes Ambrosianae. No. XLVIII', 693.

67 Symonds (1994), 386, 385; *Works*, 7. 51, 65.

[68] *Works*, 7. 302; Wellek (1931), 173.

[69] *Works*, 7. 161.

[70] Symonds (1994), 394.

[71] Goldman (1965), 32; *Works*, 7. 317, 157, 159.

[72] Forward (1937), 252; Moir (1955), 2. 541.

[73] Derry (1966), xi, 78; Symonds (1994), 400.

[74] Symonds (1994), 409–10, 404.

[75] Eaton (1936), 335; Symonds (1994), 390–2, 397.

[76] Symonds (1994), 398.

[77] Japp (1890), 460–1, 278.

[78] Forward (1939), 517; Symonds (1994), 399, 419.

[79] Japp (1890), 281; Symonds (1994), 418–19.

[80] Eaton (1936), 370.

[81] BPL MS: Acc. 28; Eaton (1936), 340–1, 519.

[82] NLS MS: 4717, f. 23; NLS MS: 4717, ff. 46/47.

[83] *Works*, 8. 101; Symonds (1994), 422.

[84] Symonds (1994), 423.

[85] *Works*, 12. 15; Armitt (1916), 700; BLO MS: Eng. Lett. E. 28, ff. 95/6.

[86] NLS MS: 4035, ff. 178/179; Eaton (1936), 341; Symonds (1994), 439.

[87] Forward (1939), 519; Symonds (1994), 439.

[88] Espinasse (1877), 446; Symonds (1994), 432.

[89] Symonds (1994), 432, 441.

[90] Eaton (1936), 519; Symonds (1994), 454, 460.

[91] Eaton (1936), 519.

[92] Forward (1939), 515–16; Symonds (1994), 462, 465.

[93] Symonds (1994), 457–8.

[94] Symonds (1994), 459; Eaton (1936), 346; BL MS: 10568/3.

[95] Symonds (1994), 432; Knight (1864–5), 2. 248.

[96] Symonds (1994), 427.

[97] Jonathan Wordsworth (1993), 233.

[98] Robinson (1938), 2. 482; Coleridge (1956–71), 6. 911.

[99] *Works*, 9. 135, 450.

[100] *Works*, 9. 4, 63.

[101] NLS MS: 4717, ff. 5/6.

CHAPTER ELEVEN: Tales of Terror

[1] NLS MS: 4060, f. 248; NLS MS: 4060, f. 232.

[2] Eaton (1936), 405, 418–19, 286; Symonds (1994), 274.

[3] Knight (1864–5), 1. 329; Hill (1878), 494.

[4] Priestley (1908), 56; Hogg (1895), 256.

[5] BL MS: Dep. 10568/2; Jordan (1963), 36.

[6] *Works*, 2. 65; 10. 109; Eaton (1936), 374.

[7] Japp (1890), 430; *Works*, 10. 262; Eaton (1936), 374.

[8] *Works*, 15. 184–5.

[9] Japp (1890), 460; *Works*, 11. 261; Sedgwick (1986), 37–96.

[10] *Works*, 11. 110; McDonagh (1994), 180; Milligan (1995), 68.

[11] *Works*, 11. 369.

[12] Eaton (1936), 519–20; *Works*, 9. 209.

[13] NLS MS: 1670, ff. 35/36.

[14] NLS MS: 1670, ff. 35/36; BL MS: Add. 37215, ff. 10–12.

[15] Carlyle (1970–continuing), 6. 371.

[16] Jordan (1963), 302; Robinson (1922), 60.

[17] NLS MS: 4035, ff. 176/177; BPL MS: Acc. 28.

[18] NLS MS: 4717, ff. 13/14; Eaton (1936), 519; Gray (1926), 181–4.

[19] BC MS: De Quincey MS (H).

[20] Carlyle (1970–continuing), 6. 348.

[21] Forward (1939), 518–19.

[22] Forward (1939), 522–3.

[23] BC MS: De Quincey MS (H).

[24] BC MS: De Quincey MS (H).

[25] Armitt (1916), 704; BC MS: De Quincey MS (H); Eaton (1936), 322.

[26] Robinson (1922), 58.

[27] Japp (1890), 144.

[28] DCL MS: WLMS A / De Quincey, Thomas / 1 / 58 /.

[29] Catford (1975), 102; Woof (1985), 109; BC MS: De Quincey MS (H).

[30] Eaton (1936), 519.

[31] Halkerston (1831), 1–66.

32 NLS MS: 4717, ff. 15/16; RUL MS: De Quincey Collection.

33 NLS MS: Acc. 12725.

34 Scott (1892), 1. 98.

35 Gray (1926), 182; NLS MS: 4717, ff. 15/16; *Works*, 10. 367; Eaton (1936), 374; Jong (2009), 55.

36 NLS MS: 972, f. 47; Eaton (1936), 519.

37 Eaton (1936), 374, 519; NLS MS: 972, f. 47; Lindop (1981), 311.

38 *Works*, 10. 367; Japp (1890), 460.

39 Thin (1905), 33; Symonds (1994), 438.

40 *Works*, 11. 585–6.

41 Tait (1832), 64; Tait (1833), ix.

42 Easley (2005), 263–79; Weinstein (1983), 401–5; Bertram (1893), 30.

43 *Works*, 20. 11; Japp (1891), 2. 174.

44 DWL MS: Thomas Robinson to Henry Crabb Robinson, 21 November 1834, f. 67.

45 Bertram (1893), 35–6; NLS MS: 4035, ff. 176/177.

46 NLS MS: 4717, ff. 13/14.

47 *Works*, 9. 337; 11. 584.

48 Barrell (1991); Kebbel (1861), 32.

49 *Works*, 7. 219; 9. 384.

50 *Works*, 8. 111–12; 10. 194.

51 *Works*, 8. 107; 10. 340–1.

52 *Works*, 7. 161; 11. 194; 10. 343.

53 *Works*, 10. 212.

54 *Works*, 11. 205; 10. 205; 11. 257.

55 *Works*, 10. 21, 262.

56 *Works*, 10. 338.

57 *Works*, 10. 338, 287.

58 Emerson (1960–82), 5. 59; Roberts (2000), 12.

59 Hare (1835), 25; Robinson (1938), 1. 451.

60 Coleridge (1990), 2. 28, 18; Carlyle (2000), 391.

61 Carlyle (2000), 391; Wordsworth (1979), 740.

62 Coleridge (1847), 2. 772.

63 Parsons (1934), 193.

64 Balfour (1835), 319–21.

65 Parsons (1934), 193–4.

66 Balfour (1835), 323.

67 Balfour (1835), 323–4.

68 *Works*, 15. 146; Balfour (1835), 325.

69 *Works*, 20. 269.

70 Woof (1985), 99.

71 Woof (1985), 97–8.

72 Woof (1985), 98–9; Armitt (1916), 677.

73 *Works*, 20. 269–70.

74 Eaton (1936), 519; *Works*, 10. 367.

75 NLS MS: 1670, f. 13; BC MS: De Quincey MS (H).

76 BC MS: De Quincey MS (H).

77 BLO MS: Eng lett c. 461, ff. 90/91.

78 *Works*, 11. 177, 182; BLO MS: Eng lett c. 461, f. 90.

79 Japp (1891), 2. 171.

80 HL MS: HM 37740; Wordsworth (1958), 226.

81 Wordsworth (1958), 226; Eaton (1936), 519; Forward (1939), 522–3; BL MS: Dep. 10568/2.

82 Eaton (1936), 365, 367.

83 NLS MS: 1670, f. 21; *Works*, 9. 381, 395.

84 *Works*, 9. 390, 404, 407, 402.

85 *Works*, 9. 475–513.

86 Eaton (1936), 367–8; *Works*, 14. 71.

87 Japp (1891), 2. 177–8.

88 Eaton (1936), 519.

89 Japp (1890), 279; Catford (1975), 102.

90 *Works*, 10. 366–7.

91 *Works*, 10. 195; Shepherd (1837), 340; Johnstone (1837), 337–8.

92 Symonds (1994), 358.

93 *Works*, 9. 204.

94 Eaton (1936), 368, 519; HLH MS: bMS Eng 1009/64.

95 Eaton (1936), 519–20; HLH MS: bMS Eng 1009/64.

96 ESDL MS: De Quincey collection.

97 DCL MS: 1989.161.59; ESDL MS: De Quincey collection.

98 Japp (1980), 219; Bertram (1893), 70.

99 *Works*, 11. 94, 135.

100 *Works*, 15. 577, 579; 11. 94–5.

101 *Works*, 11. 192–3; 20. 269.

102 *Works*, 11. 135, 64, 590.

103 Owen (1990), 72–6.

104 *Works*, 9. 210, 212, 218, 229.

105 *Works*, 9. 232, 245, 259, 214, 263.
106 Leighton (1992), 170–1.
107 Eaton (1936), 519–20; DCL MS: 1989.161.59.
108 NLS MS: 1670, f. 35; Eaton (1936), 483–4; GROS MS: Census 1841 685/02 059/02 015.
109 Eaton (1936) 378.
110 Japp (1890), 249.
111 DCL MS: 1989.161.59; NLS MS: 4717, f. 36; Eaton (1936), 483–4.
112 *Works*, 17. 84; Eaton (1936), 375.
113 Moore (1933), 176.
114 BLYU MS: Osborn Manuscript Files: 'D', 4331.
115 NLS MS: 1670, f. 32.
116 NLS MS: 4717, ff. 18/19.
117 Brockway and Winer (1950), 351; Eaton (1936), 375.
118 Bertram (1893), 63, 62.
119 Bertram (1893), 72, 71.
120 NLS MS: 972. f. 47; Brockway and Winer (1950), 352.
121 NLS MS: 1670, ff. 23/24; NLS MS: 4046, ff. 144/145; DCL MS: 1989.161.28.
122 NLS MS: 1670, f. 31; NLS MS 1670, f. 32.
123 NLS MS: MS 1670, f. 33.
124 Eaton (1936), 520; NLS MS: 4046, f. 141.
125 Brockway and Winer (1950), 351–3; Eaton (1936), 377.
126 Eaton (1936), 520; BLYU MS: Osborn Manuscript Files: 'D', 4331.
127 *Works*, 10. 377–8.
128 NLS MS: 1670, f. 34; BLYU MS: Osborn Manuscript Files: 'D', 4331.
129 Bertram (1893), 75; BLYU MS: Osborn Manuscript Files: 'D', 4331.
130 NLS MS: 1670, f. 36; BLYU MS: Osborn Manuscript Files: 'D', 4331.
131 NLS MS: 1670, f. 51; DCL MS: 1989.161.59.
132 DCL MS: 1989.161.59; *Works*, 2. 250.
133 NLS MS: 21240, ff. 157/158.
134 *Works*, 13. 273, 238.
135 Willmott [?] (1841), 49.
136 NLS MS: 3112, ff. 287/288; PCSC MS: Misc MS 104.
137 NLS MS: 1670, ff. 74/75; *Works*, 21. 147.
138 Bertram (1893), 69–70.
139 *Works*, 11. 108; Wilson (2008), 246–7.
140 *Works*, 11. 73, 79, 85.
141 Wells (1941), 1–24; *Works*, 11. 42–3; Emerson (1960–82), 10. 220, 535.
142 *Works*, 11. 256.
143 *Works*, 11. 71, 64, 61–3.
144 *Works*, 11. 118.
145 *Works*, 11. 60, 52, 56, 55.
146 NLS MS: 1670, f. 57; Jordan (1963), 349.
147 PCSC MS: Misc MS 104.
148 FitzGerald (1980), 1. 236.
149 MacFarlane (1917), 82; Martineau (1969), 98, 100; Jordan (1963), 347.
150 Robinson (1922), 59; Robinson (1938), 1. 273.
151 *Works*, 11. 219, 253, 256, 181.
152 NLS MS: 1670, ff. 83/84.
153 NLS MS: 4051, f. 111.
154 NLS MS: 4937, ff. 39/40.
155 NLS MS: 4048, ff 224/225; NLS MS: 30007.
156 NLS MS: 30007; NLS MS: 4051, f. 175.
157 NLS MS: 30007.
158 *Works*, 9. 264–5.
159 *Works*, 9. 275, 278, 298; Morrison (2001), 424–41.
160 NLS MS: 21240, ff. 157/158.
161 Gray (1926), 183; NLS MS: 1670, f. 19; NLS MS: 4048, f. 219.
162 NLS MS: 4048, f. 219.
163 *Works*, 11. 339, 502.
164 NLS MS: 4049, ff. 308/309; NLS MS: 4729, ff. 95/96.
165 *Works*, 11. 493, 438–41; 12. 73.
166 *Works*, 20. 285.
167 *Works*, 12. 132.
168 *Works*, 11. 400.
169 Japp (1890), 281; Eaton (1936), 467.
170 Japp (1890), 281.
171 Eaton (1936), 520, 384–5; Brown (1889), 33–5.
172 Gray (1926), 183; Priestley (1908), 58.

173 Watson and Watson (1892), 62–3; Japp (1980), 432–3.

174 Willmott [?] (1841), 49; Hogg (1895), 55; Hill (1896), 99–100.

175 NLS MS: 4051, ff. 122/23; NLS MS: 4051, f. 175.

176 NLS MS: 4048, ff. 240/241; NLS MS: 4051, f. 110; NLS MS: 4051, f. 111.

177 NLS MS: 4051, ff. 137/138.

178 Priestley (1908), 57; NLS MS: 21240, ff. 157/158; BLYU MS: Osborn Manuscript Files: 'D', 4331.

179 BLYU MS: Osborn Manuscript Files: 'D', 4331; NLS MS: 1670, ff. 69/70; NLS MS: 4048, f. 236.

180 Eaton (1936), 520.

181 NLS MS: 4051, ff. 128/129.

182 BLYU MS: Osborn Manuscript Files: 'D', 4331; NLS MS: 4048, ff. 224/225; EUL MS: DC.4. 102; De Quincey (1937), 44; NLS MS: 4048, f. 243.

183 NLS MS: 4051, ff. 108/109; NLS MS: 4051, f. 114; NLS MS: 4051, ff. 122/123; NLS MS: 4051, f. 161; NLS MS: 4051, f. 175.

184 NLS MS: 4055, ff. 141/142.

185 NLS MS: 4055, f. 147; Works, 10. 377.

186 Nisbet (1860), 37; Symonds (1994), 364.

187 NLS MS: 4048, f. 243; NLS MS: 4048, ff. 224/225.

188 NLS MS: 4052, ff. 48/49; Priestley (1908), 60.

189 Fairbrother (1915), 273.

190 NLS MS: 4048, ff. 220/221; Japp (1890), 511; Eaton (1936), 408, 410.

191 Eaton (1936), 368; NLS MS: 4051, f. 144.

192 NLS MS: 4051, f. 145; Eaton (1936), 375.

193 NLS MS: 4052, ff. 48/49.

194 NLS MS: 4051, f. 119; NLS MS: 4051, ff. 124/125.

195 NLS MS: 4051, ff. 172/173; NLS MS: 4055, f. 147.

196 Works, 20. 409; NLS MS: 4051, ff. 172/173.

197 NLS MS: 4055, f. 146; NLS MS: 4055, f. 147.

198 Eaton (1936), 520; NLS MS: 4055, f. 147.

CHAPTER TWELVE: Lasswade

1 Woof (1985), 99.

2 Sawyer (1969), 403–8.

3 Prod'homme (1946), 98–106.

4 Simmons (1931), 445–50.

5 Emerson (1971–continuing), 5. 1.

6 Colton (1836), 421.

7 Poe (1969–78), 2. 339.

8 Hayter (1968), 136; Snyder (1984), 103–10.

9 Blair (1842), 50.

10 Gerin (1961), 159–74.

11 Brontë (1997–9), 3. 290; Gerin (1961), 278–301; Gaskell (2005–6), 8. 181.

12 Mackay (1887), 171; Works, 15. 394, 411.

13 NLS MS: 4055, f. 149.

14 NLS MS: 4055, f. 149.

15 Woof (1985), 110–11.

16 Eaton (1936), 397; NLS MS: 4055, f. 153.

17 NLS MS: 4055, f. 154; NLS MS: 4055, ff. 156/157.

18 NLS MS: 4055, ff. 156/157; Works, 12. 283.

19 NLS MS: 4055, ff. 156/157; NLS MS: 4060, f. 272.

20 Gilfillan (1881), 32.

21 Fairbrother (1915), 273–4.

22 NLS MS: 4055, f. 175; NLS MS: 4055, f. 161; BL MS: Dep. 10568/2.

23 NLS MS: 4055, f. 140; NLS MS: 4055, f. 148.

24 NLS MS: 4055, ff. 173/174.

25 Emerson (1960–82), 10. 537.

26 Mackay (1877), 324; Japp (1890), 281; Emerson (1960–82), 10. 537.

27 Works, 12. 299, 306.

28 Eaton (1936), 411; NLS MS: 4055, f. 160.

29 NLS MS: 4055, f. 191; Hogg (1895), 70.

30 Works, 13. 79–81.

31 NLS MS: 4060, f. 225.

32 NLS MS: 4060, f. 228; NLS MS: 4060, f. 229.

33 NLS MS: 4060, f. 243.

34 NLS MS: 4060, f. 232; NLS MS: 4060, f. 229.

[35] NLS MS: 4060, f. 243; NLS MS: 4060, f. 244.

[36] NLS MS: 4060, ff. 256/257.

[37] NLS MS: 4060, f. 236; NLS MS: 4060, f. 243.

[38] NLS MS: 21239, f. 3.

[39] NLS MS: 4060, f. 245; NLS MS: 4060, f. 246; NLS MS: 4060, f. 243.

[40] NLS MS: 4060, f. 247.

[41] *Works*, 13. 139, 142, 156.

[42] *Works*, 14. 5, 20; NLS MS: 4060, ff. 262/263.

[43] *Works*, 14. 187, 65.

[44] NLS MS: 4048, ff. 208/209.

[45] Fairbrother (1915), 273; Japp (1890), 511.

[46] NLS MS: 4065, ff. 162/163.

[47] NLS MS: 4065, ff. 11/12.

[48] Cranbrook (1884), 158.

[49] NLS MS: 4065, f. 170; NLS MS: 4065, f. 171.

[50] NLS MS: 4065, ff. 172/173; NLS MS: 4065, f. 177.

[51] Knight (1864–5), 2. 306; Hogg (1895), 61.

[52] NLS MS: 4065, ff. 176/177.

[53] NLS MS: 4060, ff. 260/261.

[54] NLS MS: 4065, ff. 179/180.

[55] Japp, (1890), 246.

[56] Eaton (1936), 455; Hogg (1895), 229; Japp (1890), 282.

[57] Japp, (1890), 279.

[58] *Works*, 15. 252–3.

[59] NLS MS: 4065, f. 196; NLS MS: 4065, ff. 184/185.

[60] Japp, (1890), 243; *Works*, 15. 252.

[61] NLS MS: 4065, ff. 197/198.

[62] NLS MS: 4070, ff. 211/212; NLS MS: 4065, ff. 202/203.

[63] NLS MS: 5509, ff. 113/114.

[64] NLS MS: 4065, ff. 186/187; NLS MS: 4065, ff. 197/198.

[65] NLS MS: 4070, ff. 196/197; TCLC MS: Cullum M. 46, item 1.

[66] Fairbrother (1915), 273–5.

[67] NLS MS: 4717, f. 53.

[68] Woof (1985), 100–1.

[69] NLS MS: 4070, f. 195; NLS MS: 4070, ff. 207/208.

[70] Japp (1890), 247.

[71] UKL MS: W. Hugh Peal Collection.

[72] DCL MS: 2002.1.7.

[73] Eaton (1936), 420.

[74] *Works*, 14. 189.

[75] Carlyle (1896–9), 20. 44, 151; *Works*, 14. 220, 229, 203–4, 278.

[76] *Works*, 14. 298, 304, 283.

[77] Mill (1963–91), 4. 401, 404.

[78] Murray (1970), 7–12; Mill (1963–91), 3. 456–7, 462–4, 466, 468, 474.

[79] Marx (1974), 420.

[80] *Works*, 14. 174, 160, 170, 162, 156.

[81] *Works*, 15. 30.

[82] *Works*, 14. 138.

[83] *Works*, 14. 136, 182; 15. 207.

[84] *Works*, 15. 114; NLS MS: 4073, ff. 145/146.

[85] NLS MS: 4074, ff. 181/182.

[86] NLS MS: 4068, ff. 232/233; NLS MS: 4073, ff. 149/150; NLS MS: 4074, ff. 179/180.

[87] NLS MS: 4073, ff. 145/146; Gilfillan (1845), 154–5.

[88] Masson (1865), 89; Gilfillan (1845), 154–5.

[89] Japp (1890), 242–3.

[90] Japp (1890), 242–4.

[91] NLS MS: 4070, ff. 205/206.

[92] Japp (1890), 245.

[93] Japp (1890), 244–5.

[94] Japp (1890), 245, 241–2.

[95] *Works*, 15. 121, 124.

[96] *Works*, 15. 580, 584.

[97] NLS MS: 5509, ff. 113/114.

[98] NLS MS: 10998, ff. 142/143; HLH MS: bMS Am 1631 (107).

[99] NLS MS: 10998, ff. 142/143.

[100] *Works*, 15. 130–1.

[101] Ford (2007), 229–49.

[102] *Works*, 15. 131–3.

[103] *Works*, 15. 187–8.

[104] *Works*, 15. 179–82; Barrett Browning (1984–continuing), 10. 125.

[105] Eaton (1936), 421.

[106] Eaton (1936), 422, 520.

[107] Oliphant (1877), 739–40.

[108] NLS MS: 10998, ff. 140/141.

[109] NLS MS: 4074, ff. 181/182; NLS MS: 4074, f. 184.

[110] NLS MS: 4074, ff. 187/188; NLS MS: 4074, ff. 185/186.

[111] *Works*, 15. 607, 567, 579–81.

[112] Finkelstein (2002), 10–11; NLS MS: 4074, ff. 189/190.

[113] NLS MS: 4073, ff. 216/217.

[114] NLS MS: 4073, ff. 224/225; NLS MS: 10998, ff. 142/143.

[115] *Works*, 15. 236, 237.

[116] *Works*, 15. 262–3, 272–3.

[117] Webb (1977), 20–1; *Works*, 15. 284.

[118] *Works*, 15. 378, 363–4, 234–5.

[119] *Works*, 15. 411.

[120] Mackay (1887), 175; Mackay (1877), 324; Hogg (1895), 117.

[121] *Works*, 15. 245, 246, 251; Hopkins (1937), 40.

[122] Mackay (1877), 314; Japp (1890), 244.

[123] HRC MS: Drake MS.

[124] *Works*, 15. 328–9; Martin (1900), 155.

[125] De Quincey (1937) American Art Association, Jan. 13–14, 1937; cat. 4289, lot 152.

[126] NLS MS: 4055, f. 175.

[127] De Quincey (1937) American Art Association, Jan. 13–14, 1937; cat. 4289, lot 152.

[128] Eaton (1936), 429–30; Woof (1985), 97.

[129] DCL MS: 1989: L332; Lonsdale (1868), 1. 118–21.

[130] BLO MS: Autogr. B.3, f. 45b.

[131] Japp (1890), 252; Eaton (1936), 441.

[132] NLS MS: 1670, f. 98; NLS MS: 1670, ff. 96/97.

[133] Mackay (1877), 317.

[134] Mackay (1877), 316; Japp (1890), 251.

[135] Barrell (1991), 106–13; *Works*, 15. 404–5.

[136] Smith (1993), 205; *Works*, 15. 400–1, 403.

CHAPTER THIRTEEN: The End of Night

[1] *Works*, 15. 316; 20. 387.

[2] *Works*, 3. 22; 16. 316; Japp (1890), 266.

[3] *Works*, 15. 527; 18. 4–5; 16. 16–17.

[4] Troup (1881), 40.

[5] Hogg (1895), 111–12.

[6] Japp (1890), 274; Kilpatrick (1898), 217.

[7] Hogg (1895), 114, 116; Japp (1890), 275.

[8] Hogg (1895), 113, 119; Eaton (1936), 433–4.

[9] Watson and Watson (1892), 120.

[10] Eaton (1936), 434; Japp (1890), 258.

[11] Troup (1881), 14.

[12] PCSC MS: Misc. MS 1782.

[13] Brown (1889), 118.

[14] Mackay (1877), 315, 324–5.

[15] Hogg (1895), 116, 113, 117, 118.

[16] BLO MS: Eng. Lett. E.28, ff. 95/96.

[17] Japp (1890), 263, 266.

[18] Brontë (1995–2004), 1. 529–30; Japp (1890), 439–40.

[19] Japp (1890), 260–1.

[20] LRO MS: 920 MD 424.

[21] Japp (1890), 266; *Works*, 16. 169.

[22] *Works*, 16. 48, 6; Japp (1890), 262.

[23] Anonymous (1854), 398; Morrison (2001), 426–7.

[24] Japp (1890), 266; Leighton (1992), 172.

[25] *Works*, 16. 258, 256; Newman (1970), 54.

[26] Hogg (1895), 114–15; Troup (1881), 14.

[27] Japp (1891), 2. 180–1; *Works*, 16. 246.

[28] Japp (1891), 2. 180–1; Hogg (1895), 121.

[29] *Works*, 16. 506, 503.

[30] De Quincey (1922), 123; Dickens (1965–2002), 5. 216.

[31] Herbert (1974), 247; Japp (1890), 265.

[32] Landreth (1894), 481, 489.

[33] Emerson (1960–82), 10. 220–1, 534–7.

[34] Emerson (1939), 4. 22; Japp (1890), 310; Landreth (1894), 491.

[35] HLH MS: bMS Am 1280. 226 (3340); *Works*, 16. 511–13.

[36] Japp (1890), 310.

[37] Emerson (1939), 4. 19; Scott (1850), 320–1.

[38] Emerson (1960–82), 10. 536, 534.

[39] Landreth (1894), 486–7; *Works*, 16. 268, 286, 279.

[40] *Works*, 16. 291–7.

[41] *Works*, 16. 307–9; 19. 170.

[42] *Works*, 16. 317–18.

[43] *Works*, 16. 359; Bate (1993), 149.

[44] *Works*, 16. 337; Jordan (1952), 38.

[45] *Works*, 16. 391, 370.

[46] NLS MS: 21239, ff. 6/7; *Works*, 20. 363, 268.

[47] BL MS: Dep. 10568/1; Silverman (2009), [33]; Lindop (1981), 380; Hopkins (1937), 40.

[48] Jong (2009), 41.

[49] Japp (1890), 282–3; BL MS: Dep. 10568/3; BL MS: Dep. 10568/2.

[50] NLS MS: 21239, ff. 6/7; Jordan (1963), 333.

[51] *Works*, 20. 78; Japp (1890), 270–1.

[52] Japp (1890), 271.

[53] Eaton (1936), 520; NLS MS: 30315, ff. 190 a–c.

[54] *Works*, 21. 43, 58; NLS MS: 30315, ff. 226/227.

[55] *Works*, 16. 401–3; 20. 34, 317–20.

[56] *Works*, 16. 421.

[57] *Works*, 16. 432–3; Maniquis (1976), 70.

[58] *Works*, 16. 421, 419, 422–3.

[59] Lindop (1995), 'De Quincey and the Cursed Crocodile', 136–9.

[60] *Works*, 16. 422.

[61] Hopkins (1967), 147; *Works*, 16. 417.

[62] Maniquis (1976), 68.

[63] *Works*, 16. 446; Hopkins (1967), 147–8.

[64] *Works*, 16. 448–9.

[65] Tredrey (1954), 236.

[66] *Works*, 16. 406; Rockwell (1954), 161–8; Cohen (1983), 19–20.

[67] Tryon (1963), 130; Gilfillan (1857), 2. 161–2.

[68] Tryon (1963), 302–7; Mitford (1870), 2. 310.

[69] Tryon (1963), 131–2, 157; Fields (1881), 48.

[70] *Works*, 17. 3–4.

[71] *Works*, 17. 27, 151, 23, 174–5.

[72] Houghton (1966–89), 4. 481–2.

[73] *Works*, 17. 197, 357, 220, 211.

[74] Eaton (1936), 440.

[75] Eaton (1936), 459; GROS MS: 30/03/1851 De Quincey, Thomas (Census 1851 691/00 004/00 029).

[76] Eaton (1936), 459–60.

[77] GROS MS: 30/03/1851 De Quincey, Thomas (Census 1851 691/00 004/00 029); Japp (1890), 246.

[78] Japp (1890), 255–6.

[79] DCL MS: 1989.161.57.

[80] Calkins (1871), 91; Bertram (1893), 77.

[81] Saville (1971), 327; Hogg (1895), 230.

[82] Japp (1890), 319, 336.

[83] Hogg (1895), 251, 253, 260.

[84] Hogg (1895), 128, 130–4.

[85] Hogg (1895), 226–7.

[86] Hogg (1895), 221–32.

[87] Hogg (1895), 233–4.

[88] Fields (1894), 111–12; Chavkin and Oehlschlaeger (1978), 131.

[89] Chavkin and Oehlschlaeger (1978), 131–2.

[90] Chavkin and Oehlschlaeger (1978), 132; Fields (1894), 114, 112.

[91] Silverman (2009), [30–1]; Fields (1894), 115, 117; Chavkin and Oehlschlaeger (1978), 132.

CHAPTER FOURTEEN: Recollected

[1] *Works*, 20. 129.

[2] *Works*, 20. 4–5.

[3] Japp (1890), 331.

[4] Eaton (1936), 473.

[5] DCL MS: 1986.3.2; *Works*, 18. 196.

[6] Eaton (1936), 477; *Works*, 20. 10–11.

[7] *Works*, 20. 12, 13, 16.

[8] *Works*, 19. 206.

[9] UIL MS: MsL D426.

[10] Lewes (1853), 571; Eliot (1954–78), 2. 111.

[11] Mitford (1870), 2. 342.

[12] Bright (1854), 520.

[13] Fields (1884), 62; Hawthorne (1962–97), 17. 198.

[14] Japp (1891), 2. 187; *Works*, 21. 148.

[15] *Works*, 20. 47, 51.

[16] *Works*, 15. 122.

[17] BL MS: Dep. 10568/2; Hodgson (1881), 7, 30, 61; Japp (1891), 2. 83.

[18] Hogg (1895) 172; *Works*, 17. 172; Japp (1891), 2. 190–2; *Works*, 7. 393; PUL MS: Rtcol 6/7.

[19] Japp (1890), 328.

[20] L'Estrange (1882), 115; Hogg (1895), 235–7; Fields (1884), 337.

[21] Eaton (1936), 464, 466; Japp (1890), 293.

[22] Japp (1890), 360; BL MS: Dep. 10568/2.

[23] GROS MS: 13/12/1853 De Quincey, Margaret Thomasiana (O.P.R. Marriages 676/ 0030 0391 Cockpen); BL MS: Dep. 10568/3.

[24] BL MS: Dep. 10568/2; Bonner (1936), 30.

[25] Japp (1890), 362.

[26] Hawthorne (1962–97), 17. 296; Hogg (1895), 139.

[27] Masson (1881), 117.

[28] Japp (1890), 373; Bonner (1936), 66; DCL MS: 2004.88.12.

[29] Hogg (1895), 147; Japp (1890), 368.

[30] Japp (1890), 430, 420.

[31] Priestley (1908), 58; Hogg (1895), 252.

[32] Watson and Watson (1892), 206; Hogg (1895), 151; Gilfillan (1881), 34.

[33] Hogg (1895), 157, 146, 129, 145.

[34] Hogg (1895), 141, 143, 146.

[35] Japp (1890), 368; Eaton (1936), 378; Japp (1877), 2. 269.

[36] Japp (1877), 2. 269; Japp (1890), 325.

[37] Bonner (1936), 72–3; BL MS: Dep. 10568/2; Japp (1890), 324.

[38] Eaton (1936), 391; Japp (1890), 326–7.

[39] DCL MS: 2004.88.7.

[40] Japp (1890), 359, 376; BL MS: Dep. 10568/3; Hogg (1895), 155.

[41] PUL MS: Rtcol 6/7.

[42] Hogg (1890), 456; Lindop (1981), 380; PUL MS: Rtcol 6/7.

[43] Bonner (1936), 33, 31; Japp (1890), 386; Lindop (1981), 385.

[44] Barrell (1991), 188–9; Bonner (1936), 39; BL MS: Dep. 10568/1.

[45] Bonner (1936), 31–2; BL MS: Dep. 10568/1; Vetch, rev. Stearn, 'Smith' (2004), 51. 279.

[46] Japp (1890), 372–3, 375; Hogg (1895), 156.

[47] Japp (1890), 375; Eaton (1936), 454; Hogg (1895), 157.

[48] Japp (1890), 334, 383, 286.

[49] NLS MS: 21239, ff. 11/13.

[50] Sellar (1907), 71; TRC MS: Letter 2484.

[51] *Works*, 2. 93; BL MS: Dep. 10568/1; Bonner (1936), 30; Eaton (1936), 495.

[52] Woof (1985), 106.

[53] Bonner (1936), 65–7, 70, 75, 68.

[54] Bonner (1936), 73, 69.

[55] *Works*, 2. 100.

[56] *Works*, 2. 100; Japp (1890), 387–8.

[57] *Works*, 2. 136, 96.

[58] *Works*, 2. 253, 182, 107, 101–2.

[59] *Works*, 2. 244.

[60] *Works*, 2. 252.

[61] *Works*, 2. 246, 251, 99.

[62] *Works*, 2. 98. 242.

[63] Bonner (1936), 68, 75; Hogg (1895), 154, 183–4.

[64] Hogg (1895), 158–9, 194.

[65] HLH MS: bMS Eng 1009 (143).

[66] Silverman (2009), [28]; BL MS: Dep. 10568/1; Japp (1890), 429.

[67] BC MS: De Quincey Manuscript; BC MS: De Quincey Manuscript (Y).

[68] Japp (1890), 329, 393.

[69] Japp (1890), 411, 410.

[70] *Works*, 18. 93.

[71] *Works*, 18. 111, 141, 136; Roberts (2008), 37.

[72] Japp (1890), 407.

[73] Sellar (1907), 71; Bonner (1936), 39.

[74] DCL MS: WLMS A / De Quincey, Thomas / 2 / 18.

[75] Japp (1890), 409.

[76] *Works*, 18. 162.

[77] *Works*, 18. 164, 186, 180, 178, 176, 169, 165.

[78] *Works*, 18. 182, 172.

[79] Japp (1890), 408.

[80] HLH MS: bMS Eng 1009 (5); Eaton (1936), 478.

[81] Bonner (1936), 83, 95; MPL MS: De Quincey Collection, BR Box 349/351 (6).

[82] Hogg (1895), 162.

83 Hogg (1895), 160, 175; Japp (1890), 351; MPL MS: De Quincey Collection, BR Box 349/351 (5); Bonner (1936), 39.
84 Lindop (1981), 383–4; Bonner (1936), 41.
85 Bonner (1936), 39.
86 Bonner (1936), 91–2, 101, 39; Eaton (1936), 500.
87 PC MS: Frederick Burwick Collection; Symonds (1994), 226; BL MS: Dep. 10568/2; BL MS: Dep. 10568/3; Silverman (2009), [37–8].
88 Works, 18. 53; Japp (1890), 333–4.
89 Hogg (1895), 178, 185, 188, 198, 178–9, 174.
90 Hogg (1895), 176.
91 Eaton (1936), 477; Bonner (1936), 100–1.
92 Japp (1890), 447, 443–5.
93 Japp (1890), 445, 448–9; Eaton (1936), 507.
94 Bonner (1936), 42.
95 TRC MS: Letter 2527.
96 Bonner (1936), 42–4.
97 Bonner (1936), 43; Japp (1890), 447.

98 Japp (1890), 450–1; Bonner (1936), 43–4; Works, 15. 145, 585.
99 Hogg (1895), 163; Bonner (1936), 44.
100 GROS MS: 1859 De Quincey, Thomas (Statutory Deaths 685/04 0588); Japp (1890), 447; Lindop (1981), 387.
101 Works, 2. 86–7; BL MS: Dep. 10568/1.
102 Anonymous, The Athenaeum (1859), 814; Anonymous, The Scotsman (1859), 6; Anonymous, The Times (1859), 6.
103 NAS MS: SC70 / 1 / 103; Eaton (1936), 509.
104 Nisbet (1860), 36–48; Eaton (1936), 477.
105 Japp (1891), 2. 239, 241; McFarland (1987), 95.

EPILOGUE

Works, 10. 29; MacFarlane (1917), 81–2; Gordon (1863), 326; Woolf (1986–continuing), 4. 367; Chesterton (1913), 24–5; Burroughs (2001), 507; Borges (1974), 38.

Bibliography

1775   Quincey, Thomas, *A Short Tour in the Midland Counties of England*, London: Printed by M. Lewis, for the Author.

1802   Jeffrey, Francis, '*Thalaba, the Destroyer: A Metrical Romance*, by Robert Southey', *Edinburgh Review*, 1. 63–83.

1820   Wilson, John, 'An Hour's Tete-a-Tete with the Public', *Blackwood's Magazine*. 8. 78–105.

Scott, John, 'Preface and Prospectus of the London Magazine', *London Magazine*, 1. iii–viii.

Scott, John, 'Lord Byron: His French Critics: The Newspapers; and The Magazines', *London Magazine*, 1. 492–7.

Scott, John, '*Blackwood's Magazine*', *London Magazine*, 2. 509–21.

1821   Hood, Thomas, 'The Lion's Head', *London Magazine*, 4. 583–4.

1822   Anonymous, '*Confessions of an English Opium Eater*', *The Album*, 2. 177–207.

Anonymous, 'Review of Christen on the Nature of Opium', *Medical Intelligencer*, 3. 287–90.

Maginn, William, 'Noctes Ambrosianae. No. IV', *Blackwood's Magazine*, 12. 100–14.

Wilson, John, 'Noctes Ambrosianae. No. II', *Blackwood's Magazine*, 11. 475–89.

1823   Advertisement, 'This day is published', *The Times*, 24 December, page 4, column 2.

Anonymous, *Advice to Opium Eaters*, London: Goodluck.

Anonymous, '*Confessions of an English Opium Eater*', *Eclectic Review*, New Series 19. 366–71.

Anonymous, '*Confessions of an English Opium Eater*', *Imperial Magazine*, 5. 89–95.

De Quincey, Thomas [?], 'The Raven', *Knight's Quarterly Magazine*, 1. 349–52.

De Quincey, Thomas [?], 'The Black Chamber', *Knight's Quarterly Magazine*, 1. 353–61.

Hazlitt, William, 'To the Editor of the *London Magazine*', 8. 459–60.

Wilson, John, 'The General Question', *Blackwood's Magazine*, 14. 332–42.

Wilson, John and Lockhart, John Gibson [?], 'Noctes Ambrosianae. No. XII', *Blackwood's Magazine*, 14. 484–503.

1824   Advertisement, 'This day is published', *The Times*, 3 July, page 4, column 5.

Knight, Charles, 'The Anniversary', *Knight's Quarterly Magazine*, 3. 178–238.

Lockhart, John Gibson and Wilson, John, 'Noctes Ambrosianae. No. XVI', *Blackwood's Magazine*, 16. 231–50.

Maginn, William, 'THE HUMBUGS OF THE AGE. *No. I – The Opium Eater*', *John Bull Magazine*, 1. 21–4.

Wilson, John, 'Noctes Ambrosianae. No. XIV', *Blackwood's Magazine*, 15. 367–90.

1825   Anonymous, *'Confessions of an English Opium Eater'*, *United States Literary Gazette*, 1. 38–40.

Bailey, Samuel, *A Critical Dissertation on the Nature, Measures, and Causes of Value*, London: Hunter.

1828   Anonymous, 'Mr De Quincy and the London University', *The Athenaeum*, 61. 24 December. 969.

1829   Wilson, John, 'Noctes Ambrosianae. No. XLVII', *Blackwood's Magazine*, 27. 845–78.

1830   Wilson, John, 'Noctes Ambrosianae. No. XLVIII', *Blackwood's Magazine*, 27. 659–94.

Wilson, John, 'Noctes Ambrosianae. No. XLIX', *Blackwood's Magazine*, 27. 802–32.

1831   Halkerston, Peter, *A Treatise of the History, Law, and Privileges of the Palace and Sanctuary of Holyroodhouse*, Edinburgh: Maclachlan and Stewart.

1832   Tait, William, 'The Spirit of the Time', *Tait's Edinburgh Magazine*, 1. 57–64.

1833   Tait, William, 'To our Readers', *Tait's Edinburgh Magazine*, 3. ix–x.

1835   Balfour, J. H., 'Case of Peculiar Disease of the Skull and Dura Mater', *The Edinburgh Medical and Surgical Journal*, 43. 319–25.

Hare, Julius, 'Samuel Taylor Coleridge and the English Opium-Eater', *British Magazine*, 7. 15–27.

1836   Colton, Walter, 'Turkish Sketches', *The Knickerbocker Magazine*, 7. 421–3.

1837   Johnstone, Christian, 'Mr De Quincey, and the Literary Society of Liverpool in 1801', *Tait's Edinburgh Magazine*, 8. 337–40.

Shepherd, William, 'To the Editor of Tait's Magazine', *Tait's Edinburgh Magazine*, 8. 340.

1838   Gillman, James, *The Life of Samuel Taylor Coleridge*, London: Pickering.

Johnstone, Christian, 'Animal Magnetism', *Tait's Edinburgh Magazine*, 9. 460–7.

1839   Hood, Thomas, *Hood's Own*, London: Baily.

1841   Willmott, Robert Aris [?], 'The last new life of Shakespeare', *Fraser's Magazine*, 24. 48–57.

1842   Blair, William, 'An Opium-Eater in America', *The Knickerbocker Magazine*, 20. 47–57.

1844   Grant, J. P. (ed.), *Memoirs and Correspondence of Mrs Grant of Laggan*, 3 vols, London: Longman, Brown, Green, and Longmans.

1845   Gilfillan, George, *Gallery of Literary Portraits*, Tait: Edinburgh.

McCulloch, John Ramsay, *The Literature of Political Economy*, London: Longman, Brown, Green, and Longmans.

1847   Coleridge, Sara (ed.), *Biographia Literaria . . . by Samuel Taylor Coleridge*, 2 vols, New York: Wiley and Putnam.

1848   Cottle, Joseph, *Reminiscences of Samuel Taylor Coleridge and Robert Southey*, Second Edition, London: Houlston and Stoneman.

1850   Scott, William Bell, *Memoir of David Scott*, Edinburgh: Adam and Charles Black.

1851   Gillies, Robert Pearse, *Memoirs of a Literary Veteran*, 3 vols, London: Bentley.

1853   Lewes, George Henry, 'Thomas De Quincey', *The Leader*, 4. 571–2.

1854   Bright, Henry Arthur, 'Thomas De Quincey and his Works', *The Westminster Review*, New Series, 5. 519–37.

1854–   Warren, Samuel, 'A Few Recollections of Christopher North', *The
5   Works of Samuel Warren*, 5 vols, Edinburgh: Blackwood, 5. 495–501.

1856   Southey, Robert, *Selections from the Letters*, ed. John Wood Warter, 4 vols, London: Longman, Brown, Green, and Longmans.

1857   Gilfillan, George, *Gallery of Literary Portraits*, 2 vols, Edinburgh: James Hogg.

1859   Anonymous, 'Thomas De Quincey', *The Athenaeum*, 17 December, 814–15.

Anonymous, 'Death of Thomas De Quincey', *The Scotsman*, 10 December, 6.

Anonymous, 'Death of Thomas De Quincey', *The Times*, 14 December, 6.

1860   Nisbet, Thomas, *Catalogue of an extensive and valuable collection of books ... including the library of the late Thomas De Quincey, Esq*, Edinburgh: Nisbet. 36–48.

1861   Kebbel, Thomas E., 'Selections, Grave and Gay', *The Quarterly Review*, 110. 1–35.

1863   Gordon, Mary, *'Christopher North'. A Memoir of John Wilson*, New York: W. J. Widdleton.

1864   Mancuniensis, 'Thomas De Quincey', *Notes and Queries*, 3rd Series, 6. 125.

1864–   Knight, Charles, *Passages of a Working Life*, 3 vols, London: Bradbury
5   and Evans.

1865   Masson, David, 'Dead Men Whom I Have Known', *Macmillan's Magazine*, 12. 74–90.

        Neal, John, 'William Blackwood', *The Atlantic Monthly*, 16. 660–72.

1866   Procter, Bryan Waller, *Charles Lamb: A Memoir*, London: Moxon.

1866–   Smith, Jeremiah Finch, *The Admission Register of the Manchester
74   School*, 3 vols, Manchester: Chetham Society.

1868   Lonsdale, Henry, 'Biographical Memoir', *The Anatomical Memoirs of John Goodsir*, ed. William Turner, 2 vols, Edinburgh: Adam and Charles Black. 1. 1–203.

1869   Martineau, Harriet, *Biographical Sketches*, New York: Leypoldt & Holt.

1870   Mitford, Mary Russell, *The Life*, ed. A. G. K. L'Estrange, 2 vols, New York: Harper.

1871   Calkins, Alonzo, *Opium and the Opium-Appetite*, Philadelphia: Lippincott.

1872   Stockdale, James, *Annales Caermoelenses, or Annals of Cartmel*, Ulverston: Kitchin.

1873   Coleridge, Sara, *Memoirs and Letters*, 2 vols, London: King.

1874   Procter, Richard Wright, *Memorials of Manchester Streets*, Manchester: Sutcliffe.

1877   Espinasse, Francis, *Lancashire Worthies*, London: Simpkin, Marshall, and Company.

        Japp, Alexander H., *Thomas De Quincey: His Life and Writings*, 2 vols, New York: Scribner, Armstrong and Company.

        Mackay, Charles, *Forty Years' Recollections of Life, Literature, and Public Affairs*, London: Chapman and Hall.

Procter, Bryan Waller, *An Autobiographical Fragment and Biographical Notes*, Boston: Roberts.

Oliphant, Margaret, 'The Opium-Eater', *Blackwood's Magazine*, 122. 717–41.

1878   Hill, Rosamond and Davenport, Florence, *A Memoir of Matthew Davenport Hill*, London: Macmillan.

1879   Anonymous, 'Thomas De Quincey: His Father and his Birthplace', *Manchester Literary Club Papers*, 5. 244–5.

1881   Fields, James T., *Biographical Notes and Personal Sketches*, Boston: Houghton, Mifflin and Company.

Gilfillan, George, *Sketches Literary and Theological*, ed. Frank Henderson, Edinburgh: Douglas.

Gray, G. J., '*Knight's Quarterly Magazine*', *Notes and Queries*, 6th Series, 4. 261–3.

Hodgson, Shadworth, *Outcast Essays*, London: Longmans, Green, and Company.

Masson, David, *De Quincey*, London: Macmillan.

Shepherd, Richard Herne (ed.), *Memoirs of the Life and Writings of Thomas Carlyle*, 2 vols, London: Allen.

Troup, George Elmslie, *Life of George Troup, Journalist*, Edinburgh: MacNiven and Wallace.

1882   L'Estrange, A. G. (ed.), *The Friendships of Mary Russell Mitford*, London: Hurst and Blackett.

1884   Cranbrook, Lord, 'Christopher North', *National Review*, 3. 151–60.

Fields, James T., *Yesterday With Authors*, Boston: Houghton, Mifflin and Company.

1885   Carne, John, *Letters*, Edinburgh: Privately Printed.

1887   Mackay, Charles, *Through the Long Day*, London: Allen.

1889   Brown, James, *Life of William B. Robertson*, Glasgow: MacLehose and Sons.

Clayden, P. W., *Rogers and his Contemporaries*, London: Smith, Elder.

1889–   Masson, David (ed.), *The Collected Writings of Thomas De Quincey*,
90   14 vols, London: Black.

1890   Bain, Joseph, 'Thomas De Quincey and his Supposed Descent from the Earls of Winchester', *The Genealogist*, New Series, 7. 17–21.

Hogg, James, 'Nights and Days with De Quincey', *Harper's New Monthly Magazine*, 80. 446–56.

Japp, Alexander H., *Thomas De Quincey: His Life and Writings*, London: Hogg.

1891   Japp, Alexander H., *De Quincey Memorials*, 2 vols, London: Heinemann.

1892   Clowes, Alice, *Charles Knight: A Sketch*, London: Bentley.

Scott, William Bell, *Autobiographical Notes*, ed. W. Minto, 2 vols, London: Osgood, McIlvaine, and Company.

Watson, Robert A. and Watson, Elizabeth S., *George Gilfillan: Letters and Journals, with Memoir*, London: Hodder and Stoughton.

1893   Daniel, W. E., *Our Memories: Shadows of Old Oxford*, Oxford: Daniel.

Bertram, James, *Some Memories of Books, Authors, and Events*, London: Constable.

1894   Beddoes, Thomas Lovell, *The Letters*, ed. Edmund Gosse, London: Elkin Mathews and John Lane.

Fields, Annie Adams, *A Shelf of Old Books*, London: Osgood, McIlvaine.

Landreth, Peter, 'Emerson's Meeting with De Quincey', *Blackwood's Magazine*, 155. 480–91.

1895   Hogg, James, *De Quincey and his Friends*, London: Sampson Low, Marston and Company.

1896   Hill, George Birkbeck, *Talks about Autographs*, London: T. Fisher Unwin.

1896– Carlyle, Thomas, *The Works*, ed. H. D. Traill, 30 vols, London:
9   Chapman and Hall.

1897   Landor, Walter Savage, *Letters and Other Unpublished Writings*, ed. Stephen Wheeler, London: Bentley.

Lang, Andrew, *The Life and Letters of John Gibson Lockhart*, London: Nimmo.

Oliphant, Margaret, *Annals of a Publishing House: William Blackwood and his Sons*, 2 vols, Edinburgh: Blackwood.

1898   Kilpatrick, James A., *Literary Landmarks of Glasgow*, Glasgow: Saint Mungo Press.

Le Gallienne, Richard, 'Introduction', *The Opium-Eater and Essays by Thomas De Quincey*, London: Ward, Lock, and Company.

1899   Axon, William E. A., *Echoes of Old Lancashire*, London: Andrews.

1900   Axon, William E. A., 'Some De Quincey Documents', *The Manchester Guardian*, 10 December. 10.

Hughes, Henry, 'De Quincey, a Chymru, a'r Methodistiaid', *Y Trysorfa*, 292–9.

Martin, Theodore, *Helena Faucit (Lady Martin)*, Edinburgh: Blackwood.

Mortimer, John, 'Some Notes on Thomas Quincey', *The Manchester Quarterly*, 19. 146–62.

1905 Lucas, E. V., *The Life of Charles Lamb*, 2 vols, London: Dent.

Thin, James, *Reminiscences of Booksellers and Bookselling in Edinburgh in the Time of William IV*, Edinburgh: Oliver and Boyd.

1907 Axon, William E. A., 'Thomas De Quincey', *The Bookman*, 31. 207–12.

Sellar, E. M., *Recollections and Impressions*, Edinburgh: Blackwood.

1908 Green, J. A., *Thomas De Quincey: A Bibliography Based Upon the De Quincey Collection in the Moss Side Library*, Manchester: Moss Side Library.

Priestley, Eliza, *The Story of a Lifetime*, London: Kegan Paul, Trench, Trübner, and Company.

1913 Chesterton, G. K., *The Victorian Age in Literature*, New York: Holt.

Rayment, Henry, 'De Quincey and 4, York Street, Covent Garden', *Notes and Queries*, 11th Series, 8. 104–5.

1915 Fairbrother, E. H., 'Lieut. Horatio De Quincey', *Notes and Queries*, 11th Series, 12. 273–5.

1916 Armitt, Mary L., *Rydal*, ed. Willingham F. Rawnsley, Kendal: Wilson.

1917 MacFarlane, Charles, *Reminiscences of a Literary Life*, London: Murray.

1920 Duckers, J. Scott, 'The De Quincey Family', *Times Literary Supplement*, 21 October, 684.

1922 De Quincey, Thomas, 'Lasswade, December 27, 1847', *Catalogue of Valuable Illuminated Manuscripts, Printed Books, and Autograph Letters*, London: Sotheby, Wilkinson and Hodge, 19–21 June, 123.

Robinson, Henry Crabb, *Blake, Coleridge, Wordsworth, Lamb, etc*, ed. Edith J. Morley, Manchester: University of Manchester Press.

1923 Austen, Jane, *The Novels*, ed. R. W. Chapman, 5 vols, Oxford: Oxford University Press.

Wilson, David Alec, *Carlyle Till Marriage*, London: Kegan Paul.

1925 Taylor, Olive M., 'John Taylor, Author and Publisher', *The London Mercury*, 12. 258–67.

1926 Gray, W. Forbes, 'De Quincey as Lady Nairne's Tenant', *Chambers's Journal*, 7th Series, 16. 181–4.

1927   Eaton, Horace (ed.), *A Diary of Thomas De Quincey, 1803*, London: Douglas.

Morley, Edith J. (ed.), *The Correspondence of Henry Crabb Robinson with the Wordsworth Circle*, 2 vols, Oxford: Clarendon Press.

1928   Terry, Charles E. and Pellens, Mildred, *The Opium Problem*, New York: Bureau of Social Hygiene.

1929   Adcock, A. St John, *Famous Houses and Literary Shrines of London*, London: Dent.

Stockley, Violet, *German Literature as Known in England*, London: Routledge.

1931   Simmons, E. J., 'Gogol and English Literature', *Modern Language Review*, 26. 445–50.

Wellek, René, *Immanuel Kant in England*, Princeton, NJ: Princeton University Press.

1932–   Scott, Sir Walter, *The Letters*, ed. H. J. C. Grierson, 12 vols, London:
7   Constable.

Moore, E. Hamilton, 'Some Unpublished Letters of Thomas De Quincey', *Review of English Studies*, 9. 176–85.

1934   Parsons, Coleman O., 'The Woes of Thomas De Quincey', *Review of English Studies*, 10. 190–99.

Potter, Stephen (ed.), *Minnow Among Tritons: Mrs S. T. Coleridge's Letters to Thomas Poole*, London: Nonesuch Press.

Swann, Elsie, *Christopher North <John Wilson>*, Edinburgh: Oliver and Boyd.

1935   Lamb, Charles and Mary, *The Letters*, ed. E. V. Lucas, 3 vols, London: Dent.

1936   Blunden, Edmund, *Keats's Publisher: A Memoir of John Taylor*, London: Cape.

Bonner, Willard Hallam, *De Quincey at Work*, Buffalo, NY: Airport Publishers.

Eaton, Horace, *Thomas De Quincey: A Biography*, New York: Oxford University Press.

1937   De Quincey, Thomas, 'A Remarkable Series of Thirty-Seven Letters by Thomas De Quincey to William Tait, his Publisher', *Books and Autographs*, Sale Number 4289, American Art Association, Anderson Galleries, Inc., 43–4.

Forward, Kenneth, '"Libellous Attack" on De Quincey', *PMLA*, 52. 244–60.

Hopkins, Gerard Manley, *The Note-Books and Papers*, ed. Humphry House, London: Oxford University Press.

1938   Robinson, Henry Crabb, *On Books and Their Writers*, ed. Edith J. Morley, 3 vols, London: Dent.

1939   Emerson, Ralph Waldo, *The Letters*, ed. Ralph L. Rusk, 6 vols, New York: Columbia University Press.

Forward, Kenneth, 'De Quincey's *Cessio Bonorum*', *PMLA*, 54. 511–25.

1941   Wells, John Edwin, 'De Quincey and *The Prelude* in 1839', *Philological Quarterly*, 20. 1–24.

1944   Wordsworth, Dora, *The Letters*, ed. Howard P. Vincent, Chicago: Packard and Company.

1945   Simmons, Jack, *Southey*, London: Collins.

1946   Prod'homme, J.-G., 'Berlioz, Musset, and Thomas De Quincey', *The Musical Quarterly*, 32. 98–106.

1947   Parker, W. M., 'Charles Ollier to William Blackwood', *Times Literary Supplement*, 7 June, 288.

1950   Brockway, Wallace and Winer, Bart Keith, *A Second Treasury of the World's Great Letters*, London: Heinemann.

1952   Jordan, John E., *Thomas De Quincey, Literary Critic*, Berkeley: University of California Press.

1954   Hutchinson, Sara, *The Letters*, ed. Kathleen Coburn, Toronto: University of Toronto Press.

Musgrove, S. (ed.), *Unpublished Letters of Thomas De Quincey and Elizabeth Barrett Browning*, Auckland University College, Bulletin 44.

Rockwell, Frederick S., 'De Quincey and the Ending of *Moby Dick*', *Nineteenth-Century Fiction*, 9. 161–8.

Tredrey, F. D., *The House of Blackwood, 1804–1954*, Edinburgh: William Blackwood and Sons.

1954– George Eliot, *The Letters*, ed. Gordon S. Haight, 9 vols, New Haven,
78   CT: Yale University Press.

1955   Moir, David Macbeth, 'The Letters to William Blackwood', ed. Eugene A. Nolte, 2 vols, Unpublished Ph.D. thesis, Texas Technological College.

1956– Coleridge, Samuel Taylor, *The Collected Letters*, ed. Earl Leslie
71   Griggs, 6 vols, Oxford: Clarendon Press.

1957– Coleridge, Samuel Taylor, *The Notebooks*, 5 vols, ed. Kathleen
2002   Coburn, Princeton, NJ: Princeton University Press.

1958   Wordsworth, Mary, *The Letters*, ed. Mary E. Burton, Oxford: Clarendon Press.

Keats, John, *The Letters*, ed. H. E. Rollins, 2 vols, Cambridge, MA: Harvard University Press.

1958–
78 Burke, Edmund, *The Correspondence*, gen. ed. T. W. Copeland, 10 vols, Cambridge: Cambridge University Press.

1960–
82 Emerson, Ralph Waldo, *The Journals and Miscellaneous Notebooks*, ed. Ronald A. Bosco, William H. Gilman, Alfred R. Ferguson, Merton M. Sealts, et al., 16 vols, Cambridge, MA: Harvard University Press.

1961 Gerin, Winifred, *Branwell Brontë*, London: Thomas Nelson.

1962–
97 Hawthorne, Nathaniel, *The Centenary Edition of the Works*, ed. William Charvat, Thomas Woodson, et al., 23 vols, Columbus: Ohio State University Press.

1963 Jordan, John E. (ed.), *De Quincey to Wordsworth*, Berkeley: University of California Press.

Miller, J. Hillis, *The Disappearance of God*, Cambridge, MA: Harvard University Press.

Tryon, W. S., *Parnassus Corner: A Life of James T. Fields*, Boston: Houghton Mifflin Company.

1963–
91 Mill, John Stuart, *Collected Works*, gen. ed. J. M. Robson, 33 vols, Toronto: University of Toronto Press.

1964 Shelley, Percy Bysshe, *The Letters*, ed. Frederick L. Jones, 2 vols, Oxford: Clarendon Press.

Thomas, Lionel, *Willibald Alexis*, Oxford: Blackwell.

1965 Goldman, Albert, *The Mine and the Mint: Sources for the Writings of Thomas De Quincey*, Carbondale: Southern Illinois University Press.

Rollins, H. E. (ed.), *The Keats Circle*, 2 vols, Cambridge, MA: Harvard University Press.

Southey, Robert, *New Letters*, ed. Kenneth Curry, 2 vols, New York: Columbia University Press.

1965–
2002 Dickens, Charles, *The Letters*, gen. ed. Madeline House, Graham Storey, and Kathleen Tillotson, 12 vols, Oxford: Clarendon Press.

1966 Derry, Warren, *Dr Parr: A Portrait of the Whig Dr Johnson*, Oxford: Clarendon Press.

Tave, Stuart (ed.), *New Essays by De Quincey*, Princeton, NJ: Princeton University Press.

1966–
89 Houghton, Walter E. (gen. ed.), *The Wellesley Index to Victorian Periodicals*, 5 vols, Toronto: University of Toronto Press.

1967 Hopkins, Robert, 'De Quincey on War and the Pastoral Design of *The English Mail-Coach*', *Studies in Romanticism*, 6. 129–51.

Schiller, Friedrich, *On the Aesthetic Education of Man*, ed. Elizabeth M. Wilkinson and L. A. Willoughby, Oxford: Clarendon Press.

Wordsworth, William and Dorothy, *The Letters: The Early Years, 1787–1805*, ed. Chester L. Shaver, Oxford: Clarendon Press.

1968 Hayter, Alethea, *Opium and the Romantic Imagination*, London: Faber.

Podmore, Frank, *Robert Owen: A Biography*, New York: Kelley.

1969 Coleridge, Samuel Taylor, *The Friend*, ed. Barbara E. Rooke, 2 vols, Princeton, NJ: Princeton University Press.

Sawyer, Paul, 'Musset's Translation of *Confessions of an English Opium-Eater*', *French Review*, 42. 403–8.

Wordsworth, William and Dorothy, *The Letters: The Middle Years, Part I, 1806–1811*, ed. Mary Moorman, Oxford: Clarendon Press.

1969– Poe, Edgar Allan, *The Collected Works*, ed. T. O. Mabbott, 3 vols,
78 Cambridge, MA: Harvard University Press.

1970 Abrams, M. H., *The Milk of Paradise*, New York: Harper and Row.

Murray, James G., 'Mill on De Quincey: *Esprit Critique* Revoked', *The Victorian Newsletter*, 37. 7–12.

Newman, John Henry, *The Letters and Diaries, Volume XX*, ed. Charles Stephen Dessain, London: Nelson.

Wordsworth, William and Dorothy, *The Letters: The Middle Years, Part II, 1812–1820*, ed. Mary Moorman and Alan G. Hill, Oxford: Clarendon Press.

1970– Carlyle, Thomas and Jane Welsh, *The Collected Letters*, ed. C. R.
cont. Saunders, Kenneth Fielding, et al., Durham, NC: Duke University Press.

1971 Saville, John (ed.), *The Life of Thomas Cooper*, New York: Humanities Press.

1971– Emerson, Ralph Waldo, *The Collected Works*, ed. Joseph Slater,
cont. Alfred R. Ferguson, Douglas Emory Wilson, et al., Cambridge, MA: Harvard University Press.

1972 Chilcott, Tim, *A Publisher and his Circle: The Life and Work of John Taylor, Keats's Publisher*, London: Routledge.

1973 Reynolds, John Hamilton, *The Letters*, ed. Leonidas M. Jones, Lincoln: University of Nebraska Press.

1973– Byron, Lord, *Letters and Journals*, ed. Leslie A. Marchand, 13 vols,
94 Cambridge, MA: Harvard University Press.

1974 Borges, Jorge Luis, *An Introduction to English Literature*, Lexington: University Press of Kentucky.

Clubbe, John (ed.), *Two Reminiscences of Thomas Carlyle*, Durham, NC: Duke University Press.

Herbert, Christopher, 'De Quincey and Dickens', *Victorian Studies*, 17. 247–63.

Marx, Karl, *Capital*, ed. G. D. H. Cole, London: Dent.

Sackville West, Edward, *A Flame in Sunlight: The Life and Work of Thomas De Quincey*, ed. John E. Jordan, London: The Bodley Head.

Wordsworth, William, *The Prose Works*, ed. W. J. B. Owen and Jane Worthington Smyser, 3 vols, Oxford: Clarendon Press.

1975   Catford, E. D., *Edinburgh: The Story of a City*, London: Hutchinson.

Reed, Mark L., *Wordsworth: The Chronology of the Middle Years, 1800–1815*, Cambridge, MA: Harvard University Press.

1976   Maniquis, Robert, 'Lonely Empires: Personal and Public Visions of Thomas De Quincey', *Literary Monographs, Volume 8*, ed. Eric Rothstein and Joseph Anthony Wittreich, Madison: University of Wisconsin Press, 47–127.

1977   Webb, Timothy, *Shelley: A Voice Not Understood*, Atlantic Highlands, NJ: Humanities Press.

1978   Chavkin, Allan and Oehlschlaeger, Fritz, 'In Europe with Carlyle, De Quincey, and Samuel Rogers: Five Letters of James T. Fields to Edwin P. Whipple', *The American Transcendental Quarterly*, 38. 121–35.

Wordsworth, William and Dorothy, *The Letters: The Later Years, Part I, 1821–1828*, ed. Alan G. Hill, Oxford: Clarendon Press.

1979   Wordsworth, William and Dorothy, *The Letters: The Later Years, Part II, 1829–1834*, ed. Alan G. Hill, Oxford: Clarendon Press.

1980   Ashton, Rosemary, *The German Idea*, Cambridge: Cambridge University Press.

FitzGerald, Edward, *The Letters*, ed. Alfred McKinley Terhune and Annabelle Burdick Terhune, 4 vols, Princeton, NJ: Princeton University Press.

1981   Berridge, Virginia and Edwards, Griffith, *Opium and the People: Opiate Use in Nineteenth-Century England*, London: Allen Lane.

Butler, Marilyn, *Romantics, Rebels, and Reactionaries: English Literature and its Background, 1760–1830*, Oxford: Oxford University Press.

Lindop, Grevel, *The Opium-Eater: A Life of Thomas De Quincey*, London: Dent.

Maddux, James F. and Desmond, David P., *Careers of Opioid Users*, New York: Praeger.

1983   Cohen, Susan R., 'Avoiding the High Prophetic Strain: De Quincey's Mail-Coach and *Felix Holt*', *Victorian Newsletter*, 64. 19–20.

Coleridge, Samuel Taylor, *Biographia Literaria*, ed. James Engell and Walter Jackson Bate, 2 vols, Princeton, NJ: Princeton University Press.

Morris, Douglas K., '*Knight's Quarterly Magazine*', *British Literary Magazines: The Romantic Age, 1789–1836*, ed. Alvin Sullivan, Westport, CN: Greenwood Press, 208–15.

Parssinen, Terry M., *Secret Passions, Secret Remedies: Narcotic Drugs in British Society, 1820–1930*, Manchester: Manchester University Press.

O'Leary, Patrick, *Regency Editor: The Life of John Scott*, Aberdeen: Aberdeen University Press.

Snyder, Robert Lance, 'A De Quinceyan Source for Poe's "The Masque of the Red Death"', *Studies in Short Fiction*, 21. 103–10.

Weinstein, Mark A., '*Tait's Edinburgh Magazine*', *British Literary Magazines: The Romantic Age, 1789–1836*, ed. Alvin Sullivan, Westport, CN: Greenwood Press, 401–5.

1984   Butler, Marilyn, 'Satire and the Images of Self in the Romantic Period: The Long Tradition of Hazlitt's *Liber Amoris*', *English Satire and the Satiric Tradition*, ed. Claude Rawson and Jenny Mezciems, Oxford: Blackwell, 209–25.

1984– Barrett Browning, Elizabeth and Browning, Robert, *The Brownings'*
cont.   *Correspondence*, ed. Philip Kelley, Scott Lewis, et al., Winfield, KS: Wedgestone Press.

1985   Caseby, Richard, *The Opium-Eating Editor: Thomas De Quincey and the Westmorland Gazette*, Kendal: Westmorland Gazette.

Clare, John, *The Letters*, ed. Mark Storey, Oxford: Clarendon Press.

Lindop, Grevel, 'Pursuing the Throne of God: De Quincey and the Evangelical Revival', *The Charles Lamb Bulletin*, New Series, 52. 97–111.

Woof, Robert, *Thomas De Quincey: An English Opium-Eater, 1785–1859*, Cumbria: CN Print Ltd.

1986   Sedgwick, Eve Kosofsky, *The Coherence of Gothic Conventions*, New York: Methuen.

Sutherland, L. S. and Mitchell, L. G. (ed.), *The History of the University of Oxford: The Eighteenth Century*, Oxford: Clarendon Press.

Waller, John O., *A Circle of Friends: The Tennysons and the Lushingtons of Park House*, Columbus: Ohio State University Press.

Wright, David, 'Introduction', *Thomas De Quincey: Recollections of the Lakes and the Lake Poets*, London: Penguin, 7–27.

1986– Woolf, Virginia, *The Essays*, ed. Andrew McNeillie and Stuart N.
cont. Clarke, 5 vols, London: The Hogarth Press.

1987 Coleridge, Samuel Taylor, *Lectures 1808–1819: On Literature*, 2 vols, ed. R. A. Foakes, Princeton, NJ: Princeton University Press.

McFarland, Thomas, *Romantic Cruxes: The English Essayists and the Spirit of the Age*, Oxford: Clarendon Press.

1990 Baxter, Edmund, *De Quincey's Art of Autobiography*, Edinburgh: Edinburgh University Press.

Bentley, James, *Dare to be Wise: A History of the Manchester Grammar School*, London: James and James.

Coleridge, Henry Nelson, 'Preface to *Specimens of the Table Talk of Samuel Taylor Coleridge*', Coleridge, Samuel Taylor, *Table Talk*, ed. Carl Woodring, 2 vols, Princeton, NJ: Princeton University Press, 2. 1–305.

Foucault, Michel, *The History of Sexuality: An Introduction*, trans. Robert Hurley, New York: Vintage Books.

Owen, W. J. B., 'De Quincey and Shoplifting', *The Wordsworth Circle*, 21. 72–6.

1991 Barrell, John, *The Infection of Thomas De Quincey: A Psychopathology of Imperialism*, New Haven, CT: Yale University Press.

1992 Groves, David, 'De Quincey, the West Indies, and the *Edinburgh Evening Post*', *The Papers of the Bibliographical Society of America*, 86. 41–56.

Leask, Nigel, *British Romantic Writers and the East*, Cambridge: Cambridge University Press.

Leighton, Angela, 'De Quincey and Women', *Beyond Romanticism: New Approaches to Texts and Contexts, 1780–1832*, ed. Stephen Copley and John Whale, London: Routledge, 160–77.

Morrison, Robert, 'De Quincey, Champion of Shelley', *Keats-Shelley Journal*, 41. 36–41.

Wordsworth, William, *Lyrical Ballads, and Other Poems, 1797–1800*, ed. James Butler and Karen Green, Ithaca, NY: Cornell University Press.

1993 Bate, Jonathan, 'The Literature of Power: Coleridge and De Quincey', *Coleridge's Visionary Language*, ed. Tim Fulford and Morton D. Paley, Cambridge: D. S. Brewer, 137–50.

Smith, Jonathan, 'De Quincey's Revisions to "The System of the Heavens"', *Victorian Periodicals Review,* 26. 203–12.

Wordsworth, Jonathan, '*Klosterheim*', *Visionary Gleam: Forty Books from the Romantic Period,* London: Woodstock, 229–35.

Wordsworth, William and Dorothy, *A Supplement of New Letters,* ed. Alan G. Hill, Oxford: Clarendon Press.

1994 Lickbarrow, Isabella, *Poetical Effusions,* intro. Jonathan Wordsworth, Oxford: Woodstock Books.

Lindop, Grevel, 'De Quincey and the Portico Library', *Bulletin of the John Rylands University Library of Manchester,* 76. 179–86.

McDonagh, Josephine, *De Quincey's Disciplines,* Oxford: Clarendon Press.

Symonds, Barry (ed.), 'De Quincey and his Publishers: The Letters of Thomas De Quincey to His Publishers, and other Letters, 1819–32', Unpublished Ph.D. thesis, University of Edinburgh.

1995 Lindop, Grevel, 'De Quincey and the Cursed Crocodile', *Essays in Criticism,* 45. 121–40.

Lindop, Grevel, 'De Quincey's Wordsworthian Quotations', *The Wordsworth Circle,* 26. 58–65.

Milligan, Barry, *Pleasures and Pains: Opium and the Orient in Nineteenth-Century British Culture,* Charlottesville: University Press of Virginia.

Rzepka, Charles J., *Sacramental Commodities: Gift, Text, and the Sublime in De Quincey,* Amherst: University of Massachusetts Press.

1995– Brontë, Charlotte, *The Letters,* ed. Margaret Smith, 3 vols, Oxford:
2004 Clarendon Press.

1996 Booth, Martin, *Opium: A History,* New York: St Martin's Press.

Hardman, Joel G. and Limbird, Lee E. (ed.), *Goodman and Gilman's The Pharmacological Basis of Therapeutics,* Ninth Edition, New York: McGraw-Hill.

1997 Brock, M. G. and Curthoys, M. C. (ed.), *The History of the University of Oxford: The Nineteenth-Century, Part I,* Oxford: Clarendon Press.

1997– Brontë, Patrick Branwell, *The Works,* ed. Victor A. Neufeldt, 3 vols,
9 New York: Garland.

1998 Groves, David, 'Climbing the *Post*: Thomas De Quincey as a Newspaper-Editor, 1827–28', *The Wordsworth Circle,* 29. 126–31.

Lindop, Grevel, 'De Quincey and the Edinburgh and Glasgow University Circles', *Grub Street and the Ivory Tower,* ed. Jeremy

Treglown and Bridget Bennett, Oxford: Clarendon Press, 41–57.

Morrison, Robert (ed.), 'Richard Woodhouse's *Cause Book*: the Opium-Eater, the Magazine Wars, and the London Literary Scene in 1821', *Harvard Library Bulletin*, 9. 1–43.

Symonds, Barry, '"Do not suppose that I am underwriting myself": The Labyrinth of De Quincey's Manuscripts', *The Wordsworth Circle*, 29. 137–40.

1999 Morrison, Robert, '"An Edinburgh surgeon of great eminence" in De Quincey's *Confessions of an English Opium-Eater*', *Notes and Queries*, 46. 47–8.

Plant, Sadie, *Writing on Drugs*, New York: Farrar, Straus and Giroux.

2000 Carlyle, Thomas, *Reminiscences*, ed. Kenneth J. Fielding and Ian Campbell, Oxford: Oxford University Press.

Groves, David, '"Disgusted with all the Cockneys": De Quincey, the *London Magazine*, and *Blackwood's Magazine*', *Notes and Queries*, 47. 326–7.

Roberts, Daniel, *Revisionary Gleam: De Quincey, Coleridge, and the High Romantic Argument*, Liverpool: Liverpool University Press.

2001 Coleridge, Samuel Taylor, *Poetical Works*, ed. J. C. C. Mays, 6 vols, Princeton, NJ: Princeton University Press.

Morrison, Robert, 'Poe's De Quincey, Poe's Dupin', *Essays in Criticism*, 51. 424–41.

Plotz, Judith, *Romanticism and the Vocation of Childhood*, New York: Palgrave.

Burroughs, William S., *Burroughs Live: The Collected Interviews of William S. Burroughs*, Los Angeles: Semiotext(e).

2002 Finkelstein, David, *The House of Blackwood: Author-Publisher Relations in the Victorian Era*, University Park: The Pennsylvania State University Press.

Robinson, Eric and Powell, David (ed.), *John Clare By Himself*, Manchester: Carcanet Press.

2003 Clark, David L., 'We "Other Prussians": Bodies and Pleasures in De Quincey and Late Kant', *European Romantic Review*, 14. 261–87.

Hogg, James, *Altrive Tales*, ed. Gillian Hughes, Edinburgh: Edinburgh University Press.

Lindop, Grevel, 'De Quincey's *Confessions* in Context', *Confessions of an English Opium-Eater: Thomas De Quincey*, ed. Jean-Pierre Naugrette, Nantes: Editions du Temps, 7–20.

Milligan, Barry (ed.), *Confessions of an English Opium-Eater and Other Writings*, London: Penguin Books.

2004 Bridgwater, Patrick, *De Quincey's Gothic Masquerade*, New York: Rodopi.

St Clair, William, *The Reading Nation in the Romantic Period*, Cambridge: Cambridge University Press.

Vetch, R. H., rev. Bowyer, T. H., 'Watson, Henry', *Oxford Dictionary of National Biography*, ed. H. C. G. Matthew and Brian Harrison, 60 vols, Oxford: Oxford University Press, 57. 616–17.

Vetch, R. H., rev. Stearn, Roger T., 'Smith, Richard Baird', *Oxford Dictionary of National Biography*, ed. H. C. G. Matthew and Brian Harrison, 60 vols, Oxford: Oxford University Press, 51. 278–81.

2004– Hogg, James, *The Collected Letters*, gen. ed. Gillian Hughes, 3 vols,
8 Edinburgh: Edinburgh University Press.

2005 Easley, Alexis, ' *Tait's Edinburgh Magazine* in the 1830s: Dialogues on Gender, Class, and Reform', *Victorian Periodicals Review*, 38. 263–79.

Milligan, Barry, 'Morphine-Addicted Doctors, The English Opium-Eater, and Embattled Medical Authority', *Victorian Literature and Culture*, 33. 541–53.

2005– Gaskell, Elizabeth, *The Works*, gen. ed. Joanne Shattock, 10 vols,
6 London: Pickering and Chatto.

2006 Dalrymple, Theodore, *Romancing Opiates: Pharmacological Lies and the Addiction Bureaucracy*, New York: Encounter Books.

DeGrandpre, Richard, *The Cult of Pharmacology*, Durham, NC: Duke University Press.

Morrison, Robert, 'Introduction', *Thomas De Quincey: On Murder*, ed. Robert Morrison, Oxford: Oxford University Press, vii–xxvii.

Morrison, Robert, 'William Blackwood and the Dynamics of Success', *Print Culture and the Blackwood Tradition*, ed. David Finkelstein, Toronto: University of Toronto Press, 21–48.

2007 Ford, Natalie, 'Beyond Opium: De Quincey's Range of Reverie', *The Cambridge Quarterly*, 36. 229–49.

Foxcroft, Louise, *The Making of Addiction: The 'Use and Abuse' of Opium in Nineteenth-Century Britain*, Aldershot: Ashgate.

Hoffman, John and Froemke, Susan, *Addiction: Why Can't They Just Stop?* New York: Rodale.

2008 Black, Joel, 'National Bad Habits: Thomas De Quincey's Geography of Addiction', *Thomas De Quincey: New Theoretical and Critical Directions*, ed. Robert Morrison and Daniel Sanjiv Roberts, London: Routledge, 143–64.

Cottle, Basil, *Joseph Cottle and the Romantics*, Bristol: Redcliffe.

McDonagh, Josephine, 'De Quincey and the Secret Life of Books', *Thomas De Quincey: New Theoretical and Critical Directions*, ed. Robert Morrison and Daniel Sanjiv Roberts, London: Routledge, 123–42.

Milligan, Barry, 'Brunonianism, Radicalism, and "The Pleasures of Opium"', *Thomas De Quincey: New Theoretical and Critical Directions*, ed. Robert Morrison and Daniel Sanjiv Roberts, London: Routledge, 45–61.

Morrison, Robert, '"Earthquake and Eclipse": Radical Energies and De Quincey's 1821 *Confessions*', *Thomas De Quincey: New Theoretical and Critical Directions*, ed. Robert Morrison and Daniel Sanjiv Roberts, London: Routledge, 63–79.

Roberts, Daniel Sanjiv, '"Mix(ing) a Little with Alien Natures": Biblical Orientalism in De Quincey', *Thomas De Quincey: New Theoretical and Critical Directions*, ed. Robert Morrison and Daniel Sanjiv Roberts, London: Routledge, 19–43.

Whale, John, 'De Quincey and Men (of Letters)', *Thomas De Quincey: New Theoretical and Critical Directions*, ed. Robert Morrison and Daniel Sanjiv Roberts, London: Routledge, 81–97.

Wilson, Francis, *The Ballad of Dorothy Wordsworth*, London: Faber.

2009 Jong, Petrus de, *De Quincey's Loved Ones*, Oosterhout: Totalprint.

Silverman, Michael, 'The Daughters of Thomas De Quincey: A Significant New Source for the Author's Life', *Catalogue Twenty-Seven: Literary and Historical Manuscripts*, London: Silverman, [26–40].

Index